THE CITY OF TH

AND

ACROSS THE ROCKY MOUNTAINS TO CALIFORNIA.

BY

RICHARD F. BURTON,

AUTHOR OF

"THE LAKE REGIONS OF CENTRAL AFRICA," ETC.

With Illustrations.

NEW YORK:

HARPER & BROTHERS, PUBLISHERS,

FRANKLIN SQUARE.

1862.

" Clear your mind of cant."—JOHNSON.

" MONTESINOS.—America is in more danger from religious fanaticism. The government there not thinking it necessary to provide religious instruction for the people in any of the new states, the prevalence of superstition, and that, perhaps, in some wild and terrible shape, may be locked for as one likely consequence of this great and portentous omission. An Old Man of the Mountain might find dupes and followers as readily as the All-friend Jemima; and the next Aaron Burr who seeks to carve a kingdom for himself out of the overgrown territories of the Union, may discern that fanaticism is the most effective weapon with which ambition can arm itself; that the way for both is prepared by that immorality which the want of religion naturally and necessarily induces, and that camp-meetings may be very well directed to forward the designs of military prophets. Were there another Mohammed to arise, there is no part of the world where he would find more scope or fairer opportunity than in that part of the Anglo-American Union into which the older states continually discharge the restless part of their population, leaving laws and Gospel to overtake it if they can, for in the march of modern colonization both are left behind."

This remarkable prophecy appeared from the pen of Robert Southey, the Poet-Laureate, in March, 1829 (" Sir Thomas More; or, Colloquies on the Progress and Prospects of Society," vol. i., Part II., " The Reformation—Dissenters—Methodists.")

Reprinted from the edition of 1862, New York
First AMS EDITION published 1971
Manufactured in the United States of America

International Standard Book Number: 0-404-08433-8

Library of Congress Catalog Number: 72-134390

AMS PRESS INC.
NEW YORK, N.Y. 10003

Dedication.

PREFACE.

UNACCUSTOMED, of late years at least, to deal with tales of twice-told travel, I can not but feel, especially when, as in the present case, so much detail has been expended upon the trivialities of a Diary, the want of that freshness and originality which would have helped the reader over a little lengthiness. My best excuse is the following extract from the lexicographer's "Journey to the Western Islands," made in company with Mr. Boswell during the year of grace 1773, and upheld even at that late hour as somewhat a feat in the locomotive line.

"These diminutive observations seem to take away something from the dignity of writing, and therefore are never communicated but with hesitation, and a little fear of abasement and contempt. But it must be remembered that life consists not of a series of illustrious actions or elegant enjoyments; the greater part of our time passes in compliance with necessities, in the performance of daily duties, in the removal of small inconveniences, in the procurement of petty pleasures, and we are well or ill at ease as the main stream of life glides on smoothly, or is ruffled by small obstacles and frequent interruptions."

True! and as the novelist claims his right to elaborate, in the "domestic epic," the most trivial scenes of household routine, so the traveler may be allowed to enlarge, when copying nature in his humbler way, upon the subject of his little drama, and, not confining himself to the great, the good, and the beautiful, nor suffering himself to be wholly engrossed by the claims of cotton, civilization, and Christianity, useful knowledge and missionary enterprise, to *desipere in loco* by expatiating upon his bed, his meat, and his drink.

The notes forming the ground-work of this volume were written on patent improved metallic pocket-books in sight of the objects which attracted my attention. The old traveler is again right when he remarks: "There is yet another cause of error not always easily surmounted, though more dangerous to the veracity of itinerary narratives than imperfect mensuration. An observer deeply impressed by any remarkable spectacle does not suppose that the traces will soon vanish from his mind, and, having commonly no great convenience for writing"—Penny and Letts are of a later date—"defers the description to a time of more leisure and better accommodation. He who has not made the experiment, or is not accustomed to require rigorous accuracy from himself, will scarcely believe how much a few hours take from certainty of knowledge and distinctness of imagery; how the succession of objects will be broken, how separate parts will be confused, and how many particular features and discriminations will be found compressed and conglobated with one gross and general idea." Brave words, somewhat pompous and diffused, yet worthy to be written in letters of gold. But, though of the same opinion with M. Charles Didier, the Miso-Albion (Séjour chez le Grand-Chérif de la Mekkeh, Preface, p. vi.), when he characterizes "un voyage de fantaisie" as "le pire de tous les romans," and with Admiral Fitzroy (Hints to Travelers, p. 3), that the descriptions should be written with the objects in view, I would avoid the other extreme, viz., that of publishing, as our realistic age is apt to do, mere photographic representations. Byron could not write verse when on Lake Leman, and the traveler who puts forth his narrative without after-study and thought will produce a kind of Persian picture, pre-Raphaelitic enough, no doubt, but lacking distance and perspective—in artists' phrase, depth and breadth—in fact, a narrative about as pleasing to the reader's mind as the sage and saleratus prairies of the Far West would be to his ken.

In working up this book I have freely used authorities well known across the water, but more or less rare in England. The books principally borrowed from are "The Prairie Traveler," by Captain Marcy; "Explorations of Nebraska," by Lieutenant G. A. Warren; and Mr. Bartlett's "Dictionary of Americanisms." To describe these regions without the aid of their first explorers, Messrs. Frémont and Stansbury, would of course have been impossible. If I have not always specified the authority for a statement, it has been rather for the purpose of not wearying the reader by repetitions than with the view of enriching my pages at the expense of others.

In commenting upon what was seen and heard, I have endeavored to assume—whether successfully or not the public will decide—the cosmopolitan character, and to avoid the capital error, especially in treating of things American, of looking at them from the fancied vantage-ground of an English point of view. I hold the Anglo-Scandinavian* of the New World to be in most things equal, in many inferior, and in many superior, to his cousin in the Old; and that a gentleman, that is to say, a man of education, probity, and honor—not, as I was once told, one who must get *on onner* and *onnest*—is every where the same, though living in separate hemispheres. If, in the present transition state of the Far West, the broad lands lying between the Missouri River and the Sierra Nevada have occasionally been handled somewhat roughly, I have done no more than I should have permitted my: self to do while treating of rambles beyond railways through the semi-civilized parts of Great Britain, with their "pleasant primitive populations"—Wales, for instance, or Cornwall.

I need hardly say that this elaborate account of the Holy City of the West and its denizens would not have seen the light so soon after the appearance of a "Journey to Great Salt Lake City," by M. Jules Remy, had there not been much left to say. The French naturalist passed through the Mormon Settlements in 1855, and five years in the Far West are equal to fifty in less conservative lands; the results of which are, that the relation of my experiences will in no way clash with his, or prove a tiresome repetition to the reader of both.

If in parts of this volume there appear a tendency to look upon things generally in their ludicrous or absurd aspects—from which nothing sublunary is wholly exempt—my excuse must be *sic me natura fecit*. Democritus was not, I believe, a whit the worse philosopher than Heraclitus. The Procreation of Mirth should be a theme far more sympathetic than the Anatomy of Melancholy, and the old Roman gentleman had a perfect right to challenge all objectors with

ridentem dicere verum
Quid vetat?

---

* The word is proposed by Dr. Norton Shaw, Secretary to the Royal Geographical Society, and should be generally adopted. Anglo-Saxon is to Anglo-Scandinavian what Indo-Germanic is to Indo-European; both serve to humor the absurd pretensions of claimants whose principal claim to distinction is pretentiousness. The coupling England with Saxony suggests to my memory a toast once proposed after a patriotic and fusional political feed in the Isle of the Knights—"Malta and England united can conquer the world."

Finally, I would again solicit forbearance touching certain errors of omission and commission which are to be found in these pages. Her most gracious majesty has been pleased to honor me with an appointment as Consul at Fernando Po, in the Bight of Biafra, and the necessity of an early departure has limited me to a single revise.

14 St. James' Square, 1st July, 1861.

CONTENTS.

LIST OF ILLUSTRATIONS.

THE CITY OF THE SAINTS.

CHAPTER I.

A TOUR through the domains of Uncle Samuel without visiting the wide regions of the Far West would be, to use a novel simile, like seeing Hamlet with the part of Prince of Denmark, by desire, omitted. Moreover, I had long determined to add the last new name to the list of " Holy Cities;" to visit the young rival, *soi-disant*, of Memphis, Benares, Jerusalem, Rome, Meccah; and after having studied the beginnings of a mighty empire "in that New World which is the Old," to observe the origin and the working of a regular go-ahead Western and Columbian revelation. Mingled with the wish of prospecting the City of the Great Salt Lake in a spiritual point of view, of seeing Utah as it is, not as it is said to be, was the mundane desire of enjoying a little skirmishing with the savages, who in the days of Harrison and Jackson had given the pale faces tough work to do, and that failing, of inspecting the line of route which Nature, according to the general consensus of guide-books, has pointed out as the proper, indeed the only practical direction for a railway between the Atlantic and the Pacific. The commerce of the world, the Occidental Press had assured me, is undergoing its grand climacteric: the resources of India and the nearer orient are now well-nigh cleared of "loot," and our sons, if they would walk in the paths of their papas, must look to Cipangri and the parts about Cathay for *their* annexations.

The Man was ready, the Hour hardly appeared propitious for other than belligerent purposes. Throughout the summer of 1860 an Indian war was raging in Nebraska; the Comanches, Kiowas, and Cheyennes were "out;" the Federal government had dispatched three columns to the centres of confusion; intestine feuds among the aborigines were talked of; the Dakotah or Sioux had threatened to "wipe out" their old foe the Pawnee, both tribes being possessors of the soil over which the road ran. Horrible accounts of murdered post-boys and cannibal emigrants, greatly exaggerated, as usual, for private and public purposes,

A

filled the papers, and that nothing might be wanting, the following positive assertion (I afterward found it to be, as Sir Charles Napier characterized one of a Bombay editor's saying, "a marked and emphatic lie") was copied by full half the press:

"Utah has a population of some fifty-two or fifty-three thousand—more or less—rascals. Governor Cumming has informed the President exactly how matters stand in respect to them. Neither life nor property is safe, he says, and bands of depredators roam unpunished through the territory. The United States judges have abandoned their offices, and the law is boldly defied every where. He requests that 500 soldiers may be retained at Utah to afford some kind of protection to American citizens who are obliged to remain here."

"Mormon" had in fact become a word of fear; the Gentiles looked upon the Latter-Day Saints much as our crusading ancestors regarded the "Hashshashiyun," whose name, indeed, was almost enough to frighten them. Mr. Brigham Young was the Shaykh-el-Jebel, the Old Man of the Hill redivivus, Messrs. Kimball and Wells were the chief of his Fidawin, and "Zion on the tops of the mountains" formed a fair representation of Alamut.

"Going among the Mormons!" said Mr. M—— to me at New Orleans; "they are shooting and cutting one another in all directions; how can *you* expect to escape?"

Another general assertion was that "White Indians"—those Mormons again!—had assisted the "Washoes," "Pah Utes," and "Bannacks" in the fatal affair near Honey Lake, where Major Ormsby, of the militia, a military frontier-lawyer, and his forty men, lost the numbers of their mess.

But sagely thus reflecting that "dangers which loom large from afar generally lose size as one draws near;" that rumors of wars might.have arisen, as they are wont to do, from the political necessity for another "Indian botheration," as editors call it; that Governor Cumming's name might have been used in vain; that even the President might not have been a Pope, infallible; and that the Mormons might turn out somewhat less black than they were painted; moreover, having so frequently and willfully risked the chances of an "I told you so" from the lips of friends, those "prophets of the past;" and, finally, having been so much struck with the discovery by some Western man of an enlarged truth, viz., that the bugbear approached has more affinity to the bug than to the bear, I resolved to risk the chance of the "red nightcap" from the bloodthirsty Indian and the poisoned bowie-dagger—without my Eleonora or Berengaria—from the jealous Latter-Day Saints. I forthwith applied myself to the audacious task with all the recklessness of a "party" from town precipitating himself for the first time into "foreign parts" about Calais.

And, first, a few words touching routes.

As all the world knows, there are three main lines proposed

for a "Pacific Railroad" between the Mississippi and the Western Ocean, the Northern, Central, and Southern.*

The first, or British, was in my case not to be thought of; it involves semi-starvation, possibly a thorough plundering by the Bedouins, and, what was far worse, five or six months of slow travel. The third, or Southern, known as the Butterfield or American Express, offered to start me in an ambulance from St. Louis, and to pass me through Arkansas, El Paso, Fort Yuma on the Gila River, in fact through the vilest and most desolate portion of the West. Twenty-four mortal days and nights—twenty-five being schedule time—must be spent in that ambulance; passengers becoming crazy by whisky, mixed with want of sleep, are often obliged to be strapped to their seats; their meals, dispatched during the ten-minute halts, are simply abominable, the heats are excessive, the climate malarious; lamps may not be used at night for fear of unexisting Indians: briefly, there is no end to

* The following table shows the lengths, comparative costs, etc., of the several routes explored for a railroad from the Mississippi to the Pacific, as extracted from the Speech of the Hon. Jefferson Davis, of Mississippi, on the Pacific Railway Bill in the United States Senate, January, 1859, and quoted by the Hon. Sylvester Maury in the "Geography and Resources of Arizona and Sonora."

ROUTES.	Distance by proposed railroad route.	Sum of ascents and descents.	Comparative cost of different routes.	No. of miles of route through arable lands.	No. of miles of route through land generally uncultivable, arable soil being found in small areas.	Altitude above the sea of the highest point on the route.
	Miles.	Feet.	Dollars.			Feet.
Route near forty-seventh and forty-ninth parallels, from St. Paul to Seattle......................	1955	18,654	135,871,000	535	1490	6,044
Route near forty-seventh and forty-ninth parallels, from St. Paul to Vancouver....................	1800	17,645	425,781,000	374	1490	6,044
Route near forty-first and forty-second parallels, from Rock Island, via South Pass, to Benicia...	2299	29,120*	122,770,000	899	1400	8,373
Route near thirty-eighth and thirty-ninth parallels, from St. Louis, via Coo-che-to-pa and Tah-ee-chay-pah passes to San Francisco.....	2325	49,985†	Impracticable.	865	1460	10,032
Route near thirty-eighth and thirty-ninth parallels, from St. Louis, via Coo-chee-to-pa and Madeline Passes, to Benicia..............	2535	56,514‡	Impracticable.	915	1620	10,032
Route near thirty-fifth parallel, from Memphis to San Francisco.......	2366	48,521†	113,000,000	916	1450	7,550
Route near thirty-second parallel, from Memphis to San Pedro	2090	48,862†	99,000,000	690	1400	7,550
Route near thirty-second parallel, near Gaines' Landing, to San Francisco by coast route........	2174	38,200§	94,000,000	984	1190	5,717
Route near thirty-second parallel, from Gaines' Landing to San Pedro	1748	30,181§	72,000,000	558	1190	5,717
Route near thirty-second parallel, from Gaines' Landing to San Diego	1683	33,454§	72,000,000	524	1150	5,717

* The ascents and descents between Rock Island and Council Bluffs are not known, and therefore not included in this sum.
† The ascents and descents between St. Louis and Westport are not known, and therefore not included in this sum.
‡ The ascents and descents between Memphis and Fort Smith are not known, and therefore not included in this sum.
§ The ascents and descents between Gaines' Landing and Fulton are not known, and therefore not included in this sum.

this Via Mala's miseries. The line received from the United States government upward of half a million of dollars per annum for carrying the mails, and its contract had still nearly two years to run.

There remained, therefore, the central route, which has two branches. You may start by stage to the gold regions about Denver City or Pike's Peak, and thence, if not accidentally or purposely shot, you may proceed by an uncertain ox-train to Great Salt Lake City, which latter part can not take less than thirty-five days. On the other hand, there is "the great emigration route" from Missouri to California and Oregon, over which so many thousands have traveled within the past few years. I quote from a useful little volume, "The Prairie Traveler,"* by Randolph B. Marcy, Captain U. S. Army. "The track is broad, well worn, and can not be mistaken. It has received the major part of the Mormon emigration, and was traversed by the army in its march to Utah in 1857."

The mail-coach on this line was established in 1850, by Colonel Samuel H. Woodson, an eminent lawyer, afterward an M. C., and right unpopular with Mormondom, because he sacrilegiously owned part of Temple Block, in Independence, Mo., which is the old original New Zion. The following are the rates of contract and the phases through which the line has passed.

1. Colonel Woodson received for carrying a monthly mail $19,500 (or $23,000?): length of contract 4 years.

2. Mr. F. M'Graw, $13,500, besides certain considerable extras.

3. Messrs. Heber Kimball & Co. (Mormons), $23,000.

4. Messrs. Jones & Co., $30,000.

5. Mr. J. M. Hockaday, weekly mail, $190,000.

6. Messrs. Russell, Majors, & Waddell, army contractors; weekly mail, $190,000.†

Thus it will be seen that in 1856 the transit was in the hands of the Latter-Day Saints: they managed it well, but they lost the contracts during their troubles with the federal government in 1857, when it again fell into Gentile possession. In those early days it had but three changes of mules, at Forts Bridger, Laramie, and Kearney. In May, 1859, it was taken up by the present firm, which expects, by securing the monopoly of the whole line between the Missouri River and San Francisco, and by canvassing at head-quarters for a bi-weekly—which they have now obtained—and even a daily transit, which shall constitutionally extinguish the Mormon community, to insert the fine edge of that

---

* Printed by Messrs. Harper & Brothers, New York, 1859, and Messrs. Sampson Low, Son, and Co., Ludgate Hill, and amply meriting the honors of a second edition.

† In the American Almanac for 1861 (p. 196), the length of routes in Utah Territory is 1450 miles, 533 of which have no specified mode of transportation, and the remainder, 977, in coaches; the total transportation is thus 170,872 miles, and the total cost $144,638.

wedge which is to open an aperture for the Pacific Railroad about to be.   At Saint Joseph (Mo.), better known by the somewhat irreverent abbreviation of St. Jo, I was introduced to Mr. Alexander Majors, formerly one of the contractors for supplying the army in Utah—a veteran mountaineer, familiar with life on the prairies.   His meritorious efforts to reform the morals of the land have not yet put forth even the bud of promise.   He forbade his drivers and employés to drink, gamble, curse, and travel on Sundays; he desired them to peruse Bibles distributed to them gratis; and though he refrained from a lengthy proclamation commanding his lieges to be good boys and girls, he did not the less expect it of them.   Results: I scarcely ever saw a sober driver; as for profanity—the Western equivalent for hard swearing—they would make the blush of shame crimson the cheek of the old Isis bargee; and, rare exceptions to the rule of the United States, they are not to be deterred from evil talking even by the dread presence of a "lady."   The conductors and road-agents are of a class superior to the drivers; they do their harm by an inordinate ambition to distinguish themselves.   I met one gentleman who owned to three murders, and another individual who lately attempted to ration the mules with wild sage.   The company was by no means rich; already the papers had prognosticated a failure, in consequence of the government withdrawing its supplies, and it seemed to have hit upon the happy expedient of badly entreating travelers that good may come to it of our evils.   The hours and halting-places were equally vilely selected; for instance, at Forts Kearney, Laramie, and Bridger, the only points where supplies, comfort, society, are procurable, a few minutes of grumbling delay were granted as a favor, and the passengers were hurried on to some distant wretched ranch,* apparently for the sole purpose of putting a few dollars into the station-master's pockets.   The travel was unjustifiably slow, even in this land, where progress is mostly on paper.   From St. Jo to Great Salt Lake City, the mails might easily be landed during the fine weather, without inconvenience to man or beast, in ten days; indeed, the agents have offered to place them at Placerville in fifteen.   Yet the schedule time being twenty-one days, passengers seldom reached their destination before the nineteenth; the sole reason given was, that snow makes the road difficult in its season, and that if people were accustomed to fast travel, and if letters were received under schedule time, they would look upon the boon as a right.

Before proceeding to our preparations for travel, it may be as well to cast a glance at the land to be traveled over.

* "Rancho" in Mexico means primarily a rude thatched hut where herdsmen pass the night; the "rancharia" is a sheep-walk or cattle-run, distinguished from a "hacienda," which must contain cultivation.   In California it is a large farm with grounds often measured by leagues, and it applies to any dirty hovel in the Mississippian Valley.

The United States territory lying in direct line between the Mississippi River and the Pacific Ocean is now about 1200 miles long from north to south, by 1500 of breadth, in 49° and 32° N. lat., about equal to Equatorial Africa, and 1800 in N. lat. 38°. The great uncultivable belt of plain and mountain region through which the Pacific Railroad must run has a width of 1100 statute miles near the northern boundary; in the central line, 1200; and through the southern, 1000. Humboldt justly ridiculed the "maddest natural philosopher" who compared the American continent to a female figure—long, thin, watery, and freezing at the 58th°, the degrees being symbolic of the year at which woman grows old. Such description manifestly will not apply to the 2,000,000 of square miles in this section of the Great Republic— she is every where broader than she is long.

The meridian of 105° 𝐧𝐨𝐫𝐭𝐡 longitude (G.)—Fort Laramie lies in 104° 31′ 26″—divides this vast expanse into two nearly equal parts. The eastern half is a basin or river valley rising gradually from the Mississippi to the Black Hills, and the other outlying ranges of the Rocky Mountains. The average elevation near the northern boundary (49°) is 2500 feet, in the middle latitude (38°) 6000 feet, and near the southern extremity (32°), about 4000 feet above sea level. These figures explain the complicated features of its water-shed. The western half is a mountain region whose chains extend, as far as they are known, in a general N. and S. direction.

The 99th meridian (G.)—Fort Kearney lies in 98° 58′ 11″ᵂᴱˢᵀ divides the western half of the Mississippian Valley into two unequal parts.

The eastern portion, from the Missouri to Fort Kearney—400 to 500 miles in breadth—may be called the "Prairie land." It is true that passing westward of the 97° meridian, the *mauvaises terres*, or Bad Grounds, are here and there met with, especially near the 42d parallel, in which latitude they extend farther to the east, and that upward to 99° the land is rarely fit for cultivation, though fair for grazing. Yet along the course of the frequent streams there is valuable soil, and often sufficient wood to support settlements. This territory is still possessed by settled Indians, by semi-nomads, and by powerful tribes of equestrian and wandering savages, mixed with a few white men, who, as might be expected, excel them in cunning and ferocity.

The western portion of the valley, from Fort Kearney to the base of the Rocky Mountains—a breadth of 300 to 400 miles—is emphatically "the desert," sterile and uncultivable, a dreary expanse of wild sage (artemisia) and saleratus. The surface is sandy, gravelly, and pebbly; cactus carduus and aloes abound; grass is found only in the rare river bottoms where the soils of the different strata are mixed, and the few trees along the borders of streams —fertile lines of wadis, which laborious irrigation and coal mining might convert into oases—are the cotton-wood and willow, to which the mezquite* may be added in the southern latitudes. The desert is mostly uninhabited, unendurable even to the wildest Indian. But the people on its eastern and western frontiers, namely, those holding the extreme limits of the fertile prairie, and those occupying the desirable regions of the western mountains, are, to quote the words of Lieutenant Gouverneur K. Warren, U. S. Topographical Engineers, whose valuable reconnaissances and explanations of Nebraska in 1855, '56, and '57 were published in the Reports of the Secretary of War, " on the shore of a sea, up to which population and agriculture may advance and no farther. But this gives these outposts much of the value of places along the Atlantic frontier, in view of the future settlements to be formed in the mountains, between which and the present frontier a most valuable trade would exist. The western frontier has always been looking to the east for a market; but as soon as the wave of emigration has passed over the desert portion of the plains, to which the discoveries of gold have already given an impetus that will propel it to the fertile valleys of the Rocky Mountains, then will the present frontier of Kansas and Nebraska become the starting-point for all the products of the Mississippi Valley which the population of the mountains will require. We see the effects of it in the benefits which the western frontier of Missouri has received from the Santa Fé tract, and still more plainly in the impetus given to Leavenworth by the operations of the army of Utah in the interior region. This flow of products has, in the last instance, been only in one direction; but when those mountains become settled, as they eventually must, then there will be a reciprocal trade materially beneficial to both."

The mountain region westward of the sage and saleratus desert, extending between the 105th and 111th meridian (G.)—a little more than 400 miles—will in time become sparsely peopled. Though in many parts arid and sterile, dreary and desolate, the long bunch grass (*Festuca*), the short curly buffalo grass (*Sisleria dactyloides*), the mesquit grass (*Stipa spata*), and the Gramma, or rather, as it should be called, " Gamma" grass (*Chondrosium fœnum*),† which clothe the slopes west of Fort Laramie, will enable it to rear an abundance of stock. The fertile valleys, according to Lieutenant Warren, "furnish the means of raising sufficient quantities of grain and vegetables for the use of the inhabitants, and beautiful healthy and desirable locations for their homes. The remarkable freedom here from sickness is one of the attractive features of the region, and will in this respect go far to com-

---

* Often corrupted from the Spanish to muskeet (*Algarobia glandulosa*), a locust inhabiting Texas, New Mexico, California, etc., bearing, like the carob generally, a long pod full of sweet beans, which, pounded and mixed with flour, are a favorite food with the Southwestern Indians.

† Some of my informants derived the word from the Greek letter; others make it Hispano-Mexican.

pensate the settler from the Mississippi Valley for his loss in the smaller amount of products that can be taken from the soil. The great want of suitable building material, which now so seriously retards the growth of the West, will not be felt there." The heights of the Rocky Mountains rise abruptly from 1000 to 6000 feet over the lowest known passes, computed by the Pacific Railroad surveyors to vary from 4000 to 10,000 feet above sea-level. The two chains forming the eastern and western rims of the Rocky Mountain basin have the greatest elevation, walling in, as it were, the other sub-ranges.

There is a popular idea that the western slope of the Rocky Mountains is smooth and regular; on the contrary, the land is rougher, and the ground is more complicated than on the eastern declivities. From the summit of the Wasach range to the eastern foot of the Sierra Nevada, the whole region, with exceptions, is a howling wilderness, the sole or bed of an inland sweetwater sea, now shrunk into its remnants—the Great Salt and the Utah Lakes. Nothing can be more monotonous than its regular succession of high grisly hills, cut perpendicularly by rough and rocky ravines, and separating bare and barren plains. From the seaward base of the Sierra Nevada to the Pacific—California—the slope is easy, and the land is pleasant, fertile, and populous.

After this *aperçu* of the motives which sent me forth, once more a pilgrim, to young Meccah in the West, of the various routes, and of the style of country wandered over, I plunge at once into personal narrative.

Lieutenant Dana (U. S. Artillery), my future *compagnon de voyage*, left St. Louis,* "the turning-back place of English sportsmen," for St. Jo on the 2d of August, preceding me by two days. Being accompanied by his wife and child, and bound on a weary voyage to Camp Floyd, Utah Territory, he naturally wanted a certain amount of precise information concerning the route, and one of the peculiarities of this line is that no one knows any thing about it. In the same railway car which carried me from St. Louis were five passengers, all bent upon making Utah with the least delay—an unexpected cargo of officials: Mr. F********, a federal judge with two sons; Mr. W*****, a state secretary; and Mr. G****, a state marshal. As the sequel may show, Dana was doubly fortunate in securing places before the list could be filled up by the unusual throng: all we thought of at the time was our good luck in escaping a septidium at St. Jo, whence the stage started on Tuesdays only. We hurried, therefore, to pay for our tickets—$175 each being the moderate sum—to reduce our luggage to its minimum approach toward 25 lbs., the price of transport for ex-

---

* St. Louis (Mo.) lies in N. lat. 28° 37' and W. long. (G.) 90° 16': its elevation above tide water is 461 feet: the latest frost is in the first week of March, the earliest is in the middle of November, giving some 115 days of cold. St. Joseph (Mo.) lies about N. lat. 39° 40', and W. long. (G.) 34° 54'.

cess being exorbitantly fixed at $1 per lb., and to lay in a few necessaries for the way, tea and sugar, tobacco and cognac. I will not take liberties with my company's "kit;" my own, however, was represented as follows:

One India-rubber blanket, pierced in the centre for a poncho, and garnished along the longer side with buttons, and corresponding elastic loops with a strap at the short end, converting it into a carpet-bag—a "sine quâ non" from the equator to the pole. A buffalo robe ought to have been added as a bed: ignorance, however, prevented, and borrowing did the rest. With one's coat as a pillow, a robe, and a blanket, one may defy the dangerous "bunks" of the stations.

For weapons I carried two revolvers: from the moment of leaving St. Jo to the time of reaching Placerville or Sacramento the pistol should never be absent from a man's right side—remember, it is handier there than on the other—nor the bowie-knife from his left. Contingencies with Indians and others may happen, when the difference of a second saves life: the revolver should therefore be carried with its butt to the fore, and when drawn it should not be leveled as in target practice, but directed toward the object by means of the right fore finger laid flat along the cylinder while the medius draws the trigger. The instinctive consent between eye and hand, combined with a little practice, will soon enable the beginner to shoot correctly from the hip; all he has to do is to think that he is pointing at the mark, and pull. As a precaution, especially when mounted upon a kicking horse, it is wise to place the cock upon a capless nipple, rather than trust to the intermediate pins. In dangerous places the revolver should be discharged and reloaded every morning, both for the purpose of keeping the hand in, and to do the weapon justice. A revolver is an admirable tool when properly used; those, however, who are too idle or careless to attend to it, had better carry a pair of "Derringers." For the benefit of buffalo and antelope, I had invested $25 at St. Louis in a "shooting-iron" of the "Hawkins" style—that enterprising individual now dwells in Denver City—it was a long, top-heavy rifle; it weighed 12 lbs., and it carried the smallest ball—75 to the pound—a combination highly conducive to good practice. Those, however, who can use light weapons, should prefer the Maynard breech-loader, with an extra barrel for small shot; and if Indian fighting is in prospect, the best tool, without any exception, is a ponderous double-barrel, 12 to the pound, and loaded as fully as it can bear with slugs. The last of the battery was an air-gun to astonish the natives, and a bag of various ammunition.

Captain Marcy outfits his prairie traveler with a "little blue mass, quinine, opium, and some cathartic medicine put up in doses for adults." I limited myself to the opium, which is invaluable when one expects five consecutive days and nights in a prairie wagon, quinine, and Warburg's drops, without which no traveler should ever face fever, and a little citric acid, which, with green tea drawn off the moment the leaf has sunk, is perhaps the best substitute for milk and cream. The "holy weed Nicotian" was not forgotten; cigars must be bought in extraordinary quantities, as the driver either receives or takes the lion's share: the most satisfactory outfit is a *quantum sufficit* of Louisiana Pirique and Lynchburg gold-leaf—cavendish without its abominations of rum and honey or molasses—and two pipes, a meerschaum for luxury, and a brier-root to fall back upon when the meerschaum shall have been stolen. The Indians will certainly pester for matches; the best lighting apparatus, therefore, is the Spanish mechero, the Oriental sukhtah—agate and cotton match—besides which, it offers a pleasing exercise, like billiards, and one at which the British soldier greatly excels, surpassed only by his exquisite skill in stuffing the pipe.

For literary purposes, I had, besides the two books above quoted, a few of the great guns of exploration, Frémont, Stansbury, and Gunnison, with a selection of the most violent Mormon and Anti-Mormon polemicals, sketching materials—I prefer the "improved metallics" five inches long, and serving for both diary and drawing-book—and a tourist's writing-case of those sold by Mr. Field (Bible Warehouse, The Quadrant), with but one alteration, a snap lock, to obviate the use of that barbarous invention called a key. For instruments I carried a pocket sextant with a double face, invented by Mr. George, of the Royal Geographical Society, and beautifully made by Messrs. Cary, an artificial horizon of black glass, and bubble tubes to level it, night and day compasses, with a portable affair attached to a watch-chain—a traveler feels nervous till he can "orienter" himself—a pocket thermometer, and a B. P. ditto. The only safe form for the latter would be a strong neckless tube, the heavy pyriform bulbs in general use never failing to break at the first opportunity. A Stanhope lens, a railway whistle, and instead of the binocular, useful things of earth, a very valueless telescope—(warranted by the maker to show Jupiter's satellites, and by utterly declining so to do, reading a lesson touching the non-advisability of believing an instrument-maker)—completed the outfit.

The prairie traveler is not particular about toilet: the easiest dress is a dark flannel shirt, worn over the normal article; no braces—I say it, despite Mr. Galton—but broad leather belt for "six-shooter" and for "Arkansas tooth-pick," a long clasp-knife, or for the rapier of the Western world, called after the hero who perished in the "red butchery of the Alamo." The nether garments should be forked with good buckskin, or they will infallibly give out, and the lower end should be tucked into the boots, after the sensible fashion of our grandfathers, before those ridiculous Wellingtons were dreamed of by our sires. In warm weather, a pair of moccasins will be found easy as slippers, but they are bad for wet places; they make the feet tender, they strain the back sinews, and they form the first symptom of the savage mania. Socks keep the feet cold; there are, however, those who should take six pair. The use of the pocket-handkerchief is unknown in the plains; some people, however, are uncomfortable without it, not liking "se emungere" after the fashion of Horace's father.

In cold weather—and rarely are the nights warm—there is nothing better than the old English tweed shooting-jacket, made with pockets like a poacher's, and its similar waistcoat, a "stomach warmer" without a roll collar, which prevents comfortable sleep, and with flaps as in the Year of Grace 1760, when men were too wise to wear our senseless vests, whose only property seems to be that of disclosing after exertions a lucid interval of linen or longcloth. For driving and riding, a large pair of buckskin gloves, or rather gauntlets, without which even the teamster will not travel, and leggins—the best are made in the country, only the straps should be passed through and sewn on to the leathers—are advisable, if at least the man at all regards his epidermis: it is almost unnecessary to bid you remember spurs, but it may be useful to warn you that they will, like riches, make to themselves wings. The head-covering by excellence is a brown felt, which, by a little ingenuity, boring, for instance, holes round the brim to admit a ribbon, you may convert into a riding-hat or night-cap, and wear alternately after the manly slouch of Cromwell and his Martyr, the funny three-cornered spittoon-like "shovel" of the Dutch Georges, and the ignoble cocked-hat, which completes the hideous metamorphosis.

And, above all things, as you value your nationality—this is written for the benefit of the home reader—let no false shame cause you to forget your hat-box and your umbrella. I purpose, when a moment of inspiration waits upon leisure and a mind at ease, to invent an elongated portmanteau, which shall be perfection—portable—solid leather of two colors, for easy distinguishment—snap lock—in length about three feet; in fact, long enough to contain without creasing "small clothes," a lateral compartment destined for a hat, and a longitudinal space where the umbrella can repose: its depth—but I must reserve that part of the secret until this benefit to British humanity shall have been duly made by Messrs. Bengough Brothers, and patented by myself.

The dignitaries of the mail-coach, acting upon the principle "first come first served," at first decided, maugre all our attempts at "moral suasion," to divide the party by the interval of a week. Presently reflecting, I presume, upon the unadvisability of leaving at large five gentlemen, who, being really in no particular hurry, might purchase a private conveyance and start leisurely westward, they were favored with a revelation of "'cuteness." On the day before departure, as, congregated in the Planter's House

Hotel, we were lamenting over our "morning glory," the necessity of parting—in the prairie the more the merrier, and the fewer the worse cheer—a youth from the office was introduced to tell, Hope-like, a flattering tale and a tremendous falsehood. This juvenile delinquent stated with unblushing front, over the hospitable cocktail, that three coaches instead of one had been newly and urgently applied for by the road-agent at Great Salt Lake City, and therefore that we could not only all travel together, but also all travel with the greatest comfort. We exulted. But on the morrow only two conveyances appeared, and not long afterward the two dwindled off to one. "The Prairie Traveler" doles out wisdom in these words: "Information concerning the route coming from strangers living or owning property near them, from agents of steam-boats and railways, or from other persons connected with transportation companies"—how carefully he piles up the heap of sorites—"should be received with great caution, and never without corroboratory evidence from disinterested sources." The main difficulty is to find the latter—to catch your hare—to know whom to believe.

I now proceed to my Diary.

THE START.

Tuesday, 7th August, 1860.

Precisely at 8 A.M. appeared in front of the Patee House—the Fifth Avenue Hotel of St. Jo—the vehicle destined to be our home for the next three weeks. We scrutinized it curiously.

The mail is carried by a "Concord coach," a spring wagon, comparing advantageously with the horrible vans which once dislocated the joints of men on the Suez route. The body is shaped somewhat like an English tax-cart considerably magnified. It is built to combine safety, strength, and lightness, without the slightest regard to appearances. The material is well-seasoned white oak—the Western regions, and especially Utah, are notoriously deficient in hard woods—and the manufacturers are the well-known coachwrights, Messrs. Abbott, of Concord, New Hampshire; the color is sometimes green, more usually red, causing the antelopes to stand and stretch their large eyes whenever the vehicle comes in sight. The wheels are five to six feet apart, affording security against capsising, with little "gather" and less "dish;" the larger have fourteen spokes and seven fellies; the smaller twelve and six. The tires are of unusual thickness, and polished like steel by the hard dry ground; and the hubs or naves and the metal nave-bands are in massive proportions. The latter not unfrequently fall off as the wood shrinks, unless the wheel is allowed to stand in water; attention must be paid to resetting them, or in the frequent and heavy "sidlins" the spokes may snap off all round like pipe-stems. The wagon-bed is supported by iron bands or perpendiculars abutting upon wooden rockers, which rest on strong leather thoroughbraces: these are found to break the jolt better than the best steel springs, which, moreover, when injured, can not readily be repaired. The whole bed is covered with stout osnaburg supported by stiff bars of white oak; there is a sun-shade or hood in front, where the driver sits, a curtain behind which can be raised or lowered at discretion, and four flaps on each side, either folded up or fastened down with hooks and eyes. In heavy frost the passengers must be half dead with cold, but they care little for that if they can go fast. The accommodations are as follows: In front sits the driver, with usually a conductor or passenger by his side; a variety of packages, large and small, is stowed away under his leather cushion; when the brake must be put on, an operation often involving the safety of the vehicle, his right foot is planted upon an iron bar which presses by a leverage upon the rear wheels; and in hot weather a bucket for watering the animals hangs over one of the lamps, whose companion is usually found wanting. The inside has either two or three benches fronting to the fore or placed *vis-à-vis;* they are movable and reversible, with leather cushions and hinged padded backs; unstrapped and turned down, they convert the vehicle into a tolerable bed for two persons or two and a half. According to Cocker, the mail-bags should be safely stowed away under these seats, or if there be not room enough, the passengers should perch themselves upon the correspondence; the jolly driver, however, is usually induced to cram the light literature between the wagon-bed and the platform, or running-gear beneath, and thus, when ford-waters wash the hubs, the letters are pretty certain to endure ablution. Behind, instead of dicky, is a kind of boot where passengers' boxes are stored beneath a stout canvas curtain with leather sides. The comfort of travel depends upon packing the wagon; if heavy in front or rear, or if the thoroughbraces be not properly "fixed," the bumping will be likely to cause nasal hemorrhage. The description will apply to the private ambulance, or, as it is called in the West, "avalanche," only the latter, as might be expected, is more convenient; it is the drosky in which the vast steppes of Central America are crossed by the government employés.

On this line mules are preferred to horses as being more enduring. They are all of legitimate race; the breed between the horse and the she-ass is never heard of, and the mysterious jumard is not believed to exist. In dry lands, where winter is not severe—they inherit the sire's impatience of cold—they are invaluable animals; in swampy ground this American dromedary is the meanest of beasts, requiring, when stalled, to be hauled out of the mire before it will recover spirit to use its legs. For sureness of foot (during a journey of more than 1000 miles, I saw but one fall and two severe stumbles), sagacity in finding the road, apprehension of danger, and general cleverness, mules are superior to their mothers: their main defect is an unhappy obstinacy derived from the other side of the house. They are great in hardihood, never sick nor sorry, never groomed nor shod, even where ice is on the ground; they have no grain, except five quarts per diem when snow conceals the grass; and they have no stable save the open corral. Moreover, a horse once broken down requires a long rest; the mule, if hitched up or ridden for short distances, with frequent intervals to roll and repose, may still, though "resté," get over 300 miles in tolerable time. The rate of travel on an average is five miles an hour; six is good; between seven and eight is the maximum, which sinks in hilly countries to three or four. I have made behind a good pair, in a light wagon, forty consecutive miles at the rate of nine per hour, and in California a mule is little thought of if it can not accomplish 250 miles in forty-eight hours. The price varies from $100 to $130 per head when cheap, rising to $150 or $200, and for fancy animals from $250 to $400. The value, as in the case of the Arab, depends upon size; "rats," or small mules, especially in California, are not esteemed. The "span"—the word used in America for beasts well matched—is of course much more expensive. At each station on this road, averaging twenty-five miles apart—beyond the forks of the Platte they lengthen out by one third—are three teams of four animals, with two extra, making a total of fourteen, besides two ponies for the express riders. In the East they work beautifully together, and are rarely mulish beyond a certain ticklishness of temper, which warns you not to meddle with their ears when in harness, or to attempt encouraging them by preceding them upon the road. In the West, where they run half wild and are lassoed for use once a week, they are fearfully handy with their heels; they flirt out with the hind legs, they rear like goats, breaking the harness and casting every strap and buckle clean off the body, and they bite their replies to the chorus of curses and blows: the wonder is that more men are not killed. Each fresh team must be ringed half a dozen times before it will start fairly; there is always some excitement in change; some George or Harry, some Julia or Sally disposed to shirk work or to play tricks, some Brigham Young or General Harney — the Trans-Vaal Republican calls his worst animal "England"—whose stubbornness is to be corrected by stone-throwing or the lash.

But the wagon still stands at the door. We ought to start at 8 30 A.M.; we are detained an hour while last words are said, and adieu—a long adieu—is bidden to joke and julep, to ice and idleness. Our "plunder"* is clapped on with little ceremony; a hat-case falls open—it was not mine, gentle reader—collars and other small gear cumber the ground, and the owner addresses to the clumsy-handed driver the universal G— d—, which in these lands changes from its expletive or chrysalis form to an adjec-

* In Canada they call personal luggage *butin*.

tival development. We try to stow away as much as possible; the minor officials, with all their little faults, are good fellows, civil and obliging; they wink at non-payment for bedding, stores, weapons, and they rather encourage than otherwise the multiplication of whisky-kegs and cigar-boxes. We now drive through the dusty roads of St. Jo, the observed of all observers, and presently find ourselves in the steam ferry which is to convey us from the right to the left bank of the Missouri River. The "Big Muddy," as it is now called—the Yellow River of old writers—venerable sire of snag and sawyer, displays at this point the source whence it has drawn for ages the dirty brown silt which pollutes below their junction the pellucid waters of the "Big Drink."* It runs, like the lower Indus, through deep walls of stiff clayey earth, and, like that river, its supplies, when filtered (they have been calculated to contain one eighth of solid matter), are sweet and wholesome as its brother streams. The Plata of this region, it is the great sewer of the prairies, the main channel and common issue of the water-courses and ravines which have carried on the work of denudation and degradation for days dating beyond the existence of Egypt.

According to Lieutenant Warren, who endorses the careful examinations of the parties under Governor Stevens in 1853, the Missouri is a superior river for navigation to any in the country, except the Mississippi below their junction. It has, however, serious obstacles in wind and frost. From the Yellow Stone to its mouth, the breadth, when full, varies from one third to half a mile; in low water the width shrinks, and bars appear. Where timber does not break the force of the winds, which are most violent in October, clouds of sand are seen for miles, forming banks, which, generally situated at the edges of trees on the islands and points, often so much resemble the Indian mounds in the Mississippi Valley, that some of them—for instance, those described by Lewis and Clarke at Bonhomme Island—have been figured as the works of the ancient Toltecs. It would hardly be feasible to correct the windage by foresting the land. The bluffs of the Missouri are often clothed with vegetation as far as the debouchure of the Platte River. Above that point the timber, which is chiefly cotton-wood, is confined to ravines and bottom lands, varying in width from ten to fifteen miles above Council Bluffs, which is almost continuous to the mouth of the James River. Every where, except between the mouth of the Little Cheyenne and the Cannon Ball rivers, there is a sufficiency of fuel for navigation; but, ascending above Council Bluffs, the protection afforded by forest growth on the banks is constantly diminishing. The trees also are injurious; imbedded in the channel by the "caving-in" of the banks, they form the well-known sawyers, or floating timbers, and snags, trunks standing like *chevaux de frise* at various

---

* A "Drink" is any river: the Big Drink is the Mississippi.

inclinations, pointing down the stream. From the mouth of the James River down to the Mississippi, it is a wonder how a steamer can run: she must lose half her time by laying to at night, and is often delayed for days, as the wind prevents her passing by bends filled with obstructions. The navigation is generally closed by ice at Sioux City on the 10th of November, and at Fort Leavenworth by the 1st of December. The rainy season of the spring and summer commences in the latitude of Kansas, Missouri, Iowa, and Southern Nebraska, between the 15th of May and the 30th of June, and continues about two months. The floods produced by the melting snows in the mountains come from the Platte, the Big Cheyenne, the Yellow Stone, and the Upper Missouri, reaching the lower river about the 1st of July, and lasting a month. Rivers like this, whose navigation depends upon temporary floods, are greatly inferior for ascent than for descent. The length of the inundation much depends upon the snow on the mountains: a steamer starting from St. Louis on the first indication of the rise would not generally reach the Yellow Stone before low water at the latter point, and if a miscalculation is made by taking the temporary rise for the real inundation, the boat must lay by in the middle of the river till the water deepens.

Some geographers have proposed to transfer to the Missouri, on account of its superior length, the honor of being the real head of the Mississippi; they neglect, however, to consider the direction and the course of the stream, an element which must enter largely in determining the channels of great rivers. It will, I hope, be long before this great ditch wins the day from the glorious Father of Waters.

The reader will find in Appendix No. I. a detailed itinerary, showing him the distances between camping-places, the several mail stations where mules are changed, the hours of travel, and the facilities for obtaining wood and water—in fact, all things required for the novice, hunter, or emigrant. In these pages I shall consider the route rather in its pictorial than in its geographical aspects, and give less of diary than of dissertation upon the subjects which each day's route suggested.

Landing in Bleeding Kansas—she still bleeds*—we fell at once into "Emigration Road," a great thoroughfare, broad and well worn as a European turnpike or a Roman military route, and undoubtedly the best and the longest natural highway in the world.

---

* And no wonder!

"I advise you, one and all, to enter every election district in Kansas and vote at the point of the bowie-knife and revolver. Neither give nor take quarter, as our case demands it."

"I tell you, mark every scoundrel among you that is the least tainted with Free-soilism or Abolitionism, and exterminate him. Neither give nor take quarter from them."

(Extracts from Speeches of General Stringfellow—happy name!—in the Kansas Legislature.)

For five miles the line bisected a bottom formed by a bend in the
river, with about a mile's diameter at the neck. The scene was
of a luxuriant vegetation. A deep tangled wood—rather a thicket or a jungle than a forest—of oaks and elms, hickory, basswood,*
and black walnut, poplar and hackberry (*Celtis crassifolia*), box elder, and the common willow (*Salix longifolia*), clad and festooned,
bound and anchored by wild vines, creepers, and huge llianas, and
sheltering an undergrowth of white alder and red sumach, whose
pyramidal flowers were about to fall, rested upon a basis of deep
black mire, strongly suggestive of chills—fever and ague. After
an hour of burning sun and sickly damp, the effects of the late
storms, we emerged from the waste of vegetation, passed through
a straggling "neck o' the woods," whose yellow inmates reminded me of Mississippian descriptions in the days gone by, and after
spanning some very rough ground we bade adieu to the valley
of the Missouri, and emerged upon the region of the Grand Prairie,† which we will pronounce "perrairey."

Differing from the card-table surfaces of the formation in Illinois and the lands east of the Mississippi, the Western prairies
are rarely flat ground. Their elevation above sea-level varies
from 1000 to 2500 feet, and the plateau's aspect impresses the eye
with an exaggerated idea of elevation, there being no object of
comparison—mountain, hill, or sometimes even a tree—to give a
juster measure. Another peculiarity of the prairie is, in places,
its seeming horizontality, whereas it is never level: on an open
plain, apparently flat as a man's palm, you cross a long ground-
swell which was not perceptible before, and on its farther incline
you come upon a chasm wide and deep enough to contain a settlement. The aspect was by no means unprepossessing. Over
the rolling surface, which, however, rarely breaks into hill and
dale, lay a tapestry of thick grass already turning to a ruddy yellow under the influence of approaching autumn. The uniformity
was relieved by streaks of livelier green in the rich soils of the
slopes, hollows, and ravines, where the water gravitates, and, in
the deeper "intervales" and bottom lands on the banks of streams
and courses, by the graceful undulations and the waving lines of

---

* The basswood (*Tilia Americana*) resembles our linden : the trivial name is derived from "bast," its inner bark being used for mats and cordage. From the pli-
ability of the bark and wood, the name of the tree is made synonymous with "dough-
face" in the following extract from one of Mr. Brigham Young's sermons : "I say,
as the Lord lives, we are bound to become a sovereign state in the Union, or an independent nation by ourselves ; and let them drive us from this place if they can—
they can not do it. I do not throw this out as a banter. You Gentiles, and hickory
and *basswood* Mormons, can write it down, if you please ; but write it as I speak it."
The above has been extracted from a "Dictionary of Americanisms," by John Russell Bartlett (London, Trübner and Co., 1859), a glossary which the author's art has
made amusing as a novel.

† The word is somewhat indefinite. Hunters apply it generally to the bare lands
lying westward of the timbered course of the Mississippi ; in fact, to the whole region
from the southern Rio Grande to the Great Slave Lake.

B

mottes or prairie islands, thick clumps and patches simulating or-
chards by the side of cultivated fields. The silvery cirri and cu-
muli of the upper air flecked the surface of earth with spots of
dark cool shade, surrounded by a blaze of sunshine, and by their
motion, as they trooped and chased one another, gave a peculiar
liveliness to the scene; while here and there a bit of hazy blue
distance, a swell of the sea-like land upon the far horizon, gladdened the sight—every view is fair from afar. Nothing, I may
remark, is more monotonous, except perhaps the African and Indian jungle, than those prairie tracts, where the circle of which
you are the centre has but about a mile of radius; it is an ocean
in which one loses sight of land. You see, as it were, the ends of
the earth, and look around in vain for some object upon which
the eye may rest: it wants the sublimity of repose so suggestive
in the sandy deserts, and the perpetual motion so pleasing in the
aspect of the sea. No animals appeared in sight where, thirty
years ago, a band of countless bisons dotted the plains; they will,
however, like the wild aborigines, their congeners, soon be followed by beings higher in the scale of creation. These prairies are
preparing to become the great grazing-grounds which shall supply the unpopulated East with herds of civilized kine, and perhaps with the yak of Tibet, the llama of South America, and the
koodoo and other African antelopes.

As we sped onward we soon made acquaintance with a tradi-
tionally familiar feature, the "pitch-holes," or "chuck-holes"—the
ugly word is not inappropriate—which render traveling over the
prairies at times a sore task. They are gullies and gutters, not
unlike the Canadian "cahues" of snow formation: varying from
10 to 50 feet in breadth, they are rivulets in spring and early summer, and—few of them remain perennial—they lie dry during the
rest of the year. Their banks are slightly raised, upon the principle, *in parvo*, that causes mighty rivers, like the Po and the Indus, to run along the crests of ridges, and usually there is in the
sole a dry or wet cunette, steep as a step, and not unfrequently
stony; unless the break be attended to, it threatens destruction to
wheel and axle-tree, to hound and tongue. The pitch-hole is more
frequent where the prairies break into low hills; the inclines along
which the roads run then become a net-work of these American
nullahs.

Passing through a few wretched shanties* called Troy—last
insult to the memory of hapless Pergamus—and Syracuse (here
we are in the third, or classic stage of United States nomenclature), we made, at 3 P.M., Cold Springs, the junction of the Leavenworth route. Having taken the northern road to avoid rough
ground and bad bridges, we arrived about two hours behind time.
The aspect of things at Cold Springs, where we were allowed an

* American authors derive the word from the Canadian *chienté*, a dog-kennel. It
is, however, I believe, originally Irish.

hour's halt to dine and to change mules, somewhat dismayed our fine-weather prairie travelers. The scene was the *rale* "Far West." The widow body to whom the shanty belonged lay sick with fever. The aspect of her family was a "caution to snakes:" the ill-conditioned sons dawdled about, listless as Indians, in skin tunics and pantaloons fringed with lengthy tags such as the redoubtable "Billy Bowlegs" wears on tobacco labels; and the daughters, tall young women, whose sole attire was apparently a calico morning-wrapper, color invisible, waited upon us in a protesting way. Squalor and misery were imprinted upon the wretched log hut, which ignored the duster and the broom, and myriads of flies disputed with us a dinner consisting of doughnuts, green and poisonous with saleratus, suspicious eggs in a massive greasy fritter, and rusty bacon, intolerably fat. It was our first sight of squatter life, and, except in two cases, it was our worst. We could not grudge 50 cents a head to these unhappies; at the same time, we thought it a dear price to pay—the sequel disabused us—for flies and bad bread, worse eggs and bacon.

The next settlement, Valley Home, was reached at 6 P.M. Here the long wave of the ocean land broke into shorter seas, and for the first time that day we saw stones, locally called rocks (a Western term embracing every thing between a pebble and a boulder), the produce of nullahs and ravines. A well 10 to 12 feet deep supplied excellent water. The ground was in places so far reclaimed as to be divided off by posts and rails; the scanty crops of corn (Indian corn), however, were wilted and withered by the drought, which this year had been unusually long. Without changing mules we advanced to Kennekuk, where we halted for an hour's supper under the auspices of Major Baldwin, whilom Indian agent; the place was clean, and contained at least one charming face.

Kennekuk derives its name from a chief of the Kickapoos, in whose reservation we now are. This tribe, in the days of the Baron la Hontan (1689), a great traveler, but "aiblins," as Sir Walter Scott said of his grandmither, "a prodigious story-teller," then lived on the Rivière des Puants, or Fox River, upon the brink of a little lake supposed to be the Winnebago, near the Sakis (Osaki, Sawkis, Sauks, or Sacs),* and the Pouteoustamies (Potawotomies). They are still in the neighborhood of their

---

* In the days of Major Pike, who, in 1805-6-7, explored, by order of the government of the United States, the western territories of North America, the Sacs numbered 700 warriors and 750 women; they had four villages, and hunted on the Mississippi and its confluents from the Illinois to the Iowa River, and on the western plains that bordered on the Missouri. They were at peace with the Sioux, Osages, Potawotomies, Menomenes or Folles Avoines, Iowas, and other Missourian tribes, and were almost consolidated with the Foxes, with whose aid they nearly exterminated the Illinois, Cahokias, Kaskaskias, and Peorians. Their principal enemies were the Ojibwas. They raised a considerable quantity of maize, beans, and melons, and were celebrated for cunning in war rather than for courage.

dreaded foes, the Sacs and Foxes,* who are described as stalwart and handsome bands, and they have been accompanied in their southern migration from the waters westward of the Mississippi, through Illinois, to their present southern seats by other allies of the Winnebagoes,† the Iowas, Nez Percés, Ottoes, Omahas, Kansas, and Osages. Like the great nations of the Indian Territory, the Cherokees, Creeks, Choctaws, and Chickasaws, they form intermediate social links in the chain of civilization between the outer white settlements and the wild nomadic tribes to the west, the Dakotahs and Arapahoes, the Snakes and Cheyennes. They cultivate the soil, and rarely spend the winter in hunting buffalo upon the plains. Their reservation is twelve miles by twenty-four; as usual with land set apart for the savages, it is well watered and timbered, rich and fertile; it lies across the path and in the vicinity of civilization; consequently, the people are greatly demoralized. The men are addicted to intoxication, and the women to unchastity; both sexes and all ages are inveterate beggars, whose principal industry is horse-stealing. Those Scottish clans were the most savage that vexed the Lowlands, it is the case here: the tribes nearest the settlers are best described by Colonel B——'s phrase, "great liars and dirty dogs." They have well-nigh cast off the Indian attire, and rejoice in the splendors of boiled and ruffled shirts, after the fashion of the whites. According to our host, a stalwart son of that soil which for generations has sent out her best blood westward, Kain-tuk-ee, the Land of the Cane, the Kickapoos number about 300 souls, of whom one fifth are braves. He quoted a specimen of their facetiousness: when they first saw a crinoline, they pointed to the wearer and cried, "There walks a wigwam." Our "vertugardin" of the 19th century has run the gauntlet of the world's jests, from the refined

---

* From the same source we learn that the Ottagamies, called by the French Les Renards, numbered 400 warriors and 500 women: they had three villages near the confluence of the Turkey River with the Mississippi, hunted on both sides of the Mississippi from the Iowa stream below the Prairie du Chien to a river of that name above the same village, and annually sold many hundred bushels of maize. Conjointly with the Sacs, the Foxes protected the Iowas, and the three people, since the first treaty of the two former with the United States, claimed the land from the entrance of the Jauflione on the western side of the Mississippi, up the latter river to the Iowa above the Prairie du Chien, and westward to the Missouri. In 1807 they had ceded their lands lying south of the Mississippi to the United States, reserving to themselves, however, the privileges of hunting and residing on them.

† The Winnebagoes, Winnipegs (turbid water), or Ochangras numbered, in 1807, 450 warriors and 500 women, and had seven villages on the Wisconsin, Rock, and Fox Rivers, and Green Bay: their proximity enabled the tribe to muster in force within four days. They then hunted on the Rock River, and the eastern side of the Mississippi, from Rock River to the Prairie du Chien, on Lake Michigan, on Black River, and in the countries between Lakes Michigan, Huron, and Superior. Lieutenant Pike is convinced, "from a tradition among themselves, and their speaking the same language as the Ottoes of the Platte River," that they are a tribe who about 150 years before his time had fled from the oppression of the Mexican Spaniards, and had become clients of the Sioux. They have ever been distinguished for ferocity and treachery.

impertinence of Mr. Punch to the rude grumble of the American Indian and the Kaffir of the Cape.

Beyond Kennekuk we crossed the first Grasshopper Creek. Creek, I must warn the English reader, is pronounced "crik," and in these lands, as in the jargon of Australia, means not "an arm of the sea," but a small stream of sweet water, a rivulet; the rivers of Europe, according to the Anglo-American of the West, are "criks." On our line there are many grasshopper creeks; they anastomose with, or debouch into, the Kansas River, and they reach the sea *viâ* the Missouri and the Mississippi. This particular Grasshopper was dry and dusty up to the ankles; timber clothed the banks, and slabs of sandstone cumbered the sole. Our next obstacle was the Walnut Creek, which we found, however, provided with a corduroy bridge; formerly it was a dangerous ford, rolling down heavy streams of melted snow, and then crossed by means of the "bouco" or coracle, two hides sewed together, distended like a leather tub with willow rods, and poled or paddled. At this point the country is unusually well populated; a house appears after every mile. Beyond Walnut Creek a dense nimbus, rising ghost-like from the northern horizon, furnished us with a spectacle of those perilous prairie storms which make the prudent lay aside their revolvers and disembarrass themselves of their cartridges. Gusts of raw, cold, and violent wind from the west whizzed overhead, thunder crashed and rattled closer and closer, and vivid lightning, flashing out of the murky depths around, made earth and air one blaze of living fire. Then the rain began to patter ominously upon the carriages; the canvas, however, by swelling, did its duty in becoming water-tight, and we rode out the storm dry. Those learned in the weather predicted a succession of such outbursts, but the prophecy was not fulfilled. The thermometer fell about 6° (F.), and a strong north wind set in, blowing dust or gravel, a fair specimen of "Kansas gales," which are equally common in Nebraska, especially during the month of October. It subsided on the 9th of August.

Arriving about 1 A.M. at Locknan's Station, a few log and timber huts near a creek well feathered with white oak and American elm, hickory and black walnut, we found beds and snatched an hourful of sleep.

8th August, to Rock Creek.

Resuming, through air refrigerated by rain, our now weary way, we reached at 6 A.M. a favorite camping-ground, the "Big Nemehaw" Creek, which, like its lesser neighbor, flows after rain into the Missouri River, *viâ* Turkey Creek, the Big Blue, and the Kansas. It is a fine bottom of rich black soil, whose green woods at that early hour were wet with heavy dew, and scattered over the surface lay pebbles and blocks of quartz and porphyritic granites. "Richland," a town mentioned in guide-books, having disappeared, we drove for breakfast to Seneca, a city consisting of a few shanties, mostly garnished with tall square lumber fronts, ineffectually, especially when the houses stand one by one, masking the diminutiveness of the buildings behind them. The land, probably in prospect of a Pacific Railroad, fetched the exaggerated price of $20 an acre, and already a lawyer has "hung out his shingle" there.

Refreshed by breakfast and the intoxicating air, brisk as a bottle of *veuve Clicquot*—it is this that gives one the "prairie fever" —we bade glad adieu to Seneca, and prepared for another long stretch of twenty-four hours. That day's chief study was of wagons, those ships of the great American Sahara which, gathering in fleets at certain seasons, conduct the traffic between the eastern and the western shores of a waste which is every where like a sea, and which presently will become salt. The white-topped wain—banished by railways from Pennsylvania, where, drawn by the "Conestoga horse," it once formed a marked feature in the landscape—has found a home in the Far West. They are not unpicturesque from afar, these long-winding trains, in early morning like lines of white cranes trooping slowly over the prairie, or in more mysterious evening resembling dim sails crossing a rolling sea. The vehicles are more simple than our Cape wagons— huge beds like punts mounted on solid wheels, with logs for brakes, and contrasting strongly with the emerald plain, white tilts of twilled cotton or osnaburg, supported by substantial oaken or hickory bows. The wain is literally a "prairie ship:" its body is often used as a ferry, and when hides are unprocurable the covering is thus converted into a "bull boat." Two stakes driven into the ground, to mark the length, are connected by a longitudinal keel and ribs of willow rods; cross-sticks are tied with thongs to prevent "caving in," and the canvas is strained over the frame-work. In this part of the country the wagon is unnecessarily heavy; made to carry 4000 lbs., it rarely carries 3000: westward I have seen many a load of 3½ tons of 2000 lbs. each, and have heard of even 6 tons. The wheels are of northern white oak, well seasoned under pain of perpetual repairs, the best material, "bow-dark" Osage orange-wood (*bois d'arc* or *Maclura aurantiaca*), which shrinks but little, being rarely procurable about Concord and Troy, the great centres of wagon manufacture. The neap or tongue (pole) is jointed where it enters the hounds, or these will be broken by the heavy jolts; and the perch is often made movable, so that after accidents a temporary conveyance can be made out of the débris. A long covered wooden box hangs behind: on the road it carries fuel; at the halt it becomes a trough, being preferred to nose-bags, which prevent the animals breathing comfortably; and in the hut, where every part of the wagon is utilized, it acts as a chest for valuables. A bucket swings beneath the vehicle, and it is generally provided with an extra chain for "coraling." The teams vary in number from six

to thirteen yoke; they are usually oxen, an "Old Country" prejudice operating against the use of cows.*   The yoke, of pine or
other light wood, is, as every where in the States, simple and effective, presenting a curious contrast to the uneasy and uncertain
contrivances which still prevail in the antiquated Campagna and
other classic parts of Europe.   A heavy cross-piece, oak or cotton-wood, is beveled out in two places, and sometimes lined with
sheet-lead, to fit the animals' necks, which are held firm in bows
of bent hickory passing through the yoke and pinned above.
The several pairs of cattle are connected by strong chains and
rings projecting from the under part of the wood-work.

THE WESTERN YOKE.

The "ripper," or driver, who is bound to the gold regions of
Pike's Peak, is a queer specimen of humanity.   He usually hails
from one of the old Atlantic cities—in fact, from settled America
—and, like the civilized man generally, he betrays a remarkable
aptitude for facile descent into savagery.   His dress is a harlequin-
ade, typical of his disposition.   Eschewing the chimney-pot or
stove-pipe tile of the bourgeois, he affects the "Kossuth," an
Anglo-American version of the sombrero, which converts felt into
every shape and form, from the jaunty little head-covering of the
modern sailor to the tall steeple-crown of the old Puritan.   He
disregards the trichotomy of St. Paul, and emulates St. Anthony
and the American aborigines in the length of his locks, whose
ends are curled inward, with a fascinating sausage-like roll not
unlike the Cockney "aggrawator."   If a young hand, he is probably in the buckskin mania, which may pass into the squaw
mania, a disease which knows no cure: the symptoms are, a leather coat and overalls to match, embroidered if possible, and finished
along the arms and legs with fringes cut as long as possible, while
a pair of gaudy moccasins, resplendent with red and blue porcelain beads, fits his feet tightly as silken hose.   I have heard of
coats worth $250, vests $100, and pants $150: indeed, the poorest
of buckskin suits will cost $75, and if hard-worked it must be re-
newed every six months.   The successful miner or the gambler
—in these lands the word is confined to the profession—will add
$10 gold buttons to the attractions of his attire.   The older hand
prefers to buckskin a "wamba" or round-about, a red or rainbow-

* According to Mormon rule, however, the full team consists of one wagon (12 ft.
long, 3 ft. 4 in. wide, and 18 in. deep), two yoke of oxen, and two milch cows.   The
Saints have ever excelled in arrangements for travel by land and sea.

colored flannel over a check cotton shirt; his lower garments, garnished *a tergo* with leather, are turned into Hessians by being thrust inside his cow-hide Wellingtons; and, when in riding gear, he wraps below each knee a fold of deer, antelope, or cow skin, with edges scalloped where they fall over the feet, and gartered tightly against thorns and stirrup thongs, thus effecting that graceful elephantine bulge of the lower leg for which " Jack ashore" is justly celebrated. Those who suffer from sore eyes wear huge green goggles, which give a crab-like air to the physiognomy, and those who can not procure them line the circumorbital region with lampblack, which is supposed to act like the surma or kohl of the Orient. A broad leather belt supports on the right a revolver, generally Colt's Navy or medium size (when Indian fighting is expected, the large dragoon pistol is universally preferred); and on the left, in a plain black sheath, or sometimes in the more ornamental Spanish scabbard, is a buck-horn or ivory-handled bowie-knife. In the East the driver partially conceals his tools; he has no such affectation in the Far West: moreover, a glance through the wagon-awning shows guns and rifles stowed along the side. When driving he is armed with a mammoth fustigator, a system of plaited cow-hides cased with smooth leather; it is a knout or an Australian stock-whip, which, managed with both hands, makes the sturdiest ox curve and curl its back. If he trudges along an ox-team, he is a grim and grimy man, who delights to startle your animals with a whip-crack, and disdains to return a salutation: if his charge be a muleteer's, you may expect more urbanity; he is then in the " upper-crust" of teamsters; he knows it, and demeans himself accordingly. He can do nothing without whisky, which he loves to call tarantula juice, strychnine, red-eye, corn juice, Jersey lightning, leg-stretcher, " tangle-leg,"* and many other hard and grotesque names; he chews tobacco like a horse; he becomes heavier " *on* the shoulder" or " *on* the shyoot," as, with the course of empire, he makes his way westward; and he frequently indulges in a " spree," which in these lands means four acts of drinking-bout, with a fifth of rough-and-tumble. Briefly, he is a post-wagon driver exaggerated.

Each train is accompanied by men on horse or mule back—oxen are not ridden after Cape fashion in these lands.† The equipment of the cavalier excited my curiosity, especially the saddle, which has been recommended by good authorities for military use. The coming days of fast warfare, when " heavies," if not wholly

---

* For instance, " whisky is now tested by the distance a man can walk after tasting it. The new liquor called ' Tangle-leg' is said to be made of diluted alcohol, nitric acid, pepper, and tobacco, and will upset a man at a distance of 400 yards from the demijohn."

† Captain Marcy, in quoting Mr. Andersson's remarks on ox-riding in South-western Africa, remarks that " a ring instead of a stick put through the cartilage of the animal's nose would obviate the difficulty of managing it." As in the case of the camel, a ring would soon be torn out by an obstinate beast : a stick resists.

banished to the limbo of things that were, will be used as mounted "beef-eaters," only for show, demand a saddle with as little
weight as is consistent with strength, and one equally easy to the
horse and the rider. In no branch of improvement, except in
hat-making for the army, has so little been done as in saddles.
The English military or hunting implement still endures without
other merit than facility to the beast, and, in the man's case, faculty of falling uninjured with his horse. Unless the rider be cop-
per-lined and iron-limbed, it is little better in long marches than
a rail for riding. As far as convenience is concerned, an Arab
pad is preferable to Peat's best. But the Californian saddle can
not supply the deficiency, as will, I think, appear in the course of
description.

The native Indian saddle is probably the degenerate offspring
of the European pack-saddle: two short forks, composing the
pommel and cantle, are nailed or lashed to a pair of narrow side-
boards, and the rude tree is kept in shape by a green skin or hide
allowed to shrink on. It remarkably resembles the Abyssinian,
the Somal, and the Circassian saddle, which, like the "dug-out"
canoe, is probably the primitive form instinctively invented by
mankind. It is the sire of the civilized saddle, which in these
lands varies with every region. The Texan is known by its circular seat; a string passed round the tree forms a ring: provided
with flaps after the European style, it is considered easy and comfortable. The Californian is rather oval than circular; borrowed
and improved from the Mexican, it has spread from the Pacific to
the Atlantic slope of the Rocky Mountains, and the hardy and
experienced mountaineer prefers it to all others: it much resembles the Hungarian, and in some points recalls to mind the old
French cavalry demipique. It is composed of a single tree of
light strong wood, admitting a freer circulation of air to the horse's
spine — an immense advantage — and, being without iron, it can
readily be taken to pieces, cleaned or mended, and refitted. The
tree is strengthened by a covering of raw-hide carefully sewed
on; it rests upon a "sweat-leather," a padded sheet covering the
back, and it is finished off behind with an "anchero" of the same
material protecting the loins. The pommel is high, like the crutch
of a woman's saddle, rendering impossible, under pain of barking
the knuckles, that rule of good riding which directs the cavalier
to keep his hands low. It prevents the inexperienced horseman
being thrown forward, and enables him to "hold on" when likely to be dismounted; in the case of a good rider, its only use is
to attach the lariat, riata, or lasso. The great merit of this "unicorn" saddle is its girthing: with the English system, the strain
of a wild bull or of a mustang "bucker" would soon dislodge the
riding gear. The "sincho" is an elastic horsehair cingle, five to
six inches wide, connected with "lariat straps," strong thongs
passing round the pommel and cantle; it is girthed well back

from the horse's shoulder, and can be drawn till the animal suffers
pain: instead of buckle, the long terminating strap is hitched
two or three times through an iron ring. The whole saddle is
covered with a machila, here usually pronounced *macheer*, two
pieces of thick leather handsomely and fancifully worked or
stamped, joined by a running thong in the centre, and open to
admit the pommel and cantle. If too long, it draws in the stirrup-leathers, and cramps the ankles of any but a bowlegged man.
The machila is sometimes garnished with pockets, always with
straps behind to secure a valise, and a cloak can be fastened over
the pommel, giving purchase and protection to the knees. The
rider sits erect, with the legs in a continuation of the body line,
and the security of the balance-seat enables him to use his arms
freely: the *pose* is that of the French schools in the last century,
heels up and toes down. The advantages of this equipment are
obvious; it is easier to horse and man probably than any yet invented. On the other hand, the quantity of leather renders it
expensive: without silver or other ornaments, the price would
vary from $25 at San Francisco to $50 at Great Salt Lake City,
and the highly got-up rise to $250=£50 for a saddle! If the
saddle-cloth slips out, and this is an accident which frequently
occurs, the animal's back will be galled. The stirrup-leathers
can not be shortened or lengthened without dismounting, and
without leggins the board-like leather *macheer* soon makes the
mollets innocent of skin. The pommel is absolutely dangerous:
during my short stay in the country I heard of two accidents, one
fatal, caused by the rider being thrown forward on his fork. Finally, the long seat, which is obligatory, answers admirably with
the Californian pacer or canterer, but with the high-trotting military horse it would inevitably lead—as has been proved before
the European stirrup-leather was shortened—to hernias and other
accidents.

To the stirrups I have but one serious objection—they can not
be made to open in case of the horse falling; when inside the
stiff leather *macheer*, they cramp the legs by bowing them inward, but habit soon cures this. Instead of the light iron contrivances which before recovered play against the horse's side,
which freeze the feet in cold, and which toast them in hot weather, this stirrup is sensibly made of wood. In the Eastern States
it is a lath bent somewhat in the shape of the dragoon form, and
has too little weight; the Californian article is cut out of a solid
block of wood, mountain mahogany being the best, then maple,
and lastly the softer pine and cotton-wood. In some parts of the
country it is made so narrow that only the toe fits in, and then
the instep is liable to be bruised. For riding through bush and
thorns, it is provided in front with zapateros or leathern curtains,
secured to the straps above, and to the wood on both sides: they
are curiously made, and the size, like that of the Turk's lantern,

denotes the owner's fashionableness; dandies may be seen with the pointed angles of their stirrup-guards dangling almost to the ground. The article was borrowed from Mexico—the land of character dresses. When riding through prickly chapparal, the leathers begin higher up, and protect the leg from the knee downward. I would not recommend this stirrup for Hyde Park, or even Brighton; but in India and other barbarous parts of the British empire, where, on a cold morning's march, men and officers may be seen with wisps of straw defending their feet from the iron, and on African journeys, where the bush is more than a match for any texture yet woven, it might, methinks, be advantageously used.

The same may be said of the spurs, which, though cruel in appearance, are really more merciful than ours. The rowels have spikes about two inches long; in fact, are the shape and size of a small starfish; but they are never sharpened, and the tinkle near the animal's sides serves to urge it on without a real application. The two little bell-like pendants of metal on each side of the rowel-hinge serve to increase the rattling, and when a poor rider is mounted upon a tricksy horse, they lock the rowels, which are driven into the sincho, and thus afford another *point d'appui.* If the rider's legs be long enough, the spurs can be clinched under the pony's belly. Like the Mexican, they can be made expensive: $25 a pair would be a common price.

The bridle is undoubtedly the worst part of the horse's furniture. The bit is long, clumsy, and not less cruel than a Chifney. I have seen the Arab ring, which, with sufficient leverage, will break a horse's jaw, and another, not unlike an East Indian invention, with a sharp triangle to press upon the animal's palate, apparently for the purpose of causing it to rear and fall backward. It is the offspring of the Mexican manége, which was derived, through Spain, from the Moors.

Passing through Ash Point at 9 30 A.M., and halting for water at Uncle John's Grocery, where hang-dog Indians, squatting, standing, and stalking about, showed that the forbidden luxury—essence of corn—was, despite regulations, not unprocurable there, we spanned the prairie to Guittard's Station. This is a clump of board houses on the far side of a shady, well-wooded creek—the Vermilion, a tributary of the Big Blue River, so called from its red sandstone bottom, dotted with granitic and porphyritic boulders.

Our conductor had sprained his ankle, and the driver, being in plain English drunk, had dashed like a Phaeton over the "chuck-holes;" we willingly, therefore, halted at 11 30 A.M. for dinner. The host was a young Alsatian, who, with his mother and sister, had emigrated under the excitement of Californian fever, and had been stopped, by want of means, half way. The improvement upon the native was palpable: the house and kitchen were clean, the fences neat; the ham and eggs, the hot rolls and coffee, were fresh and good, and, although drought had killed the salad, we had abundance of peaches and cream, an offering of French to American taste which, in its simplicity, luxuriates in the curious mixture of lacteal with hydrocyanic acid.

At Guittard's I saw, for the first time, the Pony Express rider arrive. In March, 1860, "the great dream of news transmitted from New York to San Francisco (more strictly speaking from St. Joseph to Placerville, California) in eight days was tested." It appeared, in fact, under the form of an advertisement in the St. Louis "Republican,"* and threw at once into the shade the great Butterfield Mail, whose expedition had been the theme of universal praise. Very meritoriously has the contract been fulfilled. At the moment of writing (Nov., 1860), the distance between New York and San Francisco has been farther reduced by the advance of the electric telegraph—it proceeds at the rate of six miles a day—to Fort Kearney from the Mississippi and to Fort Churchill from the Pacific side. The merchant thus receives his advices in six days. The contract of the government with Messrs. Russell, Majors, and Co., to run the mail from St. Joseph to Great Salt Lake City, expired the 30th of November, and it was proposed to continue it only from Julesburg on the crossing of the South Platte, 480 miles west of St. Joseph. Mr. Russell, however, objected, and so did the Western States generally, to abbreviating the mail-service as contemplated by the Post-office Department. His spirit and energy met with supporters whose interest it was not to fall back on the times when a communication between New

* The following is the first advertisement:

"*To San Francisco in eight days, by the Central Overland California and Pike's Peak Express Company.*

"The first courier of the 'Pony Express' will leave the Missouri River on Tuesday, April the 3d, at — o'clock P.M., and will run regularly weekly hereafter, carrying a letter mail only. The point on the Missouri River will be in telegraphic communication with the East, and will be announced in due time.

"Telegraphic messages from all parts of the United States and Canada, in connection with the point of departure, will be received up to 5 o'clock P.M. of the day of leaving, and transmitted over the Placerville and St. Joseph Telegraph-wire to San Francisco and intermediate points by the connecting Express in eight days. The letter mail will be delivered in San Francisco in ten days from the departure of the Express. The Express passes through Forts Kearney, Laramie, and Bridger, Great Salt Lake City, Camp Floyd, Carson City, the Washoe Silver Mines, Placerville, and Sacramento. And letters for Oregon, Washington Territory, British Columbia, the Pacific Mexican Ports, Russian Possessions, Sandwich Islands, China, Japan, and India, will be mailed in San Francisco.

"Special messengers, bearers of letters, to connect with the Express of the 3d April, will receive communications for the Courier of that day at No. 481 Tenth Street, Washington City, up to 2 45 P.M. on Friday, March 30th; and in New York, at the office of J.B. Simpson, Room No. 8 Continental Bank Building, Nassau Street, up to 6 50 A.M. of 31st March.

"Full particulars can be obtained on application at the above places, and from the Agents of the Company.   W. H. RUSSELL, President.
"Leavenworth City, Kansas, March, 1860.

"*Office, New York.*—J. B. Simpson, Vice-President; Samuel and Allen, Agents, St. Louis, Mo.; H. J. Spaulding, Agent, Chicago."

York and California could not be secured short of twenty-five or thirty days; and, aided by the newspapers, he obtained a renewal of his contract. The riders are mostly youths, mounted upon active and lithe Indian nags. They ride 100 miles at a time—about eight per hour—with four changes of horses, and return to their stations the next day: of their hardships and perils we shall hear more anon. The letters are carried in leathern bags, which are thrown about carelessly enough when the saddle is changed, and the average postage is $5 = £1 per sheet.

Beyond Guittard's the prairies bore a burnt-up aspect. Far as the eye could see the tintage was that of the Arabian Desert, sere and tawny as a jackal's back. It was still, however, too early; October is the month for those prairie fires which have so frequently exercised the Western author's pen. Here, however, the grass is too short for the full development of the phenomenon, and beyond the Little Blue River there is hardly any risk. The fire can easily be stopped, *ab initio*, by blankets, or by simply rolling a barrel; the African plan of beating down with boughs might also be used in certain places; and when the conflagration has extended, travelers can take refuge in a little Zoar by burning the vegetation to windward. In Texas and Illinois, however, where the grass is tall and rank, and the roaring flames leap before the wind with the stride of maddened horses, the danger is imminent, and the spectacle must be one of awful sublimity.

In places where the land seems broken with bluffs, like an iron-bound coast, the skeleton of the earth becomes visible; the formation is a friable sandstone, overlying fossiliferous lime, which is based upon beds of shale. These undergrowths show themselves at the edges of the ground-waves and in the dwarf precipices, where the soil has been degraded by the action of water. The yellow-brown humus varies from forty to sixty feet deep in the most favored places, and erratic blocks of porphyry and various granites encumber the dry water-courses and surface drains. In the rare spots where water then lay, the herbage was still green, forming oases in the withering waste, and showing that irrigation is its principal, if not its only want.

Passing by Marysville, in old maps Palmetto City, a county town which thrives by selling whisky to ruffians of all descriptions, we forded before sunset the "Big Blue," a well-known tributary of the Kansas River. It is a pretty little stream, brisk and clear as crystal, about forty or fifty yards wide by 2·50 feet deep at the ford. The soil is sandy and solid, but the banks are too precipitous to be pleasant when a very drunken driver hangs on by the lines of four very weary mules. We then stretched once more over the "divide"—the ground, generally rough or rolling, between the fork or junction of two streams, in fact, the Indian Doab—separating the Big Blue from its tributary the Little Blue. At 6 P.M. we changed our fagged animals for fresh, and the land

of Kansas for Nebraska, at Cotton-wood Creek, a bottom where
trees flourished, where the ground had been cleared for corn, and
where we detected the prairie wolf watching for the poultry.   The
fur of our first coyote was light yellow-brown, with a tinge of red,
the snout long and sharp, the tail bushy and hanging, the gait
like a dog's, and the manner expressive of extreme timidity; it
is a far more cowardly animal than the larger white buffalo-wolf
and the black wolf of the woods, which are also far from fierce.
At Cotton-wood Station we took "on board" two way-passengers,
"lady" and "gentleman," who were drafted into the wagon containing the Judiciary.   A weary drive over a rough and dusty
road, through chill night air and clouds of musquetoes, which we
were warned would accompany us to the Pacific slope of the
Rocky Mountains, placed us about 10 P.M. at Rock, also called
Turkey Creek—surely a misnomer; no turkey ever haunted so
villainous a spot!   Several passengers began to suffer from fever
and nausea; in such travel the second night is usually the crisis,
after which a man can endure for an indefinite time.   The "ranch"
was a nice place for invalids, especially for those of the softer sex.
Upon the bedded floor of the foul "doggery" lay, in a seemingly
promiscuous heap, men, women, children, lambs, and puppies, all
fast in the arms of Morpheus, and many under the influence of a
much jollier god.   The *employés*, when aroused pretty roughly,
blinked their eyes in the atmosphere of smoke and musquetoes,
and declared that it had been "merry in hall" that night—the
effects of which merriment had not passed off.   After half an
hour's dispute about who should do the work, they produced cold
scraps of mutton and a kind of bread which deserves a totally
distinct generic name.   The strongest stomachs of the party made
tea, and found some milk which was not more than one quarter
flies.   This succulent meal was followed by the usual douceur.
On this road, however mean or wretched the fare, the station-
keeper, who is established by the proprietor of the line, never
derogates by lowering his price.

The Valley of the Little Blue, 9th August.
    A little after midnight we resumed our way, and in the state
which Mohammed described when he made his famous night
journey to heaven—*bayni 'l naumi wa 'l yakzán*—we crossed the
deep shingles, the shallow streams, and the heavy vegetation of
the Little Sandy, and five miles beyond it we forded the Big
Sandy.   About early dawn we found ourselves at another station,
better than the last only as the hour was more propitious.   The
colony of Patlanders rose from their beds without a dream of ablution, and clearing the while their lungs of Cork brogue, prepared a neat *déjeûner à la fourchette* by hacking "fids" off half a
sheep suspended from the ceiling, and frying them in melted tal-
low.   Had the action occurred in Central Africa, among the Es-

quimaux, or the Araucanians, it would not have excited my attention: mere barbarism rarely disgusts; it is the unnatural co-
habitation of civilization with savagery that makes the traveler's
gorge rise.

Issuing from Big Sandy Station at 6 30 A.M., and resuming
our route over the divide that still separated the valleys of the
Big Blue and the Little Blue, we presently fell into the line of
the latter, and were called upon by the conductor to admire it.
It is pretty, but its beauties require the cosmetic which is said to
act unfailingly in the case of fairer things—the viewer should
have lately spent three months at sea, out of sight of rivers and
women.   Averaging two miles in width, which shrinks to one
quarter as you ascend, the valley is hedged on both sides by low
rolling bluffs or terraces, the boundaries of its ancient bed and
modern debordements.   As the hills break off near the river, they
show a diluvial formation; in places they are washed into a variety of forms, and being white, they stand out in bold relief.   In
other parts they are sand mixed with soil enough to support a
last-year's growth of wheat-like grass, weed-stubble, and dead
trees, that look like old corn-fields in new clearings.   One could
not have recognized at this season Colonel Frémont's description
written in the month of June—the "hills with graceful slopes
looking uncommonly green and beautiful."   Along the bluffs the
road winds, crossing at times a rough projecting spur, or dipping
into some gully washed out by the rains of ages.   All is barren
beyond the garden-reach which runs along the stream; there is
not a tree to a square mile—in these regions the tree, like the bird
in Arabia and the monkey in Africa, signifies water—and animal
life seems well-nigh extinct.   As the land sinks toward the river
bottom, it becomes less barren.   The wild sunflower (*Helianthus*)
—it seldom, however, turns toward the sun—now becomes abundant; it was sparse near the Missouri; it will wax even more
plentiful around Great Salt Lake City, till walking through the
beds becomes difficult.   In size it greatly varies according to the
quality of the soil; six feet is perhaps the maximum.   It is a
growth of some value.   The oleaginous seeds form the principal
food of half-starved Indians, while the stalks supply them with a
scanty fuel: being of rapid growth, it has been used in the States
to arrest the flow of malaria, and it serves as house and home to
the rattlesnake.   Conspicuous by its side is the sumach, whose
leaf, mixed with kinnikinik, the peel of the red willow, forms the
immemorial smoking material of the Wild Man of the North.
Equally remarkable for their strong odor are large beds of wild
onions; they are superlatively wholesome, but they affect the
eater like those of Tibet.   The predominant colors are pink and
yellow, the former a lupine, the latter a shrub, locally called the
rabbit-bush.   The blue lupine also appears with the white mallow, the eccentric putoria, and the taraxacum (dandelion), so much

used as salad in France and in the Eastern·States. This land appears excellently adapted for the growth of manioc or cassava. In the centre of the bottom flows the brownish stream, about twenty yards wide, between two dense lines of tall sweet cottonwood. The tree which was fated to become familiar to us during our wanderings is a species of poplar (*P. monilifera*), called by the Americo-Spaniards, and by the people of Texas and New Mexico, " Alamo:" resembling the European aspen, without its silver lining, the color of the leaf, in places, appears of a dull burnished hue, in others bright and refreshingly green. Its trivial name is derived, according to some, from the fibrous quality of the bark, which, as in Norway, is converted into food for cattle and even man; according to others, from the cotton-like substance surrounding the seeds. It is termed " sweet" to distinguish it from a different tree with a bitter bark, also called a cotton-wood or narrow-leaved cotton-wood (*Populus angustifolia*), and by the Canadians *liard amère*. The timber is soft and easily cut; it is in many places the only material for building and burning, and the recklessness of the squatters has already shortened the supply.

This valley is the Belgium of the adjoining tribes, the once terrible Pawnees, who here met their enemies, the Dakotahs and the Delawares: it was then a great buffalo ground; and even twenty years ago it was well stocked with droves of wild horses, turkeys, and herds of antelope, deer, and elk. The animals have of late migrated westward, carrying off with them the " bones of contention." Some details concerning the present condition of these bands and their neighbors may not be uninteresting—these poor remnants of nations which once kept the power of North America at bay, and are now barely able to struggle for existence.

In 1853, the government of the United States, which has ever acted paternally toward the Indians, treating with them — Great Britain did the same with the East Indians—as though they were a civilized people, availed itself of the savages' desire to sell lands encroached upon by the whites, and set apart for a general reservation 181,171 square miles. Here, in the Far West, were collected into what was then believed to be a permanent habitation, the indigenes of the land, and the various bands once lying east of the Mississippi. This " Indian's home" was bounded, in 1853, on the north by the Northwestern Territory and Minnesota; on the south by Texas and New Mexico; to the east lay Iowa, Missouri, and Arkansas; and to the west, Oregon, Utah, and New Mexico.

The savages' reservation was then thus distributed. The eastern portion nearest the river was stocked with tribes removed to it from the Eastern States, namely, the Iowas, Sacs and Foxes, Kickapoos, Delawares, Potawotomies, Wyandottes, Quapaws, Senecas, Cherokees, Seminoles, Creeks, Choctaws, Chickasaws, Miamis, and Ottawas. The west and part of the northeast — poor and barren lands — were retained by the aboriginal tribes, Ponkahs, Omahas or Mahas, Pawnees, Ottoes, Kansas or Konzas, and Osages. The central and the remainder of the western portion — wild countries abounding in buffalo — were granted to the Western Pawnees, the Arickarees, Arapahoes, Cheyennes, Kiowas, Comanches, Utahs, Grosventres, and other nomads.

It was somewhat a confusion of races. For instance, the Pawnees form an independent family, to which some authors join the Arickaree; the Sacs (Sauk) and Foxes, Winnebagoes, Ottoes, Kaws, Omahas, Cheyennes, Mississippi Dakotahs, and Missouri Dakotahs, belong to the Dakotan family; the Choctaws, Creeks, and Seminoles are Appalachians; the Wyandottes, like the Iroquois, are Hodesaunians; and the Ottawas, Delawares, Shawnees, Potawotomies, Peorians, Mohekuneuks, Kaskaskias, Piankeshaws, Weaws, Miamis, Kickapoos, and the Menomenes, are, like the Ojibwas, Algonquins.

The total number of Indians on the prairies and the Rocky Mountains was estimated roughly at 63,000.

Still the resistless tide of emigration swept westward: the federal government was as powerless to stem it as was General Fitzroy of New South Wales to prevent, in 1852, his subjects flocking to the "gold diggings." Despite all orders, reckless whites would squat upon, and thoughtless reds, bribed by whisky, tobacco, and gunpowder, would sell off the lands. On the 20th of May, 1854, was passed the celebrated "Kansas-Nebraska Bill," an act converting the greater portion of the "Indian Territory," and all the "Northwestern Territory," into two new territories—Kansas, north of the 37th parallel, and Nebraska, north of the 40th. In the passage of this bill, the celebrated "Missouri Compromise" of 1828, prohibiting negro slavery north of 36° 30', was repealed, under the presidency of General Pierce.* It provided that the

---

* The "Missouri Compromise" is an important event in Anglo-American history; it must be regarded as the great parent of the jangles and heart-burnings which have disunited the United States. The great Jefferson prophesied in these words: "the Missouri question is a breaker on which we lose the Missouri country by revolt, and what more God only knows. From the battle of Bunker's Hill to the treaty of Paris, we never had so ominous a question."

The origin of the trouble was this. In 1817 the eastern half of the Mississippi Territory became the Territory of Alabama, and—in those days events had wings—the 14th of Dec., 1819, witnessed the birth of Alabama as a free sovereign and independent slave state. The South, strong in wealth and numbers, thereupon moved toward legalizing slavery in the newly-acquired Territory of Missouri, and when Missouri claimed to be admitted as a state, demanded that it should be admitted as a slave state. The Free-soilers, or opposite party, urged two reasons why Missouri should be a free state. Firstly, since the date of the union eight new states had been admitted, four slave and four free. Alabama, the last, was a slave state, therefore it was the turn for a free state. Secondly—and here was the rub—that "slavery ought not to be permitted in any state or territory where it could be prohibited." This very broad principle involved, it is manifest, the ruin of the slave-ocracy. From the days of Mr. Washington to those of Mr. Lincoln, the northern or labor states have ever aimed at the ultimate abolition of servitude by means of non-extension.

C

rights and properties of the Indians, within their shrunken possessions, should be respected. By degrees the Indians sold their lands for whisky, as of old, and retired to smaller reservations. Of course, they suffered in the bargain ; the savage ever parts with his birthright for the well-known mess of pottage. The Osages, for instance, canceled $4000, claimed by unscrupulous traders, by a cession of two million acres of arable land. The Potawotomies fared even worse; under the influence of liquor, ὡς λέγουσι, their chiefs sold 100,000 acres of the best soil on the banks of the Missouri for a mere song. The tribe was removed to a bald smooth prairie, sans timber and consequently sans game ; many fled to the extreme wilds, and the others, like the Acadians of yore, were marched about till they found homes — many of them six feet by two — in Fever Patch, on the Kaw or Kansas River. Others were more fortunate. The Ottoes, Omahas, and Kansas had permanent villages near the Missouri and its two tributaries, the Platte and the Kansas. The Osages, formerly a large nation in Arkansas, after ceding 10,000,000 of acres for a stipend of $52,000 for thirty years, were settled in a district on the west bank of the Neosho or Whitewater—the Grand River. They are described as the finest and largest men of the semi-nomad races, with well-formed heads and symmetrical figures, brave, warlike, and well disposed to the whites. Early in June, after planting their maize, they move in mounted bands to the prairies, feast upon the buffalo for months, and bring home stores of smoked and jerked meat. When the corn is in milk they husk and sundry it; it is then boiled, and is said to be better flavored and more nutritious than the East Indian " butah" or the American hominy. After the harvest in October they return to the game country, and then pass the winter under huts or skin lodges. Their chief scourge is small-pox : apparently, all the tribes carry some cross. Of the settled races the best types are the Choctaws and the Cherokees; the latter have shown a degree of improv-

---

The contest about Missouri began in 1818, and raged for three years, complicated by a new feature, namely, Maine separating herself from Massachusetts, and balancing the admission of Alabama by becoming a free state. The Lower House several times voted to exclude the "peculiar institution" from the new state, and the conservative Senate — in which the Southern element was ever predominant — as often restored it. Great was the war of words among the rival legislators; at length, after repeated conferences, both Senate and House agreed upon a bill admitting Missouri, after her Constitution should be formed, free of restriction, but prohibiting slavery north of 36° 30'. Missouri acknowledged the boon by adopting a Constitution which denied the rights of citizens even to free negroes. She was not finally admitted until the 10th of August, 1821, when her Legislature had solemnly covenanted to guarantee the rights of citizenship to "the citizens of either of the states." Such is an outline of the far-famed " Missouri Compromise." The influence of the Southern slaveholders caused it to be repealed, as a slip of Texas happened to lie north of the prohibitative latitude, and the late Mr. S. A. Douglas did it to death in 1854. The Free-soilers, of course, fought hard against the "sad repeal," and what they now fight about, forty years afterward, is to run still farther south the original line of limitation. *Hinc illæ lachrymæ !*

ability, which may still preserve them from destruction; they have a form of government, churches, theatres, and schools; they read and write English; and George Guess, a well-known chief, like the negro inventor of the Vai syllabarium in West Africa, produced an alphabet of sixty-eight characters, which, improved and simplified by the missionaries, is found useful in teaching the vernacular.

Upon the whole, however, the philanthropic schemes of the government have not met with brilliant success. The chiefs are still bribed, and the people cheated by white traders, and poverty, disease, and debauchery rapidly thin the tribesmen. Sensible heads have proposed many schemes for preserving the race. Apparently the best of these projects is to introduce the Moravian discipline. Of all missionary systems, I may observe, none have hitherto been crowned with important results, despite the blood and gold so profusely expended upon them, except two—those of the Jesuits and the United Brethren. The fraternity of Jesus spread the Gospel by assimilating themselves to the heathen; the Unitas Fratrum by assimilating the heathen to themselves. The day of Jesuitism, like that of protection, is going by. The advance of Moravianism, it may safely be prophesied, is to come. These civilization societies have as yet been little appreciated, because they will not minister to that ignorant enthusiasm which extracts money from the pockets of the many. Their necessarily slow progress is irksome to ardent propagandists. We naturally wish to reap as well as to sow; and man rarely invests capital in schemes of which only his grandson will see the results.

The American philanthropist proposes to wean the Indian savage from his nomad life by turning his lodge into a log tent, and by providing him with cattle instead of buffalo, and the domestic fowl instead of grasshoppers. The hunter become a herdsman would thus be strengthened for another step—the agricultural life, which necessarily follows the pastoral. Factors would be appointed instead of vicious traders—*coureurs des bois*, as the Canadians call them; titles to land would be granted in fee-simple, practically teaching the value of property in severalty, alienation into white hands would be forbidden, and, if possible, a cordon militaire would be stretched between the races. The agricultural would lead to the mechanical stage of society. Agents and assistant craftsmen would teach the tribes to raise mills and smithies (at present there are mills without millers, stock without breeders, and similar attempts to make civilization run before she can walk), and a growing appreciation for the peace, the comfort, and the luxuries of settled life would lay the nomad instinct forever.

The project labors only under one difficulty—the one common to philanthropic schemes. In many details it is somewhat visionary—utopian. It is, like peace on earth, a "dream of the wise." Under the present system of Indian agencies, as will in a future page appear, it is simply impossible. It has terrible obstacles in the westward gravitation of the white race, which, after sweeping away the aborigines—as the gray rat in Europe expelled the black rat—from the east of the Mississippi in two centuries and a half, threatens, before a quarter of that time shall have elapsed, to drive in its advance toward the Pacific the few survivors of now populous tribes, either into the inhospitable regions north of the 49th parallel, or into the anarchical countries south of the 32d. And where, I may ask, in the history of the world do we read of a people learning civilization from strangers instead of working it out for themselves, through its several degrees of barbarism, feudalism, monarchy, republicanism, despotism? Still it is a noble project; mankind would not willingly see it die.

The Pawnees were called by the French and Canadian traders Les Loups, that animal being their totem, and the sign of the tribe being an imitation of the wolf's ears, the two fore fingers of the right hand being stuck up on the side of the head. They were in the last generation a large nation, containing many clans—Minnikajus, the Sans Arc, the Loup Fork, and others. Their territory embraced both sides of the Platte River, especially the northern lands; and they rendered these grounds terrible to the trapper, trader, and traveler. They were always well mounted. Old Mexico was then, and partially is still, their stable, and a small band has driven off horses by hundreds. Of late years they have become powerless. The influenza acts as a plague among them, killing off 400 or 500 in a single season, and the nation now numbers little more than 300 braves, or rather warriors, the latter, in correct parlance, being inferior to the former, as the former are subservient to the chief. A treaty concluded between them and the United States in the winter of 1857 sent them to a reserve on the Loup Fork, where their villages were destroyed by the Sioux. They are Ishmaelites, whose hand is against every man. They have attempted, after the fashion of declining tribes, to strengthen themselves by alliances with their neighbors, but have always failed in consequence of their propensity to plunder developing itself even before the powwow was concluded. They and the northern Dakotahs can never be trusted. Most Indian races, like the Bedouin Arabs, will show hospitality to the stranger who rides into their villages, though no point of honor deters them from robbing him after he has left the lodge-shade. The Pawnees, African-like, will cut the throat of a sleeping guest. They are easily distinguished from their neighbors by the scalp-lock protruding from a shaven head. After killing white men, they have insulted the corpse in a manner familiar to those who served in the Affghan war. They have given up the practice of torturing prisoners, saying that the "Great Spirit," or rather, as the expression should be translated, the "Great Father" no longer wills it. The tradition is, that a few years ago a squaw of a hostile tribe was snatched from the stake by a white trader, and the action was interpreted as a decree of heaven. It is probably a corruption of the well-known story of the rescue of the Itean woman by Petalesharoo, the son of the " Knife Chief." Like the Southern and Western Indians generally, as is truly remarked by Captain Mayne Reid,* " They possess more of that cold continence and chivalrous delicacy than characterize the Red Men of the forest." They are too treacherous to be used as soldiers. Like most pedestrian Indians, their arms and bodies are light and thin, and their legs are muscular and well developed. They are great in endurance. I have heard of a Pawnee, who, when thoroughly "stampeded" by his enemies, "loped" from Fort Laramie to Kearney—300 miles—making the distance as fast as the mail. This bad tribe is ever at war with their hereditary enemies the Sioux. They do not extend westward of Fort Kearney. The principal sub-tribe is the Arickaree, or Ree, called Pedani by the Dakotah, who attacked and conquered them. Their large villages, near the mouth of the Grand River, were destroyed by the expedition sent in 1825–26, under Colonel Leavenworth, to chastise the attack upon the trading party of General Ashley.

A more interesting people than the Pawnee is the Delaware, whose oldest tradition derives him from the region west of the Mississippi. Thence the tribe migrated to the Atlantic shores, where they took the title of Lenne Lenape, or men, and the neighboring races in respect called them " uncle." William Penn and his followers found this remnant of the great Algonquin confederacy in a depressed state: subjugated by the Five Nations, they had been compelled to take the name of " Iroquois Squaws." In those days they felt an awe of the white man, and looked upon him as a something godlike. Since their return to the West their spirit has revived, their war-path has reached through Utah to the Pacific Ocean, to Hudson's Bay on the north, and southward to the heart of Mexico. Their present abodes are principally near Fort Leavenworth upon the Missouri, and in the Choctaw territory near Fort Arbuckle, upon the eastern Colorado or Canadian River. They are familiar with the languages, manners, and customs of their pale-faced neighbors; they are so feared as rifle shots that a host of enemies will fly from a few of their warriors, and they mostly lead a vagrant life, the wandering Jews of the West, as traders, hunters, and trappers, among the other Indian tribes. For 185 years the Shawnees have been associated with them in intermarriage, yet they are declining in numbers; here and there some are lost, one by one, in travel or battle; they have now dwindled to about a hundred warriors, and the extinction of the tribe appears imminent. As hunters and guides, they are preferred to all others by the whites, and it is believed that they would make as formidable partisan soldiers as any on this conti-

* The Scalp-hunters, chap. xlii.

nent. When the government of the United States, after the fashion of France and England, begins to raise "Irregular Native Corps," the loss of the Delawares will be regretted.

Changing mules at Kiowa about 10 A.M., we pushed forward through the sun, which presently was mitigated by heavy nimbi, to Liberty Farm, where a station supplied us with the eternal eggs and bacon of these *mangeurs de lard*. It is a dish constant in the great West, as the omelet and pigeon in the vetturini days of Italy, when, prompted by the instincts of self-preservation, the inmates of the dove-cot, unless prevented in time, are said to have fled their homes at the sight of Milordo's traveling carriage, not to return until the portent had disappeared. The Little Blue ran hard by, about fifty feet wide by three or four deep, fringed with emerald-green oak groves, cotton-wood, and long-leaved willow: its waters supply catfish, suckers, and a soft-shelled turtle, but the fish are full of bones, and taste, as might be imagined, much like mud. The country showed vestiges of animal life, the prairie bore signs of hare and antelope; in the valley, coyotes, wolves, and foxes, attracted by the carcasses of cattle, stared us in the face, and near the stream, plovers, jays, the bluebird (sialia), and a kind of starling, called the swamp or redwinged blackbird, twittered a song of satisfaction. We then resumed our journey over a desert, waterless save after rain, for twenty-three miles; it is the divide between the Little Blue and the Platte rivers, a broken table-land rising gradually toward the west, with, at this season, a barren soil of sand and clay. As the evening approached, a smile from above lit up into absolute beauty the homely features of the world below. The sweet commune with nature in her fairest hours denied to the sons of cities—who must contemplate her charms through a vista of brick wall, or over a foreground of chimney-pots—consoled us amply for all the little hardships of travel. Strata upon strata of cloud-banks, burnished to golden red in the vicinity of the setting sun, and polished to dazzling silvery white above, lay piled half way from the horizon to the zenith, with a distinct strike toward a vanishing point in the west, and dipping into a gateway through which the orb of day slowly retired. Overhead floated in a sea of amber and yellow, pink and green, heavy purple nimbi, apparently turned upside down—their convex bulges below, and their horizontal lines high in the air— while in the east black and blue were so curiously blended that the eye could not distinguish whether it rested upon darkening air or upon a lowering thunder-cloud. We enjoyed these beauties in silence; not a soul said, "Look there!" or "How pretty!"

At 9 P.M., reaching "Thirty-two-mile Creek," we were pleasantly surprised to find an utter absence of the Irishry. The station-master was the head of a neat-handed and thrifty family from Vermont; the rooms, such as they were, looked cosy and clean and the chickens and peaches were plump and well "fixed." Soldiers from Fort Kearney loitered about the adjoining store, and from them we heard past fights and rumors of future wars which were confirmed on the morrow. Remounting at 10 30 P.M., and before moonrise, we threaded the gloom without other accident than the loss of a mule that was being led to the next station. The amiable animal, after breaking loose, coquetted with its pursuers for a while, according to the fashion of its kind, and when the cerne or surround was judged complete, it dashed through the circle and gave leg-bail, its hoofs ringing over the stones till the sound died away in the distant shades.

The Platte River and Fort Kearney, August 10.

After a long and chilly night—extensive evaporation making 40° F. feel excessively cold—lengthened by the atrocity of the musquetoes, which sting even when the thermometer stands below 45°, we awoke upon the hill sands divided by two miles of level green savanna, and at 4 A.M. reached Kearney Station, in the valley of La Grande Platte, seven miles from the fort of that name. The first aspect of the stream was one of calm and quiet beauty, which, however, it owed much to its accessories: some travelers have not hesitated to characterize it as "the dreariest of rivers." On the south is a rolling range of red sandy and clayey hillocks, sharp toward the river—the "coasts of the Nebraska." The valley, here two miles broad, resembles the ocean deltas of great streams; it is level as a carpet, all short green grass without sage or bush. It can hardly be called a bottom, the rise from the water's edge being, it is calculated, about 4 feet per 1000. Under a bank, from half a yard to a yard high, through its two lawns of verdure, flowed the stream straight toward the slanting rays of the rising sun, which glittered upon its broad bosom, and shed rosy light over half the heavens. In places it shows a sea horizon, but here it was narrowed by Grand Island, which is fifty-two miles long, with an average breadth of one mile and three quarters, and sufficiently elevated above the annual flood to be well timbered.

Without excepting even the Missouri, the Platte is doubtless the most important western influent of the Mississippi. Its valley offers a route scarcely to be surpassed for natural gradients, requiring little beyond the superstructure for light trains; and by following up its tributary—the Sweetwater—the engineer finds a line laid down by nature to the foot of the South Pass of the Rocky Mountains, the dividing ridge between the Atlantic and the Pacific water-beds. At present the traveler can cross the 300 or 400 miles of desert between the settlements in the east and the populated parts of the western mountains by its broad highway, with never-failing supplies of water, and, in places, fuel. Its banks will shortly supply coal to take the place of the timber that has thinned out.

The Canadian voyageurs first named it La Platte, the Flat River, discarding, or rather translating after their fashion, the musical and picturesque aboriginal term, "Nebraska," the "shallow stream:" the word has happily been retained for the Territory. Springing from the eastern slope of the Rocky Mountains, it has, like all the valley streams westward of the Mississippi, the Niobrara, or Eau qui court,* the Arkansas, and the Canadian River, a declination to the southeast. From its mouth to the junction of its northern and southern forks, the river valley is mostly level, and the scenery is of remarkable sameness: its singularity in this point affects the memory. There is not a tributary, not a ravine, in places not a tree to distract attention from the grassy intermediate bottom, which, plain as a prairie, extends from four to five and even twelve miles in width, bounded on both sides by low, rolling, sandy hills, thinly vegetated, and in few places showing dwarf bluffs. Between the forks and Fort Laramie the ground is more accented, the land near its banks often becomes precipitous, the road must sometimes traverse the tongues and ridges which project into the valley, and in parts the path is deep with sand. The stream averages about a mile in breadth, and sometimes widens out into the semblance of an estuary, flowing in eddies where holes are, and broken by far-reaching sand-bars and curlew shallows. In places it is a labyrinth of islets, variously shaped and of all sizes, from the long tongue which forms a vista to the little bouquet of cool verdure, grass, young willows, and rose-bushes. The shallowness of the bed causes the water to be warm in summer; a great contrast to the clear, cool springs on its banks. The sole is treacherous in the extreme, full of quicksands and gravel shoals, channels and cuts, which shift, like those of the Indus, with each year's flood; the site being nearly level, the river easily swells, and the banks, here of light, there of dark colored silt, based, like the floor, on sand, are, though vertical, rarely more than two feet high. It is a river willfully wasted by nature. The inundation raises it to about six feet throughout: this freshet, however, is of short duration, and the great breadth of the river causes a want of depth which renders it unfit for the navigation of a craft more civilized than the Indian's birch or the Canadian fur-boat. Colonel Frémont failed to descend it in September with a boat drawing only four inches. The water, like that of the Missouri, and for the same reason, is surcharged with mud drained from the prairies; carried from afar, it has usually a dark tinge; it is remarkably opaque after floods; if a few inches deep, it looks bottomless, and, finally, it contains little worth fishing for. From the mouth to Fort Kearney, beyond which point timber is rare, one bank, and one only, is fringed with narrow lines of well-grown cotton-wood, red wil-

* For an accurate geographical description of this little-known river, the reader is referred to Lieutenant Warren's report, published by the Secretary of War, United States.

lows, and cedars, which are disappearing before the emigrant's axe. The cedar now becomes an important tree. It will not grow on the plains, owing to the dryness of the climate and the excessive cold; even in the sheltered ravines the wintry winds have power to blight all the tops that rise above prairie level, and where the locality is better adapted for plantations, firs prevail. An interesting effect of climate upon the cedar is quoted by travelers on the Missouri River. At the first Cedar Island (43° N. lat.) large and straight trees appear in the bottom lands, those on the bluffs being of inferior growth; higher up the stream they diminish, seldom being seen in any number together above the mouth of the Little Cheyenne (45° N. lat.), and there they are exceedingly crooked and twisted. In the lignite formations above the Missouri and the Yellow Stone, the cedar, unable to support itself above ground, spreads over the hill-sides and presents the appearance of grass or moss.

Beyond the immediate banks of the Platte the soil is either sandy, quickly absorbing water, or it is a hard, cold, unwholesome clay, which long retains muddy pools, black with decayed vegetation, and which often, in the lowest levels, becomes a mere marsh. The wells deriving infiltration from the higher lands beyond are rarely more than three feet deep; the produce is somewhat saline, and here and there salt may be seen efflorescing from the soil around them. In the large beds of prêle (an equisetum), scouring rush, and other aquatic plants which garnish the banks, myriads of musquetoes find a home. Flowers of rich, warm color appear, we remark, in the sandy parts: the common wild helianthus and a miniature sunflower like chamomile, a thistle (*Carduus leucographus*), the cactus, a peculiar milk-plant (*Asclepias syrivea*), a spurgewort (*Asclepias tuberosa*), the amorpha, the tradescantia, the putoria, and the artemisia, or prairie sage. The richer soils and ravines produce in abundance the purple aster — violet of these regions — a green plant, locally known as "Lamb's Quarters," a purple flower with bulbous root, wild flax with pretty blue blossoms, besides mallow, digitalis, anemone, streptanthis, and a honeysuckle. In parts the valley of the Platte is a perfect parterre of wild flowers.

After satisfying hunger with vile bread and viler coffee—how far from the little forty-berry cup of Egypt!—for which we paid 75 cents, we left Kearney Station without delay. Hugging the right bank of our strange river, at 8 A.M. we found ourselves at Fort Kearney, so called, as is the custom, after the gallant officer, now deceased, of that name.

Every square box or block-house in these regions is a fort; no misnomer, however, can be more complete than the word applied to the military cantonments on the frontier. In former times the traders to whom these places mostly belonged erected quadrangles of sun-dried brick with towers at the angles; their forts still appear in old books of travels: the War Department, however, has been sensible enough to remove them. The position usually chosen is a river bottom, where fuel, grass, and water are readily procurable. The quarters are of various styles; some, with their low verandas, resemble Anglo-Indian bungalows or comfortable farm-houses; others are the storied houses, with the "stoop" or porch of the Eastern States in front; and low, long, peat-roofed tenements are used for magazines and out-houses. The best material is brown adobe or unburnt brick; others are of timber, whitewashed and clean-looking, with shingle roofs, glass windows, and gay green frames—that contrast of colors which the New Englander loves. The habitations surround a cleared central space for parade and drill; the ground is denoted by the tall flag-staff, which does not, as in English camps, distinguish the quarters of the commanding officer. One side is occupied by the officers' bungalows, the other, generally that opposite, by the adjutant's and quartermaster's offices, and the square is completed by low ranges of barrack and commissariat stores, while various little shops, stables, corrals for cattle, a chapel, perhaps an artillery park, and surely an ice-house—in this point India is far behind the wilds of America—complete the settlement. Had these cantonments a few more trees and a far more brilliant verdure, they would suggest the idea of an out-station in Guzerat, the Deccan, or some similar Botany Bay for decayed gentlemen who transport themselves.

While at Washington I had resolved—as has already been intimated—when the reports of war in the West were waxing loud, to enjoy a little Indian fighting. The meritorious intention — for which the severest "wig," concluding with something personally offensive about volunteering in general, would have been its sole result in the "fast-anchored isle"—was most courteously received by the Hon. John B. Floyd, Secretary of War, who provided me with introductory letters addressed to the officers commanding various "departments"*— "divisions," as they would

* The following is a list of the military departments into which the United States are divided:

MILITARY COMMANDS.

Department of the East.—The country east of the Mississippi River; head-quarters at Troy, N. Y.

Department of the West.—The country west of the Mississippi River, and east of the Rocky Mountains, except that portion included within the limits of the departments of Texas and New Mexico; head-quarters at St. Louis, Mo.

Department of Texas.—The State of Texas, and the territory north of it to the boundaries of New Mexico, Kansas, and Arkansas, and the Arkansas River, including Fort Smith. Fort Bliss, in Texas, is temporarily attached to the department of New Mexico; head-quarters at San Antonio, Texas.

Department of New Mexico.—The Territory of New Mexico; head-quarters at Santa Fé, New Mexico.

Department of Utah.—The Territory of Utah, except that portion of it lying west of the 117th degree of west longitude; head-quarters, Camp Floyd, U. T.

Department of the Pacific.—The country west of the Rocky Mountains, except

be called by Englishmen—in the West. The first tidings that saluted my ears on arrival at Fort Kearney acted as a quietus: an Indian action had been fought, which signified that there would be no more fighting for some time. Captain Sturgis, of the 1st Cavalry, U. S., had just attacked, near the Republican Fork of Kansas River, a little south of the fort, with six companies (about 350 men) and a few Delawares, a considerable body of the enemy, Comanches, Kiowas, and Cheyennes, who apparently had forgotten the severe lesson administered to them by Colonel—now Brigadier General—Edwin V. Sumner, 1st Cavalry, in 1857, and killed twenty-five with only two or three of his own men wounded. According to details gathered at Fort Kearney, the Indians had advanced under a black flag, lost courage, as wild men mostly will, when they heard the *pas de charge*, and, after making a running fight, being well mounted as well as armed, had carried off their "cripples" lashed to their horses. I had no time to call upon Captain Sully, who remained in command at Kearney with two troops (here called companies) of dragoons, or heavy cavalry, and one of infantry; the mail-wagon would halt there but a few minutes. I therefore hurriedly chose the alternative of advancing, with the hope of seeing "independent service" on the road. Intelligence of the fight had made even the conductor look grave; fifty or sixty miles is a flea-bite to a mounted war-party, and disappointed Indians upon the war-path are especially dangerous—even the most friendly can not be trusted when they have lost, or have not succeeded in taking, a few scalps. We subsequently heard that they had crossed our path, but whether the tale was true or not is an essentially doubtful matter. If this chance failed, remained the excitement of the buffalo and the Mormon; both were likely to show better sport than could be found in riding wildly about the country after runaway braves.

We all prepared for the "gravity of the situation" by discharging and reloading our weapons, and bade adieu, about 9 30 A.M., to Fort Kearney. Before dismissing the subject of forts, I am disposed to make some invidious remarks upon the army system of outposts in America.

The War Department of the United States has maintained the same system which the British, much to their loss—I need scarcely trouble the reader with a list of evils done to the soldier by outpost duty—adopted and pertinaciously kept up for so long a time in India; nay, even maintain to the present day, despite the imminent danger of mutiny. With the Anglo-Scandinavian race, the hate of centralization in civil policy extends to military or-

those portions of it included within the limits of the departments of Utah and New Mexico, and the district of Oregon; head-quarters at San Francisco, California.

District of Oregon.—The Territory of Washington and the State of Oregon, excepting the Rogue River and Umpqua districts in Oregon; head-quarters at Fort Vancouver, Washington Territory.

ganization, of which it should be the vital principle. The French, gifted with instinct for war, and being troubled with scant prejudice against concentration, civil as well as military, soon abandoned, when they found its futility, the idea of defending their Algerian frontier by extended lines, block-houses, and feeble intrenched posts. They wisely established, at the centres of action, depôts, magazines, and all the requisites for supporting large bodies of men, making them pivots for expeditionary columns, which by good military roads could be thrown in overwhelming numbers, in the best health and in the highest discipline, wherever an attack or an insurrectionary movement required crushing.

The necessity of so doing has long occurred to the American government, in whose service at present "a regiment is stationed to-day on the borders of tropical Mexico; to-morrow, the war-whoop, borne on a gale from the northwest, compels its presence to the frozen latitudes of Puget's Sound." The objections to altering their present highly objectionable system are two: the first is a civil consideration, the second a military one.

As I have remarked about the centralization of troops, so it is with their relation to civilians; the Anglo-Scandinavian blood shows similar manifestations in the Old and in the New Country. The French, a purely military nation, pet their army, raise it to the highest pitch, send it in for glory, and when it fails are to its faults a little blind. The English and Anglo-Americans, essentially a commercial and naval people, dislike the red coat; they look upon, and from the first they looked upon, a standing army as a necessary nuisance; they ever listen open-eared to projects for cutting and curtailing army expenditure; and when they have weakened their forces by a manner of atrophy, they expect them to do more than their duty, and if they can not command success, abuse them. With a commissariat, transport, and hospitals—delicate pieces of machinery, which can not run smoothly when roughly and hurriedly put together—unaccustomed to and unprepared for service, they land an army 3000 miles from home, and then make the world ring with their disappointment, and their complainings anent fearful losses in men and money. The fact is that, though no soldiers in the world fight with more bravery and determination, the Anglo-Scandinavian race, with their present institutions, are inferior to their inferiors in other points, as regards the art of military organization. Their fatal wants are order and economy, combined with the will and the means of selecting the best men—these belong to the emperor, not to the constitutional king or the president—and most of all, the habit of implicit subjection to the commands of an absolute dictator. The end of this long preamble is that the American government apparently thinks less of the efficiency of its troops than of using them as escorts to squatters, as police of the highway. Withal they fail; emigrants will not be escorted; women and children will struggle when they please, even in an Indian country, and every season has its dreadful tales of violence and starvation, massacre and cannibalism. In France the emigrants would be ordered to collect in bodies at certain seasons, to report their readiness for the road to the officers commanding stations, to receive an escort, as he should deem proper, and to disobey at their peril.

The other motive of the American outpost system is military, but also of civilian origin. Concentration would necessarily be unpalatable to a number of senior officers, who now draw what in England would be called command allowances at the several stations.* One of the principles of a republic is to pay a man only while he works; pensions, like sinecures, are left to governments less disinterested. The American army—it would hardly be believed—has no pensions, sale of commissions, off-reckonings, nor retiring list. A man hopelessly invalided, or in his second childhood, must hang on by means of furloughs and medical certificates to the end. The colonels are mostly upon the sick-list—one died lately aged ninety-three, and dating from the days of Louis XVI. —and I heard of an officer who, though practicing medicine for years, was still retained upon the cadre of his regiment. Of course, the necessity of changing such an anomaly has frequently been mooted by the Legislature; the scandalous failure, however, of an attempt at introducing a pension-list into the United States Navy so shocked the public that no one will hear of the experiment being renewed, even *in corpore vili*, the army.

To conclude the subject of outpost system. If the change be advisable in the United States, it is positively necessary to the British in India. The peninsula presents three main points, not to mention the detached heights that are found in every province, as the great pivots of action, the Himalayas, the Deccan, and the Nilgherry Hills, where, until wanted, the Sepoy and his officer, as well as the white soldier—the latter worth £100 a head—can be kept in health, drilled, disciplined, and taught the hundred arts which render an "old salt" the most handy of men. A few years ago the English soldier was fond of Indian service; hardly a regiment returned home without leaving hundreds behind it. Now, long, fatiguing marches, scant fare, the worst accommodation, and the various results of similar hardships, make him look upon the land as a Golgotha; it is with difficulty that he can be prevented from showing his disgust. Both in India and America, this will be the great benefit of extensive railroads: they will do away with single stations, and enable the authorities to carry out a system of concentration most beneficial to the country and to the service,

---

* The aggregate of the little regular army of the United States in 1860 amounted to 18,093. It was dispersed into eighty military posts, viz., thirteen in the Department of the East, nine in the West, twenty in Texas, twelve in the Department of New Mexico, two in Utah (Fort Bridger and Camp Floyd), eleven in Oregon, and thirteen in the Department of California. They each would have an average of about 225 men.

which, after many years of sore drudgery, may at last discern the good time coming.

In the United States, two other measures appear called for by circumstances. The Indian race is becoming desperate, wild-beast like, hemmed in by its enemies that have flanked it on the east and west, and are gradually closing in upon it. The tribes can no longer shift ground without inroads into territories already occupied by neighbors, who are, of course, hostile; they are, therefore, being brought to final bay.

The first is a camel corps. At present, when disturbances on a large scale occur in the Far West—the spring of 1862 will probably see them—a force of cavalry must be sent from the East, perhaps also infantry. "The horses, after a march of 500 or 600 miles, are expected to act with success"—I quote the sensible remarks of a "late captain of infantry" (Captain Patterson, U. S. Army)—"against scattered bands of mounted hunters, with the speed of a horse and the watchfulness of a wolf or antelope, whose faculties are sharpened by their necessities; who, when they get short of provisions, separate and look for something to eat, and find it in the water, in the ground, or on the surface; whose bill of fare ranges from grass-seed, nuts, roots, grasshoppers, lizards, and rattlesnakes, up to the antelope, deer, elk, bear, and buffalo, and who, having a continent to roam over, will neither be surprised, caught, conquered, overawed, or reduced to famine by a rumbling, bugle-blowing, drum-beating town passing through their country on wheels, at the speed of a loaded wagon." But the camel would in these latitudes easily march sixty miles per diem for a week or ten days, amply sufficient to tire out the sturdiest Indian pony; it requires water only after every fifty hours, and the worst soil would supply it with ample forage in the shape of wild sage, rabbit-bush, and thorns. Each animal would carry two men, with their arms and ammunition, rations for the time required, bedding and regimental necessaries, with material to make up a *tente d'abri* if judged necessary. The organization should be that of the Sindh Camel Corps, which, under Sir Charles Napier, was found so efficient against the frontier Beloch. The best men for this kind of fighting would be the Mountaineers, or Western Men, of the caste called "Pikes;" properly speaking, Missourians, but popularly any "rough" between St. Louis and California. After a sound flogging, for the purpose of preparing their minds to admit the fact that all men are *not* equal, they might be used by sea or land, whenever hard, downright fighting is required. It is understood that hitherto the camel, despite the careful selection by Mr. De Leon, the excellent Consul General of the United States in Egypt, and the valuable instructions of Hekekyan Bey, has proved a failure in the Western world. If so, want of patience has been the sole cause; the animal must be acclimatized by slow degrees before heavy loading to test its powers of strength and speed.   Some may deem this amount of delay impossible.   I confess my belief that the Anglo-Americans can, within any but the extremest limits, accomplish any thing they please—except unity.

The other necessity will be the raising of native regiments. The French in Africa have their Spahis, the Russians their Cossacks, and the English their Sepoys.   The American government has often been compelled, as in the case of the Creek battalion, which did good service during the Seminole campaign, indirectly to use their wild aborigines; but the public sentiment, or rather prejudice, which fathers upon the modern Pawnee the burning and torturing tastes of the ancient Mohawk, is strongly opposed to pitting Indian against Indian in battle.   Surely this is a false as well as a mistaken philanthropy.   If war must be, it is better that Indian instead of white blood should be shed.   And invariably the effect of enlisting savages and barbarians, subjecting them to discipline, and placing them directly under the eye of the civilized man, has been found to diminish their ferocity.   The Bashi Buzuk, left to himself, roasted the unhappy Russian; in the British service he brought his prisoner alive into camp with a view to a present or promotion.   When talking over the subject with the officers of the United States regular army, they have invariably concurred with me in the possibility of the scheme, provided that the public animus could be turned pro instead of con; and I have no doubt but that they will prove as leaders of Irregulars—it would be invidious to quote names—equal to the best of the Anglo-Indians, Skinner, Beatson, and Jacob.   The men would receive about ten dollars per man, and each corps number 300.   They would be better mounted and better armed than their wild brethren, and they might be kept, when not required for active service, in a buffalo country, their favorite quarters, and their finest field for soldierlike exercises.   The main point to be avoided is the mistake committed by the British in India, that of appointing too many officers to their Sepoy corps.

We left Kearney at 9 30 A.M., following the road which runs forty miles up the valley of the Platte.   It is a broad prairie, plentifully supplied with water in wells two to four feet deep; the fluid is cool and clear, but it is said not to be wholesome. Where the soil is clayey pools abound; the sandy portions are of course dry.   Along the southern bank near Kearney are few elevations; on the opposite or northern side appear high. and wooded bluffs.   The road was rough with pitch-holes, and for the first time I remarked a peculiar gap in the ground like an East Indian sun-crack—in these latitudes you see none of the deep fissures which scar the face of mother earth in tropical lands—the effect of rain-streams and snow-water acting upon the clay.   Each succeeding winter lengthens the head and deepens the sole of this deeply-gashed water-cut till it destroys the road.   A curious mirage appeared, doubling to four the strata of river and vegetation on the banks. The sight and song of birds once more charmed us after a desert where animal life is as rare as upon the plains of Brazil. After fifteen miles of tossing and tumbling, we made "Seventeen-mile Station," and halted there to change mules. About twenty miles above the fort the southern bank began to rise into mounds of tenacious clay, which, worn away into perpendicular and precipitous sections, composes the columnar formation called O'Fallon's Bluffs. At 1 15 P.M. we reached Plum Creek, after being obliged to leave behind one of the conductors, who had become delirious with the "shakes." The establishment, though new, was already divided into three; the little landlady, though she worked so manfully, was, as she expressed it, "enjoying bad health;" in other words, suffering from a "dumb chill." I may observe that the Prairie Traveler's opinions concerning the power of encamping with impunity upon the banks of the streams in this country must not be applied to the Platte. The whole line becomes with early autumn a hotbed of febrile disease. And generally throughout this season the stranger should not consider himself safe on any grounds save those defended from the southern trade-wind, which, sweeping directly from the Gulf of Mexico, bears with it noxious exhalations.

About Plum Ranch the soil is rich, clayey, and dotted with swamps and "slews," by which the English traveler will understand sloughs. The dryer portions were a Gulistan of bright red, blue, and white-flowers, the purple aster, and the mallow, with its parsnip-like root, eaten by the Indians, the gaudy yellow helianthus—we remarked at least three varieties—the snowy mimulus, the graceful flax, sometimes four feet high, and a delicate little euphorbia, while in the damper ground appeared the polar plant, that prairie compass, the plane of whose leaf ever turns toward the magnetic meridian. This is the "weed-prairie," one of the many divisions of the great natural meadows; grass prairie, rolling prairie, motte prairie, salt prairie, and soda prairie. It deserves a more poetical name, for

> "These are the gardens of the desert, these
> The unshorn fields, boundless and beautiful,
> For which the speech of England has no name."

Buffalo herds were behind the hills, but we were too full of sleep to follow them. The plain was dotted with blanched skulls and bones, which would have made a splendid bonfire. Apparently the expert voyageur has not learned that they form good fuel; at any rate, he has preferred to them the "chips" of which it is said that a steak cooked with them requires no pepper.*

We dined at Plum Creek on buffalo, probably bull beef, the

---

* The chip corresponds with the bois de vache of Switzerland, the tezek of Armenia, the arghol of Thibet, and the gobar of India. With all its faults, it is at least superior to that used in Sindh.

worst and dryest meat, save elk, that I have ever tasted; indeed, without the assistance of pork fat, we found it hard to swallow. As every one knows, however, the two-year old cow is the best eating, and at this season the herds are ever in the worst condition. The animals calve in May and June, consequently they are in August completely out of flesh. They are fattest about Christmas, when they find it difficult to run. All agree in declaring that there is no better meat than that of the young buffalo: the assertion, however, must be taken *cum grano salis*. Wild flesh was never known to be equal to tame, and that monarch did at least one wise thing who made the loin of beef Sir Loin. The voyageurs and travelers who cry up the buffalo as so delicious, have been living for weeks on rusty bacon and lean antelope; a rich hump with its proper menstruum, a cup of *café noir* as strong as possible, must truly be a "tit-bit." They boast that the fat does not disagree with the eater; neither do three pounds of heavy pork with the English plow-boy, who has probably taken less exercise than the Canadian hunter. Before long, buffalo flesh will reach New York, where I predict it will be held as inferior to butcher's meat as is the antelope to park-fed venison. While hunting, Indians cut off the tail to test the quality of the game, and they have acquired by habit a power of judging on the run between fat and lean.

Resuming our weary ride, we watered at "Willow Island Ranch," and then at "Cold Water Ranch"—drinking-shops all —five miles from Midway Station, which we reached at 8 P.M. Here, while changing mules, we attempted with sweet speech and smiles to persuade the landlady, who showed symptoms of approaching maternity, into giving us supper. This she sturdily refused to do, for the reason that she had not received due warning. We had, however, the satisfaction of seeing the *employés* of the line making themselves thoroughly comfortable with bread and buttermilk. Into the horrid wagon again, and "a rollin:" lazily enough the cold and hungry night passed on.*

To the Forks of the Platte. 11th August.

Precisely at 1 35 in the morning we awoke, as we came to a halt at Cotton-wood Station. Cramped with a four days' and four nights' ride in the narrow van, we entered the foul tenement, threw ourselves upon the mattresses, averaging three to each, and ten in a small room, every door, window, and cranny being shut

---

* According to Colonel Frémont, the total amount of buffalo robes purchased by the several companies, American, Hudson's Bay, and others, was an annual total of 90,000 from the eight or ten years preceding 1843. This is repeated by the Abbé Domenech, who adds that the number does not include those slaughtered in the southern regions by the Comanches and other tribes of the Texan frontier, nor those killed between March and November, when the skins are unfit for tanning. In 1847, the town of St. Louis received 110,000 buffalo robes, stags', deer, and other skins, and twenty-five salted tongues.

—after the fashion of these Western folks, who make up for a day in the open air by perspiring through the night in unventilated log huts—and, despite musquetoes, slept.

The morning brought with it no joy. We had arrived at the westernmost limit of the "gigantic Leicestershire" to which buffalo at this season extend, and could hope to see no trace of them between Cotton-wood Station and the Pacific. I can not, therefore, speak *ex cathedrâ* concerning this, the noblest "venerie" of the West: almost every one who has crossed the prairies, except myself, can. Captain Stansbury* will enlighten the sportsman upon the approved method of bryttling the beasts, and elucidate the mysteries of the "game-beef," marrow-bone and depuis, tongue and tender-loin, bass and hump, hump-rib and liver, which latter, by-the-by, is not unfrequently eaten raw, with a sprinkling of gall,† by the white hunter emulating his wild rival, as does the European in Abyssinia. The Prairie Traveler has given, from experience, the latest observations concerning the best modes of hunting the animal. All that remains to me, therefore, is to offer to the reader a few details collected from reliable sources, and which are not to be found in the two works above alluded to.

The bison (*Bison Americanus*) is trivially known as the Prairie Buffalo, to distinguish it from a different and a larger animal, the Buffalo of the Woods, which haunts the Rocky Mountains. The "Monarch of the Prairies," the "most gigantic of the indigenous mammalia of America," has, it is calculated, receded westward ten miles annually for the last 150 years. When America was discovered, the buffalo extended down to the Atlantic shore. Thirty years ago, bands grazed upon the banks of the Missouri River. The annual destruction is variously computed at from 200,000 to 300,000 head: the American Fur Company receive per annum about 70,000 robes, which are all cows; and of these not more than 5000 fall by the hands of white men. At present there are three well-known bands, which split up, at certain seasons, into herds of 2000 and 3000 each. The first family is on the head-waters of the Mississippi; the second haunts the vast crescent-shaped valley of the Yellow Stone; while the third occupies the prairie country between the Platte and the Arkansas. A fourth band, westward of the Rocky Mountains, is quite extinct. Fourteen to fifteen years ago, buffalo was found in Utah Valley, and later still upon the Humboldt River: according to some, they emigrated northward, through Oregon and the lands of the Blackfeet. It is more probable, however, that they were killed off by the severe winter of 1845, their skulls being still found scattered in heaps, as if a sudden and general destruction had come upon the doomed tribe.

* Exploration and Survey, etc., chap. ix.

† "Prairie bitters"—made of a pint of water and a quarter ot a gill of buffalo gall—are considered an *elixir vitæ* by old voyageurs.

The buffalo is partially migratory in its habits: it appears to follow the snow, which preserves its food from destruction. Like the antelope of the Cape, when on the "trek," the band may be reckoned by thousands. The grass, which takes its name from the animal, is plentiful in the valley of the Big Blue; it loves the streams of little creeks that have no bottom-land, and shelters itself under the sage. It is a small, moss-like gramen, with dark seed, and, when dry, it has been compared by travelers to twisted gray horsehair. Smaller herds travel in Indian file; their huge bodies, weighing 1500 lbs., appear, from afar, like piles erected to bridge the plain. After calving, the cows, like the African koodoo and other antelopes, herd separately from the males, and for the same reason, timidity and the cares of maternity. As in the case of the elephant and the hippopotamus, the oldsters are driven by the young ones, en charivari, from the band, and a compulsory bachelorhood souring their temper, causes them to become "rogues." The albino, or white buffalo, is exceedingly rare; even veteran hunters will confess never to have seen one. The same may be said of the glossy black accident called the "silk robe," supposed by Western men to be a cross between the parent and the offspring. The buffalo calf has been tamed by the Flatheads and others: I have never, however, heard of its being utilized.

The Dakotahs and other Prairie tribes will degenerate, if not disappear, when the buffalo is "rubbed out." There is a sympathy between them, and the beast flies not from the barbarian and his bow as it does before the face of the white man and his hot-mouthed weapon. The aborigines are unwilling to allow travelers, sportsmen, or explorers to pass through the country while they are hunting the buffalo; that is to say, preserving the game till their furs are ready for robes. At these times no one is permitted to kill any but stragglers, for fear of stampeding the band; the animal not only being timid, but also in the habit of hurrying away cattle and stock, which often are thus irretrievably lost. In due season the savages surround one section, and destroy it, the others remaining unalarmedly grazing within a few miles of the scene of slaughter. If another tribe interferes, it is a casus belli, death being the punishment for poaching. The white man, whose careless style of battue is notorious, will be liable to the same penalty, or, that failing, to be plundered by even "good Indians;" and I have heard of an English gentleman who, for persisting in the obnoxious practice, was very properly threatened with prosecution by the government agent.

What the cocoanut is to the East Indian, and the plantain and the calabash to various tribes of Africans, such is the "bos" to the carnivorous son of America. No part of it is allowed to waste. The horns and hoofs make glue for various purposes, especially for feathering arrows; the brains and part of the bowels are used for curing skins; the hide clothes the tribes from head to foot; the calf-skins form their apishamores, or saddle-blankets; the sinews make their bow-strings, thread, and finer cord; every part of the flesh, including the fœtus and placenta, is used for food. The surplus hides are reserved for market. They are prepared by the squaws, who, curious to say, will not touch a bear-skin till the age of maternity has passed; and they prefer the spoils of the cow, as being softer than those of the bull. The skin, after being trimmed with an iron or bone scraper — this is not done in the case of the "parflèche," or thick sole-leather — and softened with brain or marrow, is worked till thoroughly pliable with the hands. The fumigation, which gives the finishing touch, is confined to buckskins intended for garments. When the hair is removed, the hides supply the place of canvas, which they resemble in whiteness and facility of folding. Dressed with the hair, they are used, as their name denotes, for clothing; they serve also for rugs and bedding. In the prairies, the price ranges from $1 to $1 50 in kind; in the Eastern States, from $5 to $10. The fancy specimens, painted inside, decorated with eyes, and otherwise adorned with split porcupine quills dyed a gamboge-yellow, fetch from $8 to $35. A "buffalo" (*subaudi* robe) was shown to me, painted with curious figures, which, according to my Canadian informant, were a kind of hieroglyph or *aide-mémoire*, even ruder than the Mexican picture-writing.

The Indians generally hunt the buffalo with arrows. They are so expert in riding that they will, at full speed, draw the missile from the victim's flank before it falls. I have met but one officer, Captain Heth, of the 10th Regiment, who ever acquired the art. The Indian hog-spear has been used to advantage. Our predecessors in Eastern conquest have killed with it the tiger and nylgau; there is, therefore, no reason why it might not be efficiently applied to the buffalo. Like the Bos Caffre, the bison is dull, surly, and stupid, as well as timid and wary; it requires hard riding, with the chance of a collar-bone broken by the horse falling into a prairie-dog's home; and when headed or tired an old male rarely fails to charge.

The flies chasing away the musquetoes—even as Aurora routs the lingering shades of night—having sounded our *reveillée* at Cotton-wood Station, we proceeded by means of an "eye-opener," which even the abstemious judge could not decline, and the use of the "skillet," to prepare for a breakfast composed of various abominations, especially cakes of flour and grease, molasses and dirt, disposed in pretty equal parts. After paying the usual 50 cents, we started in the high wind and dust, with a heavy storm brewing in the north, along the desert valley of the dark, silent Platte, which here spread out in broad basins and lagoons, picturesquely garnished with broad-leafed dock and beds of *prêle*, flags and water-rushes, in which, however, we saw nothing but traces of Monsieur Maringouin.   On our left was a line of sub-conical buttes, red, sandy-clay pyramids, semi-detached from the wall of the rock behind them, with smooth flat faces fronting the river, toward which they slope at the natural angle of 45°.   The land around, dry and sandy, bore no traces of rain; a high wind blew, and the thermometer stood at 78° (F.), which was by no means uncomfortably warm.   Passing Junction-House Ranch and Frémont Slough—whisky-shops both—we halted for "dinner," about 11 A.M., at Frémont Springs, so called from an excellent little water behind the station.   The building is of a style pecul-iar to the South, especially Florida—two huts connected by a roof-work of thatched timber, which acts as the best and coolest of ve-randas.   The station-keeper, who receives from the proprietors of the line $30 per month, had been there only three weeks; and his wife, a comely young person, uncommonly civil and smiling for a "lady," supplied us with the luxuries of pigeons, onions, and light bread, and declared her intention of establishing a poul-try-yard.

An excellent train of mules carried us along a smooth road at a slapping pace, over another natural garden even more flowery than that passed on the last day's march.   There were beds of lupins, a brilliant pink and blue predominating, the green plant locally known as "Lamb's Quarters" (*Chenopodium album*); the streptanthis; the milk-weed, with its small white blossoms; the anemone; the wild flax, with its pretty blue flowers, and growths which appeared to be clematis, chamomile, and digitalis.   Distant black dots—dwarf cedars, which are yearly diminishing—lined the bank of the Platte and the long line of River Island; they elicited invidious comparisons from the Pennsylvanians of the party.   We halted at Half-way House, near O'Fallon's Bluffs, at the quarters of Mr. M——, a *compagnon de voyage*, who had now reached his home of twenty years, and therefore insisted upon "standing drinks."   The business is worth $16,000 per annum; the contents of the store somewhat like a Parsee's shop in West-ern India—every thing from a needle to a bottle of Champagne. A sign-board informed us that we were now distant 400 miles from St. Jo, 120 from Fort Kearney, 68 from the upper, and 40 from the lower crossing of the Platte.   As we advanced the valley narrow-ed, the stream shrank, the vegetation dwindled, the river islands were bared of timber, and the only fuel became buffalo chip and last year's artemisia.   This hideous growth, which is to weary our eyes as far as central valleys of the Sierra Nevada, will require a few words of notice.

The artemisia, absinthe, or wild sage differs much from the pan-acea concerning which the Salernitan school rhymed:

"Cur moriatur homo cui Salvia crescit in horto."

Yet it fills the air with a smell that caricatures the odor of the garden-plant, causing the traveler to look round in astonishment; and when used for cooking it taints the food with a taste between camphor and turpentine. It is of two kinds. The smaller or white species (*A. filifolia*) rarely grows higher than a foot. Its fetor is less rank, and at times of scarcity it forms tolerable fodder for animals. The Western men have made of it, as of the " red root," a tea, which must be pronounced decidedly inferior to corn coffee. The Indians smoke it, but they are not particular about what they inhale: like that perverse p——n of Ludlow, who smoked the bell-ropes rather than not smoke at all, or like school-boys who break themselves in upon ratan, they use even the larger sage as well as a variety of other graveolent growths. The second kind (*A. tridentata*) is to the family of shrubs what the prairie cedar is to the trees—a gnarled, crooked, rough-barked deformity. It has no pretensions to beauty except in earliest youth, and in the dewy hours when the breeze turns up its leaves that glitter like silver in the sun; and its constant presence in the worst and most desert tracts teaches one to regard it, like the mangrove in Asia and Africa, with aversion. In size it greatly varies; in some places it is but little larger than the white species; near the Red Buttes its woody stem often attains the height of a man and the thickness of his waist. As many as fifty rings have been counted in one wood, which, according to the normal calculation, would bring its age up to half a century. After its first year, stock will eat it only when threatened with starvation. It has, however, its use; the traveler, despite its ugliness, hails the appearance of its stiff, wiry clumps at the evening halt: it is easily uprooted, and by virtue of its essential oil it makes a hot and lasting fire, and ashes over. According to Colonel Frémont, " it has a small fly accompanying it through every change of elevation and latitude." The same eminent authority also suggests that the respiration of air so highly impregnated with aromatic plants may partly account for the favorable effect of the climate upon consumption.

At 5 P.M., as the heat began to mitigate, we arrived at Alkali Lake Station, and discovered some " exiles from Erin," who supplied us with antelope meat and the unusual luxury of ice taken from the Platte. We attempted to bathe in the river, but found it flowing liquid mire. The Alkali Lake was out of sight; the driver, however, consoled me with the reflection that I should " glimpse" alkali lakes till I was sick of them.

Yesterday and to-day we have been in a line of Indian " removes." The wild people were shifting their quarters for grass; when it becomes a little colder they will seek some winter abode on the banks of a stream which supplies fuel and where they can find meat, so that with warmth and food, song and chat—they are fond of talking nonsense as African negroes—and smoke and sleep, they can while away the dull and dreary winter. Before describing the scene, which might almost serve for a picture of Bedouin or gipsy life—so similar are the customs of all savages —I have something to say about the Red Man.

This is a country of misnomers. America should not, according to the school-books, have been named America, consequently the Americans should not be called Americans. A geographical error, pardonable in the fifteenth century, dubbed the old tenants of these lands Indians,* but why we should still call them the Red Men can not be conceived. I have now seen them in the north, south, east, and west of the United States, yet never, except under the influence of ochre or vermilion, have I seen the Red Man red. The real color of the skin, as may be seen under the leggins, varies from a dead pale olive to a dark dingy brown. The parts exposed to the sun are slightly burnished, as in a Tartar or an Affghan after a summer march. Between the two extremes above indicated there are, however, a thousand shades of color, and often the skin has been so long grimed in with pigment, grease, and dirt that it suggests a brick-dust tinge which a little soap or soda would readily remove. Indeed, the color and the complexion, combined with the lank hair, scant beard, and similar peculiarities, renders it impossible to see this people for the first time without the strongest impression that they are of that Turanian breed which in prehistoric ages passed down from above the Himalayas as far south as Cape Comorin.

Another mistake touching the Indian is the present opinion concerning him and his ancestors. He now suffers in public esteem from the reaction following the high-flown descriptions of Cooper and the herd of minor romancers who could not but make their heroes heroes. Moreover, men acquainted only with the degenerate Pawnees or Diggers extend their evil opinions to the noble tribes now extinct—the Iroquois and Algonquins, for instance, whose remnants, the Delawares and Ojibwas, justify the high opinion of the first settlers. The exploits of King Philip, Pontiac, Gurister Sego, Tecumseh, Keokuk, Iatan, Captain J. Brant, Black Hawk, Red Jacket, Osceola, and Billy Bowlegs, are rapidly fading away from memory, while the failures of such men as Little Thunder, and those like him, stand prominently forth in modern days. Besides the injustice to the manes and memories of the dead, this depreciation of the Indians tends to serious practical evils. Those who see the savage lying drunk about stations, or eaten up with disease, expect to beat him out of the field by merely showing their faces; they fail, and pay the penalty with

* Columbus and Vespucius both died in the conviction that they had only discovered portions of Asia. Indeed, as late as 1533, the astronomer Schöner maintained that Mexico was the Quinsai of Marco Polo. The early navigators called the aborigines of the New World "Indians," believing that they inhabited the eastern portion of "India," a term then applied to the extremity of Oriental Asia. Until the present century the Spaniards applied the names India and Indies to their possessions in America.

their lives—an event which occurs every year in some parts of America.

The remove of the village presented an interesting sight—an animated shifting scene of bucks and braves, squaws and pappooses, ponies dwarfed by bad breeding and hard living, dogs and puppies struggling over the plains westward. In front, singly or in pairs, rode the men, not gracefully, not according to the rules of Mexican *manège*, but like the Abyssinian eunuch, as if born upon and bred to become part of the animal. Some went bare-backed; others rode, like the ancient chiefs of the Western Islands, upon a saddle-tree, stirrupless, or provided with hollow blocks of wood: in some cases the saddle was adorned with bead hangings, and in all a piece of buffalo hide with the hair on was attached beneath to prevent chafing. The cruel ring-bit of the Arabs is not unknown. A few had iron curbs, probably stolen. For the most part they managed their nags with a hide thong lashed round the lower jaw and attached to the neck. A whip, of various sizes and shapes, sometimes a round and tattooed ferule, more often a handle like a butcher's tally-stick, flat, notched, one foot long, and provided with two or three thongs, hung at the wrist. Their nags were not shod with parflèche, as among the horse-Indians of the South. Their long, lank, thick, brownish-black hair, ruddy from the effects of weather, was worn parted in the middle, and depended from the temples confined with a long twist of otter or beaver's skin in two queues, or pig-tails, reaching to the breast: from the poll, and distinct from the remainder of the hair, stream-ed the scalp-lock. This style of hair-dressing, doubtless, aids in giving to the coronal region that appearance of depression which characterizes the North American Indians as a race of "Flat-heads," and which, probably being considered a beauty, led to the artificial deformities of the Peruvian and the Aztec. The parting in men, as well as in women, was generally colored with vermil-ion, and plates of brass or tin, with beveled edges, varying in size from a shilling to half a crown, were inserted into the front hair. The scalp-lock—in fops the side-locks also—was decorated with tin or silver plates, often twelve in number, beginning from the head and gradually diminishing in size as they approached the heels; a few had eagle's, hawk's, and crow's feathers stuck in the hair, and sometimes, grotesquely enough, crownless Kossuth hats, felt broadbrims, or old military casquettes, surmounted all this finery. Their scanty beard was removed; they compare the bushy-faced European to a dog running away with a squirrel in its mouth. In their ears were rings of beads, with pendants of tin plates or mother of pearl, or huge circles of brass wire not un-like a Hindoo tailor's; and their fore-arms, wrists, and fingers were, after an African fashion, adorned with the same metals, which the savage ever prefers to gold or silver. Their other decorations were cravats of white or white and blue, oval beads, and necklaces of plates like those worn in the hair. The body dress was a tight-sleeved waistcoat of dark drugget, over an American cotton shirt; others wore tattered flannels, and the middle was wrapped round with a common blanket, presented by the government agent—scarlet and blue being the colors preferred, white rare: a better stuff is the coarse broadcloth manufactured for the Indian market in the United States. The leggins were a pair of pantaloons without the body part—in their palmy days the Indians laughed to scorn their future conquerors for tightening the hips so as to impede activity—looped up at both haunches with straps to a leathern girdle, and all wore the breech-cloth, which is the common Hindoo languti or T-bandage. The cut of the leggins is a parallelogram, a little too short and much too broad for the limb; it is sewn so as to fit tight, and the projecting edges, for which the light-colored list or bordering is usually preserved, answers the effect of a military stripe. When buckskin leggins are made the outside edges are fringed, producing that feathered appearance which distinguishes in our pictures the nether limbs of the Indian brave. The garb ends with moccasins,* the American brogues, which are made in two ways. The simplest are of one piece, a cylinder of skin cut from above and below the hock of some large animal—moose, elk, or buffalo—and drawn on before shrinking, the joint forming the heel, while the smaller end is sewn together for a toe. This rough contrivance is little used but as a *pis aller*. The other kind is made of tanned hide in two pieces—a sole and an upper leather, sewn together at the junction; the last is a bit of board rounded off at the end. They are open over the instep, where also they can be laced or tied, and they fit as closely as the Egyptian mizz´ or under-slipper, which they greatly resemble. They are worn by officers in the Far West as the expatriated Anglo-Indian adopts the "Juti." The greatest inconvenience to the novice is the want of heel; moreover, they render the feet uncomfortably tender, and, unless soled with parflèche or thick leather, they are scant defense against stony ground; during dry weather they will last fairly, but they become, after a single wetting, even worse than Bombay-made Wellingtons. A common pair will cost $2; when handsomely embroidered with bead-work by the squaws they rise to $15.

The braves were armed with small tomahawks or iron hatchets, which they carried with the powder-horn, in the belt, on the right side, while the long tobacco-pouch of antelope skin hung by the left. Over their shoulders were leather targes, bows and arrows, and some few had rifles; both weapons were defended from damp in deer-skin cases, and quivers with the inevitable bead-work, and the fringes which every savage seems to love. These articles reminded me of those in use among the Bedouins of El Hejaz. Their nags were lean and ungroomed; they treat them as cruelly

---

* This Algonquin word is written *moccasson* or *mocasin*, and is pronounced *moksin*.

as do the Somal; yet nothing—short of whisky—can persuade the Indian warrior, like the man of Nejd, to part with a favorite steed. It is his all in all, his means of livelihood, his profession, his pride; he is an excellent judge of horse-flesh, though ignoring the mule and ass; and if he offers an animal for which he has ·once refused to trade, it is for the reason that an Oriental takes to market an adult slave—it has become useless. Like the Arab, he considers it dishonorable to sell a horse; he gives it to you, expecting a large present, and if disappointed he goes away grumbling that you have "swallowed" his property. He is fond of short races—spurts they are called—as we had occasion to see; there is nothing novel nor interesting in the American as there is in the Arabian hippology; the former learned all its arts from Europeans, the latter taught them.

Behind the warriors and braves followed the baggage of the village. The lodge poles, in bundles of four and five, had been lashed to pads or pack-saddles, girthed tight to the ponies' backs, the other ends being allowed to trail along the ground like the shafts of a truck; the sign easily denotes the course of travel. The wolf-like dogs were also harnessed in the same way; more lupine than canine, they are ready when hungry to attack man or mule; and, sharp-nosed and prick-eared, they not a little resemble the Indian pariah dog. Their equipments, however, were of course on a diminutive scale; a little pad girthed round the barrel, with a breastplate to keep it in place, enabled them to drag two short light lodge poles tied together at the smaller extremity. One carried only a hawk on its back—yet falconry has never, I believe, been practiced by the Indian. Behind the ponies the poles were connected by cross-sticks, upon which were lashed the lodge covers, the buffalo robes, and other bulkier articles. Some had strong frames of withes or willow basket-work, two branches being bent into an oval, garnished below with a net-work of hide thongs for a seat, covered with a light wicker canopy, and opening, like a cage, only on one side; a blanket or a buffalo robe defends the inmate from sun and rain. These are the litters for the squaws when weary, the children, and the puppies, which are part of the family till used for feasts. It might be supposed to be a rough conveyance; the elasticity of the poles, however, alleviates much of that inconvenience. A very ancient man, wrinkled as a last year's walnut, and apparently crippled by old wounds, was carried, probably by his great-grandsons, in a rude sedan. The vehicle was composed of two pliable poles, about ten feet long, separated by three cross-bars twenty inches or so apart; a blanket had been secured to the foremost and hindermost, and under the centre-bit lay Senex secured against falling out. In this way the Indians often bear the wounded back to their villages; apparently they have never thought of a horse-litter, which might be made with equal facility, and would certainly save work.

While the rich squaws rode, the poorer followed their pack-horses on foot, eying the more fortunate as the mercer's wife re-gards what she terms the "carriage lady." The women's dress not a little resembles their lords'; the unaccustomed eye often hesitates between the sexes.   In the fair, however, the waistcoat is absent, the wide-sleeved shift extends below the knees, and the leggins are of somewhat different cut.   All wore coarse shawls, or white, blue, and scarlet cloth-blankets round their bodies.   Upon the Upper Platte we afterward saw them dressed in cotton gowns, after a semi-civilized fashion, and with bowie-knives by their sides.   The grandmothers were fearful to look upon—horrid ex-crescences of nature, teaching proud man a lesson of humility, and a memento of his neighbor in creation, the "humble ape"— it is only civilization that can save the aged woman from resem-bling the gorilla.   The middle-aged matrons were homely bodies, broad and squat like the African dame after she has become *mère de famille;* their hands and feet were notably larger from work than those of the men, and the burdens upon their backs caused them to stoop painfully.   The young squaws—pity it is that all our household Indian words, pappoose, for instance, tomahawk, wigwam, and powwow, should have been naturalized out of the Abenaki and other harsh dialects of New England—deserved a more euphonious appellation.   The belle savage of the party had large and languishing eyes and dentists' teeth that glittered, with sleek, long black hair like the ears of a Blenheim spaniel, justi-fying a natural instinct to stroke or pat it, drawn straight over a low, broad, Quadroon-like brow.   Her figure had none of the fra-gility which distinguishes the higher race, who are apparently too delicate for human nature's daily food — porcelain, in fact, when pottery is wanted; nor had she the square corpulency which appears in the negro woman after marriage.   Her ears and neck were laden with tinsel ornaments, brass-wire rings adorned her wrists and fine arms, a bead-work sash encircled her waist, and scarlet leggins fringed and tasseled, ended in equally costly moccasins.   When addressed by the driver in some terms to me unintelligible, she replied with a soft clear laugh—the principal charm of the Indian, as of the smooth-throated African woman— at the same time showing him the palm of her right hand as though it had been a looking-glass.   The gesture would have had a peculiar significance in Sindh; here, however, I afterward learned, it simply conveys a refusal.   The maidens of the tribe, or those under six, were charming little creatures, with the wild-est and most piquant expression, and the prettiest doll-like fea-tures imaginable; the young coquettes already conferred their smiles as if they had been of any earthly value.   The boys once more reminded me of the East; they had black beady eyes, like snakes, and the wide mouths of young caymans.   Their only dress, when they were not in "birth-day suit," was the Indian languti.   None of the braves carried scalps, finger-bones, or notches on the lance, which serve like certain marks on saw-handled pistols farther east, nor had any man lost a limb.   They followed us for many a mile, peering into the hinder part of our traveling wigwam, and ejaculating "How! How!" the normal salutation.   It is supposed to mean "good," and the Western man, when he drinks to your health, says "Here, how!" and expects a return in kind.   The politeness of the savages did not throw us off our guard; the Dakotah of these regions are expert and daring kleptomaniacs; they only laughed, however, a little knowingly as we raised the rear curtain, and they left us after begging pertinaciously—bakhshish is an institution here as on the banks of the Nile—for tobacco, gunpowder, ball, copper caps, lucifers, and what not.   The women, except the pretty party, looked, methought, somewhat scowlingly, but one can hardly expect a smiling countenance from the human biped trudging ten or twenty miles under a load fit for a mule.   A great contrast with these Indians was a train of "Pike's Peakers," who, to judge from their grim looks, were returning disappointed from the new gold diggings.   I think that if obliged to meet one of the two troops by moonlight alone, my choice would have fallen upon "messieurs les sauvages."

At 6 P.M. we resumed our route, with a good but fidgety train, up the Dark Valley, where musquetoes and sultry heat combined to worry us.   Slowly traveling and dozing the while, we arrived about 9 15 P.M. at Diamond Springs, a bright little water much frequented by the "lightning-bug" and the big-eyed "Devil's darning-needle,"* where we found whisky and its usual accompaniment, soldiers.   The host related an event which he said had taken place but a few days before.   An old mountaineer, who had married two squaws, was drinking with certain Cheyennes, a tribe famous for ferocity and hostility to the whites.   The discourse turning upon topics stoical, he was asked by his wild boon companions if he feared death.   The answer was characteristic: "You may kill me if you like!"   Equally characteristic was their acknowledgment; they hacked him to pieces, and threw the corpse under a bank.   In these regions the opposite races regard each other as wild beasts; the white will shoot an Indian as he would a coyote.   He expects to go under whenever the "all-fired, red-bellied varmints"—I speak, oh reader, Occidentally—get the upper hand, and *vice versâ*.

The Platte River divides at N. lat. 40° 05' 05", and W. long. (G.) 101° 21' 24".   The northern, by virtue of dimensions, claims to be the main stream.   The southern, which is also called in obsolete maps Padouca, from the Pawnee name for the Iatans, whom

---

* The first is the firefly, the second is the dragon-fly, called in country parts of England "the Devil's needle."

the Spaniards term Comanches,* averages 600 yards, about 100 less than its rival in breadth, and, according to the prairie people, affords the best drinking. Hunters often ford the river by the Lower Crossing, twenty-eight miles above the bifurcation. Those with heavily-loaded wagons prefer this route, as by it they avoid the deep loose sands on the way to the Upper Crossing. The mail-coach must endure the four miles of difficulty, as the road to Denver City branches off from the western ford.

At 10 P.M., having "caught up" the mules, we left Diamond Springs, and ran along the shallow river which lay like a thin sheet of shimmer broken by clumps and islets that simulated, under the imperfect light of the stars, houses and towns, hulks and ships, wharves and esplanades. On the banks large bare spots, white with salt, glistened through the glooms; the land became so heavy that our fagged beasts groaned; and the descents, watercuts, and angles were so abrupt that holding on constituted a fair gymnastic exercise. The air was clear and fine. My companions snored while I remained awake enjoying a lovely aurora, and, Epicurean-like, reserving sleep for the Sybaritic apparatus, which, according to report, awaited us at the grand *établissement* of the Upper Crossing of La Grande Platte.

This was our fifth night in the mail-wagon. I could not but meditate upon the difference between travel in the pure prairie air, despite an occasional "chill," and the perspiring miseries of an East Indian dawk, or of a trudge in the miasmatic and pestilential regions of Central Africa. Much may be endured when, as was ever the case, the highest temperature in the shade does not exceed 98° F.

12th August.   We cross the Platte.

Boreal aurora glared brighter than a sunset in Syria. The long streamers were intercepted and mysteriously confused by a massive stratum of dark cloud, through whose narrow rifts and jagged chinks the splendors poured in floods of magic fire. Near the horizon the tint was an opaline white—a broad band of calm, steady light, supporting a tender rose-color, which flushed to crimson as it scaled the upper firmament. The mobility of the spectacle was its chiefest charm. The streamers either shot out or shrank from full to half length; now they flared up, widening till they filled the space between Lucifer rising in the east and Aries setting in the west; then they narrowed to the size of a span; now they stood like a red arch with steadfast legs and oscillating summit; then, broadening at the apex, they apparently

---

* The Kaumainsh (Comanche), a warlike and independent race, who, with the Apaches, have long been the bane of New Spain, were in the beginning of this century entirely erratic, without any kind of cultivation, subsisting, in fact, wholly by the chase and plunder. They were then bounded westward by New Mexico, where they have laid waste many a thriving settlement; eastward by the Pawnees and Osages; northward by the Utahs, Kiowas, and Shoshonees; and southward by the nations on the Lower Red River.

revolved with immense rapidity; at times the stars shone undimmed through the veil of light, then they were immersed in its exceeding brilliancy. After a full hour of changeful beauty, paling in one place and blushing in another, the northern lights slowly faded away with a blush which made the sunrise look colder than its wont. It is no wonder that the imaginative Indian, looking with love upon these beauties, connects them with the ghosts of his ancestors.

Cramped with cold and inaction—at 6 A.M. the thermometer showed only 56° F. in the sun—hungry, thirsty, and by no means in the mildest of humors, we hear with a gush of joy, at 3 15 A.M., the savage Yep! yep! yep! with which the driver announces our approach. The plank lodgings soon appear; we spring out of the ambulance; a qualm comes over us; all is dark and silent as the grave; nothing is prepared for us; the wretches are all asleep. A heavy kick opens the door of the soon-found restaurant, when a pheesy, drowsy voice from an inner room asks us, in German-English—so strong is the causality, the crapulousness of why and wherefore in this "divided, erudite race"—"And how ze komen in?" Without attempting to gratify his intellectual cravings, we ordered him out of bed, and began to talk of supper, refreshment, and repose. But the "critter" had waxed surly after securing for himself a compound epithet, of which "hunds—" is the first syllable, and his every negative answer concluded with a faint murmur of "petampt." I tried to get his bed for Mrs. Dana, who was suffering severely from fatigue. He grumbled out that his "lady and bebbé" were occupying it. At length I hit upon the plan of placing the cushions and cloaks upon the table, when the door opened for a second dog-Teuton, who objected to that article of furniture being used otherwise than for his morning meal. *Excédés*, and mastering with pain our desire to give these villain "sausage-eaters" "particular fits," we sat down, stared at the fire, and awaited the vile food. For a breakfast cooked in the usual manner, coffee boiled down to tannin (ever the first operation), meat subjected to half sod, half stew, and, lastly, bread raised with sour milk corrected with soda, and so baked that the taste of the flour is ever prominent, we paid these German rascals 75 cents, a little dearer than at the Trois Frères.

At the Upper Crossing of the South Fork there are usually tender adieux, the wenders toward Mormonland bidding farewell to those bound for the perilous gold regions of Denver City and Pike's Peak. If "fresh," they take leave of one another with sincere commiseration for one another's dooms, each deeming, of course, his own the brighter. The wagons were unloaded, thus giving us the opportunity of procuring changes of raiment and fresh caps—our felts had long disappeared under the influence of sleeping on the perch. By some means we retained our old ambulance, which, after five days and nights, we had learned to look upon as a home; the Judiciary, however, had to exchange theirs for one much lighter and far less comfortable. Presently those bound to Denver City set out upon their journey. Conspicuous among them was a fair woman who had made her first appearance at Cotton-wood Creek—fit place for the *lune de mélasse*—with an individual, apparently a well-to-do drover, whom she called "Tom" and "husband." She had forgotten her "fixins," which, according to a mischievous and scandalous driver, consisted of a reticule containing a "bishop," a comb, and a pomatumpot, a pinchbeck watch, and a flask of "Bawme"—not of Meccah. Being a fine young person of Scotch descent, she had, till dire suspicions presented themselves, attracted the attentions of her fellow-travelers, who pronounced her to be "all sorts of a gal." But virtue is rabid in these lands, and the purity of the ermine must not be soiled. It was fortunate for Mr. and Mrs. Mann—the names were *noms de voyage*—that they left us so soon. In a certain Southern city I heard of a high official who, during a trip upon one of the floating palaces of the Mississippi, had to repeat "deprendi miserum est;" the fond, frail pair was summarily ejected with bag and baggage to furnish itself with a down-stream passage on board a lumber raft.

We crossed the "Padouca" at 6 30 A.M., having placed our luggage and the mails for security in an ox cart. The South Fork is here 600 to 700 yards broad; the current is swift, but the deepest water not exceeding 250 feet, the teams are not compelled to cross diagonally. The channel was broken with sand-banks and islets; the bed was dark and gravelly; the water, though dark as hotel coffee, was clear, not, as described by Captain Stansbury, "perfectly opaque with thick yellow mud," and the earthbanks, which rise to five feet, are never inundated. The half-broken mules often halted, and seemed inclined to lie down; a youth waded on the lower side of the team, shouting and swinging his arms to keep them from turning their heads down stream; the instinct of animals to find an easy ford ended with a few desperate struggles up the black oozy mire. Having reloaded on the left bank, and cast one last look of hatred upon the scene of our late disappointment, we set out at 7 A.M. to cross the divide separating the Northern and Southern Forks of the Platte.

We had now entered upon the outskirts of the American wilderness, which has not one feature in common with the deserts of the Old World. In Arabia and Africa there is majesty in its monotony: those awful wastes so brightly sunburnished that the air above them appears by contrast black; one vast and burning floor, variegated only by the mirage-reek, with nothing below the firmament to relieve or correct the eye. Here it is a brown smooth space, insensibly curving out of sight, wholly wanting "second distance," and scarcely suggesting the idea of immensity; we seem, in fact, to be traveling for twenty miles over a convex, treeless hill-top. The air became sultry, white clouds shut in the sky, and presently arose the high south wind, which at this season blows a gale between 10 A.M. and 3 P.M. The ground, bleached where sandy, was thinly scattered here and there with wiry grass, dun and withered, and with coarse and sunburnt shrubs, among which the "leadplant" (*Amorphe canescens*) was the characteristic. A dwarf aloetic vegetation became abundant; vegetation was fast going the way of all grass; after rain, however, it is doubtless fresh and copious. The buffalo grass sought the shade of the wild sage. A small euphorbia, the cotton-weed, a thistle haunted by the Cynthia cardua, that butterfly common to the eastern and western hemispheres, and a bright putoria, mingled with mushrooms like huge bulbs. The cactus was of two kinds: the flat-leaved species is used by white men to filter water, and by the savages, who peel and toast it, as provaunt:* there is another globular variety (an *echinocactus*) lying stalkless, like a half melon, with its brilliant flowers guarded by a panoply of spines. We pursued a sandy tract, broken by beds of nullahs and fiumaras, between two ridges of hillocks, draining to the right into a low bottom denoted by a lively green, with bays and bends of lush, reed-like grass. This is the well-known Lodge-Pole Creek or Fork, a mere ditch, the longest and narrowest of its kind, rising from a mountain lakelet near the "New Bayou" or "Park," in the Black Hills, and falling into the South Fork of the Platte, about seventy miles west of the bifurcation. By following up this water along the Cherokee trail to its head in the Cheyenne Pass of the Rocky Mountains, instead of describing the arc *viâ* Fort Laramie, the mail would gain 61 miles; emigrants, indeed, often prefer the short cut. Moreover, from the Cheyenne Pass to Great Salt Lake City, there is, according to accounts, a practicable road south of the present line, which, as it would also save time and labor, has been preferred for the mail line.

In the American Sahara animal life began to appear. The coyote turned and stared at us as though we were trespassing upon his property. This is the jackal of the Western world, the small prairie-wolf, the *Canis latrans*, and the old Mexican coyotl, best depicted by the old traveler, Abbé Clavigero, in these words: "It is a wild beast, voracious like the wolf, cunning like the fox, in form like the dog, and in some qualities like the jackal." The

---

* There is another kind of cactus called by the whites "whisky-root," and by the Indian "peioke," used like the intoxicating mushroom of Siberia. "It grows in Southern Texas, in the range of sand-hills bordering on the Rio Grande, and in gravelly, sandy soil. The Indians eat it for its exhilarating effect on the system, producing precisely the same excitement as alcoholic drinks. It is sliced as you would a cucumber; the small piece is chewed and swallowed, and in about the same time as comfortably tight cocktails would 'stir the divinity within' you, this indicates itself; only its effects are what I might term a little *k-a-v-o-r-t-i-n-g*, giving rather a wilder scope to the imagination and actions."—(A Correspondent of the *New Orleans Picayune*, quoted by Mr. Bartlett.)

animal has so often been described that there is little new to say about it. The mountain men are all agreed upon one thing, namely, that the meat is by no means bad; most of them have tried "wolf-mutton" in hard times, and may expect to do so again. The civilizee shudders at the idea of eating wolf from a food-prejudice, whose consideration forms a curious chapter in human history. It is not very easy, says Dr. Johnson, to fix the principles upon which mankind have agreed to eat some animals and reject others; and as the principle is not evident, so it is not uniform. Originally invented for hygienic purposes, dietetic laws soon became tenets of religion, and passed far beyond their original intention: thus pork, for instance, injurious in Syria, would not be eaten by a Jew in Russia. An extreme arbitrariness marks the modern systems of civilized people: the Englishman, for instance, eats oysters, periwinkles, shrimps, and frogs, while he is nauseated by the snails, robins, and crows which the Frenchman uses; the Italian will devour a hawk, while he considers a rabbit impure, and has refused to touch potatoes even in a famine; and all delight in that foul feeder, the duck, while they reject the meat of the cleanly ass. The Mosaic law seems still to influence the European world, causing men to throw away much valuable provision because unaccustomed to eat it or to hear of its being eaten. The systems of China and Japan are far more sensible for densely populated countries, and the hippophagists have shown, at least, that one animal has been greatly wasted. The terrible famines, followed by the equally fearful pestilences, which have scourged mankind, are mainly owing to the prevalence of these food-prejudices, which, as might be expected, are the most deeply rooted in the poorer classes, who can least afford them.

I saw to-day, for the first time, a prairie-dog village. The little beast, hardly as large as a Guinea-pig, belongs to the family of squirrels and the group of marmots—in point of manner it somewhat resembles the monkey. "Wish-ton-Wish"*—an Indian onomatoplasm—was at home, sitting posted like a sentinel upon the roof, and sunning himself in the midday glow. It is not easy to shoot him; he is out of doors all day; but, timid and alert, at the least suspicion of danger he plunges with a jerking of the tail, and a somersault, quicker than a shy young rabbit's, into the nearest hole, peeping from the ground, and keeping up a feeble little cry (wish! ton! wish!), more like the note of a bird than a bark. If not killed outright, he will manage to wriggle into his home. The villages are generally on the brow of a hill, near a creek or pond, thus securing water without danger of drowning. The earth burrowed out while making the habitations is thrown up in heaps, which serve as sitting-places in the wet season, and give

* The name will recall to mind one of Mr. Fennimore Cooper's admirable fictions, the "Wept of Wish-ton-Wish," which was, however, a bird, the "Whip-poorwill," or American night-hawk.

E

a look-out upon the adjacent country; it is more dangerous to ride over them than to charge a field of East Indian "T'hur," and many a broken leg and collar-bone have been the result. The holes, which descend in a spiral form, must be deep, and they are connected by long galleries, with sharp angles, ascents and descents, to puzzle the pursuer. Lieutenant Pike had 140 kettles of water poured into one without dislodging the occupant. The village is always cleared of grass, probably by the necessities of the tenants, who, though they enjoy insects, are mainly graminivorous, and rarely venture half a mile from home. The limits are sometimes three miles square, and the population must be dense, as a burrow will occur every few paces. The *Cynomys Ludovicianus* prepares for winter by stopping the mouth of its burrow, and constructing a deeper cell, in which it hibernates till spring appears. It is a graceful little animal, dark brown above and white below, with teeth and nails, head and tail somewhat like the gray sciurus of the States. The Indians and trappers eat this American marmot, declaring its flesh to be fatter and better than that of the squirrel. Some travelers advise exposing the meat for a night or two to the frost, by which means the rankness of subterranean flavor is corrected. It is undoubted that the rattlesnake—both of the yellow and black species—and the small white burrowing-owl (*Strix cunicularia*) are often found in the same warren with this rodent, a curious happy family of reptile, bird, and beast, and in some places he has been seen to associate with tortoises, rattlesnakes, and horned frogs (*Phrynosoma*). According to some naturalists, however, the fraternal harmony is not so perfect as it might be: the owl is accused of occasionally gratifying his carnivorous lusts by laying open the skull of Wish-ton-Wish with a smart stroke of the beak. We sighted, not far from the prairie-dog village, an animal which I took to be a lynx; but the driver, who had often seen the beast in Minnesota and Old "Ouisconsinc," declared that they are not to be found here.

At 12 45 P.M., traveling over the uneven barren, and in a burning sirocco, we reached Lodge-Pole Station, where we made our "noonin." The hovel fronting the creek was built like an Irish shanty, or a Beloch hut, against a hill side, to save one wall, and it presented a fresh phase of squalor and wretchedness. The mud walls were partly papered with "Harper's Magazine," "Frank Leslie," and the "New York Illustrated News;" the ceiling was a fine festoon-work of soot, and the floor was much like the ground outside, only not nearly so clean. In a corner stood the usual "bunk,"* a mass of mingled rags and buffalo

---

* American writers derive this word from the Anglo-Saxon *benc*, whence the modern English "bench." It means a wooden case used in country taverns and in offices, and serving alike for a seat during the day and a bed at night. In towns it is applied to the tiers of standing bed peculiar to the lowest class of lodging-houses. In the West, it is a frame-work, in size and shape like a berth on board ship, sometimes single, sometimes double or treble.

robes; the centre of the room was occupied by a rickety table, and boxes, turned up on their long sides, acted as chairs. The unescapable stove was there, filling the interior with the aroma of meat. As usual, the materials for ablution, a "dipper" or cup, a dingy tin skillet of scanty size, a bit of coarse gritty soap, and a public towel, like a rag of gunny bag, were deposited upon a rickety settle outside.

There being no "lady" at the station on Lodge-Pole Creek, milk was unprocurable. Here, however, began a course of antelope venison, which soon told upon us with damaging effect. I well knew the consequences of this heating and bilious diet in Asia and Africa; but thinking it safe to do at Rome as the Romans do, I followed in the wake of my companions, and suffered with them. Like other wild meats, bear, deer, elk, and even buffalo, antelope will disagree with a stranger; it is, however, juicy, fat, and well-flavored, especially when compared with the hard, dry, stringy stuff which the East affords; and the hunter and trapper, like the Indian, are loud in its praise.

The habitat of the prong-horn antelope (*Antelocapra Americana*, called "le cabris" by the Canadian, and "the goat" by the unpoetic mountain man) extends from the plains west of the Missouri to the Pacific Ocean; it is also abundant on Minnesota and on the banks of the Red River; its southern limit is Northern Mexico, whence it ranges to 53° N. lat. on the Saskatchewan. It is about the size of a small deer, the male weighing 65 lbs. in good condition. The coat is coarse and wiry, yellow dun on the back, with dull white under the belly, and the tanned skin is worth three dollars. It is at once the fleetest and the wariest animal on the prairies, and its sense of hearing as acute as its power of smell. The best time for "still hunting" (*i. e.*, stalking) is at early dawn, when the little herds of four or five are busy grazing. They disappear during the midday heats of summer, and in the evening, as in India and Arabia, they are wild and wary. They assemble in larger bodies near the Rocky Mountains, where pasturage—not sage, which taints the meat—abounds, and the Indian savages kill them by surrounds, especially in winter, when the flesh is fattest. White men usually stalk them. During the migration season few are seen near the road; at other times they are often sighted. They are gifted, like the hippopotamus, with a truly feminine curiosity; they will stand for minutes to stare at a red wagon-bed, and, despite their extreme wariness, they will often approach, within shot, a scarlet kerchief tied to a stick, or any similar decoy. In manner they much resemble the Eastern gazelle. When the herd is disturbed, the most timid moves off first, followed by the rest; the walk gradually increases from a slow trot to a bounding gallop. At times they halt, one by one, and turn to gaze, but they presently resume flight, till they reach some prominent place where their keen vision can command the surrounding country. When well roused, they are thoroughly on the alert; the hunter will often find that, though he has moved toward them silently, up the wind and under cover, they have suspected sinister intentions and have shifted ground.

Besides the antelope, there are three species of deer in the regions east of the Rocky Mountains. Perhaps the most common is the red deer of the Eastern States (*Cervus Virginianus; le chevreuil*): it extends almost throughout the length of the continent, and is seemingly independent of altitude as of latitude. The venison is not considered equal to that of the antelope; travelers, however, kill off the deer to save butchers' bills, so that it is now seldom "glimpsed" from the line of route. The black-tailed or long-eared deer (*Cervus macrotis*) is confined to the higher ground; it has similar habits to the red variety, and is hunted in the same way. The long-tailed, or jumping deer (*Cervus leucrurus*, vulgarly called the roebuck), affects, like the black-tailed, the Rocky Mountains. The elk (*Cervus Canadensis*) is found in parts of Utah Territory and forty miles north of the mail-road, near the Wind-River Mountains—a perfect paradise for sportsmen. It is noble shooting, but poor eating as the Indian sambar.* The moose (*Cervus Alces*), the giant of the deer kind, sometimes rising seventeen hands high, and weighing 1200 lbs., is an inhabitant of higher latitudes—Nova Scotia, Canada, Maine, and other parts of New England.

At Lodge-Pole Station, the mules, as might be expected from animals allowed to run wild every day in the week except one, were like newly-caught mustangs.† The herdsman—each station boasts of this official—mounted a nag barebacked, and, jingling a bell, drove the cattle into the corral, a square of twenty yards, formed by a wall of loose stones, four to five feet high. He wasted three quarters of an hour in this operation, which a well-trained shepherd's dog would have performed in a few minutes. Then two men entering with lassos or lariats, thongs of flexible plaited or twisted hide, and provided with an iron ring at one end to form the noose—the best are made of hemp, Russian, not Manilla—proceeded, in a great "muss" on a small scale, to secure their victims. The lasso‡ in their hands was by no means the

---

* The elk is being domesticated in the State of New York; it is still, however, doubtful whether the animals will fatten well or supply milk, or serve for other than ornamental purposes.

† The mustang is the Spanish mesteño. The animal was introduced by the first colonists, and allowed to run at large. Its great variety of coat proves the mustang's degeneracy from the tame horse; according to travelers, cream-color, skewbald, and piebald being not uncommon. "Sparing in diet, a stranger to grain, easily satisfied whether on growing or dead grass, inured to all weathers, and capable of great labor," the mustang-pony is a treasure to the prairie-man.

‡ According to Mr. Bartlett, the lasso (Span. "lazo") is synonymous with "lariat" (Span. "lariata"). In common use, however, the first word is confined to the rope with which buffaloes, mustangs, or mules are caught; the second, which in the West is popularly pronounced "lariet," or "lariette," more generally means the article

"unerring necklace" which the Mexican *vaquéro* has taught it to be: they often missed their aim, or caught the wrong animal. The effect, however, was magical: a single haul at the noose made the most stiff-necked mule tame as a costermonger's ass. The team took, as usual, a good hour to trap and hitch up: the latter was a delicate operation, for the beasts were comically clever with their hoofs.

At 3 P.M., after a preliminary ringing, intended to soothe the fears of Madame, we set out *au grand galop*, with a team that had never worked together before. They dashed down the cahues with a violence that tossed us as in a blanket, and nothing could induce them, while fresh, to keep the path. The yawing of the vehicle was ominous: fortunately, however, the road, though self-made, was excellent; the sides were smooth, and the whole country fit to be driven over. At first the view was sadly monotonous. It was a fair specimen of the rolling prairie, in nowise differing from any other land except in the absence of trees. According to some travelers, there is in several places an apparently progressive decay of the timber, showing that formerly it was more extensive than it is now. Others attribute the phenomenon to the destruction of forests in a former era by fires or by the aborigines. It is more satisfactory to account for it by a complication of causes—a want of proper constituents, an insufficiency of rain, the depth of the water below the surface, the severity of the eight months of winter snow, the fierce winds — the hardiest growths that present their heads above the level of the prairies have dead tops—the shortness of the summers, and last, but not least, the clouds of grasshoppers. According to Lieutenant Warren, whose graphic description is here borrowed, these insects are "nearly the same as the locusts of Egypt; and no one who has not traveled on the prairie, and seen for himself, can appreciate the magnitude of the swarms. Often they fill the air for many miles of extent, so that an inexperienced eye can scarcely distinguish their appearance from that of a shower of rain or the smoke of a prairie fire. The height of their flight may be somewhat appreciated, as Mr. E. James saw them above his head, as far as their size would render them visible, while standing on the top of a peak of the Rocky Mountains, 3500 feet above the plain, and an elevation of 14,500 above that of the sea, in the region where the snow lies all the year. To a person standing in one of these swarms as they pass over and around him, the air becomes sensibly darkened, and the sound produced by their wings resembles that of the passage of a train of cars on a railroad when standing two or three hundred yards from the track. The Mormon settlements have suffered more from the ravages of these insects than

with which animals are picketed. Many authors, however, have made "lariat" the equivalent of "lasso." The Texans use, instead of the hide lasso, a hair rope called "caberes," from the Spanish "cabestro," a halter.

probably all other causes combined. They destroyed nearly all the vegetables cultivated last year at Fort Randall, and extended their ravages east as far as Iowa."

As we advanced, the horizon, every where within musket-shot —a wearying sight!—widened out, and the face of the country notably changed. A scrap of blue distance and high hills—the "Court-house" and others—appeared to the northwest. The long, curved lines, the gentle slopes, and the broad hollows of the divide facing the South Fork changed into an abrupt and precipitous descent, "gullied" like the broken ground of sub-ranges attached to a mountain chain. Deep ravines were parted by long narrow ridges, sharp-crested and water-washed, exposing ribs and backbones of sandstone and silicious lime, like the vertebræ of some huge saurian: scatters of kunker, with a detritus of quartz and granite, clothed the ground, and, after passing Lodge-Pole Creek, which bears away to the west, the rocky steps required the perpetual application of the brake. Presently we saw a dwarf cliff inclosing in an elliptical sweep a green amphitheatre, the valley of our old friend the Platte. On the far bank of its northern fork lay a forty-mile stretch of sandy, barren, glaring, heat-reeking ground, not unlike that which the overland traveler looking southward from Suez sees.* We left far to the right a noted spot, Ash Hollow, situated at the mouth of the creek of the same prenomen. It is described as a pretty bit in a barren land, about twenty acres, surrounded by high bluffs, well timbered with ash and cedar, and rich in clematis and other wild flowers. Here, in 1855, the doughty General Harney, with 700 to 800 men, "gave Jessie" to a large war-party of Brûlé Sioux under their chief Little Thunder, of whom more anon, killing 150, and capturing 60 squaws and children, with but seven or eight casualties in his own force.

Descending into the bed of a broad "arroyo,"† at this season bone dry, we reached, at 5 45 P.M., Mud-Spring Station, which takes its name from a little run of clear water in a black miry hollow. A kind of cress grows in it abundantly, and the banks are bright with the "morning-glory" or convolvulus. The station-house was not unlike an Egyptian fellah's hut. The material was sod, half peat with vegetable matter; it is taken up in large flakes after being furrowed with the plow, and is cut to proper lengths with a short-handled spade. Cedar timber,‡ brought from the neighboring hills, formed the roof. The only accommodation was an open shed, with a sort of doorless dormitory by its side.

---

* According to Lieutenant Warren, the tract called the Sand-hills occupies an area, north of the Platte, not less than 20,000 square miles: from between the Niobrara and White Rivers to the north, probably beyond the Arkansas in the south.

† The Arabo-Spanish "arroyo," a word almost naturalized by the Anglo-Americans, exactly corresponds with the Italian "fiumara" and the Indian nullah.

‡ The word "cedar," in the United States, is applied to various genera of the pine family. The red cedar (*J. Virginiana*) is a juniper. The "white cedar" of the Southern swamps is a cypress.

We dined in the shed, and amused ourselves with feeding the little brown-speckled swamp-blackbirds that hopped about us tame and "peert" as wrens, and when night drew near we sought shelter from the furious southern gale, and heard tales of Mormon suffering which made us think lightly of our little hardships.* Dreading the dormitory—if it be true that the sultan of fleas inhabits Jaffa and his vizier Grand Cairo, it is certain that his vermin officials have settled *pro tem.* on Emigration Road—I cast about for a quieter retreat. Fortune favored me by pointing out the body of a dismantled wagon, an article—like the Tyrian keels which suggested the magalia—often used as a habitation in the Far West, and not unfrequently honored by being converted into a bridal-chamber after the short and sharp courtship of the "Perraries." The host, who was a kind, intelligent, and civil man, lent me a "buffalo" by way of bedding; the water-proof completed my outfit, provided with which I bade adieu for a while to this weary world. The thermometer sank before dawn to 62° (F.). After five nights more or less in the cramping wagon, it might be supposed that we should have enjoyed the unusual rest; on the contrary, we had become inured to the exercise; we could have kept it up for a month, and we now grumbled only at the loss of time.

Past the Court-house and Scott's Bluffs. August 13th.

At 8 A.M., after breaking our fast upon a tough antelope steak, and dawdling while the herdsman was riding wildly about in search of his runaway mules—an operation now to become of daily occurrence—we dashed over the Sandy Creek with an *élan* calculated to make timid passengers look "skeery," and began to finish the rolling divide between the two forks. We crossed several arroyos and "criks" heading in the line of clay highlands to our left, a dwarf sierra which stretches from the northern to the southern branch of the Platte. The principal are Omaha Creek, more generally known as "Little Punkin,"† and Lawrence Fork.‡

* The Mormon emigrants usually start from Council Bluffs, on the left bank of the Missouri River, in N. lat. 41° 18′ 50″, opposite Kanesville, otherwise called Winter Quarters. According to the "Overland Guide," Council Bluffs is the natural crossing of the Missouri River, on the route destined by Nature for the great thoroughfare to the Pacific. This was the road selected by "Nature's civil engineers," the buffalo and the elk, for their western travel. The Indians followed them in the same trail; then the travelers; next the settlers came. After ninety-four miles' marching, the Mormons are ferried across Loup Fork, a stream thirteen rods wide, full of bars, with banks and a bottom all quicksand. Another 150 miles takes them to the Platte River, where they find good camping-places, with plenty of water, buffalo-chips, and grass. Eighty-two miles beyond that point (a total of 306), they arrive at "Last Timber," a station so called because, for the next 300 miles on the north side of the Platte, the only sign of vegetation is "Lone Tree." Many emigrants avoid this dreary "spell" by crossing the Platte opposite Ash Hollow. Others pass it at Platte-River Ferry, a short distance below the mouth of Laramie River, while others keep the old road to the north.

† Punkin (*i. e.*, pumpkin) and corn (*i. e.*, zea maize) are, and were from time immemorial, the great staples of native American agriculture.

‡ According to Webster, "forks" (in the plural)—the point where a river divides,

The latter is a pretty bubbling stream, running over sand and stones washed down from the Court-house Ridge; it bifurcates above the ford, runs to the northeast through a prairie four to five miles broad, and swells the waters of old Father Platte: it derives its name from a Frenchman slaughtered by the Indians, murder being here, as in Central Africa, ever the principal source of nomenclature. The heads of both streams afford quantities of currants, red, black, and yellow, and cherry-sticks which are used for spears and pipe-stems.

After twelve miles' drive we fronted the Court-house, the remarkable portal of a new region, and this new region teeming with wonders will now extend about 100 miles. It is the *mauvaises terres*, or Bad lands, a tract about 60 miles wide and 150 long, stretching in a direction from the northeast to the southwest, or from the Mankizitah (White-Earth) River, over the Niobrara (*Eau qui court*) and Loup Fork to the south banks of the Platte: its eastern limit is the mouth of the Keya Paha. The term is generally applied by the trader to any section of the prairie country where the roads are difficult, and by dint of an ill name the Bad lands have come to be spoken of as a Golgotha, white with the bones of man and beast. American travelers, on the contrary, declare that near parts of the White River "some as beautiful valleys are to be found as any where in the Far West," and that many places "abound in the most lovely and varied forms in endless variety, giving the most striking and pleasing effects of light and shade." The formation is the pliocene and miocene tertiary, uncommonly rich in vertebrate remains: the *mauvaises terres* are composed of nearly horizontal strata, and "though diversified by the effects of denuding agencies, and presenting in different portions striking characteristics, yet they are, as a whole, a great uniform surface, gradually rising toward the mountains, at the base of which they attain an elevation varying between 3000 and 5500 feet above the level of the sea."

The Court-house, which had lately suffered from heavy rain, resembled any thing more than a court-house; that it did so in former days we may gather from the tales of many travelers, old Canadian voyageurs, who unanimously accounted it a fit place for Indian spooks, ghosts, and hobgoblins to meet in powwow, and to "count their coups" delivered in the flesh. The Court-house lies about eight miles from the river, and three from the road; in circumference it may be half a mile, and in height 300 feet; it is, however, gradually degrading, and the rains and snows of not many years will lay it level with the ground. The material is a rough conglomerate of hard marl; the mass is apparently the flank or shoulder of a range forming the southern buttress of the Platte, and which, being composed of softer stuff, has gradually

or rather where two rivers meet and unite in one stream. Each branch is called a "fork." The word might be useful to English travelers.

melted away, leaving this remnant to rise in solitary grandeur above the plain. In books it is described as resembling a gigantic ruin, with a huge rotunda in front, windows in the sides, and remains of roofs and stages in its flanks: verily potent is the eye of imagination! To me it appeared in the shape of an irregular pyramid, whose courses were inclined at an ascendable angle of 35°, with a detached outwork composed of a perpendicular mass based upon a slope of 45°; in fact, it resembled the rugged earthworks of Sakkara, only it was far more rugged. According to the driver, the summit is a plane upon which a wagon can turn. My military companion remarked that it would make a fine natural fortress against Indians, and perhaps, in the old days of romance and Colonel Bonneville, it has served as a refuge for the harried fur-hunter. I saw it when set off by weather to advantage. A blazing sun rained fire upon its cream-colored surface—at 11 A.M. the glass showed 95° in the wagon—and it stood boldly out against a purple-black nimbus which overspread the southern skies, growling distant thunders, and flashing red threads of "chained lightning."

I had finished a hasty sketch, when suddenly appeared to us a most interesting sight—a neat ambulance,* followed by a fourgon and mounted soldiers, from which issued an officer in uniform, who advanced to greet Lieutenant Dana. The traveler was Captain, or rather Major Marcy, who was proceeding westward on leave of absence. After introduction, he remembered that his vehicle contained a compatriot of mine. The compatriot, whose length of facial hair at once told his race—for

"The larger the whisker, the greater the Tory"—

was a Mr. A——, British vice-consul at * * *'s, Minnesota. Having lately tried his maiden hand upon buffalo, he naturally concluded that I could have no other but the same object. Pleasant estimate, forsooth, of a man's brain, that it can find nothing in America worthy of its notice but bison-shooting! However, the supposition had a *couleur locale*. Every week the New York papers convey to the New World the interesting information that some distinguished Britisher has crossed the Atlantic and half crossed the States to enjoy the society of the "monarch of our prairies." Americans consequently have learned to look upon this Albionic eccentricity as "the thing." That unruly member the tongue was upon the point of putting in a something about

---

* The price of the strong light traveling wagon called an ambulance in the West is about $250; in the East it is much cheaper. With four mules it will vary from $750 to $900; when resold, however, it rarely fetches half that sum. A journey between St. Joseph and Great Salt Lake City can easily be accomplished in an ambulance within forty days. Officers and sportsmen prefer it, because they have their time to themselves, and they can carry stores and necessaries. On the other hand, "strikers"—soldier-helps—or Canadian *engagés* are necessary; and the pleasure of traveling is by no means enhanced by the nightly fear that the stock will "bolt," not to be recovered for a week, if then.

the earnest, settled purpose of shooting a prairie-dog, when the re-flection that it was hardly fair so far from home to "chaff" a com-patriot evidently big with the paternity of a great exploit, with bit and bridle curbed it fast.

Shortly after "liquoring up" and shaking hands, we found our-selves once more in the valley of the Platte, where a lively green relieved eyes which still retained retina-pictures of the barren. Sindh-like divide. The road, as usual along the river-side, was rough and broken, and puffs of simoom raised the sand and dust in ponderous clouds. At 12 30 P.M. we nooned for an hour at a little hovel called a ranch, with the normal corral; and I took occasion to sketch the far-famed Chimney Rock. The name is not, as is that of the Court-house, a misnomer: one might almost expect to see smoke or steam jetting from the summit. Like most of these queer malformations, it was once the knuckle-end of the main chain which bounded the Platte Valley; the softer

CHIMNEY ROCK.

adjacent strata of marl and earthy limestone were disintegrated by wind and weather, and the harder material, better resisting the action of air and water, has gradually assumed its present form. Chimney Rock lies two and a half miles from the south bank of the Platte. It is composed of a friable yellowish marl, yielding readily to the knife. The shape is a thin shaft, perpendicular and quasi conical. Viewed from the southeast it is not unlike a giant jack-boot based upon a high pyramidal mound, which, disposed in the natural slope, rests upon the plain. The neck of sand-stone connecting it with the adjacent hills has been distributed by the floods around the base, leaving an ever-widening gap between. This "Pharos of the prairie sea" towered in former days 150 to 200 feet above the apex of its foundation,* and was a landmark

* According to M. Preuss, who accompanied Colonel Frémont's expedition, "trav-

visible for 40 to 50 miles: it is now barely 35 feet in height.   It
has often been struck by lightning; *imber edax* has gnawed much
away, and the beginning of the end is already at hand.   It is easy
to ascend the pyramid; but, while Pompey's Pillar, Peter Botte,
and Ararat have all felt the Anglo-Scandinavian foot, no venturous scion of the race has yet trampled upon the top of Chimney
Rock.   Around the waist of the base runs a white band which
sets off its height and relieves the uniform tint.   The old sketches
of this curious needle now necessarily appear exaggerated; moreover, those best known represent it as a column rising from a
confused heap of boulders, thus conveying a completely false idea.
Again the weather served us: nothing could be more picturesque
than this lone pillar of pale rock lying against a huge black cloud,
with the forked lightning playing over its devoted head.

After a frugal dinner of biscuit and cheese we remounted and
pursued our way through airy fire, which presently changed from
our usual pest — a light dust-laden breeze — into a Punjaubian
dust-storm, up the valley of the Platte.   We passed a ranch called
" Robidoux' Fort," from the well-known Indian trader of that
name;* it is now occupied by a Canadian or a French Creole,

clers who visited it some years since placed its height at upward of 500 feet," though
in his day (1842) it had diminished to 200 feet above the river.

* From the *St. Joseph* (Mo.) *Gazette:* " Obituary.—Departed this life, at his residence in this city, on Wednesday, the 29th day of August, 1860, after a long ill-
ness, Antoine Robidoux, in the sixty-sixth year of his age.   Mr. Robidoux was born
in the city of St. Louis, in the year 1794.   He was one of the brothers of Mr. Joseph Robidoux, founder of the city of St. Joseph.   He was possessed of a sprightly
intellect and a spirit of adventure.   When not more than twenty-two years of age he
accompanied Gen. Atkinson to the then very wild and distant region of the Yellow
Stone.   At the age of twenty-eight he went to Mexico, and lived there fifteen years.
He then married a very interesting Mexican lady, who returned with him to the
States.   For many years he traded extensively with the Navajoes and Apaches.   In
1840 he came to this city with his family, and has resided here ever since.   In 1845
he went out to the mountains on a trading expedition, and was caught by the most
terrible storms, which caused the death of one or two hundred of his horses, and
stopped his progress.   His brother Joseph, the respectable founder of this city, sent
to his relief and had him brought in, or he would have perished.   He was found in
a most deplorable condition, and saved.   In 1846 he accompanied Gen. Kearney, as
interpreter and guide, to Mexico.   In a battle with the Mexicans he was lanced severely in three places, but he survived his wounds, and returned to St. Joseph in
1849.   Soon after that he went to California, and remained until 1854.   In 1855
he removed to New Mexico with his family, and in 1856 he went to Washington,
and remained there a year, arranging some business with the government.   He then
returned to St. Joseph, and has remained here ever since.   Mr. Robidoux was a very
remarkable man.   Tall, slender, athletic, and agile, he possessed the most graceful
and pleasing manners, and an intellect of a superior order.   In every company he
was affable, graceful, and highly pleasing.   His conversation was always interesting
and instructive, and he possessed many of those qualities which, if he remained in
the States, would have raised him to positions of distinction.   He suffered for several years before his death with a terrible soreness of the eyes, which defied the cura-
tive skill of the doctors; and for the past ten years he has been afflicted with drop-
sy.   A week or two ago he was taken with a violent hemorrhage of the lungs, which
completely prostrated him, and from the effects of which he never recovered.   He
was attended by the best medical skill, and his wife and many friends were with
him to the hour of his dissolution, which occurred on Monday morning, at four
o'clock, at his residence in this city.   He will be long remembered as a courteous,

who, as usual with his race in these regions, has taken to himself
a wife in the shape of a Sioux squaw, and has garnished his quiver with a multitude of whitey-reds.   The driver pointed out the
grave of a New Yorker who had vainly visited the prairies in
search of a cure for consumption.   As we advanced the storm
increased to a tornado of north wind, blinding our cattle till it
drove them off the road.   The gale howled through the pass with
all the violence of a khamsin, and it was followed by lightning
and a few heavy drops of rain.   The threatening weather caused
a large party of emigrants to "fort themselves" in a corral near
the base of Scott's Bluffs.

The corral, a Spanish and Portuguese word, which, corrupted
to "kraal," has found its way through Southern Africa, signifies
primarily a square or circular pen for cattle, which may be made
of tree-trunks, stones, or any other convenient material.   The
corral of wagons is thus formed.   The two foremost are brought
near and parallel to each other, and are followed by the rest, disposed aslant, so that the near fore wheel of the hinder touches
the off hind wheel of that preceding it, and *vice versâ* on the other
side.   The "tongues," or poles, are turned outward, for convenience of yoking, when an attack is not expected, otherwise they
are made to point inward, and the gaps are closed by ropes and
yoke and spare chains.   Thus a large oval is formed with a single opening fifteen to twenty yards across; some find it more
convenient to leave an exit at both ends.   In dangerous places
the passages are secured at night either by cords or by wheeling
round the near wagons; the cattle are driven in before sundown,
especially when the area of the oval is large enough to enable
them to graze, and the men sleep under their vehicles.   In safer
travel the tents are pitched outside the corral with their doors
outward, and in front of these the camp-fires are lighted.   The
favorite spots with teamsters for corraling are the re-entering angles of deep streams, especially where these have high and precipitous banks, or the crests of abrupt hills and bluffs—the position
for nighting usually chosen by the Australian traveler—where
one or more sides of the encampment is safe from attack, and the
others can be protected by a cross fire.   As a rule Indians avoid
attacking strong places; this, however, must not always be relied upon; in 1844 the Utah Indians attacked Uintah Fort, a
trading-post belonging to M. A. Robidoux, then at St. Louis,
slaughtered the men, and carried off the women.   The corral is
especially useful for two purposes: it enables the wagoners to
yoke up with ease, and it secures them from the prairie traveler's
prime dread—the stampede.   The Western savages are perfectly
acquainted with the habits of animals, and in their marauding
expeditions they instinctively adopt the system of the Bedouins,

cultivated, agreeable gentleman, whose life was one of great activity and public use-
fulness, and whose death will be long lamented."

the Gallas, and the Somal. Providing themselves with rattles and other implements for making startling noises, they ride stealthily up close to the cattle, and then rush by like the whirl-wind with a volley of horrid whoops and screams. When the "cavallard" flies in panic fear, the plunderers divide their party; some drive on the plunder, while the others form a rear-guard to keep off pursuers. The prairie-men provide for the danger by keeping their fleetest horses saddled, bridled, and ready to be mounted at a moment's notice. When the animals have stam-peded, the owners follow them, scatter the Indians, and drive, if possible, the madriña, or bell-marc, to the front of the herd, grad-ually turning her toward the camp, and slacking speed as the fa-miliar objects come in sight. Horses and mules appear peculiar-ly timorous upon the prairies. A band of buffalo, a wolf, or even a deer, will sometimes stampede them; they run to great distances, and not unfrequently their owners fail to recover them.

"Scott's Bluffs," situated 285 miles from Fort Kearney and 51 from Fort Laramie, was the last of the great marl formations which we saw on this line, and was of all by far the most curious. In the dull uniformity of the prairies, it is a striking and attract-ive object, far excelling the castled crag of Drachenfels or any of the beauties of romantic Rhine. From a distance of a day's march it appears in the shape of a large blue mound, distinguished only by its dimensions from the detached fragments of hill around. As you approach within four or five miles, a massive medieval city gradually defines itself, clustering, with a wonderful fullness of detail, round a colossal fortress, and crowned with a royal cas-tle. Buttress and barbican, bastion, demilune, and guard-house, tower, turret, and donjon-keep, all are there: in one place para-

SCOTT'S BLUFFS.

pets and battlements still stand upon the crumbling wall of a fortalice like the giant ruins of Château Gaillard, the "Beautiful Castle on the Rock;" and, that nothing may be wanting to the resemblance, the dashing rains and angry winds have cut the old line of road at its base into a regular moat with a semicircular sweep, which the mirage fills with a mimic river. Quaint figures develop themselves; guards and sentinels in dark armor keep watch and ward upon the slopes, the lion of Bastia crouches unmistakably overlooking the road; and as the shades of an artificial evening, caused by the dust-storm, close in, so weird is its aspect that one might almost expect to see some spectral horseman, with lance and pennant, go his rounds about the deserted streets, ruined buildings, and broken walls. At a nearer aspect again, the quaint illusion vanishes; the lines of masonry become yellow layers of boulder and pebble imbedded in a mass of stiff, tamped, bald marly clay; the curtains and angles change to the gashings of the rains of ages, and the warriors are metamorphosed into dwarf cedars and dense shrubs, scattered singly over the surface. Travelers have compared this glory of the *mauvaises terres* to Gibraltar, to the Capitol at Washington, to Stirling Castle. I could think of nothing in its presence but the Arabs' "City of Brass," that mysterious abode of bewitched infidels, which often appears at a distance to the wayfarer toiling under the burning sun, but ever eludes his nearer search.

Scott's Bluffs derive their name from an unfortunate fur-trader there put on shore in the olden time by his boat's crew, who had a grudge against him: the wretch, in mortal sickness, crawled up the mound to die. The politer guide-books call them "Capitol Hills:" methinks the first name, with its dark associations, must be better pleasing to the *genius loci*. They are divided into three distinct masses. The largest, which may be 800 feet high, is on the right, or nearest the river. To its left lies an outwork, a huge, detached cylinder whose capping changes aspect from every direction; and still farther to the left is a second castle, now divided from, but once connected with the others. The whole affair is a spur springing from the main range, and closing upon the Platte so as to leave no room for a road.

After gratifying our curiosity we resumed our way. The route lay between the right-hand fortress and the outwork, through a degraded bed of softer marl, once doubtless part of the range. The sharp, sudden torrents which pour from the heights on both sides, and the draughty winds—Scott's Bluffs are the permanent head-quarters of hurricanes—have cut up the ground into a labyrinth of jagged gulches steeply walled in. We dashed down the drains and pitch-holes with a violence which shook the nave-bands from our sturdy wheels.* Ascending, the driver showed a place

* The dry heat of the prairies in summer causes the wood to warp by the percolation of water, which the driver restores by placing the wheels for a night to stand in

where the skeleton of an "elephant" had been lately discovered. On the summit he pointed out, far over many a treeless hill and barren plain, the famous Black Hills and Laramie Peak, which has been compared to Ben Lomond, towering at a distance of eighty miles. The descent was abrupt, with sudden turns round the head of earth-cracks deepened to ravines by snow and rain; and one place showed the remains of a wagon and team which had lately come to grief. After galloping down a long slope of twelve miles, with ridgelets of sand and gravel somewhat raised above the bottom, which they cross on their way to the river, we found ourselves, at 5 30 P.M., once more in the valley of the Platte. I had intended to sketch the Bluffs more carefully from the station, but the western view proved to be disappointingly inferior to the eastern. After the usual hour's delay we resumed our drive through alternate puffs of hot and cold wind, the contrast of which was not easy to explain. The sensation was as if Indians had been firing the prairies—an impossibility at this season, when whatever herbage there is is still green. It may here be mentioned that, although the meteorology of the earlier savans, namely, that the peculiar condition of the atmosphere known as the Indian summer* might be produced by the burning of the plain-vegetation, was not thought worthy of comment, their hypothesis is no longer considered trivial. The smoky canopy must produce a sensible effect upon the temperature of the season. "During a still night, when a cloud of this kind is overhead, no dew is produced; the heat which is radiated from the earth is reflected or absorbed, and radiated back again by the particles of soot, and the coating of the earth necessary to prevent the deposition of water in the form of dew or hoar-frost is prevented." According to Professor Henry, of Washington, "it is highly probable that a portion of the smoke or fog-cloud produced by the burning of one of the Western prairies is carried entirely across the eastern portion of the continent to the ocean."

Presently we dashed over the Little Kiowa Creek, forded the Horse Creek, and, enveloped in a cloud of villainous musquetoes,

some stream. Paint or varnish is of little use. Moisture may be drawn out even through a nail-hole, and exhaust the whole interior of the wood-work.

* These remarks are borrowed from a paper by Professor Joseph Henry, Secretary of the Smithsonian Institution, entitled "Meteorology in its Connection with Agriculture."

The Indian summer is synonymous with our St. Martin's or Allhallows summer, so called from the festival held on the 11th of November. "The Indians avail themselves of this delightful time for harvesting their corn; and the tradition is that they were accustomed to say they always had a second summer of nine days before the winter set in. It is a bland and genial time, in which the birds, insects, and plants feel a new creation, and enjoy a short-lived summer ere they shrink finally from the rigor of the winter's blast. The sky, in the mean time, is generally filled with a haze of orange and gold, intercepting the direct rays of the sun, yet possessing enough of light and heat to prevent sensations of gloom or chill, while the nights grow sharp and frosty, and the necessary fires give cheerful forecast of the social winter evenings near at hand."—The *National Intelligencer*, Nov. 26th, 1857, quoted by Mr. Bartlett.

entered at 8 30 P.M. the station in which we were to pass the
night. It was tenanted by one Reynal, a French Creole—the son
of an old soldier of the Grand Armée, who had settled at St. Louis
—a companionable man, but an extortionate: he charged us a
florin for every "drink" of his well-watered whisky. The house
boasted of the usual squaw, a wrinkled old dame, who at once began to prepare supper, when we discreetly left the room. These
hard-working but sorely ill-favored beings are accused of various
horrors in cookery, such as grinding their pinole, or parched corn,
in the impurest manner, kneading dough upon the floor, using
their knives for any purpose whatever, and employing the same
pot, unwashed, for boiling tea and tripe. In fact, they are about
as clean as those Eastern pariah servants who make the knowing
Anglo-Indian hold it an abomination to sit at meat with a new
arrival or with an officer of a "home regiment." The daughter
was an unusually fascinating half-breed, with a pale face and
Franco-American features. How comes it that here, as in Hindostan, the French half-caste is pretty, graceful, amiable, coquettish, while the Anglo-Saxon is plain, coarse, gauche, and ill-tem-
pered? The beauty was married to a long, lean down-Easter,
who appeared most jealously attentive to her, occasionally hinting at a return to the curtained bed, where she could escape the
admiring glances of strangers. Like her mother, she was able to
speak English, but she could not be persuaded to open her mouth.
This is a truly Indian prejudice, probably arising from the savage, childish sensitiveness which dreads to excite a laugh; even
a squaw married to a white man, after uttering a few words in a
moment of *épanchement*, will hide her face under the blanket.

The half-breed has a bad name in the land. Like the negro,
the Indian belongs to a species, sub-species, or variety—whichever
the reader pleases—that has diverged widely enough from the
Indo-European type to cause degeneracy, physical as well as moral, and often, too, sterility in the offspring. These half-breeds are,
therefore, like the mulatto, quasi-mules. The men combine the
features of both races; the skin soon becomes coarse and wrinkled, and the eye is black, snaky, and glittering like the Indian's.
The mongrels are short-lived, peculiarly subject to infectious diseases, untrustworthy, and disposed to every villainy. The half-
breed women, in early youth, are sometimes attractive enough,
uniting the figure of the mother to the more delicate American
face; a few years, however, deprive them of all litheness, grace,
and agility. They are often married by whites, who hold them
to be more modest and humble, less capricious and less exacting,
than those of the higher type: they make good wives and affectionate mothers, and, like the Quadroons, they are more "ambitious"—that is to say, of warmer temperaments—than either of
the races from which they are derived. The so-called red is a
higher ethnic type than the black man; so, in the United States,

where all admixture of African blood is deemed impure, the aboriginal American entails no disgrace—some of the noblest of the land are descended from "Indian princesses." The half-breed girls resemble their mothers in point of industry, and they barter their embroidered robes and moccasins, and mats and baskets. made of bark and bulrush, in exchange for blankets, calicoes, glass beads—an indispensable article of dress—mirrors, needles, rings, vermilion, and other luxuries. The children, with their large black eyes, wide mouths, and glittering teeth, flattened heads, and remarkable agility of motion, suggest the idea of little serpents.

The day had been fatiguing, and our eyes ached with the wind and dust. We lost no time in spreading on the floor the buffalo robes borrowed from the house, and in defying the smaller tenants of the ranch. Our host, M. Reynal, was a study, but we deferred the lesson till the next morning.

To Fort Laramie. 14th August.

M. Reynal had been an Indian trader in his youth. Of this race there were in his day two varieties: the regular trader and the *coureur des bois*, or unlicensed peddler, who was subject to certain pains and penalties. The former had some regard for his future; he had a permanent interest in the Indians, and looked to the horses, arms, and accoutrements of his *protégés*, so that hunting might not flag. The *bois brûlé* peddler, having—like an English advertising firm—no hope of dealing twice with the same person, got all he could for what he could. These men soon sapped the foundation of the Indian's discipline. One of them, for instance, would take protection with the chief, pay presents, and by increasing the wealth, enhance the importance of his protector. Another would place himself under the charge of some ambitious aspirant to power, who was thus raised to a position of direct rivalry. A split would ensue; the weaker would secede with his family and friends, and declare independence; a murder or two would be the result, and a blood-feud would be bequeathed from generation to generation. The licensed traders have ever strenuously opposed the introduction of alcohol, a keg of which will purchase from the Indian every thing that is his, his arms, lodge, horses, children, and wives. In olden times, however, the Maine Liquor Law was not, as now, in force through the territories. The *coureur des bois*, therefore, entered the country through various avenues, from the United States and from Mexico, without other stock in trade but some kegs of whisky, which he retailed at the modest price of $36 per gallon. He usually mixed one part of fire with five of pure water, and then sold a pint-canful for a buffalo robe. "Indian liquor" became a proverbial term. According to some travelers, a barrel of "pure Cincinnati," even after running the gauntlet of railroad and lake travel, has afforded a

F

hundred barrels of "good Indian liquor." A small bucketful is poured into a wash-tub of water; a large quantity of "dog-leg" tobacco and red pepper is then added, next a bitter root common in the country is cut up into it, and finally it is colored with burnt sugar—a nice recipe for a morning's headache! The only drawback to this traffic is its danger. The Indian, when intoxicated, is ready for any outrageous act of violence or cruelty; vinosity brings out the destructiveness and the utter barbarity of his character; it makes him thirst tiger-like for blood. The *coureur des bois*, therefore, who in those days was highly respected, was placed in the Trader's Lodge, a kind of public house, like the Iwanza of Central Africa, and the village chief took care to station at the door a guard of sober youths, sometimes habited like Europeans, ready to check the unauthorized attempts of ambitious clansmen upon the whisky-vendor's scalp. The Western men, who will frequently be alluded to in these pages, may be divided, like the traders, into two classes. The first is the true mountaineer, whom the platitude and tame monotony of civilized republican life has in early youth driven, often from an honored and wealthy family, to the wilds and wolds, to become the forlorn hope in the march of civilization. The second is the offscouring and refuse of the Eastern cities, compelled by want, fatuity, or crime to exile himself from all he most loves. The former, after passing through the preliminary stage greenhorn, is a man in every sense of the term: to more than Indian bravery and fortitude, he unites the softness of woman, and a child-like simplicity, which is the very essence of a chivalrous character; you can read his nature in his clear blue eyes, his sun-tanned countenance, his merry smile, and his frank, fearless manner. The latter is a knave or a fool; it would make "bad blood," as the Frenchman says, to describe him.

M. Reynal's history had to be received with many grains of salt. The Western man has been worked by climate and its consequences, by the huge magnificence of nature and the violent contrasts of scenery, into a remarkable resemblance to the wild Indian. He hates labor—which poet and divine combine to deify in the settled states—as the dire effect of a primeval curse; "loaf" he must and will; to him one hour out of the twenty-four spent in honest industry is *satis superque*. His imagination is inflamed by scenery and climate, difficulty and danger; he is as superstitious as an old man-o'-war's-man of the olden school; and he is a transcendental liar, like his prototype the aborigine, who in this point yields nothing to the African negro. I have heard of a man riding eighty miles—forty into camp and forty out—in order to enjoy the sweet delights of a lie. His yarns and stories about the land he lives in have become a proverbial ridicule; he will tell you that the sun rises north of what it did *se puero;* he has seen mountains of diamonds and gold nuggets scattered like rocks

over the surface of our general mother.   I have been gravely told
of a herd of bison which arrested the course of the Platte River,
causing its waters, like those of the Red Sea, to stand up, wall
fashion, while the animals were crossing.   Of this Western order
is the well-known account of a ride on a buffalo's horns, delivered for the benefit of a gaping world by a popular author of the
yellow-binding category.   In this age, however, the Western man
has become sensitive to the operation of "smoking."   A popular
Joe Miller anent him is this: A traveler, informed of what he
might educe by "querying," asked an old mountaineer, who shall
be nameless, what difference he observed in the country since he
had first settled in it.

   " Wal, stranger, not much!" was the reply; "only when I fust
come here, that 'ere mountain," pointing to the tall Uinta range,
"was a hole!"

   Disembarrassing M. Reynal's recital of its mask of improbabil-
ities and impossibilities, remained obvious the naked fact that he
had led the life of a confirmed *coureur des bois*.   The French Canadian and Creole both, like the true Français de France, is loth
to stir beyond the devil-dispelling sound of his chapel-bell; once
torn from his *chez lui*, he apparently cares little to return, and,
like the Englishman, to die at home in his own land.   The adventurous Canadians—in whom extremes meet—have wandered
through the length and breadth of the continent; they have left
their mark even upon the rocks in Utah Territory.   M. Reynal
had quitted St. Louis at an early age as trader, trapper, every
thing in short, provided with a little outfit of powder, ball, and
whisky.   At first he was unfortunate.   In a war between the
Sioux and the Pawnees, he was taken prisoner by the latter, and
with much ado preserved, by the good aid of his squaw, that useful article his scalp.   Then fickle fortune turned in his favor.
He married several wives, identified himself with the braves, and
became a little brother of the tribe, while his whisky brought him
in an abundance of furs and peltries.   After many years, waxing
weary of a wandering life, he settled down into the somewhat
prosaic position in which we had the pleasure of finding him.
He was garrulous as a veteran soldier upon the subject of his old
friends the trappers, that gallant advance guard who, sixty years
ago, unconsciously fought the fight of civilization for the pure
love of fighting; who battled with the Indian in his own way,
surpassing him in tracking, surprising, ambuscading, and shooting, and never failing to raise the enemy's hair.   They are well-
nigh extinct, those old pioneers, wild, reckless, and brave as the
British tar of a century past; they live but in story; their place
knows them no longer; it is now filled by the "prospector."
Civilization and the silk hat have exterminated them.   How
many deeds of stern fight and heroic endurance have been ignored
by this world, which knows nothing of its greatest men, *carent*

quia vate sacro! We talk of Thermopylæ and ignore Texas; we have all thrilled at the account of the Mameluke Bey's leap; but how many of us have heard of Major Macculloch's spring from the cliff?

Our breakfast was prepared in the usual prairie style. First the coffee—three parts burnt beans, which had been duly ground to a fine powder and exposed to the air, lest the aroma should prove too strong for us—was placed on the stove to simmer till every noxious principle was duly extracted from it. Then the rusty bacon, cut into thick slices, was thrown into the fry-pan: here the gridiron is unknown, and if known would be little appreciated, because it wastes the "drippings," which form with the staff of life a luxurious sop. Thirdly, antelope steak, cut off a corpse suspended for the benefit of flies outside, was placed to stew within influence of the bacon's aroma. Lastly came the bread, which of course should have been "cooked" first. The meal is kneaded with water and a pinch of salt; the raising is done by means of a little sour milk, or more generally by the deleterious yeast-powders of the trade. The carbonic acid gas evolved by the addition of water must be corrected, and the dough must be expanded by saleratus or prepared carbonate of soda or alkali, and other vile stuff, which communicates to the food the green-yellow tinge, and suggests many of the properties of poison. A hundred-fold better, the unpretending chapati, flap-jack, scone, or, as the Mexicans prettily called it, "tortilla!" The dough, after being sufficiently manipulated upon a long, narrow, smooth board, is divided into "biscuits" and "dough-nuts,"[*] and finally it is placed to be half cooked under the immediate influence of the rusty bacon and graveolent antelope. "Uncle Sam's stove," be it said with every reverence for the honored name it bears, is a triumph of convenience, cheapness, unwholesomeness, and nastiness—excuse the word, nice reader. This travelers' bane has exterminated the spit and gridiron, and makes every thing taste like its neighbor: by virtue of it, mutton borrows the flavor of salmon trout, tomatoes resolve themselves into greens. I shall lose my temper if the subject is not dropped.

We set out at 6 A.M. over a sandy bottom, from which the musquetoes rose in swarms. After a twelve-mile stretch the driver pointed out on the right of the road, which here runs between high earth-banks, a spot still infamous in local story. At this place, in 1854, five Indians, concealing themselves in the bed of a dwarf arroyo, fired upon the mail-wagon, killing two drivers and one passenger, and then plundered it of 20,000 dollars.

---

[*] The Western "biscuit" is English roll; "cracker" is English biscuit. The "dough-nut" is, properly speaking, a "small roundish cake, made of flour, eggs, and sugar, moistened with milk and boiled in lard" (Webster). On the prairies, where so many different materials are unprocurable, it is simply a diminutive loaf, like the hot roll of the English passenger steamer.

"Long-chin," the leader, and the other murderers, when given up by the tribe, were carried to Washington, D. C., where—with the ultra-philanthropy which has of modern days distinguished the "Great Father's" government of his "Poor Children of the Plains"—the villains were liberally rewarded and restored to their homes.*   To cut off a bend of the Platte we once more left the valley, ascended sundry slopes of sand and clay deeply cut by dry creeks, and from the summit enjoyed a pretty view.   A little to the left rose the aerial blue cone of that noble landmark, Laramie Peak, based like a mass of solidified air upon a dark wall, the Black Hills, and lit up with the roseate hues of the morning. The distance was about sixty miles; you would have guessed twenty.   On the right lay a broad valley, bounded by brown rocks and a plain-colored distance, with the stream winding through it like a thread of quicksilver; in places it was hidden from sight by thickets of red willow, cypress clumps, and dense cool cotton-woods.   All was not still life; close below us rose the white lodges of the Ogalala tribe.

These Indian villages are very picturesque from afar when dimly seen dotting the verdure of the valleys, and when their tall white cones, half hidden by willow clumps, lie against a blue background.   The river side is the savages' favorite site; next to it the hill foot, where little groups of three or four tents are often seen from the road, clustering mysteriously near a spring.   Almost every prairie-band has its own way of constructing lodges, encamping and building fires, and the experienced mountaineer easily distinguishes them.

The Osages make their lodges in the shape of a wagon-tilt, somewhat like our gipsies' tents, with a frame-work of bent willow rods planted in the ground, and supporting their blankets, skins, or tree-basts.

The Kickapoos build dwarf hay-stack huts, like some tribes of Africans, setting poles in the earth, binding them over and lashing them together at the top; they are generally covered with clothes or bark.

The Witchetaws, Wakoes, Towakamis, and Tonkowas are described by the "Prairie Traveler" as erecting their hunting lodges of sticks put up in the form of the frustrum of a cone, and bushed over like "boweries."

All these tribes leave the frame-work of their lodges standing when they shift ground, and thus the particular band is readily recognized.

* A United States official, fresh from Columbia, informed me that the Indians there think twice before they murder a King George's man (Briton), while they hardly hesitate to kill a Boston man or American citizen.   He attributed this peculiarity principally to the over lenity of his own government, and its want of persistency in ferreting out and punishing the criminal.   Under these circumstances, it is hardly to be wondered at if the trader and traveler in Indian countries take the law in their own hands.   This excessive clemency has acted evilly in "either Ind." We may hope that its day is now gone by.

The Sacs, Foxes, Winnebagoes, and Menomenes build lodges in the form of an ellipse, some of them 30—40 feet long, by 14—15 wide, and large enough to shelter twenty people permanently, and sixty temporarily.* The covering is of plaited rush-mats bound to the poles, and a small aperture in the lodge acts as chimney.

The Delawares and Shawnees, Cherokees and Choctaws, prefer the Indian pal, a canvas covering thrown like a *tente d'abri* over a stick supported by two forked poles.

The Sioux, Arapahoes, Cheyennes, Utahs, Snakes, Blackfeet, and Kiowas use the Comanche lodge covered with bison skins, which by dressing become flexible as canvas. They are usually of a shining white, save where smoke-stained near the top; the lodges of great chiefs are sometimes decorated with horizontal stripes of alternate black and white, and ornamented with figures human and bestial, crosses, circles, and arabesques. The lodge is made of eight to twenty-four straight peeled poles or saplings of ash, pine, cedar, or other wood, hard and elastic if possible, about 20 feet long; the largest marquees are 30 feet in diameter by 35 feet high, and are comprised of 26—30 buffalo skins; and they are sometimes planted round a " basement" or circular excavation two or three feet deep. When pitching, three poles lashed to one another with a long line, somewhat below the thinner points, are raised perpendicularly, and the thicker ends are spread out in a tripod to the perimeter of the circle which is to form the lodge floor; the rest of the poles are then propped against the three first, and disposed regularly and equidistantly to make a steady and secure conical frame-work. The long line attached to the tripod is then wound several times round the point where the poles touch, and the lower end is made fast to the base of the lodge, thus securing the props in position. The covering of dressed, hairless, and water-proof cow-buffalo hide—traders prefer osnaburg—cut and sewn to fit the frame like an envelope, and sometimes pinned together with skewers, is either raised at first with the tripod, or afterward hoisted with a perch and spread round the complete structure. It is pinned to the ground with wooden pegs, and a narrow space forms a doorway, which may be closed with a blanket suspended from above and spread out with two small sticks. The apex is left open with a triangular wing or flap, like a lateen sail, and is prevented from closing by a pole inserted into a pocket at the end. The aperture points to windward when ventilation is required, and, drawing like a wind-sail, it keeps the interior cool and comfortable; when smoke is to be carried off, it is turned to leeward, thus giving draught to the fire, and making the abode warm in the severest weather; while in lodges of other forms,

* The wigwams, huts, or cabins of the Eastern American tribes were like these, large, solid, and well roofed with skins. The word "lodge" is usually applied to the smaller and less comfortable habitations of the Prairie Indians.

you must lie down on the ground to prevent being asphyxiated. By raising the lower part so as freely to admit the breeze, it is kept perfectly free from musquetoes, which are unable to resist the strong draught. The squaws are always the tent-pitchers, and they equal Orientals in dexterity and judgment. Before the lodge of each warrior stands his light spear, planted Bedouin-fashion in the ground, near or upon a tripod of thin, cleanly-scraped wands, seven to eight feet long, which support his spotless white buffalo-skin targe, sometimes decorated with his "totem"—we translate the word "crest"—and guarded by the usual prophylactic, a buckskin sack containing medicine. Readers of "Ivanhoe"—they are now more numerous in the New than in the Old Country—ever feel "a passing impulse to touch one of these spotless shields with the muzzle of the gun, expecting a grim warrior to start from the lodge and resent the challenge." The fire, as in the old Hebridean huts, is built in the centre of the hard dirt floor; a strong stick planted at the requisite angle supports the kettle, and around the walls are berths divided by matted screens; the extremest uncleanliness, however, is a feature never absent. In a quiet country these villages have a simple and patriarchal appearance. The tents, which number from fifteen to fifty, are disposed round a circular central space, where animals can be tethered. Some have attached to them corrals of wattled canes, and a few boast of fields where corn and pumpkins are raised.

The Comanche lodge is the favorite tenement of the Canadian and Creole voyageurs, on account of its coolness or warmth when wanted, its security against violent winds, and its freedom from musquetoes. While traveling in an Indian country they will use no other. It has been simplified by Major H. H. Sibley, of the United States Army, who has changed the pole frame-work for a single central upright, resting upon an iron tripod, with hooks for suspending cooking utensils over the fire; when folded up, the tripod admits the upright between its legs, thereby reducing the length to one half—a portable size. The "Sibley tent" was the only shelter of the United States Army at Fort Scott, in Utah Territory, during the hard winter of 1857–8, and gave universal satisfaction. The officers still keep to the old wall-tent. This will, however, eventually be superseded by the new form, which can accommodate comfortably twelve, but not seventeen, the usual number allotted to it. Captain Marcy is of opinion that of the tents used in the different armies of Europe, "none in point of convenience, comfort, and economy will compare with the 'Sibley tent' for campaigning in cold weather." In summer, however, it has, like all conical tents, many disadvantages: there is always a loss of room; and for comfortably disposing kit—chair, table, and camp couch—there is nothing equal to the wall-tent. The price of a "Sibley," when made of good material, is from $40 to $50 (£8—£10), and it can be procured from Baltimore, Philadelphia, and New York.

At 10 20 A.M. we halted to change mules at Badeau's Ranch, or, as it is more grandiloquently called, "Laramie City." The "city," like many a Western "town," still appertains to the category of things about to be; it is at present represented by a single large "store," with out-houses full of small half-breeds. The principal articles of traffic are liquors and groceries for the whites, and ornaments for the Indians, which are bartered for stock (*i. e.*, animals) and peltries. The prices asked for the skins were from $1—$1 30 for a fox or a coyote, $3 for wolf, bear, or deer, $6—$7 for an elk, $5 for a common buffalo, and from $8 to $35 for the same painted, pictographed, and embroidered. Some of the party purchased moccasins, for which they paid $1—$2; the best articles are made by the Snakes, and when embroidered by white women rise as high as $25. I bought, for an old friend who is insane upon the subject of pipes, one of the fine marble-like sandstone bowls brought from the celebrated Côteau (slope) des Prairies, at the head of Sioux River—

> "On the mountains of the Prairie,
> On the Great Red Pipe-stone Quarry."

This instrument is originally the gift of Gitchie Manitou, who, standing on the precipice of the Red Pipe-stone Rock, broke off a fragment and moulded it into a pipe, which, finished with a reed, he smoked over his children to the north, south, east, and west. It is of queer shape, not unlike the clay and steatite articles used by the Abyssinians and the Turi or Sinaitic Bedouins. The length of the stick is 23 inches, of the stem 9·50, and of the bowl 5 inches; the latter stands at a right angle upon the former; both are circular; but the 2·75 inches of stem, which project beyond the bowl, are beveled off so as to form an edge at the end. The peculiarity of the form is in the part where the tobacco is inserted; the hole is not more than half an inch broad, and descends straight without a bulge, while the aperture in the stem is exactly similar. The red color soon mottles and the bowl clogs if smoked with tobacco; in fact, it is fit for nothing but the "kinnikinik" of the Indians. To prepare this hard material with the rude tools of a savage must be a work of time and difficulty; also the bowls are expensive and highly valued: for mine I paid $5, and farther West I could have exchanged it for an Indian pony.

Having finished our *emplettes* at M. Badeau's, we set out at 11 30 P.M. over a barren and recking bit of sandy soil. Close to the station, and a little to the right of the road, we passed the barrow which contains the remains of Lieutenant Grattan and his thirty men. A young second lieutenant of Irish origin and fiery temper, he was marching westward with an interpreter, a small body of men, and two howitzers, when a dispute arose, it is said, about a cow, between his party and the Brûlés or Burnt-Thigh Indians. The latter were encamped in a village of 450 to 500 lodges, which, reckoning five to each, gives a total of 2200 to 2500 souls. A fight took place; the whites imprudently discharged both their cannon, overshooting the tents of the enemy; their muskets, however, did more execution, killing Matriya, "the Scattering Bear," who had been made chief of all the Sioux by Colonel Mitchell of the Indian Bureau.   The savages, seeing the fall of Ursa Major, set to in real earnest; about 1200 charged the soldiers before they could reload; the little detachment broke, and not a man survived to tell the tale.   The whites in the neighborhood narrowly preserved their scalps—M. Badeau owned that he owed his to his Sioux squaw—and among other acts of violence was the murder and highway robbery which has already been recounted.   Both these events occurred in 1854.   As has been said, in 1855, General W. S. Harney, who, whatever may be his faults as a diplomatist, is the most dreaded "Minahaska"* in the Indian country, punished the Brûlés severely at Ash Hollow.   They were led by their chosen chief Little Thunder, who, not liking the prospect, wanted to palaver; the general replied by a charge, which, as usual, scattered the "chivalry of the prairies" to the four winds. "Little Thunder" was solemnly deposed, and Mato Chigukesa, "Bear's Rib," was ordered to reign in his stead; moreover, in 1856, a treaty was concluded, giving to whites, among other things, the privilege of making roads along the Platte and White-Earth Rivers (Mankisita Wakpa—Smoking-earth Water) to Forts Pierre and Laramie, and to pass up and down the Missouri in boats.   Since that time, with the exception of plundering an English sportsman, Sir G—— G——, opposing Lieutenant Warren's expedition to the Black Hills, and slaughtering a few traders and obscure travelers, the Brûlés have behaved tolerably to their paleface rivals.

As we advanced the land became more barren; it sadly wanted rain: it suffers from drought almost every year, and what vegetable matter the soil will produce the grasshopper will devour. Dead cattle cumbered the way-side; the flesh had disappeared; the bones were scattered over the ground; but the skins, mummified, as it were, by the dry heat, lay life-like and shapeless, as in the Libyan Desert, upon the ground.   This phenomenon will last till we enter the humid regions between the Sierra Nevada and the Pacific Ocean, and men tell wonderful tales of the time during which meat can be kept.   The road was a succession of steep ascents and jumps down sandy ground.   A Sioux "buck," mounted upon a neat nag, and wrapped up, despite sun and glare, as if it had been the depth of winter, passed us, sedulously averting his eyes.   The driver declared that he recognized the horse,

---

* "Longknife." The whites have enjoyed this title since 1758, when Captain Gibson cut off with his sabre the head of Little Eagle, the great Mingo or Chief, and won the title of Big-Knife Warrior. Savages in America as well as Africa who ignore the sword always look upon that weapon with horror. The Sioux call the Americans Wasichi, or bad men.

and grumbled certain Western facetiæ concerning "hearty-chokes and caper sauce."

In these lands the horse-thief is the great enemy of mankind; for him there is no pity, no mercy; Lynch-law is held almost too good for him; to shoot him *in flagrante delicto* is like slaying a man-eating Bengal royal tiger—it entitles you to the respect and gratitude of your species. I asked our conductor whether dandiness was at the bottom of the "buck's" heavy dress. "'Guess," was the reply, "what keeps cold out, keeps heat out tew!"

At 12 15 P.M., crossing Laramie's Fork, a fine clear stream about forty yards broad, we reached Fort Laramie — another "fort" by courtesy, or rather by order — where we hoped to recruit our exhausted stores.

The straggling cantonment requires no description: it has the usual big flag, barracks, store-houses, officers' quarters, guard-houses, sutlers' stores, and groceries, which doubtless make a good thing by selling deleterious "strychnine" to passing trains who can afford to pay $6 per gallon.

Fort Laramie, called Fort John in the days of the American Fur Company, was used by them as a store-house for the bear and buffalo skins, which they collected in thousands. The old adobe *enceinte*, sketched and described by Frémont and Stansbury, soon disappeared after the place was sold to the United States government. Its former rival was Fort Platte, belonging in 1842—when the pale face first opened this road—to Messrs. Sybille, Adams, and Co., and situated immediately on the point of land at the junction of Laramie Fort with the Platte. The climate here is arid and parching in summer, but in winter tolerably mild, considering the altitude—4470 feet—and the proximity of the Black Hills; yet it has seen hard frost in September. It is also well defended from the warm, moist, and light winds, which, coming from the Mexican Gulf, cause "calentures" on the lower course of the river. The soil around the settlement is gravelly and sterile, the rocks are sand, lime, and clay, and there is a solitary, desolate look upon every thing but the bright little stream that bubbles from the dark heights. The course is from S.W. to N.E.: about half way it bifurcates, with a right fork to the west and main fork east, and near Laramie it receives its main affluent, the Chugwater.

My companion kindly introduced me to the officer commanding the fort, Colonel B. Alexander, 10th Infantry, and we were at once made at home. The amiable mistress of the house must find charitable work enough to do in providing for the wants of way-worn friends who pass through Laramie from east to west. We rested and dined in the cool comfortable quarters, with only one qualm at heart—we were so soon to leave them. On these occasions the driver seems to know by instinct that you are enjoying yourself, while he, as an outsider, is not. He becomes, therefore, unusually impatient to start; perhaps, also, time runs more rapidly than it is wont.   At any rate, after a short two hours, we were compelled to shake hands with our kind and considerate hosts, and to return to limbo—the mail-wagon.

From Fort Laramie westward the geological formation changes: the great limestone deposits disappear, and are succeeded by a great variety of sandstones, some red, argillaceous, and compact; others gray or yellow, ferruginous, and coarse.   Pudding-stones or conglomerates also abound, and the main chain of the Laramie Mountains is supposed to be chiefly composed of this rock.

Beyond the fort there are two roads.   The longer leads to the right, near the Platte River.   It was formerly, and perhaps is still, a favorite with emigrants.   We preferred the left, which, crossing the edges of the Black Hills, is rough and uneven, but is "some shorter," as the guide-book says, than the other.   The weather began to be unusually disagreeable with heat and rain-drops from a heavy nimbus, that forced us to curtain up the rattling vehicle; perhaps, too, we were a little cross, contrasting the present with the past—civilized society, a shady bungalow, and wonderfully good butter.   At 4 P.M., following the Platte Valley, after two hours' drive we halted to change mules at Ward's Station, *alias* the "Central Star," where several whites were killed by the Sioux in 1855, among them M. Montalan, a Parisian.

Again we started for another twenty-five miles at 4 P.M.   The road was rough, and the driver had a curious proclivity for losing the way.   I have often found this to be the case after passing through a station.   There was little to remark, except that the country was poor and bad, that there was clear water in a ravine to the right, and that we were very tired and surly.   But as sorrow comes to an end as well as joy, so, at 9 30 P.M., we drove in, somewhat consoled, to Horseshoe Station—the old *Fer à Cheval*—where one of the road agents, Mr. Slade, lived, and where we anticipated superior comfort.

We were *entichés* by the aspect of the buildings, which were on an extensive scale — in fact, got up regardless of expense.   An ominous silence, however, reigned around.   At last, by hard knocking, we were admitted into a house with the Floridian style of veranda previously described, and by the pretensions of the room we at once divined our misfortune—we were threatened with a "lady."   The "lady" will, alas! follow us to the Pacific: even in hymns we read,

> "Now let the Prophet's heart rejoice,
> His noble lady's too."

Our mishap was really worse than we expected — we were exposed to two "ladies," and of these one was a Bloomer.   It is only fair to state that it was the only hermaphrodite of the kind that ever met my eyes in the United States; the great founder of the order has long since subsided into her original obscurity, and her acolytes have relapsed into the weakness of petticoats. The Bloomer was an uncouth being; her hair, cut level with her eyes, depended with the graceful curl of a drake's tail around a flat Turanian countenance, whose only expression was sullen insolence. The body-dress, glazed brown calico, fitted her somewhat like a soldier's tunic, developing haunches which would be admired only in venison; and—curious *inconséquence* of woman's nature!—all this sacrifice of appearance upon the shrine of comfort did not prevent her wearing that kind of crinoline depicted by Mr. *Punch* upon "our Mary Hanne." The pantalettes of glazed brown calico, like the vest, tunic, blouse, shirt, or whatever they may call it, were in peg-top style, admirably setting off a pair of thin-soled Frenchified patent-leather bottines, with elastic sides, which contained feet large, broad, and flat as a negro's in Unyamwezi. The dear creature had a husband: it was hardly safe to look at her, and as for sketching her, I avoided it, as men are bidden by the poet to avoid the way of Slick of Tennessee. The other "lady," though more decently attired, was like women in this wild part of the world generally— cold and disagreeable in manner, full of "proper pride," with a touch-me-not air, which reminded me of a certain

> "Miss Baxter,
> Who refused a man before he axed her."

Her husband was the renowned Slade:

> "Of gougers fierce, the eyes that pierce, the fiercest gouger he."

His was a noted name for "deadly strife;" he had the reputation of having killed his three men; and a few days afterward the grave that concealed one of his murders was pointed out to me. This pleasant individual "for an evening party" wore the revolver and bowie-knife here, there, and every where. He had lately, indeed, had a strong hint not to forget his weapon. One M. Jules, a French trader, after a quarrel which took place at dinner, walked up to him and fired a pistol, wounding him in the breast. As he rose to run away Jules discharged a second, which took effect upon his back, and then, without giving him time to arm, fetched a gun and favored him with a dose of slugs somewhat larger than revolver bullets. The fiery Frenchman had two narrow escapes from Lynch-lawyers: twice he was hung between wagons, and as often he was cut down. At last he disappeared in the farther West, and took to lodge and squaw. The avenger of blood threatens to follow him up, but as yet he has taken no steps.

It at once became evident that the station was conducted upon the principle of the Western hotel-keeper of the last generation, and of Continental Europe about A.D. 1500— the innkeeper of "Anne of Geierstein"— that is to say, for his own convenience; the public there was the last thing thought of. One of our party

The Western Swell. The Sioux. INDIANS. The Arrapaho. The Crow.

The old Shoshonee. Jake the Shoshonee.

who had ventured into the kitchen was fiercely ejected by the "ladies." In asking about dormitories we were informed that "lady travelers" were admitted into the house, but that the ruder sex must sleep where it could—or not sleep at all if it preferred. We found a barn outside: it was hardly fit for a decently brought-up pig; the floor was damp and knotty; there was not even a door to keep out the night breeze, now becoming raw, and several drunken fellows lay in different parts of it. Two were in one bunk, embracing maudlingly, and freely calling for drinks of water. Into this disreputable hole we were all thrust for the night: among us, it must be remembered, was a federal judge, who had officiated for years as minister at a European court. His position, poor man! procured him nothing but a broken-down pallet. It was his first trip to the Far West, and yet, so easily are Americans satisfied, and so accustomed are they to obey the ridiculous jack-in-office who claims to be one of the powers that be, he scarcely uttered a complaint. I, for one, grumbled myself to sleep. May gracious Heaven keep us safe from all "ladies" in future! better a hundred times the squaw, with her uncleanliness and civility.

We are now about to leave the land of that great and dangerous people, the Sioux, and before bidding adieu to thém it will be advisable to devote a few pages to their ethnology.

CHAPTER II.

The Sioux or Dakotahs.

The Sioux belong essentially to the savage, in opposition to the Aztecan peoples of the New World. In the days of Major Pike (1805–1807), they were the dread of all the neighboring tribes, from the confluence of the Mississippi and the Missouri to the Raven River on the latter. According to Lieutenant Warren, they are still scattered over an immense territory extending from the Mississippi on the east to the Black Hills on the west, and from the forks of the Platte on the south to Minsi Wakan, or the Devil's Lake, on the north. Early in the winter of 1837 they ceded to the United States all their lands lying east of the Mississippi, which became the Territory of Minnesota. They are to the North American tribes what the great Anizeh race is among the Bedouins of Arabia. Their vernacular name, Dakotah, which some pronounce Lakotah, and others Nakotah, is translated "leagued" or "allied," and they sometimes speak of themselves as Osheti Shakowin, or the "Seven Council Fires." The French call them "les Coupes-gorges," from their sign or symbol, and the whites generally know them as the Sues or Sioux, from the plural form of Nadonaisi, which in Ojibwa means an enemy. The race is divided into seven principal bands, viz.:

1. Mdewakantonwan (Minowa Kantongs* or Gens du Lac), meaning "Village of the Mdewakan"—Mille Lacs or Spirit Lake. They formerly extended from Prairie du Chien to Prairie des Français, thirty-five miles up the St. Peter's River. They have now moved farther west. This tribe, which includes seven bands, is considered the bravest of the Sioux, and has even waged an internecine war with the Folles Avoines† or Menomenes, who are reputed the most gallant of the Ojibwas (Chippewas), and who, inhabiting a country intersected by lakes, swamps, water-courses, and impenetrable morasses, long bade defiance to all their neighbors. They have received annuities since 1838, and their number enrolled in 1850 was 2000 souls.

2. Wahpekute (Washpeconte, translated Gens de Feuillestirées, and by others the "Leaf Shooters"). Their habitation lies westward of the Des Moines, Cannon, and Blue-Earth Rivers. According to Major Pike, they were like the Bedouin Ghuzw, a band of vagabonds formed of refugees, who for some bad deed had been expelled their tribes. The meaning of their name is unknown; in 1850 they numbered 500 or 600 souls.

3. Sisitonwan (Sussitongs, or the Village of the Marsh). This band used to hunt over the vast prairies lying eastward of the Mississippi, and up that stream as high as Raven River. They now plant their corn about Lake Traverse (Lac Travers) and on the Côteau des Prairies, and numbered in 1850 about 2500 souls.

4. Wahpetonwans (Washpetongs, Gens des Feuilles, because they lived in woods), the "Village in the Leaves." They have moved from their old home about the Little Rapids of the Minnesota River to Lac qui Parle and Big Stone Lake. In 1850 they numbered 1000 to 1200 souls. They plant corn, have substituted the plow for the hoe, and, according to the missionaries,

---

* The first is the correct, the second is the old and incorrect form of writing the name.

† The Folles Avoines are a small tribe esteemed by the whites and respected by their own race; their hunting-grounds are the same as those of the Winnebagoes. They speak a peculiar dialect. But all understand the copious and sonorous, but difficult and complicated Algonquin or Ojibwa — the language of some of the old New England races, Pequots, Delawares, Mohicans, Abenaki, Narragansets, Penobscots, and the tribes about the Lake regions and the head-waters of the Mississippi, viz., Ottawa, Potawotomies, Menomene, Knisteneaux or Cree, Sac, Kickapoo, Maskigo, Shawnee, Miami, Kaskaskia, etc. The other great northeastern language is that of the Mohawk, spoken by the Oneida, Onondaga, Seneca, Cayuga, Tuscarora, Wyandotte, and Cherokee.

"Folles Avoines" is the Canadian French for the wild rice (*Zizania aquatica*), a tall, tubular, reedy water-plant, plentiful on the marshy margins of the northern lakes and in the plashy waters of the Upper Mississippi. Its leaves and spikes, though much larger, resemble those of oats. Millions of migrating water-fowl fatten on it before their autumnal flights to the south, while in autumn it furnishes the Northern savages and the Canadian traders and hunters with their annual supply of grain. It is used for bread by most of the tribes to the northwest.

have made some progress in reading and writing their own language.

The above four constitute the Mississippi and Minnesota Sioux, and are called by those on the Missouri "Isánti," from Isanati or Isanyati, because they once lived near Isantamde, one of the Mille Lacs. They number, according to Major Pike, 5775 souls; according to Lieutenant Warren, about 6200; and many of those on the Mississippi have long since become semi-civilized by contact with the white settlements, and have learned to cultivate the soil. Others, again, follow the buffalo in their primitive wildness, and have of late years given much trouble to the settlers of Northern Iowa.

5. Ihanktonwans (Yanctongs, meaning "Village at the End"), also sometimes called Wichiyela, or First Nation. They are found at the mouth of the Big Sioux, between it and the Missouri River, as high up as Fort Look-out, and on the opposite bank of the Missouri. In 1851 they were set down at 240 lodges = 2400 souls; they have since increased to 360 lodges and 2880 souls, of whom 576 are warriors. Distance from the buffalo country has rendered them poor; the proximity of the pale face has degenerated them, and the United States have purchased most of their lands.

6. Ihanktonwannas (Yanctannas), one of the "End Village" bands. They range between the James and the Missouri Rivers, as far north as Devil's Lake. The Dakotah Mission numbered them at 400 lodges = 4000 souls; subsequent observers at 800 lodges = 6400 souls, and 1280 warriors; and, being spirited and warlike, they give much trouble to settlers in the Dakotah Territory. A small portion live in dirt lodges during the summer. This band suffered severely from small-pox in the winter of 1856–7. They are divided into the Hunkpatidans (of unknown signification), Pabakse or Cut-heads, and Kiyuksa, deriders or breakers of law. From their sub-tribe the Wazikute, or Pine Shooters, sprang, it is said, the Assiniboin tribe of the Dakotahs. Major Pike divides the "Yanctongs" into two grand divisions, the Yanctongs of the North and the Yanctongs of the South.

7. Titonwan (Teton, "Village of the Prairies"), inhabiting the trans-Missourian prairies, and extending westward to the dividing ridge between the Little Missouri and Powder River, and thence south on a line near the 106° meridian. They constitute more than one half of the whole Dakotah nation. In 1850 they were numbered at 1250 lodges = 12,500 souls, but that number was supposed to be overestimated. They are allied by marriage with the Cheyennes and Arickarees, but are enemies of the Pawnees and Crows. The Titonwan, according to Major Pike, are, like the Yanctongs, the most erratic and independent not only of the Sioux, but "of all the Indians in the world." They follow the buffalo as chance directs, clothing themselves with the robes, and

G

making their lodges, saddles, and bridles of the same material, the flesh of the animal furnishing their food. None but the few families connected with the whites have planted corn. Possessing an innumerable stock of horses, they are here this day and five hundreds of miles off in a week, moving with a rapidity scarcely to be imagined by the inhabitants of the civilized world: they find themselves equally at home in all places. The Titonwan are divided into seven principal bands, viz.:

The Hunkpapa, "they who camp by themselves"(?). They roam from the Big Cheyenne up to the Yellow Stone, and west to the Black Hills, and number 365 lodges, 2920 souls, and 584 warriors.

The Sisahapa or Blackfeet live with the Hunkpapa, and, like them, have little reverence for the whites: they number 165 lodges, 1321 souls, and 264 warriors.

The Itazipko, Sans Arc, or "No Bows;" a curious name—like the Sans Arc Pawnees, they are good archers—perhaps given to them in olden times, when, like certain tribes of negroes, they used the spear to the exclusion of other weapons: others, however, translate the word "Bow-pith." They roam over nearly the same lands as the Hunkpapa, number about 170 lodges, 1360 souls, and 272 warriors.

The Minnikanye-wozhipu, "those who plant by the water," dwell between the Black Hills and the Platte. They number about 200 lodges, 1600 inmates, and 320 warriors: they are favorably disposed toward the whites.

The Ogalala or Okandanda are generally to be found on or about the Platte, near Fort Laramie, and are the most friendly of all the Titonwan toward the whites. They number about 460 lodges, 3680 souls, and 736 warriors.

The Sichangu, Brûlés or Burnt-Thighs, living on the Niobrara and White-Earth Rivers, and ranging from the Platte to the Cheyenne, number about 380 lodges, containing 3680 inmates.

The Oohenonpa, "Two Boilings" or "Two Kettle-band," are much scattered among other tribes, but are generally to be found in the vicinity of Fort Pierre. They number about 100 lodges, 800 inmates, and 160 warriors.

The author of the above estimate, allotting eight to ten inmates to a lodge, of whom between one fifth and one sixth are warriors, makes an ample allowance. It is usual to reckon in a population between one fourth, one fifth, and one sixth—according to the work—as capable of bearing arms, but the civilized rule will not apply to the North American Indian. The grand total of the number of the Sioux nations, including the Isánti, would amount to 30,200 souls. Half a century ago it was estimated by Major Pike at 21,675, and in 1850 the Dakotah Mission set them down at 25,000. It is the opinion of many that, notwithstanding the ravages of cholera and small-pox, the Dakotah nation, except when mingled with the frontier settlements, rather increases than diminishes. It has been observed by missionaries that whenever an account of births and deaths has been kept in a village the former usually exceed the latter. The original numbers of the Prairie Indians have been greatly overestimated both by themselves and by strangers; the only practicable form of census is the rude proceeding of counting their "tipi," or skin tents. It is still a moot question how far the Prairie Indians have diminished in numbers, which can not be decided for some years.*

The Dakotahs are mostly a purely hunting tribe in the lowest condition of human society: they have yet to take the first step, and to become a pastoral people. The most civilized are the Mdewakantonwans, who, even at the beginning of the present century, built log huts and "stocked" land with corn, beans, and pumpkins. The majority of the bands hunt the buffalo within their own limits throughout the summer, and in the winter pitch their lodges in the clumps or fringes of tree and underwood along the banks of the lakes and streams. The bark of the cotton-wood furnishes fodder for their horses during the snowy season, and to obtain it the creeks and branches have been thinned or entirely denuded of their beautiful groves. They buy many animals from the Southern Indians, who have stolen them from New Mexico, or trapped them on the plains below the Rocky Mountains. Considerable numbers are also bred by themselves. The Dakotah nation is one of the most warlike and numerous in the United States territory. In single combat on horseback they are described as having no superiors; a skill acquired by constant practice enables them to spear their game at full speed, and the rapidity with which they discharge their arrows, and the accuracy of their aim, rival the shooting which may be made with a revolver. They are not, however, formidable warriors; want of discipline and of confidence in one another render them below their mark. Like the Moroccans in their last war with Spain, they never attack when they should, and they never fail to attack when they should not.

The Dakotahs, when first visited by the whites, lived around the head-waters of the Mississippi and the Red River of the north. They have gradually migrated toward the west and southwest, guarded by their allies the Cheyennes, who have given names successively to the Cheyenne of Red River, to the Big Cheyenne of the Missouri, and to the section of the country between the Platte and the Arkansas which they now occupy. The Dakotah first moved to the land now occupied by the Ojibwa (anciently known as Chippewas, Orechipewa, or Sauteurs†), which tribe in-

---

* At the time of the first settlement of the country by the English no certain estimate was made; at the birth of the thirteen original states, the Indians, according to Dr. Trumbull, did not exceed 150,000. In 1860, the number of Indians within the limits of the United States was estimated by the Commissioner of Indian Affairs at 350,000.

† The Rev. Peter Jones (Kahkewagquody), in his history of the Ojibwa Indians,

habited the land between Sault* St. Marie and Lake Winnipeg, while their allies the Crees occupied the country from Lake Winnipeg to the Kisiskadjiwan and Assiniboin Rivers. The plains lying southward of the latter river were the fields of many a fierce and bloody fight between the Dakotahs and the other allied two tribes, until a feud caused by jealousy of the women arose among the former, and made a division which ended in their becoming irreconcilable enemies, as they are indeed to the present day. The defeated party fled to the craggy precipices of the Lake of the Woods, and received from the Ojibwa the name of Assiniboin or Dakotah of the Rocks, by which they are now universally known to the whites. They retain, however, among themselves the term Dakotah, although their kinsmen universally, when speaking of them, called them "hohe" or enemies, and they still speak the Sioux language. After this feud the Assiniboins strengthened themselves by alliance with the Ojibwa and Cree tribes, and drove the Dakotah from all the country north of the Cheyenne River, which is now regarded as the boundary-line. The three races are still friendly, and so hostile to the Dakotah that no lasting peace can be made between them; in case of troubles with either party, the government of the United States might economically and effectually employ one against the other. The common war-ground is the region about Lake Minsiwakan, where they all meet when hunting buffalo. The Assiniboin tribe now extends from the Red River westward along the Missouri as far as the mouth of Milk River: a large portion of their lands, like those of the Cree, is British territory. They suffered severely from small-pox in 1856–7, losing about 1500 of their tribe, and now number about 450 lodges, or 3600 souls. Having comparatively few horses, they rely mainly upon the dog for transportation, and they use its flesh as food.

The Dakotah, according to Lieutenant Warren, are still numerous, independent, warlike, and powerful, and have the means of prolonging an able resistance to the advance of the Western settlers. Under the present policy of the United States government —this is written by an American—which there is no reason to believe likely to be changed, encroachments will continue, and battle and murder will be the result. There are many inevitable causes at work to produce war with the Dakotah before many years.† The conflict will end in the discomfiture of the natives,

makes "Chippewa" a corrupted word, signifying the "Puckered-Moccasin People;" the Abbé Domenech (Seven Years' Residence in the Great Deserts of North America"—a mere compilation) draws an unauthorized distinction between Chippewas and Ojibwas, but can not say what it is. He explains Ojibwa, the form of Ojidwa, to mean "a singularity in the voice or pronunciation."

* Pronounced "Soo:" the word is old French, still commonly used in Canada and the North, and means rapids.

† Lieutenant Warren considered the greatest point of his explorations to be the knowledge of the proper routes by which to invade their country and to conquer them. The project may be found in the Report of the Secretary of War. I quote

who will then fast fall away. Those dispossessed of their lands can not, as many suppose, retire farther west; the regions lying beyond one tribe are generally occupied by another, with whom deadly animosity exists. Even when the white settlers advance their frontier, the natives linger about till their own poverty and vice consign them to oblivion, and the present policy adopted by the government is the best that could be devised for their extermination. It is needless to say that many of the Sioux look forward to the destruction of their race with all the feelings of despair with which the civilized man would contemplate the extinction of his nationality. How indeed, poor devils, are they to live when the pale face comes with his pestilent fire-water and small-pox, followed up with paper and pen work, to be interpreted under the gentle auspices of fire and steel?

The advance of the settlements is universally acknowledged by the people of the United States to be a political necessity in the national development, and on that ground only is the displacement of the rightful owners of the soil justifiable. But the government, instead of preparing the way for settlements by wise and just purchases from those in possession, and proper support and protection for the indigent and improvident race thus dispossessed, is sometimes behind its obligations. There are instances of Congress refusing or delaying to ratify the treaties made by its duly authorized agents. The settler and pioneer are thus precipitated into the Indian country, without the savage having received the promised consideration, and he often, in a manner that enlists the sympathies of mankind, takes up the tomahawk and perishes in the attempt. It frequently happens that the Western settlers are charged with bringing about these wars; they are now, however, fighting the battles of civilization exactly as they were fought three centuries ago upon the Atlantic shore, under circumstances that command equal admiration and approval. While, therefore, we sympathize with the savage, we can not but feel for the unhappy squatter, whose life is sacrificed to the Indian's vengeance by the errors or dilatoriness of those whose duty it is to protect him.

The people of the United States, of course, know themselves to be invincible by the hands of these half-naked savages. But the Indians, who on their own ground still outnumber the whites, are by no means so convinced of the fact. Until the army of Utah moved westward, many of them had never seen a soldier. At a grand council of the Dakotah, in the summer of 1857, on the North Fork of the Platte River, they solemnly pledged themselves to resist the encroachments of the whites, and, if necessary, to "whip" them out of the country. The appearance of the troops has undoubtedly produced a highly beneficial effect; still,

Mr. Warren's opinion concerning the future of the Dakotahs as a contrast to that of the Dakotah Mission. My own view will conclude the case in p. 102.

something more is wanted. Similarly in Hindostan, though the natives knew that the British army numbered hundreds of thousands, every petty independent prince thought himself fit to take the field against the intruder, till the failure of the attempt suggested to him some respect for *les gros bataillons*.

The Sioux differ greatly in their habits from the Atlantic tribes of times gone by. The latter lived in wigwams or villages of more stable construction than the lodge; they cultivated the soil, never wandered far from home, made their expeditions on foot, having no horses, and rarely came into action unless they could "tree" themselves. They inflicted horrid tortures on their prisoners, as every English child has read; but, Arab-like, they respected the honor of their female captives. The Prairie tribes are untamed and untamable savages, superior only to the "Arab" hordes of great cities, who appear destined to play in the history of future ages the part of Goth and Vandal, Scythian, Bedouin, and Turk. Hitherto the *rôle* which these hunters have sustained in the economy of nature has been to prepare, by thinning off its wild animals, a noble portion of the world for the higher race about to succeed them. Captain Mayne Reid somewhere derides the idea of the Indian's progress toward extinction. A cloud of authorities bear witness against him. East of the Mississippi the savage has virtually died out, and few men allow him two prospective centuries of existence in the West, unless he be left, which he will not be, to himself.

"Wolves of women born," the Prairie Indians despise agriculture as the Bedouin does. Merciless freebooters, they delight in roaming; like all equestrian and uncivilized people, they are perfect horsemen, but poor fighters when dismounted, and they are nothing without their weapons. As a rule they rarely torture their prisoners, except when an old man or woman is handed over to the squaws and pappooses "pour les amuser," as a Canadian expressed it. Near and west of the Rocky Mountains, however, the Shoshonees and the Yutas (Utahs) are as cruel as their limited intellects allow them to be. Moreover, all the Prairie tribes never fail to subject women to an ordeal worse than death. The best character given of late years to the Sioux was by a traveler in 1845, who writes that "their freedom and power have imparted to their warriors some gentlemanly qualities; they are cleanly, dignified and graceful in manners, brave, proud, and independent in bearing and deed."

The qualities of the Sioux, and of the Prairie tribes generally, are little prized by those who have seen much of them. They ignore the very existence of gratitude; the benefits of years can not win their affections. After boarding and lodging with a white for any length of time, they will steal his clothes; and, after receiving any number of gifts, they will haggle for the value of the merest trifle. They are inveterate thieves and beggars;

the Western settlers often pretend not to understand their tongue for fear of exposing themselves to perpetual pilfering and perse- cution; and even the squaws, who live with the pale faces, annoy their husbands by daily applications for beads and other coveted objects; they are cruel to one another as children. The obsti- nate revengefulness of their vendetta is proverbial; they hate with the "hate of Hell;" and, like the Highlanders of old, if the author of an injury escape them, they vent their rage upon the innocent, because he is of the same clan or color. If struck by a white man, they must either kill him or receive damages in the shape of a horse; and after the most trivial injury they can nev- er be trusted. Their punishments are Draconic; for all things death, either by shooting or burning. Their religion is a low form of fetichism. They place their women in the most de- graded position. The squaw is a mere slave, living a life of utter drudgery; and when the poor creature wishes, according to the fashion of her sex, to relieve her feelings by a domestic "scene," followed by a "good cry," or to use her knife upon a sister squaw, as the Trasteverina mother uses her bodkin, the husband, after squatting muffled up, in hope that the breeze will blow over, en- forces silence with a cudgel. The warrior, considering the chase an ample share of the labor-curse, is so lazy that he will not rise to saddle or unsaddle his pony; he will sit down and ask a white man to fetch him water, and only laugh if reproved. Like a wild beast, he can not be broken to work; he would rather die than employ himself in honest industry—a mighty contrast to the ne- gro, whose only happiness is in serving. He invariably attributes an act of kindness, charity, or forbearance to fear. Ungenerous, he extols, like the Bedouin, generosity to the skies. He never makes a present except for the purpose of receiving more than its equivalent; and an "Indian gift" has come to be a proverb, mean- ing any thing reclaimed after being given away. Impulsive as the African, his mind is blown about by storms of unaccountable contradictions. Many a white has suddenly seen the scalping- knife restored to its sheath instead of being buried in his flesh, while others have been as unexpectedly assaulted and slain by those from whom they expected kindness and hospitality. The women are mostly cold and chaste. The men have vices which can not be named: their redeeming points are fortitude and en- durance of hardship; moreover, though they care little for their wives, they are inordinately fond of their children. Of their bravery Indian fighters do not speak highly: they are notorious- ly deficient in the civilized quality called moral courage, and, though a brave will fight single-handed stoutly enough, they rare- ly stand up long in action. They are great at surprises, ambus- cades, and night attacks: as with the Arabs and Africans, their favorite hour for onslaught is that before dawn, when the enemy is most easily terrified — they know that there is nothing which tries man's nerve so much as an unexpected night attack — and when the cattle can be driven off to advantage. In some points their characters have been, it is now granted, greatly misunderstood. Their forced gravity and calmness — purely "company manners" — were not suspected to cloak merriment, sociability, and a general fondness of feasts and fun. Their apathy and sternness, which were meant for reserve and dignity among strangers, gave them an air of ungeniality which does not belong to their mental constitutions. Their fortitude and endurance of pain is the result, as in the prize-fighter, of undeveloped brain.

The Sioux are tall men, straight, and well made: they are never deformed, and are rarely crippled, simply because none but the able-bodied can live. The shoulders are high and somewhat straight; the figure is the reverse of the sailor's, that is to say, while the arms are smooth, feeble, and etiolated, the legs are tolerably muscular; the bones are often crooked or bowed in the equestrian tribes; they walk as if they wanted the ligamentum teres; there is a general looseness of limb, which promises, however, lightness, endurance, and agility, and which, contrasted with the Caucasian race, suggests the gait of a wild compared with that of a tame animal. Like all savages, they are deficient in corporeal strength: a civilized man finds no difficulty in handling them: on this road there is only one Indian (a Shoshonee) who can whip a white in a "rough and tumble." The temperament is usually bilious-nervous; the sanguine is rare, the lymphatic rarer, and I never knew or heard of an albino. The hands, especially in the higher tribes, are decidedly delicate, but this is more observable in the male than in the female; the type is rather that of the Hindoo than of the African or the European. The feet, being more used than the other extremities, and unconfined by boot or shoe, are somewhat splay, spreading out immediately behind the toes, while the heel is remarkably narrow. In consequence of being carried straight to the fore—the only easy position for walking through grass—they tread, like the ant-eater, more heavily on the outer than on the inner edge. The sign of the Indian is readily recognized by the least experienced tracker.

It is erroneously said that he who has seen a single Indian has seen them all. Of course there is a great similarity among savages and barbarians of the same race and climate. The same pursuits, habits, and customs naturally produce an identity of expression which, as in the case of husband and wife, parent and child, moulds the features into more or less of likeness. On the other hand, a practiced eye will distinguish the Indian individually or by bands as easily as the shepherd, by marks invisible to others, can swear to his sheep. I have little doubt that to the savages all white men look alike.

The Prairie Indian's hair and complexion have already been described. According to some savages the build of the former differs materially from that of the European and the Asiatic. The animal development varies in the several races: the Pawnee's and Yuta's scalp-lock rarely exceeds eighteen inches in length, while that of the Crow, like the East Indian Jatawala's, often sweeps the ground. There are salient characteristics in the cranium which bear testimony to many phrenological theories. The transverse diameter of the rounded skull between the parietal bones, where destructiveness and secretiveness are placed, is enormous, sometimes exceeding the longitudinal line from sinciput to occiput, the direct opposite of the African negro's organization. The region of the cerebellum is deficient and shrunken, as with the European in his second childhood: it sensibly denotes that the subject wants "vim." The coronal region, where the sentiments are supposed to lie, is rather flat than arched; in extreme cases the face seems to occupy two thirds instead of half the space between poll and chin. The low conical forehead recedes, as in Robespierre's head, from the region of benevolence, and rises high at the apex, where firmness and self-esteem reside: a common formation among wild tribes, as every traveler in Asia and Africa has remarked. The facial angle of Camper varies, according to phrenologists, between 70° and 80°. The projecting lower brow is strong, broad, and massive, showing that development of the perceptions which is produced by the constant and minute observation of a limited number of objects. The well-known Indian art of following the trail is one result of this property. The nose is at once salient and dilated—in fact, partaking of the Caucasian and African types. The nostrils are broad and deeply whorled; the nasal orifice is wide, and, according to osteologists, the bones that protect it are arched and expanded; the eyebrows are removed, like the beard and mustache, by vellication, giving a dull and bald look to the face; the lashes, however, grow so thickly that they often show a sooty black line, suggesting the presence of the Oriental kohl or surma. The orbits are large and square: largeness and squareness are, in fact, the general character of the features: it doubtless produces that peculiar besotted look which belongs to the Indian as to the Mongolian family. The conjunctival membrane has the whiteness and clearness of the European and the Asiatic; it is not, as in the African, brown, yellow, or red. The pupil, like the hair, is of different shades between black and brown: when the organ is blue—an accident which leads to a suspicion of mixed blood—the owner generally receives a name from the peculiarity. Travelers, for the most part, describe the organ as "black and piercing, snaky and venomous;" others as "dull and sleepy;" while some detect in its color a mingling of black and gray. The only peculiarity which I observed in the pupil was its similarity to that of the gipsy. The Indian first fixes upon you a piercing glance, which seems to look below the surface. After a few seconds, however, the eye glazes as though a film passed over it, and gazes, as it were, on vacancy. The look would at once convict him of Jattatura and Molocchio in Italy, and of El Ayn, or the Evil Eye, in the East. The mouth is at once full and compressed; it opens widely; the lips are generally *bordés* or everted— decidedly the most unpleasant fault which that feature can have —the corners are drawn down as if by ill temper, and the two seams which spring from the alæ of the nostrils are deeply traced. This formation of the oral, combined with the fullness of the circumoral regions, and the length and fleshiness of the naked upper lip, communicates a peculiar animality to the countenance. The cheek-bones are high and bony; they are not, however, expanded or spread backward, nor do they, as in the Chinese, alter the appearance of the eyes by making them oblique. The cheeks are rather lank and falling in than full or oval. The whole maxillary organ is projecting and ponderous. The wide condyles of the lower jaw give a remarkable massiveness to the jowl, while the chin—perhaps the most characteristic feature—is long, bony, large, and often parted in the centre. The teeth are faultless, full-sized and white, even and regular, strong and lasting; and they are vertical, not sloping forward like the African's. To sum up, the evanishing of the forehead, the compression of the lips, the breadth and squareness of the jaw, and the massiveness of the chin, combine to produce a normal expression of harshness and cruelty, which, heightened by red and black war-paint, locks like horsehair, plumes, and other savage decorations, form a "rouge dragon" whose *tout ensemble* is truly revolting.

The women when in their teens have often that *beauté du diable*, which may be found even among the African negresses; nothing, however, can be more evanescent. When full grown the figure becomes dumpy and *trapu;* and the face, though sometimes not without a certain comeliness, has a Turanian breadth and flatness. The best portrait of a sightly Indian woman is that of Pocahontas, the Princess, published by Mr. Schoolcraft. The drudgery of the tent and field renders the squaw cold and unimpassioned; and, like the coarsest-minded women in civilized races, her eye and her heart mean one and the same thing. She will administer "squaw medicine," a love philter, to her husband, but rather for the purpose of retaining his protection than his love. She has all the modesty of a savage, and is not deficient in sense of honor. She has no objection to a white man, but, Affghan-like, she usually changes her name to "John" or some other alias. Her demerits are a habit of dunning for presents, and a dislike to the virtue that ranks next to godliness, which nothing but the fear of the rod will subdue. She has literally no belief, not even in the rude fetichism of her husband, and consequently she has no religious exercises. As she advances in years she rapidly descends in *physique* and *morale:* there is nothing on earth more fiendlike than the vengeance of a cretin-like old squaw.

The ancient Persians taught their progeny archery, riding, and truth-telling; the Prairie Indian's curriculum is much the same, only the last of the trio is carefully omitted. The Indian, like other savages, never tells the truth; verity is indeed rather an intellectual than an instinctive virtue, which, as children prove, must be taught and made intelligible; except when "counting his coups," in other words, recounting his triumphs, his life is therefore one system of deceit, the strength of the weak. Another essential part of education is to close the mouth during sleep: the Indian has a superstition that all disease is produced by inhalation. The children, "born like the wild ass's colts," are systematically spoiled with the view of fostering their audacity; the celebrated apophthegm of the Wise King—to judge from his notable failure at home, he probably did not practice what he preached—which has caused such an expenditure of birch and cane in higher races, would be treated with contempt by the Indians. The fond mother, when chastening her child, never goes beyond dashing a little cold water in its face—for which reason to besprinkle a man is a mortal insult—a system which, perhaps, might be naturalized with advantage in some parts of Europe. The son is taught to make his mother toil for him, and openly to disobey his sire; at seven years of age he has thrown off all parental restraint; nothing keeps him in order but the fear of the young warriors. At ten or twelve he openly rebels against all domestic rule, and does not hesitate to strike his father; the parent then goes off rubbing his hurt, and boasting to his neighbors of the brave boy whom he has begotten.

The religion of the North American Indians has long been a subject of debate. Some see in it traces of Judaism, others of Sabæanism; Mr. Schoolcraft detects a degradation of Guebrism. His faith has, it is true, a suspicion of duality; Hormuzd and Ahriman are recognizable in Gitche Manitou and Mujhe Manitou, and the latter, the Bad god, is naturally more worshiped, because more feared, than the Good god. Moreover, some tribes show respect for and swear by the sun, and others for fire: there is a north god and a south god, a wood god, a prairie god, an air god, and a water god; but—they have not risen to monotheism —there is not one God. None, however, appear to have that reverence for the elements which is the first article of the Zoroastrian creed; the points of difference are many, while those of resemblance are few and feeble, and it is hard to doubt that the instincts of mankind have been pressed by controversialists into the service of argument as traditional tenets.

To judge from books and the conversation of those who best know the Indians, he is distinctly a Fetichist like the African negro, and, indeed, like all the child-like races of mankind.* The

* The reader who cares to consult my studies upon the subject of Fetichism in Africa, where it is and ever has been the national creed, is referred to "The Lake

medicine-man is his mganga, angekok, sorcerer, prophet, physician, exorciser, priest, and rain-doctor; only, as he is rarely a cultivator of the soil, instead of heavy showers and copious crops, he is promised scalps, salmon trout, and buffalo beef in plenty. He has the true Fetichist's belief—invariably found in tribes who live dependent upon the powers of Nature—in the younger brothers of the human family, the bestial creation: he holds to a metamorphosis like that of Abyssinia, and to speaking animals. Every warrior chooses a totem, some quadruped, bird, or fish, to which he prays, and which he will on no account kill or eat. Dr. Livingstone shows (chap. i.) that the same custom prevails in its entirety among the Kaffir Bakwaina, and opines that it shows traces of addiction to animal worship, like the ancient Egyptians; in the prophecies of Israel the tribes are compared with animals, a true totemic practice. The word totem also signifies a sub-clan or sub-tribe; and some nations, like the African Somal, will not allow marriage in the same totem. The medicine-men give away young children as an atonement when calamities impend: they go clothed, not in sackcloth and ashes, but in coats of mire, and their macerations and self-inflicted tortures rival those of the Hindoos: a fanatic has been known to drag about a buffalo skull with a string cut from his own skin till it is torn away. In spring-time, the braves, and even the boys, repairing to lonely places and hill-tops, their faces and bodies being masked, as if in mourning, with mud, fast and pray, and sing rude chants to propitiate the ghosts for days consecutively. The Fetichist is ever grossly superstitious; and the Indians, as might be expected, abound in local rites. Some tribes, as the Cheyennes, will not go to war without a medicine-man, others without sacred war-gourds* containing the tooth of the drum-head fish. Children born with teeth are looked upon as portents, and when gray at birth the phenomenon is attributed to evil ghosts.

I can not but think that the two main articles of belief which have been set down to the credit of the Indian, namely, the Great Spirit or Creator, and the Happy Hunting-grounds in a future world, are the results of missionary teaching, the work of Fathers Hennepin, Marquette, and their noble army of martyred Jesuit followers. In later days they served chiefly to inspire the Anglo-American muse, e. g.:

> "By midnight moons o'er moistening dews,
> In vestments for the chase arrayed,
> The hunter still the deer pursues—
> The hunter and the deer, a shade!

Regions of Central Africa," chap. xix. The modes of belief, and the manners and customs of savage and barbarous races are so similar, that a knowledge of the African is an excellent introduction to that of the American.

* This gourd or calabash is the produce of the *Cucurbita lagenaria*, or calabash vine. In Spanish, Central, and Southern America, Cuba and the West Indies, they use the large round fruit of the *Crescentia cujete*.

> And long shall timorous fancy see
> The painted chief and pointed spear,
> And Reason's self shall bow the knee
> To shadows and delusions here."

My conviction is, that the English and American's popular ideas upon the subject are unreliable, and that their embodiment, beautiful poetry, "Lo the poor Indian," down to "his faithful dog shall bear him company," are but a splendid myth. The North American aborigine believed, it is true, in an unseen power, the Manitou, or, as we are obliged to translate it, "Spirit," residing in every heavenly body, animal, plant, or other natural object. This is the very essence of that form of Fetichism which leads to Pantheism and Polytheism. There was a Manitou, as he conceived, which gave the spark from the flint, lived in every blade of grass, flowed in the streams, shone in the stars, and thundered in the waterfall; but in each example—a notable instance of the want of abstractive and generalizing power—the idea of the Deity was particular and concrete. When the Jesuit fathers suggested the unity of the Great Spirit pervading all beings, it was very readily recognized; but the generalization was not worked out by the Indian mind. He was, therefore, like all savages, atheistic in the literal sense of the word. He had not arrived at the first step, Pantheism, which is so far an improvement that it opens out a grand idea, the omnipresence, and consequently the omnipotence, of the Deity. In most North American languages the Theos is known, not as the "Great Spirit," but as the "Great Father," a title also applied to the President of the United States, who is, I believe, though sometimes a step-father, rather the more reverenced of the twain. With respect to the happy hunting-grounds, it is a mere corollary of the monotheistic theorem above proved. It is doubtful whether these savages ever grasped the idea of a human soul. The Chicury of New England, indeed, and other native words so anglicized, appear distinctly to mean the African Pepo—ghost or larva.

Certain missionaries have left us grotesque accounts of the simple good sense with which the Indians of old received the Glad Tidings. The strangers were courteously received, the calumet was passed round, and they were invited to make known their wants in a "big talk." They did so by producing a synopsis of their faith, beginning at Adam's apple and ending at the Savior's cross. The patience of the Indian in enduring long speeches, sermons, and harangues has ever been exemplary and peculiar, as his fortitude in suffering lingering physical tortures. The audience listened with a solemn demeanor, not once interrupting what must have appeared to them a very wild and curious story. Called upon to make some remark, these antipomologists simply ejaculated,

"Apples are not wholesome, and those who crucified Christ were bad men!"

In their turn, some display of oratory was required. They avoided the tedious, long-drawn style of argument, and spoke, as was their wont, briefly to the point. "It is good of you," said they, "to cross the big water, and to follow the Indian's trail, that ye may relate to us what ye have related. Now listen to what our mothers told us. Our first father, after killing a beast, was roasting a rib before the fire, when a spirit, descending from the skies, sat upon a neighboring bluff. She was asked to eat. She ate fat meat. Then she arose and silently went her way. From the place where she rested her two hands grew corn and pumpkin; and from the place where she sat sprang tobacco!"

The missionaries listened to the savage tradition with an excusable disrespect, and, not unnaturally, often interrupted it. This want of patience and dignity, however, drew upon them severe remarks. "Pooh!" observed the Indians. "When you told us what your mothers told you, we gave ear in silence like men. When we tell you what our mothers told us, ye give tongue like squaws. Go to! Ye are no medicine-men, but silly fellows!"

Besides their superstitious belief in ghosts, spirits, or familiars, and the practice of spells and charms, love-philters, dreams and visions, war-medicine, hunting-medicine, self-torture, and incantations, the Indians had, it appears to me, but three religious observances, viz., dancing, smoking, and scalping.

The war-dances, the corn-dances, the buffalo-dances, the scalp-dances, and the other multiform and solemn saltations of these savages, have been minutely depicted and described by many competent observers. The theme also is beyond the limits of an essay like this.

Smoking is a boon which the Old owes to the New World. It is a heavy call upon our gratitude, for which we have naturally been very ungrateful.

"Non epulis tantum, non Bacchi pascimur usu,
    Pascimur et fumis, ingeniosa gula est."

We began by calling our new gift the "holy herb;" it is now, like the Balm of Gilead, entitled, I believe, a weed. Among the North American Indians even the spirits smoke; the "Indian summer" is supposed to arise from the puffs that proceed from the pipe of Nanabozhoo, the Ojibwa Noah. The pipe may have been used in the East before the days of tobacco, but if so it was probably applied to the inhalation of cannabis and other intoxicants.* On the other hand, the Indian had no stimulants. He never invented the beer of Osiris, though maize grew abundantly around him;† the koumiss of the Tartar was beyond his mental

---

* The word tobacco (West Indian, tobago or tobocco, a peculiar pipe), which has spread through Europe, Asia, and Africa, seems to prove the origin of the nicotiana, and the non-mention of smoking in the "Arabian Nights" disproves the habit of inhaling any other succedaneum.

† It has long been disputed whether maize was indigenous to America or to Asia; learned names are found on both sides of the question. In Central Africa the ce-

reach; and though "Jimsen weed"* overruns the land, he neglected its valuable intoxicating properties. His is almost the only race
that has ever existed wholly without a stimulant; the fact is a
strong proof of its autochthonic origin. It is indeed incredible
that man, having once learned, should ever forget the means of
getting drunk. Instead of the social cup the Indian smoked. As
tobacco does not grow throughout the continent, he invented kinnikinik. This Indian word has many meanings. By the hunters and settlers it is applied to a mixture of half and half, or two
thirds tobacco and one of red willow bark; others use it for a
mixture of tobacco, sumach leaves, and willow rind; others, like
Ruxton ("Life in the Far West," p. 116), for the cortex of the willow only. This tree grows abundantly in copses near the streams
and water-courses. For smoking, the twigs are cut when the leaves
begin to redden. Some tribes, like the Sioux, remove the outer
and use only the highly-colored inner bark; others again, like the
Shoshonees, employ the external as well as the internal cuticle.
It is scraped down the twig in curling ringlets, without, however,
stripping it off; the stick is then planted in the ground before the
fire, and, when sufficiently parched, the material is bruised, comminuted, and made ready for use. The taste is pleasant and aromatic, but the effect is that of the puerile ratan rather than the
manly tobacco. The Indian, be it observed, smokes like all savages by inhaling the fumes into the lungs, and returning them
through the nostrils; he finds pure tobacco, therefore, too strong
and pungent. As has been said, he is catholic in his habits of
smoking; he employs indifferently rose-bark (*Rosa blanda?*)† and
the cuticle of a cornus, the lobelia,‡ the larb, a vaccinium, a Daph-
ne-like plant, and many others. ‧ The Indian smokes incessantly,
and the "calumet"§ is an important part of his household goods.

real is now called as in English, "Indian corn," proving that in that continent it first
was introduced from Hindostan. The Italians have named it Gran' Turco, showing
whence it was imported by them. The word maiz, mays, maize, or mahiz, is a Carib
word introduced by the Spaniards into Europe; in the United States, where "corn"
is universally used, maize is intelligible only to the educated.

    * Properly Jamestown weed, the *Datura stramonium*, the English thorn-apple, un-
prettily called in the Northern States of America "stinkweed." It found its way
into the higher latitudes from Jamestown (Virginia), where it was first observed
springing on heaps of ballast and other rubbish discharged from vessels. According
to Beverly ("History of Virginia," book ii., quoted by Mr. Bartlett), it is "one of the
greatest coolers in the world;" and in some young soldiers who ate plentifully of it
as a salad, to pacify the troubles of bacon, the effect was "a very pleasant remedy, for
they turned natural fools upon it for several days."

    † The wild rose is every where met with growing in bouquets on the prairies.

    ‡ The *Lobelia inflata*, or Indian tobacco, is corrupted by the ignorant Western man
to low belia in contradistinction to high belia, better varieties of the plant.

    § The calumet, a word introduced by the old French, is the red sandstone pipe,
described in a previous page, with a long tube, generally a reed, adorned with feathers. It is the Indian symbol of hatred or amity; there is a calumet of war as well
as a calumet of peace. To accept the calumet is to come to terms; to refuse it is to
reject them. The same is expressed by burying and digging up the tomahawk or
hatchet. The tomahawk and calumet are sometimes made of one piece of stone;
specimens, however, have become very rare since the introduction of the iron axe.

He has many superstitions about the practice. It is a sacred instrument, and its red color typifies the smoker's flesh. The Western travelers mention offerings of tobacco to, and smoking of pipes in honor of, the Great Spirit. Some men will vow never to use the pipe in public, others to abstain on particular days. Some will not smoke with their moccasins on, others with steel about their persons; some are pledged to abstain inside, others outside the wigwam, and many scatter buffalo chip over their tobacco. When beginning to smoke there are certain observances; some, *exempli gratiâ*, direct, after the fashion of Gitche Manitou, the first puff upward or heavenward, the second earthward, and the third and fourth over the right and left shoulders, probably in propitiation of the ghosts, who are being smoked for in proxy; others, before the process of inhaling, touch the ground with the heel of the pipe-bowl, and turn the stem upward and averted.

According to those who, like Pennant, derive the North American from the Scythians, scalping is a practice that originated in High and Northeastern Asia. The words of the Father of History are as follows: "Of the first enemy a Scythian sends down, he quaffs the blood; he carries the heads of all that he has slain in battle to the king; for when he has brought a head, he is entitled to a share of the booty that may be taken—not otherwise; to skin the head, he makes a circular incision from ear to ear, and then, laying hold of the crown, shakes out the skull; after scraping off the flesh with an ox's rib, he rumples it between his hands, and having thus softened the skin, makes use of it as a napkin; he appends it to the bridle of the horse he rides, and prides himself on this, for the Scythian that has most of these skin napkins is adjudged the best man, etc., etc. They also use the entire skins as horse-cloths, also the skulls for drinking-cups."— ("Melpomene," iv., 64, Laurent's trans.) The underlying idea is doubtless the natural wish to preserve a memorial of a foeman done to death, and at the same time to dishonor his hateful corpse by mutilation. Fashion and tradition regulate the portions of the human frame preferred.

Scalping is generally, but falsely, supposed to be a peculiarly American practice. The Abbé Em. Domenech ("Seven Years' Residence in the Great Deserts of North America," chap. xxxix.) quotes the *decalvare* of the ancient Germans, the *capillos et cutem detrahere* of the code of the Visigoths, and the annals of Flude, which prove that the "Anglo-Saxons" and the Franks still scalped about A.D. 879. And as the modern American practice is traceable to Europe and Asia, so it may be found in Africa, where aught of ferocity is rarely wanting. "In a short time after our

---

The "Song of Hiawatha" (Canto I., The Peace Pipe) and the interesting "Letters and Notes on the Manners, Customs, and Conditions of the North American Indians" (vol. ii., p. 160), have made the Red Pipe-stone Quarry familiar to the Englishman.

return," says Mr. Duncan ("Travels in Western Africa in 1845 and 1846"), "the Apadomey regiment passed, on their return, in single file, each leading in a string a young male or female slave, carrying also the dried scalp of one man supposed to have been killed in the attack. On all such occasions, when a person is killed in battle, the skin is taken from the head and kept as a trophy of valor. It must not be supposed that these female warriors kill according to the number of scalps presented; the scalps are the accumulation of many years. If six or seven men are killed during one year's war it is deemed a great thing; one party always run away in these slave-hunts; but where armies meet the slaughter is great. I counted 700 scalps pass in this manner." But mutilation, like cannibalism, tattooing, and burying in barrows, is so natural under certain circumstances to man's mind that we distinctly require no traditional derivation.

Scalp-taking is a solemn rite. In the good old times braves scrupulously awaited the wounded man's death before they "raised his hair;" in the laxity of modern days, however, this humane custom is too often disregarded. Properly speaking, the trophy should be taken after fair fight with a hostile warrior; this also is now neglected. When the Indian sees his enemy fall he draws his scalp-knife—the modern is of iron, formerly it was of flint, obsidian, or other hard stone—and twisting the scalp-lock, which is left long for that purpose, and boastfully braided or decorated with some gaudy ribbon or with the war-eagle's plume, round his left hand, makes with the right two semicircular incisions, with and against the sun, about the part to be removed. The skin is next loosened with the knife-point, if there be time to spare and if there be much scalp to be taken. The operator then sits on the ground, places his feet against the subject's shoulders by way of leverage, and, holding the scalp-lock with both hands, he applies a strain which soon brings off the spoils with a sound which, I am told, is not unlike "flop." Without the long lock it would be difficult to remove the scalp; prudent white travelers, therefore, are careful, before setting out through an Indian country, to "shingle off" their hair as closely as possible; the Indian, moreover, hardly cares for a half-fledged scalp. To judge from the long love-locks affected by the hunter and mountaineer, he seems to think lightly of this precaution; to hold it, in fact, a point of honor that the savage should have a fair chance. A few cunning men have surprised their adversaries with wigs. The operation of scalping must be exceedingly painful; the sufferer turns, wriggles, and "squirms" upon the ground like a scotched snake. It is supposed to induce brain fever; many instances, however, are known of men and even women recovering from it, as the former do from a more dreadful infliction in Abyssinia and Galla-land; cases are of course rare, as a disabling wound is generally inflicted before the bloodier work is done.

H

After taking the scalp, the Indian warrior—proud as if he had won a *médaille de sauvetage*—prepares for return to his village. He lingers outside for a few days, and then, after painting his hands and face with lampblack, appears slowly and silently before his lodge. There he squats for a while; his relatives and friends, accompanied by the elders of the tribe, sit with him dumb as himself. Presently the question is put; it is answered with truth, although these warriors at other times will lie like Cretans. The "coup" is recounted, however, with abundant glorification; the Indians, like the Greek and Arab of their classical ages, are allowed to vent their self-esteem on such occasions without blame, and to enjoy a treat for which the civilized modern hero longs ardently, but in vain. Finally the "green scalp," after being dried and mounted, is consecrated by the solemn dance, and becomes then fit for public exhibition. Some tribes attach it to a long pole used as a standard, and others to their horses' bridles, others to their targes, while others ornament with its fringes the outer seams of their leggins; in fact, its uses are many. The more scalps the more honor; the young man who can not boast of a single murder or show the coveted trophy is held in such scant esteem as the English gentleman who contents himself with being passing rich on a hundred pounds a year. Some great war-chiefs have collected a heap of these honorable spoils. It must be remembered by "curio" hunters that only one scalp can come off one head; namely, the centre lock or long tuft growing upon the coronal apex, with about three inches in diameter of skin. This knowledge is the more needful, as the Western men are in the habit of manufacturing half a dozen cut from different parts of the same head; they sell readily for $50 each, but the transaction is not considered reputable. The connoisseur, however, readily distinguishes the real article from "false scalping" by the unusual thickness of the cutis, which is more like that of a donkey than of a man. Set in a plain gold circlet it makes a very pretty brooch. Moreover, each tribe has its own fashion of scalping derived from its forefathers. The Sioux, for instance, when they have leisure to perform the operation, remove the whole headskin, including a portion of the ears; they then sit down and dispose the ears upon the horns of a buffalo skull, and a bit of the flesh upon little heaps of earth or clay, disposed in quincunx, apparently as an offering to the manes of their ancestors, and they smoke ceremoniously, begging the manitou to send them plenty more. The trophy is then stretched upon a willow twig bent into an oval shape, and lined with two semi-ovals of black or blue and scarlet cloth. The Yutas and the Prairie tribes generally, when pressed for time, merely take off the poll skin that grows the long tuft of hair, while the Chyuagara or Nez Percés prefer a long strip about two inches wide, extending from the nape to the commissure of the hair and forehead. The fingers of the slain are often reserved for sévignés and necklaces.   Indians are aware of the aversion with which the pale faces regard this barbarity. Near Alkali Lake, where there was a large Dakotah "tipi" or encampment of Sioux, I tried to induce a tribesman to go through the imitative process before me; he refused with a gesture indignantly repudiating the practice.   A glass of whisky would doubtless have changed his mind, but I was unwilling to break through the wholesome law that prohibits it.

It is not wonderful that the modern missionary should be unable to influence such a brain as the Prairie Indian's.   The old propagandists, Jesuits and Franciscans, became medicine-men: like the great fraternity in India, they succeeded by the points of resemblance which the savages remarked in their observances, such as their images and rosaries, which would be regarded as totems, and their fastings and prayers, which were of course supposed to be spells and charms.   Their successors have succeeded about as well with the Indian as with the African; the settled tribes have given ear to them, the Prairie wanderers have not; and the Europeanization of the Indian generally is hopeless as the Christianization of the Hindoo.   The missionaries usually live under the shadow of the different agencies, and even they own that nothing can be done with the children unless removed from the parental influence.   I do not believe that an Indian of the plains ever became a Christian.   He must first be humanized, then civilized, and lastly Christianized ; and, as has been said before, I doubt his surviving the operation.

As might be expected of the Indian's creed, it has few rites and ceremonies; circumcision is unknown, and it ignores the complicated observances which, in the case of the Hindoo Pantheist, and in many African tribes, wait upon gestation, parturition, and allactation.   The child is seldom named.*   There are but five words given in regular order to distinguish one from another. There are no family names.   The men, after notable exploits, are entitled by their tribes to assume the titles of the distinguished dead, and each fresh deed brings a new distinction.   Some of the names are poetical enough : the "Black Night," for instance, the "Breaker of Arrows," or the "War Eagle's Wing ;" others are coarse and ridiculous, such as "Squash-head," "Bull's-tail," "Dirty Saddle," and "Steam from a Cow's Belly ;" not a few bear a whimsical likeness to those of the African negroes, as "His Great Fire," "The Water goes in the Path," and "Buffalo Chips"—the "Mavi yá Gnombe" of Unyamwezi.   The son of a chief succeeding his father usually assumes his name, so that the little dynasty, like that of the Pharaohs, the Romuli, or the Numas, is perpetuated.   The women are not unfrequently called after the parts and properties of some admired or valued animal, as the White Mar-

* The Ojibwa and other races have the ceremony of a burnt-offering when the name is given.

tin, the Young Mink,* or the Muskrat's Paw.   In the north there have been men with as many as seven wives, all "Martins."   The Prairie Indians form the names of the women like those of men, adding the feminine suffix, as Cloud-woman, Red-earth-woman, Black-day-woman.   The white stranger is ever offending Indian etiquette by asking the savage "What's your name?"   The person asked looks aside for a friend to assist him; he has learned in boyhood that some misfortune will happen to him if he discloses his name.   Even husbands and wives never mention each other's names.   The same practice prevails in many parts of Asia.

Marriage is a simple affair with them.   In some tribes the bride, as among the Australians, is carried off by force.   In others the man who wants a wife courts her with a little present, and pickets near the father's lodge the number of horses which he supposes to be her equivalent.   As among all savage tribes, the daughter is a chattel, an item of her father's goods, and he will not part with her except for a consideration.   The men are of course polygamists; they prefer to marry sisters, because the tent is more quiet, and much upon the principle with which marriage with a deceased wife's sister is advocated in England.   The women, like the Africans, are not a little addicted to suicide.   Before espousal the conduct of the weaker sex in many tribes is far from irreproachable.   The "bundling" of Wales and of New England in a former day† is not unknown to them, and many think little of that *præguslatio matrimonii* which, in the eastern parts of the New World, goes by the name of Fanny Wrightism and Free-loveism. Several tribes make trial, like the Highlanders before the reign of James the Fifth, of their wives for a certain time — a kind of "hand-fasting," which is to morality what fetichism is to faith. There are few nations in the world among whom this practice, originating in a natural desire not to "make a leap in the dark," can not be traced.   Yet after marriage they will live, like the Spartan matrons, a life of austerity in relation to the other sex. In cases of divorce, the children, being property, are divided, and in most tribes the wife claims the odd one.   If the mother takes any care to preserve her daughter's virtue, it is only out of regard

* Putorius vison, a pretty dark-chestnut-colored animal of the weasel kind, which burrows in the banks of streams near mills and farm-houses, where it preys upon the poultry like the rest of the family.   It swims well, and can dive for a long time. Its food is small fish, mussels, and insects, but it will also devour rats and mice.

† Traces of this ancient practice may be found in the four quarters of the globe. Mr. Bartlett, in his instructive volume, quotes the Rev. Samuel Pike ("General History of Connecticut," London, 1781), who quaintly remarks: "Notwithstanding the great modesty of the females is such that it would be accounted the greatest rudeness for a gentleman to speak before a lady of a garter or a leg, yet it is thought but a piece of civility to ask her to *bundle*."   The learned and pious historian endeavored to prove that bundling was not only a Christian, but a very polite and prudent practice.   So the Rev. Andrew Barnaby, who traveled in New England in 1759–60, thinks that though bundling may "at first appear the effect of grossness of character, it will, upon deeper research, be found to proceed from simplicity and innocence."

to its market value.   In some tribes the injured husband displays all the philosophy of Cato and Socrates.   In others the wife is punished, like the native of Hindostan, by cutting, or, more generally, by biting off the nose-tip.   Some slay the wife's lover; others accept a pecuniary compensation for their dishonor, and take as damages skins or horses.   Elopement, as among the Arabs, prevails in places.   The difference of conduct on the part of the women of course depends upon the bearing of the men.   "There is no adulteress without an adulterer"—meaning that the husband is ever the first to be unfaithful — is a saying as old as the days of Mohammed.   Among the Arapahoes, for instance, there is great looseness; the Cheyennes, on the contrary, are notably correct. Truth demands one unpleasant confession, viz., on the whole, chastity is little esteemed among those Indians who have been corrupted by intercourse with whites.

The dignity of chief denotes in the Indian language a royal title.   It is hereditary as a rule, but men of low birth sometimes attain it by winning a name as warriors or medicine-men.   When there are many sons it often happens that each takes command of a small clan.   Personal prowess is a necessity in sagamore and sachem: an old man, therefore, often abdicates in favor of his more vigorous son, to whom he acts as guide and counselor. There is one chief to every band, with several sub-chiefs.   The power possessed by the ruler depends upon his individual character, and the greater or lesser capacity for discipline in his subjects.   Some are obeyed grudgingly, as the Sheikh of a Bedouin tribe.   Others are absolute monarchs, who dispose of the lives and properties of their followers without exciting a murmur. The counteracting element to despotism resides in the sub-chief and in the council of warriors, who obstinately insist upon having a voice in making laws, raising subsidies, declaring wars, and ratifying peace.

Their life is of course simple; they have no regular hours for meals or sleep.   Before eating they sometimes make a heave-offering of a bit of food toward the heavens, where their forefathers are, and a second toward the earth, the mother of all things: the pieces are then burned.   They are not cannibals, except when a warrior, after slaying a foe, eats, porcupine-like, the heart or liver, with the idea of increasing his own courage.   The women rarely sit at meals with the men.   In savage and semi-barbarous societies the separation of the sexes is the general rule, because, as they have no ideas in common, each prefers the society of its own. They are fond of adoption and of making brotherhoods, like the Africans; and so strong is the tie, that marriage with the sister of an adopted brother is within the prohibited degrees.   Gambling is a passion with them: they play at cards, an art probably learned from the Canadians, and the game is that called in the States "matching," on the principle of dominoes or beggar-my-neighbor. When excited they ejaculate Will! Will!—sharp and staccato—it is possibly a conception of the English well. But it often comes out in the place of bad, as the Sepoy orderly in India reports to his captain, "Ramnak Jamnak dead, Joti Prasad very sick—all vell!" The savages win and lose with the stoicism habitual to them, rarely drawing the "navajon," like the Mexican "lepero," over a disputed point; and when a man has lost his last rag, he rises in nude dignity and goes home. Their language ignores the violent and offensive abuse of parents and female relatives, which distinguishes the Asiatic and the African from the European Billingsgate: the worst epithets that can be applied to a man are miser, coward, dog, woman. With them good temper is good breeding—a mark of gentle blood. A brave will stand up and harangue his enemies, exulting how he scalped their sires, and squaws, and sons, without calling forth a grunt of irritation. Ceremony and manners, in our sense of the word, they have none, and they lack the profusion of salutations which usually distinguishes barbarians. An Indian appearing at your door rarely has the civility to wait till beckoned in; he enters the house, with his quiet catlike gait and his imperturbable countenance, saying, if a Sioux, "How!" or "How! How!" meaning Well? shakes hands, to which he expects the same reply, if he has learned "paddling with the palms" from the whites—this, however, is only expected by the chiefs and braves—and squats upon his hams in the Eastern way, I had almost said the natural way, but to man, unlike all other animals, every way is equally natural, the chair or the seat upon the ground. He accepts a pipe if offered to him, devours what you set before him—those best acquainted with the savage, however, avoid all unnecessary civility or generosity: Milesian-like, he considers a benefit his due, and if withheld, he looks upon his benefactor as a "mean man"—talks or smokes as long as he pleases, and then rising, stalks off without a word. His ideas of time are primitive. The hour is denoted by pointing out the position of the sun; the days, or rather the nights, are reckoned by sleeps; there are no weeks; the moons, which are literally new, the old being nibbled away by mice, form the months, and suns do duty for years. He has, like the Bedouin and the Esquimaux, sufficient knowledge of the heavenly bodies to steer his course over the pathless sage-sea. Night-work, however, is no favorite with him except in cases of absolute necessity. Counting is done upon man's first abacus, the fingers, and it rarely extends beyond ten. The value of an article was formerly determined by beads and buffaloes; dollars, however, are now beginning to be generally known.

The only arts of the Indians are medicine and the use of arms. They are great in the knowledge of simples and tisanes. The leaves of the white willow are the favorite emetic; wounds are dressed with astringent herbs, and inflammations are reduced by scarification and the actual cautery. Among some tribes, the hammam, or Turkish bath, is invariably the appendage to a village. It is an oven sunk in the earth, with room for about a score of persons, and a domed roof of tamped and timber-propped earth—often mistaken for a bulge in the ground—pierced with a little square window for ventilation when not in use. A fire is kindled in the centre, and the patient, after excluding the air, sits quietly in this rude calidarium till half roasted and stifled by the heat and smoke. Finally, like the Russian peasant, he plunges into the burn that runs hard by, and feels his ailments dropping off him with the dead cuticle. The Indians associating with the horse have learned a rude farriery which often succeeds where politer practice would fail. I heard of one who cured the bites of rattlesnakes and copperheads by scarifying the wounded beast's face, plastering the place with damped gunpowder paste and setting it on fire.

Among the Prairie tribes are now to be found individuals provided not only with the old muskets formerly supplied to them, but with yägers,* Sharp's breech-loaders, alias "Beecher's Bibles," Colt's revolvers, and other really good fire-arms. Their shooting has improved with their tools: many of them are now able to "draw a bead" with coolness and certainty. Those who can not afford shooting-irons content themselves with their ancient weapons, the lance and bow. The former is a poor affair, a mere iron spike from two to three inches long, inserted into the end of a staff about as thick as a Hindostanee's bamboo lance; it is whipped round with sinew for strength, decorated with a few bunches of gaudy feathers, and defended with the usual medicine-bag. The bow varies in dimensions with the different tribes. On the prairies, for convenient use on horseback, it seldom exceeds three feet in length; among the Southern Indians its size doubles, and in parts of South America it is like that of the Andamans, a gigantic weapon with an arrow six feet long, and drawn by bringing the aid of the feet to the hands. The best bows among the Sioux and Yutas are of horn, hickory being unprocurable; an inferior sort is made of a reddish wood, in hue and grain not unlike that called "mountain mahogany." A strip of raw-hide is fitted to the back for increase of elasticity, and the string is a line of twisted sinew. When not wanted for use the weapon is carried in a skin case slung over the shoulder. It is drawn with the two forefingers—not with the forefinger and thumb, as in the East— and generally the third or ring-finger is extended along the string to give additional purchase. Savage tribes do little in the way of handicraft, but that little they do patiently, slowly, and therefore well. The bow and arrow are admirably adapted to their purpose. The latter is either a reed or a bit of arrow-wood (*Viburnum dentatum*), whose long, straight, and tough stems are used

---

* An antiquated sort of German rifle, formerly used by the federal troops.

by the fletcher from the Mississippi to the Pacific. The piles are triangles of iron, agate, flint, chalcedony, opal, or other hard stone: for war purposes they are barbed, and bird-bolts tipped with hard wood are used for killing small game. Some tribes poison their shafts: the material is the juice of a buffalo's or an antelope's liver when it has become green and decomposed after the bite of a rattlesnake; at least this is the account which all the hunters and mountaineers give of it. They have also, I believe, vegetable poisons. The feathers are three in number; those preferred are the hawk's and the raven's; and some tribes glue, while others whip them on with tendon-thread. The stele is invariably indented from the feathers to the tip with a shallow spiral furrow: this vermiculation is intended, according to the traders, to hasten death by letting air into or letting blood out of the wound. It is probably the remnant of some superstition now obsolete, for every man does it, while no man explains why or wherefore. If the Indian works well, he does not work quickly; he will expend upon half a dozen arrows as many months. Each tribe has its own mark; the Pawnees, for instance, make a bulge below the notch. Individuals also have private signs which enable them to claim a disputed scalp or buffalo robe. In battle or chase the arrows are held in the left hand, and are served out to the right with such rapidity that one long string of them seems to be cleaving the air. A good Sioux archer will, it is said, discharge nine arrows upward before the first has fallen to the ground. He will transfix a bison and find his shaft upon the earth on the other side; and he shows his dexterity by discharging the arrow up to its middle in the quarry and by withdrawing it before the animal falls. Tales are told of a single warrior killing several soldiers; and as a rule, at short distances, the bow is considered by the whites a more effectual weapon than the gun. It is related that when the Sioux first felt the effects of Colt's revolver, the weapon, after two shots, happened to slip from the owner's grasp; when he recovered it and fired a third time all fled, declaring that a white was shooting them with buffalo chips. Wonderful tales are told of the Indians' accuracy with the bow: they hold it no great feat to put the arrow into a keyhole at the distance of forty paces. It is true that I never saw any thing surprising in their performances, but the savage will not take the trouble to waste his skill without an object.

The Sioux tongue, like the Pawnee, is easily learned; government officials and settlers acquire it as the Anglo-Indian does Hindostanee. They are assisted by the excellent grammar and dictionary of the Dakotah language, collated by the members of the Dakotah Mission, edited by the Rev. S. R. Riggs, M.A., and accepted for publication by the Smithsonian Institution, December, 1851. The Dakotah-English part contains about 16,000 words, and the bibliography (spelling-books, tracts, and translations) numbered ten years ago eighteen small volumes. The work is compiled in a scholar-like manner. The orthography, though rather complicated, is intelligible, and is a great improvement upon the old and unartistic way of writing the polysynthetic Indian tongues, syllable by syllable, as though they were monosyllabic Chinese; the superfluous *h* (as Dakota*h* for Dakota), by which the broad sound of the terminal *a* is denoted, has been justly cast out. The peculiar letters *ch*, *p*, and *t*, are denoted by a dot beneath the simple sound; similarly the *k* (or Arabic *kaf*), the *gh* (the Semitic *ghain*) and the *kh* (*khá*), which, as has happened in Franco-Arabic grammars, was usually expressed by an *R*. An apostrophe (*s'a*) denotes the hiatus, which is similar to the Arab's hamzah.

Vater long ago remarked that the only languages which had a character, if not similar, at any rate analogous to the American, are the Basque and the Congo, that is, the South African or Kaffir family. This is the case in many points: in Dakotah, for instance, as in Kisawahili, almost every word ends in a pure or a nasalized vowel. But the striking novelty of the African tongues, the inflexion of words by an initial, not, as with us, by a terminal change and the complex system of euphony, does not appear in the American, which in its turn possesses a dual unknown to the African. The Dakotah, like the Kaffir, has no gender; it uses the personal and impersonal, which is an older distinction in language. It follows the primitive and natural arrangement of speech: it says, for instance, "aguyapi maku ye," bread to me give; as in Hindostanee, to quote no other, "roti hamko do." So in logical argument it begins with the conclusion and proceeds to the premisses, which renders it difficult for a European to think in Dakotah. Like other American tongues, it is polysynthetic, which appears to be the effect of arrested development. Human speech begins with inorganic sounds, which represent symbolism by means of arrows pointed in a certain direction, bent trees, crossed rods, and other similar contrivances. Its first step is monosyllabic, which corresponds with the pictograph, the earliest attempt at writing among the uncivilized.* The next advance is polysynthesis, which is apparently built upon monosyllabism, as the idiograph of the Chinese upon a picture or glyph. The last step is the syllabic and inflected, corresponding with the Phœnico-Arabian alphabet, which gave rise to the Greek, the Latin, and their descendants. The complexity of Dakotah grammar is another illustration of the phenomenon that man in most things, in language especially, begins with the most difficult and works on toward the facile. Savages, who have no mental exercise but the cultivation of speech, and semi-barbarous people, who still retain

---

* A Kaffir girl wishing to give a hint to a friend of mine drew a setting sun, a tree, and two figures standing under it; intelligible enough, yet the Kaffirs ignore a syllabarium.

the habit, employ complicated and highly elaborate tongues, *e. g.*, Arabic, Sanscrit, Latin, Greek, Kaffir, and Anglo-Saxon. With time these become more simple; the *modus operandi* appears to be admixture of race.

The Dakotahs have a sacred language, used by medicine-men, and rendered unintelligible to the vulgar by words borrowed from other Indian dialects, and by synonyms, *e. g.*, biped for man, quadruped for wolf. A chief, asking for an ox or cow, calls it a dog, and a horse, moccasins: possibly, like Orientals, he superstitiously avoids direct mention, and speaks of the object wanted by a humbler name. Poetry is hardly required in a language so highly figurative: a hi-hi-hi-hi-hi, occasionally interrupted by a few words, composes their songs. The Rev. Mr. Pond gives the following specimen of "Blackboy's" Mourning Song for his Grandson, addressed to those of Ghostland:

> Friend, pause, and look this way;
> Friend, pause, and look this way;
> Friend, pause, and look this way;
>   Say ye,
> A Grandson of Blackboy is coming.

Their speech is sometimes metaphorical to an extent which conveys an opposite meaning: "Friend, thou art a fool; thou hast let the Ojibwa strike thee," is the highest form of eulogy to a brave who has killed and scalped a foe; possibly a Malocchio-like fear, the dread of praise, which, according to Pliny, kills in India, underlies the habit.

The funerals differ in every tribe; the Sioux expose their dead, wrapped in blankets or buffalo robes, upon tall poles—a custom that reminds us of the Parsee's "Tower of Silence." The Yutas make their graves high up the kanyons, usually in clefts of rock. Some bury the dead at full length; others sitting or doubled up; others on horseback, with a barrow or tumulus of earth heaped up over their remains. The absence of grave-yards in an Indian country is as remarkable as in the African interior; thinness of population and the savage's instinctive dislike to any *memento mori* are the causes. After deaths the "keening" is long, loud, and lasting: the women, and often the men, cut their hair close, not allowing it to fall below the shoulders, and not unfrequently gash themselves, and amputate one or more fingers. The dead man, especiallly a chief, is in almost all tribes provided with a viaticum, dead or alive, of squaws and boys—generally those taken from another tribe—horses and dogs; his lodge is burned, his arms, cooking utensils, saddles, and other accoutrements are buried with him, and a goodly store of buffalo meat or other provision is placed by his side, that his ghost may want nothing which it enjoyed in the flesh. Like all savages, the Indian is unable to separate the idea of man's immaterial spirit from man's material wants: an impalpable and invisible form of matter—called "spirit" because it is not cognizable to the senses, which are the only avenues of all knowledge—is as unintelligible to them as to a Latter-Day Saint, or, indeed, as to the mind of man generally. Hence the Indian's smoking and offerings over the graves of friends. Some tribes mourn on the same day of each moon till grief is satisfied; others for a week after the death.

A remarkable characteristic of the Prairie Indian is his habit of speaking, like the deaf and dumb, with his fingers. The pantomime is a system of signs, some conventional, others instinctive or imitative, which enables tribes who have no acquaintance with each other's customs and tongues to hold limited but sufficient communication. An interpreter who knows all the signs, which, however, are so numerous and complicated that to acquire them is the labor of years, is preferred by the whites even to a good speaker. Some writers, as Captain H. Stansbury, consider the system purely arbitrary; others, Captain Marcy, for instance, hold it to be a natural language similar to the gestures which surd-mutes use spontaneously. Both views are true, but not wholly true; as the following pages will, I believe, prove, the pantomimic vocabulary is neither quite conventional nor the reverse.

The sign-system doubtless arose from the necessity of a communicating medium between races speaking many different dialects, and debarred by circumstances from social intercourse. Its area is extensive: it prevails among many of the Prairie tribes, as the Hapsaroke, or Crows, the Dakotah, the Cheyenne, and the Shoshonee; the Pawnees, Yutas, and Shoshoko, or Diggers, being vagrants and outcasts, have lost or never had the habit. Those natives who, like the Arapahoes, possess a very scanty vocabulary, pronounced in a quasi-unintelligible way, can hardly converse with one another in the dark: to make a stranger understand them they must always repair to the camp fire for "powwow." A story is told of a man who, being sent among the Cheyennes to qualify himself for interpreting, returned in a week, and proved his competence: all that he did, however, was to go through the usual pantomime with a running accompaniment of grunts. I have attempted to describe a few of the simpler signs: the reader, however, will readily perceive that without diagrams the explanation is very imperfect, and that in half an hour, with an Indian or an interpreter, he would learn more than by a hundred pages of print.

The first lesson is to distinguish the signs of the different tribes, and it will be observed that the French voyageurs and traders have often named the Indian nations from their totemic or masonic gestures.

The Pawnees (Les Loups) imitate a wolf's ears with the two forefingers—the right hand is always understood unless otherwise specified*—extended together, upright, on the left side of the head.

The Arapahoes, or Dirty Noses, rub the right side of that organ

* The left, as a rule, denotes inversion or contradiction.

with the forefinger: some call this bad tribe the Smellers, and make their sign to consist of seizing the nose with the thumb and forefinger.

The Comanches (Les Serpents) imitate, by the waving of the hand or forefinger, the forward crawling motion of a snake.

The Cheyennes, Paikanavos, or Cut-Wrists, draw the lower edge of the hand across the left arm as if gashing it with a knife.

The Sioux (Les Coupe-gorges), by drawing the lower edge of the hand across the throat: it is a gesture not unknown to us, but forms a truly ominous salutation considering those by whom it is practiced; hence the Sioux are called by the Yutas Pámpe Chyimina, or Hand-cutters.

The Hapsaroke (Les Corbeaux), by imitating the flapping of the birds' wings with the two hands—palms downward—brought close to the shoulders.

The Kiowas, or Prairie-men, make the signs of the prairie and of drinking water. These will presently be described.

The Yutas, "they who live on mountains," have a complicated sign which denotes "living in mountains;" these will be explained under "sit" and "mountains."

The Blackfeet, called by the Yutas Paike or Goers, pass the right hand, bent spoon-fashion, from the heel to the little toe of the right foot.

The following are a few preliminaries indispensable to the prairie traveler:

Halt!—Raise the hand, with the palm in front, and push it backward and forward several times—a gesture well known in the East.

I don't know you!—Move the raised hand, with the palm in front, slowly to the right and left.

I am angry!—Close the fist, place it against the forehead, and turn it to and fro in that position.

Are you friendly?—Raise both hands, grasped, as if in the act of shaking hands, or lock the two forefingers together while the hands are raised.

These signs will be found useful upon the prairie in case of meeting a suspected band. The Indians, like the Bedouin and N. African Moslem, do honor to strangers and guests by putting their horses to speed, couching their lances, and other peculiarities which would readily be dispensed with by gentlemen of peaceful pursuits and shaky nerves. If friendly, the band will halt when the hint is given and return the salute; if surly, they will disregard the command to stop, and probably will make the sign of anger. Then—ware scalp!

Come!—Beckon with the forefinger, as in Europe, not as is done in the East.

Come back!—Beckon in the European way, and draw the forefinger toward yourself.

Go!—Move both hands edgeways (the palms fronting the breast) toward the left with a rocking-horse motion.

Sit!—Make a motion toward the ground, as if to pound it with the ferient of the closed hand.

Lie down!—Point to the ground, and make a motion as if of lying down.

Sleep!—Ditto, closing the eyes.

Look!—Touch the right eye with the index and point it outward.

Hear!—Tap the right ear with the index tip.

Colors are expressed by a comparison with some object in sight. Many things, as the blowing of wind, the cries of beasts and birds, and the roaring of the sea, are imitated by sound.

See!—Strike out the two forefingers forward from the eyes.

Smell!—Touch the nose-tip. A bad smell is expressed by the same sign, ejaculating at the same time "Pooh!" and making the sign of bad.

Taste!—Touch the tongue-tip.

Eat!—Imitate the action of conveying food with the fingers to the mouth.

Drink!—Scoop up with the hand imaginary water into the mouth.

Smoke!—With the crooked index describe a pipe in the air, beginning at the lips; then wave the open hand from the mouth to imitate curls of smoke.

Speak!—Extend the open hand from the chin.

Fight!—Make a motion with both fists to and fro, like a pugilist of the eighteenth century who preferred a high guard.

Kill!—Smite the sinister palm earthward with the dexter fist sharply, in sign of "going down;" or strike out with the dexter fist toward the ground, meaning to "shut down;" or pass the dexter index under the left forefinger, meaning to "go under."

To show that fighting is actually taking place, make the gestures as above described; tap the lips with the palm like an Oriental woman when "keening," screaming the while O-a! O-a! to imitate the war-song.

Wash!—Rub the hand as with invisible soap in imperceptible water.

Think!—Pass the forefinger sharply across the breast from right to left.

Hide!—Place the hand inside the clothing of the left breast. This means also to put away or to keep secret. To express "I won't say," make the signs of "I" and "no" (which see), and hide the hand as above directed.

Love!—Fold the hands crosswise over the breast, as if embracing the object, assuming at the same time a look expressing the desire to carry out the operation. This gesture will be understood by the dullest squaw.

Tell truth!—Extend the forefinger from the mouth ("one word").

Tell lie!—Extend the two first fingers from the mouth ("double tongue," a significant gesture).

Steal!—Seize an imaginary object with the right hand from under the left fist. To express horse-stealing they saw with the right hand down upon the extended fingers of the left, thereby denoting rope-cutting.

Trade or exchange!—Cross the forefingers of both hands before the breast—" diamond cut diamond."

This sign also denotes the Americans, and, indeed, any white men, who are generically called by the Indians west of the Rocky Mountains " Shwop," from our swap or swop, an English Romany word for barter or exchange.

The pronouns are expressed by pointing to the person designated. For " I," touch the nose-tip, or otherwise indicate self with the index. The second and third persons are similarly made known.

Every animal has its precise sign, and the choice of gesture is sometimes very ingenious. If the symbol be not known, the form may be drawn on the ground, and the strong perceptive faculties of the savage enable him easily to recognize even rough draughts. A cow or a sheep denotes white men, as if they were their totems. The Indian's high development of locality also enables him to map the features of a country readily and correctly upon the sand. Moreover, almost every grand feature has a highly significant name, Flintwater, for instance, and nothing is easier than to combine the signs.

The *bear* is expressed by passing the hand before the face to mean ugliness, at the same time grinning and extending the fingers like claws.

The *buffalo* is known by raising the forefingers crooked inward, in the semblance of horns on both sides of the head.

The *elk* is signified by simultaneously raising both hands with the fingers extended on both sides of the head to imitate palmated horns.

For the *deer*, extend the thumbs and the two forefingers of each hand on each side of the head.

For the *antelope*, extend the thumbs and forefingers along the sides of the head, to simulate ears and horns.

Mountain sheep are denoted by placing the hands on a level with the ears, the palms facing backward and the fingers slightly reversed, to imitate the ammonite-shaped horns.

For the *beaver*, describe a parenthesis, *e. g.* ( ), with the thumb and index of both hands, and then with the dexter index imitate the wagging of the tail.

The *dog* is shown by drawing the two forefingers slightly opened horizontally across the breast from right to left. This is a highly appropriate and traditional gesture: before the introduction of horses, the dog was taught to carry the tent poles, and the motion expressed the lodge trail.

To denote the *mule* or *ass*, the long ears are imitated by the indices on both sides and above the head.

For the *crow*, and, indeed, any bird, the hands are flapped near the shoulders. If specification be required, the cry is imitated or some peculiarity is introduced. The following will show the ingenuity with which the Indian can convey his meaning under difficulties. A Yuta wishing to explain that the torpedo or gymnotus eel is found in Cotton-wood Kanyon Lake, took to it thus: he made the body by extending his sinister index to the fore, touched it with the dexter index at two points on both sides to show legs, and finally sharply withdrew his right forefinger to convey the idea of an electric shock.

Some of the symbols of relationship are highly appropriate, and not ungraceful or unpicturesque. Man is denoted by a sign which will not admit of description; woman, by passing the hand down both sides of the head as if smoothing or stroking the long hair. A son or daughter is expressed by making with the hand a movement denoting issue from the loins: if the child be small, a bit of the index held between the antagonized thumb and medius is shown. The same sign of issue expresses both parents, with additional explanations: To say, for instance, "*my mother,*" you would first pantomime "*I,*" or, which is the same thing, "*my;*" then "*woman;*" and, finally, the symbol of parentage. "*My grandmother*" would be conveyed in the same way, adding to the end clasped hands, closed eyes, and like an old woman's bent back. The sign for brother and sister is perhaps the prettiest: the two first fingertips are put into the mouth, denoting that they fed from the same breast. For the wife—squaw is now becoming a word of reproach among the Indians—the dexter forefinger is passed between the extended thumb and index of the left.

Of course there is a sign for every weapon. The *knife*—scalp or other—is shown by cutting the sinister palm with the dexter ferient downward and toward one's self: if the cuts be made upward with the palm downward, meat is understood. The *tomahawk*, hatchet, or axe is denoted by chopping the left hand with the right; the *sword* by the motion of drawing it; the *bow* by the movement of bending it; and a *spear* or *lance* by an imitation of darting it. For the *gun*, the dexter thumb and fingers are flashed or scattered, *i. e.*, thrown outward or upward to denote fire. The same movement made lower down expresses a *pistol*. The *arrow* is expressed by nocking it upon an imaginary bow, and by "snapping" with the index and medius. The *shield* is shown by pointing with the index over the left shoulder, where it is slung ready to be brought over the breast when required.

The following are the most useful words:

Yes.—Wave the hands straight forward from the face.

No.—Wave the hand from right to left, as if motioning away. This sign also means "I'll have nothing to do with you." Done slowly and insinuatingly, it informs a woman that she is *charmante*—"not to be touched" being the idea.

Good.—Wave the hand from the mouth, extending the thumb from the index and closing the other three fingers. This sign means also "I know." "I don't know" is expressed by waving the right hand with the palm outward before the right breast, or by moving about the two forefingers before the breast, meaning "two hearts."

Bad.—Scatter the dexter fingers outward, as if spirting away water from them.

Now (*at once*).—Clap both palms together sharply and repeatedly, or make the sign of " to-day."

Day.—Make a circle with the thumb and forefinger of both, in sign of the sun. The *hour* is pointed out by showing the luminary's place in the heavens. The *moon* is expressed by a crescent with the thumb and forefinger: this also denotes a month. For a *year* give the sign of rain or snow.

Many Indians ignore the quadripartite division of the seasons, which seems to be an invention of European latitudes; the Persians, for instance, know it, but the Hindoos do not. They have, however, distinct terms for the month, all of which are pretty and descriptive, appropriate and poetical; *e. g.*, the moon of light nights, the moon of leaves, the moon of strawberries, for April, May, and June. The Ojibwa have a queer quaternal division, called Of sap, Of abundance, Of fading, and Of freezing. The Dakotah reckon five moons to winter and five to summer, leaving one to spring and one to autumn; the year is lunar, and as the change of season is denoted by the appearance of sore eyes and of raccoons, any irregularity throws the people out.

Night.—Make a closing movement as if of the darkness by bringing together both hands with the dorsa upward and the fingers to the fore: the motion is from right to left, and at the end the two indices are alongside and close to each other. This movement must be accompanied by bending forward with bowed head, otherwise it may be misunderstood for the freezing over of a lake or river.

To-day.—Touch the nose with the index tip, and motion with the fist toward the ground.

Yesterday.—Make with the left hand the circle which the sun describes from sunrise to sunset, or invert the direction from sunset to sunrise with the right hand.

To-morrow.—Describe the motion of the sun from east to west. Any number of days may be counted upon the fingers. The latter, I need hardly say, are the only numerals in the pantomimic vocabulary.

Among the Dakotahs, when they have gone over the fingers and thumbs of both hands, one is temporarily turned down for one ten; at the end of another ten a second finger is turned down, and so on, as among children who are learning to count. "Opawinge," one hundred, is derived from "pawinga," to go round in circles, as the fingers have all been gone over again for their respective tens; "kektopawinge" is from "ake" and "opawinge"— "hundred again"—being about to recommence the circle of their fingers already completed in hundreds. For numerals above a thousand there is no method of computing. There is a sign and word for one half of a thing, but none to denote any smaller aliquot part.

Peace.—Intertwine the fingers of both hands.

Friendship.—Clasp the left with the right hand.

Glad (pleased).—Wave the open hand outward from the breast, to express " good heart."

A Cup.—Imitate its form with both hands, and make the sign of drinking from it. In this way any utensil can be intelligibly described—of course, provided that the interlocutor has seen it.

Paint.—Daub both the cheeks downward with the index.

Looking-glass.—Place both palms before the face, and admire your countenance in them.

Bead.—Point to a bead, or make the sign of a necklace.

Wire.—Show it, or where it ought to be, in the ear-lobe.

Whisky.—Make the sign of " bad" and " drink" for " bad water."

Blanket or Clothes.—Put them on in pantomime.

A Lodge.—Place the fingers of both hands ridge-fashion before the breast.

Fire.—Blow it, and warm the hands before it. To express the boiling of a kettle, the sign of fire is made low down, and an imaginary pot is eaten from.

It is cold.—Wrap up, shudder, and look disagreeable.

Rain.—Scatter the fingers downward. The same sign denotes snow.

Wind.—Stretch the fingers of both hands outward, puffing violently the while.

A Storm.—Make the rain sign; then, if thunder and lightning are to be expressed, move, as if in anger, the body to and fro, to show the wrath of the elements.

A Stone.—If light, act as if picking it up; if heavy, as if dropping it.

A Hill.—Close the finger-tips over the head : if a mountain is to be expressed, raise them high. To denote an ascent on rising ground, pass the right palm over the left hand, half doubling up the latter, so that it looks like a ridge.

A Plain.—Wave both the palms outward and low down.

A River.—Make the sign of drinking, and then wave both the palms outward. A rivulet, creek, or stream is shown by the drinking sign, and by holding the index tip between the thumb and medius; an arroyo (dry water-course), by covering up the tip with the thumb and middle finger.

A Lake.—Make the sign of drinking, and form a basin with both hands. If a large body of water is in question, wave both palms outward as in denoting a plain. The Prairie savages have never seen the sea, so it would be vain to attempt explanation.

A Book.—Place the right palm on the left palm, and then open both before the face.

A Letter.—Write with the thumb and dexter index on the sinister palm.

A Wagon.—Roll hand over hand, imitating a wheel.

I

A Wagon-road.—Make the wagon sign, and then wave the hand along the ground.

Grass.—Point to the ground with the index, and then turn the fingers upward to denote growth. If the grass be long, raise the hand high; and if yellow, point out that color.

The pantomime, as may be seen, is capable of expressing detailed narratives. For instance, supposing an Indian would tell the following tale—"Early this morning I mounted my horse, rode off at a gallop, traversed a kanyon or ravine, then over a mountain to a plain where there was no water, sighted bison, followed them, killed three of them, skinned them, packed the flesh upon my pony, remounted, and returned home"—he would symbolize it thus:

Touches nose—"*I.*"

Opens out the palms of his hand—"*this morning.*"

Points to east—"*early.*"

Places two dexter forefingers astraddle over sinister index—"*mounted my horse.*"

Moves both hands upward and rocking-horse fashion toward the left—"*galloped.*"

Passes the dexter hand right through thumb and forefinger of the sinister, which are widely extended—"*traversed a kanyon.*"

Closes the finger-tips high over the head, and waves both palms outward—"*over a mountain to a plain.*"

Scoops up with the hand imaginary water into the mouth, and then waves the hand from the face to denote "no"—"*where there was no water.*"

Touches eye—"*sighted.*"

Raises the forefingers crooked inward on both sides of the head—"*bison.*"

Smites the sinister palm downward with the dexter fist—"*killed.*"

Shows three fingers—"*three of them.*"

Scrapes the left palm with the edge of the right hand—"*skinned them.*"

Places the dexter on the sinister palm, and then the dexter palm on the sinister dorsum—"*packed the flesh upon my pony.*"

Straddles the two forefingers on the index of the left—"*remounted;*" and, finally,

Beckons toward self—"*returned home.*"

To conclude, I can hardly flatter myself that these descriptions have been made quite intelligible to the reader. They may, however, serve to prepare his mind for a *vivâ voce* lesson upon the prairies, should fate have such thing in store for him.

After this digression I return to my prosaic Diary.

CHAPTER III.

Concluding the Route to the Great Salt Lake City.

Along the Black Hills to Box-Elder.   15th August.

I AROSE "between two days," a little before 4 A.M., and watched the dawn, and found in its beauties a soothing influence, which acted upon stiff limbs and discontented spirit as if it had been a spell.

The stars of the Great Bear—the prairie night-clock—first began to pale without any seeming cause, till presently a faint streak of pale light—*dum i gurg*, or the wolf's tail, as it is called by the Persian—began to shimmer upon the eastern verge of heaven. It grew and grew through the dark blue air: one unaccustomed to the study of the "gray-eyed morn" would have expected it to usher in the day, when, gradually as it had struggled into existence, it faded, and a deeper darkness than before once more invaded the infinitude above.   But now the unrisen sun is more rapidly climbing the gloomy walls of Koh i Kaf—the mountain rim which encircles the world, and through whose lower gap the false dawn had found its way — preceded by a warm flush of light, which chases the shades till, though loth to depart, they find neither on earth nor in the firmament a place where they can linger.   Warmer and warmer waxes the heavenly radiance, gliding up to the keystone of the vault above; fainter and fainter grows the darkness, till the last stain disappears behind the Black Hills to the west, and the stars one by one, like glow-worms, "pale their ineffectual fires"—the "Pointers" are the longest to resist—retreat backward, as it were, and fade away into endless space.   Slowly, almost imperceptibly, the marvelous hues of "glorious morn," here truly a fresh "birth of heaven and earth," all gold and sapphire, acquire depth and distinctness, till at last a fiery flush ushers from beneath the horizon the source of all these splendors,

> "Robed in flames and amber light;"

and another day, with its little life of joys and sorrows, of hopes and fears, is born to the world.

Though we all rose up early, packed, and were ready to proceed, there was an unusual *vis inertiæ* on the part of the driver: Indians were about; the mules, of course, had bolted; but that did not suffice as explanation.   Presently the "wonder leaked out:" our companions were transferred from their comfortable vehicle to a real "shandridan," a Rocky-Mountain bone-setter. They were civil enough to the exceedingly drunken youth—a runaway New Yorker—who did us the honor of driving us; for

quand on a besoin du diable on lui dit, "*Monsieur.*"   One can not
expect, however, the *diable* to be equally civil: when we asked
him to tidy our vehicle a little, he simply replied that he'd be
darned if he did.   Long may be the darning-needle and sharp to
him!   But tempers seriously soured must blow up or burst, and
a very pretty little quarrel was the result: it was settled blood-
lessly, because one gentleman, who, to do him justice, showed every
disposition to convert himself into a target, displayed such perfect
unacquaintance with the weapons—revolvers—usually used on
similar occasions, that it would have been mere murder to have
taken pistol in hand against him.

As we sat very disconsolate in the open veranda, five Indians
stalked in, and the biggest and burliest of the party, a middle-aged
man, with the long, straight Indian hair, high, harsh features, and
face bald of eyebrows and beard, after offering his paw to Mrs.
Dana and the rest of the party, sat down with a manner of natural
dignity somewhat trenching upon the impertinent.   Presently,
diving his hand into his breast, the old rat pulled out a thick fold
of leather, and, after much manipulation, disclosed a dirty brown,
ragged-edged sheet of paper, certifying him to be "Little Thunder," and signed by "General Harney."   This, then, was the chief
who showed the white feather at Ash Hollow, and of whom some
military poet sang:

> "We didn't make a blunder,
> We rubbed out Little Thunder,
> And we sent him to the other side of Jordan."

Little Thunder did not look quite rubbed out; but for poesy fiction is, of course, an element far more appropriate than fact.   I
remember a similar effusion of the Anglo-Indian muse, which consigned "Akbar Khan the Yaghi" to the tune and fate of the King
of the Cannibal Isles, with a contempt of actualities quite as refreshing.   The Western Indians are as fond of these testimonials
as the East Indians: they preserve them with care as guarantees
of their good conduct, and sometimes, as may be expected, carry
about certificates in the style of Bellerophons' letters.   Little
Thunder was *en route* to Fort Laramie, where he intended to lay
a complaint against the Indian agent, who embezzled, he said,
half the rations and presents intended for his tribe.   Even the
whites owned that the "Maje's" bear got more sugar than all the
Indians put together.

Nothing can be worse, if the *vox populi occidentalis* be taken as
the *vox Dei,* than the modern management of the Indian Bureau
at Washington.   In former times the agencies were in the hands
of the military authorities, and the officer commanding the department was responsible for malversation of office.   This was found
to work well; the papers signed were signed on honor.   But in
the United States, the federal army, though well paid, is never allowed to keep any appointment that can safely be taken away

from it. The Indian Department is now divided into six superintendencies, viz., Northern, Central, Southern, Utah, New Mexico, Washington and Oregon Territories, who report to the Indian Office or Bureau of the Commissioners of Indian Affairs at Washington, under the charge of the Department of the Interior. The bond varies from $50,000 to $75,000, and the salary from $2000 to $2500 per annum. The northern superintendency contains four agencies, the central fourteen, the southern five, the Utah three, New Mexico six, and the miscellaneous, including Washington, eight. The grand total of agents, including two specials for Indians in Texas, is forty-two. Their bond is between $5000 and $75,000, and the salary between $1000 and $1550. There are also various sub-agencies, with pay of $1000 each, and giving in bonds $2000. There ought to be no perquisites; an unscrupulous man, however, finds many opportunities of making free with the presents; and the reflection that his office tenure shall expire after the fourth year must make him but the more reckless. As fifty or sixty appointments = 50 or 60 votes, × 20 in President electioneering, fitness for the task often becomes quite a subordinate consideration; the result is, necessarily, peculation producing discontent among the Indians, and the finale, death to the whites. To become a good Indian agent, a man requires the variety of qualifications which would fit him for the guardianship of children, experience and ability, benevolence and philanthropy: it would be difficult to secure such phœnix for $200 per annum, and it is found easier not to look for it. The remedy of these evils is not far from the surface—the restoration of the office into the hands of the responsible military servant of the state, who would keep it *quamdiu se benè gesserit*, and become better capable of serving his masters, the American people, by the importance which the office would give him in the eyes of his *protégés*. This is the system of the French Bureau Arabe, which, with its faults, I love still. But the political mind would doubtless determine the cure to be worse than the disease. After venting his grievances, Little Thunder arose, and, accompanied by his braves, remounted and rode off toward the east.

While delayed by the mules and their masters, we may amuse ourselves and divert our thoughts from the battle, and, perhaps, murder and sudden death, which may happen this evening, by studying the geography of the Black Hills. The range forms nearly a right angle, the larger limb—ninety miles—running east to west with a little southing along the Platte, the shorter leg—sixty miles—trending from north to south with a few degrees of easting and westing. Forming the easternmost part of the great trans-Mississippian mountain region, in the 44th parallel and between the 103d and 105th meridians, these masses cover an area of 6000 square miles. They are supposed to have received their last violent upheaval at the close of the cretaceous period; their bases are elevated from 2500 to 3500 feet—the highest peaks attaining 6700 feet—above river level, while their eastern is from 2000 to 3000 feet below the western foundation. Their materials, as determined by Lieutenant Warren's exploration, are successively metamorphosed azoic rock, including granite, lower Silurian (Potsdam sandstone), Devonian (?), carboniferous, Permian, Jurassic, and cretaceous. Like Ida, they are abundant in springs and flowing streams, which shed mainly to the northeast and the southeast, supplying the Indians with trout and salmon trout, catfish (*Prinelodus*), and pickerel. They abound in small rich valleys, well grown with grass, and wild fruits, choke-cherries (*P. Virginiana*), currants, sand-buttes fruit (*C. pumila ?*), and buffalo berries (*Shepherdia argentea*, or grains de bœuf). When irrigated, the bottoms are capable of high cultivation. They excel in fine timber for fuel and lumber, covering an area of 1500 square miles; in carboniferous rock of the true coal measures; and in other good building material. As in most of the hill ranges which are offsets from the Rocky Mountains, they contain gold in valuable quantities, and doubtless a minute examination will lead to the discovery of many other useful minerals. The Black Hills are appropriately named: a cloak of gloomy forest, pine and juniper, apparently springing from a rock denuded of less hardy vegetation, seems to invest them from head to foot. The Laramie Hills are sub-ranges of the higher ridge, and the well-known peak, the Pharos of the prairie mariner, rises about 1° due west of Fort Laramie to the height of 6500 feet above sea level. Beyond the meridian of Laramie the country totally changes. The broad prairie lands, unencumbered by timber, and covered with a rich pasturage, which highly adapts them for grazing, are now left behind. We are about to enter a dry, sandy, and sterile waste of sage, and presently of salt, where rare spots are fitted for rearing stock, and this formation will continue till we reach the shadow of the Rocky Mountains.

At length, the mules coming about 10 45 A.M., we hitched up, and, nothing loth, bade adieu to Horseshoe Creek and the "ladies." The driver sentimentally informed us that we were to see no more specimens of ladyhood for many days—gladdest tidings to one of the party, at least. The road, which ran out of sight of the river, was broken and jagged; a little labor would have made it tolerable, but what could the good pastor of Oberlin do with a folk whose only thought in life is dram-drinking, tobacco-chewing, trading, and swapping?* The country was cut with creeks

---

* The civilized Anglo-Americans are far more severe upon their half-barbarous brethren than any stranger; to witness, the following:

A Hoosier (native of Indiana) was called upon the stand, away out West, to testify to the character of a brother Hoosier. It was as follows:

"How long have you known Bill Bushwhack?"

"Ever since he war born."

"What is his general character?"

and arroyos, which separated the several bulges of ground, and the earth's surface was of a dull brick-dust red, thinly scrubbed over with coarse grass, ragged sage, and shrublets fit only for the fire. After a desolate drive, we sighted below us the creek La Bonté—so called from a French *voyageur*—green and bisected by a clear mountain stream whose banks were thick with self-planted trees. In the labyrinth of paths we chose the wrong one: presently we came to a sheer descent of four or five feet, and after deliberation as to whether the vehicle would "take it" or not, we came to the conclusion that we had better turn the restive mules to the right-about. Then, cheered by the sight of our consort, the other wagon, which stood temptingly shaded by the grove of cotton-wood, willows, box elder (*Negundo aceroides*), and wild cherry, at the distance of about half a mile, we sought manfully the right track, and the way in which the driver charged the minor obstacles was "a caution to mules." We ought to have arrived at 2 45 P.M.; we were about an hour later. The station had yet to be built; the whole road was in a transition state at the time of our travel; there was, however, a new corral for "forting" against Indians, and a kind of leafy arbor, which the officials had converted into a "cottage near a wood."

A little after 4 P.M. we forded the creek painfully with our new cattle—three rats and a slug. The latter was pronounced by our driver, when he condescended to use other language than anathemata, "the meanest cuss he ever seed." We were careful, however, to supply him at the shortest intervals with whisky-drams, which stimulated him, after breaking his whip, to perform a tattoo with clods and stones, kicks and stamps, upon the recreant animals' haunches, and by virtue of these we accomplished our twenty-five miles in tolerable time. For want of other pleasantries to contemplate, we busied ourselves in admiring the regularity and accuracy with which our consort wagon secured for herself all the best teams. The land was a red waste, such as travelers find in Eastern Africa, which after rains sheds streams like blood. The soil was a decomposition of ferruginous rock, here broken with rugged hills, precipices of ruddy sandstone 200 feet high, shaded or dotted with black-green cedars, there cumbered by huge boulders; the ravine-like water-courses which cut the road showed that after heavy rains a net-work of torrents must add to the pleasures of traveling, and the vegetation was reduced to the dull green artemisia, the azalia, and the jaundiced potentil-

---

"Letter A, No. 1—'bove par a very great way."

"Would you believe him on oath?"

"Yes, Sir-ee, on or off, or any other way."

"What is your opinion on his qualifications to good conduct?"

"He's the best shot on the prairies or in the woods; he can shave the eye-bristles off a wolf as far as a shootin'-iron 'll carry a ball; he can drink a quart of grog any day, and he chaws tobacker like a horse."

So Bill Bushwhack passed muster.—*N. Y. Spirit of the Times.*

la. After six miles we saw on the left of the path a huge natural pile or burrow of primitive boulders, about 200 feet high, and called "Brigham's Peak," because, according to Jehu's whiskyfied story, the prophet, revelator, and seer of the Latter-Day Saints had there, in 1857 (!), pronounced a 4th of July oration in the presence of 200 or 300 fair devotees.

Presently we emerged from the red region into the normal brown clay, garnished with sage as moors are with heather, over a road which might have suggested the nursery rhyme,

> "Here we go up, up, up,
> There we go down, down, down."

At last it improved, and once more, as if we never were to leave it, we fell into the Valley of the Platte. About eight miles from our destination we crossed the sandy bed of the La Prêle River, an arroyo of twenty feet wide, which, like its brethren, brims in spring with its freight of melted snow. In the clear shade of evening we traversed the "timber," or well-wooded lands lying upon Box-Elder Creek—a beautiful little stream some eight feet broad, and at 9 P.M. arrived at the station. The master, Mr. Wheeler, was exceptionably civil and communicative; he lent us buffalo robes for the night, and sent us to bed after the best supper the house could afford. We were not, however, to be balked of our proper pleasure, a "good grumble," so we hooked it on to another peg. One of the road-agents had just arrived from Great Salt Lake City in a neat private ambulance after a journey of three days, while we could hardly expect to make it under treble that time. It was agreed on all sides that such conduct was outrageous; that Messrs. Russell and Co. amply deserved to have their contract taken from them, and—on these occasions your citizen looks portentous, and deals darkly in threatenings, as if his single vote could shake the spheres—we came to a mutual understanding that *that* firm should never enjoy our countenance or support. We were unanimous; all, even the mortal quarrel, was "made up" in the presence of the general foe, the Mail Company. Briefly we retired to rest, a miserable Public, and, soothed by the rough lullaby of the coyote, whose shrieks and screams perfectly reproduced the Indian jackal, we passed into the world of dreams.

To Platte Bridge. August 16th.

At 8 30 A.M. we were once more under way along the valley of Father Platte, whose physiognomy had now notably changed for the better. Instead of the dull, dark, silent stream of the lower course, whose muddy monotonous aspect made it a grievance to behold, we descried with astonishment a bright little river, hardly a hundred yards wide—one's ideas of potamology are enlarged with a witness by American travel! a mirrory surface, and .waters clear and limpid as the ether above them. The limestones and marls which destroy the beauty of the Lower Platte do not extend to the upper course. The climate now became truly delicious. The height above sea-level—5000 feet—subjects the land to the wholesome action of gentle winds, which, about 10—11 A.M., when the earth has had time to air, set in regularly as the sea-breezes of tropical climes, and temper the keen shine of day. These higher grounds, where the soil is barren rather for want of water than from the character of its constituents, are undoubtedly the healthiest part of the plains: no noxious malaria is evolved from the sparse growth of tree and shrub upon the banks of the river; and beyond them the plague of brûlés (sand-flies) and musquetoes is unknown; the narrowness of the bed also prevents the shrinking of the stream in autumn, at which season the Lower Platte exposes two broad margins of black infected mire. The three great elements of unhealthiness, heavy and clammy dews, moisture exhaled from the earth's surface, and the overcrowding of population—which appears to generate as many artificial diseases as artificial wants—are here unknown: the soil is never turned up, and even if it were, it probably would not have the deleterious effect which climatologists have remarked in the damp hot regions near the equator. The formation of the land begins to change from the tertiary and cretaceous to the primary—granites and porphyries—warning us that we are approaching the Rocky Mountains.

On the road we saw for the first time a train of Mormon wagons, twenty-four in number, slowly wending their way toward the Promised Land. The "Captain"—those who fill the dignified office of guides are so designated, and once a captain always a captain is the Far Western rule—was young Brigham Young, a nephew of the Prophet; a *blondin*, with yellow hair and beard, an intelligent countenance, a six-shooter by his right, and a bowie-knife by his left side. It was impossible to mistake, even through the veil of freckles and sun-burn with which a two months' journey had invested them, the nationality of the emigrants; "British-English" was written in capital letters upon the white eyelashes and tow-colored curls of the children, and upon the sandy brown hair and staring eyes, heavy bodies, and ample extremities of the adults. One young person concealed her facial attractions under a manner of mask. I thought that perhaps she might be a sultana, reserved for the establishment of some very magnificent Mormon bashaw; but the driver, when appealed to, responded with contempt, "'Guess old Briggy wont stampede many o' that 'ere lot!" Though thus homely in appearance, few showed any symptoms of sickness or starvation; in fact, their condition first impressed us most favorably with the excellence of the Perpetual Emigration Funds' traveling arrangements.

The Mormons who can afford such luxury generally purchase for the transit of the plains an emigrant's wagon, which in the West seldom costs more than $185. They take a full week be-

fore well *en route*, and endeavor to leave the Mississippi in early
May, when "long forage" is plentiful upon the prairies. Those
prospecting parties who are bound for California set out in March
or April, feeding their animals with grain till the new grass appears; after November the road over the Sierra Nevada being
almost impassable to way-worn oxen. The ground in the low
parts of the Mississippi Valley becomes heavy and muddy after
the first spring rains, and by starting in good time the worst parts
of the country will be passed before the travel becomes very laborious. Moreover, grass soon disappears from the higher and less
productive tracts; between Scott's Bluffs and Great Salt Lake
City we were seldom out of sight of starved cattle, and on one
spot I counted fifteen skeletons. Travelers, however, should not
push forward early, unless their animals are in good condition
and are well supplied with grain; the last year's grass is not quite
useless, but cattle can not thrive upon it as they will upon the
grammas, festucas, and buffalo clover (*Trifolium reflexum*) of Utah
and New Mexico. The journey between St. Jo and the Mormon
capital usually occupies from two to three months. The Latter-
Day Saints march with a quasi-military organization. Other emigrants form companies of fifty to seventy armed men—a single
wagon would be in imminent danger from rascals like the Pawnees, who, though fonder of bullying than of fighting, are ever
ready to cut off a straggler—elect their "Cap.," who holds the
office only during good conduct; sign and seal themselves to certain obligations, and bind themselves to stated penalties in case
of disobedience or defection. The "Prairie Traveler" strongly
recommends this systematic organization, without which, indeed,
no expedition, whether emigrant, commercial, or exploratory,
ought ever or in any part of the world to begin its labors; justly
observing that, without it, discords and dissensions sooner or later
arise which invariably result in breaking up the company.

In this train I looked to no purpose for the hand-carts with
which the poorer Saints add to the toils of earthly travel a semi-
devotional work of supererogation expected to win a proportionate
reward in heaven.*

After ten miles of the usual number of creeks, "Deep," "Small,"
"Snow," "Muddy," etc., and heavy descents, we reached at 10
A.M. Deer Creek, a stream about thirty feet wide, said to abound
in fish. The station boasts of an Indian agent, Major Twiss, a

---

* The following estimate of outfit was given to me by a Mormon elder, who has
frequently traveled over the Utah route. He was accompanied by his wife, and
family, and help—six persons in total; and having money to spare, he invested it in
a speculation which could hardly fail at least to quadruple his outlay at the end of
the march: the stove, for instance, bought at $28, would sell for $80 to $120. The
experienced emigrant, it may be observed, carries with him a little of every thing
that may or might be wanted, such as provisions, clothing, furniture, drugs, lint, stationery, spices, ammunition, and so forth; above all things, he looks to his weapons
as likely to be, at a pinch, his best friends:

post-office, a store, and of course a grog-shop. M. Bissonette, the owner of the two latter and an old Indian trader, was the usual Creole, speaking a French not unlike that of the Channel Islands, and wide awake to the advantages derivable from travelers: the large straggling establishment seemed to produce in abundance large squaws and little half-breeds. Fortunately stimulants are not much required on the plains: I wish my enemy no more terrible fate than to drink excessively with M. Bissonette of M. Bissonette's liquor. The good Creole, when asked to join us, naïvely refused: he reminded me of certain wine-merchants in more civilized lands, who, when dining with their pratique, sensibly prefer small-beer to their own concoctions.

A delay of fifteen minutes, and then we were hurried forward. The ravines deepened; we were about entering the region of kanyons.* Already we began to descry bunch-grass clothing the hills. This invaluable and anomalous provision of nature is first found, I believe, about fifty miles westward of the meridian of Fort Laramie, and it extends to the eastern slope of the Sierra Nevada. On the Pacific water-shed it gives way to the wild oats (*Avena fatua*), which are supposed to have been introduced into California by the Spaniards. The festuca is a real boon to the land, which, without it, could hardly be traversed by cattle. It grows by clumps, as its name denotes, upon the most unlikely ground, the thirsty sand, and the stony hills; in fact, it thrives best upon the poorest soil. In autumn, about September, when all other grasses turn to hay, and their nutriment is washed out by the autumnal rains, the bunch-grass, after shedding its seed, begins to put forth a green shoot within the apparently withered sheath. It remains juicy and nutritious, like winter wheat in April, under the snows, and, contrary to the rule of the *gramineæ*,

2 yokes oxen...........at $180 to $200 00		100 lbs. ham and bacon	$14 00
1 cow (milch)........................	25 00	150 lbs. crackers (sea biscuits)....	13 13
1 wagon	87 30	100 lbs. sugar........................	9 50
1 double cover........................	8 50	25 lbs. crystallized ditto...........	3 00
2 ox yokes	8 00	24 lbs. raisins........................	4 00
1 ox chain..............................	1 50	20 lbs. currants......................	3 00
1 tar-bucket	1 00	25 lbs. rice	2 25
1 large tent ($9 for smaller sizes)	15 00	1 bushel dried apples...............	6 00
Camp equipment, axes, spades, } shovels, triangles for fires, etc. }	10 00	1 " " peaches............. 1 " " beans........................	4 30 2 00
600 lbs. flour	25 50	1 stove	28 00
		Grand total...............$490 98	

* The Spanish cañon—Americanized to kanyon—signifies, primarily, a cannon or gun-barrel; secondarily, a tube, shaft of a mine, or a ravine of peculiar form, common in this part of America. The word is loosely applied by the Western men, but properly it means those gorges through a line of mountains whose walls are high and steep, even to a tunnel-like overhanging, while their soles, which afford passages to streams, are almost flat. In Northern Mexico the kanyon becomes of stupendous dimensions; it is sometimes a crack in the plains 2000 feet deep, exposing all the layers that clothe earth's core, with a stream at the bottom, in sight, but impossible for the traveler dying of thirst to drink at.

it pays the debt of nature, drying and dying about May; yet, even when in its corpse-like state, a light yellow straw, it contains abundant and highly-flavored nutriment; it lasts through the summer, retiring up the mountains, again becomes grass in January, thus feeding cattle all the year round. The small dark pyriform seed, about half the size of an oat, is greedily devoured by stock, and has been found to give an excellent flavor to beef and mutton. It is curious how little food will fatten animals upon the elevated portions of the prairies and in the valleys of the Rocky Mountains. I remarked the same thing in Somaliland, where, while far as the eye could see the country wore the semblance of one vast limestone ledge, white with desolation, the sheep and bullocks were round and plump as stall-fed animals. The idea forces itself upon one's mind that the exceeding purity and limpidity of the air, by perfecting the processes of digestion and assimilation, must stand in lieu of quantity. I brought back with me a small packet of the bunch-grass seed, in the hope that it may be acclimatized: the sandy lands about Aldershott, for instance, would be admirably fitted for the growth.

We arrived at a station, called the " Little Muddy Creek," after a hot drive of twenty miles. It was a wretched place, built of " dry stones," viz., slabs without mortar, and the interior was garnished with certain efforts of pictorial art, which were rather *lestes* than otherwise. The furniture was composed of a box and a trunk, and the negative catalogue of its supplies was extensive —whisky forming the only positive item.

We were not sorry to résume our journey at 1 15 P.M. After eight miles we crossed the vile bridge which spans "Snow Creek," a deep water, and hardly six feet wide. According to the station-men, water here was once perennial, though now reduced to an occasional freshet after rain: this phenomenon, they say, is common in the country, and they attribute it to the sinking of the stream in the upper parts of the bed, which have become porous, or have given way. It is certain that in the Sinaitic regions many springs, which within a comparatively few years supplied whole families of Bedouins, have unaccountably dried up; perhaps the same thing happens in the Rocky Mountains.

After about two hours of hot sun, we debouched upon the bank of the Platte at a spot where once was the Lower Ferry.* The river bed is here so full of holes and quicksands, and the stream is so cold and swift, that many have been drowned when bathing, more when attempting to save time by fording it. A wooden bridge was built at this point some years ago, at an expense of $26,000, by one Regshaw, who, if report does not belie him, has gained and lost more fortunes than a Wall Street professional

---

* The first ferry, according to the old guide-books, was at Deer Creek; the second was at this place, thirty-one miles above the former; and the third was four miles still farther on.

"lame duck." We halted for a few minutes at the indispensable store—the *tête de pont*—and drank our whisky with ice, which, after so long a disuse, felt unenjoyably cold. Remounting, we passed a deserted camp, where in times gone by two companies of infantry had been stationed: a few stumps of crumbling wall, broken floorings, and depressions in the ground, were the only remnants which the winds and rains had left. The banks of the Platte were stained with coal: it has been known to exist for some years, but has only lately been worked. Should the supply prove sufficient for the wants of the settlers, it will do more toward the civilization of these regions than the discovery of gold.

The lignite tertiary of Nebraska extends north and west to the British line; the beds are found throughout this formation sometimes six and seven feet thick, and the article would make good fuel. The true coal-measures have been discovered in the southeastern portion of the Nebraska prairies, and several small seams at different points of the Platte Valley. Dr. F. V. Hayden, who accompanied Lieutenant Warren as geologist, appears to think that the limestones which contain the supplies, though belonging to the true coal-measures, hold a position above the workable beds of coal, and deems it improbable that mines of any importance will be found north of the southern line of Nebraska. But, as his examination of the ground was somewhat hurried, there is room to hope that this unfavorable verdict will be canceled. The coal as yet discovered is all, I believe, bituminous. That dug out of the Platte bank runs in a vein about six feet thick, and is as hard as cannel coal: the texture of the rock is a white limestone. The banks of the Deer and other neighboring creeks are said also to contain the requisites for fuel.

Our station lay near the upper crossing or second bridge, a short distance from the town. It was also built of timber at an expense of $40,000, about a year ago, by Louis Guenot, a Quebecquois, who has passed the last twelve years upon the plains. He appeared very downcast about his temporal prospects, and handed us over, with the *insouciance* of his race, to the tender mercies of his venerable squaw. The usual toll is 50 cents, but from trains, especially of Mormons, the owner will claim $5; in fact, as much as he can get without driving them to the opposition lower bridge, or to. the ferry-boat. It was impossible to touch the squaw's supper; the tin cans that contained the coffee were slippery with grease, and the bacon looked as if it had been dressed side by side with "boyaux." I lighted my pipe, and, air-cane in hand, sallied forth to look at the country.

The heights behind the station were our old friends the Black Hills, which, according to the Canadian, extend with few breaks as far as Denver City. They are covered with dark green pine; at a distance it looks black, and the woods shelter a variety of wild beasts, the grizzly bear among the number. In the more grassy spaces mustangs, sure-footed as mountain goats, roam uncaught; and at the foot of the hills the slopes are well stocked with antelope, deer, and hares, here called rabbits. The principal birds are the sage-hen (*Tetrao urophasianus*) and the prairie-hen (*T. pratensis*). The former, also called the cock of the plains, is a fine, strong-flying grouse, about the size of a full-grown barn-door fowl, or, when younger, of a European pheasant, which, indeed, the form of the tail, as the name denotes, greatly resembles, and the neck is smooth like the partridge of the Old World.* Birds of the year are considered good eating: after their first winter the flesh is so impregnated with the intolerable odor of wild sage that none but a starving man can touch it. The prairie-hen, also called the "heath-hen" and the "pinnated grouse," affects the plains of Illinois and Missouri, and is rarely found so far west as the Black Hills: it is not a migratory bird. The pinnæ from which it derives its name are little wing-like tufts on both sides of the neck, small in the female, large in the male. The cock, moreover, has a stripe of skin running down the neck, which changes its natural color toward pairing-time, and becomes of a reddish yellow: it swells like a turkey-cock's wattles, till the head seems buried between two monstrous protuberances, the owner spreading out its tail, sweeping the ground with its wings, and booming somewhat like a bittern. Both of these birds, which are strong on the wing, and give good sport, might probably be naturalized in Europe, and the "Société d'Acclimatisation" would do well to think of it.

Returning to the station, I found that a war-party of Arapahoes had just alighted in a thin copse hard by. They looked less like warriors than like a band of horse-stealers; and, though they had set out with the determination of bringing back some Yuta scalps and fingers,† they had not succeeded. On these occasions the young braves are generally very sulky—a fact which they take care to show by short speech and rude gestures, throwing about and roughly handling, like spoiled children, whatever comes in their way. At such times one must always be prepared for a word and a blow; and, indeed, most Indian fighters justify themselves in taking the initiative, as, of course, it is a great thing to secure first chance. However we may yearn toward our "poor black brother," it is hard not to sympathize with the white in

---

* The trivial names for organic nature are as confused and confusing in America as in India, in consequence of the Old Country terms applièd, *per fas et nefas*, to New Country growths: for instance, the spruce grouse is the Canadian partridge; the ruffled grouse is the partridge of New England and New York, and the pheasant of New Jersey and the Southern States; while in the latter the common quail (*O. Virginiana*) is called "partridge."

† The enemy's fore or other finger, crooked and tied with two bits of the skin which are attached to the wrist or the forehead, is a favorite and picturesque ornament. That failing, the bear's (especially the grizzly's) talons, bored at the base, and strung upon their sinews, are considered highly honorable.

many aggressions against the ferocious and capricious so-called Red Man. The war-party consisted of about a dozen warriors, with a few limber, lither-looking lads. They had sundry lean, sore-backed nags, which were presently turned out to graze. Dirty rags formed the dress of the band; their arms were the usual light lances, garnished with leather at the handles, with two cropped tufts and a long loose feather dangling from them. They had bows shaped like the Grecian Cupid's, strengthened with sinews and tipped with wire, and arrows of light wood, with three feathers—Captain Marcy says, two intersecting at right angles; but I have never seen this arrangement—and small triangular iron piles. Their shields were plain targes—double folds of raw buffalo hide, apparently unstuffed, and quite unadorned. They carried mangy buffalo robes; and scattered upon the ground was a variety of belts, baldricks, and pouches, with split porcupine quills dyed a saffron yellow.

The Arapahoes, generally pronounced 'Rapahoes — called by their Shoshonee neighbors Sháretikeh, or Dog-eaters, and by the French Gros Ventres—are a tribe of thieves living between the South Fork of the Platte and the Arkansas Rivers. They are bounded north by the Sioux, and hunt in the same grounds with the Cheyennes. This breed is considered fierce, treacherous, and unfriendly to the whites, who have debauched and diseased them, while the Cheyennes are comparatively chaste and uninfected. The Arapaho is distinguished from the Dakotah by the superior gauntness of his person, and the boldness of his look; there are also minor points of difference in the moccasins, arrow-marks, and weapons. His language, like that of the Cheyennes, has never, I am told, been thoroughly learned by a stranger: it is said to contain but a few hundred words, and these, being almost all explosive growls or guttural grunts, are with difficulty acquired by the civilized ear. Like the Cheyennes, the Arapahoes have been somewhat tamed of late by the transit of the United States army in 1857.

Among the Prairie Indians, when a war-chief has matured the plans for an expedition, he habits himself in the garb of battle. Then, mounting his steed, and carrying a lance adorned with a flag and eagle's feathers, he rides about the camp chanting his war-song. Those disposed to volunteer join the parade, also on horseback, and, after sufficiently exhibiting themselves to the admiration of the village, return home. This ceremony continues till the requisite number is collected. The war-dance, and the rites of the medicine-man, together with perhaps private penances and propitiations, are the next step. There are also copious powwows, in which, as in the African parlance, the chiefs, elders, and warriors sit for hours in grim debate, solemn as if the fate of empires hung upon their words, to decide the momentous question whether Jack shall have half a pound more meat than Jim. Neither the chief nor the warriors are finally committed by the procession to the expedition; they are all volunteers, at liberty to retire; and jealousy, disappointment, and superstition often interpose between themselves and glory.

The war-party, when gone, is thoroughly gone; once absent, they love to work in mystery, and look forward mainly to the pleasure of surprising their friends. After an absence which may extend for months, a loud, piercing, peculiar cry suddenly announces the vanguard courier of the returning braves. The camp is thrown at once from the depths of apathy to the height of excitement, which is also the acmé of enjoyment for those whose lives must be spent in forced inaction. The warriors enter with their faces painted black, and their steeds decorated in the most fantastic style; the women scream and howl their exultation, and feasting and merriment follow with the ceremonious scalp-dance. The braves are received with various degrees of honor according to their deeds. The highest merit is to ride single-handed into the enemy's camp, and to smite a lodge with lance or bow. The second is to take a warrior prisoner. The third is to strike a dead or fallen man—an idea somewhat contrary to the Englishman's fancies of fair play, but intelligible enough where it is the custom, as in Hindostan, to lie upon the ground "playing 'possum," and waiting the opportunity to hamstring or otherwise disable the opponent. The least of great achievements is to slay an enemy in hand-to-hand fight. A Pyrrhic victory, won even at an inconsiderable loss, is treated as a defeat; the object of the Indian guerrilla chief is to destroy the foe with as little risk to himself and his men as possible; this is his highest boast, and in this are all his hopes of fame. Should any of the party fall in battle, the relatives mourn by cutting off their hair and the manes and tails of their horses, and the lugubrious lamentations of the women introduce an ugly element into the triumphal procession.

In the evening, as Mrs. Dana, her husband, and I were sitting outside the station, two of the warriors came and placed themselves without ceremony upon the nearest stones. They were exceedingly unprepossessing with their small gipsy eyes, high, rugged cheek-bones, broad flat faces, coarse sensual mouths everted as to the lips, and long heavy chins; they had removed every sign of manhood from their faces, and their complexions were a dull oily red, the result of vermilion, ochre, or some such pigment, of which they are as fond as Hindoos, grimed in for years. They watched every gesture, and at times communicated their opinions to each other in undistinguishable gruntings, with curious attempts at cachinnation. It is said that the wild dog is unable to bark, and that the tame variety has acquired the faculty by attempting to imitate the human voice; it is certain that, as a rule, only the civilized man can laugh loudly and heartily. I happened to mention to my fellow-travelers the universal dislike of savages to any thing like a sketch of their physiognomies; they expressed a doubt that the Indians were subject to the rule. Pencil and paper were at hand, so we proceeded to proof. The savage at first seemed uneasy under the operation, as the Asiatic or African will do, averting his face at times, and shifting position to defeat my purpose. When I passed the caricature round it excited some merriment; the subject, forthwith rising from his seat, made a sign that he also wished to see it. At the sight, however, he screwed up his features with an expression of intense disgust, and managing to "smudge" over the sketch with his dirty thumb, he left us with a " pooh!" that told all his outraged feelings.

Presently the warriors entered the station to smoke and tacitly beg for broken victuals. They squatted in a circle, and passed round the red sandstone calumet with great gravity, puffing like steam-tugs, inhaling slowly and lingeringly, swallowing the fumes, and with upturned faces exhaling them through the nostrils. They made no objection to being joined by us, and always before handing the pipe to a neighbor, they wiped the reed mouth-piece with the cushion of the thumb. The contents of their calumet were kinnikinik, and, though they accepted tobacco, they preferred replenishing with their own mixture. They received a small present of provisions, and when the station-people went to supper they were shut out.

We are now slipping into Mormonland; one of the station-keepers belonged to the new religion. The "madam," on entering the room, had requested him to depose a cigar which tainted the air with a perfume like that of greens'-water; he took the matter so coolly that I determined he was not an American, and, true enough, he proved to be a cabinet-maker from Birmingham. I spent the evening reading poor Albert Smith's "Story of Mont Blanc"—Mont Blanc in sight of the Rocky Mountains!—and admiring how the prince of entertainers led up the reader to what he called the crowning glory of his life, the unperilous ascent of that monarch of the Alps, much in the spirit with which one would have addressed the free and independent voters of some well-bribed English borough.

We are now about to quit the region which Nature has prepared, by ready-made roads and embankments, for a railway; all beyond this point difficulties are so heaped upon difficulties—as the sequel will prove—that we must hope against hope to see the "iron horse" (I believe he is so called) holding his way over the mountains.

17th August.   To the Valley of the Sweetwater.

The morning was bright and clear, cool and pleasant. The last night's abstinence had told upon our squeamishness: we managed to secure a fowl, and with its aid we overcame our repugnance to the massive slices of eggless bacon. At 6 30 A.M. we hitched up, crossed the rickety bridge at a slow pace, and pro-

K

ceeded for the first time to ascend the left bank of the Platte. The valley was grassy; the eternal sage, however, haunted us; the grouse ran before us, and the prairie-dogs squatted upon their house-tops, enjoying the genial morning rays. After ten miles of severe ups and downs, which, by-the-by, nearly brought our consort, the official's wagon, to grief, we halted for a few minutes at an old-established trading-post called "Red Buttes."* The feature from which it derives its name lies on the right bank of, and about five miles distant from the river, which here cuts its way through a ridge. These bluffs are a fine bold formation, escarpments of ruddy argillaceous sandstones and shells, which dip toward the west: they are the eastern wall of the mass that hems in the stream, and rear high above it their conical heads and fantastic figures. The ranch was on the margin of a cold, clear spring, of which we vainly attempted to drink. The banks were white, as though by hoar-frost, with nitrate and carbonate of soda efflorescing from the dark mould. Near Red Buttes the water is said to have a chalybeate flavor, but of that we were unable to judge.

Having allowed the squaws and half-breeds a few minutes to gaze, we resumed our way, taking off our caps in token of adieu to old Father Platte, our companion for many a weary mile. We had traced his course upward, through its various phases and vicissitudes, from the dignity and portliness of his later career as a full-grown river to his small and humble youth as a mountain rivulet, and—interest, either in man or stream, often results from the trouble we take about them—I looked upon him for the last time with a feeling akin to regret. Moreover, we had been warned that from the crossing of the North Platte to the Sweetwater all is a dry, and dreary, and desolate waste.

On the way we met a mounted Indian, armed with a rifle, and habited in the most grotesque costume. "Jack"—he was recognized by the driver—wore a suit of buckskin, and a fool's cap made out of an old blanket, with a pair of ass-ear appendages that hung backward viciously like a mule's; his mouth grinned from ear to ear, and his eyes were protected by glass and wire goggles, which gave them the appearance of being mounted on stalks like a crustacean's. He followed us for some distance, honoring us by riding close to the carriage, in hopes of a little black-mail; but we were not generous, and we afterward heard something which made us glad that we had not been tempted to liberality. He was fol-

---

* The French word is extensively used in the Rocky Mountains and Oregon, "where," says Colonel Frémont ("Expedition to the Rocky Mountains," p. 145), "it is naturalized, and which, if desirable to render into English, there is no word which would be its precise equivalent. It is applied to the detached hills and ridges which rise abruptly and reach too high to be called hills or ridges, and are not high enough" —he might have added, are not massive enough—"to be called mountains. *Knob*, as applied in the Western States, is their most descriptive term in English; but no translation or periphrasis would preserve the identity of these picturesque landmarks."

lowed by an ill-favored squaw, dressed in a kind of cotton gown, remarkable only for the shoulders being considerably narrower than the waist. She sat her bare nag cavalierly, and eyed us as we passed with that peculiarly unpleasant glance which plain women are so fond of bestowing.

After eighteen miles' drive we descended a steep hill, and were shown the Devil's Backbone. It is a jagged, broken ridge of huge sandstone boulders, tilted up edgeways, and running in a line over the crest of a long roll of land: the *tout ensemble* looks like the vertebræ of some great sea-serpent or other long crawling animal; and, on a nearer view, the several pieces resolve themselves into sphinxes, veiled nuns, Lot's pillars, and other freakish objects. I may here remark that the *aut Cæsar aut diabolus* of the medieval European antiquary, when accounting for the architecture of strange places, is in the Far West consigned without partnership to the genius loci, the fiend who, here as in Europe, has monopolized all the finest features of scenery. We shall pass successively the Devil's Gate, the Devil's Post-office, and the Devil's Hole—in fact, we shall not be thoroughly rid of his satanic majesty's appurtenances till Monte Diablo, the highest of the Californian coast-range, dips slowly and unwillingly behind the Pacific's tepid wave.

We nooned at Willow Springs, a little doggery boasting of a shed and a bunk, but no corral; and we soothed, with a drink of our whisky, the excited feelings of the rancheros. The poor fellows had been plundered of their bread and dried meat by some petty thief, who had burrowed under the wall, and they sorely suspected our goggled friend, Jack the Arapaho. Master Jack's hair might have found itself suspended near the fireplace if he had then been within rifle-shot; as it was, the two victims could only indulge in consolatory threats about wreaking their vengeance upon the first "doggond red-bellied crittur" whom good fortune might send in their way. The water was unusually good at Willow Springs; unfortunately, however, there was nothing else.

At 2 30 P.M. we resumed our way through the yellow-flowered rabbit-bush — it not a little resembled wild mustard — and a thick sage-heath, which was here and there spangled with the bright blossoms of the wilderness. After about twenty miles we passed, to the west of the road, a curious feature, to which the Mormon exodists first, *on dit*, gave the name of Saleratus Lake.*

---

* According to Dr. L. D. Gale (Appendix F. to Captain Stansbury's "Expedition to the Great Salt Lake"), who tested specimens of this saleratus, "it is composed of the sesquicarbonate of soda, mixed with the sulphate of soda and chloride of soda, and is one of the native salts called *Trona*, found in the Northern Lakes, in Hungary, Africa, and other countries."

"Three grammes of this salt in dry powder, cleared of its earthy impurities, gave carbonic acid 0·9030 of a gramme, which would indicate 1·73239 grammes of the sesquicarbonate. The other salts were found to be the muriate and sulphate of soda: the proportions were not determined."

It lies to the west of the road, and is only one of a chain of alkaline waters and springs whose fetor, without exaggeration, taints the land. Cattle drinking of the fluid are nearly sure to die; even those that eat of the *herbe salée*, or salt grass growing upon its borders, and known by its reddish-yellow and sometimes bluish tinge, will suffer from a disease called the "Alkali," which not unfrequently kills them. The appearance of the Saleratus Lake startles the traveler who, in the full blaze of midday upon this arid waste, where mirage mocks him at every turn, suddenly sees outstretched before his eyes a kind of Wenham Lake solidly over-frozen. The illusion is so perfect that I was completely deceived, nor could the loud guffaws of the driver bring me at once to the conclusion that seeing in this case is not believing. On a near inspection, the icy surface turns out to be a dust of carbonate of soda, concealing beneath it masses of the same material, washed out of the adjacent soil, and solidified by evaporation. The Latter-Day Saints were charmed with their *trouvaille*, and laid in stores of the fetid alkaline matter, as though it had been manna, for their bread and pastry. It is still transported westward, and declared to be purer than the saleratus of the shops. Near the lake is a deserted ranch, which once enjoyed the title of "Sweetwater Station."

Four miles beyond this "Waterless Lake"—Bahr bila Ma as the Bedouin would call it—we arrived at Rock Independence, and felt ourselves in a new region, totally distinct from the clay formation of the mauvaises terres over which we have traveled for the last five days. Again I was startled by its surprising like-ness to the scenery of Eastern Africa: a sketch of Jiwe la Mkoa, the Round Rock in eastern Unyamwezi,* would be mistaken, even by those who had seen both, for this grand *échantillon* of the Rocky Mountains. It crops out of an open plain, not far from the river bed, in dome shape wholly isolated, about 1000 feet in length by 400—500 in breadth; it is 60 to 100 feet in height,† and in circumference 1½ to 2 miles. Except upon the summit, where it has been weathered into a feldspathic soil, it is bare and bald; a scanty growth of shrubs protrudes, however, from its poll. The material of the stern-looking dome is granite, in enormous slabs and boulders, cracked, flaked, seared, and cloven, as if by igneous pressure from below. The prevailing tradition in the West is, that the mass derived its name from the fact that Colonel Frémont there delivered an Independence-day oration; but read a little farther. It is easily ascended at the northern side and the southeastern corner, and many climb its rugged flanks for a pe-culiarly Anglo-American purpose—Smith and Brown have held

---

* I crave the reader's pardon for referring him to my own publications; but the only account of this Round Rock which has hitherto been published is to be found in the "Lake Regions of Central Africa," chap. viii.

† Colonel Frémont gives its dimensions as 650 yards long and 40 feet high.

high jinks here. In Colonel Fremont's time (1842), every where within six or eight feet of the ground, where the surface is sufficiently smooth, and in some places sixty or eighty feet above, the rock was inscribed with the names of travelers. Hence the Indians have named it Timpe Nabor, or the Painted Rock, corresponding with the Sinaitic "Wady Mukattab." In the present day, though much of the writing has been washed away by rain, 40,000—50,000 souls are calculated to have left their dates and marks from the coping of the wall to the loose stones below this huge sign-post. There is, however, some reason in the proceeding; it does not in these lands begin and end with the silly purpose, as among climbers of the Pyramids, and *fouilleurs* of the sarcophagi of Apis, to bequeath one's few poor letters to a little athanasia. Prairie travelers and emigrants expect to be followed by their friends, and leave, in their vermilion outfit, or their white house-paint, or their brownish-black tar—a useful article for wagons—a homely but hearty word of love or direction upon any conspicuous object. Even a bull or a buffalo's skull, which, lying upon the road, will attract attention, is made to do duty at this *Poste Restante.*

I will here take the liberty of digressing a little, with the charitable purpose of admiring the serious turn with which the United States explorers perform their explorations.

Colonel Frémont* thus calls to mind the earnest deeds of a bygone day. "One George Weymouth was sent out to Maine by the Earl of Southampton, Lord Arundel, and others, and in the narrative of their discoveries he says, ' The next day we ascended in our pinnace that part of the river which lies more to the westward, carrying with us a cross—a thing never omitted by any Christian traveler—which we erected at the ultimate end of our route.' This was in the year 1605, and in 1842 I obeyed the feeling of early travelers, and left the impressions of the cross deeply engraved on the vast rock, one thousand miles beyond the Mississippi, to which discoverers have given the national name of Rock Independence."

Captain Stansbury† is not less scrupulous upon the subject of traveling proprieties. One of his entries is couched as follows: "Sunday, June 10, barometer 28·82, thermometer 70°. The camp rested: it had been determined, from the commencement of the expedition, to devote this day, whenever practicable, to its legitimate purpose, as an interval of rest for man and beast. I here beg to record, as the result of my experience, derived not only from the present journey, but from the observations of many years spent in the performance of similar duties, that, as a mere matter of pecuniary consideration, apart from all higher obligations, it is wise to keep the Sabbath."

---

* Report of the Exploring Expedition to the Rocky Mountains, p. 72.
† Stansbury's Expedition, ch. i., p. 22.

Lieutenant W. F. Lynch, United States Navy, who in 1857 commanded the United States Expedition to the River Jordan and the Dead Sea,* and published a narrative not deficient in interest, thus describes his proceedings at El Meshra, the bathing-place of the Christian pilgrims:

"This ground is consecrated by tradition as the place where the Israelites passed over with the ark of the covenant, and where the blessed Savior was baptized by John. Feeling that it would be desecration to moor the boats at a place so sacred, we passed it, and with some difficulty found a landing below.

"My first act was to bathe in the consecrated stream, thanking God, first, for the precious favor of being permitted to visit such a spot; and, secondly, for his protecting care throughout our perilous passage. For a long time after I sat upon the bank, my mind oppressed with awe, as I mused upon the great and wondrous events which had here occurred." In strange contrast with these passages stands the characteristic prophecy, "The time is coming —the beginning is come now—when the whole worthless list of kings, with all their myrmidons, will be swept from their places, and made to bear a part in the toils and sufferings of the great human family," etc., etc.

I would not willingly make light in others of certain finer sentiments—veneration, for instance, and conscientiousness—which Nature has perhaps debarred me from overenjoying; nor is it in my mind to console myself for the privation by debasing the gift in those gifted with it. But—the but, I fear, will, unlike "if," be any thing rather than a great peacemaker in this case—there are feelings which, when strongly felt, when they well from the bottom of the heart, man conceals in the privacy of his own bosom; and which, if published to the world, are apt to remind the world that it has heard of a form of speech, as well as of argument, ranking under the category of *ad captandum vulgus*.

About a mile beyond Independence Rock we forded the Sweetwater. We had crossed the divide between this stream and the Platte, and were now to ascend our fourth river valley, the three others being the Missouri, the Big Blue, and the Nebraska. The Canadian voyageurs have translated the name Sweetwater from the Indian Pina Pa; but the term is here more applicable in a metaphorical than in a literal point of view. The water of the lower bed is rather hard than otherwise, and some travelers have detected brackishness in it, yet the banks are free from the saline hoar, which deters the thirstiest from touching many streams on this line. The Sweetwater, in its calmer course, is a perfect Naiad of the mountains; presently it will be an Undine hurried by that terrible Anagké, to which Jove himself must bend his omniscient head, into the grisly marital embrace of the gloomy old Platte.

* Chap. iii. Authorized Edition. Sampson Low, Son, and Co., 47 Ludgate Hill, 1859.

Passing pleasant, after the surly ungenial silence of the Shallow River, is the merry prattle with which she answers the whisperings of those fickle flatterers, the winds, before that wedding-day when silence shall become her doom.   There is a something in the Sweetwater which appeals to the feelings of rugged men: even the drivers and the station-keepers speak of " her" with a bearish affection.

After fording the swift Pina Pa, at that point about seventy feet wide and deep to the axles, we ran along its valley about six miles, and reached at 9 15 P.M. the muddy station kept by M. Planté, the usual Canadian.   En route we had passed by the Devil's Gate, one of the great curiosities of this line of travel.   It is the beau ideal of a kanyon, our portal opening upon the threshold of the Rocky Mountains: I can compare its form from afar only with the Brêche de Roland in the Pyrenees.   The main pass of Aden magnified twenty fold is something of the same kind, but the simile is too unsavory.   The height of the gorge is from 300 to 400 feet perpendicular, and on the south side threatening to fall: it has already done so in parts, as the masses which cumber the stream-bed show.   The breadth varies from a minimum of 40 to a maximum of 105 feet, where the fissure yawns out, and the total length of the cleft is about 250 yards.   The material of the walls is a gray granite, traversed by dikes of trap; and the rock in which the deep narrow crevasse has been made runs right through the extreme southern shoulder of a ridge, which bears appropriately enough the name of "Rattlesnake Hills."   Through this wild gorge the bright stream frets and forces her way, singing, unlike Liris, with a feminine untaciturnity, that awakes the echoes of the pent-up channel—tumbling and gurgling, dashing and foaming over the snags, blocks, and boulders, which, fallen from the cliffs above, obstruct the way, and bedewing the cedars and bright shrubs which fringe the ragged staples of the gate. Why she should not have promenaded gently and quietly round, instead of through, this grisly barrier of rock, goodness only knows: however, willful and womanlike, she has set her heart upon an apparent impossibility, and, as usual with her sex under the circumstances, she has had her way.   Sermons in stones—I would humbly suggest to my gender.

Procrastination once more stole my chance; I had reserved myself for sketching the Devil's Gate from the southwest, but the station proved too distant to convey a just idea of it.   For the truest representation of the gate, the curious reader will refer to the artistic work of Mr. Frederick Piercy;* that published in Captain Marcy's "List of Itineraries" is like any thing but the Devil's Gate; even the rough lithograph in Colonel Frémont's report is more truthful.

We supped badly as mankind well could at the *cabaret*, where

* Route from Liverpool to Great Salt Lake City.

a very plain young person, and no neat-handed Phyllis withal, supplied us with a cock whose toughness claimed for it the honors of grandpaternity. Chickens and eggs there were none; butcher's meat, of course, was unknown, and our hosts ignored the name of tea; their salt was a kind of saleratus, and their sugar at least half Indian-meal. When asked about fish, they said that the Sweetwater contained nothing but suckers,* and that these, though good eating, can not be caught with a hook. They are a queer lot, these French Canadians, who have "located" themselves in the Far West. Travelers who have hunted with them speak highly of them as a patient, submissive, and obedient race, inured to privations, and gifted with the reckless *abandon*— no despicable quality in prairie traveling—of the old Gascon adventurer; armed and ever vigilant, hardy, handy, and hearty children of Nature, combining with the sagacity and the instinctive qualities all the superstitions of the Indians; enduring as mountain goats; satisfied with a diet of wild meat, happiest when it could be followed by a cup of strong milkless coffee, a "chasse café" and a "brule-gueule;" invariably and contagiously merry; generous as courageous; handsome, active, and athletic; sashed, knived, and dressed in buckskin, to the envy of every Indian "brave," and the admiration of every Indian belle, upon whom, if the adventurer's heart had not fallen into the snares of the more attractive half-breed, he would spend what remained of his $10 a month, after coffee, alcohol, and tobacco had been extravagantly paid for, in presents of the gaudiest trash. Such is the voyageur of books: I can only speak of him as I found him, a lazy dog, somewhat shy and proud, much addicted to loafing and to keeping cabarets, because, as the old phrase is, the cabarets keep him —in idleness too. Probably his good qualities lie below the surface: those who hide a farthing rush-light under a bushel can hardly expect us, in this railway age, to take the trouble of finding it. I will answer, however, for the fact, that the bad points are painfully prominent. By virtue of speaking French and knowing something of Canada, I obtained some buffalo robes, and after a look at the supper, which had all the effect of a copious feed, I found a kind of out-house, and smoked till sleep weighed down my eyelids.

Up the Sweetwater. 19th August.

We arose at 6 A.M., before the rest of the household, who, when aroused, "hifered" and sauntered about all *desœuvrés* till their wool-gathering wits had returned. The breakfast was a little picture of the supper; for watered milk, half-baked bread, and unrecognizable butter, we paid the somewhat "steep" sum of 75 cents; we privily had our grumble, and set out at 7 A.M. to as-

---

* A common fish of the genus Labio, of which there are many species—chub, mullet, barbel, horned dace, etc.: they are found in almost all the lakes and rivers of North America.

cend the Valley of the Sweetwater. The river-plain is bounded by two parallel lines of hills, or rather rocks, running nearly due east and west. Those to the north are about a hundred miles in extreme length, and, rising from a great plateau, lie perpendicular to the direction of the real Rocky Mountains toward which they lead : half the course of the Pina Pa subtends their southern base. The Western men know them as the Rattlesnake Hills, while the southern are called after the river. The former—a continuation of the ridge in which the Sweetwater has burst a gap—is one of those long lines of lumpy, misshapen, barren rock, that suggested to the Canadians for the whole region the name of Les Montagnes Rocheuses. In parts they are primary, principally syenite and granite, with a little gneiss, but they have often so regular a line of cleavage, perpendicular as well as horizontal, that they may readily be mistaken for stratifications. The stratified are slaty micaceous shale and red sandstone, dipping northward, and cut by quartz veins and trap dikes. The remarkable feature in both formations is the rounding of the ridges or blocks of smooth naked granite : hardly any angles appeared; the general effect was, that they had been water-washed immediately after birth. The upper portions of this range shelter the bighorn, or American moufflon, and the cougar,* the grizzly bear, and the wolf. The southern or Sweetwater range is vulgarly known as the Green-River Mountains : seen from the road, their naked, barren, and sandy flanks appear within cannon shot, but they are distant seven miles.

After a four-miles' drive up the pleasant valley of the little river-nymph, to whom the grisly hills formed an effective foil, we saw on the south of the road " Alkali Lake," another of the Trona formations with which we were about to become familiar; in the full glare of burning day it was undistinguishable as to the surface from the round pond in Hyde Park. Presently ascending a little rise, we were shown for the first time a real bit of the far-famed Rocky Mountains, which was hardly to be distinguished from, except by a shade of solidity, the fleecy sunlit clouds resting upon the horizon : it was Frémont's Peak, the sharp, snow-clad apex of the Wind River range. Behind us and afar rose the distant heads of black hills. The valley was charming with its bright glad green, a tapestry of flowery grass, willow copses where the grouse ran in and out, and long lines of aspen, beech, and cotton-wood, while pine and cedar, cypress and scattered evergreens, crept up the cranks and crannies of the rocks. In the midst of this Firdaus—so it appeared to us after the horrid unwithering artemisia Jehennum of last week—flowed the lovely

---

* Locally called the mountain lion. This animal (*F. unicolor*) is the largest and fiercest feline of the New World : it is a beast of many names—puma, cougar, American lion, panther or painter, etc. Its habit of springing upon its prey from trees makes it feared by hunters. It was once in the Kaatskills.

little stream, transparent as crystal, and coquettishly changing from side to side in her bed of golden sand. To see her tamely submit to being confined within those dwarf earthen cliffs, you would not have known her to be the same that had made that terrible breach in the rock-wall below. "Varium et mutabile semper," etc. : I will not conclude the quotation, but simply remark that the voyageurs have called her "She." And every where, in contrast with the deep verdure and the bright flowers of the valley, rose the stern forms of the frowning rocks, some apparently hanging as though threatening a fall, others balanced upon the slenderest foundations, all split and broken as though earthquake-riven, loosely piled into strange figures, the lion couchant, sugar-loaf, tortoise, and armadillo — not a mile, in fact, was without its totem.

The road was good, especially when hardened by frost. We are now in altitudes where, as in Tibet, parts of the country for long centuries never thaw. After passing a singular stone bluff on the left of the road, we met a party of discharged soldiers, who were traveling eastward comfortably enough in government wagons drawn by six mules. Not a man saluted Lieutenant Dana, though he was in uniform, and all looked surly as Indians after a scalpless raid. Speeding merrily along, we were shown on the right of the road a ranch belonging to a Canadian, a "mighty mean man," said the driver, "who onst gin me ole mare's meat for b'ar." We were much shocked by this instance of the awful depravity of the unregenerate human heart, but our melancholy musings were presently interrupted by the same youth, who pointed out on the other side of the path a mass of clay (conglomerate, I presume), called the Devil's Post-office. It has been lately washed with rains so copious that half the edifice lies at the base of that which is standing. The structure is not large : it is highly satisfactory—especially to a man who in this life has suffered severely, as the Anglo-Indian ever must from endless official and semi-official correspondence—to remark that the London Post-office is about double its size.

Beyond the Post-office was another ranch belonging to a Portuguese named Luis Silva, married to an Englishwoman who had deserted the Salt Lake Saints. We "staid a piece" there, but found few inducements to waste our time. Moreover, we had heard from afar of an "ole 'ooman," an Englishwoman, a Miss Moore—Miss is still used for Mrs. by Western men and negroes —celebrated for cleanliness, tidiness, civility, and housewifery in general, and we were anxious to get rid of the evil flavor of Canadians, squaws, and "ladies."

At 11 A.M. we reached "Three Crossings," when we found the "miss" a stout, active, middle-aged matron, deserving of all the praises that had so liberally been bestowed upon her. The little ranch was neatly swept and garnished, papered and ornamented.

The skull of a full-grown bighorn hanging over the doorway represented the spoils of a stag of twelve.   The table-cloth was clean, so was the cooking, so were the children; and I was reminded of Europe by the way in which she insisted upon washing my shirt, an operation which, after leaving the Missouri, *ça va sans dire*, had fallen to my own lot.   In fact, this day introduced me to the third novel sensation experienced on the western side of the Atlantic.   The first is to feel (practically) that all men are equal; that you are no man's superior, and that no man is yours.   The second—this is spoken as an African wanderer— to see one's quondam acquaintance, the Kaffir, laying by his grass kilt and coat of grease, invest himself in broadcloth, part his wool on one side, shave what pile nature has scattered upon his upper lip, chin, and cheeks below a line drawn from the ear to the mouth-corner after the fashion of the times when George the Third was king, and call himself, not Sambo, but Mr. Scott.   The third was my meeting in the Rocky Mountains with this refreshing specimen of that far Old World, where, on the whole, society still lies in strata, as originally deposited, distinct, sharply defined, and rarely displaced, except by some violent upheaval from below, which, however, never succeeds long in producing total inversion.   Miss Moore's husband, a decent appendage, had transferred his belief from the Church of England to the Church of Utah, and the good wife, as in duty bound, had followed in his wake whom she was bound to love, honor, and obey.   But when the serpent came and whispered in Miss Moore's modest, respectable, one-idea'd ear that the Abrahams of Great Salt Lake City are mere "sham Abrams"—that, not content with Sarahs, they add to them an unlimited supply of Hagars, then did our stout Englishwoman's power of endurance break down never to rise again. "Not an inch would she budge;" not a step toward Utah Territory would she take.   She fought pluckily against the impending misfortune, and—*à quelque chose malheur est bon!*—she succeeded in reducing her husband to that state which is typified by the wife using certain portions of the opposite sex's wardrobe, and in making him make a good livelihood as station-master on the wagon-line.

After a copious breakfast, which broke the fast of the four days that had dragged on since our civilized refection at Fort Laramie, we spread our buffalos and water-proofs under the ample eaves of the ranch, and spent the day in taking time with the sextant—every watch being wrong—in snoozing, dozing, chatting, smoking, and contemplating the novel view.   Straight before us rose the Rattlesnake Hills, a nude and grim horizon, frowning over the soft and placid scene below, while at their feet flowed the little river—*splendidior vitro*—purling over its pebbly bed with graceful meanderings through clover prairillons and garden-spots full of wild currants, strawberries, gooseberries, and rattlesnakes; while, contrasting with the green River Valley and the scorched and tawny rock-wall, patches of sand-hill, raised by the winds, here and there cumbered the ground. The variety of the scene was much enhanced by the changeful skies. The fine breeze which had set in at 8 A.M. had died in the attempt to thread these heat-refracting ridges, and vapory clouds, sublimated by the burning sun, floated lazily in the empyrean, casting fitful shadows that now intercepted, then admitted, a blinding glare upon the mazy stream and its rough cradle.

In the evening we bathed in the shallow bed of the Sweetwater. It is vain to caution travelers against this imprudence. *Video meliora proboque*—it is doubtless unwise—but it is also *mera stultitia* to say to men who have not enjoyed ablutions for a week or ten days, "If you do take that delicious dip you may possibly catch fever." *Deteriora sequor*—bathed. Miss Moore warned us strongly against the rattlesnakes, and during our walk we carefully observed the Indian rule, to tread upon the log and not to overstep it. The crotalus, I need hardly say, like other snakes, is fond of lurking under the shade of fallen or felled trunks, and when a heel or a leg is temptingly set before it, it is not the beast to refuse a bite. Accidents are very common, despite all precautions, upon this line, but they seldom, I believe, prove fatal. The remedies are almost endless: *e. g.*, hartshorn, used externally and drunk in dilution; scarification and irrumation of the part, preceded, of course, by a ligature between the limb and the heart; application of the incised breast of a live fowl or frog to the wound; the dried and powdered blood of turtle, of this two pinches to be swallowed and a little dropped upon the place bitten; a plaster of chewed or washed plantain-leaves—it is cooling enough, but can do little more—bound upon the puncture, peppered with a little finely-powdered tobacco; pulverized indigo made into a poultice with water; cauterization by gunpowder, hot iron, or lunar caustic; cedron, a nut growing on the Isthmus of Panama —of this remedy I heard, *in loco*, the most wonderful accounts, dying men being restored, as if by magic, after a bit about the size of a bean had been placed in their mouths. As will be seen below, the land is rich in snakeroots, but the superstitious snakestone of Hindostan—which acts, if it does act, as an absorbent of the virus by capillary attraction—is apparently unknown. The favorite remedy now in the United States is the "whisky cure," which, under the form of arrack, combined in the case of a scorpion-sting with a poultice of chewed tobacco, was known for the last fifty years to the British soldier in India. It has the advantage of being a palatable medicine; it must also be taken in large quantities, a couple of bottles sometimes producing little effect. With the lighted end of a cigar applied as moxa to the wound, a *quantum sufficit* of ardent spirits, a couple of men to make me walk about when drowsy by the application of a stick, and, above all, with the serious resolution not to do any thing so mean as to "leap the twig," I should not be afraid of any snake yet created. The only proviso is that our old enemy must not touch an artery, and that the remedies must be at hand. Fifteen minutes lost, you are "down among the dead men." The history of fatal cases always shows some delay.*

We supped in the evening merrily. It was the best coffee we had tasted since leaving New Orleans; the cream was excellent, so was the cheese. But an antelope had unfortunately been brought in; we had insisted upon a fry of newly-killed flesh, which was repeated in the morning, and we had bitterly to regret it. While I was amusing myself by attempting to observe an immersion of Jupiter's satellites with a notable failure in the shape of that snare and delusion, a portable telescope, suddenly there arose a terrible hubbub. For a moment it was believed that the crotalus horridus had been taking liberties with one of Miss Moore's progeny. The seat of pain, however, soon removed the alarming suspicion, and—the rattlesnake seldom does damage at night—we soon came to the conclusion that the dear little fellow who boo-hoo'd for forty had been bitten by a musqueto somewhat bigger than its fellows. The poor mother soon was restored to her habits of happiness and hard labor. Not contented with supporting her own family, she was doing supererogation by feeding a little rat-eyed, snub-nosed, shark-mouthed half-breed girl, who was, I believe, in the market as a "chattel." Mrs. Dana pointed out to me one sign of demoralization on the part of Miss Moore. It was so microscopic that only a woman's acute eye could detect it. Miss Moore was teaching her children to say "Yes, surr!" to every driver.

To the Foot of South Pass. 19th August.

With renewed spirit, despite a somewhat hard struggle with the musquetoes, we set out at the respectable hour of 5 45 A.M. We had breakfasted comfortably, and an interesting country lay before us. The mules seemed to share in our gayety. Despite a long ringing, the amiable animals kicked and bit, bucked and backed, till their recalcitrances had almost deposited us in the first ford of the Sweetwater. For this, however, we were amply consoled by the greater misfortunes of our consort, the official wagon. After long luxuriating in the pick of the teams, they were to-day so thoroughly badly "muled" that they were compelled to apply for our assistance.

We forded the river twice within fifty yards, and we recognized with sensible pleasure a homely-looking magpie (*Pica Hud-*

---

* The author of " The Quadroon" (chap. xxxii., etc.) adduces a happy instance of a "hero" who, after a delay and an amount of exertion which certainly would have cost him his life, was relieved by tobacco and cured by the snakeroot (*Polygala Senega*). The popular snakeroots quoted by Mr. Bartlett are the Seneca snakeroot above alluded to, the black snakeroot (*Cimicifuga racemosa*), and the Virginia snakeroot (*Aristolochia serpentaria*).

sonica), and a rattlesnake, not inappropriately, considering where we were, crossed the road. Our path lay between two rocky ridges, which gradually closed inward, forming a regular kanyon, quite shutting out the view. On both sides white and micaceous granite towered to the height of 300 or 400 feet, terminating in jagged and pointed peaks, whose partial disruption covered the angle at their base. Arrived at Ford No. 5, we began an ascent, and reaching the summit, halted to enjoy the fine back view of the split and crevassed mountains.

A waterless and grassless track of fifteen to sixteen miles led us to a well-known place—the Ice Springs—of which, somewhat unnecessarily, a marvel is made. The ground, which lies on the right of the road, is a long and swampy trough between two waves of land which permit the humidity to drain down, and the grass is discolored, suggesting the presence of alkali. After digging about two feet, ice is found in small fragments. Its presence, even in the hottest seasons, may be readily accounted for by the fact that hereabouts water will freeze in a tent during July, and by the depth to which the wintry frost extends. Upon the same principle, snow gathering in mountain ravines and hollows long outlasts the shallower deposits. A little beyond Ice Springs, on the opposite side of, and about a quarter of a mile distant from the road, lie the Warm Springs, one of the many alkaline pans which lie scattered over the face of the country. From the road nothing is to be seen but a deep cunette full of percolated water.

Beyond the Warm Springs lay a hopeless-looking land, a vast slope, barren and desolate as Nature could well make it. The loose sands and the granite masses of the valley had disappeared; the surface was a thin coat of hard gravelly soil. Some mosses, a scanty yellow grass, and the dark gray artemisia, now stunted and shrunk, were sparsely scattered about. It had already begun to give way before an even hardier creation, the rabbit-bush and the greasewood. The former, which seems to thrive under the wintry snow, is a favorite food with hares, which abound in this region; the latter (*Obione*, or *Atriplex canescens*, the chamizo of the Mexicans) derives its name from the oleaginous matter abundant in its wood, and is always a sign of a poor and sterile soil. Avoiding a steep descent by a shorter road, called "Landers' Cut-off," we again came upon the Sweetwater, which was here somewhat broader than below, and lighted upon good grass and underbrush, willow copses, and a fair halting-place. At Ford No. 6 —three followed one another in rapid succession—we found the cattle of a traveling trader scattered over the pasture-grounds. He proved to be an Italian driven from the low country by a band of Sioux, who had slain his Shoshonee wife, and at one time had thought of adding his scalp to his squaw's. After Ford No. 8, we came upon a camping-ground, usually called in guide-books "River Bank and Stream." The Sweetwater is here twenty-five feet wide. About three miles beyond it lay the "Foot of Ridge Station," near a willowy creek, called from its principal inhabitants the Muskrat.* The ridge from which it derives its name is a band of stone that will cross the road during to-morrow's ascent. Being a frontier place, it is a favorite camping-ground with Indians. To-day a war party of Sioux rode in, *en route* to provide themselves with a few Shoshonee scalps.

We made a decided rise to-day, and stood at least 6000 feet above the level of the sea. The altitude of St. Louis being in round numbers 500 feet, and reckoning the diminution of temperature at $1°$ F.$=100$ yards, we are already $19°$ to $20°$ F. colder than before. The severity of the atmosphere and the rapid evaporation from the earth cause an increase of frigidity, to which the salts and nitrates upon the surface of the soil, by absorbing the hydrogen of the atmosphere — as is shown by the dampness of the ground and the absence of dust around the Saleratus Lakes— greatly add. Another remark made by every traveler in these regions is the marked influence upon the temperature caused by the presence and the absence of the sun. The day will be sultry and oppressive, and a fire will be required at night. In the morning, about 11 A.M., the thermometer showed $80°$ Fahrenheit; at 4 P.M., the sky being clouded over, it fell $25°$; before dawn, affected by the cold north wind from the snows about the Pass, it stood at $40°$.

The lowering firmament threatened rain, of which, however, the thirsty land was disappointed. Moreover, all were agreed that snow was to be expected in another fortnight, if not sooner. Glacial storms occasionally occur in July and August, so that in some years the land may be said to have no summer. In winter the sharpness of the cold is such that it can be kept out only by clothes of the closest texture; the mountain-men, like the Esquimaux, prefer to clothe themselves cap-a-piè in the prepared skins of animals. We were all animated with a nervous desire for travel, but there was the rub. The station-master declared that he had no driver, no authority to forward two wagonsful, and no cattle; consequently, that the last comers must be last served, and wait patiently at Rocky Ridge till they could be sent on. They would find antelopes in plenty, perhaps a grizzly, and plenty of plover, crows, and delicate little ground-squirrels† by the burrowful, to "keep their hands in." We being the first comers, a title to preference rarely disputed in this law-and-rule-abiding land, prudently held ourselves aloof. The Judiciary, however, was

---

* *Fiber zibeticus*, a beaver-like animal that inhabits the banks of ponds and streams: it has a strong musky odor in summer only, and is greedily eaten by the Indians.

† I had no opportunity of observing this clean, pretty, and vivacious little animal, whose chirruping resembles that of a bird; but it appeared to be quite a different species from the common striped and spotted prairie-squirrel (*Spermophilus tredecimlineatus*), or the chipmonk or chipmuk (*S. striatus*).

sorely "exercised." Being a "professor," that is, a serious person, he could not relieve his mind by certain little *moyens* which naturally occurred to the rest of the party. Many and protracted were the powwows that took place on this momentous occasion. Sometimes our quondam companions—we now looked upon them as friends lost to us—would mysteriously disappear as though the earth had opened and swallowed them, and presently they would return with woe-begone step and the wrinkled brow of care, simulating an ease which they were far from feeling.

The station rather added to than took from our discomfort: it was a terrible unclean hole; milk was not procurable within thirty-five miles; one of the officials was suffering sorely from a stomach-ache; there was no sugar, and the cooking was atrocious. With a stray title-pageless volume of some natural history of America, and another of agricultural reports—in those days, before reform came, these scientific and highly elaborate compositions, neatly printed and expensively got up at the public expense, were apparently distributed to every ranch and station in the line of road—I worked through the long and tedious afternoon. We were not sorry when the night came, but then the floor was knobby, the musquetoes seemed rather to enjoy the cold, and the banks swarmed with "chinches."* The coyotes and wolves made night vocal with their choruses, and had nearly caused an accident. One of the station-men arose, and, having a bone to pick with the animals for having robbed his beef-barrel, cocked his revolver, and was upon the point of firing, when the object aimed at started up and cried out in the nick of time that he was a federal marshal, not a wolf.

To the South Pass. August 20th.

We rose with the daybreak; we did not start till nearly 8 A.M., the interim having been consumed by the tenants of our late consort in a vain palaver. We bade adieu to them and mounted at last, loudly pitying their miseries as they disappeared from our ken. But the driver bade us reserve our sympathy and humane expressions for a more fitting occasion, and declared—it was probably a little effort of his own imagination—that those faithless friends had spent all their spare time in persuading him to take them on and to leave us behind. I, for one, will never believe that any thing of the kind had been attempted; a man must be created with a total absence of the bowels of compassion who would leave a woman and a young child for days together at the foot of Ridge Station.

The road at once struck away from the Sweetwater, winding up and down rugged hills and broken hollows. From Fort Lara-

---

* The chinch or chints is the Spanish *chinche*—the popular word for the *Cimex lectularius* in the Southern States. In other parts of the United States the English bug is called a bed-bug: without the prefix it is applied to beetles and a variety of Coleopters, as the May-bug, June-bug, golden-bug, etc.

mie the land is all a sandy and hilly desert where one can easily starve, but here it shows its worst features. During a steep descent a mule fell, and was not made to regain its footing without difficulty. Signs of wolves, coyotes, and badgers were abundant, and the *coqs de prairie* (sage-chickens), still young and toothsome at this season, were at no pains to get out of shot. After about five miles we passed by "Three Lakes," dirty little ponds north of the road, two near it and one distant, all about a quarter of a mile apart, and said by those fond of tasting strange things to have somewhat the flavor, as they certainly have the semblance, of soap-suds. Beyond this point we crossed a number of influents of the pretty Sweetwater, some dry, others full: the most interesting was Strawberry Creek: it supplies plenty of the fragrant wild fruit, and white and red willows fringe the bed as long as it retains its individuality. To the north a mass of purple nimbus obscured the mountains—on Frémont's Peak it is said always to rain or snow—and left no visible line between earth and sky. Quaking-Asp Creek was bone dry. At MacAchran's Branch of the Sweetwater we found, pitched upon a sward near a willow copse, a Provençal Frenchman—by what "hasard que les sceptiques appellent l'homme d'affaires du bon Dieu" did he come here?—who begged us to stop and give him the news, especially about the Indians: we could say little that was reassuring. Another spell of rough, steep ground placed us at Willow Creek, a pretty little prairillon, with verdure, water, and an abundance of the larger vegetation, upon which our eyes, long accustomed to artemisia and rabbit-bush, dwelt with a compound sense of surprise and pleasure. In a well-built ranch at this place of plenty were two Canadian traders, apparently settled for life; they supplied us, as we found it necessary to "liquor up," with a whisky which did not poison us, and that is about all that I can say for it. At Ford No. 9, we bade adieu to the Sweetwater with that natural regret which one feels when losing sight of the only pretty face and pleasant person in the neighborhood; and we heard with a melancholy satisfaction the driver's tribute to departing worth, viz., that its upper course is the "healthiest water in the world." Near this spot, since my departure, has been founded "South-Pass City," one of the many mushroom growths which the presence of gold in the Rocky Mountains has caused to spring up.

Ten miles beyond Ford No. 9, hilly miles, ending in a long champaign having some of the characteristics of a rolling prairie, with scatters of white, rose, and smoky quartz, granite, hornblende, porphyry, marble-like lime, sandstone, and mica slate—the two latter cropping out of the ground and forming rocky ridges—led us to the South Pass, the great *Wasserscheide* between the Atlantic and the Pacific, and the frontier points between the territory of Nebraska and the State of Oregon. From the mouth of the Sweetwater, about 120 miles, we have been rising so gradually, almost

L

imperceptibly, that now we unexpectedly find ourselves upon the summit. The distance from Fort Laramie is 320 miles, from St. Louis 1580, and from the mouth of the Oregon about 1400 : it is therefore nearly midway between the Mississippi and the Pacific. The dimensions of this memorial spot are 7490 feet above sea-level, and 20 miles in breadth. The last part of the ascent is so gentle that it is difficult to distinguish the exact point where the versant lies : a stony band crossing the road on the ridge of the table-land is pointed out as the place, and the position has been fixed at N. lat. 48° 19′, and W. long. 108° 40′.* The northern limit is the noble chain of Les Montagnes Rocheuses, which goes by the name of the Wind River; the southern is called Table Mountain, an insignificant mass of low hills.

A pass it is not : it has some of the features of Thermopylæ or the Gorge of Killiecrankie; of the European St. Bernard or Simplon; of the Alleghany Passes or of the Mexican *Barrancas*. It is not, as it sounds, a ghaut between lofty mountains, or, as the traveler may expect, a giant gateway, opening through Cyclopean walls of beetling rocks that rise in forbidding grandeur as he passes onward to the Western continent. And yet the word "Pass" has its significancy. In that New World where Nature has worked upon the largest scale, where every feature of scenery, river and lake, swamp and forest, prairie and mountain, dwarf their congeners in the old hemisphere, this majestic level-topped bluff, the highest steppe of the continent, upon whose iron surface there is space enough for the armies of the globe to march over, is the grandest and the most appropriate of avenues.

A water-shed is always exciting to the traveler. What shall I say of this, where, on the topmost point of American travel, you drink within a hundred yards of the waters of the Atlantic and the Pacific Oceans—that divides the "doorways of the west wind" from the "portals of the sunrise?" On the other side of yon throne of storms, within sight, did not the Sierra interpose, lie separated by a trivial space the fountain-heads that give birth to the noblest rivers of the continent, the Columbia, the Colorado, and the Yellow Stone, which is to the Missouri what the Missouri is to the Mississippi, whence the waters trend to four opposite directions : the Wind River to the northeast; to the southeast the Sweetwater and the Platte; the various branches of the Snake River to the northeast; and to the southwest the Green River, that finds its way into the Californian Gulf.† It is a suggestive

* Some guide-books place the water-shed between two small hills, the "Twin Peaks," about fifty or sixty feet high; the road, however, no longer passes between them.

† As early as A.D. 1772 (Description of the Province of Carolana, etc., etc., by Daniel Cox) it was suggested that there was a line of water communication by means of the "northern branch of the Great Yellow River, by the natives called the River of the Massorites" (Missouri River), and a branch of the Columbia River, which, however, was erroneously supposed to disembogue through the Great Salt

spot, this "divortia aquarum:" it compels Memory to revive past scenes before plunging into the mysterious "Lands of the Hereafter," which lie before and beneath the feet. The Great Ferry, which steam has now bridged, the palisaded banks of the Hudson, the soft and sunny scenery of the Ohio, and the kingly course of the Upper Mississippi, the terrible beauty of Niagara, and the marvels of that chain of inland seas which winds its watery way from Ontario to Superior; the rich pasture-lands of the North, the plantations of the semi-tropical South, and the broad cornfields of the West; finally, the vast meadow-land and the gloomy desert-waste of sage and saleratus, of clay and *mauvaise terre*, of red *butte* and tawny rock, all pass before the mind in rapid array ere they are thrust into oblivion by the excitement of a new departure.

But we have not yet reached our destination, which is two miles below the South Pass. Pacific Springs is our station; it lies a little down the hill, and we can sight it from the road. The springs are a pond of pure, hard, and very cold water, surrounded by a strip of shaking bog, which must be boarded over before it will bear a man. The hut would be a right melancholy abode were it not for the wooded ground on one hand, and the glorious snow-peaks on the other side of the "Pass." We reached Pacific Springs at 3 P.M., and dined without delay, the material being bouilli and potatoes—unusual luxuries. About an hour afterward the west wind, here almost invariable, brought up a shower of rain, and swept a vast veil over the forms of the Wind-River Mountains. Toward sunset it cleared away, and the departing luminary poured a flood of gold upon the majestic pile—I have seldom seen a view more beautiful.

From the south, the barren rolling table-land that forms the Pass trends northward till it sinks apparently below a ridge of offsets from the main body, black with timber—cedar, cypress, fir, and balsam pine. The hand of Nature has marked, as though by line and level, the place where vegetation shall go and no farther. Below the waist the mountains are robed in evergreens; above it, to the shoulders, they would be entirely bare but for the atmosphere, which has thrown a thin veil of light blue over their tawny gray, while their majestic heads are covered with ice and snow, or are hidden from sight by thunder-cloud or the morning mist. From the south, on clear days, the cold and glittering ra-

---

Lake into the Pacific. The idea has been revived in the present day. Some assert that the upper waters of the Yellow Stone, which approach within three hundred miles of Great Salt Lake City, are three feet deep, and therefore navigable for flat-bottomed boats during the annual inundation. Others believe that, as in the case of the Platte, shallowness would be an insuperable obstacle, except for one or two months. This point will doubtless be settled by Captain W. F. Raynolds, of the United States Topographical Engineers, who, accompanied by Colonel J. Bridger, was, at the time of my visit to Great Salt Lake City, exploring the Valley of the Yellow Stone.

diance may be seen at a distance of a hundred miles. The monarch of these mountains is "Frémont's Peak;" its height is laid down at 13,570 feet above sea level; and second to it is a hoary cone called by the station-people Snowy Peak.

That evening the Wind-River Mountains appeared in marvelous majesty. The huge purple hangings of rain-cloud in the northern sky set off their huge proportions, and gave prominence, as in a stereoscope, to their gigantic forms, and their upper heights, hoar with the frosts of ages. The mellow radiance of the setting sun diffused a charming softness over their more rugged features, defining the folds and ravines with a distinctness which deceived every idea of distance. And as the light sank behind the far western horizon, it traveled slowly up the mountain side, till, reaching the summit, it mingled its splendors with the snow — flashing and flickering for a few brief moments, then wasting them in the dark depths of the upper air. Nor was the scene less lovely in the morning hour, as the first effulgence of day fell upon the masses of dew-cloud—at this time mist always settles upon their brows — lit up the peaks, which gleamed like silver, and poured its streams of light and warmth over the broad skirts reposing upon the plain.

This unknown region was explored in August, 1842, by Colonel, then Brevet Captain, J. C. Frémont, of the United States Topographical Engineers; and his eloquent descriptions of the magnificent scenery that rewarded his energy and enterprise prove how easily men write well when they have a great subject to write upon. The concourse of small green tarns, rushing waters, and lofty cascades, with the gigantic disorder of enormous masses, the savage sublimity of the naked rock, broken, jagged cones, slender minarets, needles, and columns, and serrated walls, 2000 to 3000 feet high, all naked and destitute of vegetable earth; the vertical precipices, chasms, and fissures, insecure icy passages, long moraines, and sloping glaciers — which had nearly proved fatal to some of the party; the stern recesses, shutting out from the world dells and ravines of exquisite beauty, smoothly carpeted with soft grass, kept green and fresh by the moisture of the atmosphere, and sown with gay groups of brilliant flowers, of which yellow was the predominant color: all this glory and grandeur seems to be placed like a picture before our eyes. The reader enjoys, like the explorer, the fragrant odor of the pines, and the pleasure of breathing, in the bright, clear morning, that "mountain air which makes a constant theme of the hunter's praise," and which causes man to feel as if he had been inhaling some exhilarating gas. We sympathize with his joy in having hit upon "such a beautiful entrance to the mountains," in his sorrow, caused by accidents to barometer and thermometer, and in the honest pride with which, fixing a ramrod in the crevice of "an unstable and precarious slab, which it seemed a breath would hurl into the abyss below," he unfurled the Stars and the Stripes, to wave in the breeze where flag never waved before—over the topmost crest of the Rocky Mountains.   And every driver upon the road now can tell how, in the profound silence and terrible stillness and solitude that affect the mind as the great features of the scene, while sitting on a rock at the very summit, where the silence was absolute, unbroken by any sound, and the stillness and solitude were completest, a solitary "humble-bee"* winging through the black-blue air his flight from the eastern valley, alit upon the knee of one of the men, and, helas! " found a grave in the leaves of the large book, among the flowers collected on the way."

The Wind-River Range has other qualities than mere formal beauty to recommend it.   At Horseshoe Creek I was shown a quill full of large gold-grains from a new digging.   Probably all the primitive masses of the Rocky Mountains will be found to contain the precious metal.   The wooded heights are said to be a very paradise of sport, full of elk and every kind of deer; pumas; bears, brown† as well as grizzly; the wolverine;‡ in parts the mountain buffalo—briefly, all the noble game of the Continent. The Indian tribes, Shoshonees and Blackfeet, are not deadly to whites.   Washiki, the chief of the former, had, during the time of our visit, retired to hilly ground, about forty miles north of the Foot of Ridge Station.   This chief—a fine, manly fellow, equal in point of physical strength to the higher race—had been a firm friend, from the beginning, to emigrant and settler; but he was complaining, according to the road officials, that the small amount of inducement prevented his affording good conduct any longer —that he must rob, like the rest of the tribe.   Game, indeed, is not unfrequently found near the Pacific Springs; they are visited, later in the year, by swans, geese, and flights of ducks.   At this season they seem principally to attract coyotes — five mules have lately been worried by the little villains—huge cranes, chicken-hawks, a large species of trochilus, and clouds of musquetoes, which neither the altitude, the cold, nor the eternal wind-storm that howls through the Pass can drive from their favorite breeding-bed.   Near nightfall a flock of wild geese passed over us, audibly threatening an early winter.   We were obliged, before resting, to insist upon a smudge,§ without which fumigation sleep would have been impossible.

* A species of *bromus* or *bombus*.   In the United States, as in England, the word is often pronounced bumble-bee.   Johnson says we call a bee an humble bee that wants a sting; so the States call black cattle without horns "humble cows."   It is the general belief of the mountaineers that the bee, the partridge, the plantain, and the " Jamestown weed" follow the footsteps of the white pioneers westward.

† Some authorities doubt that the European brown bear is found in America.

‡ The wolverine (*Gulo luscus*), carcajou, or glutton, extends throughout Utah Territory: its carnivorous propensities render it an object of peculiar hatred to furhunters.   The first name is loosely used in the States: the people of Michigan are called Wolverines, from the large number of *mischievous prairie wolves* found there (Bartlett).

§ This old North of England word is used in the West for a heap of green bush

The shanty was perhaps a trifle more uncomfortable than the average; our only seat was a kind of trestled plank, which suggested a certain obsolete military punishment called riding on a rail. The station-master was a *bon enfant;* but his help, a Mormon lad, still in his teens, had been trained to go in a "sorter" jibbing and somewhat uncomfortable "argufying," "highfalutin'" way. He had the furor for fire-arms that characterizes the ingenuous youth of Great Salt Lake City, and his old rattletrap of a revolver, which always reposed by his side at night, was as dangerous to his friends as to himself. His vernacular was peculiar; like Mr. Boatswain Chucks (Mr. D——s), he could begin a sentence with polished and elaborate diction, but it always ended, like the wicked, badly. He described himself, for instance, as having lately been "slightly inebriated;" but the euphuistic periphrasis concluded with an asseveration that he would be "Gord domned" if he did it again.

The night was, like the day, loud and windy, the log hut being somewhat. crannied and creviced, and the door had a porcelain handle, and a shocking bad fit—a characteristic combination. We had some trouble to keep ourselves warm. At sunrise the thermometer showed 35° Fahrenheit.

To Green River. August 21st.

We rose early, despite the cold, to enjoy once more the lovely aspect of the Wind-River Mountains, upon whose walls of snow the rays of the unrisen sun broke with a splendid effect; breakfasted, and found ourselves *en route* at 8 A.M. The day did not begin well: Mrs. Dana was suffering severely from fatigue, and the rapid transitions from heat to cold; Miss May, poor child! was but little better, and the team was re-enforced by an extra mule returning to its proper station: this four-footed Xantippe caused us, without speaking of the dust from her hoofs, an immensity of trouble.

At the Pacific Creek, two miles below the springs, we began the descent of the Western water-shed, and the increase of temperature soon suggested a lower level. We were at once convinced that those who expect any change for the better on the counter-slope of the mountains labor under a vulgar error. The land was desolate, a red waste, dotted with sage and greasebush, and in places pitted with large rain-drops. But, looking backward, we could admire the Sweetwater's Gap heading far away, and the glorious pile of mountains which, disposed in crescent shape, curtained the horizon; their southern and western bases wanted, however, one of the principal charms of the upper view: the snow had well-nigh been melted off. Yet, according to the explorer, they supply within the space of a few miles the Green River with a

or other damp combustibles, placed inside or to windward of a house or tent, and partially lighted, so as to produce a thick, pungent steam.

number of tributaries, which are all called the New Forks.   We kept them in sight till they mingled with the upper air like immense masses of thunder-cloud gathering for a storm.

From Pacific Creek the road is not bad, but at this season the emigrant parties are sorely tried by drought, and when water is found it is often fetid or brackish.   After seventeen miles we passed the junction of the Great Salt Lake and Fort Hall roads.   Near Little Sandy Creek—a feeder of its larger namesake—which after rains is about 2·5 feet deep, we found nothing but sand, caked clay, sage, thistles, and the scattered fragments of camp-fires, with large ravens picking at the bleaching skeletons, and other indications of a halting-ground, an eddy in the great current of mankind, which, ceaseless as the Gulf Stream, ever courses from east to west.   After a long stage of twenty-nine miles we made Big Sandy Creek, an important influent of the Green River; the stream, then shrunken, was in breadth not less than five rods, each = 16·5 feet, running with a clear, swift current through a pretty little prairillon, bright with the blue lupine, the delicate pink malvacea, the golden helianthus, purple aster acting daisy, the white mountain heath, and the green Asclepias tuberosa,* a weed common throughout Utah Territory.   The Indians, in their picturesque way, term this stream Wágahongopá, or the Glistening Gravel Water.†   We halted for an hour to rest and dine; the people of the station, man and wife, the latter very young, were both English, and of course Mormons; they had but lately become tenants of the ranch, but already they were thinking, as the Old Country people will, of making their surroundings "nice and tidy."

Beyond the Glistening Gravel Water lies a *mauvaise terre*, sometimes called the First Desert, and upon the old road water is not found in the dry season within forty-nine miles—a terrible *jornada*‡ for laden wagons with tired cattle.   We prepared for drought by replenishing all our canteens—one of them especially, a tin flask, covered outside with thick cloth, kept the fluid deliciously cold—and we amused ourselves by the pleasant prospect of seeing wild mules taught to bear harness.   The tricks of equine viciousness and asinine obstinacy played by the mongrels were so distinct, that we had no pains in determining what was inherited from the father and what from the other side of the house.   Before they could be hitched up they were severally hustled into some-

---

* Locally called milkweed.   The whites use the silky cotton of the pods, as in Arabia, for bed-stuffings, and the Sioux Indians of the Upper Platte boil and eat the young pods with their buffalo flesh.   Colonel Frémont asserts that he never saw this plant without remarking "on the flower a large butterfly, so nearly resembling it in color as to be distinguishable at a little distance only by the motion of its wings."

† Similarly the Snake River, an eastern influent of the Colorado, is called Yampa Pa, or Sweet Root (*Anethum graveolens*) Water.

‡ The Spanish-Mexican term for a day's march.   It is generally applied to a waterless march, *e. g.*, "Jornada del Muerto" in New Mexico, which, like some in the Sahara, measures ninety miles across.

thing like a parallel line with the pole, and were then forced into their places by a rope attached to the fore wheel, and hauled at the other end by two or three men. Each of these pleasant animals had a bell: it is sure, unless corraled, to run away, and at night sound is necessary to guide the pursuer. At last, being "all aboord," we made a start, dashed over the Big Sandy, charged the high stiff bank with an impetus that might have carried us up an otter-slide or a Montagne Russe, and took the right side of the valley, leaving the stream at some distance.

Rain-clouds appeared from the direction of the hills: apparently they had many centres, as the distant sheet was rent into a succession of distinct streamers. A few drops fell upon us as we advanced. Then the fiery sun "ate up" the clouds, or raised them so high that they became playthings in the hands of the strong and steady western gale. The thermometer showed 95° in the carriage, and 111° exposed to the reflected heat upon the black leather cushions. It was observable, however, that the sensation was not what might have been expected from the height of the mercury, and perspiration was unknown except during severe exercise; this proves the purity and salubrity of the air. In St. Jo and New Orleans the effect would have been that of India or of a Turkish steam-bath. The heat, however, brought with it one evil—a green-headed horsefly, that stung like a wasp, and from which cattle must be protected with a coating of grease and tar. Whenever wind blew, tourbillons of dust coursed over the different parts of the plain, showing a highly electrical state of the atmosphere. When the air was unmoved the mirage was perfect as the sarab in Sindh or Southern Persia; earth and air were both so dry that the refraction of the sunbeams elevated the objects acted upon more than I had ever seen before. A sea lay constantly before our eyes, receding of course as we advanced, but in all other points a complete *lusus naturæ*. The color of the water was a dull cool sky-blue, not white, as the "looming" generally is; the broad expanse had none of that tremulous upward motion which is its general concomitant; it lay placid, still, and perfectly reflecting in its azure depths—here and there broken by projecting capes and bluff headlands—the forms of the higher grounds bordering the horizon.

After twelve miles' driving we passed through a depression called Simpson's Hollow, and somewhat celebrated in local story. Two semicircles of black still charred the ground; on a cursory view they might have been mistaken for burnt-out lignite. Here, in 1857, the Mormons fell upon a corraled train of twenty-three wagons, laden with provisions and other necessaries for the federal troops, then halted at Camp Scott awaiting orders to advance. The wagoners, suddenly attacked, and, as usual, unarmed—their weapons being fastened inside their awnings—could offer no resistance, and the whole convoy was set on fire except two conveyances, which were left to carry back supplies for the drivers till they could reach their homes. On this occasion the *dux facti* was Lot Smith, a man of reputation for hard riding and general gallantry. The old Saint is always spoken of as a good man who lives by "Mormon rule of wisdom." As at Fort Sumter, no blood was spilled. So far the Mormons behaved with temper and prudence; but this their first open act of rebellion against, or secession from, the federal authority nearly proved fatal to them; had the helm of government been held by a firmer hand than poor Mr. Buchanan's, the scenes of Nauvoo would have been acted again at Great Salt Lake City. As it was, all turned out *à merveille* for the saints militant. They still boast loudly of the achievement, and on the marked spot where it was performed the juvenile emigrants of the creed erect dwarf graves and nameless "wooden" tomb-"stones" in derision of their enemies.

As sunset drew near we approached the banks of the Big Sandy River. The bottom through which it flowed was several yards in breadth, bright green with grass, and thickly feathered with willows and cotton-wood. It showed no sign of cultivation; the absence of cereals may be accounted for by its extreme cold; it freezes there every night, and none but the hardiest grains, oats and rye, which here are little appreciated, could be made to grow. We are now approaching the valley of the Green River, which, like many of the rivers in the Eastern States, appears formerly to have filled a far larger channel. Flat tables and elevated terraces of horizontal strata—showing that the deposit was made in still waters—with layers varying from a few lines to a foot in thickness, composed of hard clay, green and other sandstones, and agglutinated conglomerates, rise like islands from barren plains, or form escarpments that buttress alternately either bank of the winding stream. Such, according to Captain Stansbury, is the general formation of the land between the South Pass and the "Rim" of the Utah Basin.

Advancing over a soil alternately sandy and rocky—an iron flat that could not boast of a spear of grass—we sighted a number of coyotes, fittest inhabitants of such a waste, and a long, distant line of dust, like the smoke of a locomotive, raised by a herd of mules which were being driven to the corral. We were presently met by the Pony Express rider; he reined in to exchange news, which *de part et d'autre* were simply *nil*. As he pricked onward over the plain, the driver informed us, with a portentous rolling of the head, that Ichabod was an a'mighty fine "shyoot." Within five or six miles of Green River we passed the boundary stone which bears Oregon on one side and Utah on the other. We had now traversed the southeastern corner of the country of Long-eared men,* and were entering Deserét, the Land of the Honey-bee.

* Oregon is supposed by Mr. Edward to have been named by the Spaniards from the immensely lengthened ears (*orejones*) of the Indians who inhabited it.

At 6 30 P.M. we debouched upon the bank of the Green River. The station was the home of Mr. Macarthy, our driver. The son of a Scotchman who had settled in the United States, he retained many signs of his origin, especially freckles, and hair which one might almost venture to describe as sandy; perhaps also, at times, he was rather o'er fond of draining "a cup o' kindness yet." He had lately taken to himself an English wife, the daughter of a Birmingham mechanic, who, before the end of her pilgrimage to "Zion on the tops of the mountains," had fallen considerably away from grace, and had incurred the risk of being buffeted by Satan for a thousand years—a common form of commination in the New Faith—by marrying a Gentile husband.* The station had the indescribable scent of a Hindoo village, which appears to result from the burning of *bois de vache* and the presence of cattle: there were sheep, horses, mules, and a few cows, the latter so lively that it was impossible to milk them. The ground about had the effect of an oasis in the sterile waste, with grass and shrubs, willows and flowers, wild geraniums, asters, and various *cruciferæ*. A few trees, chiefly quaking asp, lingered near the station, but dead stumps were far more numerous than live trunks. In any other country their rare and precious shade would have endeared them to the whole settlement; here they were never safe when a log was wanted. The Western man is bred and perhaps born—I believe devoutly in transmitted and hereditary qualities—with an instinctive dislike to timber in general. He fells a tree naturally as a bull-terrier worries a cat, and the admirable woodsman's axe which he has invented only serves to whet his desire to try conclusions with every more venerable patriarch of the forest.† Civilized Americans, of course, lament the destructive mania, and the Latter-Day Saints have learned by hard experience the inveterate evils that may arise in such a country from disforesting the ground. We supped comfortably at Green-River Station, the stream supplying excellent salmon trout. The kichimichi, or buffalo berry,‡ makes tolerable jelly, and alongside of the station is a store where Mr. Burton (of Maine) sells "Valley Tan" whisky.§

* Mr. Brigham Young, one of the most tolerant of a people whose motto is toleration, would not, I believe, offer any but an official objection to a Mormon member marrying a worthy Gentile; but even he—and it could hardly be expected that he should—can not overlook the sin of apostasy. The order of the faith runs thus: "We believe that it is not right to prohibit members of the Church from marrying out of the Church, if it be their determination so to do, but such persons will be considered weak in the faith of our Lord and Savior Jesus Christ." The same view of the subject is taken, I need hardly say, by the more rigid kind of Roman Catholic.

† Many of the blades, being made by convicts at the state prisons, are sold cheap. The extent of the timber regions necessitated this excellent implement, and the saving of labor on the European article is enormous.

‡ A shrub 10–15 feet high, with a fruit about the size of a pea, red like a wild rose-hip, and with a pleasant sub-acid flavor: the Indians eat it with avidity, and it is cultivated in the gardens at Great Salt Lake City.

§ Tannery was the first technological process introduced into the Mormon Valley: hence all home industry has obtained the sobriquet of "Valley Tan."

The Green River is the Rio Verde of the Spaniards, who named it from its timbered shores and grassy islets: it is called by the Yuta Indians Piya Ogwe, or the Great Water; by the other tribes Sitskidiágí, or " Prairie-grouse River." It was nearly at its lowest when we saw it; the breadth was not more than 330 feet. In the flood-time it widens to 800 feet, and the depth increases from three to six. During the inundation season a ferry is necessary, and when transit is certain the owner sometimes nets $500 a week, which is not unfrequently squandered in a day. The banks are in places thirty feet high, and the bottom may average three miles from side to side. It is a swift-flowing stream, running as if it had no time to lose, and truly it has a long way to go. Its length, volume, and direction entitle it to the honor of being called the head water of the great Rio Colorado, or Colored River, a larger and more important stream than even the Columbia. There is some grand exploration still to be done upon the line of the Upper Colorado, especially the divides which lie between it and its various influents, the Grand River and the Yaquisilla, of which the wild trapper brings home many a marvelous tale of beauty and grandeur. Captain T. A. Gove, of the 10th Regiment of Infantry, then stationed at Camp Floyd, told me that an expedition had often been projected: a party of twenty-five to thirty men, well armed and provided with inflatable boats, might pass without unwarrantable risk through the sparsely populated Indian country: a true report concerning regions of which there are so many false reports, all wearing more or less the garb of fable—beautiful valleys inclosed in inaccessible rocks, Indian cities and golden treasures—would be equally interesting and important. I can not recommend the undertaking to the European adventurer: the United States have long since organized and perfected what was proposed in England during the Crimean war, and which fell, as other projects then did, to the ground, namely, a corps of Topographical Engineers, a body of well-trained and scientific explorers, to whose hands the task may safely be committed.*

* The principal explorers under the United States government of the regions lying west of the Mississippi, and who have published works upon the subject, are the following:

1. Messrs. Lewis and Clarke, in 1804–6, first explored the Rocky Mountains to the Columbia River.

2. Major Z. M. Pike, in 1805–7, visited the upper waters of the Mississippi and the western regions of Louisiana.

3. Major, afterward Colonel S. H. Long, of the United States Topographical Engineers, made two expeditions, one in 1819–20 to the Rocky Mountains, another in 1823 to the Sources of the St. Peter and the Lake of the Woods, whereby four volumes octavo were filled.

4. Governor Cass and Mr. Schoolcraft in 1820 explored the Sources of the Mississippi and the regions west and south of Lake Superior.

5. Colonel H. Dodge, U. S. Army, in 1835 traveled 1600 miles from Fort Leavenworth, and visited the regions between the Arkansas and the Platte Rivers.

6. Captain Canfield, United States Topographical Engineers, in 1838 explored the country between Forts Leavenworth and Snelling.

We passed a social evening at Green-River Station. It boasted of no less than three Englishwomen, two married, and one, the help, still single. Not having the Mormonite *retenue*, the dames were by no means sorry to talk about Birmingham and Yorkshire, their birthplaces. At 9 P.M. arrived one of the road-agents, Mr. Cloete, from whom I gathered that the mail-wagon which once ran from Great Salt Lake City had lately been taken off the road. The intelligence was by no means consolatory, but a course of meditation upon the saying of the sage, " in for a penny, in for a pound," followed by another visit to my namesake's grog-shop, induced a highly philosophical turn, which enabled me—with the aid of a buffalo—to pass a comfortable night in the store.

22d August.   To Ham's Fork and Millersville.

We were not under way before 8 A.M. Macarthy was again to take the lines, and a *Giovinetto* returning after a temporary absence to a young wife is not usually rejoiced to run his course. Indeed, he felt the inconveniences of a semi-bachelor life so severely, that he often threatened in my private ear, *chemin faisant*, to throw up the whole concern.

After the preliminary squabble with the mules, we forded the pebbly and gravelly bed of the river—in parts it looks like a lake exhausted by drainage—whose swift surging waters wetted the upper spokes of the wheels, and gurgled pleasantly around the bags which contained the mail for Great Salt Lake City.*

---

7. Mr. M'Cox, of Missouri, surveyed the boundaries of the Indian reservations: his work was in part revised by the late Captain Hood, United States Topographical Engineers.

8. Mr. Nicollet (French) in 1833–38 mapped the country west of the Upper Mississippi: he was employed in 1838–9 to make a similar scientific reconnoissance between the Mississippi and the Missouri, on which occasion he was accompanied by Mr. Frémont. He died in 1842.

The explorations of Colonel Frémont, Captain Howard Stansbury, Lieutenant Gunnison, and Lieutenant Warren have been frequently alluded to in these pages.

9. Lieutenant, afterward Captain Charles Wilkes, U. S. Navy, set out in 1838, and, after a long voyage of discovery in South America, Oceanica, and the Antarctic continent, made San Francisco on August 11, 1841. It is remarkable that this officer's party were actually pitched upon the spot (New Helvetia, afterward called Sacramento City) where Californian gold was dug by the Mormons.

10. Captain R. B. Marcy, U. S. Army, "discovered and explored, located and marked out the wagon-road from Fort Smith, Arkansas, to Santa Fé, New Mexico." The road explorers, however, are too numerous to specify.

11. Governor I. I. Stevens, of Washington Territory, surveyed in 1853 the northern land proposed for a Pacific railway near the 47°–49° parallels, from St. Paul to Puget Sound. No portion of that line had been visited since the days of Lewis and Clarke, except a small portion toward the Pacific Ocean.

12. Captain Raynolds, United States Topographical Engineers, accompanied by Colonel Bridger as guide and interpreter, is still (1860) exploring the head-waters of the Yellow Stone River.

* Sticklers for strict democracy in the United States maintain, on the principle that the least possible power should be delegated to the federal government, that the transmission of correspondence is no more a national concern than the construction of railways and telegraphs, or the transit of passengers and goods. The present system was borrowed from the monopolies of Europe, and was introduced into Amer-

We then ran down the river valley, which was here about one mile in breadth, in a smooth flooring of clay, sprinkled with water-rolled pebbles, overgrown in parts with willow, wild cherry, buffalo berries, and quaking asp. Macarthy pointed out in the road-side a rough grave, furnished with the normal tomb-stone, two pieces of wagon-board: it was occupied by one Farren, who had fallen by the revolver of the redoubtable Slade. Presently we came to the store of Michael Martin, an honest Creole, who vended the staple of prairie goods, Champagne, bottled cocktail, " eye-opener," and other liquors, dry goods—linen drapery—a few fancy goods, ribbons, and finery ; brandied fruits, jams and jellies, potted provisions, buckskins, moccasins, and so forth. Hearing that Lieutenant Dana was *en route* for Camp Floyd, he requested him to take charge of $500, to be paid to Mr. Livingston, the sutler, and my companion, with the obligingness that marked his every action, agreed to deliver the dollars, *sauve* the judgment of God in the shape of Indians, or " White Indians."* At the store we noticed a paralytic man. This original lived under the delusion that it was impossible to pass the Devil's Gate : his sister had sent for him to St. Louis, and his friends tried to transport him eastward in chairs; the only result was that he ran away before reaching the Gate, and after some time was brought back by Indians.

Resuming our journey, we passed two places where trains of fifty-one wagons were burned in 1857 by the Mormon Rangers: the black stains had bitten into the ground like the blood-marks

ica at a time when individual enterprise was inadequate to the task ; in the year one of the Republic it became, under the direction of Benjamin Franklin, a state department, and, though men argue in the abstract, few care to propose a private mail system, which would undertake the management of some 27,000 scattered offices and 40,000 poorly paid clerks.

On this line we saw all the evils of the contract system. The requisite regularity and quickness was neglected, letters and papers were often lost, the mail-bags were wetted or thrown carelessly upon the ground, and those intrusted to the conductors were perhaps destroyed. Both parties complain—the postmaster that the contractors seek to drive too hard a bargain with the department, and the contractors that they are carrying the mails at a loss. Since the restoration (in 1858) of the postal communication with the United States which was interrupted in 1857, the Mormons attempt to secure good service by advertising their grievances, and with tolerable success. Postmaster Morrill—a Gentile—complained energetically of the mail service during the last year, that letters were wetted and jumbled together, two of one month perhaps and one of another ; that magazines often arrived four months after date, and that thirty sacks left at Rocky Ridge were lost. The consequence was that during my stay at Great Salt Lake City the contractors did their duty.

When salaries are small and families large, post-office robberies must at times be expected. The postal department have long adopted the system of registered letters : upon payment of five cents instead of three, the letter is placed in a separate bag, entered separately in the office books, forwarded with certain precautions, and delivered to the address only after a receipt from the recipient. But the department disclaims all responsibility in case of loss or theft, and the only value of the higher stamp is a somewhat superior facility of tracking the document that bears it.

* A cant term for white thieves disguised as savages, which has a terrible significancy a little farther West.

in the palace of Holyrood—a neat foundation for a structure of superstition. Not far from it was a deep hole, in which the plunderers had "cached" the iron-work which they were unable to carry away. Emerging from the river plain we entered upon another *mauvaise terre*, with knobs and elevations of clay and green gault, striped and banded with lines of stone and pebbles: it was a barren, desolate spot, the divide between the Green River and its western influent, the shallow and somewhat sluggish Black's Fork. The name is derived from an old trader: it is called by the Snakes Ongo Ogwe Pa, or "Pine-tree Stream;" it rises in the Bear-River Mountains, drains the swamps and lakelets on the way, and bifurcates in its upper bed, forming two principal branches, Ham's Fork and Muddy Fork.

Near the Pine-tree Stream we met a horse-thief driving four bullocks: he was known to Macarthy, and did not look over comfortable. We had now fallen into the regular track of Mormon emigration, and saw the wayfarers in their worst plight, near the end of the journey. We passed several families, and parties of women and children trudging wearily along: most of the children were in rags or half nude, and all showed gratitude when we threw them provisions. The greater part of the men were armed, but their weapons were far more dangerous to themselves and their fellows than to the enemy. There is not on earth a race of men more ignorant of arms as a rule than the lower grades of English; becoming an emigrant, the mechanic hears that it may be necessary to beat off Indians, so he buys the first old fire-arm he sees, and probably does damage with it. Only last night a father crossed Green River to beg for a piece of cloth; it was intended to shroud the body of his child, which during the evening had been accidentally shot, and the station people seemed to think nothing of the accident, as if it were of daily recurrence. I was told of three, more or less severe, that happened in the course of a month. The Western Americans, who are mostly accustomed to the use of weapons, look upon these awkwardnesses with a profound contempt. We were now in a region of graves, and their presence in this wild was not a little suggestive.

Presently we entered a valley in which green grass, low and dense willows, and small but shady trees, an unusually vigorous vegetation, refreshed, as though with living water, our eyes, parched and dazed by the burning glare. Stock strayed over the pasture, and a few Indian tents rose at the farther side; the view was probably *pas grand' chose*, but we thought it splendidly beautiful. At midday we reached Ham's Fork, the northwestern influent of Green River, and there we found a station. The pleasant little stream is called by the Indians Turugempa, the "Blackfoot Water."

The station was kept by an Irishman and a Scotchman—"Dawvid Lewis:" it was a disgrace; the squalor and filth were worse almost than the two—Cold Springs and Rock Creek—which we called our horrors, and which had always seemed to be the *ne plus ultra* of Western discomfort.   The shanty was made of dry stone piled up against a dwarf cliff to save back wall, and ignored doors and windows.   The flies—unequivocal sign of unclean living!—darkened the table and covered every thing put upon it; the furniture, which mainly consisted of the different parts of wagons, was broken, and all in disorder; the walls were impure, the floor filthy.   The reason was at once apparent.   Two Irishwomen, sisters,* were married to Mr. Dawvid, and the house was full of "childer," the noisiest and most rampageous of their kind. I could hardly look upon the scene without disgust.   The fair ones had the porcine Irish face—I need hardly tell the reader that there are three orders of physiognomy in that branch of the Keltic family, viz., porcine, equine, and simian—the pig-faced, the horse-faced, and the monkey-faced.   Describing one I describe both sisters; her nose was "pugged," apparently by gnawing hard potatoes before that member had acquired firmness and consistency; her face was powdered with freckles; her hair, and, indeed, her general costume, looked, to quote Mr. Dow's sermon, as though she had been rammed through a bush fence into a world of wretchedness and woe.   Her dress was unwashed and in tatters, and her feet were bare; she would not even take the trouble to make for herself moccasins.   Moreover, I could not but notice that, though the house contained two wives, it boasted only of one cubile, and had only one cubiculum.   Such things would excite no surprise in London or Naples, or even in many of the country parts of Europe; but here, where ground is worthless, where building material is abundant, and where a few hours of daily labor would have made the house look at least respectable, I could not but wonder at it.   My first impulse was to attribute the evil, uncharitably enough, to Mormonism; to renew, in fact, the stock-complaint of nineteen centuries' standing—

> "Fœcunda culpæ secula nuptias
> Primùm inquinavere, et genus et domus."

A more extended acquaintance with the regions west of the Wasach taught me that the dirt and discomfort were the growth of the land.   To give the poor devils their due, Dawvid was civil and intelligent, though a noted dawdler, as that rare phenomenon, a Scotch idler, generally is.   Moreover, his wives were not deficient in charity; several Indians came to the door, and none went away without a "bit" and a "sup."   During the process of sketching one of these men, a Snake, distinguished by his vermilion'd hair-parting, eyes blackened, as if by lines of soot or surma, and delicate Hindoo-like hands, my eye fell upon the German-silver

* A man (Mormon) may even marry a mother and her daughters: usually the relationship with the former is Platonic; the tie, however, is irregular, and has been contracted in ignorance of the prohibited degrees.

handle of a Colt's revolver, which had been stowed away under the blankets, and a revolver in the Lamanite's hands breeds evil suspicions.

Again we advanced. The air was like the breath of a furnace; the sun was a blaze of fire—accounting, by-the-by, for the fact that the human nose in these parts seems invariably to become cherry-red—all the nullahs were dried up, and the dust-pillars and mirage were the only moving objects on the plain. Three times we forded Black's Fork, and then debouched once more upon a long flat. The ground was scattered over with pebbles of granite, obsidian, flint, and white, yellow, and smoky quartz, all water-rolled. After twelve miles we passed Church Butte, one of many curious formations lying to the left hand or south of the road. This isolated mass of stiff clay has been cut and ground by wind and rain into folds and hollow channels which from a distance perfectly simulate the pillars, groins, and massive buttresses of a ruinous Gothic cathedral. The foundation is level, except where masses have been swept down by the rain, and not a blade of grass grows upon any part. An architect of genius might profitably study this work of Nature: upon that subject, however, I shall presently have more to say. The Butte is highly interesting in a geological point of view; it shows the elevation of the adjoining plains in past ages, before partial deluges and the rains of centuries had effected the great work of degradation.

Again we sighted the pretty valley of Black's Fork, whose cool clear stream flowed merrily over its pebbly bed. The road was now populous with Mormon emigrants; some had good teams, others hand-carts, which looked like a cross between a wheel-barrow and a tax-cart. There was nothing repugnant in the demeanor of the party; they had been civilized by traveling, and the younger women, who walked together and apart from the men, were not too surly to exchange a greeting. The excessive barrenness of the land presently diminished; gentian and other odoriferous herbs appeared, and the greasewood, which somewhat reminded me of the Sindhian camel-thorn, was of a lighter green than elsewhere, and presented a favorable contrast with the dull glaucous hues of the eternal prairie sage. We passed a dwarf copse so strewed with the bones of cattle as to excite our astonishment: Macarthy told us that it was the place where the 2d Dragoons encamped in 1857, and lost a number of their horses by cold and starvation. The wolves and coyotes seemed to have retained a predilection for the spot; we saw troops of them in their favorite "location"—the crest of some little rise, whence they could keep a sharp look-out upon any likely addition to their scanty larder.

After sundry steep inclines we forded another little stream, with a muddy bed, shallow, and about thirty feet wide: it is called Smith's Fork, rises in the "Bridger Range" of the Uinta Hills,

and sheds into Black's Fork, the main drain of these parts. On
the other side stood Millersville, a large ranch with a whole row
of unused and condemned wagons drawn up on one side. We
arrived at 5 15 P.M., having taken three hours and fifteen minutes to get over twenty miles. The tenement was made of the
component parts of vehicles, the chairs had backs of yoke-bows,
and the fences which surrounded the corral were of the same material. The station was kept by one Holmes, an American Mormon, and an individual completely the reverse of genial; he dispensed his words as if shelling out coin, and he was never—by us
at. least—seen to smile. His wife was a pretty young Englishwoman, who had spent the best part of her life between London
and Portsmouth; when alone with me she took the opportunity
of asking some few questions about old places, but this most innocent *tête-à-tête* was presently interrupted by the protrusion through
the open door of a *tête de mari au naturel*, with a truly *renfrogné*
and vinegarish aspect, which made him look like a calamity.
After supplying us with a supper which was clean and neatly
served, the pair set out for an evening ride, and toward night we
heard the scraping of a violin, which reminded me of Tommaso
Scarafaggio:

> "Detto il sega del villagio
> Perché suona il violino."

The "fiddle" was a favorite instrument with Mr. Joseph Smith,
as the harp with David; the Mormons, therefore, at the instance
of their prophet, are not a little addicted to the use of the bow.
We spent a comfortable night at Millersville. After watching
the young moon as she sailed through the depths of a firmament
unstained by the least fleck of mist, we found some scattered volumes which rendered us independent of our unsocial Yankee
host.

23d August.   Fort Bridger.

We breakfasted early the next morning, and gladly settled accounts with the surly Holmes, who had infected — probably by
following the example of Mr. Caudle in later life—his pretty wife
with his own surliness. Shortly after starting—at 8 30 A.M.—
we saw a little clump of seven Indian lodges, which our experience soon taught us were the property of a white; the proprietor
met us on the road, and was introduced with due ceremony by
Mr. Macarthy. "Uncle Jack" (Robinson, really) is a well-known
name between South Pass and Great Salt Lake City; he has
spent thirty-four years in the mountains, and has saved some
$75,000, which have been properly invested at St. Louis; as
might be expected, he prefers the home of his adoption and his
Indian spouse, who has made him the happy father of I know not
how many children, to good society and bad air farther east.

Our road lay along the valley of Black's Fork, which here flows
from the southwest to the northeast; the bottom produced in

M

plenty luxuriant grass, the dandelion, and the purple aster, thickets of a shrub-like hawthorn (cratœgus), black and white currants, the willow and the cotton-wood. When almost in sight of the military post we were addressed by two young officers, one of them an assistant surgeon, who had been engaged in the healthful and exciting pursuit of a badger, whose markings, by-the-by, greatly differ from the European; they recognized the uniform, and accompanied us to the station.

Fort Bridger lies 124 miles from Great Salt Lake City; according to the drivers, however, the road might be considerably shortened. The position is a fertile basin cut into a number of bits by Black's Fork, which disperses itself into four channels about 1·5 mile above the station, and forms again a single bed about two miles below. The fort is situated upon the westernmost islet. It is, as usual, a mere cantonment, without any attempt at fortification, and at the time of my visit was garrisoned by two companies of foot, under the command of Captain F. Gardner, of the 10th Regiment. The material of the houses is pine and cedar brought from the Uinta Hills, whose black flanks supporting snowy cones rise at the distance of about thirty-five miles. They are a sanitarium, except in winter, when under their influence the mercury sinks to —20° F., not much less rigorous than Minnesota, and they are said to shelter grizzly bears and an abundance of smaller game.

The fort was built by Colonel James Bridger, now the oldest trapper on the Rocky Mountains, of whom Messrs. Frémont and Stansbury have both spoken in the highest terms. He divides with Christopher Carson, the Kit Carson of the Wind River and the Sierra Nevada explorations, the honor of being the best guide and interpreter in the Indian country: the palm for prudence is generally given to the former; for dash and hard fighting to the latter, although, it is said, the mildest mannered of men. Colonel Bridger, when an Indian trader, placed this post upon a kind of neutral ground between the Snakes and Crows (Hapsaroke) on the north, the Ogalalas and other Sioux to the east, the Arapahoes and Cheyennes on the south, and the various tribes of Yutas (Utahs) on the southwest. He had some difficulties with the Mormons, and Mrs. Mary Ettie Smith, in a volume concerning which something will be said at a future opportunity, veraciously reports his barbarous murder, some years ago, by the Danite band. He was at the time of my visit absent on an exploratory expedition with Captain Raynolds.

Arrived at Fort Bridger, our first thought was to replenish our whisky-keg: its emptiness was probably due to the "rapid evaporation in such an elevated region imperfectly protected by timber;" but, however that may be, I never saw liquor disappear at such a rate before. *Par parenthèse*, our late friends the officials had scarcely been more fortunate: they had watched their whis-

ky with the eyes of Argus, yet, as the driver facetiously remarked, though the quantity did not diminish too rapidly, the quality
lost strength every day.   We were conducted by Judge Carter to
a building which combined the function of post-office and sutler's
store, the judge being also sutler, and performing both parts, I
believe, to the satisfaction of every one.   After laying in an ample provision of biscuits for Miss May and korn-schnapps for ourselves, we called upon the commanding officer, who introduced us
to his officers, and were led by Captain Cumming to his quarters,
where, by means of chat, "solace-tobacco," and toddy—which in
these regions signifies "cold with"—we soon worked our way
through the short three quarters of an hour allowed us.   The officers complained very naturally of their isolation and unpleasant
duty, which principally consists in keeping the roads open for, and
the Indians from cutting off, parties of unmanageable emigrants,
who look upon the federal army as their humblest servants.   At
Camp Scott, near Bridger, the army of the federal government
halted under canvas during the severe winter of 1857–1858, and
the subject is still sore to military ears.

We left Bridger at 10 A.M.   Macarthy explained away the disregard for the comfort of the public on the part of the contractors
in not having a station at the fort by declaring that they could
obtain no land in a government reservation; moreover, that forage there would be scarce and dear, while the continual influx of
Indians would occasion heavy losses in cattle.   At Bridger the
road forks: the northern line leads to Soda or Beer Springs,* the
southern to Great Salt Lake City.   Following the latter, we crossed the rough timber bridges that spanned the net-work of streams,
and entered upon another expanse of degraded ground, covered
as usual with water-rolled pebbles of granite and porphyry, flint
and greenstone.   On the left was a butte with steep bluff sides,
called the Race-course: the summit, a perfect *mesa*, is said to be
quite level, and to measure exactly a mile round—the rule of the
American hippodrome.   Like these earth formations generally,
it points out the ancient level of the land before water had washed away the outer film of earth's crust.   The climate in this part,
as indeed every where between the South Pass and the Great Salt

---

* These springs of sadly prosaic name are the greatest curiosity to be seen on the
earth.   They lie but a short distance east of the junction of the Fort Hall and the
California roads, and are scattered over, perhaps, 40 acres of volcanic ground.   They
do not, like most springs, run out of the sides of hills, but boil up directly from a level plain.   The water contains a gas, and has quite an acid taste: when exposed to
the sun or air, it passes but a short distance before it takes the formation of a crust
or solid coat of scarlet hue, so that the continued boiling of any of these fountains
will "create a stone to the height of its source (15 or twenty feet) some 10 to 20 feet
in diameter at the bottom, and from 2 to 3 feet at the top."   After arriving at a uniform height, the water has ceased to run from several of the "eyes" to burst out in
some other place.   The water spurts from some of these very beautifully.—Horn's
"Overland Guide to California," p. 38.   They are also described by Colonel Frémont: "Expedition to Oregon and North California (1843–44)," p. 136.

Lake Valley, was an exaggeration of the Italian, with hot days, cool nights, and an incomparable purity and tenuity of atmosphere. We passed on the way a party of emigrants, numbering 359 souls and driving 39 wagons. They were commanded by the patriarch of Mormondom, otherwise Captain John Smith, the eldest son of Hyrum Smith, a brother of Mr. Joseph Smith the Prophet, and who, being a child at the time of the murderous affair at Carthage, escaped being coiffe'd with the crown of martyrdom. He rose to the patriarchate on the 18th of February, 1855; his predecessor was "old John Smith"—uncle to Mr. Joseph, and successor to Mr. Hyrum Smith—who died the 23d of May, 1854. He was a fair-complexioned man, with light hair. His followers accepted gratefully some provisions with which we could afford to part.

After passing the Mormons we came upon a descent which appeared little removed from an angle of 35°, and suggested the propriety of walking down. There was an attempt at a zigzag, and, for the benefit of wagons, a rough wall of stones had been run along the sharper corners. At the foot of the hill we remounted, and, passing through a wooded bottom, reached at 12 15 P.M.—after fording the Big Muddy—Little Muddy Creek, upon whose banks stood the station. Both these streams are branches of the Ham's Fork of Green River; and, according to the well-known "rule of contrary," their waters are clear as crystal, showing every pebble in their beds.

Little Muddy was kept by a Canadian, a chatty, lively, good-humored fellow blessed with a sour English wife. Possibly the heat —the thermometer showed 95° F. in the shade—had turned her temper; fortunately, it had not similarly affected the milk and cream, which were both unusually good. Jean-Baptiste, having mistaken me for a *Française de France*, a being which he seemed to regard as little lower than the angels—I was at no pains to disabuse him—was profuse in his questionings concerning his imperial majesty, the emperor, carefully confounding him with the first of the family; and so pleased was he with my responses, that for the first time on that route I found a man ready to spurn *cet animal féroce qu'on appelle la pièce de cinq francs*—in other words, the "almighty dollar."

We bade adieu to Little Muddy at noon, and entered a new country, a broken land of spurs and hollows, in parts absolutely bare, in others clothed with a thick vegetation. Curiously shaped hills, and bluffs of red earth capped with a clay which much resembled snow, bore a thick growth of tall firs and pines whose sombre uniform contrasted strangely with the brilliant leek-like, excessive green foliage, and the tall, note-paper-colored trunks of the ravine-loving quaking asp (*Populus tremuloides*). The mixture of colors was bizarre in the extreme, and the lay of the land, an uncouth system of converging, diverging, and parallel ridges, with deep divisions—in one of these ravines, which is unusually broad and grassy, rise the so-called Copperas Springs—was hardly less striking. We ran winding along a crest of rising ground, passing rapidly, by way of farther comparison, two wretched Mormons, man and woman, who were driving, at a snail's pace, a permanently lamed ox, and after a long ascent stood upon the summit of Quaking-Asp Hill.

Quaking-Asp Hill, according to the drivers, is 1000 feet higher than the South Pass, which would exalt its station to 8400 feet; other authorities, however, reduce it to 7900. The descent was long and rapid—so rapid, indeed, that oftentimes when the block of wood which formed our brake dropped a bit of the old shoe-sole nailed upon it to prevent ignition, I felt, as man may be excused for feeling, that catching of the breath that precedes the first five-barred gate after a night of "heavy wet." The sides of the road were rich in vegetation, stunted oak, black-jack, and box elder of the stateliest stature; above rose the wild cherry, and the service-tree formed the bushes below. The descent, besides being decidedly sharp, was exceedingly devious, and our frequent "shaves"—a train of Mormon wagons was crawling down at the same time—made us feel somewhat thankful that we reached the bottom without broken bones.

The train was commanded by a Captain Murphy, who, as one might expect from the name, had hoisted the Stars and Stripes—it was the only instance of such loyalty seen by us on the Plains. The emigrants had left Council Bluffs on the 20th of June, an unusually late date, and, though weather-beaten, all looked well. Inspirited by our success in surmounting the various difficulties of the way, we "poked fun" at an old Yorkshireman, who was assumed, by way of mirth, to be a Cœlebs in search of polygamy at an epoch of life when perhaps the blessing might come too late; and at an exceedingly plain middle-aged and full-blooded negro woman, who was fairly warned—the children of Ham are not admitted to the communion of the Saints, and consequently to the forgiveness of sins and a free seat in Paradise—that she was "carrying coals to Newcastle."

As the rays of the sun began to slant we made Sulphur Creek; it lies at the foot of a mountain called Rim Base, because it is the eastern wall of the great inland basin; westward of this point the waters can no longer reach the Atlantic or the Pacific; each is destined to feed the lakes,

"Nec Oceani pervenit ad undas."

Beyond Sulphur Creek, too, the face of the country changes; the sedimentary deposits are no longer seen; the land is broken and confused, upheaved into huge masses of rock and mountains broken by deep kanyons, ravines, and water-gaps, and drained by innumerable streamlets. The exceedingly irregular lay of the land makes the road devious, and the want of level ground, which is found only in dwarf parks and prairillons, would greatly add to the expense of a railway. We crossed the creek, a fetid stagnant water, about ten feet wide, lying in a bed of black infected mud: during the spring rains, when flowing, it is said to be wholesome enough. On the southern side of the valley there are some fine fountains, and on the eastern are others strongly redolent of sulphur; broad seams of coal crop out from the northern bluffs, and about a mile distant in the opposite direction are the Tar Springs, useful for greasing wagon-wheels and curing galled-backed horses.

Following the valley, which was rough and broken as it well could be, we crossed a small divide, and came upon the plain of the Bear River, a translation of the Indian Kuiyápá. It is one of the most important tributaries of the Great Salt Lake. Heading in the Uinta Range to the east of Kamas Prairie,* it flows with a tortuous course to the northwest, till, reaching Beer Springs, it turns sharply round with a horseshoe bend, and sets to the southwest, falling into the general reservoir at a bight called Bear-River Bay. According to the mountaineers, it springs not far from the sources of the Weber River and of the Timpanogos Water. Coal was found some years ago upon the banks of the Bear River, and more lately near Weber River and Silver Creek. It is the easternmost point to which Mormonism can extend *main forte;* for fugitives from justice "over Bear River" is like "over Jordan." The aspect of the valley, here half a mile broad, was prepossessing. Beyond a steep terrace, or step which compelled us all to dismount, the clear stream, about 400 feet in width, flowed through narrow lines of willows, cotton-wood, and large trees, which waved in the cool refreshing western wind; grass carpeted the middle levels, and above all rose red cliffs and buttresses of frowning rock.

We reached the station at 5 30 P.M. The valley was dotted with the tents of the Mormon emigrants, and we received sundry visits of curiosity; the visitors, mostly of the sex conventionally termed the fair, contented themselves with entering, sitting down, looking hard, tittering to one another, and departing with Parthian glances that had little power to hurt. From the men we heard tidings of "a massacre" of emigrants in the north, and a defeat of Indians in the west. Mr. Myers, the station-master, was an English Saint, who had lately taken to himself a fifth wife, after severally divorcing the others; his last choice was not without comeliness, but her reserve was extreme; she could hardly be coaxed out of a "Yes, sir." I found Mr. Myers diligently perusing a translation of "Volney's Ruins of Empire;" we had a chat about the Old and the New Country, which led us to sleeping-teme. I had here a curious instance of the effect of the associa-

---

* So called from the *Camassia esculenta*, the Pomme des Prairies or Pomme Blanche of the Canadians, and the prairie turnip and breadroot of the Western hunters. The Kamas Prairie is a pretty little bit of clear and level ground near the head of the Timpanogos River.

tion of words, in hearing a by-stander apply to the Founder of Christianity the "Mr." which is the "*Kyrios*" of the West, and is always prefixed to "Joseph Smith:" he stated that the mission of the latter was "far ahead of" that of the former prophet, which, by-the-by, is not the strict Mormon doctrine.   My companion and his family preferred as usual the interior of the mail-wagon, and it was well that they did so; after a couple of hours entered Mr. Macarthy, very drunk and "fighting mad."   He called for supper, but supper was past and gone, so he supped upon "fids" of raw meat.   Excited by this lively food, he began a series of caprioles, which ended, as might be expected, in a rough-and-tumble with the other three youths who occupied the hard floor of the ranch.   To Mr. Macarthy's language on that occasion *horresco referens ;* every word was apparently English, but so perverted, misused, and mangled, that the home reader would hardly have distinguished it from High-Dutch: *e. g.*, "I'm intire mad as a meat-axe; now du don't, I tell ye; say, *you*, shut up in a winkin', or I'll be chawed up if I don't run over *you;* 'can't come that 'ere tarnal carryin' on over *me*," and—*O si sic omnia!*   As no weapons, revolvers, or bowie-knives were to the fore, I thought the best thing was to lie still and let the storm blow over, which it did in a quarter of an hour.   Then, all serene, Mr. Macarthy called for a pipe, excused himself ceremoniously to himself for taking the liberty with the "Cap's." meerschaum solely upon the grounds that it was the only article of the kind to be found at so late an hour, and presently fell into a deep slumber upon a sleeping contrivance composed of a table for the upper and a chair for the lower portion of his person.   I envied him the favors of Morpheus: the fire soon died out, the cold wind whistled through the crannies, and the floor was knotty and uneven.

Echo Kanyon.   August 24th.

At 8 15 A.M. we were once more *en voyage.*   Mr. Macarthy was very red-eyed as he sat on the stool of penitence: what seemed to vex him most was having lost certain newspapers directed to a friend and committed to his private trust, a mode of insuring their safe arrival concerning which he had the day before expressed the highest opinion.   After fording Bear River—this part of the land was quite a grave-yard—we passed over rough ground, and, descending into a bush, were shown on a ridge to the right a huge Stonehenge, a crown of broken and somewhat lanceolate perpendicular conglomerates or cemented pudding-stones called not inappropriately Needle Rocks.   At Egan's Creek, a tributary of the Yellow Creek, the wild geraniums and the willows flourished despite the six feet of snow which sometimes lies in these bottoms.   We then crossed Yellow Creek, a water trending northeastward, and feeding, like those hitherto forded, Bear River: the bottom, a fine broad meadow, was a favorite camping-ground, as

the many fire-places proved. Beyond the stream we ascended
Yellow-Creek Hill, a steep chain which divides the versant of the
Bear River eastward from that of Weber River to the west. The
ascent might be avoided, but the view from the summit is a fine
panorama. The horizon behind us is girt by a mob of hills,
Bridger's Range, silver-veined upon a dark blue ground; nearer,
mountains and rocks, cones and hog-backs, are scattered about in
admirable confusion, divided by shaggy rollers and dark ravines,
each with its own little water-course. In front the eye runs down
the long bright red line of Echo Kanyon, and rests with astonishment upon its novel and curious features, the sublimity of its
broken and jagged peaks, divided by dark abysses, and based
upon huge piles of disjointed and scattered rock. On the right,
about half a mile north of the road, and near the head of the kanyon, is a place that adds human interest to the scene. Cache
Cave is a dark, deep, natural tunnel in the rock, which has sheltered many a hunter and trader from wild weather and wilder
men: the wall is probably of marl and earthy limestone, whose
whiteness is set off by the ochrish brick-red of the ravine below.

Echo Kanyon has a total length of twenty-five to thirty miles,
and runs in a southeasterly direction to the Weber River. Near
the head it is from half to three quarters of a mile wide, but its
irregularity is such that no average breadth can be assigned to it.
The height of the buttresses on the right or northern side varies
from 300 to 500 feet; they are denuded and water-washed by the
storms that break upon them under the influence of southerly
gales; their strata here are almost horizontal; they are inclined
at an angle of 45°, and the strike is northeast and southwest. The
opposite or southern flank, being protected from the dashing and
weathering of rain and wind, is a mass of rounded soil-clad hills,
or sloping slabs of rock, earth-veiled, and growing tussocks of
grass. Between them runs the clear, swift, bubbling stream, in
a pebbly bed now hugging one, then the other side of the chasm:
it has cut its way deeply below the surface; the banks or benches
of stiff alluvium are not unfrequently twenty feet high; in places
it is partially dammed by the hand of Nature, and every where
the watery margin is of the brightest green, and overgrown with
grass, nettles, willow thickets, in which the hop is conspicuous,
quaking asp, and other taller trees. Echo Kanyon has but one
fault: its sublimity will make all similar features look tame.

We entered the kanyon in somewhat a serious frame of mind;
our team was headed by a pair of exceedingly restive mules; we
had remonstrated against the experimental driving being done
upon our vile bodies, but the reply was that the animals must be
harnessed at some time. We could not, however, but remark the
wonderful picturesqueness of a scene—of a nature which in parts
seemed lately to have undergone some grand catastrophe. The
gigantic red wall on our right was divided into distinct blocks or

quarries by a multitude of minor lateral kanyons, which, after rains, add their tribute to the main artery, and each block was subdivided by the crumbling of the softer and the resistance of the harder material—a clay conglomerate. The color varied in places from white and green to yellow, but for the most part it was a dull ochrish red, that brightened up almost to a straw tint where the sunbeams fell slantingly upon it from the strip of blue above. All served to set off the curious architecture of the smaller masses. A whole Petra was there, a system of projecting prisms, pyramids, and pagoda towers, a variety of form that enabled you to see whatever your peculiar vanity might be—columns, porticoes, façades, and pedestals. Twin lines of bluffs, a succession of buttresses all fretted and honeycombed, a double row of steeples slipped from perpendicularity, frowned at each other across the gorge. And the wondrous variety was yet more varied by the kaleidoscopic transformation caused by change of position: at every different point the same object bore a different aspect.

And now, while we are dashing over the bouldered crossings; while our naughty mules, as they tear down the short steep pitches, swing the wheels of the mail-wagon within half a foot of the high bank's crumbling edge; while poor Mrs. Dana closes her eyes and clasps her husband's hand, and Miss May, happily unconscious of all peril, amuses herself by perseveringly perching upon the last toe that I should have been inclined to offer, the monotony of the risk may be relieved by diverting our thoughts to the lessons taught by the scenery around.

An American artist might extract from such scenery as Church Butte and Echo Kanyon a system of architecture as original and national as Egypt ever borrowed from her sandstone ledges, or the North of Europe from the solemn depths of her fir forests. But Art does not at present exist in America; as among their forefathers farther east, of artists they have plenty, of Art nothing. We can explain the presence of the phenomenon in England, where that grotesqueness and bizarrerie of taste which is observable in the uneducated, and which, despite collections and art-missions, hardly disappears in those who have studied the purest models, is the natural growth of man's senses and perceptions exposed for generation after generation to the unseen, unceasing, ever-active effect of homely objects, the desolate aspects of the long and dreary winters, and the humidity which shrouds the visible world with its dull gray coloring. Should any one question the fact that Art is not yet English, let him but place himself in the centre of the noblest site in Europe, Trafalgar Square, and own that no city in the civilized world ever presented such a perfect sample of barbarous incongruity, from mast-headed Nelson with his coil behind him, the work of the Satirist's "one man and small boy," to the two contemptible squirting things that throw

water upon the pavement at his feet. Mildly has the "Thunder-
er" described it as the "chosen home of exquisite dullness and
stilted mediocrity." The cause above assigned to the fact is at
least reasonable. Every traveler, who, after passing through the
fruitful but unpicturesque orchard grounds lying between La
Manche and Paris, and the dull flats, with their melancholy poplar lines, between Paris and Lyons, arrives at Avignon, and observes the picturesqueness which every object, natural or artificial,
begins to assume, the grace and beauty which appear even in the
humblest details of scenery, must instinctively feel that he is entering the land of Art. Not of that Art which depends for development upon the efforts of a few exceptional individuals, but
the living Art which the constant contemplation of a glorious
nature,

> "That holy Virgin of the sage's creed,"

makes part of a people's organization and development. Art,
heavenly maid, is not easily seduced to wander far from her place
of birth. Born and cradled upon the all-lovely shores of that inland sea, so choicely formed by Nature's hand to become the
source and centre of mankind's civilization, she loses health and
spirits in the frigid snowy north, while in the tropical regions—
Nubia and India—her mind is vitiated by the rank and luxuriant scenery around her. A "pretty bit of home scenery," with
dumpy church tower — battlemented as the house of worship
ought *not* to be — on the humble hill, red brick cottages, with
straight tiled roofs and parallelogramic casements, and dwelling-
houses all stiff-ruled lines and hard sharp angles, the straight
road and the trimmed hedgerow — such scenery, I assert, never
can make an artistic people; it can only lead, in fact, to a nation's last phase of artistic bathos—a Trafalgar Square.

The Anglo-Americans have other excuses, but not this. Their
broad lands teem with varied beauties of the highest order, which
it would be tedious to enumerate. They have used, for instance,
the Indian corn for the acanthus in their details of architecture
—why can not they try a higher flight? Man may not, we readily grant, expect to be a great poet because Niagara is a great
cataract; yet the presence of such objects must quicken the imagination of the civilized as of the savage race that preceded him.
It is true that in America the class that can devote itself exclusively to the cultivation and the study of refinement and art is
still, comparatively speaking, small; that the care of politics, the
culture of science, mechanical and theoretic, and the pursuit of
cash, have at present more hold upon the national mind than
what it is disposed to consider the effeminating influences of the
humanizing studies; that, moreover, the efforts of youthful genius in the body corporate, as in the individual, are invariably
imitative, leading through the progressive degrees of reflection
and reproduction to originality. But, valid as they are, these

reasons will not long justify such freaks as the Americo-Grecian capitol at Richmond, a barn with the tritest of all exordiums, a portico which is original in one point only, viz., that it wants the portico's only justification—steps; or the various domes originally borrowed from that bulb which has been demolished at Washington, scattered over the country, and suggesting the idea that the shape has been borrowed from the butt end of a sliced cucumber. Better far the warehouses of Boston, with their monoliths and frontages of rough Quincy granite; they, at least, are unpretending, and of native growth: no bad test of the native mind.

After a total of eighteen miles we passed Echo Station, a half-built ranch, flanked by well-piled haystacks for future mules. The ravine narrowed as we advanced to a mere gorge, and the meanderings of the stream contracted the road and raised the banks to a more perilous height. A thicker vegetation occupied the bottom, wild roses and dwarfish oaks contending for the mastery of the ground. About four miles from the station we were shown a defile where the Latter-Day Saints, in 1857, headed by General D. H. Wells, now the third member of the Presidency, had prepared modern Caudine Forks for the attacking army of the United States. Little breastworks of loose stones, very like the "sangahs" of the Affghan Ghauts, had been thrown up where the precipices commanded the road, and there were four or five remains of dams intended to raise the water above the height of the soldiers' ammunition pouches. The situation did not appear to me well chosen. Although the fortified side of the bluff could not be crowned on account of deep chasms that separated the various blocks, the southern acclivities might have been occupied by sharpshooters so effectually that the fire from the breastworks would soon have been silenced; moreover, the defenders would have risked being taken in rear by a party creeping through the chapparal* in the sole of the kanyon. Mr. Macarthy related a characteristic trait concerning two warriors of the Nauvoo Legion. Unaccustomed to perpendicular fire, one proposed that his comrade should stand upon the crest of the precipice and.see if the bullet reached him or not; the comrade, thinking the request highly reasonable, complied with it, and received a yäger-ball through his forehead.

Traces of beaver were frequent in the torrent-bed; the "broad-tailed animal" is now molested by the Indians rather than by the whites. On this stage magpies and ravens were unusually numerous; foxes slunk away from us, and on one of the highest

---

* The Spanish "chapparal" means a low oak copse. The word has been naturalized in Texas and New Mexico, and applied to the dense and bushy undergrowth, chiefly of briers and thorns, disposed in patches from a thicket of a hundred yards to the whole flank of a mountain range (especially in the Mexican Tierra Caliente), and so closely entwined that nothing larger than a wolf can force a way through it.

bluffs a coyote stood as on a pedestal; as near Baffin Sea, these craggy peaks are their favorite howling-places during the severe snowy winters. We longed for a thunder-storm: flashing lightnings, roaring thunders, stormy winds, and dashing rains—in fact, a tornado—would be the fittest setting for such a picture, so wild, so sublime as Echo Kanyon. But we longed in vain. The day was persistently beautiful, calm and mild as a May forenoon in the Grecian Archipelago. We were also disappointed in our natural desire to hold some converse with the nymph who had lent her name to the ravine—the reverberation is said to be remarkably fine—but the temper of our animals would not have endured it, and the place was not one that admitted experiments. Rain had lately fallen, as we saw from the mud-puddles in the upper course of the kanyon, and the road was in places pitted with drops which were not frequent enough to allay the choking dust. A fresh yet familiar feature now appeared. The dews, whose existence we had forgotten on the prairies, were cold and clammy in the early mornings; the moist air, condensed by contact with the cooler substances on the surface of the ground, stood in large drops upon the leaves and grasses. As we advanced the bed of the ravine began to open out, the angle of descent became more obtuse; a stretch of level ground appeared in front, where for some hours the windings of the kanyon had walled us in, and at 2 30 P.M. we debouched upon the Weber-River Station. It lies at the very mouth of the ravine, almost under the shadow of lofty red bluffs, called "The Obelisks;" and the green and sunny landscape, contrasting with the sterile grandeur behind, is exceedingly pleasing.

After the emotions of the drive, a little rest was by no means unpleasant. The station was tolerably comfortable, and the welcome addition of potatoes and onions to our usual fare was not to be despised. The tenants of the ranch were Mormons, civil and communicative. They complained sadly of the furious rain-storms, which the funnel-like gorge brings down upon them, and the cold draughts from five feet deep of snow which pour down upon the milder valley.

At 4 30 we resumed our journey along the plain of the Weber or Webber River. It is second in importance only to the Bear River: it heads near the latter, and, flowing in a devious course toward the northwest, falls into the Great Salt Lake a few miles south of its sister stream, and nearly opposite Frémont's Island. The valley resembles that described in yesterday's diary; it is, however, narrower, and the steep borders, which, if water-washed, would be red like the kanyon rocks, are well clothed with grass and herbages. In some places the land is defended by snake-fences in zigzags,* to oppose the depredations of emigrants' cattle

---

* This is the simplest of all fences, and therefore much used in the West. Tree-trunks are felled, and either used whole or split into rails; they are then disposed in

upon the wheat, barley, and stunted straggling corn within. After fording the river and crossing the bottom, we ascended steep banks, passed over a spring of salt water five miles from the station, and halted for a few minutes to exchange news with the mail-wagon that had left Great Salt Lake City this (Friday) morning. Followed a rough and rugged tract of land apparently very trying to the way-worn cattle; many deaths had taken place at this point, and the dead lay well preserved as the monks of St. Bernard. After a succession of chuck-holes, rises, and falls, we fell into the valley of Bauchmin's Creek. It is a picturesque hollow; at the head is a gateway of red clay, through which the stream passes; the sides also are red, and as the glow and glory of the departing day lingered upon the heights, even artemisia put on airs of bloom and beauty, blushing in contrast with the sharp metallic green of the quaking asp and the duller verdure of the elder (*Alnus viridis*). As the evening closed in, the bottom-land became more broken, the path less certain, and the vegetation thicker: the light of the moon, already diminished by the narrowness of the valley, seemed almost to be absorbed by the dark masses of copse and bush. We were not sorry to make, at 7 45 P.M., the "Carson-House Station" at Bauchmin's Fork—the traveling had been fast, seven miles an hour—where we found a log hut, a roaring fire, two civil Mormon lads, and some few "fixins" in the way of food. We sat for a time talking about matters of local importance, the number of emigrants, and horse-thieves, the prospects of the road, and the lay of the land. Bauchmin's Fork, we learned, is a branch of East Kanyon Creek, itself a tributary of the Weber River;* from the station an Indian trail leads over the mountains to Provo City. I slept comfortably enough upon the boards of an inner room, not, however, without some apprehensions of accidentally offending a certain skunk (*Mephitis mephitica*), which was in the habit of making regular nocturnal visits. I heard its puppy-like bark during the night, but escaped what otherwise might have happened.

And why, naturally asks the reader, did you not shut the door? Because there was none.

The End—Hurrah! August 25th.

To-day we are to pass over the Wasach,† the last and highest chain of the mountain mass between Fort Bridger and the Great

a long serrated line, each resting upon another at both ends, like the fingers of a man's right hand extended and inserted between the corresponding fingers of the left. The zigzag is not a picturesque object: in absolute beauty it is inferior even to our English trimmed hedgerow; but it is very economical, it saves space, it is easily and readily made, it can always serve for fuel, and, therefore, is to be respected, despite the homeliness of its appearance.

* In Captain Stansbury's map, Bauchmin's Fork is a direct influent, and one of the largest, too, of the Weber River.

† The word is generally written *Wasatch* or *Wahsatch*. In the latter the *h* is, as usual, *de trop;* and in both the *t*, though necessary in French, is totally uncalled for in English.

Salt Lake Valley, and—by the aid of St. James of Compostella, who is, I believe, bound over to be the patron of pilgrims in general—to arrive at our destination, New Hierosolyma, or Jerusalem, alias Zion on the tops of the mountains, the future city of Christ, where the Lord is to reign over the Saints, as a temporal king, in power and great glory.

So we girt our loins, and started, after a cup of tea and a biscuit, at 7 A.M., under the good guidance of Mr. Macarthy, who, after a whiskyless night, looked forward not less than ourselves to the run in. Following the course of Bauchmin's Creek, we completed the total number of fordings to thirteen in eight miles. The next two miles were along the bed of a water-course, a complete fiumara, through a bush full of tribulus, which accompanied us to the end of the journey. Presently the ground became rougher and steeper: we alighted, and set our beasts manfully against "Big Mountain,'' which lies about four miles from the station. The road bordered upon the wide arroyo, a tumbled bed of block and boulder, with water in places oozing and trickling from the clay walls, from the sandy soil, and from beneath the heaps of rock—living fountains these, most grateful to the parched traveler. The synclinal slopes of the chasm were grandly wooded with hemlocks, firs, balsam-pines, and other varieties of abies, some tapering up to the height of ninety feet, with an admirable regularity of form, color, and foliage. The varied hues of the quaking asp were there; the beech, the dwarf oak, and a thicket of elders and wild roses; while over all the warm autumnal tints already mingled with the bright green of summer. The ascent became more and more rugged: this steep pitch, at the end of a thousand miles of hard work and semi-starvation, causes the death of many a wretched animal, and we remarked that the bodies are not inodorous among the mountains as on the prairies. In the most fatiguing part we saw a hand-cart halted, while the owners, a man, a woman, and a boy, took breath. We exchanged a few consolatory words with them and hurried on. The only animal seen on the line, except the grasshopper, whose creaking wings gave forth an ominous note, was the pretty little chirping squirrel. The trees, however, in places bore the marks of huge talons, which were easily distinguished as the sign of bears. The grizzly does not climb except when young: this was probably the common brown variety. At half way the gorge opened out, assuming more the appearance of a valley; and in places, for a few rods, were dwarf stretches of almost level ground. Toward the Pass-summit the rise is sharpest: here we again descended from the wagon, which the four mules had work enough to draw, and the total length of its eastern rise was five miles. Big Mountain lies eighteen miles from the city. The top is a narrow crest, suddenly forming an acute based upon an obtuse angle.

From that eyrie, 8000 feet above sea level, the weary pilgrim first sights his shrine, the object of his long wanderings, hardships, and perils, the Happy Valley of the Great Salt Lake. The western horizon, when visible, is bounded by a broken wall of light blue mountain, the Oquirrh, whose northernmost bluff buttresses the southern.end of the lake, and whose eastern flank sinks in steps and terraces into a river basin, yellow with the sunlit golden corn, and somewhat pink with its carpeting of heath-like moss. In the foreground a semicircular sweep of hill-top and an inverted arch of rocky wall shuts out all but a few spans of the valley. These heights are rough with a shaggy forest, in some places black-green, in others of brownish-red, in others of the lightest ash-color, based upon a ruddy soil; while a few silvery veins of snow still streak the bare gray rocky flanks of the loftiest peak.

After a few minutes' delay to stand and gaze, we resumed the footpath way, while the mail-wagon, with wheels rough-locked, descended what appeared to be an impracticable slope. The summit of the Pass was well-nigh cleared of timber; the woodman's song informed us that the evil work was still going on, and that we are nearly approaching a large settlement. Thus stripped of their protecting fringes, the mountains are exposed to the heat of summer, that sends forth countless swarms of devastating crickets, grasshoppers, and blue-worms; and to the wintry cold, that piles up, four to six feet high—the mountain-men speak of thirty and forty—the snows drifted by the unbroken force of the winds. The Pass from November to February can be traversed by nothing heavier than "sleighs," and during the snow-storms even these are stopped. Falling into the gorge of Big Kanyon Creek, after a total of twelve hard miles from Bauchmin's Fork, we reached at 11 30 the station that bears the name of the water near which it is built. We were received by the wife of the proprietor, who was absent at the time of our arrival; and half stifled by the thick dust and the sun, which had raised the glass to 103°, we enjoyed copious draughts—*tant soit peu* qualified—of the cool but rather hard water that trickled down the hill into a trough by the house side. Presently the station-master, springing from his light "sulky," entered, and was formally introduced to us by Mr. Macarthy as Mr. Ephe Hanks. I had often heard of this individual as one of the old triumvirate of Mormon desperadoes, the other two being Orrin Porter Rockwell and Bill Hickman—as the leader of the dreaded Danite band, and, in short, as a model ruffian. The ear often teaches the eye to form its pictures: I had eliminated a kind of mental sketch of those assassin faces which one sees on the Apennines and Pyrenees, and was struck by what met the eye of sense. The "vile villain," as he has been called by anti-Mormon writers, who verily do not try to *ménager* their epithets, was a middle-sized, light-haired, good-looking man, with regular features, a pleasant and humorous countenance, and the manly manner of his early sailor life, touched with the rough cordiality of the mountaineer. " Frank as a bear-hunter" is a proverb in these lands. He had, like the rest of the triumvirate, and like most men (Anglo-Americans) of desperate courage and fiery, excitable temper, a clear, pale blue eye, verging upon gray, and looking as if it wanted nothing better than to light up, together with a cool and quiet glance that seemed to shun neither friend nor foe.

The terrible Ephe began with a facetious allusion to all our new dangers under the roof of a Danite, to which, in similar strain, I made answer that Danite or Damnite was pretty much the same to me. After dining, we proceeded to make trial of the air-cane, to which he took, as I could see by the way he handled it, and by the nod with which he acknowledged the observation, " almighty convenient sometimes not to make a noise, Mister," a great fancy. He asked me whether I had a mind to " have a slap" at his name-sake,* an offer which was gratefully accepted, under the promise that " cuffy" should previously be marked down so as to save a long ride and a troublesome trudge over the mountains. His battery of " killb'ars" was heavy and in good order, so that on this score there would have been no trouble, and the only tool he bade me bring was a Colt's revolver, dragoon size. He told me that he was likely to be in England next year, when he had set the " ole woman" to her work. I suppose my look was somewhat puzzled, for Mrs. Dana graciously explained that every Western wife, even when still, as Mrs. Ephe was, in her teens, commands that vener-able title, venerable, though somehow not generally coveted.

From Big Kanyon Creek Station to the city, the driver " reck-oned," was a distance of seventeen miles. We waited till the bright and glaring day had somewhat burned itself out; at noon heavy clouds came up from the south and southwest, casting a grateful shade and shedding a few drops of rain. After taking friendly leave of the " Danite" chief—whose cordiality of manner had prepossessed me strongly in his favor—we entered the mail-wagon, and prepared ourselves for the finale over the westernmost ridge of the stern Wasach.

After two miles of comparatively level ground we came to the foot of " Little Mountain," and descended from the wagon to re-lieve the poor devils of mules. The near slope was much short-er, but also it was steeper far than " Big Mountain." The coun-terslope was easier, though by no means pleasant to contemplate with the chance of an accident to the brake, which in all incon-venient places would part with the protecting shoe-sole. Beyond the eastern foot, which was ten miles distant from our destina-tion, we were miserably bumped and jolted over the broken ground at the head of Big Kanyon. Down this pass, whose name is a translation of the Yuta name Obitkokichi, a turbulent little mountain stream tumbles over its boulder-bed, girt with the usual sunflower, vines of wild hops, red and white willows, cotton-wood,

* " Ole Ephraim" is the mountain-man's *sobriquet* for the grizzly bear.

quaking asp, and various bushes near its cool watery margin, and upon the easier slopes of the ravine, with the shin or dwarf oak (*Quercus nana*), mountain mahogany, balsam, and other firs, pines, and cedars.   The road was a narrow shelf along the broader of the two spaces between the stream and the rock, and frequent fordings were rendered necessary by the capricious wanderings of the torrent.   I could not but think how horrid must have been its appearance when the stout-hearted Mormon pioneers first ventured to thread the defile, breaking their way through the dense bush, creeping and clinging like flies to the sides of the hills.   Even now accidents often occur; here, as in Echo Kanyon, we saw in more than one place unmistakable signs of upsets in the shape of broken spokes and yoke-bows.   At one of the most ticklish turns Macarthy kindly pointed out a little precipice where four of the mail passengers fell and broke their necks, a pure invention on his part, I believe, which fortunately, at that moment, did not reach Mrs. Dana's ears.   He also entertained us with many a tale, of which the hero was the redoubtable Hanks: how he had slain a buffalo bull single-handed with a bowie-knife; and how, on one occasion, when refused hospitality by his Lamanite brethren, he had sworn to have the whole village to himself, and had redeemed his vow by reappearing *in cuerpo*, with gestures so maniacal that the sulky Indians all fled, declaring him to be "bad medicine."   The stories had at least local coloring.

In due time, emerging from the gates, and portals, and deep serrations of the upper course, we descended into a lower level: here Big, now called Emigration Kanyon, gradually bulges out, and its steep slopes of grass and fern, shrubbery and stunted brush, fall imperceptibly into the plain.   The valley presently lay full before our sight.   At this place the pilgrim emigrants, like the hajjis of Mecca and Jerusalem, give vent to the emotions long pent up within their bosoms by sobs and tears, laughter and congratulations, psalms and hysterics.   It is indeed no wonder that the children dance, that strong men cheer and shout, and that nervous women, broken with fatigue and hope deferred, scream and faint; that the ignorant should fondly believe that the "Spirit of God pervades the very atmosphere," and that Zion on the tops of the mountains is nearer heaven than other parts of earth. In good sooth, though uninfluenced by religious fervor—beyond the natural satisfaction of seeing a bran-new Holy City — even I could not, after nineteen days in a mail-wagon, gaze upon the scene without emotion.

The sublime and the beautiful were in present contrast.   Switzerland and Italy lay side by side.   The magnificent scenery of the past mountains and ravines still floated before the retina, as emerging from the gloomy depths of the Golden Pass—the mouth of Emigration Kanyon is more poetically so called—we came suddenly in view of the Holy Valley of the West.

N

The hour was about 6 P.M.; the atmosphere was touched with a dreamy haze, as it generally is in the vicinity of the lake; a little bank of rose-colored clouds, edged with flames of purple and gold, floated in the upper air, while the mellow radiance of an American autumn, that bright interlude between the extremes of heat and cold, diffused its mild soft lustre over the face of earth.

The sun, whose slanting rays shone full in our eyes, was setting in a flood of heavenly light behind the bold, jagged outline of "Antelope Island," which, though distant twenty miles to the northwest, hardly appeared to be ten. At its feet, and then bounding the far horizon, lay, like a band of burnished silver, the Great Salt Lake, that still innocent Dead Sea. Southwestward also, and equally deceptive as regards distance, rose the boundary of the valley plain, the Oquirrh Range, sharply silhouetted by a sweep of sunshine over its summits, against the depths of an evening sky, in that direction so pure, so clear, that vision, one might fancy, could penetrate behind the curtain into regions beyond the confines of man's ken. In the brilliant reflected light, which softened off into a glow of delicate pink, we could distinguish the lines of Brigham's, Coon's, and other kanyons, which water has traced through the wooded flanks of the Oquirrh down to the shadows already purpling the misty benches at their base. Three distinct and several shades, light azure, blue, and brown-blue, graduated the distances, which extended at least thirty miles.

The undulating valley-plain between us and the Oquirrh Range is 12·15 miles broad, and markedly concave, dipping in the centre like the section of a tunnel, and swelling at both edges into benchlands, which mark the ancient bed of the lake. In some parts the valley was green; in others, where the sun shot its oblique beams, it was of a tawny yellowish-red, like the sands of the Arabian desert, with scatters of trees, where the Jordan of the West rolls its opaline wave through pasture-lands of dried grass dotted with flocks and herds, and fields of ripening yellow corn. Every thing bears the impress of handiwork, from the bleak benches behind to what was once a barren valley in front. Truly the Mormon prophecy had been fulfilled: already the howling wilderness —in which twelve years ago a few miserable savages, the half-naked Digger Indians, gathered their grass-seed, grasshoppers, and black crickets to keep life and soul together, and awoke with their war-cries the echo of the mountains, and the bear, the wolf, and the fox prowled over the site of a now populous city—"has blossomed like the rose."

This valley—this lovely panorama of green, and azure, and gold —this land, fresh, as it were, from the hands of God, is apparently girt on all sides by hills: the highest peaks, raised 7000 to 8000 feet above the plain of their bases, show by gulches veined with lines of snow that even in this season winter frowns upon the last smile of summer.

Advancing, we exchanged the rough cahues and the frequent fords of the ravine for a broad smooth highway, spanning the easternmost valley-bench—a terrace that drops like a Titanic step from the midst of the surrounding mountains to the level of the present valley-plain.   From a distance—the mouth of Emigration Kanyon is about 4·30 miles from the city—Zion, which is not on a hill, but, on the contrary, lies almost in the lowest part of the river-plain, is completely hid from sight, as if no such thing existed.   Mr. Macarthy, on application, pointed out the notabilia of the scene.

Northward, curls of vapor ascending from a gleaming sheet—the Lake of the Hot Springs—set in a bezel of emerald green, and bordered by another lake-bench upon which the glooms of evening were rapidly gathering, hung like a veil of gauze around the waist of the mountains.   Southward for twenty-five miles stretched the length of the valley, with the little river winding its way like a silver thread in a brocade of green and gold.   The view in this direction was closed by "Mountain Point," another formation of terraced range, which forms the water-gate of Jordan, and which conceals and separates the fresh water that feeds the Salt Lake—the Sea of Tiberias from the Dead Sea.

As we descend the Wasach Mountains, we could look back and enjoy the view of the eastern wall of the Happy Valley.   A little to the north of Emigration Kanyon, and about one mile nearer the settlement, is the Red Butte, a deep ravine, whose quarried sides show mottlings of the light ferruginous sandstone which was chosen for building the Temple wall.*   A little beyond it lies the single City of the Dead, decently removed three miles from the habitations of the living, and farther to the north is City-Creek Kanyon, which supplies the Saints with water for drinking and for irrigation.   Southeast of Emigration Kanyon are other ravines, Parley's, Mill Creek, Great Cotton-wood, and Little Cotton-wood, deep lines winding down the timbered flanks of the mountains, and thrown into relief by the darker and more misty shading of the farther flank-wall.

The "Twin Peaks," the highest points of the Wasach Mountains, are the first to be powdered over with the autumnal snow. When a black nimbus throws out these piles, with their tilted-up rock strata, jagged edges, black flanks, rugged brows, and bald heads gilt by a gleam of sunset, the whole stands boldly out with that phase of sublimity of which the sense of immensity is the principal element.   Even in the clearest of weather they are rarely free from a fleecy cloud, the condensation of cold and humid air rolling up the heights and vanishing only to be renewed.

The bench-land then attracted our attention.   The soil is poor;

---

* At first a canal was dug through the bench to bring this material: the gray granite now used for the Temple is transported in carts from the southern part of the valley.

sprinkled with thin grass, in places showing a suspicious white-ness, with few flowers, and chiefly producing a salsolaceous plant like the English samphire. In many places lay long rows of bare circlets, like deserted tent-floors; they proved to be ant-hills, on which light ginger-colored swarms were working hard to throw up the sand and gravel that every where in this valley underlie the surface. The eastern valley-bench, upon whose western de-clivity the city lies, may be traced on a clear day along the base of the mountains for a distance of twenty miles: its average breadth is about eight miles.

After advancing about 1·50 mile over the bench ground, the city by slow degrees broke upon our sight. It showed, one may readily believe, to special advantage after the succession of Indian lodges, Canadian ranchos, and log-hut mail-stations of the prairies and the mountains. The site has been admirably chosen for drain-age and irrigation—so well, indeed, that a "Deus ex machinâ" must be brought to account for it.* About two miles north, and overlooking the settlements from a height of 400 feet, a detached cone, called Ensign Peak or Ensign Mount, rises at the end of a chain which, projected westward from the main range of the heights, overhangs and shelters the northeastern corner of the valley. Upon this "big toe of the Wasach range," as it is called by a local writer, the spirit of the martyred prophet, Mr. Joseph Smith, appeared to his successor, Mr. Brigham Young, and pointed out to him the position of the New Temple, which, after Zion had "got up into the high mountain," was to console the Saints for the loss of Nauvoo the Beautiful. The city—it is about two miles broad—runs parallel with the right bank of the Jordan, which forms its western limit. It is twelve to fifteen miles distant from the western range, ten from the debouchure of the river, and eight to nine from the nearest point of the lake—a respectful distance, which is not the least of the position's merits. It occupies the roll-ing brow of a slight decline at the western base of the Wasach—in fact, the lower, but not the lowest level of the eastern valley-bench; it has thus a compound slope from north to south, on the line of its water supplies, and from east to west, thus enabling it to drain off into the river.

The city revealed itself, as we approached, from behind its screen, the inclined terraces of the upper table-land, and at last it lay stretched before us as upon a map. At a little distance the

---

* I have frequently heard this legend from Gentiles, never from Mormons; yet even the Saints own that as early as 1842 visions of the mountains and kanyons, the valley and the lake, were revealed to Mr. Joseph Smith, jun., who declared it privily to the disciples whom he loved. Thus Messrs. O. Pratt and E. Snow, apostles, were enabled to recognize the Promised Land, as, the first of the pioneers, they issued from the ravines of the Wasach. Of course the Gentiles declare that the exodists hit upon the valley by the purest chance. The spot is becoming classical: here Judge and Apostle Phelps preached his "Sermon on the Mount," which, anti-Mor-mons say, was a curious contrast to the first discourse so named.

aspect was somewhat Oriental, and in some points it reminded me of modern Athens without the Acropolis. None of the buildings, except the Prophet's house, were whitewashed. The material— the thick, sun-dried adobe, common to all parts of the Eastern world*—was of a dull leaden blue, deepened by the atmosphere to a gray, like the shingles of the roofs. The number of gardens and compounds—each tenement within the walls originally received 1·50 square acre, and those outside from five to ten acres, according to their distance—the dark clumps and lines of bitter cotton-wood, locust, or acacia, poplars and fruit-trees, apples, peaches, and vines—how lovely they appeared, after the baldness of the prairies!—and, finally, the fields of long-eared maize and sweet sorghum strengthened the similarity to an Asiatic rather than to an American settlement. The differences presently became as salient. The farm-houses, with their stacks and stock, strongly suggested the Old Country. Moreover, domes and minarets— even churches and steeples—were wholly wanting, an omission that somewhat surprised me. The only building conspicuous from afar was the block occupied by the present Head of the Church. The court-house, with its tinned Muscovian dome, at the west end of the city; the arsenal, a barn-like structure, on a bench below the Jebel Nur of the valley—Ensign Peak; and a saw-mill, built beyond the southern boundary, were the next in importance.

On our way we passed the vestiges of an old moat, from which was taken the earth for the bulwarks of Zion. A Romulian wall, of puddle, mud, clay, and pebbles, six miles—others say 2600 acres —in length, twelve feet high, six feet broad at the base, and two and three quarters at the top, with embrasures five to six feet above the ground, and semi-bastions at half musket range, was decided, in 1853–54, to be necessary, as a defense against the Lamanites, whose name in the vulgar is Yuta Indians. Gentiles declare that the bulwarks were erected because the people wanting work were likely to "strike" faith, and that the amount of labor expended upon this folly would have irrigated as many thousand acres. Anti-Mormons have, of course, detected in the proceeding treacherous and treasonable intentions. Parenthetically, I must here warn the reader that in Great Salt Lake City there are three distinct opinions concerning, three several reasons for, and three diametrically different accounts of, every thing that happens, viz., that of the Mormons, which is invariably one-sided; that of the Gentiles, which is sometimes fair and just; and that of the anti-Mormons, which is always prejudiced and violent. A glance will show that this much-talked-of fortification is utterly harmless; it is commanded in half a dozen places; it could not

---

* The very word is Spanish, derived from the Arabic الطوب, meaning "the brick·" it is known throughout the West, and is written *adobies*, and prononnced *dobies*.

keep out half a dozen sappers for a quarter of an hour; and now, as it has done its work, its foundations are allowed to become salt, and to crumble away.

The road ran through the Big Field, southeast of the city, six miles square, and laid off in five-acre lots. Presently, passing the precincts of habitation, we entered, at a slapping pace, the second ward, called Denmark, from its tenants, who mostly herd together. The disposition of the settlement is like that of the nineteenth century New-World cities—from Washington to the future metropolis of the great Terra Australis—a system of right angles, the roads, streets, and lanes, if they can be called so, intersecting one another. The advantages or disadvantages of the rectangular plan have been exhausted in argument; the new style is best suited, I believe, for the New, as the old must, perforce, remain in the Old World. The suburbs are thinly settled; the mass of habitations lie around and south of Temple Block. The streets of the suburbs are mere roads, cut by deep ups and downs, and by gutters on both sides, which, though full of pure water, have no bridge save a plank at the *trottoirs*. In summer the thoroughfares are dusty, in wet weather deep with viscid mud.

The houses are almost all of one pattern—a barn shape, with wings and lean-tos, generally facing, sometimes turned endways to the street, which gives a suburban look to the settlement; and the diminutive casements show that window-glass is not yet made in the Valley. In the best abodes the adobe rests upon a few courses of sandstone, which prevent undermining by water or ground-damp, and it must always be protected by a coping from the rain and snow. The poorer are small, low, and hut-like; others are long single-storied buildings, somewhat like stables, with many entrances. The best houses resemble East Indian bungalows, with flat roofs, and low, shady verandas, well trellised, and supported by posts or pillars. All are provided with chimneys, and substantial doors to keep out the piercing cold. The offices are always placed, for hygienic reasons, outside; and some have a story and a half—the latter intended for lumber and other stores. I looked in vain for the out-house harems, in which certain romancers concerning things Mormon had informed me that wives are kept, like any other stock. I presently found this but one of a multitude of delusions. Upon the whole, the Mormon settlement was a vast improvement upon its contemporaries in the valleys of the Mississippi and the Missouri.

The road through the faubourg was marked by posts and rails, which, as we advanced toward the heart of the city, were replaced by neat palings. The garden-plots were small, as sweet earth must be brought down from the mountains; and the flowers were principally those of the Old Country—the red French bean, the rose, the geranium, and the single pink; the ground or winter ·cherry was common; so were nasturtiums; and we saw tansy, but

STORES IN MAIN STREET.

not that plant for which our souls, well-nigh weary of hopes of juleps long deferred, chiefly lusted—mint. The fields were large and numerous, but the Saints have too many and various occupations to keep them, Moravian-like, neat and trim; weeds overspread the ground; often the wild sunflower-tops outnumbered the heads of maize. The fruit had suffered from an unusually nipping frost in May; the peach-trees were barren; the vines bore no produce; only a few good apples were in Mr. Brigham Young's garden, and the watermelons were poor, yellow, and tasteless, like the African. On the other hand, potatoes, onions, cabbages, and cucumbers were good and plentiful, the tomato was ripening every where, fat full-eared wheat rose in stacks, and crops of excellent hay were scattered about near the houses. The people came to their doors to see the mail-coach, as if it were the "Derby dilly" of old, go by. I could not but be struck by the modified English appearance of the colony, and by the prodigious numbers of the white-headed children.

Presently we debouched upon the main thoroughfare, the centre of population and business, where the houses of the principal Mormon dignitaries and the stores of the Gentile merchants combine to form the city's only street which can be properly so called. It is, indeed, both street and market, for, curious to say, New Zion has not yet built for herself a bazar or market-place. Nearly opposite the Post-office, in a block on the eastern side, with a long veranda, supported by trimmed and painted posts, was a two-storied, pent-roofed building, whose sign-board, swinging to a tall, gibbet-like flag-staff, dressed for the occasion, announced it to be the Salt Lake House, the principal, if not the only establishment of the kind in New Zion. In the Far West, one learns not to expect much of the hostelry;* I had not seen aught so grand for many a day. Its depth is greater than its frontage, and behind it, secured by a *porte cochère*, is a large yard for corraling cattle. A rough-looking crowd of drivers, drivers' friends, and idlers, almost every man openly armed with revolver and bowie-knife, gathered round the doorway to greet Jim, and "prospect" the "new lot;" and the host came out to assist us in transporting our scattered effects. We looked vainly for a bar on the ground floor; a bureau for registering names was there, but (temperance, in public at least, being the order of the day) the usual tempting array of bottles and decanters was not forthcoming; up stairs we found a Gentile ballroom, a tolerably furnished sitting-room, and bedchambers, apparently made out of a single apartment by partitions too thin to be strictly agreeable. The household had its deficiencies; blacking, for instance, had run out, and servants

---

* I subjoin one of the promising sort of advertisements:
"Tom Mitchell!!! dispenses comfort to the weary (!), feeds the hungry (!!), and cheers the gloomy (!!!), at his old, well-known stand, thirteen miles east of Fort Des Moines. *Don't pass by me.*"

could not be engaged till the expected arrival of the hand-cart train.   However, the proprietor, Mr. Townsend, a Mormon, from the State of Maine—when expelled from Nauvoo, he had parted with land, house, and furniture for $50—who had married an Englishwoman, was in the highest degree civil and obliging, and he attended personally to our wants, offered his wife's services to Mrs. Dana, and put us all in the best of humors, despite the closeness of the atmosphere, the sadness ever attending one's first entrance into a new place, the swarms of "emigration flies"—so called because they appear in September with the emigrants, and, after living for a month, die off with the first snow—and a certain populousness of bedstead, concerning which the less said the better. Such, gentle reader, are the results of my first glance at Zion on the tops of the mountains, in the Holy City of the Far West.

Our journey had occupied nineteen days, from the 7th to the 25th of August, both included; and in that time we had accomplished not less than 1136 statute miles.

CHAPTER IV.

First Week at Great Salt Lake City.—Preliminaries.

BEFORE entering upon the subject of the Mormons I would fain offer to the reader a few words of warning. During my twenty-four days at head-quarters, ample opportunities of surface observation were afforded me. I saw, as will presently appear, specimens of every class, from the Head of the Church down to the field-hand, and, being a stranger in the land, could ask questions and receive replies upon subjects which would have been forbidden to an American of the States, more especially to an official. But there is in Mormondom, as in all other exclusive faiths, whether Jewish, Hindoo, or other, an inner life into which I can not flatter myself or deceive the reader with the idea of my having penetrated. At the same time, it is only fair to state that no Gentile, even the unprejudiced, who are *raræ aves*, however long he may live or intimately he may be connected with Mormons, can expect to see any thing but the superficies. The writings of the Faithful are necessarily wholly presumed. And, finally, the accounts of Life in the City of the Saints published by anti-Mormons and apostates are venomous, and, as their serious discrepancies prove, thoroughly untrustworthy. I may therefore still hope, by recounting honestly and truthfully as lies in my power what I heard, and felt, and saw, and by allowing readers to draw their own conclusions, to take new ground.

The Mormons have been represented, and are generally believed to be, an intolerant race; I found the reverse far nearer the fact. The best proof of this is that there is hardly one anti-Mormon publication, however untruthful, violent, or scandalous, which I did not find in Great Salt Lake City.* The extent of the sub-

* A list of works published upon the subject of Mormonism may not be uninteresting. They admit of a triple division—the Gentile, the anti-Mormon, and the Mormon.

Of the Gentiles, by which I understand the comparatively unprejudiced observer, the principal are,

1. The Exploration and Survey of the Great Salt Lake by Captain Stansbury, who followed up Colonel Frémont's flying survey in 1849, or two years before the Mormons had settled in the basin, and found the young colony about 2—3 years old. Anti-Mormons find fault with Captain Stansbury for expending upon their adversaries too much of the milk of human kindness.

2. The Mormons or Latter-Day Saints, by Lieutenant J. W. Gunnison, of the U. S. Topographical Engineers. This officer was second in command of the exploration under Captain Stansbury, and has recorded, in unpretending style and with great impartiality, his opinions concerning the "rise and progress, peculiar doctrines, personal conditions and prospects" of the Mormons, "derived from personal observation." Like his commanding officer, Lieutenant Gunnison is accused of having favored the New

joined bibliographical list would deter me from a theme so used up by friend and foe, were it not for these considerations.   In the

Faith, and yet, with all the inconsistency of the odium theologicum, the Faithful are charged with his subsequent murder; the only motive of the foul deed being that the Saints dreaded future disclosures, and were determined, though one of their number had been sent to accompany Captain Stansbury as assistant, to prevent other expeditions.   Upon Lieutenant Gunnison's volume is founded "Les Mormons" of M. Étourneau, first printed in the "Presse," and afterward republished, Paris, 1856.

3. The Mormons; a Discourse delivered before the Historical Society of Pennsylvania, March 26th, 1850, by Colonel T. L. Kane (U. S. Militia): this gentleman, an eye-witness, who has touchingly, and, I believe, truthfully related the details of the Nauvoo Exodus, is called by anti-Mormons an "apologist," and is suspected of being a Latter-Day Saint—baptized under the name of Dr. Osborne—in Christian disguise.   Arrived at Fort Bridger in 1857, he found assembled there the three heads of departments, Governor Cumming, Chief Justice Eccles, and General Johnston. According to the Saints, he was watched, spied, treated as a Mormon emissary, and nearly shot by a mistake made on purpose; he was, however, supported by the governor against the general, and the result was a coolness most favorable to the New Faith.   Colonel Kane is said to have preserved an affectionate and respectful remembrance of his friends the Mormons.

4. History of the Mormons, by Messrs. Chambers, Edinburgh.

5. An Excursion to California, over the Prairies, Rocky Mountains, and Great Sierra Nevada, by W. Kelly, Esq., J. P.   Mr. Kelly, whose work shared at the time of its appearance the interest and admiration of the public with Messrs. Huc and Gabet's Travels in Tartary, Tibet, and the Chinese Empire, visited Great Salt Lake City in 1849, an important epoch in the annals of the infant colony, and leaves the reader only to regret that he devoted so little of his time and of his two volumes to the history of the Saints.

6. The Mormons or Latter-Day Saints, with Memoirs of the Life of Joseph Smith, the American Mahomet.   Office of the National Illustrated Library, 198 Strand, London.   This little compilation, dealing with facts rather than theories, borrows from the polemics of both parties, and displays the calmness of judgment which results from studying the subject at a distance; though Gentile, it is somewhat in favor with Mormons because it shows some desire to speak the truth.   This solid merit has won it the honor of an abridged translation with the title "Les Mormons" (292 pages in 12mo, Messrs. Hachette, Paris, 1854), by M. Amédée Pichot, and a brilliant review by M. Prosper Mérimée in the "Moniteur," and reprinted in "Les Mélanges Historiques et Littéraires" (p. 1–58, Michel Levy, 1855).

7. A Visit to Salt Lake, and a Residence in the Mormon Settlements at Utah, by William Chandless.   London: Smith, Elder, and Co., 1857.   Mr. Chandless, about the middle of July, 1855, crossed the prairies in the character of a "teamster for pay," spent the end of the year at Great Salt Lake City, and thence traveled viâ Fillmore and San Bernardino to California.   The book is exceedingly lively and picturesque, combining pleasant reading with just observation, impartiality, and good sense.

8. Voyage au Pays des Mormons, par Jules Remy (2 vols., E. Dentu, Paris, 1860). The author, accompanied by Mr. Brenchley, M.A., traveled in July and the autumn of 1855 from San Francisco along the line of the Carson and Humboldt Rivers to Great Salt Lake City, and returned, like Mr. Chandless, by the southern road.   The two volumes are more valuable for the observations on the natural history of the little-known basin, than for the generalisms, more or less sound, with which the subject of the New Faith is discussed.

Not a few anomalies appear in the judgments passed by M. Remy upon the Saints: while in some places they are represented as fervent and full of faith, we also read: "Le Mormonisme n'a pas caractère de spontanéité des religions primitives, ce qui va, du reste, de soi, ni la naïveté des religions qui suivirent, ni la sincérité des révélations ou des réformes religieuses qui, durant les siècles derniers, ont pris place dans l'histoire;" and while Mr. Joseph Smith is in parts tenderly treated, he is ruthlessly characterized in p. 24 as un fourbe et un imposteur, a "savage and gigantic Tartuffe."   An excellent English translation of this work has lately appeared, under the auspices of Mr. Jeffs, Burlington Arcade, but an account of Great Salt Lake City in 1855 is as archæological as a study of London life in A.D. 1800.

first place, I have found, since my return to England, a prodigious general ignorance of the "Mormon rule;" the mass of the public has heard of the Saints, but even well-educated men hold theirs

9. Incidents of Travel and Adventure in the Far West, by M. Carvalho, who accompanied Colonel Frémont in his last exploration. According to anti-Mormons, the account of the Saints is far too favorable (1856).

10. Geological Survey of the Territory of Utah, by H. Englemann. Washington, 1860.

The principal anti-Mormon works are the following, ranged in the order of their respective dates. The *Cons*, it will be observed, more than treble the *Pros*.

1. A brief History of the Church of Christ of Latter-Day Saints (commonly called Mormons), including an Account of their Doctrine and Discipline, with the reason of the Author for leaving the said Church, by John Corrill, a member of the Legislature of Missouri (50 pages, 8vo, St. Louis, 1839). I know nothing beyond the name of this little work, or of the nine following.

2. Addresses on Mormonism, by the Rev. Hays Douglas (Isle of Man, 1839).

3. Mormonism weighed in the Balances of the Sanctuary and found Wanting, by Samuel Haining (66 pages, Douglas, Isle of Man, 1839).

4. The Latter-Day Saints and Book of Mormon. By W. J. Morrish, Ledbury.

5. An Exposure of the Errors and Fallacies of the Self-named Latter-Day Saints. By W. Hewitt, Staffordshire.

6. Tract on Mormonism. By Capt. D. L. St. Clair. (1840.)

7. Mormonism Unveiled. By E. D. Howe. (1841.)

8. Mormonism Exposed. By the Rev. L. Sunderland. (1841.)

9. Mormonism Portrayed; its Errors and Absurdities Exposed, and the Spirit and Designs of its Author made Manifest. By W. Harris (64 pages, Warsaw, Illinois, 1841).

10. Mormonism in all Ages; or, the Rise, Progress, and Causes of Mormonism; with the Biography of its Author and Founder, Joseph Smith, junior. By Professor J. B. Turner, Illinois College, Jacksonville. (304 pages, 12mo, New York, 1842.)

11. Gleanings by the Way. By the Rev. John A. Clark, D.D. (352 pages in 12mo, Philadelphia, 1842), Minister at Palmyra in New York at the time when the New Faith arose.

12. The History of the Saints, or an Exposé of Joe Smith and Mormonism. By John C. Bennett (344 pages, 12mo, Boston, 1842). This is the work of a celebrated apostate, who for a season took a prominent propagandist part in the political history of Mormondom. Defeated in his hopes of dominion, he has revenged himself by a volume whose title declares the character of its contents, and which wants nothing but the confidence of the reader to be highly interesting. The Mormons speak of him as the Musaylimat el Kazzáb—Musaylimat the Liar, who tried, and failed to enter into partnership with Mohammed—of their religion.

The four following works were written by the Rev. Henry Caswall, a violent anti-Mormon, who solemnly and apparently honestly believes all the calumnies against the "worthless family" of the Prophet; unhesitatingly adopts the Solomon Spaulding story, discovers in Mormon Scripture as many "anachronisms, contradictions, and grammatical errors" as ever Celsus and Porphyry detected in the writings of the early Christians, and designates the faith in which hundreds of thousands live and die as a "delusion in some respects worse than paganism, and a system destined perhaps to act like Mohammedanism (!) as a scourge upon corrupted Christianity" (sub. the American?). The Mormons speak of this gentleman as of a 19th century Torquemada: he appears by his own evidence to have combined with the heart of the great inquisitor some of the head qualities of Mr. Coroner W—— when insisting upon the unhappy Fire-king's swallowing his (Mr. W.'s) prussic acid instead of the pseudo-poison provided for the edification of the public. Mr. Caswall went to Nauvoo holding in his hand an ancient MS. of the Greek Psalter, and completely, according to his account, puzzled the Prophet, who decided it to be "reformed Egyptian." Moreover, he convicted of falsehood the "wretched old creature," viz., the maternal parent of Mr. Joseph Smith, called a mother in Israel, looked upon as one of the holiest of women, and who, at any rate, was a good and kind-hearted mother, that could not be reproached, like Luther's, with "chastising her son so severely about a nut that the blood came." It is no light proof of Mormon tolerance that so truculent a

to be a kind of socialistic or communist concern, where, as in the world to come, there is no marrying nor giving in marriage.

divine and opponent *par voie de fait* should have been allowed to depart from among a people whom he had offended and insulted without loss of liberty or life.

13. The City of the Mormons, or three Days in Nauvoo in 1842 (87 pages, Messrs. Rivingtons, London, 1843).

14. The Prophet of the 19th Century; or, the Rise, Progress, and Present State of the Mormons (277 pages, 8vo, published by the same, London, 1843).

15. Joseph Smith and the Mormons. Chapter xiii. of America and the American Church (John and Charles Mozley, Paternoster Row, London, 1851).

16. Mormonism and its Author; or, a Statement of the Doctrines of the Latter-Day Saints. London: Tract Society, No. 866 (16 pages, 1858).

17. Narrative of some of the Proceedings of the Mormons, giving an Account of their Iniquities, with Particulars concerning the Training of the Indians by them; Descriptions of their Mode of Endowment, Plurality of Wives, &c. By Catharine Lewis Lynn (24 pages, 8vo, 1848). As will presently appear, when the fair sex enters upon the subject of polygamy, it apparently loses all self-control, not to say its senses.

18. Friendly Warnings on the Subject of Mormonism. By a Country Clergyman (London, 1850).

19. The Mormon Imposture: an Exposure of the Fraudulent Origin of the Book of Mormon (8vo, Newbury, London, 1851).

20. Mormonism Exposed. By Mr. Bowes. (1851.)

21. Mormonism or the Bible; a Question for the Times. By a Cambridge Clergyman (12mo, Cambridge and London, 1852). According to Mormon view, the title should have been Mormonism *and* the Bible.

22. History of Illinois. By Governor Ford (Chicago, 1854). The author was a determined opponent of the New Faith, and gives his own version of the massacres at Carthage and Nauvoo: it is valuable only on the venerable principle "audi alteram partem."

23. Mormonism. By J. W. Conybeare, first printed in the "Edinburgh Review" (No. ccii., April, 1854, and reprinted in 112 pages, 12mo, by Messrs. Longman, London, 1854).

24. Utah and the Mormons; the History, Government, Doctrines, Customs, and Prospects of the Latter-Day Saints, from Personal Observations during a Six-months' Residence at Great Salt Lake City. By Benjamin G. Ferris, late Secretary of Utah Territory (347 pages, 12mo, Messrs. Harper, New York, 1854). The author being married, appears to have lived among them to as little purpose—for observation—as possible. Every thing is considered from an anti-Mormon point of view, and some of the accusations against the Saints, as in the case of the Eldridges and the Howards, I know to be not founded on fact. The calmness of the work, upon a highly exciting subject, contrasts curiously with the feminine violence—the natural result of contemplating polygamy—of another that issued under the same name.

25. Mormonism Unveiled; or, a History of Mormonism to the Present Time (235 pages, 8vo, London, 1855).

26. Mormonism Examined: a few Kind Words to a Mormon (8vo, Birmingham, 1855).

27. Female Life among the Mormons, published anonymously for the demand of the New York market, and especially intended for the followers of Miss Lucy Stone and of the Rev. Miss Antoinette Brown, but known to be by Mrs. Maria Ward, who subsequently edited another work. The authoress, who professes to have escaped from the Mormons, was manifestly never among them. This "tissu de mensonges et de calomnies," as M. Remy somewhat ungallantly, but very truthfully styles it, has had extensive currency. M. Révoil has given a free translation of it, under the name of "Les Harems du Nouveau Monde" (308 pages, Paris, 1856). Its success was such that its writeress was in 1858 induced to repeat the experiment.

28. The Mormons at Home; in a Series of Letters, by Mrs. Ferris, wife of the late United States Secretary for Utah Territory (Dix and Edwards, Broadway, New York, 1856). The reasons for this lady's rabid hate may be found in polygamy, which is calculated to astound, perplex, and enrage fair woman in America even more than her strong-opinioned English sister, and in the somewhat contemptuous

Even where this is not the case, the reader of travels will not dislike to peruse something more of a theme with which he is al-

estimation of a sex—which is early taught and soon learns to consider itself crea- tion's cream—conveyed in these words of Mr. Brigham Young: "If I did not con- sider myself competent to transact business without asking my wife, or any other woman's counsel, I think I ought to let *that* business alone."

Accordingly, Mrs. Ferris finds herself in the hands and of a "society of fanatics," controlled by a "gang of licentious villains"—an unpleasant predicament *pour cette vertu*—in fact, for virtue at any time of life—characterizes the land as a "Botany Bay" for society in general, and a "region of moral pestilence;" and while she lav- ishes the treasures of her pity upon the "poor, poor wife," holds her spiritual rival to be *tout bonnement* a "concubine," and consigns the wretches assembled here (*scil.* in Zion on the tops of the Mountains) to the "very hottest part of the infernal tor- rid zone." Tantæne animis cœlestibus iræ?

The Mormons declare that they incurred this funny amount of feminine wrath and suffered from its consequent pin-pricks by their not taking sufficient interest in, or notice of the writer, especially by the fact that on one occasion—it is made much of in the book—some rude men actually did walk over a bridge before her. But com- ing direct from the land of woman's rights' associations, lecturesses on propagand- ism and voluntary celibatarians, whose "mission" it is to reform, purify, and exalt the age, especially our wicked selves, what else could be expected of outraged deli- cacy and self-esteem? Not being "vivisectors," we can not, however, quite join with Mrs. Ferris in the complacency with which she relates her "probing the hearts" of her Mormon guests and visitors "with ruthless questions" about their domestic af- fairs; and we remark with pleasure that in more than one place she has most un- willingly confessed the kindness and civility of the Latter-Day Saints.

29. Adventures among the Mormons, by Elder Hawthornthwaite, an Apostate Missionary. (1857.)

30. The Mormons, the Dream and the Reality; or, Leaves from the Sketch- book of Experience. Edited by a Clergyman. W. B. F. (8vo, London, 1857).

31. The Husband in Utah; or, Sights and Scenes among the Mormons. By Aus- tin N. Ward. Edited by Mrs. Maria Ward, Author of "Female Life among the Mormons" (212 pages, 8vo, Derby and Jackson, Nassau Street, New York, 1857). It is regretable that a respectable publisher should lend his name to a volume like this. The authoress professes to edit the MS. left by a nephew of her husband, who lived among the Mormons en route to California, went on to the gold regions and died. I can not but characterize it as a pure invention. The writer who describes markets where not one ever existed, and "the tall spires of the Mormon temples glittering in the rich sunlight" (p. 15), there being no spires and no temples at Utah, can hardly expect to be believed, even when, with all the eloquence of Mr. Potts, of the "Eatanswill Gazette," she dwells upon the "fanaticism and diabolism that ever attends (?) the hideous and slimy course of Mormonism in its progress over the world." The imposture, too, is not "white;" it is premeditatedly mischievous. Al- though Brother Underwood is a fancy personage, Miss Eliza R. Snow, with whose name improper liberties are taken, is no myth, but a well educated and highly re- spectable reality.

32. Fifteen Years among the Mormons, being the Narrative of Mrs. Mary Ettie V. Smith, late of the Great Salt Lake City, a Sister of one of the Mormon High- Priests, she having been personally acquainted with most of the Mormon leaders, and long in the confidence of the Prophet Brigham Young. By Nelson Winch Green. (Charles Scribner, Broadway, New York, 1858, and unhappily republished by Messrs. Routledge, London.) This work, whose exceedingly clap-trap title is a key to the "popular" nature of the contents, is, *par excellence, the* most offensive pub- lication of the kind, and bears within it marks of an exceeding untruthfulness. The human sacrifices and the abominable rites performed in the Endowment House are reproductions of the accounts of hidden orgies in the Nauvoo Temple, invented and promulgated by Mr. Bowes. The last words placed in the mouth of Mr. Joseph Smith, "My God! my God! have mercy upon us, if there is a God!"—a palpable plagiarism from Lord P——'s will—may be a pious fraud to warn stray lambs from the fold of Mormonism, but as a history shows, it is wholly destitute of fact. The murder in Mr. Jones', the butcher's house, so circumstantially related, never took

ready perhaps familiar; for in this department of literature, as in history and biography, the more we know of a subject, the more

place. Colonel Bridger, who is killed off by the Danites at the end of the book, still lives; and a dream (ch. xxxviii.) seems to be the only proof of Lieutenant Gunnison having been slaughtered by the Latter-Day Saints, not, as is generally supposed, by the Indians. "Milking the Gentiles," coining "Bogus-money," "whistling and whittling" anti-Mormons out of the town, the dangers of competition in love-matters with an apostle, and the imminent peril of being scalped by white Indians, are stock accusations copied from book to book, and rendered somewhat harmless by want of novelty. But nothing will excuse the reckless accusations with which Mrs. Smith takes away the characters of her Mormon sisters, and the abominations with which she charges the wives of the highest dignitaries. Among those thus foully defamed is Miss Snow, who also appears as a leading actress in Mrs. Ward's fiction. The "poetess of the Mormons," now married to the Prophet, has ever led a life of exceptional asceticism—cold in fact as her name. The Latter-Day Saints retort upon Mrs. Smith, of course, in kind, quoting Chaucer (but whether truthfully or not I can not say):

> "A woman she was the most discrete alive,
> Husbandes at chirche-dore had she had five."

33. Mormonism; its Leaders and Designs, by John Hyde, Jun., formerly a Mormon Elder, and resident of Great Salt Lake City. (385 pages, 8vo, W. P. Fetridge & Co., Broadway, New York, 1857.) This is the work of an apostate Mormon, now preaching, I believe, Swedenborgianism in England: it has some pretensions to learning, and it attacks the Mormons upon all their strongest grounds. It is also satisfactory to see that in the circumstantial description of the mysteries of the Endowment House, Mrs. Smith and Mr. Hyde, whose account has apparently been borrowed by M. Remy, disagree, thus justifying us in doubting both; and it is curious to remark, that while the lady leans to the erotic, the gentleman dwells upon the treasonous and mutinous tendency of the ceremony. According to Mr. Hyde, he left the Mormons from conscientious motives. The Mormons, who, however, never fail thoroughly to denigrate the character of an enemy, especially of an apostate, declare that the author, when a missionary at Havre de Grâce, proved useless, always shirking his duty; and that, since dismissal from the ministry, he has left a wife unprovided for at Great Salt Lake City.

The now almost forgotten polemical and anti-Mormon works are,

M. Favez. Fragments sur J. Smith et les Mormons. A methodistical brochure.

Mr. Gray. Principles and Practices of Mormons.

M. Guers. L'Irvingisme et le Mormonisme jugés par la parole de Dieu.

Dr. Hurlburt's Mormonism Unveiled. This work first set on foot the story of "Solomon Spaulding" having composed the Book of Mormon, concerning which more anon.

Mormonism a Delusion. By the Rev. E. B. Chalmers.

Mormonism Unmasked. By R. Clarke.

Mormonism, its History, Doctrine, etc. By the Rev. S. Simpson.

Mormonism an Imposture. By P. Drummond.

The Latter-Day Saints and their Spiritual Views. By H. S. J.

Tracts on Mormonism. A brochure by the Rev. Edmund Clay.

A Country Clergyman's Warning to his Parishioners. (Wertheim & M'Intosh, London.)

The Materialism of the Mormons, or Latter-Day Saints, Examined and Exposed. By S. W. P. Taylder.

The Book of Mormon Examined, and its Claims to be a Revelation from God proved to be False. (12mo, Anonymous.)

The principal notices of Mormonism in periodical literature are,

Archives du Christianisme: articles de MM. Agénor de Gasparin et Monod sur le Mormonisme. Nos. of the 11th of December, 1852, and 14th of May, 1853, quoted in the "Bibliographie Universelle" of MM. Ferdinand Denis, Pinçon et De Narbonne, under the article "Utah."

Sectes religieuses au xixme siècle; Les Irvingiens et les Saints du Dernier Jour, par M. Alfred Maury. Revue des Deux-Mondes. Vol. iii. of the 23d year (A.D. 1853), 1st of September, pages 961–995.

we want to know. Moreover, since 1857, no book of general interest has appeared, and the Mormons are a progressive people.

History and Ideas of the Mormons. "Westminster Review," vol. iii., pages 196–230. (1853.)

Le Mormonisme et sa valeur morale—La Société et la Vie des Mormons, by M. Émile Montégut, "Revue des Deux-Mondes," vol. i. of the 26th year, pages 689–725, 15th of February, 1856.

Visite aux Mormons du Lac Salé par Jules Remy. Articles in the "Echo du Pacifique," San Francisco, January and February, 1856.

L'Illustration, Journal Universel. Vols. xv. and xxi. Articles by M. Depping. "Sur les Mormons" (1858).

Biographie Générale du Dr. Hæfer, publiée chez MM. Didot frères : a long article upon Mr. Brigham Young, by M. Isambert (1858).

Une Campagne des Américains contre les Mormons. By M. Auguste Laugel. "Revue des Deux-Mondes," 1er Septembre, 1859, pages 194–211.

Magasin Pittoresque. Several articles upon the Great Salt Lake, by M. Ferdinand Denis. Vol. xxvii., pages 172–239. Vol. xxviii., page 207. (1859–1860.)

Le Mormonisme et les Etats-Unis. "Revue des Deux-Mondes," 15th April, 1861, signed by M. Elisée Reclus ; an article formed chiefly upon the work of M. Remy. It is an able article, but written by one who, unfortunately, was never in the country—a sine quâ non for correct description. The "Revue" had already undertaken the subject in the number of the 1st of September, 1853, the 15th of February, 1856, and the 1st of September, 1859.

The foreign works omitted in the catalogue at the end of this note are,

Mormonismen och Swedenborgianismen. Upsala (8vo, 1854).

Geschichte der Mormonen, oder Jüngsten, Tages-Heiligen in Nord-Amerika, von Theodor Olshausen. (Göttingen, 244 pages, 8vo, 1856.)

Geographische Wanderungen. Die Mormonen und ihr Land, von Karl Andree. Dresden, 1859.

The Mormons have published at their General Repository only one purely laical book, "The Route from Liverpool to Great Salt Lake Valley," illustrated with steel engravings and wood-cuts, from sketches made by Frederick Piercy. Edited by James Linworth. It is a highly creditable volume, especially in the artistic department, but the letter-press is uninteresting, and appears a mere peg upon which to hang copious notes and official returns. The price varies from £1 to £1 3s., and the three first parts, containing an accurate history of the Latter-Day Saints' emigration from Europe up to 1854, may be had separately, 1s. each.

So good a theme for romance could not fail to fall into the hands of Captain Mayne Reid, who is to Mormonism what Alexander Dumas was to Mesmerism. In his pages the exaggerated anti-Mormon feeling attains its acme ; the explorer Stansbury, who spoke fairly of the Saints, is thus qualified : "the captain is at best but a superficial observer"—quite a glass-house stone-throwing critique. Mr. Brigham Young is a "vulgar Alcibiades ;" the City of the Saints is a "modern Gomorrah," and the Saints themselves are "sanctified forbans ;" the plurality wife is a "femme entretenue." In the tale of the "Wild Huntress," a young person married by foul means to Josh. Stebbing, the Mormon, and rescued mainly by a young hero—of course a Mexican volunteer—we have a sound abuse of the many-wife-system, despotism, theocracy, Danites, tithes, "plebbishness," and the "vulgar ring which smacks (!) of ignoble origin." On the other hand, the rascal Wakara, an ignoble sub-chief of the Yutas, known mainly as a horse-thief, contrasts splendidly by his valor, by his "delicate attentions" to the pretty half-caste, and by his chivalry and hospitality, which make him a very "Rolla of the North !" And this is "fact taught through fiction !"

The Mormon Scriptures, corresponding with the Old Testament, the Evangels, and the epistles of Christianity, consist of the following works : purely bibliographical notices are here given ; the contents will be the subject of a future page.

1. The Book of Mormon, an Account written by the hand of Mormon, upon plates taken from the Plates of Mormon. Translated by Joseph Smith, Jun. The first edition was printed in 1830, at Palmyra, New York, and consisted of 5000 copies. Since that time it has frequently been republished in England and America : it was translated into French in 1852 (Marc Ducloux, Rue Saint Benoît 7, Paris, 1852), and versions have appeared in the German, Italian, Danish, Welsh, and Hawaïan tongues.

O

whose "go-a-headitiveness" in social growth is only to be compared with their obstinate conservatism in adhering to institutions

2. The Book of Doctrine and Covenants of the Church of Jesus of Latter-Day Saints, selected (!) from the Revelations of God. By Joseph Smith, President (336 pages, 12mo). The first American edition was printed in 1832, or ten years after the Book of Mormon, and was published at Mr. Joseph Smith's expense. Many translations of this important work have appeared.

3. The Pearl of Great Price; being a Choice Selection from the Revelations, Translations, and Narratives of Joseph Smith (56 pages, 8vo, Liverpool, first published in 1851). This little volume contains the Book of Abraham, "translated from some records that have fallen into our hands from the catacombs of Egypt, purporting to be the writings of Abraham while he was in Egypt, called the Book of Abraham, written by his own hand on papyrus. With a fac-simile of three papyri."

4. The Latter-Day Saints' Millennial Star, begun in 1839, Manchester, United States, and now published 42 Islington, Liverpool, every Saturday. It has reached its 21st volume. The periodical is a single sheet (16 pages), and the price is one penny. It is an important publication, embracing the whole history of Mormonism; the hebdomadal issue now contains polemical papers, vindications of the Faith, with a kind of appendix, such as emigration reports, quarterly lists of marriages and deaths, varieties, and money lists.

5. Journal of Discourses by Brigham Young and others. First published in 1854 (8vo, Liverpool). It now appears in semi-monthly numbers, 1st and 15th, costing 2d., making up one volume per annum. The above-mentioned and the writings of "Joseph the Seer and Parley P. Pratt, wherever found," are considered by the authorities of the Church as direct revelations.

The Mormons do not hold the "Biographical Sketches of Joseph Smith the Prophet and his Progenitors, for many Generations, by Lucy Smith, mother of the Prophet," to be entirely trustworthy. Beyond its two pages of preface by Orson Pratt, it is deep below criticism. This work, 18mo, of 297 pages (including "Elegies" by Miss E. R. Snow), was first printed in 1853.

The Controversialist works, not usually included in the London catalogue, are the following. They are characterized by abundant earnestness and enthusiasm, and are purposely written in a style intelligible to the classes addressed:

The Word of our Lord to the Citizens of London, by H. C. Kimball and W. Woodruff (1839).

The Millennium, and other Poems; to which is annexed a Treatise on the Regeneration and Eternal Duration of Matter, by Parley P. Pratt, New York, 1840.

A Cry out of the Wilderness, by Elder Hyde. This book was first published in Germany and in German (120 pages, in 1842).

Three Nights' Public Discourse at Boulogne-sur-Mer, by Elder John Taylor (46 pages in 8vo, Liverpool, 1850).

Three Letters to the "New York Herald," of James Gordon Bennett, Esq., from J. M. Grant (Mayor and President of the Quorum of Seventies), of Utah, March, 1852. These epistles have been reprinted in pamphlet form; they chiefly set forth Mormon grievances, especially the injury done by the federal officials.

History of the Persecutions endured by the Church of Jesus of Latter-Day Saints in America, compiled from Public Documents and drawn from Authentic Sources, by C. W. Wandell, Minister of the Gospel (without date, but subsequent to the 64 pp. 8vo edition, printed at Sydney).

Journal of the House of Representatives, Council and Joint Sessions of the First Annual Special Sessions of the Legislative Assembly of the Territory of Utah, held at Great Salt Lake City, 1851–1852. (Printed by Brigham Young, 175 pages 12mo, 1852.)

Defense of Polygamy, by a Lady of Utah (Mrs. Belinda Marden Pratt) to her Sister in New Hampshire (11 pages, 8vo, first printed at Great Salt Lake City in 1854, and subsequently republished in the "Millennial Star" of the 29th of July in the same year). I shall presently quote this curious work.

Acts and Resolutions of the Legislative Assembly of the Territory of Utah, Great Salt Lake City, 40 pages, 12mo. First printed in 1854, and now published for every Annual Session (that of '60–'61 being the 10th) at Great Salt Lake City. Printed at the "Mountaineer" Office, by John S. Davis, Public Printer.

that date from the days of Abraham.   Secondly, the natural history of the New Faith—for such it is—through the several periods

Acts, Resolutions, and Memorials passed at the several Annual Sessions (the 9th in 1859-60) of the Legislative Assembly of the Territory of Utah.   Published by virtue of an Act approved January 19th, 1855, Great Salt Lake City, Joseph Cain, afterward J. S. Davis, Public Printer, 1855–1860.   460 pages, 12mo.   It contains the Territorial Code of Deseret, and is purely secular.

Report of the First General Festival of the Renowned Mormon Battalion, Great Salt Lake City.   39 pages in 8vo.

Discourses delivered by Joseph Smith (30th of June, 1843) and Brigham Young (18th of February, 1855) on the Relations of the Mormons to the Government of the United States.   Great Salt Lake City, 16 pages.

Marriage and Morals in Utah, by Parley P. Pratt.   8 pages, 8vo, Liverpool, 1856.

Twenty-four Miracles, by O. Pratt.   Liverpool, 16 pages, 8vo, 1857.

Latter-Day Kingdom ; or, the Preparation for the Second Advent, by O. Pratt. Liverpool, 16 pages, 8vo, 1857.

Spiritual Gifts, by Orson Pratt.   Liverpool and London, 80 pages, 8vo, 1857.

Universal Apostasy ; or, the Seventeen Centuries of Darkness, by O. Pratt, Liverpool, 16 pages in 8vo, 1857.

Compendium of the Faith and Doctrines of the Church of Jesus of Latter-Day Saints, compiled from the Bible, and also from the Book of Mormon, Doctrines and Covenants, and other publications of the Church ; with an Appendix, by Franklin D. Richards, one of the Twelve Apostles of said Church.   42 Islington, Liverpool, 243 pages, long 18mo.   (1857.)   A concordance and compilation of the chief doctrinal works and seven sermons.

The following is the Catalogue of English Works published by the Church of Jesus Christ of Latter-Day Saints, and for sale by Orson Pratt, at their General Repository and "Millennial Star" Office, 42 Islington, Liverpool, and removed from 35 Jewin Street, City, to 30 Florence Street, Islington, London.

Hymn-Book, first edition in 1851.   Morocco extra, 4s. ; calf, gilt edges, 2s. 6d. ; calf grained, 2s.; roan embossed, 1s. 6d.

The Harp of Zion.   Poems by John Lyon.   Published for the benefit of the Perpetual Emigrating Fund.   First printed in 1853.   Morocco extra, 6s. 6d. ; cloth, gilt extra, 3s. 6d. ; cloth embossed, 2s. 6d.

Poems, Religious, Historical, and Political.   By Eliza R. Snow.   Vol. I.   Morocco extra, 6s. 6d.; calf gilt, 5s.; cloth gilt, 3s. 6d.; cloth embossed, 2s. 6d.

The Government of God, by John Taylor, one of the Twelve Apostles.   First printed in 1852.   Stiff covers, 1s. 9d.

Latter-Day Saints in Utah.   Opinion of Judge Snow upon the Official Course of His Excellency Gov. B. Young—Trial of Howard Egan on Indictment, for the Murder of James Monroe, verdict—A Bill to Establish a Territorial Government for Utah.   The Territorial Officers, etc.   9d.

One Year in Scandinavia.   Results of the Gospel in Denmark and Sweden, by Erastus Snow, one of the Twelve Apostles.   3d.

Reports of Three Nights' Public Discussion in Bolton, between William Gibson, H. P., Presiding Elder of the Manchester Conference of the Church of Jesus Christ of Latter-Day Saints, and the Rev. Woodville Woodman, Minister of the New Jerusalem Church.   First published in 1851.   6d.

Assassination of Joseph and Hyrum Smith ; also a condensed History of the Expulsion of the Saints from Nauvoo, by Elder John S. Fullmer, Pastor of the Manchester, Liverpool, and Preston Conferences.   First printed in 1856.   5d.

Testimonies for the Truth ; a Record of Manifestations of the Power of God—miraculous and providential—witnessed in the travels and experience of Benjamin Brown, H. P., Pastor of the London, Reading, Kent, and Essex Conferences.   It is a list of the Miracles performed by the first Mormons.   Printed in Liverpool, 1853.   4d.

.Works by Parley P. Pratt, one of the Twelve Apostles.

Key to the Science of Theology ; designed as an Introduction to the First Principles of Spiritual Philosophy, Religion, Law, and Government, as delivered by the Ancients, and as restored in this Age, for the Final Development of Universal Peace, Truth, and Knowledge.   First published in 1855.   It is a volume far superior in

of conception, birth, and growth to vigorous youth, with fair promise of stalwart manhood, is a subject of general and no small im-

matter and manner to the average run of Mormon composition. Morocco extra, 5s. 6d.; calf grained, 3s. 6d.; cloth embossed, 2s.

The Voice of Warning; or, an Introduction to the Faith and Doctrine of the Church of Jesus Christ of Latter-Day Saints. This work has been translated into French. Morocco extra, 4s.; calf, gilt edges, 3s.; calf grained, 2s. 6d.; cloth embossed, 1s. 6d.

Works by Orson Pratt, A.M., one of the Twelve Apostles.

Absurdities of Immaterialism; or, a Reply to T. W. P. Taylder's Pamphlet, entitled "The Materialism of the Mormons, or Latter-Day Saints, Examined and Exposed." First edition in 1849. 4d.

Great First Cause; or, the Self-moving Forces of the Universe. 2d.

Divine Authenticity of the Book of Mormon, in 6 parts. Each part 2d.

Divine Authority, or the Question, was Joseph Smith sent of God? First published in 1848. 2d.

Remarkable Visions. First published in 1849. 2d.

The Kingdom of God, in 4 parts. First edition in 1849. Parts 1, 2, 3, each 1d. Part 4, 2d.

Reply to a Pamphlet printed at Glasgow, with the approbation of Clergymen of different denominations, entitled, "Remarks on Mormonism." First edition in 1849. 2d.

New Jerusalem; or, the Fulfillment of Modern Prophecy. First published in 1849. 3d.

Title and Index to the above Works, ½d.

The Seer. Vol. I., 12 numbers; II., 8 numbers. Each number 2d. The two volumes bound in one, in half calf, 5s.

A Series of Pamphlets, now being published on the first Principles of the Gospel.

The following numbers are already out: Chap. 1, The True Faith. Chap. 2, True Repentance. Chap. 3, Water Baptism. Chap. 4, The Holy Spirit. Chap. 5, Spiritual Gifts. First printed in 1857. Each number, 2d.

Works by Lorenzo Snow, one of the Twelve Apostles.

The Voice of Joseph. A brief Account of the Rise, Progress, and Persecutions of the Church of Jesus Christ of Latter-Day Saints, with their present Position and Prospects in Utah Territory; together with American Exiles' Memorial to Congress. First published in 1852. 3d.

The Only Way to be Saved. An Explanation of the First Principles of the Doctrine of the Church of Jesus Christ of Latter-Day Saints. 1d.

The Italian Mission. 4d.

Works by Elder Orson Spencer, A.B.

Letters exhibiting the most prominent Doctrines of the Church of Jesus Christ of Latter-Day Saints, in reply to the Rev. William Crowel, A.M., Boston, Mass., U.S.A. First printed in 1852. Morocco extra, 4s.; calf grained, 2s. 6d.; cloth embossed, 1s. 6d.

Patriarchal Order, or Plurality of Wives. (Being the Fifteenth Letter in Correspondence with the Rev. William Crowel, A.M.) 2d. ·

The Prussian Mission of the Church of Jesus Christ of Latter-Day Saints. Report of Elder Orson Spencer, A.B., to President Brigham Young. 2d.

Works by Elder John Jacques.

Catechism for Children. Cloth, gilt edges, 10d.; stiff covers, 6d.

Exclusive Salvation, 1d.

Salvation. A Dialogue in two parts. Each part 1d.

I will conclude this long enumeration with Catalogue of the principal Works in foreign languages.

Works in French.

Le Livre de Mormon (Book of Mormon), 3s. 6d.

Une Voix d'Avertissement (Voice of Warning). Par Parley P. Pratt. Morocco. gilt edges, 4s.; roan, 1s. 9d.; cloth, 1s. 6d.; paper covers, 1s. 3d.

portance. It interests the religionist, who looks upon it as the "scourge of corrupted Christianity," as much as the skeptic, that

Les Mormons et leurs Enemis (The Latter-Day Saints and their Enemies). Par T. B. H. Stenhouse, President des Missions Suisse et Italienne.   1s. 6d.
Autorité Divine (Divine Authority).   Par L. A. Bertrand, Elder.   4d.
De la Necessité de Nouvelles Révélations prouvée par la Bible.   Par John Taylor, un des Douze Apôtres.   4d.
Aux Amis de la Vérité Religieuse.   Par John Taylor, Elder.   2d.
Epitre du President de la Mission Française à l'Eglise des Saints des Derniers-jours en France et dans les Iles de la Manche (Epistle of the President of the French Mission, etc.), 1½d.
Traité sur le Baptême.   Par John Taylor, un des Douze Apôtres.   2d.

Works in German.

Das Buch Mormon (The Book of Mormon), 3s. 6d.
Eine Gottliche Offenbarung; und Belehrung uber den Chestand (Revelation on Marriage; and Patriarchal order or Plurality of Wives).   Stiff covers, 6d.
Zion's Panier (Zion's Pioneer).   No. 1, 3d.

Works in Italian.

Il Libro di Mormon (The Book of Mormon).   Morocco extra, 6s. 6d.; grained roan, 4s. 6d.

Works in Danish.

Mormons Bog (The Book of Mormon).   Grained roan, 4s.

Works in Welsh.

Llyfr Mormon (Book of Mormon).   Grained roan, 4s.; roan, gilt edges, 4s. 6d.
Athrawiaeth a Chyfammodau (Doctrine and Covenants).   Grained roan, 3s. 6d.; roan, gilt edges, 3s. 6d.
Llfyr Hymnau (Hymn Book).   Marble calf, 2s.; grained roan, 2s. 3d.; calf, gilt edges, 2s. 6d.
Y Perl o Fawr Bris (Pearl of Great Price), 1s. 2d.
Priodas a Moesau yn Utah, gan Parley P. Pratt (Marriage and Morals in Utah, by Parley P. Pratt), 1d.
Prophwyd y Jubili (The Millennial Prophet).   Vol. III. unbound, 2s. 0½d.

By Elder Dan Jones.

Yr Eurgrawn Ysgrythyrol (Casket, or Treatises on upward of 100 subjects).   Half calf, 3s. 3d.; unbound, 2s. 6d.
Pwy yw Duw y Saint? (Who is the God of the Saints?), 2½d.
Yr Hen Grefydd Newydd (The old Religion anew), 6d.
Annerchiad i'r Peirch, etc. (Proclamation to the Reverends, etc.), 1½d.
Gwrthbrofion i'r Spaulding Story am Lyfr Mormon (Spaulding Story, etc., refuted), 2d.
Anmhoblogrwydd Mormoniaeth (Unpopularity of Mormonism), 1d.
Arweinydd i Seion (Guide to Zion), 1½d.
Pa beth yw Mormoniaeth? (What is Mormonism?), ½d.
Pa beth yw gras Cadwedigol? (What is saving Grace?), ½d.
Dadl ar Mormoniaeth? (Discussion on Mormonism), 2d.
Anffyddiaeth Sectyddiaeth (Skepticism of Sectarianism), 1d.
Amddiffyniad rhag Cam-gyhuddiadau (Replies to False Charges), 1d.
Y Lleidr ar y Groes (The Thief on the Cross), ½d.
"Peidiwch a'u Gwrando" ("Don't go to hear them"), ½d.
Egwyddorion Cyntaf a Gwahoddiadau (First Principles and Invitations), ¼d.
Ai duw a Ddanfonodd Joseph Smith (Divinity of Joseph's Mission), 1d.
Llofruddiad Joseph a Hyrum Smith (Assassination of Joseph and Hyrum Smith), 1d.
Tarddiad Llfyr Mormon (Origin of the Book of Mormon), 1d.
Dammeg y Pren Ffrwythlawn (Parable of the Fruitful Tree), ½d.
Darlun o'r Byd Crefyddol (The Religious World Illustrated), ½d.
Traethodau D. Jones, yn rhwyn mewn hanner croen llo (D. Jones' Works bound in half calf), 6s. 4d.

admires how, in these days of steam-traveling, printing, and tele-gramming, when "many run to and fro," and when "knowledge" has been "increased," human credulity will display itself in the same glaring colors which it wore ere the diffusion of knowledge became a part of social labor.   The philosophic observer will de-tect in it a notable example of how *mens agitat molem*, the "pow-erful personal influence of personal character," and the "effect that may be produced by a single mind inflexibly applied to the pursuit of a single object;" and another proof that "it is easier to extend the belief of the multitude than to contract it — a cir-cumstance which proceeds from the false but prevalent notion that too much belief is at least an error on the right side."   The statist will consider it in its aspect as a new system of coloniza-tion.   In America the politician will look with curiosity at a despotism thriving in the centre of a democracy, and perhaps with apprehension at its future efforts, in case of war or other troubles, upon the destinies of the whilom Great Republic.   In England, which principally supplies this number of souls, men, instead of regarding it as one of many safety-valves, will be re-minded of their obligations toward the classes by which Mormon-ism is fed, and urged to the improvement of education, religion, and justice.   And I hope to make it appear that the highly-col-ored social peculiarities of the New Faith have been used as a tool by designing men to raise up enmity against a peaceful, in-dustrious, and law-abiding people, whose whole history has been a course of cruel persecution, which, if man really believed in his own improvement, would be a disgrace to a self-styled enlighten-ed age.   The prejudice has naturally enough extended from America to England.   In 1845, when the Mormons petitioned for permission to retire to Vancouver's Island, they met with

---

By Elder John Davies.

Yr hyn sydd o ran, etc. (That which is in part, etc.), 1*d.*
Epistol Cyffredinol Cyntaf (First General Epistle of the first Presidency), 1*d.*
Traethawd ar Wyrthiau (Treatise on Miracles), 1*d.*
Etto Adolygiad, etc., Chwech Rhifyn (Do. in reply to Anti-Mormon Lectures). Six Nos.   (Each No. 1*d.*)
Pregethu i'r Ysbrydion yn Ngharchar, etc. (Preaching to the Spirits in Prison, etc.), 1*d.*
Ewch a Dysgwch (Go and Teach), ½*d.*
Darlithiau ar Ffydd, gan Joseph Smith (Joseph Smith's Lectures on Faith), 4*d.*
Y Doniau Ysbrydol yn Mrawdlys y Gelyn (The Spiritual Gifts before their Ene-mies' Tribunal), 2*d.*
Traethawd ar Fedydd (Treatise on Baptism), 1*d.*
Corff Crist, neu yr Eglwys (The Body or Church of Christ), 1*d.*
Ffordd y Bywyd Tragywyddol (The Way of Eternal Life), 1*d.*
Yr Achos Mawr Cyntaf, gan O. Pratt (Great First Cause, by O. Pratt), 2*d.*
Profwch Bob Peth, etc. (Prove all things, etc.), ½*d.*
Athrawiaeth Iachus (Sound Doctrine), ½*d.*
Ymddyddanion yn Gymraeg a Saesonaeg (Dialogues in Welsh and English), ½*d.*
Llythyron Capt. Jones o Ddyffryn y li. H. Mawr, yn desgrifio arderchawgrwydd Seion (Beauties of Zion described by Captain Jones, in a Series of Letters from Great Salt Lake Valley), 2*d.*

nothing but discouragement. And even in 1860, I am told, when
a report was raised that Mr. Brigham Young would willingly
have taken refuge with his adherents in the valley of the Sas-
katchawan, the British minister was instructed to oppose the useful emigration to the utmost of his power.

On the evening of our arrival Lieutenant Dana and I proceeded
to the store of Messrs. Livingston, Bell, and Co.—formerly Livingston and Kinkhead—the sutlers of Camp Floyd, and the most
considerable Gentile merchants in Great Salt Lake City; he to
learn the readiest way of reaching head-quarters, I to make inquiries about the San Francisco road. We were cordially received
by both these gentlemen, who, during the whole period of my
stay, did all in their power to make the place pleasant. Governor
Bell, as he is generally called, presently introduced me to his wife,
a very charming person, of English descent, whose lively manners
contrasted strongly and agreeably with the almost monastic gloom
which the *régime* of the "lady-saints" casts over society. Lieutenant Dana was offered seats in Mr. Livingston's trotting-wagon
on the ensuing Monday. I was less fortunate. Captain Miller,
of Millersville, the principal agent and director at this end of the
road, informed me that he had lately ceased to run the wagon,
which had cost the company $15,000 a month, returning but
$30,000 per annum, and was sending the mails on mule-back.
However, my informants agreed that a party would probably be
starting soon, and that, all things failing, I could ride the road,
though with some little risk of scalp. We ended with a bottle of
Heidseck, and with cigars which were not unpleasant even after
the excellent "gold-leaf tobacco" of the States.

On the next day, Sunday, we walked up the main street northward, and doubling three corners of Temple Block, reached the
large adobe house, with its neat garden, the abode of the then
governor, Hon. Alfred Cumming. This gentleman, a Georgian
by birth, after a long public service as Indian agent in the northern country, was, after several refusals, persuaded by the then
president, who knew his high honor and tried intrepidity, to assume the supreme executive authority at Great Salt Lake City.
The conditions were that polygamy should not be interfered with,
nor forcible measures resorted to except in extremest need. Governor Cumming, accompanied by his wife, and an escort of 600
dragoons, left the Mississippi in the autumn of 1857, at a time
when the Mormons were in arms against the federal authority,
and ended his journey only in April of the ensuing year. By
firmness, prudence, and conciliation, he not only prevented any
collision between the local militia and the United States army,
which was burning to revenge itself for the terrible hardships of
the campaign, but succeeded in restoring order and obedience
throughout the Territory. He had been told before entering that
his life was in danger; he was not, however, a man to be deterred

from a settled purpose, and experiment showed that, so far from being molested, he was received with a salute and all the honors. Having been warned that he might share the fate of Governor Boggs, who in 1843 was shot through the mouth when standing at the window, he enlarged the casements of his house in order to give the shooter a fair chance. His determination enabled him to issue, a few days after his arrival, a proclamation offering protection to all persons illegally restrained of their liberty in Utah. The scrupulous and conscientious impartiality which he has brought to the discharge of his difficult and delicate duties, and, more still, his resolution to treat the Saints like Gentiles and citizens, not as Digger Indians or felons, have won him scant favor from either party. The anti-Mormons use very hard language, and declare him to be a Mormon in Christian disguise. The Mormons, though more moderate, can never, by their very organization, rest contented without the combination of the temporal with the spiritual power. The governor does not meet his predecessor, the ex-governor, Mr. Brigham Young, from prudential motives, except on public duty. Mrs. Cumming visits Mrs. Young, and at the houses of the principal dignitaries, this being nearly the only society in the place. As, among Moslems, a Lady M. W. Montague can learn more of domestic life in a week than a man can in a year, so it is among the Mormons. I can not but express a hope that the amiable Mrs. Cumming will favor us with the results of her observation and experience, and that she will be as disinterested and unprejudiced as she is talented and accomplished. The kindness and hospitality which I found at the governor's, and, indeed, at every place in New Zion, is "ungrateful to omit," and would be "tedious to repeat."

We dined with his excellency at the usual hour, 2 P.M. On the way I could dwell more observantly upon the main features of the city, which, after the free use of the pocket-compass, were becoming familiar to me. The first remark was, that every meridional street is traversed on both sides by a streamlet of limpid water, verdure-fringed, and gurgling with a murmur which would make a Persian Moollah long for improper drinks. The supplies are brought in raised and hollowed water-courses from City Creek, Red Buttes, and other kanyons lying north and east of the settlement. The few wells are never less than forty-five feet deep; artesians have been proposed for the benches, but the expense has hitherto proved an obstacle. Citizens can now draw with scanty trouble their drinking water in the morning, when it is purest, from the clear and sparkling streams that flow over the pebbly beds before their doors. The surplus is reserved for the purposes of irrigation, without which, as the "distillation from above" will not suffice, Deserét would still be a desert, and what is not wanted swells the City Creek, and eventually the waves of the Jordan. The element, which flows at about the rate of four miles an hour, is under a chief water-master or commissioner, assisted by a water-master in each ward, and by a deputy in each block, all sworn to see the fertilizing fluid fairly distributed. At the corners of every ward there is a water-gate which controls the supplies that branch off to the several blocks, and each lot of one and a quarter acres is allowed about three hours' irrigation during the week. For repairs and other expenses a property tax of one mill per dollar is raised, and the total of the impost in 1860 was $1163 25. The system works like clock-work. "The Act to Incorporate the Great Salt Lake City Water-works" was approved January 21, 1853.

Walking in a northward direction up Main, otherwise called Whisky Street, we could not but observe the "magnificent distances" of the settlement, which, containing 9000—12,000 souls, covers an area of three miles. This broadway is 132 feet wide, including the side-walks, which are each twenty, and, like the rest of the principal avenues, is planted with locust and other trees. There are twenty or twenty-one wards or cantons, numbered from the S.E. "boustrophedon" to the N.W. corner. They have a common fence and a bishop apiece. They are called after the creeks, trees, people, or positions, as Mill-Creek Ward, Little Cotton-wood, Denmark, and South Ward. Every ward contains about nine blocks, each of which is forty rods square. The area of ten acres is divided into four to eight lots, of two and a half to one and a quarter acres each, 264 feet by 132. A city ordinance places the houses twenty feet behind the front line of the lot, leaving an intermediate place for shrubbery or trees. This rule, however, is not observed in Main Street.

The streets are named from their direction to the Temple Block. Thus Main Street is East Temple Street No. 1; that behind it is State Road, or East Temple Street 2, and so forth, the ward being also generally specified. Temple Block is also the point to which latitude and longitude are referred. It lies in N. lat. 40° 45' 44", W. long. (G.) 112° 6' 8", and 4300 feet above sea level.

Main Street is rapidly becoming crowded. The western block, opposite the hotel, contains about twenty houses of irregular shape and size. The buildings are intended to supply the principal wants of a far-Western settlement, as bakery, butchery, and blacksmithery, hardware and crockery, paint and whip warehouse, a "fashionable tailor"—and "fashionable" in one point, that his works are more expensive than Poole's — shoe-stores, tannery and curriery; the Pantechnicon, on a more pretentious style than its neighbors, kept by Mr. Gilbert Clements, Irishman and orator; dry-goods, groceries, liquors, and furniture shops, Walker's agency, and a kind of restaurant for ice-cream, a luxury which costs 25 cents a glass; saddlers, dealers in "food, flour, and provisions," hats, shoes, clothing, sash laths, shingles, timber, copper, tin, crockery-ware, carpenters' tools, and mouse-traps; a watchmaker and repairer, a gunsmith, locksmith, and armorer, soap and candle maker, nail-maker, and venders of "Yankee notions." On the eastern side, where the same articles are sold on a larger scale, live the principal Gentile merchants, Mr. Gilbert and Mr. Nixon, an English Saint; Mr. R. Gill, a "physiological barber;" Mr. Godbe's "apothecary and drug stores;" Goddard's confectionery; Messrs. Hockaday and Burr, general dealers, who sell every thing, from a bag of potatoes to a yard of gold lace; and various establishments, Mormon and others. Crossing the street that runs east and west, we pass on the right hand a small block, occupied by Messrs. Dyer and Co., sutlers to a regiment in Arizona, and next to it the stores of Messrs. Hooper and Cronyn, with an ambrotype and daguerrean room behind. The stores, I may remark, are far superior, in all points, to the shops in an English country town that is not a regular watering-place. Beyond this lies the adobe house, with its wooden Ionic stoop or piazza (the portico is a favorite here), and well-timbered garden, occupied by Bishop Hunter; and adjoining it the long tenement inhabited by the several relicts of Mayor Jedediah M. Grant. Farther still, and facing the Prophet's Block, is the larger adobe house belonging to General Wells and his family. Opposite, or on the western side, is the well-known store of Livingston, Bell, and Co., and beyond it the establishment now belonging to the nine widows and the son of the murdered apostle, Parley P. Pratt. Still looking westward, the Globe bakery and restaurant, and a shaving saloon, lead to the "Mountaineer Office," a conspicuous building, forty-five feet square, two storied, on a foundation of cut stone stuccoed red to resemble sandstone, and provided with a small green-balconied belvidere. The cost was $20,000. It was formerly the Council House, and was used for church purposes. When purchased by the Territory the Public Library was established in the northern part; the office of the "Deserét News" on the first story, and that of the "Mountaineer" on the ground floor. This brings us to the 1st South Temple Street, which divides the "Mountaineer" office from the consecrated ground. In this vicinity are the houses of most of the apostles, Messrs. Taylor, Cannon, Woodruff, and O. Pratt.

Crowds were flocking into Temple Block for afternoon service: yet I felt disappointed by the scene. I had expected to see traces of "workmen in abundance, hewers and workers of stone and timber, and all manner of cunning men for every manner of work," reposing from their labors on the Sabbath. I thought, at any rate, to find

"pars ducere muros
Molirique arcem, et manibus subvolvere saxa."

It seemed hardly in accordance with the energy and devotedness of a new faith that a hole in the ground should represent the House of the Lord, while Mr. Brigham Young, the Prophet, thinking of his own comfort before the glory of God, is lodged, like Solomon of old, in what here appears a palace. Nor, reflecting that without a Temple the dead can not be baptized out of Purgatory, was I quite satisfied when reminded of the fate of Nauvoo (according to Gentiles the Mormons believe that they must build nine temples before they will be suffered to worship in peace), and informed that the purely provisional works, which had been interrupted by the arrival of the army in 1858, would shortly be improved.

The lines of Temple Block—which, as usual, is ten acres square = forty rods each way—run toward the cardinal points. It stands clear of all other buildings, and the locust-trees, especially those on the sunny south side, which have now been planted seven years, will greatly add to its beauties. It is surrounded with a foundation wall of handsomely dressed red sandstone, raised to the height of ten feet by adobe stuccoed over to resemble a richer material. Each facing has thirty flat pilasters, without pedestal or entablature, but protected, as the adobe always should be, by a sandstone coping. When finished, the whole will be surmounted by an ornamental iron fence. There are four gates, one to each side—of these, two, the northern and western, are temporarily blocked up with dry stone walls, while the others are left open—which in time will become carriage entrances, with two side ways for foot passengers. According to accounts, the wall and the foundations have already cost one million of dollars, or a larger sum than that spent upon the entire Nauvoo Temple.

Temple Block—the only place of public and general worship in the city—was consecrated and a Tabernacle was erected in September, 1847, immediately after the celebrated exodus from "Egypt on the banks of the Mississippi," on a spot revealed by the past to the present Prophet and his adherents. Two sides of the wall having been completed, ground was broken on the 14th of February, 1853, for the foundation of the building. One part of the ceremony consisted of planting a post at the central point, the main "stake for the curtains of Zion:" every successive step in advance was commemorated by imposing ceremonies, salvos of guns, bands playing, crowds attending, addresses by the governor, Mr. Brigham Young, prayers and pious exercises. The foundations of the Temple, which are sixteen feet deep, and composed of hard gray granite, in color like that of Aberdeen or Quincy, are now concealed from view; and the lumber huts erected for the workmen were, when the Mormons made their minor Hegira to Provo City, removed to the Sugar-house Ward, three miles southeast of the city.

The Temple Block is at present a mere waste. A central excavation, which resembles a large oblong grave, is said by Gentiles to be the beginning of a baptismal font twenty feet deep. The southwestern corner is occupied by the Tabernacle, an adobe building 126 feet long from N. to S., and 64 wide from E. to W.: its interior, ceilinged with an elliptical arch—the width being its span —can accommodate 2000—3000 souls. It urgently requires enlarging. Over the entrances at the gable ends, which open to the N. and S., is a wood-work representing the sun, with his usual coiffure of yellow beams, like a Somali's wig, or the symbol of the Persian empire. The roof is of shingles: it shelters under its projecting eaves a whole colony of swallows, and there are four chimneys—a number insufficient for warmth at one season, or for ventilation at the other. The speaker or preacher stands on the west side of the building, which is reserved for the three highest dignities, viz., the First Presidency, the "Twelve" (Apostles), and the President of the State of Zion: distinguished strangers are also admitted. Of late, as in the old Quaker meeting-houses at Philadelphia, the brethren in the Tabernacle have been separated from the "sistern," who sit on the side opposite the preacher's left; and, according to Gentiles, it is proposed to separate the Christians from the Faithful, that the "goats" may no longer mingle with the sheep.

Immediately north of the Tabernacle is the Bowery—in early spring a canopy of green leafy branches, which are left to wither with the year, supported on wooden posts. The interior will be described when we attend the house of worship next Sunday.

In the extreme northwest angle of the block is the Endowment, here pronounced *On-dewment House*, separated from the Tabernacle by a high wooden paling. The building, of which I made a pen and ink sketch from the west, is of adobe, with a pent roof and four windows, one blocked up: the central and higher portion is flanked by two wings, smaller erections of the same shape. The Endowment House is the place of great medicine, and all appertaining to it is carefully concealed from Gentile eyes and ears: the result is that human sacrifices are said to be performed within its walls. Mrs. Smith and Mr. Hyde have described the mysterious rites performed within these humble walls, but, for reasons given before, there is reason to doubt the truth of their descriptions; such orgies as they describe could not coexist with the respectability which is the law of the land. M. Remy has detailed the programme with all the exactitude of an eye-witness, which he was not. The public declare that the ceremonies consist of some show, which in the Middle Ages would be called a comedy or mystery—possibly Paradise Lost and Paradise Regained—and connect it with the working of a mason's lodge. The respectable Judge Phelps, because supposed to take the place of the Father of Sin when tempting Adam and Eve, is popularly known as "the Devil." The two small wings are said to contain fonts for the two sexes, where baptism by total immersion is performed. According to Gentiles, the ceremony occupies eleven or twelve hours. The neophyte, after bathing, is anointed with oil, and dressed in clean white cotton garments, cap and shirt, of which the latter is

ENDOWMENT HOUSE AND TABERNACLE. (From the West.)

rarely removed—Dr. Richards saved his life at the Carthage massacre by wearing it — and a small square masonic apron, with worked or painted fig-leaves : he receives a new name and a distinguishing grip, and is bound to secrecy by dreadful oaths. Moreover, it is said that, as in all such societies, there are several successive degrees, all of which are not laid open to initiation till the Temple shall be finished.   But—as every mason knows—the "red-hot poker" and other ideas concerning masonic institutions have prevailed when juster disclosures have been rejected.   Similarly in the Mormonic mystery, it is highly probable that, in consequence of the conscientious reserve of the people upon a subject which it would be indelicate to broach, the veriest fancies have taken the deepest root.

The other features of the inclosure are a well near the Tabernacle, an arched sewer in the western wall for drainage, and at the eastern entrance a small habitation for concierge and guards. The future Temple was designed by an Anglo-Mormon-architect, Mr. Truman O. Angell.   The plan is described at full length in the Latter-Day Saints' "Millennial Star," December 2, 1854, and drawings, apparently copied from the original in the historian's office, have been published at Liverpool, besides the small sketches in the works of Mr. Hyde and M. Remy.   It is hardly worth while here to trouble the general reader with a lengthy description of a huge and complicated pile, a syncretism of Greek and Roman, Gothic and Moorish, not revealed like that of Nauvoo, but planned by man, which will probably never be completed.   It has been transferred to the Appendix (No. II.), for the benefit of students : after briefly saying that the whole is symbolical, and that it is intended to dazzle, by its ineffable majesty, the beholder's sight, I will repeat the architect's concluding words, which are somewhat in the style of Parr's Life Pills advertisements : "For other particulars, wait till the house is done, then come and see it."

After dining with the governor, we sat under the stoop enjoying, as we might in India, the cool of the evening.   Several visitors dropped in, among them Mr. and Mrs. Stenhouse.   He—Elder T. B. H. Stenhouse — is a Scotchman by birth, and has passed through the usual stages of neophyte (larva), missionary (pupa), and elder or fully-developed Saint (imago).   Madame was from Jersey, spoke excellent French, talked English without nasalization or cantalenation, and showed a highly cultivated mind.   She had traveled with her husband on a propagandist tour to Switzerland and Italy, where, as president of the missions for three years, he was a "diligent and faithful laborer in the great work of the last dispensation."   He became a Saint in 1846, at the age of 21; lived the usual life of poverty and privation, founded the Southampton Conference, converted a lawyer among other great achievements, and propagated the Faith successfully in Scotland as in England. The conversation turned—somehow in Great Salt Lake City it generally does—upon polygamy, or rather plurality, which here is the polite word, and for the first time I heard that phase of the family tie sensibly, nay, learnedly advocated on religious grounds by fair lips. Mr. Stenhouse kindly offered to accompany me on the morrow, as the first hand-cart train was expected to enter, and to point out what might be interesting. I saw Elder and High-Priest Stenhouse almost every day during my stay at Great Salt Lake City, and found in his society both pleasure and profit. We of course avoided those mysterious points, into which, as an outsider, I had no right to enter; the elder was communicative enough upon all others, and freely gave me leave to use his information. The reader, however, will kindly bear in mind that, being a strict Mormon, Mr. Stenhouse could enlighten me only upon one side of the subject; his statements were therefore carefully referred to the "other part;" moreover, as he could never see any but the perfections of his system, the blame of having pointed out what I deem its imperfections is not to be charged upon him. His power of faith struck me much. I had once asked him what became of the Mormon Tables of the Law, the Golden Plates which, according to the Gentiles, were removed by an angel after they had done their work. He replied that he knew not; that his belief was independent of all such accidents; that Mormonism is and must be true to the exclusion of all other systems. I saw before me an instance how the brain or mind of man can, by mere force of habit and application, imbue itself with any idea.

Long after dark I walked home alone. There were no lamps in any but Main Street, yet the city is as safe as at St. James's Square, London. There are perhaps not more than twenty-five or thirty constables or policemen in the whole place, under their captain, a Scotchman, Mr. Sharp, "by name as well as nature so;" and the guard on public works is merely nominal. Its excellent order must be referred to the perfect system of private police, resulting from the constitution of Mormon society, which in this point resembles the caste system of Hindooism. There is no secret from the head of the Church and State; every thing, from the highest to the lowest detail of private and public life, must be brought to the ear and submitted to the judgment of the father-confessor-in-chief. Gentiles often declare that the Prophet is acquainted with their every word half an hour after it is spoken: and from certain indices, into which I hardly need enter, my opinion is that, allowing something for exaggeration, they are not very far wrong. In London and Paris the foreigner is subjected, though perhaps he may not know it, to the same surveillance, and till lately his letters were liable to be opened at the Post-office. We can not, then, wonder that at Great Salt Lake City, a stranger, before proving himself at the least to be harmless, should begin by being an object of suspicion.

On Monday, as the sun was sloping toward the east, Mr. Stenhouse called to let me know that the train had already issued from Emigration Kanyon; no time to spare. We set out together " down town" at once. Near the angle of Main Street I was shown the place where a short time before my arrival a curious murder was committed. Two men, named Johnston and Brown, *mauvais sujets*, who had notoriously been guilty of forgery and horse-stealing, were sauntering home one fine evening, when both fell with a bullet to each, accurately placed under the heart-arm. The bodies were carried to the court-house, which is here the morgue or dead-house, to be exposed, as is the custom, for a time: the citizens, when asked if they suspected who did the deed, invariably replied, with a philosophical *sangfroid*, that, in the first place, they didn't know, and, secondly, that they didn't care. Of course the Gentiles hinted that life had been taken by " counsel" —that is to say, by the secret orders of Mr. Brigham Young and his Vehm. But, even had such been the case—of course it was the merest suspicion—such a process would not have been very repugnant to that wild huntress, the Themis of the Rocky Mountains. In a place where, among much that is honest and respectable, there are notable exceptions, this wild, unflinching, and unerring justice, secret and sudden, is the rod of iron which protects the good. During my residence at the Mormon City not a single murder was, to the best of my belief, committed : the three days which I spent at Christian Carson City witnessed three. Moreover, from the Mississippi to Great Salt Lake City, I noticed that the crimes were for the most part of violence, openly and unskillfully committed; the arsenic, strychnine, and other dastardly poisonings of Europe are apparently unknown, although they might be used easily and efficiently with scant chance of detection. That white emigrants have sometimes wiped off the Indian, as the English settler settled with corrosive sublimate the hapless denizen of the great Southern Continent, is scarcely to be doubted; at the same time, it must be owned that they have rarely tried that form of assassination upon one another.

As we issued from the city, we saw the smoke-like column which announced that the emigrants were crossing the benchland; and people were hurrying from all sides to greet and to get news of friends. Presently the carts came. All the new arrivals were in clean clothes, the men washed and shaved, and the girls, who were singing hymns, habited in Sunday dresses. The company was sunburned, but looked well and thoroughly happy, and few, except the very young and the very old, who suffer most on such journeys, troubled the wains. They marched through clouds of dust over the sandy road leading up the eastern portion of the town, accompanied by crowds, some on foot, others on horseback, and a few in traps and other " locomotive doin's," sulkies, and buckboards. A few youths of rather a rowdyish appearance

P

were mounted in all the tawdriness of Western trappings—Rocky Mountain hats, tall and broad, or steeple-crowned felts, covering their scalp-locks, embroidered buckskin garments, huge leggins, with caterpillar or millepede fringes, red or rainbow-colored flannel shirts, gigantic spurs, bright-hilted pistols, and queer-sheathed knives stuck in red sashes with gracefully depending ends. The *jeunesse dorée* of the Valley Tan was easily distinguished from imported goods by the perfect ease with which they sat and managed their animals. Around me were all manner of familiar faces—heavy English mechanics, discharged soldiers, clerks, and agricultural laborers, a few German students, farmers, husbandmen, and peasants from Scandinavia and Switzerland, and correspondents and editors, bishops, apostles, and other dignitaries from the Eastern States. When the train reached the public square—at Great Salt Lake City the "squares" are hollow as in England, not solid as in the States—of the 8th ward, the wagons were ranged in line for the final ceremony. Before the invasion of the army the First President made a point of honoring the entrance of hand-cart trains (but these only) by a greeting in person. Of late he seldom leaves his house except for the Tabernacle: when inclined for a picnic, the day and the hour are kept secret. It is said that Mr. Brigham Young, despite his powerful will and high moral courage, does not show the remarkable personal intrepidity of Mr. Joseph Smith: his followers deny this, but it rests on the best and fairest Gentile evidence. He has guards at his gates, and he never appears in public unattended by friends and followers, who are of course armed. That such a mental anomaly often exists, those familiar with the biographies of the Brahmin officials at the courts of Poonah, Sattara, and other places in India, well know: many a "Pant," whose reckless audacity in intrigue conducted under imminent danger of life, argued the courage of a Cœur de Lion, was personally fearful as Hobbes, and displayed at the death the terrors of Robespierre. A moment of fear is recounted of St. Peter; Erasmus was not the stuff of which martyrs are made, and even the *beau sabreur* once ran. However, in the case of the Prophet there is an absolute necessity for precautions: as Gentiles have themselves owned to me, many a ruffian, if he found an opportunity, would, from pure love of notoriety, even without stronger incentive, try his revolver or his bowie-knife upon the "Big Mormon."

On this occasion the place of Mr. Brigham Young was taken by President Bishop Hunter, a Pennsylvanian, whom even the most fanatic and intentionally evil-speaking anti-Mormon must regard with respect. Preceded by a brass band—"this people" delight in

"Sonorous metal blowing martial sounds"—

and accompanied by the City Marshal, he stood up in his conveyance, and, calling up the Captains of Companies, shook hands with them and proceeded forthwith to business. In a short time ar rangements were made to house and employ all who required work, whether men or women. Having read certain offensive accounts about "girl-hunting elders," "gray-headed gallants," and "ogling apostles," I was somewhat surprised to see that every thing was conducted with the greatest decorum. The Gentiles, however, declare that Mr. Brigham Young and the high dignitaries have issued an order against "pre-emption" on the part of their followers, who escort and accompany the emigrant trains across the prairies.

Mr. Stenhouse circulated freely among the crowd, and introduced me to many whose names I do not remember; in almost every case the introduction was followed by some invitation. He now exchanged a word with this "brother," then a few sentences with that "sister," carefully suppressing the Mr. and Madam of the Eastern States. The fraternal address gives a patriarchal and somewhat Oriental flavor to Mormon converse; like other things, however, it is apt to run into extremes. If a boy in the streets be asked, "What's your name?" he will reply—if he condescends to do so—"I'm brother such-and-such's son." In order to distinguish children of different mothers, it is usual to prefix the maternal to the paternal parent's name, suppressing the given or Christian name of monogamic lands. Thus, for instance, my sons by Miss Brown, Miss Jones, and Miss Robinson, would call themselves Brother Brown Burton, Brother Jones Burton, and so on. The Saints—even the highest dignitaries—wave the Reverend and the ridiculous Esquire; that "title much in use among vulgar people," which in Old and New England applies to every body, gentle or simple, has not yet extended to Great Salt Lake City. The Mormon pontiff and the eminences around him are simply Brother or Mister—they have the substance, and they disdain the shadow of power. *En revanche*, among the crowd there are as many colonels and majors—about ten being the proportion to one captain—as in the days when Mrs. Trollope set the Mississippi on fire. Sister is applied to women of all ages, thus avoiding the difficulty of addressing a dowager, as in the Eastern States, Madam, in contradistinction to Mrs., her daughter-in-law, or, what is worse, of calling her after the English way, old Mrs. A., or, *Scotticè*, Mrs. A. senior.

The dress of the fair sex has, I observed, already become peculiar. The article called in Cornwall a "gowk," in other parts of England a "cottage bonnet," and in the United States a "sunbonnet," is here universally used, with the difference, however, that the Mormons provide it with a long thick veil behind, which acts like a cape or shawl. A loose jacket and a petticoat, mostly of calico or of some inexpensive stuff, compose the *tout visible*. The wealthier affect silks, especially black. The merchants are careful to keep on hand a large stock of fancy goods, millinery, and other feminine adornments. Love of dress is no accident in the mental organization of that sex which some one called ζῷον φιλοκόσμον; the essential is a pleasing foible, in which the semi-nude savage and the crinolined " civilizee," the nun and Quaker-ess, the sinner and the saint, the *biche*, the *petite maîtresse*, and the *grande dame*, all meet for once in their lives pretty much on a par, and on the same ground. Great Salt Lake City contains three " millinery stores," besides thirteen of dry goods and two of fancy goods, or varieties; and some exchange their merchandise for grain.

The contrast of *physique* between the new arrivals and the older colonists, especially those born in the vicinity of the prairies, was salient. While the fresh importations were of that solid and sometimes clumsy form and dimensions that characterize the En-glish at home—where " beauty is seldom found in cottages or workshops, even when no real hardships are suffered"—the others had much of the delicacy of figure and complexion which distin-guishes the American women of the United States. Physiologists may perhaps doubt so rapid and perceptible an operation of cli-mate, but India proves clearly enough that a very few years suffice to deteriorate form and color, especially in the weaker half of hu-manity; why, then, should we think it impossible that a climate of extremes, an air of exceeding purity and tenuity, and an arid position 4000 feet above sea level, can produce the opposite results in as short a space of time? But, whether my theory stand or fall, the fact remains the same. I remarked to my companion the change from the lymphatic and the sanguine to the bilious-nervous and the purely nervous temperament, and admired its results, the fining down of redundancy in wrist, ankle, and waist, the superior placidness and thoughtfulness of expression, and the general ap-pearance of higher caste blood. I could not but observe in those born hereabouts the noble regular features, the lofty, thoughtful brow, the clear, transparent complexion, the long silky hair, and, greatest charm of all, the soft smile of the American woman when she does smile. He appeared surprised, and said that most other Gentiles had explained the thinness of form and reflective look by the perpetual fretting of the fair under the starveling *régime* of polygamy. The belle of the crowd was Miss Sally A——, the daughter of a lawyer, and of course a *ci devant* judge. Strict Mor-mons, however, rather wag the head at this pretty person; she is supposed to prefer Gentile and heathenish society, and it is whis-pered against her that she has actually vowed never to marry a Saint.

I " queried" of my companion how the new arrivals usually behave at Great Salt Lake City, when the civilization, or rather the humanization of a voyage, a long journey, and the sense of helplessness caused by new position, have somewhat mitigated their British bounce and self-esteem. " Pretty well," he replied;

" all expect to be at the top of the tree at once, and they find themselves in the wrong box; no man gets on here by pushing; he begins at the lowest seat; a new hand is not trusted; he is first sent on mission, then married, and then allowed to rise higher if he shows himself useful." This bore a *cachet* of truth:

> Les sots sont un peuple nombreux,
> Trouvant toutes choses faciles;
> Il faut le leur passer; souvent ils sont heureux,
> Grand motif de se croire habiles.
> (*L'Ane et la Flûte.*)

Many of these English emigrants have passed over the plains without knowing that they are in the United States, and look upon Mr. Brigham Young much as Roman Catholics of the last generation regarded the Pope. The Welsh, Danes, and Swedes have been seen on the transit to throw away their blankets and warm clothing, from a conviction that a gay summer reigns throughout the year in Zion. The mismanagement of the inexperienced travelers has become a matter of Joe Miller. An old but favorite illustration, told from the Mississippi to California, is this: A man rides up to a standing wagon, and seeing a wretched-looking lad nursing a starving baby, asks him what the matter may be: " Wal, now," responds the youth, " guess I'm kinder streakt — ole dad's drunk, ole marm's in hy-sterics, brother Jim be playing poker with two gamblers, sister Sal's down yonder a' courtin' with an in-tire stranger, this 'ere baby's got the diaree, the team's clean guv out, the wagon's broke down, it's twenty miles to the next water, I don't care a —— if I never see Californy."

We returned homeward by the States Road, in which are two of the principal buildings. On the left is the Council Hall of the Seventies, an adobe tenement of the usual barn shape, fifty feet long by thirty internally, used for the various purposes of deliberation, preaching, and dancing; I looked through the windows, and saw that it was hung with red. It is a provisional building, used until a larger can be erected. A little beyond the Seventies' Hall, and on the other side of the road, was the Social Hall, the usual scene of Mormon festivities; it resembled the former, but it was larger—73 × 33 feet—and better furnished. The gay season had not arrived; I lost, therefore, an opportunity of seeing the beauty and fashion of Great Salt Lake City in ballroom toilette, but I heard enough to convince me that the Saints, though grave and unjovial, are a highly sociable people. They delight in sleighing and in private theatricals, and boast of some good amateur actors, among whom Messrs. B. Snow, H. B. Clawson, and W. C. Dunbar are particularly mentioned. Sir E. L. Bulwer will perhaps be pleased to hear that the " Lady of Lyons" excited more furore here than even in Europe. It is intended, as soon as funds can be collected, to build a theatre which will vie

with those of the Old Country.   Dancing seems to be considered
an edifying exercise.   The Prophet dances, the Apostles dance,
the Bishops dance.   A professor of this branch of the fine arts
would thrive in Zion, where the most learned of pedagogues
would require to eke out a living after the fashion of one Aristo-
cles, surnamed the "broad-shouldered."   The saltation is not in
the languid, done-up style that polite Europe affects; as in the
days of our grandparents, "positions" are maintained, steps are
elaborately executed, and a somewhat severe muscular exercise
is the result.   I confess to a prejudice against dancing after the
certain, which we are told is the uncertain, epoch of life, and have
often joined in the merriment excited among French folks by the
aspect of some bald-headed and stiff-jointed "Anglais" mingling
crabbed age with joyful youth in a public ball.   Yet there is high
authority for perseverance in the practice: David danced, we are
told, with all his might, and Scipio, according to Seneca, was wont
thus to exercise his heroic limbs.

Besides the grand fêtes at the Social Hall and other subscription establishments, there are "Ward Parties," and "Elders'
Weekly Cotillon Parties," where possibly the seniors dance together, as the Oxford dons did drill—in private.   Polkas, as at
the court of St. James's, are disapproved of.   It is generally asserted that to the New Faith Terpsichore owes a fresh form of
worship, the Mormon cotillon—alias quadrille—in which the cavalier leads out, characteristically, two dames.   May I not be allowed to recommend the importation of this decided improvement into Leamington and other watering-places, where the proportion of the sexes at "hops" rarely exceeds one to seven?

The balls at the Social Hall are highly select, and are conducted on an expensive scale; invitations are issued on embossed
bordered and gilt-edged white paper, say to 75—80 of the *élite*,
including a few of the chief Gentiles.   The ticket is in this form
and style:

PARTY AT SOCIAL HALL.

———◆———

Mr. _____ and Ladies are respectfully invited to attend a
Party at the SOCIAL HALL,

ON TUESDAY, FEBRUARY 7, 1860.

Tickets, $10 (£2) *per Couple.*

Mayor A. O. SMOOT, ⎱ Managers.
Marshal J. C. LITTLE, ⎰

Committee of Arrangements.

| William C. Staines, | William Eddington, | John T. Caine, |
| H. B. Clawson, | Robert T. Burton, | David Candland. |

Great Salt Lake City,
Feb. 1, 1860.

The $10 tickets will admit only one lady with the gentleman; for all extra $2 each must be paid. In the less splendid fêtes $2 50 would be the total price. Premiums are offered when the time draws nigh, but space is limited, and many a Jacob is shorn of his glory by appearing with only Rachel for a follower, and without his train of Leahs, Zilpahs, and Billahs.

An account of the last ball may be abridged. The hall was tastefully and elegantly decorated; the affecting motto, "Our Mountain Home," conspicuouly placed among hangings and evergreens, was highly effective. At 4 P.M. the Prophet and ex-President entered, and "order was called." (N.B.—Might not this be tried to a purpose in a London ball-room?) Ascending a kind of platform, with uplifted hands he blessed those present. Farther East I have heard of the reverse being done, especially by the *maître du logis*. He then descended to the boards and led off the first cotillon. At 8 P.M. supper was announced; covers for 250 persons had been laid by Mr. Candland, "mine host" of "The Globe." On the following page will be found the list of the somewhat substantial goodies that formed the *carte*.

It will be observed that the *cuisine* in Utah Territory has some novelties, such as bear and beaver. The former meat is a favorite throughout the West, especially when the animal is fresh from feeding; after hibernation it is hard and lean. In the Himalayas many a sportsman, after mastering an artificial aversion to eat bear's grease, has enjoyed a grill of "cuffy." The paws, which not a little resemble the human hand, are excellent—*experto crede*. I can not pronounce *ex cathedrâ* upon beavers' tails; there is no reason, however, why they should be inferior to the appendage of a Cape sheep. "Slaw"—according to my informants—is synonymous with sauer-kraut. Mountain, Pioneer, and Snowballs are unknown to me, except by their names, which are certainly patriotic, if not descriptive.

After supper dancing was resumed with spirit, and in its intervals popular songs and duets were performed by the best musicians. The "finest party of the season" ended as it began, with prayer and benediction, at 5 A.M.—thirteen successive mortal hours—it shows a solid power of enduring enjoyments! And, probably, the revelers wended their way home chanting some kind of national hymn like ⌐nis, to the tune of the "Ole Kentucky shore:"

> "Let the chorus still be sung,
> Long live Brother Brigham Young.
> And blessed be the Vale of Deserét—rét—rét!
> And blessed be the Vale of Deserét."

Returning to the hotel, we found the justiciary and the official party safely arrived; they had been delayed three days at Foot of Ridge Station, but they could not complain of the pace at which they came in. The judge was already in confab with a Pennsyl-

TERRITORIAL AND CIVIL BALL,

SOCIAL HALL, February 7, 1860.

BILL OF FARE.

First Course.

SOUPS.

Oyster,   Vermicelli,
Ox-tail,   Vegetable.

Second Course.

MEATS.

Roast.	*Boiled.*
Beef,	Sugar-corned beef,
Mutton,	Mutton,
Mountain Mutton,	Chickens,
Bear,	Ducks,
Elk,	Tripe,
Deer,	Turkey,
Chickens,	Ham,
Ducks,	Trout,
Turkeys.	Salmon.

STEWS AND FRICASSEES.

Oysters and Ox Tongues,	Chickens,
Beaver Tails,	Ducks,
Collard Head,	Turkeys.

VEGETABLES.

Boiled.	*Baked.*
Potatoes,	Potatoes,
Cabbage (*i. e.*, greens),	Parsnips,
Parsnips,	Beans.
Cauliflower,	
Slaw.	

Hominy.

Third Course.

Pastry.	*Puddings.*
Mince Pies,	Custards,
Green Apple Pie,	Rice,
Pineapple Pie,	English Plum,
Quince Jelly Pie,	Apple Soufflé,
Peach Jelly Pie,	Mountain,
Currant Jelly Pie.	Pioneer.
Blancmange.	Jellies.

Fourth Course.

Cakes.	*Fruits.*
Pound,	Raisins,
Sponge,	Grapes,
Gipsy,	Apples,
Varieties.	Snowballs.
Candies.	Nuts.
Tea.	Coffee.

vanian compatriot, Colonel S. C. Stambaugh, of the Militia, Surveyor General of Utah Territory. This gentleman is no great favorite with the Saints: they accuse him of a too great skillfulness in "mixing"—cocktails, for instance—and a degree of general joviality that swears (*qui jure*) with the grave and reverend seigniory around him. His crime, it appears to me, chiefly consists in holding a fat appointment. I need hardly say that at Great Salt Lake City party feeling rises higher, perhaps, than in any other small place, because religious acrimony is superadded to the many conflicting interests. Every man's concerns are his neighbor's; no one, apparently, ever heard of that person who "became immensely rich"—to quote an Americanism—by "minding his own business." As often happens, religion is made, like slavery in the Eastern States and opium in China, the *cheval de bataille;* the root of the quarrel must be sought deeper; in other words, interest, and interest only, is the Tisiphone that shakes the brand of war. As Mormonism grows, its frame becomes more strongly knit. Thus the Gentile merchants, who have made from 120 to 600 per cent. on capital, were, at the time of my visit, preparing to sell off, because they found the combination against them overpowering. For the most part they vowed that there is no people with whom they would rather do business than with the Mormons; praised their honesty and punctuality in payments, and compared them advantageously in such matters with those of the older faith. Yet they had resolved to remove. The total number of Gentiles in the city is probably not more than 300, a small proportion to a body of at least 9000.

A stranger, especially an official, is kindly warned, on his first arrival at Great Salt Lake City, of its inveterate cliquism, and is amicably advised to steer a middle course, without turning to the right or to the left, between the Scylla and Charybdis of Christianity and Mormonism. This mezzo-termine may be possible in official matters; in society it is not. I soon saw that, though a traveler on the wing might sit alternately in the tents of Shem and Japhet, a resident would soon be obliged to dwell exclusively in either one or the other. When Gentile and Mormon meet, they either maintain a studied or surly silence, or they enter into a dialogue which, on a closer acquaintance with its formation, proves to be a conglomerate of "rile" and "knagg"—an unpleasant predicament for those *en tiers*. Such, at least, was my short experience, and I believe that of my companions.

Colonel Stambaugh, a day or two after the introduction, offered to act cicerone through the settlement, and I was happy to accept his kindness. One fine evening we drove along the Tooele Road westward, and drank of the waters of the New Jordan, which, to the unregenerate palate, tasted, I must say, somewhat brackish and ill-flavored. The river is at this season about one hundred feet broad, and not too deep below its banks to be useless for irrigation, which, as the city increases, will doubtless be extended. It is spanned by a wooden bridge so rickety that it shakes with a child's tread—the governor has urgently but unavailingly represented the necessity of reconstruction. But, although the true Western, or rather Keltic recklessness of human life—which contrasts so strongly with the sanctity attached to it by the old Roman and the modern Anglo-Scandinavian—here still displays itself, in some points there is no disregard for improvement. Mr. Brigham Young has seen the evils of disforesting the land, and the want of plantations; he has lately contracted for planting, near Jordan and elsewhere, a million of young trees at the rate of one cent each. On the way we saw several fine Durhams and Devons, which are driven out every morning and back every evening under the charge of a boy, who receives one and a half cent *per mensem* a head. The animals have been brought across the prairies at great trouble and expense: stock-breeding is one of the Prophet's useful hobbies, and the difference between the cattle in Utah Territory and the old Spanish herds still seen in the country parts of California is remarkable. The land, as will presently appear, is better calculated for grazing than for agriculture, and a settlement of 500 souls rarely has less than 500 head of cattle.

Returning from Jordan, we re-entered the city by the western road, and drove through Mr. Brigham Young's block toward the Northern Kanyon. The gateway was surmounted by a plaster group, consisting of a huge vulturine eagle, perched, with wings outspread, neck bended as if snuffing the breeze of carrion from afar, and talons clinging upon a yellow bee-hive—a most uncomfortable and unnatural position for the poor animal. The device is doubtless highly symbolical, emblematical, typical—in fact, every thing but appropriate and commonsensical. The same, however, may be said of one of the most picturesque ensigns in the civilized world—what have stars to do with stripes or stripes with stars? It might be the device of the British or Austrian soldier — only in their case, unlike the flag of the United States, the stripes should be many and the stars few. *En passant* we remarked a kind of guard-room at the eastern doorway of the White House—a presidential title which the house of prophecy in New Zion shares with the house of politication* at Washington: my informants hinted that, in case of an assault upon head-quarters by roughs, marshals, or other officials, fifty rifles could at once be brought to bear upon the spot, and 1000 after the first hour. On the eastern side of the compound were the stables; a lamb in effigy surmounted the entrance, and meekly reposed under the humane injunction, "Take care of your flocks." Beyond this point lay a number of decrepit emigrant wagons, drawn up to form a fence, a young plantation of fruitless peaches, and the remnants of the falling wall.

* The Western press uses to "politicate," *v. n.* to make a trade of politics, and the participle politicating—why not, then, politication?

We then struck into "City," usually known as "Brigham's" Kanyon, the Prophet having a saw-mill upon the upper course. It is the normal deep narrow gorge, with a beautiful little stream, which is drawn off by raised water-courses at different altitudes to supply the settlement. The banks are margined with dwarf oaks and willows; limestone, sandstone, and granite, all of fine building quality, lie scattered about in profusion, while high above rise the acclivities of the gash, thinly sprinkled with sage and sun-flower. Artemisia in this part improves like the population in appearance, nor is it always a sign of sterility; in parts wheat grows well where the shrub has been uprooted. The road along the little torrent was excellent; it would have cost $100,000 in Pennsylvania, but here much is done by tithe-work; moreover, the respect for the Prophet is such that men would rather work for him on credit than take pay from others.

Being in want of local literature, after vainly ransacking the few book-stalls which the city contains, I went to the Public Library, and, by sending in a card, at once obtained admission. As usual in the Territories of the United States, this institution is supported by the federal government, which, besides $1500 for books, gave $5000 for the establishment, and $400 from the treasury of Utah is paid to the Territorial librarian, Mr. John Lyon, who is also a poet. The management is under the Secretary of the Territory, and the public desire to see an extra grant of $500 per annum.* The volumes, about 1000 in number, are placed in

---

* An Act in relation to Utah Library:

Sec. 1. Be it enacted by the Governor and Legislative Assembly of the Territory of Utah, That a librarian shall be elected by a joint vote of the Legislative Assembly of the Territory of Utah, whose duty it shall be to take charge of the library (known in law as the Utah Library), as hereinafter prescribed.

Sec. 2. Said librarian shall hold his office during the term of two years, or until his successor is appointed, and shall give bonds for the faithful discharge of his duties in the sum of $6000, and file the same in the office of Secretary of the Territory before entering upon his duties, who may also appoint a deputy, as occasion requires, to act in his stead, under the same restrictions as the principal librarian.

Sec. 3. It shall be the duty of the librarian to cause to be printed, at as early a date as practicable, a full and accurate catalogue of all books, maps, globes, charts, papers, apparatus, and valuable specimens in any way belonging to said library; also to use diligent efforts to preserve from waste, loss, or damage, any portion of said library.

Sec. 4. It shall be the duty of the librarian, for and in behalf of the Territory of Utah, to plant suits, collect fines, prosecute, or defend the interests of said library, or otherwise act as a legal plaintiff or defendant in behalf of the Territory, where the interests of the library are concerned.

Sec. 5. The location of the library shall be at the seat of government of the Territory of Utah, and it shall be the duty of the librarian to have all the books of the library orderly and properly arranged within the library-room, for the use of such officers and persons as are named in the fourteenth section of the Organic Act for Utah Territory, during each session of the Legislative Assembly of Utah; provided, however, that nothing herein contained shall debar the librarian, in vacation of the Legislative Assembly, from permitting books, maps, and papers being drawn from said library, for professional and scientific purposes, by officers of the United States and of Utah Territory, and other citizens of Utah, where the librarian shall judge the public good may justify.

a large room on the north side of the "Mountaineer" office, and the librarian attends every Thursday, when books are "loaned" to numerous applicants. The works are principally those of reference, elementary, and intended for the general reader, such as travels, popular histories, and novels. The "Woman in White" had already found her way across the prairies, and she received the honors and admiration which she deserved.

On the evening of the 30th of August, after dining with the governor, I accompanied him to the Thermal Springs, one of the lions of the place. We struck into the north road, and soon issued from the town. On the right hand we passed a large tumble-down tenement which has seen many vicissitudes. It began life as a bath-house and bathing-place, to which the white sulphury waters of the Warm Springs,* issuing from below Ensign Peak, were brought in pine-log pipes. It contained also a ballroom, two parlors for clubs and supper-parties, and a double kitchen. It afterward became a hotel and public house for emigrants to California and Oregon. These, however, soon learned to prefer more central quarters, and now it has subsided into a tannery of low degree. About two and a half miles beyond the northern suburb are the Hot Springs,† which issue from the western slope

---

Sec. 6. It shall be the duty of the librarian to let out books for a specified time, and call in the same when due, inflict fines for damage or loss of books, and collect the same, and keep an accurate account of all his official doings in a book kept for that purpose, and make an annual report of the same to the Legislative Assembly of Utah; provided that no fine shall be excessive, or more than four times the purchase price of the book or books for the loss or damage of which the fine may be inflicted.

Sec. 7. The librarian is hereby entitled to draw from the treasury of Utah for the current year as compensation for his services the sum of $400, not otherwise appropriated; also the sum of $200 to defray the expenses of stationery, printing catalogue, and other contingencies.

Approved March 6, 1852.

* The following is the analysis of the warm spring by Dr. L. D. Gale, printed by Captain Stansbury in Appendix F. It dates from 1851, but apparently more detailed trials have not yet been made. One hundred parts of the water (whose specific gravity was 1·0112) give the following results:

Sulphureted hydrogen absorbed in the water	0·037454
"　　　　　" 　combined with bases	0·000728
Carbonate of lime precipitated by boiling	0·075000
"　　　" 　magnesia	0·022770
Chloride of calcium	0·005700
Sulphate of soda	0·064835
Chloride of sodium	0·861600
	1·023087

The usual temperature is laid down at 102° F.

† The water of the Hot Springs was found to have the specific gravity of 1·0130, and 100 parts yielded solid contents 1·1454.

Chloride of sodium	0·8052
"　　　magnesia	0·0288
"　　　calcium	0·1096
Sulphate of lime	0·0806
Carbonate of lime	0·0180
Silica	0·0180
	1·0602

The usual temperature is laid down at 128° F.

of the hills lying behind Ensign Peak. A generous supply of water, gushing from the rock into a basin below, drains off and forms a lakelet, varying according to season from one to three miles in circumference. Where the water first issues it will boil an egg; a little below it raises the mercury to 128° F. Even at a distance from the source it preserves some heat, and, accordingly, it is frequented throughout the winter by flights of water-fowl and camping Indians, whose children sit in it to thaw their half-frozen limbs. These springs, together with the fresh-water lake and the Jordan, are held to be more purifying than Abana and Pharphar, rivers of Damascus; and, being of the Harrowgate species, they will doubtless be useful to the Valley people as soon as increased luxury requires such appliances. When the wind sets in from the north, the decided perfume of sulphureted hydrogen and saleratus is any thing but eau de Cologne. An anti-Mormon writer, describing these springs and other evidences of igneous and volcanic action, dwells with complacency upon the probability that at some no distant time New Zion may find herself in a quandary, and—like the Cities of the Plain, to which she is thus insinuatingly compared—fuel for the flames. On our way home the governor pointed out the remains of building and other works upon a model farm, which had scarcely fared better than that of Niger celebrity. The land around is hoar with salt, and bears nothing but salsolæ and similar hopeless vegetation.

CHAPTER V.

Second Week at Great Salt Lake City.—Visit to the Prophet.

SHORTLY after arriving, I had mentioned to Governor Cumming my desire to call upon Mr., or rather, as his official title is, President Brigham Young, and he honored me by inquiring what time would be most convenient to him. The following was the answer: the body was in the handwriting of an amanuensis—similarly Mr. Joseph Smith was in the habit of dictation—and the signature, which would form a fair subject for a Warrenologist, was the Prophet's autograph.

" Governor A. Cumming.

" Great Salt Lake City, Aug. 30, 1860.

" Sir,—In reply to your note of the 29th inst., I embrace the earliest opportunity since my return to inform you that it will be agreeable to me to meet the gentleman you mention in my office at 11 A.M. to-morrow, the 31st.   Brigham Young."

The " President of the Church of Jesus Christ of Latter-Day Saints all over the World" is obliged to use caution in admitting strangers, not only for personal safety, but also to defend his dignity from the rude and unfeeling remarks of visitors, who seem to think themselves entitled, in the case of a Mormon, to transgress every rule of civility.

About noon, after a preliminary visit to Mr. Gilbert—and a visit in these lands always entails a certain amount of "smiling" —I met Governor Cumming in Main Street, and we proceeded together to our visit. After a slight scrutiny we passed the guard —which is dressed in plain clothes, and to the eye unarmed—and walking down the veranda, entered the Prophet's private office. Several people who were sitting there rose at Mr. Cumming's entrance. At a few words of introduction, Mr. Brigham Young advanced, shook hands with complete simplicity of manner, asked me to be seated on a sofa at one side of the room, and presented me to those present.

Under ordinary circumstances it would be unfair in a visitor to draw the portrait of one visited. But this is no common case. I have violated no rites of hospitality. Mr. Brigham Young is a "seer, revelator, and prophet, having all the gifts of God which he bestows upon the Head of the Church:" his memoirs, lithographs, photographs, and portraits have been published again and again; I add but one more likeness; and, finally, I have nothing to say except in his favor.

The Prophet was born at Whittingham, Vermont, on the 1st of June, 1801; he was consequently, in 1860, fifty-nine years of age; he looks about forty-five. *La célébrité vieillit* — I had expected to see a venerable-looking old man. Scarcely a gray thread appears in his hair, which is parted on the side, light colored, rather thick, and reaches below the ears with a half curl. He formerly wore it long, after the Western style; now it is cut level with the ear-lobes. The forehead is somewhat narrow, the eyebrows are thin, the eyes between gray and blue, with a calm, composed, and somewhat reserved expression: a slight droop in the left lid made me think that he had suffered from paralysis; I afterward heard that the ptosis is the result of a neuralgia which has long tormented him. For this reason he usually covers his head, except in his own house or in the Tabernacle. Mrs. Ward, who is followed by the "Revue des Deux-Mondes," therefore errs again in asserting that "his Mormon majesty never removes his hat in public." The nose, which is fine and somewhat sharp-pointed, is bent a little to the left. The lips are close like the New Englander's, and the teeth, especially those of the under jaw, are imperfect. The cheeks are rather fleshy, and the line between the alæ of the nose and the mouth is broken; the chin is somewhat peaked, and the face clean shaven, except under the jaws, where the beard is allowed to grow. The hands are well made, and not disfigured by rings. The figure is somewhat large, broad-shouldered, and stooping a little when standing.

The Prophet's dress was neat and plain as a Quaker's, all gray homespun except the cravat and waistcoat. His coat was of antique cut, and, like the pantaloons, baggy, and the buttons were black. A neck-tie of dark silk, with a large bow, was loosely passed round a starchless collar, which turned down of its own accord. The waistcoat was of black satin—once an article of almost national dress—single-breasted, and buttoned nearly to the neck, and a plain gold chain was passed into the pocket. The boots were Wellingtons, apparently of American make.

Altogether the Prophet's appearance was that of a gentleman farmer in New England—in fact, such as he is: his father was an agriculturist and revolutionary soldier, who settled "down East." He is a well-preserved man; a fact which some attribute to his habit of sleeping, as the Citizen Proudhon so strongly advises, in solitude. His manner is at once affable and impressive, simple and courteous: his want of pretension contrasts favorably with certain pseudo-prophets that I have seen, each and every of whom holds himself to be a "Logos" without other claim save a semi-maniacal self-esteem. He shows no signs of dogmatism, bigotry, or fanaticism, and never once entered—with me at least —upon the subject of religion. He impresses a stranger with a certain sense of power; his followers are, of course, wholly fascinated by his superior strength of brain. It is commonly said there is only one chief in Great Salt Lake City, and that is "Brigham." His temper is even and placid; his manner is cold—in fact, like his face, somewhat bloodless; but he is neither morose nor methodistic, and, where occasion requires, he can use all the weapons of ridicule to direful effect, and "speak a bit of his mind" in a style which no one forgets. He often reproves his erring followers in purposely violent language, making the terrors of a scolding the punishment in lieu of hanging for a stolen horse or cow. His powers of observation are intuitively strong, and his friends declare him to be gifted with an excellent memory and a perfect judgment of character. If he dislikes a stranger at the first interview, he never sees him again. Of his temperance and sobriety there is but one opinion. His life is ascetic: his favorite food is baked potatoes with a little buttermilk, and his drink water: he disapproves, as do all strict Mormons, of spirituous liquors, and never touches any thing stronger than a glass of thin Lager-bier; moreover, he abstains from tobacco. Mr. Hyde has accused him of habitual intemperance: he is, as his appearance shows, rather disposed to abstinence than to the reverse. Of his education I can not speak: "men, not books—deeds, not words," has ever been his motto; he probably has, as Mr. Randolph said of Mr. Johnston, "a mind uncorrupted by books." In the only discourse which I heard him deliver, he pronounced impĕtus, impētus. Yet he converses with ease and correctness, has neither snuffle nor pompousness, and speaks as an authority upon certain subjects, such as agriculture and stock-breeding. He assumes no airs of extra sanctimoniousness, and has the plain, simple manners of honesty. His followers deem him an angel of light, his foes a goblin damned: he is, I presume, neither one nor the other. I can not pronounce about his scrupulousness: all the world over, the sincerest religious belief and the practice of devotion are sometimes compatible not only with the most disorderly life, but with the most terrible crimes; for mankind mostly believes that

"Il est avec le ciel des accommodements."

He has been called hypocrite, swindler, forger, murderer. No one looks it less. The best authorities—from those who accuse Mr. Joseph Smith of the most heartless deception, to those who believe that he began as an impostor and ended as a prophet—find in Mr. Brigham Young "an earnest, obstinate egotistic enthusiasm, fanned by persecution and inflamed by bloodshed." He is the St. Paul of the New Dispensation: true and sincere, he gave point, and energy, and consistency to the somewhat disjointed, turbulent, and unforeseeing fanaticism of Mr. Joseph Smith; and if he has not been able to create, he has shown himself great in controlling circumstances. Finally, there is a total absence of pretension in his manner, and he has been so long used to power that he cares nothing for its display. The arts by which he rules the heterogeneous mass of conflicting elements are indomitable will, profound secrecy, and uncommon astuteness.

Such is His Excellency President Brigham Young, "painter and glazier"—his earliest craft—prophet, revelator, translator, and seer; the man who is revered as king or kaiser, pope or pontiff never was; who, like the Old Man of the Mountain, by holding up his hand could cause the death of any one within his reach; who, governing as well as reigning, long stood up to fight with the sword of the Lord, and with his few hundred guerrillas, against the then mighty power of the United States; who has outwitted all diplomacy opposed to him; and, finally, who made a treaty of peace with the President of the Great Republic as though he had wielded the combined power of France, Russia, and England.

Remembering the frequent query, "What shall be done with the Mormons?" I often asked the Saints, Who will or can succeed Mr. Brigham Young? No one knows, and no one cares. They reply, with a singular disdain for the usual course of history, with a perfect faith that their Cromwell will know no Richard as his successor, that, as when the crisis came the Lord raised up in him, then unknown and little valued, a fitting successor to Mr. Joseph Smith—of whom, by-the-by, they now speak with a respectful reverential *sotto voce*, as Christians name the Founder of their faith—so, when the time for deciding the succession shall arrive, the chosen Saints will not be left without a suitable theocrat to exalt the people Israel. The Prophet professes, I believe, to hold office in a kind of spiritual allegiance to the Smith family, of which the eldest son, Mr. Joseph Smith, the third of that dynasty, has of late years, though blessed by his father, created a schism in the religion. By the persuasions of his mother, who, after the first Prophet's death, gave him a Gentile stepfather, he has abjured polygamy and settled in the Mansion House at Nauvoo. The Mormons, though ready to receive back the family at Great Salt Lake City when manifested by the Lord, hardly look to him as their future chief. They all, however, and none more than Mr. Brigham Young, show the best of feeling toward the descendants of their founder, and expect much from David Smith, the second and posthumous son of him martyred at Carthage. He was called David, and choicely blessed before his birth by his father, who prophesied that the Lord will see to his children. Moreover, all speak in the highest terms of Mr. Joseph A. Young, the dweller at the White House, the eldest son of the ex-governor, who traveled in Europe and England, and distinguished himself in opposition to the federal troops.

After finishing with the "Lion of the Lord," I proceeded to observe his companions. By my side was seated Daniel H., whose title is "General," Wells, the Superintendent of Public Works, and the commander of the Nauvoo Legion. He is the third President of the Mormon triumvirate, and having been a justice of the peace and an alderman in Illinois, when the Mormons dwelt there in 1839, he is usually known as Squire Wells: he became a Saint when the Mormons were driven from Nauvoo in 1846, and took their part in battles against the mob. In appearance he is a tall, large, bony, rufous man, and his conduct of the affair in 1857–'8 is spoken of with admiration by Mormons. The second of the Presidency, Mr. Heber C. Kimball, was not present at that time, but on another occasion he was: Mr. Brigham Young introduced me to him, remarking, with a quiet and peculiar smile, that during his friend's last visit to England, at a meeting of the Methodists, one of the reverends attempted to pull his chair from under him; at which reminiscence the person alluded to looked uncommonly grim. Mr. Kimball was born in the same year as Mr. Brigham Young, and was first baptized in 1832: he is a devoted follower of the Prophet, a very Jonathan to this David, a Umar to the New Islam. He is a large and powerful man, not unlike a blacksmith, which I believe he was, and is now the owner of a fine block, with houses and barns, garden and orchard, north of and adjoining that of Mr. Brigham Young. The third person present was the apostle Mr. George A. Smith, the historian and recorder of the Territory, and a cousin of the first Prophet: he is a walking almanac of Mormon events, and is still full of fight, strongly in favor of rubbing out the "wretched Irishmen and Dutchmen sent from the East to try whether the Mormons would receive federal officers."

Q

Mr. Willford Woodruff, like Mr. Smith, one of the original apostles, has visited England as a missionary, appeared before the public as polemic and controversialist, and has now settled down as an apostle at Great Salt Lake City. Mr. Albert O. Carrington, a graduate of Dartmouth College, had acted as second assistant on the topographical survey to Captain Stansbury, who speaks of him as follows: " Being a gentleman of liberal education, he soon acquired, under instruction, the requisite skill, and by his zeal, industry, and practical good sense materially aided us in our subsequent operations. He continued with the party till the termination of the survey, accompanied it to the city (Washington), and has since returned to his mountain home, carrying with him the respect and good wishes of all with whom he was associated." Of Mr. F. Little, who completed the *septem contra Christianitatem* then present, I shall have more to say in a future chapter.

The Prophet received us in his private office, where he transacts the greater part of his business, corrects his sermons, and conducts his correspondence. It is a plain, neat room, with the usual conveniences, a large writing-desk and money-safe, table, sofas, and chairs, all made by the able mechanics of the settlement. I remarked a pistol and a rifle hung within ready reach on the right-hand wall; one of these is, I was told, a newly-invented twelve-shooter. There was a look of order, which suited the character of the man: it is said that a door badly hinged, or a curtain hung awry, " puts his eye out." His style of doing business at the desk or in the field—for the Prophet does not disdain handiwork—is to issue distinct, copious, and intelligible directions to his *employés*, after which he dislikes referring to the subject. It is typical of his mode of acting, slow, deliberate, and conclusive. He has the reputation of being wealthy. He rose to power a poor man. The Gentiles naturally declare that he enriched himself by the tithes and plunder of his followers, and especially by preying upon and robbing the Gentiles. I believe, however, that no one pays Church-dues and alms with more punctuality than the Prophet, and that he has far too many opportunities of coining money, safely and honestly, to be guilty, like some desperate destitute, of the short-sighted folly of fraud. In 1859 he owned, it is said, to being possessed of $250,000, equal to £50,000, which makes a millionaire in these mountains—it is too large a sum to jeopardize. His fortunes were principally made in business: like the late Imaum of Muscat, he is the chief merchant as well as the high priest. He sends long trains of wagons freighted with various goods to the Eastern States, and supplies caravans and settlements with grain and provisions. From the lumber which he sold to the federal troops for hutting themselves at Camp Floyd, he is supposed to have netted not less than $200,000. This is one of the sorest points with the army: all declare that the Mormons would have been in rags or sackcloth if soldiers had not been sent; and they naturally grudge discomfort, hardship, and expatriation, whose only effect has been to benefit their enemies.

After the few first words of greeting, I interpreted the Prophet's look to mean that he would not dislike to know my object in the City of the Saints. I told him that, having read and heard much about Utah as it is said to be, I was anxious to see Utah as it is. He then entered briefly upon the subjects of stock and agriculture, and described the several varieties of soil. One delicate topic was touched upon: he alluded to the "Indian wars," as they are here called: he declared that when twenty are reported killed and wounded, that two or three would be nearer the truth, and that he could do more with a few pounds of flour and yards of cloth than all the sabres of the camp could effect. The sentiment was cordially seconded by all present. The Israelitic origin of "Lemuel," and perhaps the prophecy that "many generations shall not pass away among them save they shall be a white and delightsome people,"* though untenable as an ethnologic theory, has in practice worked at least this much of good, that the Mormons treat their step-brethren with far more humanity than other Western men: they feed, clothe, and lodge them, and attach them by good works to their interests. Slavery has been legalized in Utah, but solely for the purpose of inducing the Saints to buy children, who otherwise would be abandoned or destroyed by their starving parents.† During my stay in the city I did not see more

* Second Book of Nephi, chap. xii., par. 12. Lemuel was the brother of Nephi; and the word is used by autonomasia for the Lamanites or Indians.

† The wording of the following act shows the spirit in which slavery was proposed:

A PREAMBLE AND AN ACT FOR THE FARTHER RELIEF OF INDIAN SLAVES AND PRISONERS.

"Whereas, by reason of the acquisition of Upper California and New Mexico, and the subsequent organization of the Territorial Governments of New Mexico and Utah by the acts of the Congress of the United States, these territories have organized governments within and upon what would otherwise be considered Indian territory, and which really is Indian territory so far as the right of soil is involved, thereby presenting the novel feature of a white legalized government on Indian lands; and

"Whereas the laws of the United States in relation to intercourse with Indians are designed for, and only applicable to, territories and countries under the sole and exclusive jurisdiction of the United States; and

"Whereas, from time immemorial, the practice of purchasing Indian women and children of the Utah tribe of Indians by Mexican traders has been indulged in and carried on by those respective people until the Indians consider it an allowable traffic, and frequently offer their prisoners or children for sale; and

"Whereas it is a common practice among these Indians to gamble away their own children and women; and it is a well-established fact that women and children thus obtained, or obtained by war, or theft, or in any other manner, are by them frequently carried from place to place, packed upon horses or mules, larieted out to subsist upon grass, roots, or starve, and are frequently bound with thongs made of raw-hide until their hands and feet become swollen, mutilated, inflamed with pain, and wounded; and when with suffering, cold, hunger, and abuse they fall sick, so as to become troublesome, are frequently slain by their masters to get rid of them; and

"Whereas they do frequently kill their women and children taken prisoners, either in revenge, or for amusement, or through the influence of tradition, unless they

than half a dozen negroes; and climate, which, disdaining man's interference, draws with unerring hand the true and only compromise line between white and black labor, has irrevocably decided that the African in these latitudes is valueless as a chattel,

are tempted to exchange them for trade, which they usually do if they have an opportunity; and

"Whereas one family frequently steals the children and women of another family, and such robberies and murders are continually committed, in times of their greatest peace and amity, thus dragging free Indian women and children into Mexican servitude and slavery, or death, to the almost entire extirpation of the whole Indian race; and

"Whereas these inhuman practices are being daily enacted before our eyes in the midst of the white settlements, and within the organized counties of the Territory; and when the inhabitants do not purchase or trade for those so offered for sale, they are generally doomed to the most miserable existence, suffering the tortures of every species of cruelty, until death kindly relieves them and closes the revolting scenery:

"Wherefore, when all these facts are taken into consideration, it becomes the duty of all humane and Christian people to extend unto this degraded and downtrodden race such relief as can be awarded to them, according to their situation and circumstances; it therefore becomes necessary to consider,

"First, the circumstances of our location among these savage tribes under the authority of Congress, while yet the Indian title to the soil is left unextinguished; not even a treaty having been held, by which a partition of territory or country has been made, thereby bringing them into our door-yards, our houses, and in contact with our every avocation.

"Second, their situation, and our duty toward them, upon the common principles of humanity.

"Third, the remedy, or what will be the most conducive to ameliorate their condition, preserve their lives and their liberties, and redeem them from a worse than African bondage; it suggests itself to your committee that to memorialize Congress to provide by some act of national legislation for the new and unparalleled situation of the inhabitants of this Territory, in relation to their intercourse with these Indians, would be one resource, prolific in its results for our mutual benefit; and, farther, that we ask their concurrence in the following enactment, passed by the Legislature of the Territory of Utah, January 31, A.D. 1852, entitled,

"'An Act for the Relief of Indian Slaves and Prisoners.

"'Sec. 1. Be it enacted by the Governor and Legislative Assembly of the Territory of Utah, That whenever any white person within any organized county of this Territory shall have any Indian prisoner, child, or woman, in his possession, whether by purchase or otherwise, such person shall immediately go, together with such Indian prisoner, child, or woman, before the selectmen or probate judge of the county. If, in the opinion of the selectmen or probate judge, the person having such Indian prisoner, child, or woman, is a suitable person, and properly qualified to raise or retain and educate said Indian prisoner, child, or woman, it shall be his or their duty to bind out the same, by indenture, for the term of not exceeding twenty years, at the discretion of the judge or selectmen.

"'Sec. 2. The probate judge or selectmen shall cause to be written in the indenture the name and age, place where born, name of parents if known, tribe to which said Indian person belonged, name of the person having him in possession, name of Indian from whom said person was obtained, date of the indenture—a copy of which shall be filed in the probate clerk's office.

"'Sec. 3. The selectmen in their respective counties are hereby authorized to obtain such Indian prisoners, children, or women, and bind them to some useful avocation.

"'Sec. 4. The master to whom the indenture is made is hereby required to send said apprentice to school, if there be a school in the district or vicinity, for the term of three months in each year, at a time when said Indian child shall be between the ages of seven years and sixteen. The master shall clothe his apprentice in a comfortable and becoming manner, according to his said master's condition in life.

"'Approved March 7, 1852.'"

because his keep costs more than his work returns. The negro, however, is not admitted to the communion of Saints — rather a hard case for the Hamite, if it be true that salvation is nowhere to be found beyond the pale of the Mormon Church — and there are severe penalties for mixing the blood of Shem aad Japhet with the accursed race of Cain and Canaan. The humanity of the Prophet's followers to the Lamanite has been distorted by Gentiles into a deep and dangerous project for "training the Indians" to assassinate individual enemies, and, if necessary, to act as guerrillas against the Eastern invaders. That the Yutas—they divide the white world into two great classes, Mormon and Shwop, or American generally—would, in case of war, "stand by" their patrons, I do not doubt; but this would only be the effect of kindness, which it is unfair to attribute to no worthier cause.

The conversation, which lasted about an hour, ended by the Prophet asking me the line of my last African exploration, and whether it was the same country traversed by Dr. Livingstone. I replied that it was about ten degrees north of the Zambezi. Mr. A. Carrington rose to point out the place upon a map which hung against the wall, and placed his finger too near the equator, when Mr. Brigham Young said, " A little lower down." There are many educated men in England who could not have corrected the mistake as well: witness the "London Review," in which the gentleman who "does the geography"—not having the fear of a certain society in Whitehall Place before his eyes—confounds, in all the pomp of criticism upon the said exploration, lakes which are not less than 200 miles apart.

When conversation began to flag, we rose up, shook hands, as is the custom here, all round, and took leave. The first impression left upon my mind by this short *séance*, and it was subsequently confirmed, was, that the Prophet is no common man, and that he has none of the weakness and vanity which characterize the common uncommon man. A desultory conversation can not be expected to draw out a master spirit, but a truly distinguished character exercises most often an instinctive—some would call it a mesmeric—effect upon those who come in contact with it; and as we hate or despise at first sight, and love or like at first sight, so Nature teaches us at first sight what to respect. It is observable that, although every Gentile writer has represented Mr. Joseph Smith as a heartless impostor, few have ventured to apply the term to Mr. Brigham Young. I also remarked an instance of the veneration shown by his followers, whose affection for him is equaled only by the confidence with which they intrust to him their dearest interests in this world and in the next. After my visit many congratulated me, as would the followers of the Tien Wong, or heavenly King, upon having at last seen what they consider "a per se" the most remarkable man in the world.

Before leaving the Prophet's Block I will describe the rest of the building. The grounds are surrounded by a high wall of large pebble-like stones and mortar—the lime now used is very bad—and strengthened with semicircular buttresses. The main entrance faces south, with posts and chains before it for tethering horses. The "Lion House," occupied by Mrs. Young and her family, is in the eastern part of the square: it is so called from a stone lion placed over the large pillared portico, the work of a Mr. William Ward, who also cut the block of white limestone, with "Deserét" beneath a bee-hive, and other symbols, forwarded for the Washington Monument in 1853. It is lamentable to state that the sculptor is now an apostate. The house resembles a two-storied East Indian tenement, with balcony and balustrade, here called an observatory, and is remarkable by its chunamed coat; it cost $65,000—being the best in the city, and was finished in one year. Before building it the Prophet lived in the White House, a humbler bungalow farther to the east; he has now given it up to his son, Joseph A. Young.

On the west of the Lion House lies the private office in which we were received, and farther westward, but adjoining and connected by a passage, is the public office, where the Church and other business is transacted. This room, which is larger than the former, has three desks on each side, the left on entering being those of the public, and the right those of the private clerks. The chief accountant is Mr. Daniel O'Calder, a Scotchman, whose sagacity in business makes him an *alter ego* of the President. At the end opposite the door there is a larger *pupitre* railed off, and a gallery runs round the upper wall. The bookcases are of the yellow box-elder wood, which takes a fine polish; and all is neat, clean, and business-like.

Westward of the public office is the Bee House, so named from the sculptured bee-hive in front of it. The Hymenopter is the Mormon symbol of industry; moreover, Deserét (pronounced Deserétt) is, in "reformed Egyptian," the honey-bee; the term is applied with a certain violence to Utah, where, as yet, that industrious insect is an utter stranger.* The Bee House is a large building, with the long walls facing east and west. It is double storied, with the lower windows, which are barred, oblong: the upper, ten in number, are narrow, and shaded by a small acute ogive or gable over each. The color of the building is a yellowish-white, which contrasts well with the green blinds, and the roof, which is acute, is tiled with shingles. It was finished in 1845, and is tenanted by the "plurality wives" and their families, who each have a bedroom, sitting-room, and closet simply and similarly furnished. There is a Moslem air of retirement about the Bee

* "And they (*scil.* Jared and his brother) did also carry with them Deserét, which by interpretation is a honey-bee; and they did carry with them swarms of bees, and all manner of that which was upon the face of the land, seeds of every kind."—*Book of Ether*, chap. i., par. 3.

THE PROPHET'S BLOCK.

House; the face of woman is rarely seen at the window, and her voice is never heard from without. Anti-Mormons declare it to be, like the state-prison at Auburn, a self-supporting establishment, for not even the wives of the Prophet are allowed to live in idleness.

I was unwilling to add to the number of those who had annoyed the Prophet by domestic allusions, and therefore have no direct knowledge of the extent to which he carries polygamy; some Gentiles allow him seventeen, others thirty-six out of a household of seventy members; others an indefinite number of wives scattered through the different settlements. Of these, doubtless, many are but wives by name, such, for instance, as the widows of the late Prophet; and others are married more for the purpose of building up for themselves spiritual kingdoms than for the normal purpose of matrimony. When treating of Mormon polygamy I shall attempt to show that the relation between the sexes as lately regulated by the Mormon faith necessitates polygamy. I should judge the Prophet's progeny to be numerous from the following circumstance: On one occasion, when standing with him on the belvidere, my eye fell upon a new erection: it could be compared externally to nothing but an English gentleman's hunting stables, with their little clock-tower, and I asked him what it was intended for. " A private school for my children," he replied, " directed by Brother E. B. Kelsey." The harem is said to have cost $30,000.

On the extreme west of this block, backed by a pound for estrays, which is no longer used, lies the Tithing House and Deserét Store, a long, narrow, upper-storied building, with cellars, store-rooms, receiving-rooms, pay-rooms, and writing offices. At this time of the year it chiefly contains linseed, and rags for paper-making; after the harvest it is well stuffed with grains and cereals, which are taken instead of money payment. There is nothing more unpopular among the American Gentiles, or, indeed, more unintelligible to them, than these Mosaic tithes, which the English converts pay, from habit, without a murmur. They serve for scandalous insinuations, viz., that the chiefs are leeches that draw the people's golden blood; that the imposts are compulsory, and that they are embezzled and peculated by the principal dignitaries. I have reason to believe that the contrary is the case. The tithes which are paid into the " Treasury of the Lord" upon the property of a Saint on profession, and afterward upon his annual income, or his time, or by substitute, are wholly voluntary. It sometimes happens that a man casts his all into the bosom of the Church; in this case the all is not refused, but—may I ask—by what Church body, Islamitic, Christian, or pagan, would it be? If the Prophet takes any thing from the Tithing House, he pays for it like other men. The writers receive stipends like other writers, and no more; of course, if any one—clerk or lawyer— wishes to do the business of the Church gratis, he is graciously permitted; and where, I repeat, would he not be? The Latter-Day Saints declare that if their first Presidency and Twelve Apostles—of whom some, by-the-by, are poor—grow rich, it is by due benevolence, not by force or fraud. Much like the primitive college, and most unlike their successors in this modern day, each apostle must have some craft, and all live by handiwork, either in house, shop, or field, no drones being allowed in the social hive. The tithes are devoted in part to Church works, especially to "building up temples or otherwise beautifying and adorning Zion, as they may be directed from on high," and in part to the prosperity of the body politic, temporal, and spiritual; by aiding faithful and needy emigrants, and by supporting old and needy Saints. Perhaps the only true charge brought by the Gentiles against this, and, indeed, against all the public funds in the Mormon City, is, that a large portion finds its way eastward, and is expended in "outside influence," or, to speak plain English, bribes. It is believed by Mormons as well as Gentiles that Mr. Brigham Young has in the States newspaper spies and influential political friends, who are attached to him not only by the ties of business and the natural respect felt for a wealthy man, but by the strong bond of a regular stipend. And such is their reliance upon this political dodgery—which, if it really exists, is by no means honorable to the public morality of the Gentiles—that they deride the idea of a combined movement from Washington ever being made against them. In 1860 Governor Cumming proposed to tax the tithing fund; but the Saints replied that, as property is first taxed and then tithed, by such proceeding it would be twice taxed.

"This people"—a term reiterated at Great Salt Lake City *usque ad nauseam*—declares its belief "in being subject to kings, queen, presidents, rulers, and magistrates; in obeying, honoring, and sustaining the law." They are not backward in open acts of loyalty —I beg America's pardon—of adhesion to the Union, such as supplying stones for the Washington Monument and soldiers for the Mexican War. But they make scant pretension of patriotism. They regard the States pretty much as the States regarded England after the War of Independence, and hate them as the Mexican Criollo does the Gachupin—very much also for the same reason. Theirs is a deep and abiding resentment, which time will strengthen, not efface: the deeds of Missouri and Illinois will bear fruit for many and many a generation. The federal government, they say, has, so far from protecting their lives and property, left them to be burned out and driven away by the hands of a mob, far more cruel than the "red-coated minions" of poor King George; that Generals Harney and Johnston were only seeking the opportunity to act Burgoyne and Cornwallis. But, more galling still to human nature, whether of saint or sinner, they are despised, "treated, in fact, as nobodies"—and that last of insults who can bear? Their petitions to become a sovereign state have been unanswered and ignored.   They have been served with "small-fry" politicians and "one-horse" officials : hitherto the phrase has been, "Any thing is good enough for Utah!"   They return the treatment in kind.

"The Old Independence," the "glorious" 4th of July, '76, is treated with silent contempt: its honors are transferred to the 24th of July, the local Independence Day of their *annus mirabilis* 1847, when the weary pioneers, preceding a multitude, which, like the Pilgrim fathers of New England, left country and home for conscience' sake, and, led by Captain John Brown, whose unerring rifle saved them from starvation when the Indians had stampeded their horses, arrived in the wild waste of valley.   Their form of government, which I can describe only as a democratic despotism with a leaven of the true Mosaic theocracy, enables them to despise a political system in which they say—quoting Hamilton—that "every vital interest of the state is merged in the all-absorbing question of 'who shall be the next president.'"   There is only one "Yankee gridiron" in the town, and that is a private concern.   I do not remember ever seeing a liberty-pole, that emblem of a tyrant majority, which has been bowed to from New York to the Rhine.*   A favorite toast on public occasions is, "We can rock the cradle of Liberty without Uncle Sam to help us," and so forth.   These sentiments show how the wind sets. In two generations hence—perhaps New Zion has a prophet-making air—the Mormons in their present position will, on their own ground, be more than a match for the Atlantic, and, combined with the Chinese, will be dangerous to the Pacific States.

The Mormons, if they are any thing in secular politics, are Democrats.   It has not been judged advisable to cast off the last rags of popular government, but, as will presently appear, theocracy is not much disguised by them.   Although not of the black or extreme category, they instinctively feel that polygamy and slavery are sister institutions, claiming that sort of kindness which arises from fellow-feeling, and that Congress can not attack one without infringing upon the other.   Here, perhaps, they may be mistaken, for nations, like individuals, however warmly and affectionately they love their own peculiar follies and prejudices, sins and crimes, are not the less, indeed perhaps they are rather more, disposed to abominate the follies and prejudices, the sins and crimes of others.   The establishment of slavery, however, though here it serves a humanitarian rather than a private end,

* The first liberty-pole was erected on the open space between the Court-house and Broadway, New York.   It is a long flag-staff, often of several pieces, like the "mast of some tall ammiral," surmounted by a liberty-cap, that Phrygian or Mithridatic coiffure with which the Goddess of Liberty is supposed to disfigure herself. With a peculiar inconsequence, "the whole is" said to be "an allusion to Gesler's cap which Tell refused to do homage to, leading to the freedom of Switzerland."— *Bartlett.*   The French soon made of their *peuplier* a *peuple lié.*   The Americans, curious to say, still believe in it.

necessarily draws the Mormons and the Southern States together. Yet the Saints preferred as President the late Mr. Senator Douglas, a Northern Democrat, to his Southern rival, Mr. Breckinridge. They looked with apprehension of the rise to power of the Republican party, which, had not a weightier matter fallen into their hands, was pledged to do them a harm. I can not but think that absolute independence is and will be, until attained, the principal end and aim of Mormon *haute politique*, and when the disruption of the Great Republic shall have become a *fait accompli*, that Deserét will arise a free, sovereign, and independent state.

Should this event ever happen, it will make the regions about Great Salt Lake as exclusive as Northern China or Eastern Tibet. The obsolete rigors of the sanguinary Mosaic code will be renewed in the middle of the nineteenth century, while the statute-crime "bigamy" and unlimited polygamy will be legalized. Stripes, or, at best, fine and imprisonment, will punish fornication, and the penalty of adultery will be death by lapidation or beheading. As it is, even under the shadow of the federal laws, the self-convicted breaker of the seventh commandment, it is said, offer up his life in expiation of his crime to the Prophet, who, under present circumstances, dismisses him with a penance that may end in the death which he has legally incurred. The offenses against chastity, morality, and decency are exceptionally severe.*

* Sec. 32 (of an " Act in relation to Crimes and Punishment"). Every person who commits the crime of adultery shall be punished by imprisonment not exceeding twenty years, and not less than three years; or by fine not exceeding one thousand dollars, and not less than three hundred dollars; or by both fine and imprisonment, at the discretion of the court. And when the crime is committed between parties any one of whom is married, both are guilty of adultery, and shall be punished accordingly. No prosecution for adultery can be commenced but on the complaint of the husband or wife.

Sec. 33. If any man or woman, not being married to each other, lewdly and lasciviously associate and cohabit together; or if any man or woman, married or unmarried, is guilty of open and gross lewdness, and designedly make any open and indecent, or obscene exposure of his or her person, or of the person of another, every such person so offending shall be punished by imprisonment not exceeding ten years, and not less than six months, and fine not more than one thousand dollars, and not less than one hundred dollars, or both, at the discretion of the court.

Sec. 34. If any person keep a house of ill-fame, resorted to for the purpose of prostitution or lewdness, he shall be punished by imprisonment not exceeding ten years, and not less than one year, or by fine not exceeding five hundred dollars, or both fine and imprisonment. And any person who, after being once convicted of such offense, is again convicted of the like offense, shall be punished not more than double the above specified penalties.

Sec. 35. If any person inveigle or entice any female, before reputed virtuous, to a house of ill-fame, or knowingly conceal, aid, or abet in concealing such female so deluded or enticed, for the purpose of prostitution or lewdness, he shall be punished by imprisonment not more than fifteen years, nor less than five years.

Sec. 36. If any person without lawful authority willfully dig up, disinter, remove, or carry any human body, or the remains thereof, from its place of interment, or aid or assist in so doing, or willfully receive, conceal, or dispose of any such human body, or the remains thereof; or if any person willfully or unnecessarily, and in an improper manner, indecently exposes those remains, or abandons any human body, or the remains thereof, in any public place, or in any river, stream, pond, or other place, every such offender shall be punished by imprisonment not exceeding one year, or

The penalty attached to betting of any kind is a fine not exceeding $300, or imprisonment not exceeding six months.   The importation of spirituous liquors is already burdened with an octroi of half its price, raising cognac and whisky to $12 and $8 per gallon.   If the state could make her own laws, she would banish "poteen," hunt down the stills, and impose a prohibitory duty upon every thing stronger than Lager-bier.*

On the saddest day of the year for the bird which has lost so much good fame by condescending to appear at table *aux choux*, I proceeded with my *fidus Achates* — save the self-comparison to pious Æneas — on a visit to Mr. W. W., alias Judge Phelps, alias "the Devil."   He received me with great civility, and entered without reserve upon his hobbies.   His house, which lies west of Temple Block, bears on the weathercock הננו (Job, xxxviii., 35, "Adsumus:" "Here we are").   Besides Hebrew and other linguistic studies, the judge is a meteorologist, and has been engaged for some years in observations upon the climate of the Territory. An old editor at Independence, he now superintends the Utah Almanac, and gave me a copy for the year 1860, "being the 31st year of the Church of Jesus Christ of Latter-Day Saints."   It is a small duodecimo, creditably printed by Mr. J. M'Knight, Utah, and contains thirty-two pages.   The contents are the usual tables

by fine not exceeding one thousand dollars, or by both fine and imprisonment, at the discretion of the court.

Sec. 37. If any person torture or cruelly beat any horse, ox, or other beast, whether belonging to himself or another, he shall be punished by fine not more than one hundred dollars.

Sec. 38. If any person import, print, publish, sell, or distribute any book, pamphlet, ballad, or any printed paper containing obscene language, or obscene prints, pictures, or descriptions manifestly tending to corrupt the morals of youth, or introduce into any family, school, or place of education, or buy, procure, receive, or have in his possession any such book, pamphlet, ballad, printed paper, picture, or description, either for the purpose of loan, sale, exhibition, or circulation, or with intent to introduce the same into any family, school, or place of education, he shall be punished by fine not exceeding four hundred dollars.

Sec. 39. If any person keep a house, shop, or place resorted to for the purpose of gambling, or permit or suffer any person in any house, shop, or other place under his control or care to play at cards, dice, faro, roulette, or other game for money or other things, such offender shall be fined not more than eight hundred dollars, or imprisonment not exceeding one year, or both, at the discretion of the court.   In a prosecution under this section, any person who has the charge of, or attends to any such house, shop, or place, may be deemed the keeper thereof.

* I quote as an authority,

An Ordinance regulating the Manufacturing and Vending of Ardent Spirits.

Sec. 1. Be it ordained by the General Assembly of the State of Deserét, That it shall not be lawful for any person or persons in this state to establish any distillery or distilleries for the manufacture of ardent spirits except as hereafter provided for ; and any person or persons who shall violate this ordinance, on conviction thereof, shall forfeit all property thus invested to the state, and be liable to a fine at the discretion of the court having jurisdiction.

Sec. 2. Be it farther ordained, That when the governor shall deem it expedient to have ardent spirits manufactured within this state, he may grant a license to some person or persons to make and vend the same, and impose such restrictions thereon as he may deem requisite.

Approved Feb. 12, 1851.

of days, sunrises, sunsets, eclipses, etc., with advertisements on the alternate pages; and it ends with the denominations and value of gold and silver coins, original poetry, "scientific" notes concerning the morning and evening stars, a list of the United States officers at Utah, the number of the planets and asteroids, diarrhœa, and "moral poetry," and an explanation of the word "almanac," concluding with the following observation:

"A person without an almanac is somewhat like a ship at sea without a compass; he never knows what to do nor when to do it."

> "So Mormon, other sects, and Quaker,
> Buy Almanacs, and pay the maker.—K. J."

The only signs of sanctity are in the events appended to the days of the week; they naturally record the dates of local interest, and the births and deaths of prophets and patriarchs, presidents and apostles. Under the head of "Time," however, some novel information is provided for the benefit of the benighted chronologist.

"TIME.—There is a great mystery about time as recorded in the Bible. Authors differ as to what length of time this world has occupied since it came into being. Add 4004 to 1860, and we have 5864 years.

"Again, some authors allow, before the birth of the Savior, 5509 years, which, added to 1860, gives 7369 years since the beginning.

"The book of Abraham, as translated by Joseph Smith, gives 7000 years for the creation by the gods, one day of the Lord being a thousand years of man's time, or a day in Kolob. This important revelation of 7000 years at first shows 5960 years since the transgression of Adam and Eve, and 40 years to the next 'day of rest,' if the year 1900 commences the return of the 'ten tribes,' and the first resurrection; or 13,000 years since the gods said, 'Let there be light, and there was light,' so that the fourteen thousandth year will be the second Sabbath since creation.

"A day of the Moon is nearly thirty of our days, or more than ten thousand of earth's time. Verily, verily,

> "Man knows but little,
> Nor knows that little right."

The judge then showed me an instrument upon which he had expended the thought and labor of years: it was that grand desideratum, a magnetic compass, which, pointing with a second needle to the true north, would indicate variation so correctly as to show longitude by inspection. The article, which was as rough-looking as it could be, was placed upon the table; but it would not, as the inventor explained, point to the true north unless in a particular position. I refrain from recording my hundred doubts as to the feasibility of the operation, and my own suspicions concerning the composition of the instrument. I presently took leave of Judge Phelps, pleased with his quaint kindness, but somehow suspecting him of being a little *tête-montée* on certain subjects.

As it was newspaper day, we passed by the "Mountaineer" office and bought a copy. The press is ably and extensively represented in Great Salt Lake City, as in any other of its Western coevals.* Mormonism, so far from despising the powers of pica, has a more than ordinary respect for them.† Until lately there were three weekly newspapers. The "Valley Tan," however, during the last winter expired, after a slow and lingering dysthesis, induced by overindulgence in Gentile tendencies. It was established in 1858; the proprietor was Mr. J. Hartnett, the late federal secretary; the editor was Mr. Kirk Anderson, followed by Mr. De Wolf and others; the issue hebdomadal, and the subscription high = $10 per annum. The recognized official organ of the religion, which first appeared on the 15th of June, 1850, is the "Deserét News," whose motto is "Truth and Liberty" under a hive, over which is a single circumradiated eye in disagreeable proximity to the little busy bee. It has often changed its size, and is now printed in small folio, of eight pages, each containing four columns of close type: sometimes articles are clothed in the

* According to the "Elgin Courant," there are between 700 and 800 of a fishing population in Hopeness who never see a newspaper.

† The first Mormon newspaper was the "Latter-Day Saints' Messenger and Advocate," published at Kirtland, Ohio, in the time of Mr. Joseph Smith.

The "Evening and Morning Star," published at Independence, Mo., and edited by W. W. Phelps.

"Elders' Journal," published in 1838, in the time of Mr. Joseph Smith.

"The Upper Missouri Advertiser," published about the same time; it did not last long.

"The Nauvoo Neighbor" disappeared in the days of the Exodus.

"The Times and Seasons," containing a compendium of intelligence pertaining to the upbuilding of the kingdom of God, and the signs of the Times, together with a great variety of information in regard to the history, principles, persecutions, deliverances, and onward progress of the Church of Jesus Christ of Latter-Day Saints. Nauvoo 1839–1843. It was edited by Elder John Taylor (now one of the "Twelve") under the direction of Mr. Joseph Smith, and arrived at the fourth volume (octavo): this journal is full of interesting matter to Mormons.

"The Wasp," begun at Nauvoo in 1842.

"The Frontier Garden," published at Council Bluffs during the Exodus from Nauvoo.

"The Seer," edited at Washington, by Elder Orson Pratt, reached the second volume.

"The Gospel Reflector," published at Philadelphia, lasted for a short time.

"The Prophet," published at New York.

"Le Reflecteur," in French, published at Geneva.

"Etoile du Deserét, Organe de l'Eglise de Jésus-Christ des Saints des Derniers Jours," par John Taylor, Paris. It lasted from May, 1851, to April, 1852, and forms 1 vol. large 8vo, containing 192 pages.

"The Western Standard," edited and published weekly at San Francisco, California, United States of America, by Elder George Q. Cannon, now an Apostle and President of the Church in Great Britain. This paper, which was distinguished by the beauty of its type and the character of its composition, lasted through 1856 and 1857; in 1858 it ceased for want of funds.

"Zion's Watchman," published in Australia.

"Udgorn Seion" (the Trump of Zion), published in Wales, a bi-monthly print, which has reached the ninth volume.

"The Luminary," St. Louis, Mo.

"The Mormon," published in New York, a hebdomadal print.

Mormon alphabet. It had reached in 1860 its tenth volume; it appears every Wednesday; costs at Utah $6 per annum, in England £1 13s. 8d. per annum, in advance; single number 9d.; and is superintended by Mr. Brigham Young. It is edited by Mr. Elias Smith, also a Probate judge; he is assisted by Mr. M'Knight, formerly the editor of a paper in the United States, and now the author of the important horticultural, agricultural, and other georgic articles in the "Deserét News." This "Moniteur" also contains corrected reports of the sermons spoken at the Tabernacle. An account of a number may not be uninteresting.

No. 28, vol. x., begins with a hymn of seven stanzas, by C. W. Bryant. Follow remarks by President Brigham Young, at Provo and in the Bowery, Great Salt Lake City; the three sermons, which occupy four columns and a half, are separated by "Modern Germany, II.," by Alexander Ott. There is an article from the "New York Sun," entitled the "Great Eastern in Court." It is followed by nearly half a page of "Clippings," those little recognized piracies which make the American papers as amusing as magazines. Then come advertisements, estray notices, and others, which nearly fill the third and sixth pages, and the column at the eighth, which is the conclusion. I subjoin terms for advertising.* The fourth page contains "News by Eastern Mail" —Doings of the Probate Court—Special term of the Probate Court —Another excusable homicide—The season—Imprisoning convicts without labor—Discharge of the city police—Swiss Saints (lately arrived)—Arrival of missionaries at Liverpool—Drowned, Joseph Vest, etc.—Deserét Agriculturing and Manufacturing Society — Information wanted — and Humboldt's opinion of the United States (comparing it to a Cartesian vortex, liberty a dead machinery in the hands of Utilitarianism, etc.). The fifth and sixth pages detail news from Europe, the Sicilies, Damascus, and India, proceedings of a missionary meeting in the Bowery, and tidings from Juab and Iron County, with a few stopgaps, such as an explanation of the word Zouave, and the part conversion of the fallen Boston elm into a "Mayor's seat." The seventh page is agricultural, and opens with the "American Autumn," by Fanny Kemble, four stanzas. Then comes Sheep-husbandry No. iii., treating of change of pasture, separation of the flock, and fall

---

* ADVERTISING.—Ten lines or less constitute one square.

Regular Advertisements.

One quarter column (four squares or less), for each insertion	$1 50
Half column (seven squares or less), each insertion	3 00
One column (fourteen squares or less)	6 00

Sundry Advertisements.

One square, each insertion	$1 00
Two " "	1 50
Three " "	2 00

Thus upward, with half a dollar to the additional square for each insertion.

management. The other *morceaux* are "Training the peach-tree,"
"Stick to the Farm," an article concluding with "We shall always sign 'speed the plow;' we shall always regard the American farmer, dressed for his employment (!) and tilling his grounds,
as belonging to the order of real noblemen"—the less aristocratic
Englander would limit himself to "Nature's gentleman;" "Why
pork shrinks in the pot," and "Wheat-straw, its value as fodder."
The eighth and last page opens with "Correspondence," and a
letter signed Joseph Hall, headed "More results of 'civilization,'"
and dated Ogden City, Sept. 8, 1860. It contains an account of
occurrences resulting in the "death of one John Cornwell, a discharged government teamster, and, as is often the case with those
Christians who are sent to civilize the 'Mormons' of these mountains, a corrupt, profane, and quarrelsome individual, who doted
on belonging to the 'bully tribe.'" Then follows more news
from San Pete County. A test of love (that capital story out of
C. R. Leslie's autobiography). Siege of Magdeburg. A hard-
shell sermon (preached at Oxford, England), a scrap illustrating
the marvelous growth of Quincy, Illinois, and the Legend of the
origin of the Piano-forte. The latter is followed by a valuable
abstract containing a summary of meteorological observations,
barometric and thermometric, for the month of August, 1860, at
Great Salt Lake City, Utah, by W. W. Phelps, and concluding
with a monthly journal.* Then follow the deaths, six in number, and after one of them is inserted [Millennial Star, copy].
There are no marriages, and the Western papers, like those of
the East, are still *béqueules* enough to consider advertising the
birth of a child indelicate; at least that was the reason given to
me. The last column contains the terms for advertising and the
"fill-up" advertisements.

The "Mountaineer," whose motto is "Do what is right, let the
consequence follow," is considered rather a secular paper. It appears on Saturdays, and the terms of subscription are $6 per an-
num; the occasional supplement is issued gratis. It formerly
belonged to three lawyers, Messrs. Stout, Blair, and Ferguson; it
has now passed into the hands of the two latter. Mr. Hosea Stout
distinguished himself during the Nauvoo troubles; he was the
captain of forty policemen who watched over the safety of Mr.
Joseph Smith, and afterward went on missions to India and China. Major S. M. Blair served under General Sam. Houston in
the Texan war of independence, and was a distinguished lawyer
in the Southern States. A description of the "Deserét News"
will apply to the "Mountaineer." I notice in the issue of Sep-

---

* The maximum of the barometer during the month is 26·100; min. 25·400
    "   "   " thermometer "   " 95° F.; " 60° F.
There fell of rain water 0·670 inches during five days marked showery. Fifteen
days are marked clear and pleasant, or hot and dry, or hot and very dry, the 22d
being the hottest; and the others are partially clear, or clear and cloudy, or hazy
and cloudy.

R

tember 15, 1860, that a correspondent, quoting an extract from the "New York Tribune"—the great Republican organ, and therefore no favorite with the Mormons—says, outspokenly enough to please any amount of John Bull, "The author of the above is a most consummate liar"—so far, so good—"and a contemptible dastardly poltroon"—which is invidious.

I passed the morning of the ensuing Sunday in a painful but appropriate exercise, reading the Books of Mormon and of Moroni the Prophet. Some writers tell me that it is the best extant imitation of the Old Testament; to me it seems composed only to emulate the sprightliness of some parts of Leviticus. Others declare that it is founded upon a romance composed by a Rev. Mr. Spaulding; if so, Mr. Spaulding must have been like Prince Puckler-Muskau of traveling notoriety, a romancer utterly without romance. Surely there never was a book so thoroughly dull and heavy: it is monotonous as a sage-prairie. Though not liable to be terrified by dry or hard reading, I was, it is only fair to own, unable to turn over more than a few chapters at a time, and my conviction is that very few are so highly gifted that they have been able to read it through at a heat. In Mormonism it now holds the same locus as the Bible in the more ignorant Roman Catholic countries, where religious reading is chiefly restricted to the Breviary, to tales of miracles, and to legends of Saints Ursula and Bridget. It is strictly proper, does not contain a word about materialism and polygamy*—in fact, more than one wife is strictly forbidden even in the Book of Doctrines and Covenants.† The Mormon Bible, therefore, is laid aside for later and lighter reading. In one point it has done something. America, like Africa, is a continent of the future; the Book of Mormon has created for it an historical and miraculous past.

At 9 45 A.M. we entered the Bowery; it is advisable to go early if seats within hearing are required. The place was a kind of "hangar," about a hundred feet long by the same breadth, with a roofing of bushes and boughs supported by rough posts, and open for ventilation on the sides; it can contain about 3000 souls. The congregation is accommodated upon long rows of benches, opposite the dais, rostrum, platform, or tribune, which looked like a long lane of boarding open to the north, where it faced the audience, and entered by steps from the east. Between the people and the platform was a place not unlike a Methodist "pen" at a camp-meeting: this was allotted to the orchestra, a violin, a bass, two women and four men performers, who sang the sweet songs of Zion tolerably well—decidedly well, after a moment's reflec-

---

* Behold the Lamanites (North American Indians), your brethren, whom ye hate because of their filthiness, and the cursings which hath come upon their skins, are more righteous than you, for they have not forgotten the commandment of the Lord, which was given unto our fathers, that they should have, save it were one wife; and concubines they should have none; and there should not be whoredoms committed among them.—*Book of Jacob*, chap. ii., par. 9.   * See Chap. IX.

tion as to latitude and longitude, and after reminiscences of country and town chapels in that land where it is said, had the Psalmist heard his own psalms,

"In furious mood he would have tore 'em."

I was told that "profane"—*i. e.*, operatic and other—music is performed at worship, as in the Italian cathedrals, where they are unwilling that Sathanas should monopolize the prettiest airs; on this occasion, however, only hymns were sung.

SOUTH END OF THE TABERNACLE.

We—the judge's son and I—took our seats on the benches of the eighth ward, where we could see the congregation flocking in, a proceeding which was not over—some coming from considerable distances—till 10 15 A.M. The people were all *endimanchés;* many a pretty face peeped from the usual sun-bonnet with its long curtain, though the "mushroom" and the "pork-pie" had found their way over the plains, and trim figures were clad in neat stuff dresses, sometimes silk: in very few cases there was a little faded finery—gauze, feathers, and gaudy colors—such as one may see on great festivals in an Old-Country village. The men were as decently attired: the weather, being hot, had caused many of them to leave their coats at home, and to open their vests; the costume, however, looked natural to working-men, and there was no want of cleanliness, such as sometimes lurks behind a bulwark of buttons. The elders and dignitaries on the platform affected coats of black broadcloth, and were otherwise respectably dress-

ed. All wore their hats till the address began, and then all uncovered. By my side was the face of a blear-eyed English serv-
ant-girl; *en revanche* in front was a charming American mother
and child : she had, what I have remarked in Mormon meetings
at Saville House and other places in Europe, an unusual development of the organ which phrenologists call veneration. I did not
see any Bloomers " displaying a serviceable pair of brogues," or
" pictures of Grant Thorburn in petticoats." There were a few
specimens of the " Yankee woman," formerly wondrous grim,
with a shrewd, thrifty gray eye, at once cold and eager, angular
in body and mind, tall, bony, and square-shouldered, now softened and humanized by transplantation and transposition to her
proper place. The number of old people astonished me ; half a
dozen were sitting on the same bench ; these broken-down men
and decrepit crones had come to lay their bones in the Holy City :
their presence speaks equally well for their faith and for the kind-
heartedness of those who had brought the encumbrance. I remarked some Gentiles in the Bowery ; many, however, do not
care to risk what they may hear there touching themselves.

At 10 A.M. the meeting opened with a spiritual song. Then
Mr. Wallace—a civilized-looking man lately returned from foreign travel—being called upon by the presiding elder for the day,
opened the meeting with prayer, of which the two short-hand
writers in the tribune proceeded to take notes. The matter, as
is generally the case with returned missionaries delivering their
budget, was good ; the manner was somewhat Hibernian ; the
" valleys of the mountains"—a stock phrase, appeared and reap-
peared like the speechifying Patlander's eternal " emerald green
hills and beautiful pretty valleys." He ended by imploring a
blessing upon the (Mormon) President, and all those in authority; Gentiles of course were included. The conclusion was an
amen, in which all hands joined : it reminded me of the historical
practice of " humming" in the seventeenth century, which caused
the universities to be called " *Hum et Hissimi auditores.*"

Next arose Bishop Abraham O. Smoot, second mayor of Zion,
and successor to the late Jedediah M. Grant, who began with
" Brethering," and proceeded at first in a low and methody tone
of voice, " hardly audible in the gallery," to praise the Saints,
and to pitch into the apostates. His delivery was by no means
fluent, even when he warmed. He made undue use of the regular Wesleyan organ—the nose ; but he appeared to speak excellent sense in execrable English. He recalled past persecutions
without over-asperity, and promised future prosperity without
over-prophecy. As he was in the midst of an allusion to the
President, entered Mr. Brigham Young, and all turned their faces,
even the old lady—

" Peut-on si bien prêcher qu'elle ne dorme au sermon ?"—-

who, dear soul! from Hanover Square to far San Francisco, placidly reposes through the discourse.

The Prophet was dressed, as usual, in gray homespun and home-woven: he wore, like most of the elders, a tall, steeple-crowned straw hat, with a broad black ribbon, and he had the rare refinement of black kid gloves. He entered the tribune covered and sat down, apparently greeting those near him. A man in a fit was carried out pumpward. Bishop Smoot concluded with informing us that we should live for God. Another hymn was sung. Then a great silence, which told us that something was about to happen: *that* old man held his cough; *that* old lady awoke with a start; *that* child ceased to squall. Mr. Brigham Young removed his hat, advanced to the end of the tribune, expectorated stooping over the spittoon, which was concealed from sight by the boarding, restored the balance of fluid by a glass of water from a well-filled decanter on the stand, and, leaning slightly forward upon both hands propped on the green baize of the tribune, addressed his followers.

The discourse began slowly; word crept titubantly after word, and the opening phrases were hardly audible; but as the orator warmed, his voice rose high and sonorous, and a fluency so remarkable succeeded falter and hesitation, that—although the phenomenon is not rare in strong speakers—the latter seemed almost to have been a work of art. The manner was pleasing and animated, and the matter fluent, impromptu, and well turned, spoken rather than preached: if it had a fault it was rather rambling and unconnected. Of course, colloquialisms of all kinds were introduced, such as "he become," "for you and I," and so forth. The gestures were easy and rounded, not without a certain grace, though evidently untaught; one, however, must be excepted, namely, that of raising and shaking the forefinger; this is often done in the Eastern States, but the rest of the world over it is considered threatening and bullying. The address was long. God is a mechanic. Mormonism is a great fact. Religion had made him (the speaker) the happiest of men. He was ready to dance like a Shaker. At this sentence the Prophet, who is a good mimic, and has much of the old New English quaint humor, raised his right arm, and gave, to the amusement of the congregation, a droll imitation of Anne Lee's followers. The Gentiles had sent an army to lay waste Zion, and what had they done? Why, hung one of their own tribe! and that, too, on the Lord's day!*

---

* Alluding to one Thos. H. Ferguson, a Gentile; he killed, on Sept. 17th, 1859, in a drunken moment, A. Carpenter, who kept a boot and shoe store. Judge Sinclair, according to the Mormons, was exceedingly anxious that somebody should be *sus. per coll.*, and, although intoxication is usually admitted as a plea in the Western States, he ignored it, and hanged the man on Sunday. Mr. Ferguson was executed in a place behind the city; he appeared costumed in a Robin Hood style, and complained bitterly to the Mormon troops, who were drawn out, that his request to be shot had not been granted.

The Saints have a glorious destiny before them, and their morality is remarkable as the beauty of the Promised Land: the soft
breeze blowing over the Bowery, and the glorious sunshine outside, made the allusion highly appropriate. The Lamanites, or
Indians, are a religious people. All races know a God and may
be saved. After a somewhat lengthy string of sentences concerning the great tribulation coming on earth—it has been coming for
the last 1800 years—he concluded with good wishes to visitors
and Gentiles generally, with a solemn blessing upon the President
of the United States, the territorial governor, and all such as be
in authority over us, and, with an amen which was loudly re-ech-
oed by all around, he restored his hat and resumed his seat.

Having heard much of the practical good sense which characterizes the Prophet's discourse, I was somewhat disappointed:
probably the occasion had not been propitious. As regards the
concluding benedictions, they are profanely compared by the Gentiles to those of the slave, who, while being branded on the hand,
was ordered to say thrice, "God bless the State." The first was
a blessing. So was the second. But at the third, natural indignation having mastered Sambo's philosophy, forth came a certain
naughty word not softened to "darn." During the discourse, a
Saint, in whose family some accident had occurred, was called
out, but the accident failed to affect the riveted attention of the
audience.

Then arose Mr. Heber C. Kimball, the second President. He
is the model of a Methodist, a tall and powerful man, a "gentleman in black," with small, dark, piercing eyes, and clean-shaven
blue face. He affects the Boanerges style, and does not at times
disdain the part of Thersites: from a certain dislike to the Non-
conformist rant and whine, he prefers an every-day manner of
speech, which savors rather of familiarity than of reverence. The
people look more amused when he speaks than when others harangue them, and they laugh readily, as almost all crowds will, at
the thinnest phantom of a joke. Mr. Kimball's movements contrasted strongly with those of his predecessor; they consisted now
of a stone-throwing gesture delivered on tiptoe, then of a descending movement, as

> "When pulpit, drum ecclesiastic,
> Was beat with fist and not with stick."

He began with generalisms about humility, faithfulness, obeying
counsel, and not beggaring one's neighbor. Addressing the hand-
cart emigrants, newly arrived from the "sectarian world," he warned them to be on the look-out, or that every soul of them would
be taken in and shaved (a laugh). Agreeing with the Prophet—
Mr. Kimball is said to be his echo—in a promiscuous way concerning the morality of the Saints, he felt it notwithstanding his
duty to say that among them were "some of the greatest rascals
in the world" (a louder laugh, and N.B., the Mormons are never

spared by their own preachers). After a long suit of advice, *à propos de rien*, to missionaries, he blessed, amen'd, and sat down.

I confess that the second President's style startled me. But presently I called to mind Luther's description* of Tetzel's sermon, in which he used to shout the words Bring! bring! bring! with such a horrible bellowing, that one would have said it was a mad bull rushing on the people and goring them with his horns: and D'Aubigné's neat apology for Luther,† who, "in one of those homely and quaint, yet not undignified similitudes which he was fond of using, that he might be understood by the people," illustrated the idea of God in history by a game of cards! " . . . Then came our Lord God. He dealt the cards: . . . This is the Ace of God. . . . " Mormons also think it a merit to speak openly of " those things we know naturally:" they affect what to others appears coarseness and indelicacy. The same is the case with Oriental nations, even among the most modest and moral. After all, taste is in its general development a mere affair of time and place; what is apt to *froisser* us in the nineteenth may have been highly refined in the sixteenth century, and what may be exceedingly unfit for Westminster Abbey and Notre Dame is often perfectly suited to the predilections and intelligence of Wales or the Tessin. It is only fair to both sides to state that Mr. Kimball is accused by Gentiles of calling his young wives, from the pulpit, "little heifers;" of entering into physiological details belonging to the Dorcas Society, or the clinical lecture-room, rather than the house of worship; and of transgressing the bounds of all decorum when reproving the sex for its *penchants* and *ridicules*. At the same time, I never heard, nor heard of, any such indelicacy during my stay at Great Salt Lake City. The Saints abjured all knowledge of the "fact," and—in this case, *nefas ab hoste doceri*—so gross a scandal should not be adopted from Gentile mouths.

After Mr. Kimball's address, a list of names for whom letters were lying unclaimed was called from the platform. Mr. Eldridge, a missionary lately returned from foreign travel, adjourned the meeting till 2 P.M., delivered the prayer of dismissal, during which all stood up, and ended with the benediction and amen. The Sacrament was not administered on this occasion. It is often given, and reduced to the very elements of a ceremony; even water is used instead of wine, because the latter is of Gentile manufacture. Two elders walk up and down the rows, one carrying a pitcher, the other a plate of broken bread, and each Saint partakes of both.

Directly the ceremony was over, I passed through the thirty carriages and wagons that awaited at the door the issuing of the congregation, and returned home to write my notes. Before appearing in the "Deserét News" the discourses are always recom-

---

* History of the Reformation of the Sixteenth Century. Book iii., chap. i.

† Ditto, Preface.

posed; the reader, therefore, is warned against the following report, which appeared in the " News" of Wednesday, the 5th of September.

"BOWERY.—*Sunday, Sept.* 2, 10 A.M., Bishop Abraham O. Smoot addressed the congregation. He said he rejoiced in the opportunity he had been favored with of testing both principles and men in the Church of Jesus Christ of Latter-Day Saints; he was fully satisfied that those who do right are constantly filled with joy and gladness by the influence of the Holy Ghost. Every man must know God for himself, and practice the principles of righteousness for himself; learn the truth and the light, and walk therein. Men are too much in the habit of patterning after their neighbors' actions instead of following the dictates of the Spirit of God; if the Saints do right they are filled with light, truth, and the power of God. It has been a matter of astonishment to many how we could so much rejoice in the things of God, but the reason is our religion is true, and we know it, for God has revealed it unto us, and hence we can rejoice in the midst of calamities that would make our enemies very cross, and cause them to swear about their troubles. Nine tenths of those who have apostatized have done it on account of prosperity, like Israel of old, but the Lord desires to use us for the advancement of his kingdom, and the spreading abroad of light and truth. We should live for God, and prepare ourselves for all the temporal and spiritual blessings of his kingdom.

" President Brigham Young said if our heavenly Father could reveal all he wishes to his Saints, it would greatly hasten their perfection, and asked the question, Are the people prepared to receive those communications and profit by them, that would bring about their speedy perfection? He discovered a very great variety of degrees of intelligence in the people; he also observed a manifest stupidity in the people attempting to learn the principles of natural life. Observed that God is just and equal in his ways, and that no man will dare to dispute; also that there is no man in our government who will speak truthfully, and according to his honest convictions, but who will admit that we are the most law-abiding people within its jurisdiction. Remarked that all the heathen nations have devotional instincts, and none more than the natives of this vast continent; and they all worship according to the best of their knowledge. The whole human family can be saved in the kingdom of God if they are disposed to receive and obey the Gospel. Reasoned on the subject of fore-ordination, and said the religion of Jesus Christ is designed to make the bad good and the good better. Argued that there is a feeling in every human breast to acknowledge the supremacy of the Almighty Creator. God is just, he is true, and if this were not the case no mortal could be exalted in his presence; advised all to improve upon the knowledge they had received of the things of God. Referred briefly to the birth of Christ, and the attendant opposition and threatening of the governments of the nations of the earth.

" President Heber C. Kimball followed with appropriate remarks on the practical duties of life, the necessity of humility and faithfulness among the Saints, and admonished all to be obedient to the mandates of heaven, and to the counsels of the living oracles. In giving advice to the elders who are expected to go on missions to preach the Gospel, he said : ' The commandment of Jesus to his apostles anciently has been renewed unto us, viz., Go ye therefore, and teach all nations, baptizing them in the name of the Father, and of the Son, and of the Holy Ghost ; teaching them to observe all things whatsoever I have commanded you ; and lo, I am with you alway, even unto the end of the world.' "

The student of the subject may desire to see how one of these sermons reads; I therefore extract from the " Deserét News " one spoken by Mr. Brigham Young during my stay in the city ; it is chosen impartially, neither because it is better nor because it is worse than its fellows. The subject, it will be observed, is uninteresting ; in fact, what negroes call " talkee-talkee"—*pour passer le temps*. But Mr. Brigham Young can, all admit, when occasion serves ability, " bring the house down," and elicit thundering amens.

REMARKS by President BRIGHAM YOUNG, *Bowery*, A.M., *August* 12, 1860. (*Reported by G. D. Watt.*)—" I fully understand that all Saints constantly, so to speak, pray for each other. And when I find a person who does not pray for the welfare of the kingdom of God on the earth, and for the honest in heart, I am skeptical in regard to believing that person's religion to be genuine, and his faith I should consider not the faith of Jesus. Those who have the mind of Christ are anxious that it should spread extensively among the people, to bring them to a correct understanding of things as they are, that they may be able to prepare themselves to dwell eternally in the heavens. This is your desire, and is what we continually pray for.

" Brother J. V. Long's discourse this morning was sweet to my taste ; and the remarks of Brother T. B. H. Stenhouse were very congenial to my feelings and understanding. Brother Long has good command of language, and can readily choose such words as best suit him to convey his ideas.

" Brother Stenhouse remarked that the Gospel of salvation is the great foundation of this kingdom ; that we have not built up this kingdom, nor established this organization, we have merely embraced it in our faith ; that God has established this kingdom, and has bestowed the priesthood upon the children of men, and has called upon the inhabitants of the earth to receive it, to repent of their sins, and return to him with all their hearts. This portion of his remarks I wish you particularly to treasure up.

" If the Angel Gabriel were to descend and stand before you, though he said not a word, the influence and power that would proceed from him, were he to look upon you in the power he possesses, would melt this congregation. His eyes would be like flaming fire, and his countenance would be like the sun at midday. The countenance of an holy angel would tell more than all the language in the world. If men who are called to speak before a congregation rise full of the Holy Spirit and power of God, their countenances are sermons to the people. But if their affections, feelings, and desires are like the fool's eye to the ends of the earth, looking for this, that, and the other, and the kingdom of God is far from them and not in all their affections, they may rise here and talk what they please, and it is but like sounding brass or a tinkling cymbal—mere empty, unmeaning sounds to the ears of the people. I can not say this of what I have heard to-day.

"Those faithful elders who have testified of this work to thousands of people on the continents and islands of the sea will see the fruits of their labors, whether they have said five words or thousands. They may not see these fruits immediately, and perhaps in many cases not until the millennium, but the savor of their testimony will pass down from father to son. Children will say, 'The words of life were spoken to my grandfather and grandmother; they told me of them, and I wish to become a member of the Church; I also wish to be baptized for my father, and mother, and grandparents;' and they will come and keep coming, the living and the dead, and you will be satisfied with your labors, whether they have been much or little, if you continue faithful.

"Brother Long remarked that before he gathered to Zion he had imbibed an idea that the people were all pure here. This is a day of trial for you. If there is any thing that should give us sorrow and pain, it is that any of the brethren and sisters come here and neglect to live their religion. Some are greedy, covetous, and selfish, and give way to temptation; they are wicked and dishonest in their dealings with one another, and look at and magnify the faults of every body, on the right and on the left. 'Such a sister is guilty of pilfering; such a brother is guilty of swearing,' etc., 'and we have come a long distance to be joined with such a set; we do not care a dime for "Mormonism," nor for any thing else.' The enemy takes the advantage of such persons, and leads them to do that for which they are afterward sorry. This is a matter of great regret to those who wish to be faithful. But no matter how many give themselves up to merchandising and love it better than their God, how many go to the gold mines, how many go back on the road to trade with the wicked, nor how many take their neighbors' wood after it is cut and piled up in the kanyons, or steal their neighbors' axes, or any thing that is their neighbors', you live your religion, and we shall see the day when we shall tread iniquity under foot. But if you listen to those who practice iniquity, you will be carried away by it, as it has carried away thousands. Let every one get a knowledge for himself that this work is true. We do not want you to say that it is true until you know that it is; and if you know it, that knowledge is as good to you as though the Lord came down and told you. Then let every person say, 'I will live my religion, though every other person goes to hell; I will walk humbly before God, and deal honestly with my fellow-beings.' There are now scores of thousands in this Territory who will do this, and who feel as I do on this subject, and we will overcome the wicked. Ten filthy, dirty sheep in a thousand cause the whole flock to appear defiled, and a stranger would pronounce them all filthy; but wash them, and you will find nine hundred and ninety pure and clean. It is so with this people; half a dozen horse-thieves tend to cause the whole community to appear corrupt in the eyes of a casual observer.

" Brother Long said that the Lord will deal out correction to the evil-doer, but that he would have nothing to do with it. I do not know whether I shall or not, but I shall not ask the Lord to do what I am not willing to do; and I do not think that Brother Long is any more or less ready to do so than I am. Ask any earthly king to do a work that you would not do, and he would be insulted. Were I to ask the Lord to free us from ungodly wretches, and not lend my influence and assistance, he would look upon me differently to what he now does.

" You have read that I had an agent in China to mix poison with the tea to kill all the nations; that I was at the head of the Vigilance Committee in California; that I managed the troubles in Kansas, from the beginning to the end; that there is not a liquor-shop or distillery but what Brigham Young dictates it: so state the newspapers. In these and all other accusations of evil-doing I defy them to produce the first show of evidence against me. It is also asserted that President Buchanan and myself concocted the plan for the army to come here, with a view to make money. By-and-by the poor wretches will come bending and say, ' I wish I was a " Mormon." ' All the army, with its teamsters, hangers-on, and followers, with the judges, and nearly all the rest of the civil officers, amounting to some seventeen thousand men, have been searching diligently for three years to bring one act to light that would criminate me; but they have not been able to trace out one thread or one particle of evidence that would criminate me; do you know why? Because I walk humbly with my God, and do right so far as I know how. I do no evil to any one; and as long as I can have faith in the name of the Lord Jesus Christ to hinder the wolves from tearing the sheep and devouring them, without putting forth my hand, I shall do so.

" I can say honestly and truly before God, and the holy angels and all men, that not one act of murder or disorder has occurred in this city or Territory that I had any knowledge of, any more than a babe a week old, until after the event has transpired; that is the reason they can not trace any crime to me. If I have faith enough to cause the devils to eat up the devils, like the Kilkenny cats, I shall certainly exercise it. Joseph Smith said that they would eat each other up as did those cats. They will do so here, and throughout the world. The nations will consume each other, and the Lord will suffer them to bring it about. It does not require much talent or tact to get up opposition in these days; you see it rife in communities, in meetings, in neighborhoods, and in cities; that is the knife that will cut down this government. The axe is laid at the root of the tree, and every tree that bringeth not forth good fruit will be hewn down.

" Out of this Church will grow the kingdom which Daniel saw. This is the very people that Daniel saw would continue to grow, and spread, and prosper; and if we are not faithful, others will take our places, for this is the Church and people that will possess the kingdom forever and ever. Will we do this in our present condition as a people? No; for we must be pure and holy, and be prepared for the presence of our Savior and God, in order to possess the kingdom. Selfishness, wickedness, bickering, tattling, lying, and dishonesty must depart from the people before they are prepared for the Savior; we must sanctify ourselves before our God.

"I wanted to ask Brother Long a question this morning—what he had learned in regard to the original sin. Let the elders, who like speculation, find out what it is, if they can, and inform us next Sabbath; or, if you have any thing else that is good, bring it along. I wish to impress upon your minds to live your religion, and, when you come to this stand to speak, not to care whether you say five words or five thousand, but to come with the power of God upon you, and you will comfort the hearts of the Saints. All the sophistry in the world will do no good. If you live your religion, you will live with the Spirit of Zion within you, and will try, by every lawful means, to induce your neighbors to live their religion. In this way we will redeem Zion, and cleanse it from sin.

"God bless you. Amen."

The gift of unknown tongues—which is made by some physiologists the result of an affection of the epigastric region, and by others an abnormal action of the organ of language—is now apparently rarer than before. Anti-Mormon writers thus imitate the "blatant gibberish" which they derive directly from Irvingism: "Eli, ele, elo, ela—come, coma, como—reli, rele, rela, relo—sela, selo, sele, selum—vavo, vava, vavum—sero, seri, sera, serum." Lieutenant Gunnison relates* a facetious story concerning a waggish youth, who, after that a woman had sprung up and spoken "in tongues" as follows, "Mela, meli, melee," sorely pressed by the "gift of interpretation of tongues," translated the sentence into the vernacular, "My leg, my thigh, my knee." For this he was called before the Council, but he stoutly persisted in his "interpretation" being "by the Spirit," and they dismissed him with admonition. Gentiles have observed that whatever may be uttered "in tongues," it is always translated into very intelligible English.

That evening, when dining out, I took a lesson in Mormon modesty. The mistress of the house, a Gentile, but not an anti-Mormon, was requested by a saintly visitor, who was also a widow, to instruct me that on no account must I propose to see her home. "Mormon ladies," said my kind informant, "are very strict;" unnecessarily so on this occasion, I could not but think. Something similar occurred on another occasion: a very old lady, wishing to return home, surreptitiously left the room and sidled out of the garden gate, and my companion, an officer from Camp Floyd, at once recognized the object of the retreat. I afterward learned at dinner and elsewhere among the Mormons to abjure the Gentile practice of giving precedence to that sex than which, according to Latin grammar, the masculine is nobler. The lesson, however,

* The Mormons. Chap. vi. Social Condition.

was not new; I had been taught the same, in times past, among certain German missionaries who assumed precedence over their wives upon a principle borrowed from St. Paul.

I took the earliest opportunity of visiting, at his invitation, the Prophet's gardens. The grounds were laid out by Mr. W. C. Staines, now on Church business in London.* Mr. Staines arrived at Great Salt Lake City an exceptionally poor emigrant, and is now a rich man, with house and farm, all the proceeds of his own industry. This and many other instances which I could quote prove that although, as a rule, the highest dignitaries are the wealthiest, and although the polygamist can not expect to keep a large family and fill at the same time a long purse, the Gentiles somewhat exaggerate when they represent that Church discipline keeps the lower orders in a state of pauperdom. Mr. Staines is also the "son of 'Brigham' by adoption." This custom is prevalent among the Mormons as among the Hindoos, but with this difference, that while the latter use it when childless, the former employ it as the means of increasing their glory in the next world. The relationship is truly one of parent and child, by choice, not only by the mere accident of birth, and the "son," if necessary, lives with and receives the necessaries of life from his "father." Before entering the garden we were joined by Mr. Mercer, who, long after my departure from India, had missionarized at Kurrachee in "Scinde, or the Unhappy Valley."

The May frost had injured the fruit. Grapes were but quarter-grown, while winter was fast approaching. I suggested to the civil and obliging English gardener that it would be well to garnish the trellised walls, as is done in Tuscany, with mats which roll up and can be let down at night. Bacchus appeared in three forms: the California grape, which is supposed to be the Madeira introduced into the New World by the Franciscan Missions; the Catawba—so called from an Indian people on a river of the same name—a cultivated variety of the *Vitis labrusca*, and still the wine-grape in the States. The third is the inferior Isabella, named after his wife by "ole man Gibbs,"† who first attempted to civilize the fox-grape (*Vitis vulpina*), growing on banks of streams in most of the temperate states. A vineyard is now being planted on the hill-side near Mr. Brigham Young's block, and home-made wine will soon become an item of produce in Utah. Pomology is carefully cultivated; about one hundred varieties of apples have been imported, and of these ninety-one are found to thrive as seedlings: in good seasons their branches are bowed down by fruit, and must be propped up, or they will break under their load. The peaches were in all cases unpruned: upon this important

---

* I have to thank Mr. Staines for kind assistance in supplying me with necessary items of information.

† Similarly, the Constantia of the Cape was named after Madam Van Stell, the wife of the governor.

point opinions are greatly divided.   The people generally believe
that the foliage is a protection to the fruit during the spring frosts.
The horticulturists declare that the "extremes of temperature render proper pruning even more necessary than in France, and that
the fervid summers often induce a growth of wood which must
suffer severely during the inclement months, unless checked and
hardened by cutting back.   Besides grapes and apples, there were
walnuts, apricots and quinces, cherries and plums, currants, rasp-
berries, and gooseberries.   The principal vegetables were the Irish
and the sweet potato, squashes, peas—excellent—cabbages, beets,
cauliflowers, lettuce, and broccoli; a little rhubarb is cultivated,
but it requires too much expensive sugar for general use, and
white celery has lately been introduced.   Leaving the garden,
we walked through the various offices, oil-mill, timber-mill, and
smithy: in the latter oxen are shod, according to the custom of
the country, with half shoes.   The animal is raised from the
ground by a broad leather band under the belly, and is liable to
be lamed by any but a practiced hand.

On the evening of the 3d of September, while sauntering about
the square in which a train of twenty-three wagons had just bivouacked, among the many others to whom Mr. Staines introduced
me was the Apostle John Taylor, the "Champion of Rights,"
Speaker in the House, and whilom editor.   I had heard of him
from the best authorities as a man so morose and averse to Gentiles, "who made the healing virtue depart out of him," that it
would be advisable to avoid his "fierceness."   The *véridique* Mr.
Austin Ward describes him as "an old man deformed and crippled," and Mrs. Ferris as a "heavy, dark-colored, beetle-browed
man."   Of course, I could not recognize him from these descriptions—a stout, good-looking, somewhat elderly personage, with a
kindly gray eye, pleasant expression, and a forehead of the superior order; he talked of Westmoreland his birthplace, and of his
European travels for a time, till the subject of Carthage coming
upon the *tapis*, I suspected who my interlocutor was.   Mr. Staines
burst out laughing when he heard my mistake, and I explained
the reason to the apostle, who laughed as heartily.   Wishing to
see more of him, I accompanied him in the carriage to the Sugar-
house Ward, where he was bound on business, and *chemin faisant*
we had a long talk.   He pointed out to me on the left the mouths
of the several kanyons, and informed me that the City Creek and
the Red Buttes on the northeast, and the Emigration, Parley's,
Mill Creek, Great Cotton-wood and Little Cotton-wood Kanyons
to the east and southeast, all head together in two points, thus enabling troops and provisions to be easily and readily concentrated
for the defense of the eastern approaches.   When talking about
the probability of gold digging being developed near Great Salt
Lake City, he said that the Mormons are aware of that, but that
they look upon agriculture as their real wealth.   The Gentiles,

however—it is curious that they do not form a company among themselves for prospecting—assert that the Church has very rich mines, which are guarded by those dragons of Danites more fiercely than the Hesperidian Gardens, and which will never be known till Miss Utah becomes Mistress Deserét. Arriving at the tall, gaunt Sugar-house — its occupation is gone, while the name remains—we examined the machinery employed in making threshing and wool-carding machines, flanges, wheels, cranks, and similar necessaries. After a visit to a nail manufactory belonging to Squire Wells, and calling upon Mrs. Harris, we entered the Penitentiary. It is a somewhat Oriental-looking building, with a large quadrangle behind the house, guarded by a wall with a walk on the summit, and pepper-caster sentry-boxes at each angle. There are cells in which the convicts are shut up at night, but one of these had lately been broken by an Indian, who had cut his way through the wall; a Hindoo "gonnoff" would soon "pike" out of a "premonitory" like this. We found in it besides the guardians only six persons, of whom two were Yutas. When I remarked to Gentiles how few were the evidences of crime, they invariably replied that, instead of half a dozen souls, half the population ought to be in the place. On our return we resumed the subject of the massacre at Carthage, in which it will be remembered that Mr. John Taylor was severely wounded, and escaped by a miracle, as it were. I told him openly that there must have been some cause for the furious proceedings of the people in Illinois, Missouri, and other places against the Latter-Day Saints; that even those who had extended hospitality to them ended by hating and expelling them, and accusing them of all possible iniquities, especially of horse-thieving, forgery, larceny, and offenses against property, which on the borders are never pardoned — was this smoke quite without fire? He heard me courteously and in perfect temper; replied that no one claimed immaculateness for the Mormons; that the net cast into the sea brought forth evil as well as good fish, and that the Prophet was one of the laborers sent into the vineyard at the eleventh hour. At the same time, that when the New Faith was stoutly struggling into existence, it was the object of detraction, odium, persecution—so, said Mr. Taylor, were the Christians in the days of Nero — that the border ruffians, forgers, horse-thieves, and other vile fellows followed the Mormons wherever they went; and, finally, that every fraud and crime was charged upon those whom the populace were disposed, by desire for confiscation's sake, to believe guilty. Besides the theologic odium there was also the political: the Saints would vote for their favorite candidates, consequently they were never without enemies. He quoted the Mormon rules: 1. Worship what you like. 2. Leave your neighbor alone. 3. Vote for whom you please; and compared their troubles to the Western, or, as it is popularly called, the Whisky insurrection in 1794, whose "dread-

ful night" is still remembered in Pennsylvania.   Mr. Taylor remarked that the Saints had been treated by the United States as
the colonies had been treated by the crown: that the persecuted
naturally became persecutors, as the Pilgrim fathers, after flying
for their faith, hung the Quakers on Bloody Hill at Boston ; and
that even the Gentiles can not defend their own actions.   I heard
for the first time this view of the question, and subsequently obtained from the apostle a manuscript account, written *in extenso*,
of his experience and his sufferings.   It has been transferred in
its integrity to Appendix No. III., the length forbidding its insertion in the text: a tone of candor, simplicity, and honesty renders
it highly attractive.

ANCIENT LAKE BENCH-LAND.

CHAPTER VI.

Descriptive Geography, Ethnology, and Statistics of Utah Territory.

UTAH Territory, so called from its Indian owners, the Yuta—
"those that dwell in mountains"—is still, to a certain extent, *terra
incognita*, not having yet been thoroughly explored, much less
surveyed or settled.

The whole Utah country has been acquired, like Oregon, by
conquest and diplomacy.   By the partition of 1848, the parallel
of N. lat. 42°, left unsettled, between the Rocky Mountains and
the Pacific, by the treaties of the 22d of October, 1818, and the
12th of February, 1819, was prolonged northward to N. lat. 49°,
thus adding to the United States California, Oregon, and Wash-

ington, while to Britain remained Vancouver's Island and the joint navigation of the Columbia River. Under the Hispano-Americans the actual Utah Territory formed the northern portion of Alta California, and the peace of Guadalupe Hidalgo, concluded in 1848 between the United States and Mexico, transferred it from the latter to the former.

The present boundaries of Utah Territory are, northward (42° N. lat.), the State of Oregon; and southward, a line pursuing the parallel of N. lat. 37°, separating it from New Mexico to the southeast and from California to the southwest. The eastern portion is included between 106° and 120° W. long. (G.); a line following the crest of the Green River, the Wasach, the Bear River, and other sections of the Rocky Mountains, whose southern extremities anastomose to form the Sierra Nevada, separate it from Nebraska and Kansas. On the west it is bounded, between 116° and 120° W. long., by the lofty crest of the Sierra Nevada; the organization, however, of a new territory, the "Nevada," on the landward slope of the Snowy Range, has diminished its dimensions by about half. Utah had thus 5° of extreme breadth, and 14° of total length; it was usually reckoned 650 miles long from east to west, and 350 broad from north to south. The shape was an irregular parallelogram, of which the area was made to vary from 188,000 to 225,000 square miles, almost the superficies of France.

The surface configuration of Utah Territory is like Central Equatorial Africa, a great depression in a mountain land: a trough elevated 4000 to 5000 feet above sea level, subtended on all sides by mountains 8000 to 10,000 feet high, and subdivided by transverse ridges. The "Rim of the Basin" is an uncontinuous line formed by the broken chains of Oregon to the north, and to the south by the little-known sub-ranges of the Rocky Mountains; the latter also form the eastern wall, while the Sierra Nevada hems in the west. Before the present upheaval of the country the Great Interior Basin was evidently a sweetwater inland sea; the bench formation, a system of water-marks, is found in every valley, while detached and parallel blocks of mountain, trending almost invariably north and south, were in geological ages rock-islands protruding from the lake surface like those that now break the continuity of that "vast and silent sea" the Great Salt Lake. Between these primitive and metamorphic ridges lie the secondary basins, whose average width may be 15—20 miles; they open into one another by kanyons and passes, and are often separated longitudinally, like "waffle-irons," by smaller divides running east and west, thus converting one extended strip of secondary into a system of tertiary valleys. The Great Basin, which is not less than 500 miles long by 500 broad, is divided by two large chains, which run transversely from northeast to southwest. The northernmost is the range of the Humboldt River, rising 5000—6000 feet

S

above the sea. The southern is the prolongation of the Wasach, whose southwestern extremity abuts upon the Pacific coast range; it attains a maximum elevation of nearly 12,000 feet. Without these mountains, whose gorges are fed during the spring, and even in the summer, by melted snow, there would be no water. The levels of the valleys are still unknown; it is yet a question how far they are irregular in elevation, whether they have formed detached lakes, or whether they slope uniformly and by steps toward the Great Salt Lake and the other reservoirs scattered at intervals over the country.

The water-shed of the Basin is toward the north, south, east, and west: the affluents of the Columbia and the Colorado rivers carry off the greatest amount of drainage. One of the geographical peculiarities of the Territory is the "sinking," as it is technically called, of the rivers. The phenomenon is occasioned by the porous nature of the soil. The larger streams, like the Humboldt and the Carson rivers, form terminating lakes. The smaller are either absorbed by sand, or sink, like the South African fountains, in ponds and puddles of black mire, beneath which is peaty earth that burns as if by spontaneous combustion, and smoulders for a long time in dry weather: the waters either reappear, or, escaping under the surface—a notable instance of the "subterranean river"—feed the greater drains and the lakes. The potamology is more curious than useful; the streams, being unnavigable, play no important part in the scheme of economy.

Utah Territory is well provided with lakes; of these are two nearly parallel chains extending across the country. The easternmost begins at the north, with the Great Salt Lake, the small tarns of the Wasach, the Utah, or Sweetwater Reservoir, the Nicollet, and the Little Salt Lake, complete the line which is fed by the streams that flow from the western counterslope of the Wasach. The other chain is the drainage collected from the eastern slope of the Sierra Nevada; it consists of Mud, Pyramid, Carson, Mono, and Walker's lakes. Of these, Pyramid Lake, so called by Colonel Frémont, its explorer, from a singular rock in the centre, is the most beautiful — a transparent water, 700 feet above the level of the Great Salt Lake, and walled in by precipices nearly 3000 feet high.

The principal thermal features of Utah Territory are the Bear Springs, near the Fort Hall Road. The Harrowgate Springs, near Great Salt Lake City, have already been alluded to. Between the city and Bear River there is a fountain of strong brine, described as discharging a large volume of water. There are sulphurous pools at the southern extremity of the Great Salt Lake Valley. Others are chalybeate, coating the earth and the rocks with oxide of iron. Almost every valley has some thermal spring, in which various confervæ flourish; the difficulty is to find good cold water.

Another curious geographical peculiarity of the Territory is the formation of the mountains. For the most part the ridges, instead of presenting regular slopes, more or less inclined, are formed of short but acute angular cappings superimposed upon flatter prisms. It often happens that after easily ascending two thirds from the base, the upper part suddenly becomes wall-like and insurmountable.

Utah Territory is situated in the parallel of the Mediterranean; the southern boundary corresponds with the provinces along the Amoor lately acquired by Russia, and with Tasmania in the southern hemisphere. But the elevation, that grand modifier of climate, renders it bleak and liable to great vicissitudes of temperature. The lowest valley rises 4000 feet above sea level; the mountains behind Great Salt Lake City are 6000 feet high; Mount Nebo is marked 8000, and the Twin Peaks, that look upon the "Happy Valley," were ascertained barometrically by Messrs. O. Pratt and A. Carrington to be 11,660 feet in height: in the western part of the Territory the Sierra Nevada averages 2000 feet above the South Pass, and it has peaks that tower thousands of feet above that altitude. These snowy masses, in whose valleys thaw is seldom known, exercise a material effect upon the climate, and cause the cultivator to wage fierce war with the soil. The air is highly rarefied by its altitude. Captain Stansbury's barometrical observations for May, June, July, and August, give as a maximum 27·80 at 9 A.M. on the 4th of August, and minimum 22·86 at sunrise on the 19th of June, with a general range between 25° and 26°. New-comers suffer from difficulty of breathing; often after sudden and severe exercise, climbing, or running, the effect is like the nausea, sickness, and fainting experienced upon Mont Blanc and in Tibet; even horses feel it, and must pass two or three months before they are acclimatized.*

* Subjoined is an abstract of meteorology kindly forwarded to me by Judge Phelps:

"Great Salt Lake City, Utah, Oct. 24th, 1860.

"Dear Sir,—The following is an abstract of meteorological observations for the past year, from October, 1859, to October, 1860, inclusive:

Yearly mean of barometer	25·855
Highest range	26·550
Lowest range	25·205
Thermometer attached (mean)	60°
Thermometer (open air) "	71°
Thermometer, dry bulb "	64°
Thermometer, wet bulb "	58°

(All Fahrenheit.)

"The amount of fair days, 244. The remaining 121 were 31 stormy and the residue cloudy and foggy.

"The course of the wind more than two thirds of the year goes round daily with the sun; strongest wind south; worst for stock, north.

"Highest range of the thermometer, 96° in July; lowest range in December—22° below 0.

"The amount of snow and rain water was 12·257, which is somewhat over 1 foot.

The climate of the Basin has been compared with that of the Tartar plains of High Asia. Spring opens in the valleys with great suddenness; all is bloom and beauty below, while the snow-line creeps lingeringly up the mountain side, and does not disappear till the middle of June. Thus there are but three months of warmth in the high lands; the low lands have four, beginning with a May-day like that of England. At the equinoxes, both vernal and autumnal, there are rains in the bottoms, which in the upper levels become sleet or snow. Between April and October showers are rare; there are, however, exceptions, heavy downfalls, with thunder, lightning, and hail. "Clouds without water" is a proverbial expression; a dark, heavy pall, which in woodland countries would burst with its weight, here sails over the arid, sun-parched surface, and discharges its watery stores in the kanyons and upon the mountains. During the first few years after the arrival of the Saints there was little rain either in spring or autumn; in 1860 it extended to the middle of June. The change may be attributed to cultivation and plantation; thus also may be explained the North American Indian's saying that the pale-face brings with him his rain. The same has been observed in Kansas and New Mexico, and is equally remarked by the natives of Cairo, the Aden Coal-hole, and Kurrachee. Seed-time lasts from April to the 10th of June.

The summer is hot, but the lightness and the aridity of the air prevent its being unwholesome. During my visit the thermometer (F.) placed in a room with open windows showed at dawn 63—66°; at noon, 75°; and at sunset, 70°: the greatest midday heat was 105°. The mornings and evenings, cooled by breezes from the mountains, were deliciously soft and pure. The abundant electricity was proved, as in Sindh and Arabia, by frequent devils or dust-pillars, like huge columns of volcanic smoke, that careered over the miraged plains, violently excited where they touched the negative earth, and calm in the positive strata of the upper air, whence their floating particles were precipitated. Dust-storms and thunder-storms are frequent and severe. Clouds often gather upon the peaks, and a heavy black nimbus rises behind the Wasach wall, setting off its brilliant sunlit side, but there is seldom rain. Showers are preceded, as in Eastern Africa, by puffs and gusts of cold air, and are expected in Great Salt Lake City when the clouds come from the west and southwest, opposite and over the "Black Rock;" otherwise they will cling to the hills. Even in the hottest weather, a cold continuous wind, as from the nozzle of a forge-bellows, pours down the deep damp

---

"All the snow in the Valley was less than 3 feet, while perhaps in the mountains it was more than 10 feet, which gives ample water for irrigation.

"The weather during the year was steady, without extremes.

"Such was Utah in 1860.

"Respectfully, I have the honor to be, etc.,   W. W. PHELPS."

kanyons, where the snow lingers, and travelers, especially at night, prepare to pass across the ravine mouths with blankets and warm clothing. Where the federal troops encamped on the stony bench opposite the Provo Kanyon, it was truly predicted that they would soon be blown out. When summer is protracted, severe droughts are the result. Harvest-time is in the beginning of July.

About early September the heat ends. In 1860, the first snow fell upon the Twin Peaks and their neighborhood on the 12th of September. Rains then usually set in for a fortnight or three weeks, and mild weather often lasts till the end of October. November is partially a fine month; after two or three snowy days, the Indian summer ushers in the most enjoyable weather of the year, which, when short, ends about the middle of November.

Winter has three very severe months, reckoned from December. Icy winds blow hard, and gales are sometimes so high that spray is carried from the Great Salt Lake to the City, a distance of 10—12 miles. In 1854–5 hundreds of cattle perished in the snow. Usually in mid-winter, snow falls every day with a high westerly wind, veering toward the north, and thick with poudré— dry icy spiculæ, hard as gravel. The thermometer is not often below zero in the bottoms; on the 13th of December, 1859, however, the thermometer at daylight, with the barometer at 26·250, showed —22° (F.); 5° or 6° lower than it had ever been before. The snow seldom lies in the valleys deeper than a man's knee; it is dry, and readily thawed by the sun. A vast quantity is drifted into the kanyons and passes, where the people, as in Styria, often become prisoners at home. These crevasses, hundreds of feet deep, retain their icy stores throughout the year. It is asserted by those who believe in a Pacific Railway upon this line* that the Wasach can be traversed at all seasons; at present, however, sledge transit only is practicable, and at times even that is found impossible.

It can not be doubted that this climate of arid heat and dry cold is eminently suited to most healthy and to many sickly constitutions: children and adults have come from England apparently in a dying state, and have lived to be strong and robust men. I have elsewhere alluded to the effect of rarefaction upon

---

* The Pacific Railroad in 1852 was unknown to the political world: in 1856 it began to be necessary, and shortly afterward it appeared in both "platforms," because without it no one could expect to carry the Mississippian and Pacific States, Texas, for instance, and California. The Diary will show the many difficulties which it must encounter after crossing the South Pass; as the West can afford no assistance, provisions and material must all come from the East—an additional element of expense and delay. The estimate is roughly laid down at $100,000,000: it may safely be doubled. The well-known contractor, Mr. Whitney, offered to build it for a reservation of thirty miles on both sides: the idea was rejected as that of a crazy man. It is promised in ten years, and will probably take thirty. England, then, had better look to her line through Canada and Columbia—it would be worth a hundred East Indian railroads.

the English *physique:* another has been stated, namely, that the atmosphere is too fine and dry to require, or even to permit, the free use of spirituous liquors. Paralysis is rare; scrofula and phthisis are unknown, as in Nebraska—the climate wants that humidity which brings forward the predisposition. It is also remarkable that, though all drink snow-water, and though many live in valleys where there is no free circulation of air, goître and cretinism are not yet named. The City Council maintains an excellent sanitary supervision, which extends to the minutest objects that might endanger the general health. The stream of emigrants which formerly set copiously westward is now dribbling back toward its source, and a quarantine is established for those who arrive with contagious diseases. Great Salt Lake City is well provided with disciples of Æsculapius, against whom there is none of that prejudice founded upon superstition and fanaticism which anti-Mormon writers have detected. Dr. Francis, an English Mormon, lately died, leaving Dr. Anderson, a graduate of Maryland College, to take his place: Dr. Bernhisel prefers politics to physic, and Dr. Kay is the chief dentist.

The normal complaints are easily explained by local peculiarities—cold, alkaline dust, and overindulgence in food.

Neuralgia is by no means uncommon. Many are compelled to wear kerchiefs under their hats; and if a head be not always uncovered, there is some reason for it. Rheumatism, as in England, affects the poorer classes, who are insufficiently fed and clothed. Pneumonia, in winter, follows exposure and hard work. The pleuro-pneumonia, which in 1860 did so much damage to stock in New England, did not extend to Utah Territory: the climate, however, is too like that of the Cape of Storms to promise lasting immunity. Catarrhs are severe and lasting; they are accompanied by bad toothaches and sore throats, which sometimes degenerate into bronchitis. Diphtheria is not yet known. The measles have proved especially fatal to the Indians: in 1850, "Old Elk," the principal war-chief of the Timpanogos Yutas, died of it: erysipelas also kills many of the wild men.

For ophthalmic disease, the climate has all the efficients of the Valley of the Nile, and, unless suitable precautions are taken, the race will, after a few generations, become tender-eyed as Egyptians. The organ is weakened by the acrid irritating dust from the alkaline soil, which glistens in the sun like hoar-frost. Snow-blindness is common on the mountains and in the plains: the favorite preventive, when goggles are unprocurable, is to blacken the circumorbital region and the sides of the nose with soot—the kohl, surmah, or collyrium of the Far West: the cure is a drop of nitrate of silver or laudanum. The mucous membrane in horses, as among men, is glandered, as it were, by alkali, and the chronic inflammation causes frequent hemorrhage: the nitrous salts in earth and air exasperate to ulcers sunburns on the nose and mouth:

it is not uncommon to see men riding or walking with a bit of paper instead of a straw between their lips.   Wounds must be treated to great disadvantage where the climate, like that of Abyssinia, renders a mere scratch troublesome.   The dryness of the air produces immunity from certain troublesome excrescences which cause shooting pains in humid regions, and the pedestrian requires no vinegar and water to harden his feet: on the other hand, horses' hoofs, as in Sindh and Arabia, must be stuffed with tar, to prevent sun-crack.

Under the generic popular name "mountain fever" are included various species of febrile affections, intermittent, remittent, and typhoid: they are treated successfully with quinine.

Emigrants are advised to keep up hard work and scanty fare after arrival, otherwise the sudden change from semi-starvation and absence of fruit and vegetables upon the prairies to plenty in the settlements may cause dyspepsia, dysentery, and visceral inflammation.   Some are attacked by "liver complaint," the trivial term for the effects of malaria, which, when inhaled, affects successively the lungs, blood, liver, and other viscera.   The favorite, and, indeed, the only known successful treatment is by mineral acids, nitric, muriatic, and others.*   Scurvy is unknown to the settlers; when brought in after long desert marches, it yields readily to a more generous diet and vegetables, especially potatoes, which, even in the preserved form, act as a specific.   The terrible scorbutic disease, called the "black canker of the plains," has not extended so far west.

There is not much sport with fur, feather, and fin in this part of the Far West: the principal carnivors of the Great Basin are the cougar (*F. unicolor*) and the cat-o'-mountain, the large and small wolf, a variety of foxes, the red (*V. fulvus*), the great-tailed (*V. macrourus*), and the silver (*V. argentatus*), whose spoils were once worth their weight in silver.   There are minks, ermines, skunks, American badgers, and wolverines or gluttons, which ferret out caches of peltries and provisions, and are said sometimes to attack man.   Of rodents the principal are the beaver, a burrowing hare, the jackass-rabbit (*L. callotis*), porcupines, the geomys or gophar, a sand-rat peculiar to America, the woodchuck or ground-hog, many squirrels, especially the Spermophilus tredecim lineatus, which swarms in hilly ground, and muskrat (*F. zibeticus*), which, like other vermin, is eaten by Indians.   The principal pachyderm is the hyrax, called by the settlers "cony."   Of the ruminants we find the antelope, deer, elk, and the noble bighorn,

---

* The following is the favorite cure: it is upon the principle of the medicinal bath well known in Europe.

R Acid. Nit. ʒi.
Acid. Mur. ʒii.   Mis.

Of this fifteen drops are to be taken in a tumbler of water twice a day before meals. The local application to the hepatic region is one ounce of the nitro-muriatic acid in a quart of water, and applied upon a compress every night.

or Rocky Mountain sheep, the moufflon or argali of the New World.

Of the raptors the principal are the red-tailed hawk (*B. borealis*), the sharp-shinned hawk (*A. fuscus*), the sparrow-hawk, and the vulturine turkey-buzzard. Of game-birds there are several varieties of quail, called partridges, especially the beautiful blue species (*O. Californica*), and grouse, especially the sage-hen (*T. urophasianus*): the water-fowl are swans (*C. Americanus*), wild geese in vast numbers, the white pelican, here a migrating bird, the cormorant (*Phalacrocorax*), the mallard or greenhead (*A. boschas*), which loves the water of Jordan and the western Sea of Tiberias, the teal, red-breasted and green-winged, the brant (*A. bernicla*), the plover and curlew, the gull (a small *Larus*), a blue heron, and a brown crane (*G. Canadensis*), which are found in the marshes throughout the winter. The other members of the family are the bluebird (*A. sialia*), the humming-bird (*Trochilus*), finches, woodpeckers, the swamp blackbird, and the snowbird, small passerines: there is also a fine lark (*Sturnella*) with a harsh note, which is considered a delicacy in autumn.

Besides a variety of gray and green lizards, the principal Saurian is the Phrynosoma, a purely American type, popularly called the horned frog—or toad, although its tail, its scaly body, and its inability to jump disprove its title to rank as a batrachian—and by the Mexicans chameleon, because it is supposed to live on air. It is of many species, for which the naturalist is referred to the Appendix of Captain Stansbury's Exploration. The serpents are chiefly rattlesnakes, swamp-adders, and water-snakes. The fishes are perch, pike, bass, chub, a mountain trout averaging three pounds, and salmon trout which has been known to weigh thirty pounds. There are but few mollusks, periwinkles, snails, and fresh-water clams.*

The botany of the Great Basin has been investigated by Messrs. Frémont and Stansbury, who forwarded their collections for description to Professor John Torrey, of New York: M. Remy has described his own herbarium. To these valuable works the reader may be referred for all now known upon the subject.

* Mr. W. Baird, in the absence of Mr. S. Woodward, of the British Museum, has kindly favored me with the following list of a little collection from the Great Basin which I placed in his hands.

"British Museum, August 3d, 1861.

"DEAR SIR,—The Helix (with open umbilicus) is, I think, *H. solitaria;* the large Physa is very near, if not identical with the *P. elliptica* of our collection; the next largest Physa comes very near *P. gyrina;* the larger Lymnœa is *L. catascopium*, the smaller ditto *L. modicella.* There are two species of the genus *Lithoglyphus*, the one resembling very much the *L. naticoides* of Europe, but most probably new; the other I should imagine to be undescribed. There is a small *Paludina* looking shell which comes very near the *Paludina piscium* of D'Orbigny. There is a species of *Anodonta* which corresponds with a shell we have from the Columbia River, but of which I do not know the name. There is also a species of *Cyclas* which may be new, as I do not know at present any species from North America exactly like it. Believe me, yours truly,   W. BAIRD.

"Capt. R. F. Burton."

The rocks in Utah Territory are mostly primitive—granite, brick-red jasper, syenite, hornblende, and porphyry, with various quartzes, of which the most curious is a white nodule surrounded by a crystalline layer of satin spar. The presence of obsidian, scoriæ, and lava—apparently a dark brown mud tinged with iron, and so vitrified by heat that it rings—evidences volcanic action. Many of the ridges are a carboniferous limestone threaded by calcareous spar, and in places rich with encrinites and fossil corallines; it rests upon or alternates with hard and compact grits and sandstone. The kanyons in the neighborhood of Great Salt Lake City supply boulders of serpentine, fine gray granite, coarse red ochrish pœcilated crystalline-white and metamorphic sandstones, a variety of conglomerates, especially granitic, with tufa in large masses, talcose and striated slates, some good for roofing, gypsum (plaster of Paris), pebbles of alabaster and various kinds of limestones, some dark and fetid, others oolitic, some compact and massive, black, blue, or ash-colored, seamed with small veins of white carbonate of lime, others light gray and friable, cased with tufa, or veneered with jade. The bottom-soil in most parts is fitted for the adobe, and the lower hills contain an abundance of fossilless chalky lime, which makes tolerable mortar: the best is that near Deep Creek, the worst is in the vicinity of Great Salt Lake City. Near Fort Hall, in the northeast corner of the basin, there is said to be a mountain of marble displaying every hue and texture: marble is also found in large crystalline nodules like arragonite.

Utah Territory will produce an ample supply of iron.* According to the Mormons, it resembles that of Missouri, and the gangue contains eighty per cent. of pure metal, which, to acquire the necessary toughness, must be alloyed with imported iron. Gold, according to Humboldt, is constant in meridional mountains, and we may expect to find it in a country abounding with crystalline rocks cut by dikes of black and gray basalt and porous trap, gneiss, micaceous schists, clayey and slaty shales, and other argillaceous formations. It is generally believed that gold exists upon the Wasach Mountains, within sight of Great Salt Lake City, and in 1861 a traveling party is reported to have found a fine digging in the north. Lumps of virgin silver are said to have been discovered upon the White Mountains, in the south of the Territory, and Judge Ralston, I am informed, has lately hit upon a mine near the western route. Copper, zinc, and lead have been brought from Little Salt Lake Valley and sixty miles east of the Vegas de Santa Clara. Coal, principally bituminous—like that nearer the Pacific—is found mostly in the softer limestones south of the city, in a country of various marls, indurated clays, and earthy sandstones. In 1855 a vein of five feet thick, in quality

---

* Magnetic iron ore is traced in the basaltic rock; cubes of bisulphuret of iron are found in the argillaceous schists, and cubic crystals of iron pyrites are seen in white ferruginous quartz.

resembling that of Maryland, was discovered west of the San Pete Creek, on the road to Manti.   In Iron County, 250 to 280 miles south of Great Salt Lake City, inexhaustible coal-beds as well as iron deposits are said to line the course of the Green River, and, that nothing may be wanting, considerable affluents supply abundant water-power.   A new digging had been discovered shortly before my arrival on a tributary of the Weber River, east of the City of the Saints, and upon the western route many spots were pointed out to me as future coal-mines.   Timber being principally required for building, fencing, and mechanical purposes, renders firewood expensive: in the city a cartage of fifteen miles is necessary, and the price is thereby raised from $7 in summer to a maximum of $20 in the hard season per cord of sixteen by four feet. Unless the Saints would presently be reduced to the necessity of "breakfasting with Ezekiel," they must take heart and build a tramroad to the south.

Saltpetre is found—upon paper: here, as in other parts of America, it is deficient: a reward of $500 offered for a sample of gunpowder manufactured from Valley Tan materials produced no claimants.   Sulphur is only too common.   Saleratus or alkaline salts is the natural produce of the soil.   Borax and petroleum or mineral tar have been discovered, and the native alum has been analyzed and pronounced good by Dr. Gale.*   Rubies, emeralds, and other small but valuable stones are found in the chinks of the primitive rocks throughout the western parts of the Territory. I have also seen chalcedony, sardonyx, carnelian, and various agates.

Utah Territory is pronounced by immigrants from the Old Country to be a "mean land," hard, dry, and fit only for the steady, sober, and hard-working Mormon.   Scarcely one fiftieth part is fit for tillage; farming must be confined to rare spots, in which, however, an exceptional fertility appears.   Even in the arable lands there is a great variety: some do not exceed 8—10 bushels per acre, while Captain Stansbury mentions 180 bushels† of wheat being raised upon 3·50 acres of ground from one bushel of seed, and estimates the average yield of properly-cultivated land at 40 bushels, whereas rich Pennsylvania rarely gives 30 per acre.‡   I have heard of lands near the fresh-water lake which bear from 60 to 105 bushels per acre.

The cultivable tracts are of two kinds, bench-land and bottom-land.

* 100 grammes of the freshly crystallized salt gave,

Water	73·0
Protoxide of manganese	08·9
Alumina	04·0
Sulphuric acid	18·0

† In the United States the bushel of wheat or clover-seed is 60 lbs. ; of corn, barley, and rye, 56 lbs. ; of oats, 35—36 lbs.

‡ The yield in Egypt varies from 25 to 150 grains for one planted.

The soil of the bench-lands is fertile, a mixture of the highland feldspath with the débris of decomposed limestone. It is comparatively free from alkalines, the bane of the valleys; but as rain is wanting, it depends, like the Basses-Pyrénées, upon irrigation, and must be fertilized by the mountain torrents that issue from the kanyons. As a rule, the creeks dwindle to rivulets and sink in the porous alluvium before they have run a mile from the hill-foot, and reappear in the arid plains at a level too low for navigation: in such places artesian wells are wanted. The soil, though fertile, is thin, requiring compost: manure is here allowed to waste, the labor of the people sufficing barely for essentials. I am informed that two bushels of semence are required for each acre, and that the colonists sow too scantily: a judicious rotation of crops is also yet to come. The benches are sometimes extensive: a strip, for instance, runs along the western base of the Wasach Mountains, with a varying breadth of 1—3 miles, from 80 miles north of Great Salt Lake City to Utah Lake and Valley, the southern terminus of cultivation, a total length of 120 miles. These lands produce various cereals, especially wheat and buckwheat, oats, barley, and a little Indian corn, all the fruits and vegetables of a temperate zone, and flax, hemp, and linseed in abundance. The wild fruits are the service berry, choke-cherry, buffalo berry, gooseberry, an excellent strawberry, and black, white, red, and yellow mountain currants, some as large as ounce bullets.

The bottom-lands, where the creeks extend, are better watered than the uplands, but they are colder and salter. The refrigerated air seeks the lowest levels; hence in Utah Territory the benches are warmer than the valleys, and the spring vegetation is about a fortnight later on the banks of Jordan than above them. Another cause of cold is the presence of saleratus or alkaline salts, the natural effect of the rain being insufficient to wash them out. Experiment proved in Sindh that nothing is more difficult than to eradicate this evil from the soil: the sweetest earth brought from afar becomes tainted by it: sometimes the disease appears when the crop is half grown; at other times it attacks irregularly—one year, for instance, will see a fine field of wheat, and the next none. When inveterate, it breaks out in leprous eruptions, and pieces of efflorescence can be picked up for use: a milder form induces a baldness of growth, with an occasional birth of chenopodiaceæ. Many of the streams are dangerous to cattle, and often in the lower parts of the valleys there are ponds and pools of water colored and flavored like common ley. According to the people, a small admixture is beneficial to vegetation; the grass is rendered equal for pasturage to the far-famed salt-marshes of Essex and of the Atlantic coast; potatoes, squashes, and melons become sweeter, and the pie-plant loses its acidity. On the other hand, the beet has been found to deteriorate, no small misfortune at such a distance from the sugar-cane.

Besides salt-drought and frost, the land has to contend against an Asiatic scourge. The cricket (*Anabrus simplex?*) is compared by the Mormons to a "cross between the spider and the buffalo:" it is dark, ungainly, wingless, and exceedingly harmful. The five red-legged grasshopper (*Œdipoda corallipes*), about the size of the English migratory locust, assists these "black Philistines," and, but for a curious provision of nature, would render the land well-nigh uninhabitable. A small species of gull flocks from its resting-place in the Great Salt Lake to feed upon the advancing host; the "glossy bird of the valley, with light red beak and feet, delicate in form and motion, with plumage of downy texture and softness," stayed in 1848 the advance of the "frightful bug," whose onward march nor fires, nor hot trenches, nor the cries of the frantic farmer could arrest. We can hardly wonder that the Mormons, whose minds, so soon after the exodus, were excited to the highest pitch, should have seen in this natural phenomenon a miracle, a special departure from the normal course of events, made by Providence in their favor, or accuse them, as anti-Mormons have done, of forging signs and portents.

But, while many evils beset agriculture in Utah Territory, grazing is comparatively safe, and may be extended almost *ad libitum*. The valleys of this land of Goshen supply plentiful pasturage in the winter; as spring advances cattle will find gamma and other grasses on the benches, and as, under the influence of the melting sun, the snow-line creeps up the hills, flocks and herds, like the wild graminivorants, will follow the bunch-grass, which, vivified by the autumnal rains, breeds under the snow, and bears its seed in summer. In the basin of the Green River, fifty miles south of Fillmore City, is a fine wool-producing country 7000 square miles in area. Even the ubiquitous sage will serve for camels. As has been mentioned, Durhams, Devons, and Merino tups have found their way to Great Salt Lake City, and the terrible milk-sickness* of the Western States has not.

In 1860 the Valley of the Great Salt Lake alone produced 306,000 bushels of grain, of which about 17,000 were oats. Lieutenant Gunnison, estimating the average yield of each plowed acre at 2000 lbs. (33½ bushels), a fair estimate, and "drawing the meat part of the ration, or one half," from the herds fed elsewhere, fixes the maximum of population in Utah Territory at 4000 souls to a square mile, and opines that it will maintain with ease one million of inhabitants.

Timber, I have said, is a growing want throughout the country; the "hair of the earth-animal" is by no means luxuriant. Great Cotton-wood Kanyon is supposed to contain supplies for twenty years, but it is chiefly used for building purposes. The

---

* A fatal spasmodic disease produced in the Western States by astringent salts in the earth and water: it first attacks cattle, and then those who eat the infected meat or drink the milk. Travelers tell of whole villages being destroyed by it.

Mormons, unlike the Hibernians, of whom it was said in the last century that no man ever planted an orchard, have applied themselves manfully to remedying the deficiency, and the next generation will probably be safe.   At present, "hard woods," elm, hackberry, pecan or button-wood, hickory, mulberry, basswood, locust, black and English walnut, are wanted, and must be imported from the Eastern States.   The lower kanyons and bottoms are clothed with wild willow, scrub maple, both hard and soft, box elder, aspen, birch, cotton-wood, and other amentaciæ, and in the south with spruce and dwarf ash.   The higher grounds bear stunted cedars white and red, balsam and other pines, the dwarf oak, which, like the maple, is a mere scrub, and the mountain mahogany, a tough, hard, and strong, but grainless wood, seldom exceeding eight inches in diameter.   Hawthorn (a *Cratægus*) also exists, and in the southern and western latitudes the piñon (*P. monophyllus*), varying from the size of an umbrella to twenty feet in height, feeds the Indians with its oily nut, which not a little resembles the seed of the pinaster and the Mediterranean *P. Pinea*, and supplies a rich gum for strengthening plasters.

The present state of agriculture in the vicinity of Great Salt Lake City will best be explained by the prospectus of the annual show for 1860.*   Wheat thrives better than maize, which in the

---

* List of premiums to be awarded by the Deserét Agricultural and Manufacturing Society, at the Annual Exhibition, October 3d and 4th, 1860.

CLASS A.—CATTLE.

Awarding Committee—Hector C. Haight, Wm. Jennings, Wm. Miller, Alex. Baron.

Best Durham bull $10 00	3d best Devon cow and calf dip.	2d best blooded and wooled	
2d do. 5 00	Best native or cross cow	buck $3 00	
3d do. .... dip.	and calf.............. $5 00	3d do. do. dip.	
Best Devon bull 10 00	2d do. do. 3 00	Best 2 ewes for blood and	
2d do. 5 00	3d do. do. dip.	wool 4 00	
3d do. .... dip.	Best 2 year old heifer 3 00	2d do. do. 2 00	
Best bull under 1 year.... 5 00	2d do. do. dip.	3d do. do. dip.	
2d do. do. .... dip.	Best 1 year old heifer 2 00	Best boar............... 3 00	
Best Durham cow and calf 5 00	2d do. do. ..... dip.	2d do................. 2 00	
2d do. do. 3 00	Best matched native cattle. 5 00	3d do. .... dip.	
3d do.. do. dip.	2d do. do. 3 00	Best sow and pigs........ 3 00	
Best Devon cow and calf.. 5 00	3d do. do. dip.	2d do. 2 00	
2d do. do. .. 3 00	Best blooded & wooled buck 5 00	3d do. .... dip.	

CLASS B.—FIELD CROPS.

Awarding Committee—A. P. Rockwood, Joseph Holbrook, L. E. Harrington, John Rowberry.

Best fenced and cultivated farm not less than twenty acres........ $5 00	Best 5 acres of corn $5 00	3d best 1 acre of peas ..... dip.
2d do. dip.	2d do. 3 00	Best 1 acre of flax........ $5 00
Best fenced and cultivated garden	3d do. ...... dip.	2d do. 3 00
2d do. dip.	Best 5 acres of turnips.... 5 00	Best 1 acre of hemp 5 00
Best 5 acres of sugar-cane 15 00	2d do. 3 00	2d do. 3 00
2d do. 10 00	3d do. ..... dip.	3d do. ...... dip.
3d do. 5 00	Best 5 acres of beets...... 5 00	Best 1 acre of red clover .. 5 00
4th do. 5 00	2d do. 3 00	2d do. 3 00
Best 1 acre of sugar-cane. 5 00	3d do. ..... dip.	3d do. .. dip.
2d do. 3 00	Best 5 acres of carrots 5 00	Best 1 acre of potatoes.... 3 00
3d do. dip.	2d do. 3 00	2d do. .... dip.
Best 5 acres of wheat 5 00	3d do. .... dip.	Best 1 acre of Hungarian
2d do. ,.... 3 00	Best 1 acre of white beans. 3 00	grass................. 3 00
3d do. .... dip.	2d do. ..... dip.	2d do. 2 00
	Best 1 acre of peas 5 00	3d do. dip.
	2d do. 3 00	Best acre of rye.......... 3 00

northern parts suffers from the late frosts, and requires a longer summer. Until oats and barley can be grown in sufficient quantities, horses are fed upon heating wheat, which only the hardest

CLASS B.—FIELD CROPS—Continued.

2d best acre of rye.......	dip.	3d best 100 lbs. of flax	dip.	3d best 20 lbs. manufactured tobacco........	dip.
Best acre of turnips	$3 00	Best 100 lbs. hemp........	$5 00	Best 6 canes of Chinese sugar-cane..........	$3 00
2d do.	dip.	2d do.	2 00	2d do.	2 00
Best acre of beets	3 00	3d do.	dip.	3d do.	dip.
2d do.	dip.	Best 10 lbs. manufactured tobacco..............	3 00	Best 6 canes of field-corn..	2 00
Best acre of carrots	3 00	2d best 20 lbs. manufactured tobacco	2 00	2d do. ..	1 00
2d do.	dip.			3d do. ..	dip.
Best 100 lbs. flax........	5 00				
2d do.	2 00				

Awarding Committee on Cotton and Tobacco—William Crosby, Robert D. Covington, Joshua T. Willis, Jacob Hamblin, Jas. R. M'Cullough.

Best 10 acres of cotton....	$30 00	3d best 2 acres of cotton..	$10 00	4th best ¼ acre of cotton..	$4 00
2d do.	20 00	4th do. ..	5 00	5th do. ..	dip.
3d do.	15 00	5th do. ..	dip.	Best 5 acres of tobacco ...	25 00
4th do.	10 00	Best 1 acre of cotton.....	15 00	2d do. ...	20 00
5th do.	dip.	2d do.	10 00	3d do. ...	15 00
Best 5 acres of cotton	25 00	3d do.	8 00	4th do. ...	10 00
2d do.	20 00	4th do.	5 00	5th do. ...	dip.
3d do.	15 00	5th do.	dip.	Best 1 acre of tobacco ...	15 00
4th do.	10 00	Best ¼ acre of cotton.....	10 00	2d do.	10 00
5th do.	dip.	2d do.	8 00	3d do.	5 00
Best 2 acres of cotton	20 00	3d do.	6 00	4th do.	dip.
2d do.	15 00				

CLASS C.—VEGETABLES.

Awarding Committee—Sidney A. Knowlton, Charles H. Oliphant, Thos. Woodbury.

Best brace cucumbers	$3 00	2d best 6 stalks of celery..	dip.	Best quart of Lima beans.	$2 00
2d do.	dip.	Best 6 blood beets........	$2 00	2d do.	2 00
Best 3 squashes..........	2 00	2d do.	dip.	Best quart of bush beans..	2 00
2d do.	dip.	Best 6 sugar beets........	2 00	2d do. ..	2 00
Best 3 pumpkins.........	2 00	2d do.	dip.	Best quart of peas........	2 00
2d do.	dip.	Best 6 carrots...........	2 00	2d do.	dip.
Best 3 water melons	2 00	2d do.	dip.	Best 6 stalks of rhubarb..	2 00
2d do.	dip.	Best 6 parsnips	2 00	2d do. ..	dip.
Best 3 cantaloupes.......	2 00	2d do.	dip.	Best 4 heads of cauliflower	1 00
2d do.	dip.	Best 6 turnips	2 00	2d do.	dip.
Best peck of tomatoes....	2 00	2d do.	dip.	Best 4 heads of brocoli....	1 00
2d do.	1 00	Best peck of silver onions.	2 00	2d do.	dip.
3d do.	dip.	2d do.	dip.	Best 4 heads of lettuce....	1 00
Best 3 early cabbages.....	1 50	Best peck of yellow onions	2 00	2d do.	dip.
2d do.	dip.	2d do.	dip.	Best bunch of parsley	1 00
Best 3 late cabbages......	1 50	Best peck of red onions...	2 00	2d do.	dip.
2d do.	dip.	2d do. ...	dip.	Best collection of radishes	1 00
Best 3 red cabbages	1 50	Best peck of potatoes.....	2 00	2d do.	dip.
2d do.	dip.	2d do.	dip.	Best collection of peppers..	1 00
Best 3 Savoy cabbages....	1 50	Best peck of sweet potatoes	5 00	2d do. ..	dip.
2d do.	dip.	2d do.	2 00	Best egg-plant	1 00
Best 6 stalks of celery	2 00	3d do.	dip.	2d do.	dip.

CLASS D.—FRUITS AND FLOWERS.

Awarding Committee—Edward Sayres, George A. Niel, Daniel Graves.

Best 6 apples	$3 00	Best 6 quinces............	$3 00	Best specimen of English cherries..............	$3 00
2d do.	2 00	2d do.	2 00	2d do.	2 00
3d do.	1 00	3d do.	1 00	3d do.	dip.
4th do.	dip.	4th do.	dip.	Best bed or hills of strawberries................	3 00
Best 6 peaches...........	3 00	Best 3 bunches of grapes...	3 00	2d do.	2 00
2d do.	2 00	2d do. ...	2 00	3d do.	1 00
3d do.	1 00	3d do. ...	1 00	4th do.	dip.
4th do.	dip.	4th do. ...	dip.	Best raspberries	2 00
Best 6 pears..............	3 00	Best quart of native grafted plums..............	2 00	2d do.	1 00
2d do.	2 00	2d do.	1 00	3d do.	dip.
3d do.	1 00	3d do.	dip.	Best gooseberries	2 00
4th do.	dip.	Best pint of currants......	1 00	2d do.	1 00
Best 6 apricots...........	3 00	2d do.	1 00	3d do.	dip.
2d do.	2 00	3d do.	dip.		
3d do.	1 00				
4th do.	dip.				

riding enables them to digest. *Holcus saccharatum*, or Chinese millet, succeeds where insufficient humidity is an obstacle to the sugar-cane. The fault of the vegetables here, as in California, is excessive size, which often renders them insipid; the Irish potato, however, is superior to that of Nova Scotia and Charleston; the onions are large and mild as those of Spain. The white carrot, the French bean, and the cucumber grow well, and the "multicaulis mania" has borne good fruit in the shape of cabbage. The size of the beets suggested in 1853 the project originated in France by Napoleon the Great: $100,000 were expended upon sugar-making machinery; the experiment, however, though directed by a Frenchman, failed, it is said, on account of the alkali contained in the root, and the Saints are accused of having distilled for sale bad spirit from the useless substance. The deserts skirting the Western Holy Land have also their manna; the leaves of poplars and other trees on the banks of streams distill, at divers seasons of the year, globules of honey-dew, resembling in color gum Arabic, but of softer consistence and less adhesiveness: the people collect it with spoons into saucers. Cotton thrives in the southern and southwestern part of Utah Territory when the winter is mild: at the meeting-place of waters near the Green and Grand Rivers that unite to form the Colorado, the shrub has been grown with great success.

The principal value of Utah Territory is its position as a great half-way station—a Tadmor in the wilderness—between the Valley of the Mississippi and the Western States, California and Oregon; it has thus proved a benefit to humanity. The Mormons, "flying from civilization and Christianity," attempted to isolate themselves from the world in a mountain fastness; they were foiled by an accident far beyond human foresight. They had retired to a complete oasis, defended by sterile volcanic passes, which in winter are blocked up with snow, girt by vast waterless and uninhabitable deserts, and unapproachable from any settled country save by a painful and dangerous march of 600—1000 miles. Presently, in 1850, the gold fever broke out on the Pacific sea-board; thousands of people not only passed through Utah Territory, but were also compelled to remain there and work for a livelihood. The transit received a fresh impulse in 1858 by the gold discovered at Pike's Peak, and in 1859 by the rich silver mines found in the Carson and Washoe Valleys, on the eastern slopes of the Sierra Nevada. Carson Valley, which was settled by Colonel Reece in 1852, and colonized in 1855 by 500 Mormons, was soon cleared of Saints by the influx of prospectors and diggers, and the other El Dorados drew off much

FLOWERS.		
Best collection of China asters...............$1 00	2d best collection of dahlias dip.	2d best collection of cut flowers............... dip.
	Best collection of roses.....$2 00	
2d do. dip.	2d do. ..... dip.	Best collection of pot flowers $1 00
Best collection of dahlias .. 2 00	Best collection of cut flowers 1 00	2d do. dip.

Gentile population, which was an incalculable boon to the Mormons. They thus rid themselves of the "thriving lawyers, gamblers, prostitutes, criminals, and desperadoes, loafers, and drunkards," who made New Jerusalem a carnival of horrors. The scene is now shifted to Denver and Carson cities, where rape and robbery, intoxication and shooting are attributed to their true causes, the gathering together of a lawless and excited crowd, not to the "baleful shade of that deadly Upas-tree, Mormonism."

The Mormons, having lost all hopes of safety by isolation, now seek it in the reverse: mail communication with the Eastern and Western States is their present hobby: they look forward to markets for their produce, and to a greater facility and economy of importing. They have dreamed of a water-line to the East by means of the Missouri head-waters, which are said to be navigable for 350—400 miles, and to the West by the tributaries of the Snake River, that afford 400. Shortly after the foundation of Great Salt Lake City, they proceeded to establish, under the ecclesiastical title "Stakes of Zion in the Wilderness," settlements and outposts, echelonned in skeleton, afterward to be filled in, from Temple Block along the southern line to San Diego. The importance of connecting the Atlantic with the Pacific by a shorter route than the 24,000 miles of navigation round Cape Horn, has produced first a monthly, then a weekly, and lastly a daily mail, and has opened up a route from the Holy City to Carson Valley. So far from opposing the Pacific Railroad, the local Legislature petitioned for it in 1849, and believe that it would increase the value of their property tenfold. But as equal parts of Mormon and Gentile never could dwell together in amity, extensive communication would probably result in causing the Saints to sell out, and once more to betake themselves to their "wilderness work" in Sonora, or in other half-settled portions of Northern Mexico. This view of the question is taken by the federal authorities, who would willingly, if they could, confer upon the petitioners the fatal boon.

The Mormon pioneers, 143 in number, when sent westward under several of the apostles to seek for settlements, fixed upon the Valley of the Great Salt Lake. The advance colony of 4000 souls, expelled from Nauvoo on the Mississippi, and headed by "Brigham the Seer," arrived there on the 24th of July, 1847, the anniversary of which is their 4th of July—Independence Day. Before the end of the first week a tract of land was ditched, plowed, and planted with potatoes. City-Creek Kanyon was dammed for irrigation; an area of forty acres was fortified after the old New England fashion by facing log houses inward, and by a palisade of timber hauled from the ravines; the city was laid out upon the spot where they first rested, the most eligible site in the Valley, and prayers, with solemn ceremonies, consecrated the land.

Early in 1849, the Mormons, irritated by the contemptuous silence of the federal government, assembled themselves in Convention, and, with the boldness engendered by a perfect faith, duly erected themselves into a free, sovereign, and independent people, with a vast extent of country.* Disdaining to remain in *statu pupillari*, they dispensed with a long political minority, and rushed into the conclave of republics like California, whose sons are fond of comparing her to Minerva issuing full-grown from the cranium of Jupiter into the society of Olympus. Roused by this liberty, the Senate and House of Representatives of the United States of America, in Congress assembled, on the 9th of Septem-

* The following is the preamble to the Constitution: it is a fair specimen of Mormon plain-dealing.

Provisional Government of the State of Deserét.—Abstract of Convention Minutes. On the 15th of March, 1849, the Convention appointed the following persons a Committee to draft a Constitution for the State of Deserét, viz.: Albert Carrington, Joseph L. Heywood, William W. Phelps, David Fullmer, John S. Fullmer, Charles C. Rich, John Taylor, Parley P. Pratt, John M. Bernhisel, Erastus Snow.

March 18th, 1849. Albert Carrington, chairman of the Committee, reported the following Constitution, which was read and unanimously adopted by the Convention:

CONSTITUTION OF THE STATE OF DESERÉT.

PREAMBLE.—Whereas a large number of the citizens of the United States, before and since the Treaty of Peace with the Republic of Mexico, emigrated to, and settled in that portion of the territory of the United States lying west of the Rocky Mountains, and in the great interior Basin of Upper California; and

Whereas, by reason of said treaty, all civil organization originating from the Republic of Mexico became abrogated; and

Whereas the Congress of the United States has failed to provide a form of civil government for the territory so acquired, or any portion thereof; and

Whereas civil government and laws are necessary for the security, peace, and prosperity of society; and

Whereas it is a fundamental principle in all republican governments that all political power is inherent in the people, and governments instituted for their protection, security, and benefit should emanate from the same:

Therefore your committee beg leave to recommend the adoption of the following CONSTITUTION until the Congress of the United States shall otherwise provide for the government of the Territory hereinafter named and described by admitting us into the Union. WE, THE PEOPLE, grateful to the SUPREME BEING for the blessings hitherto enjoyed, and feeling our dependence on Him for a continuation of those blessings, DO ORDAIN AND ESTABLISH A FREE AND INDEPENDENT GOVERNMENT, by the name of the STATE OF DESERÉT, including all the territory of the United States within the following boundaries, to wit: commencing at the 33° of north latitude, where it crosses the 108° of longitude, west of Greenwich; thence running south and west to the boundary of Mexico; thence west to and down the main channel of the Gila River (or the northern line of Mexico), and on the northern boundary of Lower California to the Pacific Ocean; thence along the coast northwesterly to the 118° 30′ of west longitude; thence north to where said line intersects the dividing ridge of the Sierra Nevada mountains; thence north along the summit of the Sierra Nevada mountains to the dividing range of mountains that separate the waters flowing into the Columbia River from the waters running into the Great Basin; thence easterly along the dividing range of mountains that separate said waters flowing into the Columbia River on the north, from the waters flowing into the Great Basin on the south, to the summit of the Wind River chain of mountains; thence southeast and south by the dividing range of mountains that separate the waters flowing into the Gulf of Mexico from the waters flowing into the Gulf of California, to the place of beginning, as set forth in a map drawn by Charles Preuss, and published by order of the Senate of the United States in 1848.

T

ber, 1850, sheared the self-constituted republic of its fair proportions, and reduced it to the infant condition of New Mexico, with
the usual proviso in the organic act that when qualified for admission as states they shall become slave or free, as their respective Constitutions may prescribe. At present one of the principal
Mormon grievances is that, although their country can, by virtue
of population, claim admission into the Union, which has lately
been overrun with a mushroom growth, like Michigan, Minnesota,
and Oregon, their prayers are not only rejected, but even their
petitions remain unnoticed. The cause is, I believe, polygamy,
which, until the statute law is altered, would not and could not
be tolerated, either in America or in England. To the admission
of other Territories, Kansas, for instance, the slavery question was
the obstacle. The pro party will admit none who will not support the South, and *vice versâ*. Perhaps it is well so, otherwise
the old and civilized states would soon find themselves swamped
by batches of peers in rapidly succeeding creations.

The Mormons have another complaint, touching the tenure of
their land. The United States have determined that the Indian
title has not been extinguished. The Saints declare that no tribe
of aborigines could prove a claim to the country, otherwise they
were ready to purchase it in perpetuity by pay, presents, and provisions, besides establishing the usual reservations. Moreover,
the federal government has departed from the usual course. The
law directs that the land, when set off into townships, six miles
square with subdivisions,* must be sold at auction to the highest
bidder. The Mormons represent that although a survey of considerable tracts has been completed by a federal official, they are
left to be mere squatters that can be ejected like an Irish tenant-
ry, because the government, knowing their ability and readiness
to pay the recognized pre-emption price ($1 25 per acre), fear lest
those now in possession should become lawful owners and permanent proprietors of the soil.† Polygamy is here again to blame.

The Mormon settlements resemble those of the French in Canada and elsewhere rather than the English in Australia, the Dutch
at the Cape, or the American squatters on the Western frontier.
They eschew solitude, and cluster together round the Church and
the succedaneum for the priest. In establishing these "stakes"
they proceed methodically. A tentative expedition, sent out to
select the point presenting the greatest facilities for settlements,
is followed by a volunteer band of Saints, composed of farmers,

---

* Viz., the section of one square mile, the half section =320 acres, and the quarter section of 160 acres: the latter is the legal grant to military settlers. The pre-
emption laws in the United States are just and precise; but in the mountains it is
about as easy to eject a squatter as to collect "rint" from Western Galway in the
days of Mr. Martin.
† In England and Scotland the rent for use of land averages one quarter of the
gross produce; in France, one third; unhappy India gives one half; and the Territories of the United States nearly nothing.

mechanics, and artisans, headed by an apostle, president, elder, or some other dignitary. The foundations are laid with long ceremonies. The fort or block-house is first built, and when the people are lodged the work of agriculture begins. The cities of Utah Territory are somewhat like the "towns" of Cornwall. At present there are three long lines of these juvenile settlements established as caravanserais in the several oases. The first is along the Humboldt River to Carson Valley; the second is by the southern route, *via* Fillmore; and the third is betwixt the two, along "Egan's Route," the present mail line.

The counties, originally 5, increased in 1855 to 12, are now (1860) 19 in number, viz.:

1. Great Salt Lake County: the chief town is Great Salt Lake City; the sub-settlements are the Sugar-House, 4 miles S. of Temple Block—the invariable *point de départ;* Mill Creek, 7 miles; Great Cotton-wood, 8—9 miles; West Jordan, Jordan Mills, Herriman, and Union, or Little Cotton-wood Creek, 12 miles; Drapersville, 20—21 miles S.; all small villages, with good farming lands.

2. Utah County: the chief town is Provo or Provaux, on the Timpanogos River, 45 miles; David City, on Dry Creek, 28 miles; Lake City, on American Fork, 32 miles S.; Lehi City, 35 miles S.; Lone City, 37 miles S.; Pleasant Grove or Battle Creek, 41 miles S.; Springville or Hobble Creek, 53—54 miles; Palmyra, a small place east of the Lake, and north of Spanish Fork, 59—60 miles; Spanish-Fork City, 61 miles S.; Pondtown, 64 miles S.; Payson City, on both banks of the Peet-Neet Creek, 64—65 miles S.; and Santa Quin, 74 miles S.

3. Davis County: chief town Farmington; others, Stoker, Centreville, 12·50 miles N., and Kaysville, 22 miles N.

4. Weber County: chief town Ogden City, on both sides of Ogden River, 40 miles E.; also North Ogden.

5. Iron County: chief town Parovan, so called from the Pavant Indians; built on Centre Creek, 255 miles S. of Great Salt Lake City, and 96 miles from Fillmore, and incorporated in 1851. Also Cedar City, near Little Salt Lake, 275 miles S.; St. Joseph's Springs and Vegas de Santa Clara, 200 miles from Cedar City. The Aztecs, as their rock inscriptions prove, once extended to Little Salt Lake Valley.

6. Tooele County: chief town Tooele City, 32 miles W.; also "Eastern Tooele City," 26 miles W.; Grantsville, 27 miles W.; Richville and Cedar Valley, 40 miles W.

7. San Pete Valley County and City, 131 miles, laid out by the presidency in 1849, and incorporated in 1850; Fort Ephraim, 130 miles; Manti City, 140 miles, on the southern declivity of Mount Nebo. Aztecan pictographs have been found upon the cliffs in San Pete Valley.

8. Juab County: chief town Salt Creek, in a valley separated from Utah Valley by a ridge, on which runs Summit Creek.

9. Box-Elder County and City, 60 miles N.; also Willow Creek and Brigham's City.

10. Washington County: chief town Fort Harmony, on Ash Creek, 291 miles S., and 20 miles N. of Rio Virgen.*

* I annex a description of Washington County, which lately appeared in the "Deserét News:"

"Yesterday afternoon I met in the library of the University the Hon. Wm. Crosby, the representative from Washington County to our Legislature, who furnishes me with some items of information respecting the county he represents worthy a passing notice, especially as there is so little known of that county. The inhabitants are estimated at about 1500 persons, chiefly engaged in farming and grazing. The county of Washington in area is as large as the State of Connecticut, generally of a barren, desert character, broken and mountainous. On the borders of the Rio Virgen and the Santa Clara there are narrow strips of land exceedingly fertile, on which every thing grows with great richness, and at a cost of very little labor. During the present year only 50,000 pounds of cotton have been raised, but, properly cultivated and attended to, the inhabitants there could raise all the cotton ever required by the inhabitants of this Territory. At present its cultivation is almost neglected for the want of proper facilities for its manufacture. The entrance also of the army in 1857, followed by immense trains of goods—which, by-the-by, some of the merchants never paid a cent for, and it is very doubtful if they ever will—was also a crushing competition to the people of Washington County.

"Every kind of fruit that has been tried there grows with great luxuriance. The apple, pear, plum, apricot, peach, and fig trees do exceedingly well. The English walnut-tree grew this year nine feet, and the Catawba grape grew nineteen feet and a half before the 6th of September. The bunches of those grapes, many of them, measured nineteen inches in length. At Tocqueville, one of the small towns in that county, one man raised this year two water-melons from one vine that weighed, the one sixty, and the other fifty pounds.

"At the Agricultural Exhibition, held there last September, the fine grapes which I have mentioned were on exhibition. At the same time there was exhibited a stalk of cotton containing three hundred and seven forms; a radish measuring eighteen inches in circumference; a sunflower head thirty-six inches; and a monster castor-bean stalk; a sweet potato-vine five feet and a half long; and one Isabella grape-vine twenty-five feet long. One man had in his garden trees which in six months grew as follows:

	ft. in.		ft. in.
Washington Plum	8 6	Almond	7 2
Apple-trees	6 6	Peach	8 6
Apricots	7 0	Pears	6 0
Figs	7 0		

"In climate, Washington embraces all the varieties from frigid to torrid, from regions of perpetual frost to an eternal spring. Every kind of out-door work, plowing, ditching, building, etc., can be pursued throughout winter in some parts of the county, while in others there are killing frosts throughout the whole year.

"I had almost forgotten to mention that the soil is excellent for the grape, and during the present year very fine tobacco has been grown there, as well as madder and indigo. The sorghum raised there has a magnificent flavor, and without the 'patent fixings,' with very little labor, and that of the simplest character, good sugar is made from it. At the late exhibition the sorghum took the two highest prizes. I believe the honorable member from Washington has brought with him a few gallons of this very fine molasses as a *cadeau* to the Prophet. To readers who have every luxury in abundance and at very moderate figures, these items may have little interest, but to those who watch the progress of the people here, and the reclaiming of the desert, this information has great significance. In a few years every thing that the people require will be raised from their own soil, and manufactured by their own hands.

"Mr. Crosby, from whom I elicited these facts, was born in Indiana, but 'brought up' in the Southern States. Mormonism got hold of him in 1843, in the State of Mississippi. Following the fortunes of Brigham, he brought some nine or ten slaves, 'very select niggers.' In 1851 he went over to San Bernardino, and was bishop

11. Millard County: chief town, which is also the capital of Utah Territory, Fillmore, in N. lat. 38° 58′ 40″, in a central position, 152 miles S. of Great Salt Lake City, 600 miles E. of San Francisco, and 1200 miles W. of St. Louis. The sum of $20,000 was expended upon public buildings, but the barrenness of the soil has reduced the population from 100 to a dozen families.

12. Green River County: Fort Supply.

13. Cedar County: chief town Cedar City. It is built upon an old Aztecan foundation, rich in pottery and other remains.

14. Malad County: chief town Fort Malad, properly so called from its slow, brackish, and nauseous river.

15. Cache County, the granary of Mormonland, and the most fertile spot in the Great Basin; well settled and much valued: chief town Cache Valley, 80 miles N.

16. Beaver County: chief town Beaver Creek, 220 miles S.

17. Shambip County: Rich Valley and Deep Creek.

18. Salt Lake Islands.

19. St. Mary's County: west of Shambip City, extending to the Humboldt River; chief settlement, Deep Creek.

I found it impossible to arrive at a true estimate of the population. Like the earlier English numberings of the people, which originated in bitter political controversies—the charge of unfairness was brought as late as 1831 against the enumerators in Ireland—the census is a purely party measure. The Mormons, desiring to show the 100,000 persons which entitle them to claim admission as a state into the Union, are naturally disposed to exaggerate their numbers; they are, of course, accused of "cooking up" schedules, of counting cattle as souls, and of making every woman a mother in *esse* as in *posse*. On the other hand, the anti-

over there. The state soon liberated the ebony folks, and Mr. Crosby, of course, lost his $9000 or $10,000 by the operation.

"The Superintendent of the Church Public Works and a few others went out exploring for coal about the Weber some time in August last, and found a splendid bed of mineral. It promises to be the greatest blessing that has yet fallen to the lot of the Saints. Of course I do not look at things with 'an eye of faith;' that is their business. But among people paying $10 per cord for wood, scarce at that, and sure to be scarcer, the discovery of coal is an important matter. The present coal-bed is about fifty miles distant; but, nevertheless, paying $3 per ton at the mouth of the pit, at which it is now sold, it can be brought into the city and sold for $20. Last year it was sold here to blacksmiths for $40. The Pacific Railroad folks should have an eye on this. The apprehension that the absence of coal and wood in the Territory would be a serious obstacle need not now exist. Though the wood is scarce and high priced as an article of daily household consumption, railroad companies can get all the lumber they require for money, though they may have to haul it far and pay a good price for it. I believe that the whole country is full of coal, and what is not coal is gold and silver ; but I earnestly hope that the day is far distant before the Mormons or any body else discover the precious metals. The coal discovery, however, is very important. The bishops of the city have been instructed to urge upon their flocks the hauling of it, and it is hoped that by constant travel the snow will be kept down and the roads clear all the winter. A Scotch miner, who had just returned from the coal-bed, told me the other day that it far exceeded any thing that he had ever seen in his own country, or in the States, both in quality and abundance."

Mormons are as naturally inclined to underestimate: moreover, as the "census marshals" receive but three halfpence per head, they are by no means disposed to pay a shilling for the trouble of ransacking every ranch and kanyon where the people repair for grazing and other purposes. The nearest approach to truth will probably be met by assuming the two opposite extremes, and by "splitting the difference."

In 1849 Mr. Kelly estimated the Mormons to be "about 5000 inhabitants in the town, and 7000 more in the settlements." In 1850 the seventh official census of the United States numbered the inhabitants of Utah Territory at 11,354 free + 26 slaves = 11,380 souls. In 1853 the Saints were reckoned at 25,000 by the Gentiles, and 30,000 to 35,000 by Mr. O. Pratt, in the "Seer." In 1854 Dr. S. W. Richards estimated the number at "probably from 40,000 to 50,000" in the United States, and in Great Britain at 29,797. In 1856 the Mormon census gave 76,335 souls. I subjoin a synopsis of the official papers.* In 1858 the Peace Commissioners sent to Utah Territory reported that the Saints did not exceed 40,000 to 50,000 souls, half of them foreigners, and that they could bring 7000 men, of whom 1000 were valuable for cavalry, into the field. In 1859 M. Remy made the number of Saints in Utah Territory, not including Nevada, 80,000 souls, and the total in the world 186,000. The last official census, in 1860, was taken under peculiar disadvantages. General Burr, of the firm

* The following is a condensed Report of the enumeration of the inhabitants of Utah Territory, taken February, 1856:

Counties.	Males.	Females.	Total.
Great Salt Lake County....	12,730	13,074	25,804
Utah "	6,951	7,614	14,565
Davis "	4,765	4,575	9,340
Weber "	3,486	3,585	7,071
Iron "	2,474	2,943	5,417
Tooele "	1,315	1,673	2,988
San Pete "	1,110	1,133	2,243
Juab "	807	1,034	1,841
Box-Elder "	822	717	1,539
Washington "	742	778	1,520
Millard "	544	512	1,056
Green River "	394	345	739
Cedar "	312	369	681
Malad "	259	208	467
Cache "	240	223	463
Beaver "	118	126	244
Shambip "	83	64	147
Salt Lake Islands	125	85	210
	37,277	39,058	76,335

"Great Salt Lake City, March 1st, 1856.

"I do hereby certify that the above is a correct enumeration of the white inhabitants of Utah Territory, according to the reports furnished by my assistants, and which are now on file in my office.   LEONARD W. HARDY, Census Agent."

"Great Salt Lake City, September 13th, 1860.

"The above is a correct transcript from the originals on file in the Historian's Office.   THOMAS BULLOCK, Clerk."

of Hockaday and Burr, was appointed to that duty by Mr. Dotson, the anti-Mormon federal marshal. But as the choice excited loud murmurs, the task was committed to a clerk in the general's store, and deputies for the rest of the Territory were similarly chosen. The consequence is that the Gentile marshal's census of 1860 offers a number of 40,266 free + 29 slaves = a total of 40,295 souls; while the Mormons assert their Territory to contain from 90,000 to 100,000, and the world to hold from 300,000 to 400,000 Saints. Their rise is remarkable, even if we take the statistics of the enemy, which show nearly a quadrupling of the population in ten years, while Great Britain creeps on at a rate of about ten per cent.: a similar increase will in the ninth census of 1870 give in round numbers 160,000 persons. Utah Territory now ranks second in the eight minor states: New Mexico (93,541) and District of Columbia (75,076) take precedence of it, and it is followed by Colorado (34,197), Nebraska (28,842), Washington (11,578), Nevada (6857), and Dakotah (4839).

I have vainly attempted to discover the proportion of native Anglo-Americans to the foreign-born. The late Mr. Stephen A. Douglas, who was supposed to know and to befriend the Saints, asserted it to be one to ten. This will not hold good if applied to the authorities, and if it fails at the head it will be inapplicable to the baser part of the body politic, for the American in Mormondom is the prophet, president, apostle, bishop, or other high dignitary who leavens the lump of ignorance and superstition kneaded together in the old countries. Of the thirteen members of the Upper House, there were, in 1860, ten Americans, two English, and one Irishman: of the officers, viz., secretary and his assistant, sergeant-at-arms, messenger, fireman, and chaplain, four were Americans, one English, and one Irishman. The members of the Lower House, twenty-six in number, consisted of twenty-four Americans and two Englishmen, including the speaker, Mr. John Taylor: of its six officers, four were Americans, one English, and one Scotchman. Both houses were thus distributed:

New York.........13	Tennessee.......... 3	Ireland............ 2
Massachusetts.... 6	Kentucky........... 2	Scotland........... 1
Vermont.......... 5	New Hampshire.. 2	Isle of Man....... 1
England........... 4	Pennsylvania...... 2	Virginia........... 1
Ohio............... 4	Indiana 2	Rhode Island 1
		Grand total...........49

The Mormon emigration is without exception the most interesting feature in their scheme. There is an evident selection of species in the supply: a man must be superior to many in "grit" and energy who voluntarily leaves his native land. As regards the national classification of the converts, it may be observed that the supply depends upon the freedom of religious discussion at home. Great Britain supplies five times more than all the rest of the world, excepting Denmark. France must be proselytized through the Channel Islands, and there are few converts of the Latin race, which speaks a strange language, and is too much attached to the soil for extensive colonization. Sweden sends forth few (67)—a fine of twenty-six rix-dollars has there been imposed upon all who harbor, let rooms to, or hold to service a Mormon; Denmark supplies many (502), because the Constitution of 1849 guaranteed to her religious liberty; Switzerland is, after a fashion, Republican; Germany gives the fewest. Propagandism has not yet been thoroughly organized east of Father Rhine; moreover, the Teuton, whose faith is mostly subordinate to his fancy, finds superior inducements to settle while passing through the Eastern States. All the "diverts" long retain their motherlandish characteristics, and, associating together, are often unable to understand the English sermon at the Tabernacle. The work of proselytizing is slow in the United States; the analytic Anglo-American prefers the rôle of knave to that of fool, besides un saint n'est pas honoré dans son pays, upon the principle that no man is a hero to his valet. At Great Salt Lake City I saw neither Kanaka, Hindoo, nor Chinese; these "exotics" have probably withered out since the days of M. Remy; only one negro met my sight, and though a few Yutas, principally Weber River, were seen in the streets, none of them had Mormonized.

Emigration in Mormondom, like El Hajj in El Islam, is the fulfillment of a divine command. As soon as the Saints could afford it, they established, under the direction of the First Presidency, a fund for importing poor converts, appointed a committee for purchasing transports, and established in Europe and elsewhere agents, who collected $5000 in the first, and $20,000 in the second year. In September, 1850, a committee of three officers was appointed to transact the business of the poor fund, and an ordinance was passed incorporating the "Perpetual Emigration Fund Company," consisting of thirteen members, including the First President. The Saint whose passage is thus defrayed works out his debt in the public ateliers of the Tithing Office Department, under the superintendence of the Third President; he is supplied with food from the "Deserét Store," and receives half the value of his labor, besides which a tithe of his time and toil is free. The anti-Mormons declare that by this means the faces of the poor are ground: I doubt that so far-seeing a people as the Mormons would attempt so suicidal a policy.

According to the late agent at Liverpool, and publisher of the "Millennial Star," Dr. S. W. Richards (Select Committee on Emigrant Ships, 1854, No. 12, p. 8), the Mormon emigration, under its authorized agent and passenger-broker, is better regulated than under the provisions of the Passengers' Act; the sexes are berthed apart, and many home comforts are provided for the emigrants. In 1854 it was estimated not to exceed 3000 souls per annum, and of 2600 the English were 1430, 250 Welsh, 200 Scotch, and about a score of Irish, making a total of 1900 Britons to 700 from the Continent. The classes preferred by the Fund are agriculturists and mechanics—the latter being at a premium—moral, industrious, and educated people, " qualified to increase and enhance the interest of the community they go among." From Liverpool, whence all the emigration proceeds, to New Orleans, the passage-money varied from £3 12s. 6d. to £4, and from New Orleans to Great Salt Lake City £20 each. Of late years that line has been abandoned as unhealthy: the route now lies by rail through New York and Chicago to Florence, on the Missouri River. The emigration season is January, February, and March, and the passage can be made at the quickest in twenty-two days.

I now proceed to figures, which are given in full detail, and can easily be verified by a reference to Liverpool. The official reports are subjoined, because they speak well for Mormon accuracy.* From 1840–54 they reckon 17,195 souls, and from

* No. I.—*List of Latter-Day Saints' Emigration, from January 6th, 1851, to May 15th, 1861.*

Date of Sailing.	Vessel.	Captain.	No. of Souls.
1851, January 6.....	Ellen	Phillips.............	466
" 22...	G. W. Bourne...........	Williams..........	281
February 2....	Ellen Maria..............	Whitmore.........	378
March 4.......	Olympus.................	Wilson.............	245
1852, January 10 ...	Kennebec.................	Smith...............	333
February 10..	Ellen Maria..............	Whitmore.........	369
March 6.......	Rockaway		30
1853, January 17 ...	Ellen Maria..............	Whitmore.........	332
" 23 ...	Golconda...............	Kerr................	321
February 5....	Jersey..................	Day.................	314
" 15...	Elvira Owen............	Owen..............	345
" 28...	International............	Brown.............	425
March 26......	Falcon...................	Wade..............	324
April 6.........	Camillus.................	Day.................	228
	(Miscellaneous).........		23
1854, January 22 ...	Benjamin Adams.......	Drummond.......	6
February 4....	Golconda...............	Kerr................	464
" 22..	Windermere............	Fairfield..........	477
March 5.......	Old England............	Barstow...........	45
" 12...	John M. Wood..........	Hartley...........	393
April 4.........	Germanicus.............	Fales..............	220
" 8.........	Marshfield	Torrey............	366
" 24.......	Clara Wheeler.........	Nelson.............	29
	(Miscellaneous).........		34
November 27.	Clara Wheeler.........	Nelson.............	422
1855, January 6.....	Rockaway...............	Mills..............	440
" 7.....	James Nesmith	Goodwin	24
" 9.....	Neva....................	Brown.............	13
" 17...	Charles Buck..........	Smalley...........	403
February 3...	Isaac Jeans	Chipman..........	16
" 27..	Siddons..................	Taylor.............	430
March 31......	Jurenta	Watts..............	573
April 17	Chimborazo.............	Vesper............	431
" 22	Samuel Curling........	Curling...........	581
" 26	William Stetson........	Jordan	293
June 29........	Cynosure.................	Pray...............	159
November 30.	Emerald Isle.............	Cornish...........	350

1854–55, 4716 souls; the total in fifteen years (1840–55) being 21,911. From 1855–56 they number 4395 souls, and from the

No. I.—*Continued.*

Date of Sailing.	Vessel.	Captain.	No. of Souls.
1855, December 12..	John J. Boyd............	Austin............	512
1856, February 19 ..	Caravan..................	W. A. Sands.....	457
March 23......	Enoch Train.............	H. P. Rich........	534
April 19.......	S. Curling..............	S. Curling........	707
May 4...........	Thornton................	Collins............	764
May 25........	Horizon.................	Reed............	856
June 1	Wellfleet................	Westcott...........	146
	(Miscellaneous Ships)..	....	69
November 17.	Columbia................	Hutchinson.......	223
1857, March 28......	George Washington....	J. S. Comings....	817
April 25.......	Westmoreland..........	R. R. Decan......	544
May 30........	Tuscarora...............	Dunlery...........	547
	(Miscellaneous)........	....	50
July 18........	Wyoming	Brooks............	36
1859, April 11.......	William Tapscott.......	J. B. Bell.........	725
July 10........	Antarctic................	....	30
August 20.....	Emerald Isle............	Cornish...........	54
1860, March 30......	Underwriter.............	J. W. Roberts....	594
May 11........	William Tapscott......	J. B. Bell.........	731
	(Miscellaneous)........	....	263
1861, April 15.......	Manchester.............	Trask.............	379
" 22.......	Underwriter.............	J. W. Roberts....	624
May 15........	Monarch of the Sea....	Gardner...........	950
		Total.........	21,195

"Latter-Day Saints' European Publishing and Emigration Office,
"42 Islington, Liverpool.

"The above are the numbers of the Latter-Day Saints who have taken passage on ships chartered at this port by the Church Emigration Agent. Besides these, there are many who engage passages at other offices—not being able to arrange their affairs to go when we have ships chartered—whose numbers we do not have. The bulk of our emigration, for the past few years, has left here in the spring. This is the only time we have ships chartered. The scattering few who go over in the summer and autumn, with the intention of remaining in the United States until another spring, we do not keep any account of.   Geo. Q. Cannon."

No. II.—*General Summary of Emigration, from Nov. 30th, 1855, to July 6th, 1856.*
(*It was discontinued in 1858, owing to troubles with the U. S. Government.*)

Ship.	Captain.	President of Company.	Date of Sailing.	Port of Disembarkation.	P. E. Fund.	Ordinary.	Totals.
Emerald Isle....	G. P. Cornish..	P. C. Merrill ..	Nov. 30, 1855..	New York..	...	350	350
John J. Boyd....	Austin	C. Peterson ...	Dec. 12, 1855..	New York..	34	478	512
Caravan........	W. A. Sands...	D. Tyler	Feb. 19, 1856..	New York..	...	457	457
Enoch Train....	H. P. Rich.....	J. Ferguson ...	Mar. 23, 1856.	Boston......	431	103	534
S. Curling......	S. Curling.....	D. Jones	April 19, 1856.	Boston......	428	279	707
Thornton.......	Collins........	J. G. Willie ...	May 14, 1856..	New York..	484	280	764
Horizon	Reed..........	E. Martin	May 25, 1856..	Boston......	635	221	856
Wellfleet	Westcott	J. Aubray.....	June 1, 1856 ..	Boston.....	...	146	146
Miscellaneous Ships (U. S.)	....	....	....	....	...	69	69
				Total..	2012	2383	4395

Of this number, as the table shows, 2012 are P. E. Fund passengers, of whom 333 were ordered out by their friends in Utah; also 780 members of many years' standing in the Church have been forwarded to Utah under the P. E. Fund Co.'s arrangements, and 28 are elders returning home from missions. We have not the means of ascertaining definitely, but the approximate numbers of those who started to go

1st of July, 1857, to the 30th of June, 1860, they count 2433, making for the five subsequent years (1855–60) a total of 6828. Thus, in the twenty years between 1840–60, they show a grand

through to Utah on their own means is 385, making a total of those who started from here, with 'the intention of going through to the Valley this season, about 2397, which will leave 1998 who have located for the present in various parts of the United States, in order to obtain means to complete their journey whenever circumstances will permit.

Latter-Day Saints' Emigration Report, from July 1st, 1857, to June 30, 1860.

Ship.	Captain.	President of Company.	Port of Embarkation.	Date of Sailing.	Port of Disembarkation.	P. E. Fund	Hand-cart.	Team.	States.	Total.
Wyoming....	— Brooks ...	Chas. Harman.	Liverpool	July 18, 1857	Philadel.				36	36
Wm. Tapscott	J. B. Bell....	Robt. F. Neslen	Liverpool	Apr. 11, 1859	N. York..	54	196	149	326	725
Antarctic....	....	Jas. Chaplow..	Liverpool	July 10, 1859	N. York..				30	30
Emerald Isle.	— Cornish...	Henry Hugg ..	Liverpool	Aug. 20, 1859	N. York..				54	54
Underwriter .	J. W. Roberts	Jas. D. Ross ...	Liverpool	Mar. 30, 1860	N. York..	1	140	106	347	594
Wm. Tapscott	J. B. Bell....	Asa Calkin....	Liverpool	May 11, 1860	N. York..	17	128	246	340	731
Miscellane- ⎱ ous Ships ⎰	....	....	....	....	....				263	263
						72	464	501	1396	2433

Of this number, as the table shows, 1037 purposed going through to Utah under P. E. Fund, hand-cart, and team arrangements. But we have good cause to presume that a large number of those who left here with the intention of settling for a short time in the States (and are included in the table under that head) have also gone through to Utah, without settling on the way.

The number of natives of the various countries may be classified as follows: From the United Kingdom of Great Britain and Ireland—English, 1074; Scotch, 126; Welsh, 173; Irish, 12. The total number from the Scandinavian Mission is 762, of which there are 528 Danes, 193 Swedes, and 41 Norwegians. The total number from the Swiss and Italian Mission is 211, of which 209 are from the Swiss Cantons, and 2 from Italy. There are also 2 French, 3 Germans, and 70 elders returning home from missions, making a grand total, as per table, of 2433 souls.

Countries.—The number of natives of the various countries may be classified as follows:

```
England.....................................2611
   (Principal counties—Lancashire,
    Yorkshire, and Staffordshire.)
Scotland..................................  367
Wales.....................................  667 ——3645
Ireland ..................................   54
America...................................   19
French Mission (Channel Islands)...    9
Denmark...... ⎱                    ⎰ 505
Sweden........ ⎬ Scandinavian .....⎨  67
Norway........ ⎰                    ⎰  46
Swiss Cantons...........................   19
Piedmont, Italy.........................   31
East India Mission......................    2
Germany ................................    1 ——750
          Total...................4395 souls.
```

The emigration in 1861 is progressing satisfactorily, as the following extract proves:

"A party of Mormonites, consisting of 17 men, 25 women, and 11 children, left London lately by the Northwestern Railway for Liverpool, *en route* for the Salt Lake settlement. The emigration of Mormonites from Great Britain, particularly from the southern district of Wales, has during the past ten weeks been on a large scale. Their number embraces all classes; one gentleman, an inhabitant of Merthyr, Gla-

total of 28,739 immigrants. They expect for the present year an emigration of 1500 to 2000 souls from the British Isles, independent of some hundreds from the Scandinavian, Swiss, and other missions. Already 200 teams have been dispatched from Great Salt Lake City to assist with transport and provisions the poor emigrants from Florence. The Holy Land of the West would soon be populous were it not for two obstacles: first, the expense and difficulty of the outward journey; secondly, the facility of emigration to the gold regions of Pike's Peak and the silver mines of the Nevada.

The London Conference has seventeen places of worship, and numbers a little over 2000 men, scattered throughout Great Britain. In these isles there is a general Presidency of the Church, assisted by a counselor: these preside over the pastors or presidents of districts, ten in number, who also, assisted by counselors in their turn, direct and counsel the presidents of the twenty-four

morganshire, having contributed £1000, and joined the 'brethren,' 200 of whom, including an old woman upward of eighty years of age, have just left Wales."

No. III.—*Latter-Day Saints' Emigration, Spring of* 1861.

42 Islington, Liverpool, June 29th, 1861.

Per Ship Manchester, Captain Frask.	Males.	Females.	Per Ship Underwriter, Captain Roberts.	Males.	Females.
English	132	124	English	234	278
Scotch	3	2	Scotch	32	43
Irish	2	0	Irish	3	0
Welsh	54	57	Welsh	16	14
Danes	5	0	Norwegian	1	0
Americans	1	0	Americans	3	0
	197	183		289	335

Per Ship Monarch of the Sea, Captain Gardner.

	Males.	Females.		Males.	Females.
English	97	105	Brought forward	182	198
Scotch	25	27	Italian	1	3
Irish	2	1	French	1	2
Welsh	17	17	Danish	175	210
German	1	0	Norwegian	24	43
Swiss	40	48	Swedish	61	68
Carried forward	182	198	Total	444	524

Summary.

	Males.	Females.	Total.	
English	463	507	970	
Scotch	60	72	132	
Irish	7	1	8	
Welsh	87	88	175	1285
German	1	0	1	
Swiss	40	48	88	
Italian	1	3	4	
French	1	2	3	
Danes	180	210	390	
Swedes	61	68	129	
Norwegians	25	43	68	
Americans	4	0	4	687
	930	1042	1972	=1972

Conferences, while these superintend the presidents of the 400 branches. The total of members in the whole European mission is not less than 40,000. I subjoin a list of the various places—kindly furnished to me by an influential Saint—which the Mormons have selected for worship in London.*

Two points in this subject are truly remarkable. The first is the difference between Utah Territory and all other Anglo-Scandinavian colonies, in which males are usually far more numerous than females. The latter, at Utah, by the census of 1856, are 1781 in excess of the former; almost as great a disproportion as the extra three quarters of a million in England. The second is the rapid growth of the New Faith, and the deep hold which it has taken upon Great Britain. Few Englishmen are aware that their metropolis contains seventeen places of Mormon worship, and their fatherland an army of 4000 volunteer missionaries. In the United States it is also the fashion to ignore the Mormons. The subject, however, will grow in importance, and it is easy to predict that before two decades shall have elapsed, Deserét, unless sent once more upon her travels, will have forced herself into the position of an independent state.

The Mormon polity is, in my humble opinion—based upon the fact that liberty is to mankind in mass a burden far heavier than slavery—the perfection of government. It is the universal suffrage of the American States, tempered by the despotism of France and Russia: in moderate England men have nothing of it but that Tory-Radicalism to which the few of extremest opinions belong. At the semi-annual Conferences, which take place on the 6th of April and the 6th of October, and last for four days, all officers, from the President to the constable, are voted in by direction and counsel—i. e., of the Lord through his Prophet; consequently, re-election is the rule, unless the chief dictator determine otherwise. Every adult male has a vote, and all live under an

---

*   *Latter-Day Saints' Meeting Rooms in London and vicinity:*

Somers Town—Euston Hall, 8 George Street, Hampstead Road.
Holborn—148 Holborn, near Gray's Inn Lane.
Goswell Hall—46 Goswell Street.
Holloway—1 Cornwall Place, Holloway Road.
Whitechapel—Pisgah Chapel, North Street, Sydney Street, Mile End.
Poplar—28 Penny Fields.
Barking—Latter-Day Saints' Chapel, North Street.
Paddington—Hope Hall, Bell Street.
Chelsea—Lloyd's Assembly Rooms, 1 George Street, Sloane Square.
Shepherd's Bush—Latter-Day Saint's Chapel, Shepherd's Bush Green.
Camden Town—Beulah Cottage, King's Road, Camden Town.

On the Surrey Side of the Thames.

Walworth Common—Latter-Day Saints' Meeting Room, 2 King Street, Old Kent Road.
Lambeth—St. George's Hall, St. George's Road, near the Elephant and Castle.
Deptford—Latter-Day Saints' Meeting Room, Tanner's Hill.
Woolwich—Latter-Day Saints' Chapel, Prospect Row.
Welling—Latter-Day Saints' Meeting Room, Wickham Lane, near Welling.
Eltham—Latter-Day Saints' Meeting Room, at Mr. J. Baily's, Pound Place.

iron sway. His poor single vote—from which even the sting of ballot has been drawn—gratifies the dignity of the man, and satisfies him with the autocracy which directs him in the way he should go. He has thus all the harmless pleasure of voting, without the danger of injuring himself by his vote. The reverse, duly carried out, frees mankind from king and kaiser, and subjects them to snobs and mobs. Mormon society is modeled upon a civilized regiment: the Prophet is the colonel commanding, and the grades are nicely graduated down to the last neophyte or recruit. I know no form of rule superior to that of Great Salt Lake City; it might supply the author of "Happy Years at Hand" with new ideas for the "Outlines of the Coming Theocracy." It exerts its beneficial effects equally upon the turbulent and independent American; the sensible and self-sufficient Englishman; the Frenchman, ever lusting after new things; the Switzer, with his rude love of a most problematic liberty; the outwardly cold, inwardly fiery Scandinavian; the Italian, ready to bow down before any practice, with the one proviso that it must be successful; and the German, who demands to be governed by theories and Utopianisms, "worked" by professors "out of the depths of their self-consciousness."

The following description of a Conference is extracted at length from the "Daily Missouri Republican" of May 4, 1861:

Great Salt Lake City, April 12, 1861.

On the 6th of April, 1830, in a small room about fifteen feet square, in the town of Fayette, Seneca County, New York, a young country lad—Joseph Smith—and five other persons organized that movement now known throughout Christendom as "The Church of Jesus Christ of Latter-Day Saints," or Mormonism. How the units have each increased to tens of thousands, and where those disciples have been found, and how they have been converted, is not the task I assign myself. I *assisted*, as the Frenchmen say, at the thirty-first anniversary Conference of that obscure movement, and propose to give the readers of the "Republican" its picture, and "nothing extenuate nor set down aught in malice."

Twice a year the Mormons assemble in Conference, on the 6th of April and on the 6th of October, for the purpose of re-electing their presiding authorities, or making such changes among them as are deemed "wisdom" or "necessary"—the chiefs, also, making these periods seasonable for general instruction to the "body"—and in April electing and sending out missionaries to the nations of the earth, where Mormonism is flourishing, or where the New Faith has yet to be introduced.

As the settlements in the Territory are widely scattered, and communication between them rare—except where business or family purposes invite—the Conferences are looked forward to with peculiar interest by the people generally as a time of renewing acquaintance and friendship with those they have known and been associated with in the Old World. To this add the curiosity to see and hear again the "Prophet" and his associates, and the influences that draw the multitude to Conference is comprehended.

Up to within a few years this country has, I am told,* been rarely visited by showers of rain, the husbandmen depending almost entirely upon the melting snows of the mountains for irrigating fields and gardens. Very recently the snow and rain had fallen in great abundance, and the muddy roads were rendered almost impassable. Notwithstanding this obstacle, the faithful screwed up courage and traveled in droves from every part of the Territory, and filled the streets of the city during Conference like a county fair.

Early on Saturday morning the carriages and wagons, equestrians and pedestrians, thronged into the city, and long before the opening of the Tabernacle doors the people were gathering in groups, eager for admission to obtain a good seat, fearing the general rush. On the Sunday preceding, Brigham had requested the citizens here to stay at home, and afford their country brethren and sisters an opportunity of getting within the Tabernacle; otherwise there would have been a poor show for the strangers, and as it was they were themselves vastly too many for the dimensions of the building.

THE CONFERENCE—FIRST DAY—MORNING SESSION.

At 10 o'clock there were on the stand, according to technical rank and authority:

Of the First Presidency—Presidents Brigham Young, Heber C. Kimball, and Daniel H. Wells.

Of the Twelve Apostles—Orson Hyde, Willford Woodruff, John Taylor, George A. Smith, Ezra T. Benson, Lorenzo Snow, and Franklin D. Richards.

Of the First Presidency of the Seventies—Joseph Young, Levi W. Hancock, Henry Herriman, Zera Pulsipher, Albert P. Rockwood, and Horace S. Eldredge.

Of the Presidency of the High Priests—Edwin D. Woolley and Samuel W. Richards.

Of the Presidency of the Stake—Daniel Spencer, David Fullmer, and George B. Wallace.

Of the Presidency of the Bishopric—Edward Hunter, Leonard W. Hardy, and Jesse C. Little.

Of the Patriarchs—John Smith and Isaac Morley.

Apostle Hyde called the meeting to order, and in a moment all talking was hushed, and a choir of about a dozen persons, accompanied by a fine-toned organ in the centre of the building, sung:

> The morning breaks, the shadows flee,
> Lo! Zion's standard is unfurled!
> The dawning of a brighter day
> Majestic rises on the world.
>
> The clouds of error disappear
> Before the rays of truth divine;
> The glory bursting from afar,
> Wide o'er the nations soon will shine.

---

* The article is probably written by a Mormon elder. It is the fashion, however, in newspaper correspondence—as the columns of the "New York Herald" prove—to assume Gentilism for the nonce.

The Gentile fullness now comes in,
    And Israel's blessings are at hand;
Lo! Judah's remnant, cleansed from sin,
    Shall in their promised Canaan stand.

Jehovah speaks! let earth give ear,
    And Gentile nations turn and live;
His mighty arm is making bare,
    His cov'nant people to receive.

Angels from heaven and truth from earth
    Have met, and both have record borne;
Thus Zion's light is bursting forth,
    To bring her ransomed children home.

Apostle Lorenzo Snow offered prayer, and the choir sung, "Praise ye the Lord; 'tis good to praise."

Apostle Benson was first invited to address the Conference. "Brother Ezra" is generally called a son of thunder—great preacher, I suppose. On this occasion he aimed at being modest, and after expressing his gratitude for the privilege of being permitted to attend Conference, to come and see the Prophet, his counselors, and the twelve apostles, and the good brothers and sisters, he was prepared to bear his testimony.

He knew that Joseph Smith was a prophet; that his predictions had been fulfilled, and were daily fulfilling, to the joy of all the Saints. He would not stop there in his testimony; he would bear testimony to the teachings of President Brigham Young. His counselors—Heber C. Kimball and Daniel H. Wells—were also true as the revelations of Joseph, and he rejoiced in them. Oh, what a joy it was to know that they had such men to lead them! What would be the condemnation of those who rejected their testimony? Ezra was quite serious—yea, serious to shuddering.

The fearfulness of apostasy was eloquently portrayed. False spirits attending it, and false revelations bestowed on the backslider, and every other ugly, disagreeable business was the certain lot of the apostate, and from which the brethren were decently warned.

President Daniel H. Wells was much pleased with the Latter-Day work; it was a great blessing to live in the light of the Gospel. It had been but a few years proclaimed to the world. The channel of communication between heaven and earth was again open to the children of men. Brother Wells referred to the state of the nation. The present trouble was the result of bad treatment to the Saints. The people of God had been driven into the wilderness—thousands might have perished, and the government was indifferent. It was a political axiom, that when governments ceased to protect, the people were released from their obligations. The government had never protected the Saints as other citizens. They had been driven from place to place, and the murderers of Joseph Smith had gone unpunished. Fault had been found with the Mormons because they had asked the government to appoint good men as federal officers—men in whom they had confidence. They were for this called rebels; but they were probably the only people that would yet stand by the Constitution and uphold it.

The government had fallen in the eyes of the civilized world; it had become corrupt and debased. Nowadays nobody expected any thing from public servants but corruption. These things were well known to every body. The Saints had been molested and could get no redress. The Prophet Joseph, moved by the Spirit of the Most High, told their enemies there that they would see mobbing to their heart's content, for the measure that they meted to the Saints should be meted to them back again.

The Saints could now see the distracted state of the nations, and the confusion of all governments. If they were wise men and women, they would appreciate the blessed inheritance that the Lord had brought them to. He had but one request to make, and that was, that the people should not only believe in the counselings of President Young, but be diligent, and see that his counseling prospered.

President Heber C. Kimball got up with the invocation of "God bless the Saints, and peace be multiplied unto them." He respected and loved good men and women who were striving to do the will of Heaven. The Mormons were united, and he wanted them to continue so, and be of one heart and of one mind, and to do as they were told. The South had seceded from the North, but the Mormons would never secede from either. He had sometimes a kind of notion that North and South would secede from them, and if they did so the Mormons couldn't help it, and the Lord would yet make a great people of them, just as fast as they were able to bear it.

Heber had a fling at "the miserable creatures who had been sent here one time and another to rule and judge them." The yoke was off their neck; they were away out from the confusion, and the yoke was on the neck of their enemies, and the bow-key was in. Many were engaged in trying to have the Mormons associate with them in a national capacity; but they would have nothing to do with them. "No, gentlemen and ladies, we are free from them, and will keep free." Heber was satisfied with their position in the mountains. Brigham was their governor; had always been so, and would always be so. He went around about with his hands in his pocket, and governed the people. They had the Lord for ruler, and the men whom he delegated could govern the people. He had no fear, for he lived above the law; he transgressed no law, and had nothing to apprehend. With an exhortation to go to and make themselves happy and independent by their own industry, Heber's racy discourse terminated with a hearty *amen* from the congregation.

President Brigham Young was much pleased to meet with the Saints. The Church was that day thirty-one years old—it seemed but a short time, yet a great work had been done. He remembered when he had a great anxiety to see some person of foreign birth embrace the faith. For the first few years it was only Americans who received it, but he could now gaze upon tens of thousands from the nations of the Old World. He discarded miracles as being any evidence of the divinity of any man's mission: men might be astonished by them, but the spirit only could convince and satisfy the mind. Referred to Aaron's operations: turning his stick into a serpent, filling the air with life, and turning the rivers into blood, did not satisfy. He alluded to the troubles in the States, and warned the people

U

against too great anxiety; thought the nation was breaking up quite fast enough. All he was anxious about was the Saints being prepared for every event in the providence of the Lord. He sometimes wondered if the great men of the nation ever asked themselves the question, "How can a republican government stand?" There was but one way in which it could endure—as the government of heaven endures upon the basis of eternal truth and virtue. Had Martin Van Buren redressed the wrongs committed against the Saints—had he ordered the State of Missouri to restore them to their property, the nation would be stronger to-day than it is. He mourned to see the corruption, and he sometimes felt a blush for being an American. He had been reared by the green mountains of Vermont, and could look down upon the nation and mourn that he had no power to save it. Although he had no reason to doubt that President Lincoln was as good a man as ever sat in the chair of state, he had little hope of his accomplishing much. He was powerless, because of the corruptions that had been introduced and fostered by the chief men of the nation. "Abraham's" authority and power was like a rope of sand: he was weak as water. The governments that had been had put aside the innocent, justified thieving and every species of debauchery, and had fostered every one that plundered the coffers of the people, and said let it be so.

The choir sung, "Arise, oh glorious Zion," and with a benediction from President Joseph Young we got home for dinner.

AFTERNOON SESSION.

At 2 P.M. the choir sung,
"Great God attend while Zion sings,"
and Bishop Lorenzo D. Young prayed.
The choir sung,
"All hail the glorious day, by prophets long foretold."

Attention was requested from the congregation, and Apostle John Taylor was to put all the presiding authorities before the people for re-election. Twice a year, in April and October, all the presidents are presented and voted on separately, and such dismissals or changes made that are deemed proper. On this occasion there were some additions made, but not a dissentient voice heard. The present presiding authorities in Mormondom are:

Brigham Young as President of the Church of Jesus Christ of Latter-Day Saints; Heber C. Kimball, his first, and Daniel H. Wells, his second counselors.

Orson Hyde as President of the Quorum of the Twelve Apostles; and Orson Pratt, sen., Willford Woodruff, John Taylor, George A. Smith, Amasa Lyman, Ezra T. Benson, Charles C. Rich, Lorenzo Snow, Erastus Snow, Franklin D. Richards, and George Q. Cannon, as members of the said Quorum.

John Smith, Patriarch of the whole Church.

Daniel Spencer as President of this Stake of Zion; and David Fullmer and George B. Wallace, his counselors.

William Eddington, James A. Little, John V. Long, John L. Blythe, George Nebeker, John T. Caine, Joseph W. Young, Gilbert Clements,

Brigham Young, jun., Franklin B. Woolley, Orson Pratt, jun., and Howard Spencer, as members of the High Council.

John Young as President of the High Priests' Quorum; Edwin D. Woolley and Samuel W. Richards, his counselors.

Joseph Young, President of the first seven Presidents of the Seventies; and Levi W. Hancock, Henry Herriman, Zera Pulsipher, Albert P. Rockwood, Horace S. Eldredge, and Jacob Gates, as members of the first seven Presidents of the Seventies.

John Nebeker as President of the Elders' Quorum; and Elnathan Eldredge and Joseph Felt, his counselors.

Edward Hunter as Presiding Bishop; Leonard W. Hardy and Jesse C. Little, his counselors.

Lewis Wight as President of the Priests' Quorum; William Whiting and Samuel Moore, his counselors.

M'Gee Harris as President of the Teachers' Quorum; Adam Speirs and David Bowman, his counselors.

John S. Carpenter as President of the Deacon's Quorum; William F. Cook and Warren Hardy, his counselors.

Brigham Young was presented as Trustee in Trust for the Church of Jesus Christ of Latter-Day Saints.

Daniel H. Wells as Superintendent of Public Works.

Truman O. Angell, Architect for the Church.

Brigham Young, President of the Perpetual Emigrating Fund to gather the poor.

Heber C. Kimball, Daniel H. Wells, and Edward Hunter, his assistants and agents for said fund.

George A. Smith, Historian and general Church Recorder; and Willford Woodruff, his assistant.

Besides the time consumed in putting every name separately for the action of the assembly, there was a good deal of instruction given about the severities, which is of no outside interest.

Apostles John Taylor and George A. Smith, and Patriarch Assac Morley, addressed the audience.

The apostle Taylor thought the Mormons the freest people on the earth. They could, if they would, reject their rulers twice a year: they had the opportunity. The unity of the Saints pleased them. He questioned *Vox populi, vox Dei*. He got facetious, and wondered how they would get along, both North and South, with that doctrine. If the voice of the people in the North was the voice of God, and the voice of the people in the South was the voice of God, he was a little interested to know with which of them he would really be. [*A Voice in the stand:* "Not either of them."]

With the Saints it was *Vox Dei, vox populi;* the voice of God first, and the voice of the people afterward. The Spirit dictated and the Saints sustained it. But what were they after? Did they seek to subdue and put their feet on the necks of men? to rule and dictate nations? No. It was only the "little stone cut out of the mountains," growing into the kingdom that the prophets foresaw that would be established in the last days. The Mormons had never troubled their neighbors, but their neighbors kept meddling with them. They had sent an army here, but the Mormons did not seek to harm them when they had the chance. They came here with the intention to kill the Mormons if they could; but they couldn't, for the Lord wouldn't let them. Their enemies had hunted them like wolves; but the Lord had said, "Touch not mine anointed, and do my prophets no harm." They had kept the army out at Ham's Fork shaking and shivering till they cooled down. "Brother Taylor" was real well pleased with things in general, and concluded with Hallelujah.

Apostle George A. Smith was exceedingly humorous over the democracy. There was no head to it; the centre of its intelligence was the belly, and the principal portion of the body was in the boots. Several plundering operations were alluded to, and Uncle Sam had been sadly victimized by his boys. The government had been a miserable goose for politicians to pluck. Abe Lincoln had now the honor of presiding over a portion of what was once the United States; he had been elected by the religious portion of the States. "George A." remembered when the folks of New York sold her slaves to Virginia. Their conscience would not allow them to retain their fellow-beings in bondage—oh, they were mighty squeamish! They could take the money from Virginia, and as they got more religion and more conscience they were exceedingly anxious for Virginia to set them loose!

That religious fanaticism that had been mixed up with politics would lead to bloodshed. They were more to be dreaded than infidels. They were cruel in their fanaticism. The Republicans first whipped old Buck* into the Utah war, and they whipped him for getting into it, and whipped him awfully for getting out of it—he got out of it too soon. Politicians were in confusion, and the Lord would keep them there. He labored to show the folly of men worshiping a God without body, parts, or passions, for such being, if being he might be called, must be destitute of principles and power. He argued that the God worshiped by sectarians could not be the being that wrestled with Jacob, that conversed with Moses, and wrote with his finger upon tables of stone. He said that Joseph Smith had prophesied when the Saints were driven from Jackson County, Missouri, that if the government did not redress our wrongs, they should have mob upon mob until mob power, and that alone, should govern the whole land.

He bore-testimony to the truth of the work in which he was engaged, and said if the Latter-Day Saints would listen to President Young's instructions as they ought to do, they would soon be the wealthiest people upon the face of the earth.

The choir sung "The Standard of Zion."

Air—"*Star Spangled Banner.*"

Oh see! on the tops of the mountains unfurled,
  The ensign of promise, of hope, and salvation,
From their summits how nobly it waves to the world,
  And spreads its broad folds o'er the good of each nation;
A signal of light for the lovers of right,
To rally where truth will soon triumph in might.
'Tis the ensign of Israel streaming abroad,
And ever shall wave o'er the people of God.

* Mr. Buchanan.

By an angel's strong hand to the earth it was brought
  From the regions of glory, where long it lay folded;
And holy ones here, for the arduous work taught
  By the priesthood unflinching and faithful uphold it;
Its crown pierces heav'n, and 'twill never be riv'n,
'Till the rule of the earth will to Jesus be given.
  For the ensign of Israel's streaming abroad,
  And ever shall wave o'er the people of God.

'Tis the emblem of peace and good-will to mankind,
  That prophets have sung of when freed by the spirit,
And a token which God has for Israel designed,
  That their seed may the land of their fathers inherit;
Many nations will say, when they see its bright ray,
To the mountains of God let us hasten away;
  For the ensign of Israel's streaming abroad,
  And ever shall wave o'er the people of God.

Its guardians are sending their ministers forth,
  To tell when the Latter-Day kingdom is founded,
And invite all the lovers of truth on the earth,
  . Jew, Christian, and Gentile, to gather around it;
The cause will prevail, though all else may assail,
For God has decreed that his works shall not fail;
  Oh! the ensign of Israel's streaming abroad,
  And ever shall wave o'er the people of God.

Patriarch Morley pronounced the benediction, and the first day's conference terminated.

SECOND DAY.

The crowd on the Sunday far exceeded that of the preceding day. The streets around the Temple Block were literally filled with people and carriages. The Tabernacle could not hold a third of those who were anxious to hear. Every seat and standing-place was occupied long before the opening of proceedings. As soon as Brigham reached the inside vestry, he sent out some of the apostles and elders to preach to the outsiders, sufficiently distant from the Tabernacle as not to disturb each other with their preaching.

I have already filled so much paper that I fear trespassing too much upon your columns with the details of the second day at the present time, as Brigham was very explicit on the subject of plurality of wives, and it was the only time I ever heard him on the "peculiar institution."

Altogether it was a great conference, and, as the foregoing exhibits, the apostles enjoyed a particular free and easy time of it.

In its territorial status an anomaly has been forced upon the Mormon population. It must receive officers appointed and salaried by the federal government, viz.:

A governor, with a salary of $2500 (£500) per annum, payable quarterly.

A secretary to government, $1000.

A chief justice to the Supreme Court, $2500.

An associate   do.   do. $1000.

Do.   do.   do. $1000.

A district attorney, $400.

A marshal, $400 (not including perquisites).

A superintendent of Indian affairs, $2500.
A surveyor general, $2500.*

The governor, who is also commander-in-chief of the militia, holds office for four years, unless sooner removed by the President of the United States, or until appointment of a successor. He has the usual right of pardoning territorial offenses, and of reprieving offenders against the federal government. He approves all laws passed by the Legislative Assembly before they can take effect; he commissions all officers appointed under the laws, and takes care that the laws are faithfully executed.

The secretary holds office for the same time: his duty is to record, preserve, and transmit copies of all laws and proceedings of the Legislative Assembly, and all acts and proceedings of the governor in his executive department. In case of death, removal, resignation, or necessary absence of the governor from the Territory, he acts temporarily until the vacancy is filled up; and practically he looks forward to being a member of Congress in the House of Representatives of the United States.

The marshal holds office for a similar term: his duty is to execute all processes issued by the courts when exercising their functions as Circuit and District Courts of the United States. In disturbed countries, as California of the olden time, the marshal's principal office seems to have been that of being shot at.

The executive arm would, in any other Territory, be found to work easily and well: it is, in fact, derived, with certain modifications, from that original Constitution which has ever remained to new states the great old model. Among the Mormons, however, there is necessarily a division and a clashing of the two principles: one, the federal, republican, and laical; the other, the theocratic, despotic, and spiritual. The former is the State, under which is the Church. The latter is the Church, under which is the State, and hence complications which call for a cutting solution. As long as the Prophet and President was also the temporal governor, so long the Mormons were contented: now they must look forward to a change.

The Legislative Assembly consists of an "Upper House," a President and Council of thirteen, and a House of Representatives, or Lower House, of twenty-six members, whose term of office is one year. An appointment of the representation based upon a census is made in the ratio of population: the candidates, however, must be bonâ fide residents of the counties or districts for which they stand. No member of the Legislative Assembly is allowed to hold any appointment created while he was in office, " or for one year thereafter," and the United States officials —post-masters alone excepted—can not become either senators or representatives. The legislative pover extends to the usual

---

* The delegate to Washington receives " $8 per diem, not including ' mileage.' "

rightful and constitutional limits. "No law shall be passed interfering with the primary disposal of the soil; no tax shall be imposed upon the property of the United States, nor shall the lands or other property of non-residents be taxed higher than the lands or other property of residents. All the laws passed by the Legislative Assembly and government shall be submitted to the Congress of the United States, and, if disapproved, shall be null and of no effect."

Every free male (white) inhabitant* above the age of twenty-one, who has resided in the county for sixty days before the election, is entitled to vote, and is eligible for office; the right is limited to citizens of the United States, including those recognized by treaty with the Mexican Republic (2d of Feb., 1848), and excluding, as usual, the military servants of the federal government. Great fault was found by anti-Mormons with the following permissions in the act regulating elections (Jan., 1853), because they artistically enough abolish the ballot while they retain the vote.†

Sec. 5. Each elector shall provide himself with a vote, containing the names of the persons he wishes elected, and the offices he would have them to fill, and present it neatly folded (!) to the judge of the elections, who shall number and deposit it in the ballot-box; the clerk shall then write the name of the elector, and opposite it the number of his vote.

Sec. 6. At the close of the election the judge shall seal up the ballot-box, and the list of the names of the electors, and transmit the same without delay to the county clerks.

"In a Territory so governed," remarks Mr. Secretary Ferris, "it will not excite surprise that cases of extortion, robbery, murder, and other crimes should occur, and defy all legal redress, or that the law should be made the instrument of crime."

The deduction is unfair. The real cause why crime goes unpunished must, as will presently appear, be sought in an unfriendly and conflicting judiciary. The act itself can produce nothing

* When the vexed passage, "We hold these truths to be self-evident, that all men are created equal," written in 1776, is interpreted in 1860, it must be read, "all (free white) men" to be consistent and intelligible. Similarly "persons bound to labor" must be considered a euphuism for slaves. The "American Mirabeau," Jefferson, who framed the celebrated Declaration, certainly did not consider, as the context of his life proves, slaves to be his equals. What he intended the Mormons have expressed.

Again, what can be clearer than that the Constitution contemplated secession? If an adult citizen is allowed to throw off his allegiance, surely the body of citizens called a state have, à majori, a right to withdraw from a "federal union."

† The first Legislative Assembly was elected in the summer of 1851, and held a session in the following autumn and winter. An historian's office was established, courts were organized, cities incorporated, and a small body of Territorial laws were passed. The second Legislative Assembly met on the 15th of January, 1852, at the Council House, and after the organization of the two houses, they came together to receive the message of the governor, Mr. Brigham Young. The archon, when notified of the hour, entered, sat down in the speaker's chair, and on being asked if he had any communication to make, handed his message to the President of the Council, who passed it for reading to the Clerk of the House. The message was a lengthy and creditable document; of course, it was severely criticised, but the gravamen of the charges was the invidious phrase used by the Prophet to his lieges, "for your guidance."

but good; it enables the wise few to superintend the actions of the unwise many, and it subjects the "tyrant majority," as ever should be the case, to the will of the favored minority. As the Conqueror of Sindh often said, "When noses are counted, the many are those without brains."

The bad working of a divided executive is as nothing compared with the troubles occasioned by the opposition judiciaries, federal and territorial.

An act (19th of Jan., 1855) provides that a Supreme Court of the United States be held annually on the first Monday in January, at Fillmore City; each session to be kept open at least one day, and no session to be legal except on adjournment in the regular term. Another act (4th of Feb., 1852) directed that the District Courts, now three in number, shall exercise original jurisdiction both in civil and criminal cases when not otherwise provided by law, and also have a general supervision over all inferior courts, to prevent and correct abuses where no other remedy is provided. The above are officered by the federal government.

Section 23d of the same act provides for a Judge of Probate— of course a Mormon—*elected by the joint vote of the Legislative Assembly and commissioned by the governor.* His tenure of office is four years, and he holds regular sessions on the second Mondays of March, June, September, and December of each year. The Probate Court, besides the duties which its name suggests, has the administration of estates, and the guardianship of minors, idiots, and insane persons; with these its proper offices, however, it combines power to *exercise original jurisdiction, both civil and criminal,* regulated only by appeal under certain conditions to the District Courts. Of late the anomaly has been acknowledged by the Supreme Court.* Inferior to the Probate Court, and subject to its revision, are the Justices of the Peace, the Municipal Court, and

---

* The Court held, First. That the 9th section of the Organic Act vested all judicial power in the Supreme, District, and Probate Courts, and in Justices of the Peace.

Second. That the only restriction placed upon these courts was as to Justices of the Peace, refusing them jurisdiction to try any case involving the title or boundary to land, or any suit where the claim or demand exceeded one hundred dollars.

Third. That by virtue of that clause of the Organic Act which provides that "the jurisdiction of the several courts therein provided for," including the Probate Courts, "*shall be as limited by law,*" that the Legislature had the right to provide by law for the exercise by the Probate Courts of jurisdiction in civil and criminal cases.

Fourth. That as the Organic Act conferred common law and chancery jurisdiction upon the Supreme and District Courts respectively, that this jurisdiction belonged to these courts exclusively, and that the Probate Courts were confined to the jurisdiction conferred by statute, and such jurisdiction might be exercised concurrently with the District Courts to the extent provided by statute.

Fifth. That as the Legislature had passed a law conferring upon the Probate Courts concurrent jurisdiction with the District Courts to hear and determine civil as well as criminal cases within their respective counties, and had provided the manner in which this jurisdiction should be exercised, that the trial, conviction, and sentence of the prisoner were valid and binding in law until reversed by an appellate court.

Although Judge Shaver, one of the best of jurists, tacitly acknowledged the jurisdiction of Probate Courts, Judge Kinney is the first who has dared assert his decision judicially.

the three selectmen in each organized county. Besides the Probate Courts, the Mormons have instituted, as will presently appear, Ecclesiastical High Council under the Church authorities and the President, provided with ample powers of civil and criminal jurisdiction, and fully capable of judging between Saint and Saint.

In describing the operations of the two conflicting judiciaries, I shall borrow the words of both parties.

According to the Mormons, the increased chicanery of the federal government has arrived at full development in their Territory.* The phrase has been, "Any thing is good enough for Utah." The salary is too inconsiderable to satisfy any but the worst kind of jack-in-office, and the object of those appointed is to secure notoriety in the Eastern States by obstructing justice, and by fomenting disturbances in the West. The three judges first appointed from Washington in June, 1851, became so unpopular, that in the autumn of the same year they were obliged to leave Utah Territory—one of them with a "flea in his ear" duly inserted by Mr. Brigham Young. I shall not quote names, nor will the reader require them. Another attempted to break the amnesty in 1858, and when asked for suggestions by the Legislative Assembly, proposed an act for the prevention and punishment of polygamy, and urged the Senate to divide the land between the proposed Territories; finally, this excellent Christian hung a Gentile brother on the Lord's day. Another killed himself with opium; another was a notorious drunkard; and another was addicted to gambling in his cellar. A judge disgraced himself with an Indian squaw, who entered his court, and, *coram publico*, demanded her honorarium, and another seated on the bench his mistress —*la maîgre Ada*, as she is termed by M. Remy, the Gentile traveler—and the Mormons have not yet learned to endure Alice Peirce, or to worship the Goddess of Reason in that shape. Another attempted to convict Mr. Brigham Young of forgery. The marshal was, in one case, a *ci-devant* teamster, who could hardly write his own name. Besides the vileness of their characters, their cliqueism and violent hostility have led to prostitution of justice; a Mormon *accusé* was invariably found guilty by them, a Gentile was invariably acquitted. Thus the Probate Courts, properly jurisdictors of the dead, were made judges of the living in all civil and criminal cases, because justice was not obtainable from the Supreme District and the Circuit judges appointed by the federal government. To the envenomed reports of these officials the Saints attribute all the disturbances in 1857-58, and sun-

* The Utah correspondent of the "New York Herald," writing from Salt Lake under date of April 26th, states that the fall of Fort Sumter and the secession of Virginia had created intense interest among the "Saints." The news was read in the Tabernacle by Brigham Young, and the disciples were asked to believe that this was merely the prediction of Mr. Joseph Smith about the breaking up of the American Union.

dry high-handed violations of the constitutional liberties and the dearest rights of American citizenship. For instance, the Indian war of 1852 cost them $200,000; they repeatedly memorialized Congress to defray, strictly according to precedent, these expenditures, and yet, from 1850 to 1855, they have received, in payment of expenses and treaties, grants. and presents, only the sum of $95,940. Though Utah Territory has practiced far more economy than Oregon or California, the drafts forwarded by the Superintendent of Indian Affairs to the Treasury at Washington are totally neglected, or are subjected to delays and frivolous annoyances. The usual treaties with the Indians have not been held by the federal government. The Mormons' requisition for becoming a state is systematically ignored, and this ignoble minorhood is prolonged, although they can show five head of souls for three possessed by California at the time of her admittance—another instance of a "rancorous persecuting spirit, excited by false and malicious representations." He who lifteth up an ensign on the mountains is now "about to destroy a certain nation under the name of the sour grape (Catawba?);" and the Mormons see in the present civil war at once retribution for their injuries, and the fulfillment of the denunciations of Joseph the Seer against the "Gentile land of strife and wickedness." Assuredly Fate has played marvelously into their hands.

The federal officials retort with a counter charge against the Saints of systematically obstructing the course of justice. A Mormon must be tried by his peers; however guilty, he will be surely acquitted, as a murdering fugitive slave in the North, or a thievish filibuster in the South; that it is vain to attempt jurisdiction over a people who have an ecclesiastical Star-Chamber and Vigilance Committee working out in darkness a sectarian law; that no civilized government could or would admit into a community of Christian states a power founded on prophethood and polygamy, a theodemocracy, with a Grand Lama presiding over universal suffragators; that all accusations of private immorality proceed from a systematic attack upon the federal Union through its officers; and, finally, that, so thin-skinned is Mormon sensibility, a torrent of vituperation follows the least delay made with respect to their "ridiculous pretensions."

The author speaks. Of course there are faults on both sides, and each party has nothing better to do than to spy out the other's sins of omission and commission. The Americans (i. e., anti-Mormons), never very genial or unprejudiced, are not conciliatory; they rage violently when called Gentiles, and their "respectability," a master-passion in Columbian lands, is outraged, maiden-modesty-like, by the bare mention of polygamy. On the other hand, the Latter-Day Saints, who now flourish in the Mountain Territory, and who expect eventually to flourish over the whole earth, "are naturally prepared to hate and denigrate all beyond the pale of their own faith." If the newly-arrived judge fails, within the first week, to wait upon Mr. President, he or his may expect to be the subject of an offensive newspaper article. If another live among his co-religionists at Camp Floyd, he is convicted of cliqueism, and is forthwith condemned as a foe. Whatever proceeds from the federal government is and must be distasteful to them; to every address they reply, "To your tents, O Israel!" "Their nobles shall be of themselves, and their governor shall proceed from the midst of them," is the shaft which they level against the other party, and which recoils upon themselves. The result is that if the territorial judiciary sentences a criminal, he appeals to the federals, and at once obtains cassation —and *vice versâ.* The usual procedure in criminal cases is to make oath before a magistrate, who thereupon commands the marshal to take the accused into custody, and "them safely keep," so that he may produce their bodies before the first sessions of the United States District Courts; if the magistrate be a Mormon, he naturally refuses to prosecute and persecute a brother Saint—and *vice versâ.* Thus many notorious offenders, whom the Mormons would, for their own sakes, willingly see cut off from the congregation—in simple words, hung—escape with impunity after the first excitement has settled down: the most terrible crimes are soon forgotten in the party fight, and in the race to "go ahead;" after five years they become pabulum for the local antiquary.

I have thus attempted, with feeble hand, to divide the blame between both the great contending parties, and may fairly, I hope, expect to be unanimously rejected by both.

The ordinance to incorporate Great Salt Lake City was approved by the General Assembly of the State of Deserét on the 19th of January, 1851, and the body municipal was constituted, like Fillmore, Ogden, and other cities in the Territory. The City Council consists of a mayor, four aldermen, and one common councilor per ward—formerly there were but nine; they are elected by votes, with the usual qualifications; are sworn or affianced to support the federal and territorial Constitution, and retain office for two years. They collect the taxes, which, however, must not exceed 1·50 per cent. per annum upon the assessed value of all taxable property, real and personal.* They appoint

---

* The property-tax, like tithes, forming the Church funds and the revenue of the civil government, are general; the octroi ($20 for 100 lbs. of every thing entering the Territory from the east, and $25 from the west) and water-tax are local, and confined to towns. I can not find any other recognized imposts. The anti-Mormons declare that the Saints are overburdened with taxation. The Saints assert that their burden is light, especially when compared with the Mormons' taxation of the Atlantic cities, which averages from double to treble that of London and Paris —a little drawback to Liberty when she must be bought for her weight in gold.

In the Auditor's report accompanying the Governor's Message of 1860, there are some items of general interest to people outside, as well as to those in the Territory. The report states that "the total valuation of property assessed in the Territory for

their recorder, treasurer, assessor, collector, marshal, and supervisor of streets, and have sole charge of the police. They establish and support schools and hospitals, regulate "hacking," "tippling houses," and gambling and billiard-tables; inspect lumber, hay, bread and provisions, and provide against fires—which here, contrary to the rule throughout England and the Eastern States, are rare and little to be feared; direct night-lighting and the storage of combustibles, and regulate streets, bridges, and fences. They have power to enforce their ordinances by fines and penalties. Appeals from the decisions of the mayor and aldermen are made to the Municipal Court, composed of the mayor as chief justice, and the aldermen as associate justices, and from the Municipal Court to the Probate Court of Great Salt Lake City.

In the young settlements of the Far West there is a regular self-enforced programme of manufacturing progress. The first step is to establish flouring or grist mills, and lumber or saw mills, to provide for food and shelter. After these *sine quâ nons* come the comforts of cotton-spinning, wool-carding, cloth-weaving, tailoring, and shoemaking. Lastly arise the luxuries of life, which penetrate slowly into this Territory on account of the delay and expense of transporting heavy machinery across the "wild desert plains." The minor mechanical contrivances, the remarkable inventions of the Eastern States—results of a necessity which removes every limit to human ingenuity—such as sewing-machines, cataract washing-machines, stump-extracting machines, and others, which, but for want of hands, would never have been dreamed of, are not unknown at Great Salt Lake City.

The subjoined extract from the list of premiums of the Deserét Agricultural Society* will explain the industry at Great Salt Lake

the year 1860 (Green River and Carson counties excepted) amounts to $4,673,900." Assessors in Utah are, I presume, like assessors every where, not likely to obtain an exaggerated estimate of the value of property, as on that estimate assessments are made. Property, therefore, may be set down at a much larger figure than that given in the above extract. The Territorial tax at one half of one per cent. is $23,369 50. As an evidence of the increase of population and of improvement in property, the excess of Territorial tax is over that of last year $13,278 33—five sixths of which is collected in Great Salt Lake County, and that chiefly in this city. Of the other counties, the report states, "The counties of Weber, Box-Elder, and Juab each show a decrease in the valuation of property, compared with the assessment for 1859, of 16 per cent., and Iron County a decrease of 33 per cent., while the counties of Beaver, San Pete, and Cache show a more than corresponding increase in the following ratio, viz.: Beaver, 36; San Pete, 50; and Cache, 900 per cent. The increase in the three last-named counties, especially Cache, may account in some measure for the decrease in the other counties named, from the fact that, during the fall of 1859 and the spring of 1860, very many wealthy families moved with their stock and effects to form new settlements in Cache and San Pete counties, and probably the same may be said of Beaver."

The tax of all the counties amounts to $23,369 50; the totals of auditor's awards issued $19,184 88, which, together with $5450 95 payable on appropriations heretofore made, shows that the Mormons have the good sense to keep clear of a Territorial debt.

* The act incorporating the society, which was established "with a view of promoting the arts of domestic industry, and to encourage the production of articles

City in 1860—will prove that the infant colony has supplied all its actual wants, and will show what energy and perseverance can

from the native elements in this Territory,' was approved on January 17, 1856. The Board consists of a President, six Directors, a Treasurer, and a Secretary—the latter, my friend Mr. Thomas Bullock.

CLASS E.—FARMING IMPLEMENTS MADE IN THE TERRITORY.

Awarding Committee—Ira Eldredge, Daniel Carter, Levi E. Ritter.

Best plow	$5 00	Best horse-rake	$5 00	2d best spade	dip.
2d do.	3 00	2d do.	dip.	Best hoe	$2 00
3d do.	dip.	Best garden-rake	1 00	2d do.	dip.
Best subsoil plow	5 00	2d do.	dip.	Best wheel-barrow	2 00
2d do.	3 00	Best hay-rake	1 00	2d do.	dip.
3d do.	dip.	2d do.	dip.	Best cheese-press	2 00
Best harrow	5 00	Best hay-fork	1 00	2d do.	dip.
2d do.	3 00	2d do.	dip.	Best churn	2 00
3d do.	dip.	Best manure-fork	1 00	2d do.	dip.
Best field-roller	5 00	2d do.	dip.	Best butter tub and firkin.	2 00
2d do.	dip.	Best scythe-snath	2 00	2d do.	dip.
Best drill and irrigator	5 00	2d do.	dip.	Best washing machine	3 00
2d do.	dip.	Best set of garden tools	3 00	2d do.	2 00
Best corn-planter	5 00	2d do.	1 00	3d do.	dip.
2d do.	dip.	3d do.	dip.	Best spinning-wheel	2 00
Best 1 horse corn cultivator	5 00	Best shovel	2 00	2d do.	dip.
2d do.	dip.	2d do.	dip.	Best 6 corn brooms	2 00
Best grain-cradle	5 00	Best spade	2 00	2d do.	dip.
2d do.	dip.				

AGRICULTURAL MACHINES.

Best reaping machine	$10 00	2d best fanning mill	$2 00	Best hemp and flax dressing machine	$5 00
2d do.	5 00	3d do.	dip.	2d do.	dip.
3d do.	dip.	Best corn-sheller	3 00	Best hay and straw cutter	5 00
Best threshing machine	10 00	2d do.	2 00	2d do.	dip.
2d do.	5 00	3d do.	dip.	Best vegetable root-cutter.	5 00
3d do.	dip.	Best corn and cob mill	5 00	2d do.	dip.
Best fanning-mill	3 00	2d do.	dip.		

CLASS F.—MACHINERY.

Awarding Committee—Frederick Kesler, John Kay, William J. Silver.

Best steam-engine	$10 00	Best lath machine	$5 00	2d best stone-sawing machine	dip.
2d do.	dip.	2d do.	dip.	Best pump for a well	$5 00
Best fire-engine	10 00	Best stave machine	5 00	2d do.	dip.
2d do.	dip.	2d do.	dip.	Best water-wheel for raising water for irrigation	5 00
Best garden-engine	5 00	Best stone-dressing machine	5 00	2d do.	3 00
2d do.	dip.			3d do.	dip.
Best balance	5 00	2d do.	dip.		
2d do.	dip.	Best stone-sawing machine	5 00		

CLASS G.—LEATHER.

Awarding Committee—Seth Taft, John Lowe, Francis Platte.

Best side sole leather	$3 00	Best side skirting	$2 00	Best pair gentlemen's stoga boots	$1 00
2d do.	dip.	2d do.	dip.	2d do.	dip.
Best side upper cowhide	3 00	Best saddle	5 00	Best pair gentlemen's fine shoes	1 00
2d do.	dip.	2d do.	dip.	2d do.	dip.
Best kip-skin	3 00	Best light harness	5 00	Best pair ladies' bootees	1 00
2d do.	dip.	2d do.	dip.	2d do.	dip.
Best calf-skin	3 00	Best heavy harness	5 00	Best pair ladies' shoes	1 00
2d do.	dip.	2d do.	dip.	2d do.	dip.
Best Morocco-skin	3 00	Best bridle	3 00	Best blacking or polish	1 00
2d do.	dip.	2d do.	dip.	2d do.	dip.
Best side harness	3 00	Best pair gentlemen's fine boots	1 00		
2d do.	dip.	2d do.	dip.		

CLASS H.—CLOTHES, DRY-GOODS, AND DYE-STUFFS.

Awarding Committee—E. R. Young, John Needham, N. H. Felt.

Best made suit of clothes	$5 00	3d best made suit of buckskin	dip.	3d best 5 yards of colored flannel	dip.
2d do.	3 00	Best 5 yards of colored flannel	$2 00	Best 5 yards of white flannel	$2 00
3d do.	dip.	2d do.	1 00	2d do.	1 00
Best made suit of buckskin	5 00				
2d do.	3 00				

effect against time and all manner of obstructions. Besides the industries mentioned below, there are stores, cutlery shops, watch-

---

CLASS II.—CLOTHES, DRY-GOODS, AND DYE-STUFFS—Continued.

3d best 5 yards of white flannel	dip.	3d best 5 yards of woolen cloth	dip.	Best cloth cap	$1 00
Best 5 yards of white jeans	$2 00	Best pair of woolen blankets	$3 00	2d do.	dip.
2d do.	1 00	2d do.	dip.	Best fur muff	1 00
3d do.	dip.	Best piece of woolen carpet	2 00	2d do.	dip.
Best 5 yards of colored jeans	2 00	2d do.	dip.	Best fur cape	1 00
2d do.	1 00	Best piece of rag carpet	2 00	2d do.	dip.
3d do.	dip.	2d do.	dip.	Best 1 lb. indigo	10 00
Best 5 yards of white Linsey	2 00	Best coverlet	2 00	2d do.	5 00
2d do.	1 00	2d do.	dip.	3d do.	3 00
3d do.	dip.	Best hearth-rug	2 00	4th do.	dip.
Best 5 yards of colored Linsey	2 00	2d do.	dip.	Best 1 lb. madder	10 00
2d do.	1 00	Best woolen shawl	2 00	2d do.	5 00
3d do.	dip.	Best 5 yards of linen	2 00	3d do.	3 00
Best 5 yards of kersey	2 00	2d do.	dip.	4th do.	dip.
2d do.	1 00	Best 1 lb. of linen thread	1 00	Best colored cloth from any materials produced in this Territory, aside from indigo or madder	10 00
3d do.	dip.	2d do.	dip.	2d do.	5 00
Best 5 yards of woolen cloth	2 00	Best fur hat	2 00	3d do.	3 00
2d do.	1 00	2d do.	dip.	4th do.	dip.
		Best fur cap	2 00		
		2d do.	dip.		

CLASS I.—FURNITURE, COOPER-WARE, ETC.

Awarding Committee—Miles Romney, Archibald N. Hill, Thomas Allman.

Best bureau	$3 00	Best office-desk	$3 00	Best gallon of varnish	$2 00
2d do.	dip.	2d do.	dip.	2d do.	dip.
Best sofa	3 00	Best rocking-chair	2 00	Best gallon of castor-oil	2 00
2d do.	dip.	2d do.	dip.	2d do.	dip.
Best bedstead	3 00	Best specimen of wood carving	2 00	Best gallon of linseed-oil	2 00
2d do.	dip.	2d do.	dip.	2d do.	dip.
Best six chairs	3 00	Best specimen French polish	2 00	Best gallon of turpentine	3 00
2d do.	dip.	2d do.	dip.	2d do.	2 00
Best centre-table	3 00	Best specimen cooper's ware	2 00	3d do.	dip.
2d do.	dip.	2d do.	dip.	Best 5 lbs. of rosin	2 00
Best dining-table	3 00	Best specimen of glue	1 00	2d do.	1 00
2d do.	dip.	2d do.	dip.	3d do.	dip.
Best ladies' work-stand	2 00			Best 5 lbs. of lampblack	2 00
2d do.	dip.			2d do.	1 00
				3d do.	dip.

CLASS J.—PAINTING, ENGRAVING, ETC.

Awarding Committee—James M. Barlow, James Beck, John H. Rumell.

Best specimen of sign-painting	$3 00	Best specimen of paper	$3 00	2d best piece of sculpture	dip.
2d do.	2 00	2d do.	2 00	Best specimen of turning	$2 00
3d do.	dip.	3d do.	dip.	2d do.	dip.
Best specimen of graining	3 00	Best landscape of Great Salt Lake Valley	3 00	Best specimen of engraving	2 00
2d do.	2 00	2d do.	dip.	2d do.	dip.
3d do.	dip.	Best bird's-eye view of Salt Lake City	3 00	Best specimen of penmanship	3 00
Best specimen of printing	3 00	2d do.	2 00	2d do.	2 00
2d do.	2 00	3d do.	dip.	3d do.	dip.
3d do.	dip.	Best oil painting	2 00	Best specimen of penmanship in Deseret character	3 00
Best specimen of book-binding	3 00	2d do.	dip.	2d do.	2 00
2d do.	2 00	Best transparent window-blinds	2 00	3d do.	dip.
3d do.	dip.	2d do.	dip.		
		Best piece of sculpture	2 00		

CLASS K.—CUTLERY, HARDWARE, ETC.

Awarding Committee—Levi Richards, Zechariah B. Derrick, Jonathan Pugmire.

Best specimen of cutlery on a card	$3 00	3d best rifle	dip.	3d best axe	dip.
2d do.	2 00	Best revolving pistol	$5 00	Best door-lock	$2 00
3d do.	dip.	2d do.	3 00	2d do.	1 00
Best pruning shears	1 00	3d do.	dip.	3d best door-lock	dip.
2d do.	dip.	Best 5 lbs. gunpowder—sil. med.		Best shovel and tongs	2 00
Best rifle	5 00	2d do.	dip.	2d do.	1 00
2d do.	2 00	Best axe	2 00	3d do.	dip.
		2d do.	1 00	Best andirons	2 00

makers and jewelers, painters and glaziers, brush-makers, cabinet-makers, and skillful turners—for the most part English.   Iron and brass founderies are in contemplation, and a paper-mill is

Class K.—Cutlery, Hardware, etc.—*Continued.*

2d best andirons	$1 00	Best specimen of twine and		3d best specimen of combs		
3d do.	dip.	cord	$1 00	made of horn, bone, and		
Best 5 lbs. of cut nails	3 00	2d do.	dip.	mountain mahogany	dip.	
2d do.	2 00	Best specimen of whips	1 00	Best specimen of glass—sil. med.		
3d do.	dip.	2d do.	dip.	2d do.	dip.	
Best 5 lbs. of wrought nails	2 00	Best specimen of baskets	2 00	Best specimen of earthen-		
2d do.	1 00	2d do.	1 00	ware	$3 00	
3d do.	dip.	3d do.	dip.	2d do.	2 00	
Best 50 yards of rope	2 00	Best specimen of combs		3d do.	dip.	
2d do.	1 00	made of horn, bone, and		Best sand-paper	2 00	
3d do.	dip.	mountain mahogany	2 00	2d do.	1 00	
		2d do.	1 00	3d do.	dip.	

Class L.—Women's Work.

Awarding Committee—Mrs. Fanny Little, —— Taft, Marion Beatie, Sarah Brown.

Best ornamental needle-		Best lace cap	$1 00	2d best embroidered shawl	dip.
work	$1 00	2d do.	0 50	Best variety of crochet-	
2d do.	0 50	3d do.	dip.	work	$1 00
3d do.	dip.	Best group of flowers	1 00	2d do.	0 50
Best specimen of Ayrshire		2d do.	0 50	3d do.	dip.
needlework	1 00	3d do.	dip.	Best worked quilt	1 00
2d do.	0 50	Best specimen of wax		2d do.	0 50
3d do.	dip.	flowers	1 00	3d do.	dip.
Best ottoman cover	1 00	2d do.	0 50	Best patch-work quilt	1 00
2d do.	0 50	3d do.	dip.	2d do.	0 50
3d do.	dip.	Best ornamental shell-work	1 00	3d do.	dip.
Best table cover	1 00	2d do.	0 50	Best specimen of knitting.	1 00
2d do.	0 50	3d do.	dip.	2d do.	0 50
3d do.	dip.	Best pair worked slippers.	1 00	3d do.	dip.
Best worked shawl	1 00	2d do.	0 50	Best straw hat	2 00
2d do.	0 50	3d do.	dip.	2d do.	1 00
3d do.	dip.	Best pair woolen hose	1 00	3d do.	dip.
Best worked collar and		2d do.	0 50	Best straw bonnet	2 00
handkerchief	1 00	3d do.	dip.	2d do.	1 00
2d do.	0 50	Best pair cotton hose	1 00	3d do.	dip.
3d do.	dip.	2d do.	0 50	Best specimen of braid	
Best worked cushion	1 00	3d do.	dip.	straw or grass	1 00
2d do.	0 50	Best embroidered shawl	1 00	2d do.	0 50
3d do.	dip.	2d do.	0 50	3d do.	dip.

Class M.—Produce.

Awarding Committee—Richard Golightly, George Goddard, Eli B. Kelsey.

Best 5 lbs. of butter	$2 00	2d best gallon of molasses.	$1 00	Best pickles, tomatoes	$1 00
2d do.	1 00	3d do.	dip.	2d do.	dip.
3d do.	dip.	Best home-made wine	3 00	Best pickles, cabbages	1 00
Best cheese	2 00	2d do.	2 00	2d do.	dip.
2d do.	1 00	3d do.	dip.	Best pickles, onions	1 00
3d do.	dip.	Best preserves, pumpkins.	1 00	2d do.	dip.
Best ham	2 00	2d do.	dip.	Best 5 lbs. of soap	3 00
2d do.	1 00	Best preserves, tomatoes..	1 00	2d do.	2 00
3d do.	dip.	2d do.	dip.	3d do.	dip.
Best 10 lbs. of sugar	10 00	Best preserves of any kind	1 00	Best 3 lbs. of starch	2 00
2d do.	5 00	2d do.	dip.	2d do.	1 00
3d do.	dip.	Best pickles, cucumbers ..	1 00	3d do.	dip.
Best gallon of molasses	2 00	2d do.	dip.		

Class N.—Essays.

Awarding Committee—President and Board of Directors.

Best essay on agriculture	$10 00	Best essay on horticulture	$10 00	Best essay on home manu-
2d do.	sil. med.	2d do.	sil. med.	factures	$10 00
				2d do.	sil. med.

By order of the Board of the Deserét Agricultural and Manufacturing Society.

EDWARD HUNTER, President.

THOMAS BULLOCK, Secretary.
Great Salt Lake City, May 13, 1860.

coming across the prairies. The cutlery is good, the swords, spears, and Congress knives, the pruning-hooks, saws, and locks are yearly improving, and the imitations of Colt's revolvers can hardly be distinguished from the originals. The distilleries, of course, can not expect prizes. The whisky of Utah Territory, unlike the Monongahela or rye of Pennsylvania, and the Bourbon, or maize brandy of Kentucky, is distilled from wheat only; it is, in fact, the korn schnapps of the trans-Rhenine region. This "Valley Tan," being generally pure, is better than the alcohol one part and water one part, colored with burnt sugar and flavored with green tea, which is sold under the name of Cognac. Ale and cakes are in higher flavor than the "villainous distillation:" there are two large and eight small breweries in which a palatable Lager-bier is made. The hop grows wild and luxuriant in every kanyon; and there is no reason why in time the John Barleycorn of the Saints should not rival that of the sinners in lands where no unfriendly legislation tries, or will, it is hoped, ever try,

"To rob a poor man of his beer."

Hand-labor obtains $2 per diem, consequently much work is done at home. The fair sex still cards, spins, and weaves, as in Cornwall and Wales, and the plurality system supplies them with leisure for the exercise of the needle. Excellent blankets, the finest linens, and embroidered buckskin garments, varying in prices from $75 to $500—a splendid specimen was, at the time of my stay, being worked for that "Champion of oppressed nationalities," M. Louis Kossuth—are the results.

As in India, the mere necessaries of life at Great Salt Lake City are cheap: the foreign luxuries, and even comforts, are exorbitantly dear. A family may live almost for nothing upon vegetables grown in their own garden, milk from their own cows, wheaten bread, and butter which derives a peculiar sweetness from the bunch-grass. For some reason, which no one can explain, there is not, and there never has been, a market at Great Salt Lake City; consequently, even meat is expensive. Freight upon every article, from a bar of soap to a bar of iron, must be reckoned at 14 cents (7d.) per lb. coming from the East, and 25–30 cents from the West. Groceries and clothing are inordinately high-priced. Sugar, worth 6 cents in the United States, here fetches from 37½ to 45 cents per lb. Tea is seldom drunk, and as coffee of 10 cents per lb. in the States here costs 40–50 cents, burnt beans or toasted corn, a caricature of chicory, is the usual succedaneum. Counterblasters will be pleased to hear that tobacco fetches $1 per lb., and cigars from 5 to 6 cents each—a London price. Servants' wages vary from $30 to $40 per mensem—nearly £100 per annum; consequently, master has a strong inducement to marry the "missus's" Abigail. Thus the expense of living in Utah Territory is higher than in the Eastern States, where again it exceeds that of England.   In Great Salt Lake City $10,000 (=£2000) per annum would be equal to about £500 in London.   Fortunately for the poor, the excessive purity of the air, as in the Arabian Desert, enables them to dispense with, and not to miss, many articles, such as stimulants, which are elsewhere considered necessaries.   The subjoined "nerrick" of prices current at the General Tithing Office in Great Salt Lake City will best explain the state of things in 1860.   A remarkable feature, it will be observed, is the price of wheat—$1 50 per bushel—more than double its current value in the Mississippian States.*

* General Tithing Office Prices Current, Great Salt Lake City:

Wheat, extra produce tithing.....	$1 50 ℔ bush.	Mutton....................	$0 08 @0 12½ ℔.	
" labor and produce tithing.	2 00 "	Veal	0 03 @0 05 "	
Barley	1 50 "	Bear......................	0 08 @0 12½ "	
Corn	1 50 "	Tea.......................	1 50 @3 50 "	
Rye..............................	1 50 "	Coffee	0 40 @0 60 "	
Oats.............................	1 00 "	Sugar.....................	0 35 @0 60 "	
Buckwheat	1 25 "	Milk......................	0 10 ℔ qt.	
Peas and beans	2 00 "	Eggs	0 18 ℔ doz.	
Potatoes.........................	0 75 "	Butter	0 25 ℔ lt.	
Beets............................	0 50 "	Cheese....................	0 12½@0 25 "	
Carrots..........................	0 50 "	Salt, fine.................	0 04 "	
Parsnips.........................	0 50 "	Salt, coarse...............	0 10 "	
Onions	2 00 "	Cast steel, warranted.......	0 37½@0 50 "	
Turnips..........................	0 25 "	Spring steel	0 37½ "	
Tomatoes........................	1 00 "	Blister steel	0 18 @0 30 "	
Cabbages.................$0 02 @0 10 each.		Iron	0 10 "	
Pumpkins and squash ...... 0 02 @0 08 "		Molasses, good	3 00 ℔ gall.	
Melons.................... 0 02 @0 10 "		Vinegar...................	0 50 @0 75 "	
Cucumbers	0 01 "	Lumber, extra produce tithing	4 00 ℔ 100.	
Pigs, four weeks old........	3 00 "	" labor tithing	5 00 "	
Chickens.................. 0 10 @0 25 "		Shingles, best..............	10 00 ℔ 1000.	
Ducks .... 0 15 @0 25 "		" 2d quality........	8 00 "	
Beef, 6½ average.		Shingles, cotton-wood.......	8 00 "	
Hind quarter	0 07 ℔ lb.	" 2d quality........	6 00 "	
Fore "	0 06 "	Doves	0 12½ each.	
Tallow .... 0 10 @0 20 "		Turkeys................... 1 50 @2 50 "	
Pork...................... 0 12½@0 20 "		Fox and wolf skins	0 75 "	
Lard...................... 0 15 @0 20 "		Ox hair....................	0 50 ℔ bush.	

EDWARD HUNTER, Presiding Bishop.

X

THE DEAD SEA.

CHAPTER VII.

Third Week at Great Salt Lake City.—Excursions.

Governor Cumming had asked me to accompany Madam and himself to the shores of the lake, with an ulterior view to bathing and picnicking.

One fine morning, at 10 A.M., duly provided with the *nécessaire* and a thermometer—which duly snapped in two before immersion—we set out down the west road, crossed the rickety two-laned bridge that spans the holy stream, and debouched upon a mirage-haunted and singularly ugly plain. Wherever below the line of debordement of the lake's spring freshet, it is a mere desert; where raised, however, the land is cultivable, from the Wasach Mountains to Spring Point, at the north of the Oquirrh, giving about eighty square miles of fertile land. The soil, as near the lake generally, is a thin layer of saline humus, overspreading gravel and pebbles. The vegetation is scattered artemisia, rose-bushes, the *Euphorbia tuberosa* and other varieties of milk-weed, the greasewood, salicornias, and several salsolaceæ. There are numerous salt deposits, all wet and miry in the rainy season; and the animals that meet the sight are the coyote, the badger, and the hideous Phrynosoma. A few blue cranes and sage-chickens, which are eatable till October, were seen; and during winter the wild-fowl are found in large flocks, and the sweet-water streams are stocked with diminutive fish. In contrast with the bald and shaven aspect of the plain, rose behind us the massive forms of

the Wasach Mountains, robed in forests, mist-crowned, and showing a single streak of white, which entitles them to the poetical
boast of eternal snow—snow apparently never being respectable
without eternity.

After fifteen miles of good road we came to the Point o' the
Mountain—the head of the Oquirrh, also called West Mountain
—where pyramidal buttes bound the southern extremity of the
lake. Their horizontal lines are cleanly cut by the action of water, and fall in steps toward the plain. Any appearance of regularity in the works of Nature is always pleasing—firstly, because
it contrasts with her infinite diversty; and, secondly, because it
displays her grandeur by suggesting comparison with the minor
works of mankind. Ranches and corrals, grass and cattle, now
began to appear, and the entrance of a large cave was pointed out
to me in the base of the buttes. We drove on, and presently
emerged upon the shores of this "dead and desert"—this "still
and solitary" sea. It has not antiquity enough to have become
the scene of fabulous history; the early Canadian *voyageurs*, however, did their best to ennoble it, and recounted to wondering
strangers its fearful submarine noises, its dark and sudden storms,
and the terrible maelstrom in its centre, which, funnel-like, descended into the bowels of the earth. I believe that age is its
only want; with *quasi*-lifeless waters, a balance of evaporation
and supply—ever a mystery to the ignorant—and a horned frog,
the Dead Sea of the New World has claims to preternaturalism
at least equal to those of its sister feature, the volcano of depression, in the Old Hemisphere.

The first aspect of Mare Mortuum was by no means unprepossessing. As we stood upon the ledge, at whose foot lies the selvage of sand and salt that bounds the wave, we seemed to look
upon the sea of the Cyclades. The sky was light and clear, the
water of a deep lapis-lazuli blue, flecked here and there with the
smallest of white horses—tiny billows, urged by the warm soft
wind; and the feeble tumble of the surf upon the miniature sands
reminded me, with the first surveyor, "of scenes far, far away,
where mightier billows pay their ceaseless tribute to the strand."
In front of us, and bounding the extreme northwest, lay Antelope
or Church Island, rising in a bold central ridge. This rock forms
the western horizon to those looking from the city, and its delicate pink—the effect of a ruddy carpet woven with myriads of
small flowers—blushing in the light of the setting sun, is ever an
interesting and beautiful object. Nearer, it has a brown garb,
almost without a tinge of green, except in rare, scattered spots;
its benches, broken by gashes and gullies, rocks and ravines, are
counterparts to those on the main land; and its form and tintage,
softened by the damp overhanging air, and contrasting with the
light blue sky and the dark ultramarine streak of sea at its base,
add greatly to the picturesqueness of the view. The foreground

is a strip of sand, yellow where it can be seen, incrusted with flakes of salt like the icing of a plum-cake, and bearing marks of submergence in the season of the spring freshets. At the water's edge is a broken black line of a peculiar drift, which stands boldly out from the snowy whiteness around. Where my sketch was taken I looked as through a doorway, whose staples were two detached masses of stone. On the right rose an irregular heap of conglomerate and sandstone, attached to the ledge behind, and leaning forward as if about to fall. On the left, the "Black Rock," which can be seen as a dot from the city, a heap of flint conglomerate, imbedded in slaty, burnt, and altered clay, formed the terminating bluff to a neck of light sand and dark stone.

Before proceeding to our picnic, I will briefly resume the history and geography of this Mare Mortuum. The Baron de la Hontan, the French governor of Placentia, in Newfoundland, about 1690, heard from Indians of a Great Salt Water, which he caused to disembogue through a huge river into the South Sea or Pacific Ocean. Like the Lake Tanganyika, in Central Africa, it was arrayed in the garb of fable, 300 leagues of length, 30 of breadth, with "100 towns about it," like Mr. Cooley's highly imaginative "Zanganica," and navigated in large boats by the savage Mozeemleks, who much remind one of the old semi-mythical "Mono-moezi." Doubtless many a trapper and obscure trader has since that time visited it; a name or two has been found upon the adjacent rocks, but those were braves who, to speak metaphorically, lived before the age of Agamemnon. In 1845, Colonel Frémont, then engaged with his second expedition, made a partial flying survey, which, in 1849–50, was scientifically completed by Captain Howard Stansbury.

In geologic ages the lake occupied the space between the Sierra Madre on the east, and the ranges of Goose Creek and Humboldt River on the west. The length is roughly computed at 500 miles from north to south, the breadth from 350 to 500, and the area at 175,000 square miles. The waters have declined into the lowest part of the basin by the gradual upheaval of the land, in places showing thirteen successive steps or benches. A freshet of a few yards would submerge many miles of flat shore, and a rise of 650 feet would in these days convert all but the highest peaks of the surrounding eminences into islands and islets, the kanyons into straits, creeks, and sea-arms, and the bluffs into slightly elevated shores. Popular opinion asserts that the process of desiccation is going on at the rate of about half a mile in ten years. But the limits of beach and drift line laid down by Captain Stansbury are still well defined, and the shrinking of the volume may be ranked with its "sinking"—like the sink of the Humboldt and other rivers—an empirical explanation, by which the mountaineer removes the difficulty of believing that evaporation can drain off the supplies of so many rivers.

The lake, which is about the size of the African Chad, occupies the northeastern corner of Utah Territory, and lies to the northwest of the Great Salt Lake Valley, which is forty miles long by about twelve in breadth. The major axis of the irregular parallelogram is sixty to seventy miles in length from north to south, by thirty to thirty-five from east to west. Its altitude has been laid down at 4200 feet above, while the Dead Sea of Palestine is 1300 feet below sea level. The principal influents, beginning from the north, are the Bear River, the Weber River, and the Jordan. They supply the balance of evaporation, which from water is greater, and from high lands is usually less, than the rain. The western side is a perfect desert—a salt and arid waste of clay and sand, with the consistence of mortar when wet, which can not boast of a single stream; even the springs are sometimes separated by "jornadas" of seventy miles. When the rivers are in flood, the lake, it is said, rises to a maximum of four feet, overflowing large tracts of level saline plain, winding between the broken walls of rock which surround it on all sides. Near its shores the atmosphere is reeking, bluish, and hazy, from the effects of active evaporation, and forms a decided change from the purity and transparency of the air elsewhere. Surveyors have observed that it is a labor to use telescopes for geoditic purposes, and that astronomical observations are very imperfect. The quantity of vapor is less, and evaporation has less tension and density from the surface of salt than of fresh water; here, however, the operation is assisted by sunheat sufficient to produce an aeriform state, and by a wind brisk enough to prevent the vapor accumulating over the surface.

The water of this remarkable feature, which so curiously reproduces the marvels of Judea, contains nearly one quarter of solid matter, or about six times and a half more than the average solid constituents of sea-water, which may be laid down roughly at three and a half per cent. of its weight, or about half an ounce to the pound.* The Dead Sea is its sole known superior. The specific

---

* "One hundred parts by weight were," says Dr. Gale, "evaporated to dryness in a water-bath below the boiling-point, and then heated to about 300° of the thermometer, and retained at that heat till the mass ceased to lose any weight. It gave solid contents 22·422 (?), and consisted of

Chloride of sodium (common salt)............... 20·196	In the Abbé Domenech's work the analysis is taken from Col. Frémont: thus—	Chloride of sodium..... 97·80	
Sulphate of soda......... 1·834		" " calcium.... 0·61	
Chloride of magnesium. 0·252		" " magnesium 0·24	
Chloride of calcium..... a trace		Sulphate of soda......... 0·23	
		" " lime......... 1·12	
Total............... 22·282(?)"		Total.......... .... 100·00	

The waters of the Dead Sea give solid contents 24·580, and consist of

Chloride of sodium.....................................	10·360
" " calcium	3·920
" " magnesium...................	10·246
Sulphate of soda...	·054
Total...................................	24·580

gravity is 1·170, distilled water being 1·000; the North Atlantic, between latitude 25° N. and longitude 52° W. (G.), 1·020; and the Dead Sea, at 60° Fahrenheit, from 1·22742 to 1·130. The vulgar estimate of its saltness is exaggerated. I have heard at Salt Lake City of one bucket of saline matter being produced by the evaporation of three; and that meat can be salted, and corned beef converted into junk, after twelve or fourteen hours in the natural unevaporated brine. It is used without preparation by the citizens, who have not adopted the precautions recommended by Dr. Gale.* It is collected by boys, shoveled into carts at the points of the beach where the winds dash up the waves—forming a regular wind-tide—and is sold in retail at half a cent per pound, or two shillings per hundred pounds. The original basin of geological ages was, doubtless, as the shells have proved, fresh water. The saline substances are brought down by rain, which washes the soil and percolates through the rocky ledges, and by the rivers, which are generally estimated to contain from ten to one hundred grains of salt per gallon,† and here probably more, owing to the abundance of soda. The evaporation is, of course, nearly pure, containing but very minute traces of salts.

It has been generally stated that the water is fatal to organic life. The fish brought down the rivers perish at once in the concentrated brine; but, according to the people, there is a univalve, like a periwinkle, found at certain seasons within the influence of its saline waves; and I observed, floating near the margin, delicate moss-like algæ. Governor Cumming mentioned his having seen a leaf, of a few inches in length, lined with a web, which shelters a vermicular animal, of reddish color, and about the length of the last joint of the little finger. Near the shore, also, muci-

---

The strongest natural brine in the United States, according to Professor Beck, is that of the Syracuse Saline, New York, which contains 17·35 per cent. of chloride of sodium.

* "The salt water" (it is elsewhere called "one of the purest and most concentrated brines known in the world") "yields about 20 per cent. of pure common salt, and about 2 per cent. of foreign salts; most of the objectionable parts of which are the chloride of lime and the chloride of magnesia, both of which, being very deliquescent, attract moisture from the damp atmosphere, which has the effect to moisten and partially dissolve the common salt, and then, when the mass is exposed to dry air or heat, or both, a hard crust is formed. I believe I have found a remedy for the caking, which is cheap and easily used. It consists in sprinkling over the salt obtained by the evaporation of the water, and heaped up in a bin or box containing a porous bottom of blankets or other like material, a cold solution of the salt as it is concentrated from the lake till crystals begin to be deposited. This concentrated brine, while it will dissolve none of the common salt, will dissolve all the chlorides of calcium and magnesium, and carry them down through the porous bottom, and thus leave the salt purer and better than any now found in our markets. For persons who are obliged to prepare temporarily the salt, as travelers passing through the country, the water of the lake, without concentration, may be used for washing out the deliquescent chlorides, sprinkling the heap of salt by a watering-pot at intervals of two or three hours during a single day, and allowing it to drain and dry at night, and be spread to the sun an hour or two the following morning."

† "The Physical Geography of the Sea" (by Captain Maury), chap. ix., § 502, quoted from "Youmans' Chemistry."

laginous matter, white, pink, and rusty, like macerated moss, adheres to the rocky bed, and lies in coagulated spots upon the sand. We may fairly doubt the travelers' assertion that this Dead Sea contains no living thing; whereas neither animalculæ nor vestige of animal matter were, according to Lieutenant Lynch, detected by a powerful microscope in the waters of the Asphaltite Lake.

The Great Salt Lake is studded with an archipelago of islands, which would greatly add to its charms were their size commensurate with its diminutive limits. These, beginning from the north, are,

1. Dolphin Island, so called from its shape, a knoll of rock and shoal near the northwestern end, surrounded by about three feet of water.

2. Gunnison's Island, a large rock and small outlier, southeast of the former, and surrounded with water from nine to twelve feet deep.

3. Hat Island, southeast of Gunnison's, the smallest of the isles, with a reef sunk about seven feet: it was probably part of the following, and is separated from it by a narrow channel nowhere more than six feet in depth.

4. Carrington Island, so named from the Mormon surveyor, a circular mass with a central peak: the water is from three to six feet deep on every side except the western and southwestern, which are shoals and shallows. It contains no springs, but is rich in plants and flowers, as the sego, also spelled sigo, seacoe, and segose (*Calochortus luteus*, an onion-like bulb or tuber about the size of a walnut, more nutritious than palatable, much eaten as a table vegetable by the early Mormons and the root-digging Indians, and even now by white men when half starved), a *cleome*, a *malvastrum*, a new species of *malacothrix*, and several others.

5. Stansbury Island, the second largest in the lake, an ovate mass, with a high central ridge, dome-shaped above, and rising 3000 feet, twenty-seven miles in circumference, and about twelve in length. During the dry season it is formed into a peninsula by a sand-bank connecting it with the lake's western shore. Thus antelopes, deer, and coyotes pass over to browse upon the plants and to attack the young of the ducks, geese, plover, gulls, and pelicans, that make their homes upon the cliffs: it is also used for grazing purposes. The principal plants are a *comandra*, and sundry new species of *heuchera*, *perityle*, and *stenactis*. Fossils and shells are found in scatters.

6. Antelope, also called Church Island, because the stock of the Saints is generally kept there. Lying to the east and northeast of the preceding, and in shape an irregular and protracted conoid, it is the largest of the islands, sixteen miles long by six of extreme width, with a western ridge and an eastern line of broken peaks, which attain a maximum of 3000 feet above the lake and

7200 above sea level.   It lies twenty miles to the northwest of the
city, and the narrow passage between it and the opposite plain is
fordable.   This island is surrounded on the north by a tufa bed
twelve feet deep; eastward by six feet of water; southeast and
south by shoals; and westward by a deposit of black mud: the
deepest sounding in the lake, thirty-five feet, is found between it
and Stansbury Island.   Off the northwestern coast is a rock, called, after its principal peculiarity, Egg Island: in the eastern cliff
there is said to be a cave, described to resemble the Blue Grotto
at Capri, which has been partially explored.   Formerly there was
a small pinnace on the "Big Shallow;" it has either been wreck-
ed or broken up for fuel.*   Antelope Island contains arid ravines
and a few green valleys, besides a spring of pure water, and, being
safe from Indians, it is much esteemed as a grazing-place.
   7. Frémont Island, so named by Captain Stansbury from the
first explorer, who called it, after the rude dissipation of a dream
of "tangled wilderness of trees and shrubbery, teeming with game
of every description that the neighboring region afforded," "Disappointment Island."   The Mormons have preferred "Castle Isl-
and," suggested by its mural and turreted peak, that rises above
the higher levels.   It lies north and northeast from Antelope Isl-
and, parallel with the mouth of the Weber River, and south of
Promontory Point, the bluff termination of a rocky tongue which
separates Bear-River Bay from the body of the lake.   Its shape
is a semilune, fifteen miles in circumference, abounding in plants,
especially the Indian onion, but destitute of wood and water.
Here, on the summit, Captain Frémont lost the "brass cover to
the object-end of his spy-glass"—disdain not, gentle reader, these
little reminiscences! — and Captain Stansbury failed to find the
relic.
   I was surprised by the want of freshness and atmospheric elasticity in the neighborhood of the lake: the lips were salted as by
sea air, but there the similarity ended.   We prepared for bathing
by unhitching the mules upon the usual picnicking place, a patch
of soft white sand between the raised shore of the lake and the
water brink.   The bank supplies a plentiful stream of water, pota-
ble, though somewhat brackish, bitter, and sulphurous: it shows
its effects, however, in a clump of plants, wild roses, and the euphorbia of many names, silk-plant, *vache à lait*, *capote de sacarte*,
and milk-plant.   The familiar magpie prevented the solitude of
the scene being too impressive.   Here was also a vestige of humanity, a kind of "lean-to" of dry stone wall, with the bank for a
back-bone: you might have ridden over it without knowing that
it belonged to Mrs. Smith of Vermont, now departed, unless warn-

* In the "Revue des Deux-Mondes" (April, 1861) we are told that, "Pendant
l'été un petit bateau à vapeur fait un service régulier sur le Lac Salé." Fresh proof,
if it be required, how difficult, or rather how impossible, it is for any amount of talent
or ingenuity in a reviewer to supply the want of actual eye-seeing information. The
"Lac Salé" is not yet come.

ed off by the sudden appearance of what your superior sagacity
would have discovered to be a chimney.

The bathing-place is behind the Black Rock. The approach is
first over the fine soft white sand, like that of the sea-shore, but
shell-less, soppy where it receives the spring-water, and almost a
quicksand near the lake. The foot crunches through caked and
crusty salt-flakes, here white, there dark green, there dun-colored
ilke *bois de vache,* and every where the reverse of aromatic, and
sinks deep into the everlastingly wet sand below. This leads to
the neck of broken, riven stone pavement, whose head is the Black
Rock. As the lake is neared, the basalt-like surface becomes red
and rusty, the points are diamonded by sparkling spiculæ, and in
the hollows and crevices where the waters have dried to salt it
gathers in the form of icy lumps. A dreadful shock then awaits
the olfactory nerves. The black mud of peculiar drift before alluded to proves to be an aceldama of insects: banks a full foot
high, composed of the *larvæ, exuviæ,* and mortal coils of myriads
of worms, musquetoes, gnats, and gallinippers, cast up by the
waves, and lining the little bay, as they ferment and fester in the
burning sun, or pickle and preserve in the thick brine.* Escaping
from this mass of fetor, I reached the farther end of the promontory where the Black Rock stood decorously between the bathing-place and the picnic ground, and in a pleasant frame of curiosity descended into the new Dead Sea.

I had heard strange accounts of its buoyancy. It was said to
support a bather as if he were sitting in an arm-chair, and to float
him like an unfresh egg. My experience differs in this point
from that of others. There was no difficulty in swimming, nor
indeed in sinking. After sundry immersions of the head, in order
to feel if it really stang and removed the skin, like a mustard
plaster—as described—emboldened by the detection of so much
hyperbole, I proceeded to duck under with open eyes, and smart-
ed "for my pains." The sensation did not come on suddenly;
at first there was a sneaking twinge, then a bold succession of
twinges, and lastly a steady, honest burning like what follows a
pinch of snuff in the eyes. There was no fresh water at hand;
so, scrambling upon the rock, I sat there for half an hour, presenting to Nature the ludicrous spectacle of a man weeping flowing tears. A second experiment upon its taste was equally satisfactory; I can easily believe, with Captain Stansbury, that a man
overboard has little chance against asphyxiation; *vox faucibus
hæsit* was the least that could be said concerning its effects upon
my masticators. Those who try such experiments may be warned that a jug filled at the fresh spring is necessary in more ways
than one. The hair on emersion is powdered like the plastered

* According to Mr. T. R. Peale (quoted by Captain Stansbury, Appendix C),
"More than $\frac{9}{10}$ths of the mass is composed of the larvæ and exuviæ of the *Chirono-
mus,* or some species of musqueto, probably undescribed."

locks of the knights of flamingo-plush and bell-hanging shoulder-knots, and there is a clammy stickiness, which is exceedingly unpleasant. Salt, moreover, may be scraped from the skin—imaginative bathers have compared themselves to Lot's wife—and the Ethiop, now prosaically termed "nigger," comes out after a bath bleached, whitewashed, and with changed epidermis.

Notwithstanding the *fumet* from the kitchen of that *genius loci* whom I daurna name, we dined with excellent appetite. While the mules were being hitched to, I found an opportunity of another survey from below the Black Rock: this look-out station is sometimes ascended by those gifted with less than the normal modicum of common sense. The lands immediately about the lake are flat, rising almost imperceptibly to the base of abrupt hills, which are broken in places by soft and sandy barriers, irreclaimable for agriculture, but here and there fit for grazing; where springs exist, they burst out at too low a level for irrigation. The meridional range of the Oquirrh, at whose northern point we were standing, divides the Great Salt Lake Valley from its western neighbor Tooele or Tuilla, which in sound curiously resembles the Arabic Tawîleh—the Long Valley. It runs like most of these formations from north to south: it is divided by a transverse ridge declining westward, and not unaptly called Traverse Mountain, from Rush Valley, which again is similarly separated from Cedar Valley. From the point where we stood, the only way to Tooele settlement is round the north point of West Mountain, a bold headland, rugged with rocks and trees. Westward of Tooele Valley, and separated by a sister range to the Oquirrh, lies Spring Valley, so called because it boasts a sweet fountain, and south of this "Skull Valley"—an ominous name, but the evil omen was to the bison.

Bidding a long farewell to that inland briny sea, which apparently has no business there, we turned our faces eastward as the sun was declining. The view had memorable beauties. From the blue and purple clouds, gorgeously edged with celestial fire, shot up a fan of penciled and colored light, extending half way to the zenith, while in the south and southeast lightnings played among the darker mist-masses, which backed the golden and emerald bench-lands of the farther valley. The splendid sunset gave a reflex of its loveliness to the alkaline and artemisia barrens before us. Opposite, the Wasach, vast and voluminous, the storehouse of storms, and of the hundred streams that cool the thirsty earth, rose in stern and gloomy grandeur, which even the last smile of day failed to soften, over the subject plain. Northward, to a considerable distance, the lake-lands lay uninterrupted save by an occasional bench and a distant swell, resembling the upper convexity of a thunder-cloud. As we advanced, the city became dimly discernible beyond Jordan, built on ground gently rising away from the lake, and strongly nestling under its protecting mountains. A little to its northeast, a thin white vapor, like the spray of a spouting whale, showed the direction of the Hot Springs: as time wore on it rolled away, condensed by the cooling air, like the smoke of a locomotive before the evening breeze. Then the prominent features of the city came into view, the buildings separated themselves from their neighbors by patches and shades of several green, the streets opened out their regular rows and formal lines; once more we rolled over Jordan's rickety bridge, and found ourselves again in the Holy City of the Far West.

The ultimate destination of the Judiciary whom I had accompanied was Carson Valley, in the Sierra Nevada, a distance of some hundreds of miles through a wild country where "lifting of hair" is by no means uncommon. The judge, though not a sucking diplomat, had greenly relied upon *bona verba* at Washington for transportation, escort, and other necessaries which would be easily procurable at Camp Floyd. It was soon found advisable to apply to the military authorities at the cantonment. The coach, as I have said, had ceased to run beyond Great Salt Lake City. In May, 1858, a contract had been made with Major George Chorpenning to transport mails and passengers — the fare being $120—from Utah to California, he receiving $130,000. This lasted till September, 1859, when the drivers, complaining that the road-agents charged with paying them for eighteen months had expended the "rocks" in the hells of San Francisco, notably evinced their race's power of self-government by seizing and selling off by auction wagons and similar movable property. On the 20th of March, 1860, it came into the hands of the proprietors of the Eastern line, Messrs. Russell and Co., who ran a mail-wagon first to California, then to Camp Floyd, and lastly, on the 1st of June, finding their expenditure excessive, packed the mails on mules.* Single travelers were sometimes thus pushed through, starting on the Wednesdays, once a fortnight; for a party like ours such a proceeding would have been impossible. Consequently, the judge and I set out for Camp Floyd to see what could be done by "Uncle Sam" and his "eagles."

Mr. Gilbert — of the firm of Gilbert, Gerrish, and Co., general (Gentile) merchants—offered us seats in his trotting wagon, drawn by a fine tall pair of iron-gray mules, that cost $500 the twain, and were christened Julia and Sally, after, I believe, the fair daughters of the officer who had lately commanded the district. With a fine clear day and a breeze which veiled us with dust-hangings —the highway must be a sea of mud in wet weather—we set out along the county road, leading from the southeastern angle of the Holy City. Our route lay over the strip of alluvium that separates the Wasach Mountains from the waters of Jordan: it is cut by a multitude of streamlets rising from the kanyons; the prin-

* They carry 50 to 60 lbs.; and the schedule time to Placerville is sixteen days.

cipal are Mill Creek, Big Cotton-wood, Little Cotton-wood, Dry Cotton-wood, and Willow Creek.   The names are translated from the Indians, and we saw from the road traces of the aborigines, who were sweeping crickets and grass-seed into their large conical baskets—among these ragged gleaners we looked in vain for a Ruth.   Near Big Cotton-wood, where there is a settlement distant seven miles from the city, an English woman came across the fields and complained that she had been frightened by four Indian braves who had been riding by to bring in a stolen horse. The waters of the kanyons are exceedingly cool, sweet, and clear, and suggested frequent reference to a superior kind of tap which had been stored away within the trap.   In proportion as we left the city, the sterility of the River Valley increased; cultivation was unseen except upon the margins of the streams, and the look of the land was " real mean."   In front of us lay the denticulated bench bounding the southern end of the valley.

After twenty miles from the city we reached a ranch on rising ground, near the water-gate of the Jordan.   It was built at an expense of $17,000, and was called the Utah Brewery.   Despite, however, the plenty of hop and barley, the speculation proved a failure, and the house had become a kind of mail-station.   Between it and the river were a number of little rush-girt "eyes"— round pools, some hot, others cold—and said to be unfathomable: that is to say, from twenty to thirty fathoms deep.   They related that a dragoon, slipping with his charger into one of them, found a watery grave, where a drier death might have been expected. At the ranch we rested for an hour, but called in vain for food. From the Utah Brewery, which is about half way, drivers reckon twenty-two miles to Camp Floyd, making a total of forty-two to forty-three miles between the head-quarters of the saint and the sinner, and we therefore looked forward to a " banian day."

About noon we hitched to and proceeded to ascend Traverse Mountain, a ridge-like spur of the Wasach, running east and west. It separates the Valley of the Northern or Great Salt Lake from the basin of the Utah, or Sweetwater Lake, to the southward, and is broken through by the waters of Jordan.   The young river— called Piya Ogwap, or the Big Water, by the Shoshonees—here rushes in a foaming shallow stream, that can barely float a dugout, over a rocky, pebbly bed, in the sole of a deep but short kanyon, which winds its way through the cross range.   The descent is about 100 feet in two miles, after which the course serpentines, the banks fall, and the current becomes gentle.

As we toiled up the Dug-way, the graded incline that runs along the shoulder of the mountain, we saw a fine back view of the Happy Valley through an atmosphere clear as that of the English littoral before rain.   Advancing higher, we met, face to face, an ambulance full of uniform *en route* to the Holy City, drawn by four neat mules, and accompanied by strikers—military servants. We drew up, the judge was readily recognized, and I was introduced to Captains Heth, Clarke, and Gibson, and to Lieutenant Robinson. They began with an act of charity, supplying ham sandwiches to half-starved men, and I afterward spent pleasant evenings with them at Great Salt Lake City, and became Captain Heth's guest at Camp Floyd. Their kindness and hospitality lasted to the end of my stay. After the usual "liquoring up," they pointed to Ash Hollow, the depths below, where the Mormons had intended to make a new Thermopylæ. Promising to meet them again, we then shook hands and resumed our road.

The steep descent on the counterslope of Traverse Mountain disclosed to us the first sight of Utah Lake, which is to its sister what Carmel is to Lebanon. It was a soft and sunny, a placid and beautiful landscape, highly refreshing after the arid lands on the other side. A panorama of lake, plain, and river lay before us. On the east, south, and west were rugged walls and peaks of mountain and hill; and northward a broad grassy slope rose to the divide between the valleys of the Fresh and of the Salt Lake. From afar the binding of plain round the basin appeared so narrow that the mountains seemed to dip their feet into the quiet reservoir; and beyond the southern point the lone peak of lofty Nebo stood, to adopt the Koranic comparison, like one of the pins which fasten down the plains of earth. A nearer approach discovers a broad belt of meadow, rich alluvial soil, in parts marshy, and in others arable, wheat and root-crop flourishing in the bottom, and bunch-grass upon the acclivities. The breadth is greater to the west and south of the lake than in other parts. It is cut by many a poplar-fringed stream that issues from the tremendous gorges around—the American Fork, the Timpanogos* or Provo River, and the Spanish Fork. On the near side, beyond the winding Jordan, lay little Lehi, whose houses were half hid by black trees; and eastward of the Utah Water, dimly visible, was Provo City, on a plain watered by four creeks. Such were the environs of the Sea of Tiberias.

The Utah Lake, another Judean analogue, derives its supplies from the western versant of the Wasach. It is in shape an irregular triangle, the southern arm forming a very acute angle. The extreme length is thirty miles, and the greatest breadth is fifteen. It owes its sweetness, which, however, is by no means remarkable, to its northern drainage, the Piya Ogwap, alias Utah Outlet, alias Jordan River. Near the shores the water soon deepens to fifteen feet; the bottom is said to be smooth, uniform, and very profound in places; but probably it has never been sounded. The bed,

---

* From Timpa, a rock, and ogwabe, contracted to oge, a river, in the Yuta dialect. In English maps published as late as seven years ago, "Timpanogos" is applied to the Great Salt Lake! Provo or Provaux is the name of a Canadian trapper and trader, who in past times defeated with eighty men a thousand Indians, and was killed at the moment of victory. The Mormons call the City Provo, and Gentiles prefer as a "rile" Timpanogos.

where it shows, is pebbly; a white, chalky incrustation covers the shallower bottom; shells, especially the fresh-water clam, are numerous upon the watery margin; the flaggy "Deserét weed" in the tulares is ten feet high,* and thicket is dense in places where rock does not occupy the soil. The western side is arid for want of influents; there is a "lone tree," a solitary cotton-wood, conspicuous amid the grazing-ground of bunch-grass, sage, and grease-wood, and the only inhabitants, excepting a single ranch—Evan's—are, apparently, the Phrynosoma and the lizard, the raven and the jackass-rabbit. The Utah Lake freezes in December, January, and February. At these months the Jordan rolls down floes of ice, but it is seldom to be traversed on foot. In the flood season it rises two, and the wind tide extends to about three feet. It is still full of fish, which in former times were carried off in barrels. The white trout weigh thirty pounds. There are many kinds of mountain trout averaging three pounds, while salmon trout, suckers, and mudfish are uncommonly large and plentiful; water-snakes and "horsehair fish" are also found.

After descending the steep incline we forded the Jordan, at that point 100 feet broad, and deep to the wagon-hubs. The current was not too swift to prevent the growth of weeds. The water was of sulphury color, the effect of chalk, and the taste was brackish, but not unpleasant; cattle are said to like it. The fording was followed by a long ascent, the divide between Utah Valley and its western neighbor Cedar Valley. About half way between the Brewery and the Camp is a station, held by a Shropshire Mormon, whose only name, as far as I could discover, was Joe Dugout, so called, like the Watertons de Waterton, from the style of his habitation. He had married a young woman, who deterred him from giving her a sister—every Oriental language has a word to express what in English, which lacks the thing, is rudely translated "a rival wife"—by threatening to have his ears cut off by the "horfficers." Joe, however, seemed quite resigned to the pains and penalties of monogamy, and, what was more to our purpose, had a good brew of porter and Lager-bier.

Having passed on the way a road that branches off to the old camp, which was deserted for want of water, we sighted from afar the new cantonment. It lies in a circular basin, surrounded by irregular hills of various height, still wooded with black cedar, where not easily felled, and clustering upon the banks of Cedar Creek, a rivulet which presently sinks in a black puddly mud. For a more thoroughly detestable spot one must repair to Gharra, or some similar purgatorial place in Lower Sindh. The winter is long and rigorous, the summer hot and uncomfortable, the alkaline water curdles soap, and the dust-storms remind one of the

---

* Tulare is a marsh of bulrush (*Scirpus lacustris*), which is found extending over immense tracts of river valley in Western America. "Tooly" water, as it is pronounced, is that which is flavored or tainted by it.

Punjaub. I lost no time in suggesting to my *compagnon de voyage*, Lieutenant Dana, as a return for his kindness in supplying me with a "Bayonet Exercise," and other papers, our old campaigning habit of hanging wet canvas before every adit, and received the well-merited thanks of Madam. The hardest part of these hardships is that they are wholly purposeless. Every adobe brick in the place has been estimated to have cost a cent, as at Aden each cut stone was counted a rupee; and the purchase of lumber has enriched the enemy. In 1858 the Peace Commissioners sent by the supreme government conceded to the Mormons a point which saved the Saints. The army was not to be "located" within forty miles of Great Salt Lake City; thus the pretty sites about Utah Lake were banned to them, and the Mormons, it is said, "jockeyed" them out of the rich and fertile Cache Valley, eighty miles north of the head-quarters.

A broken wall surrounds this horrid hole. Julia and Sally carried us in with unflagging vigor. We passed through Fairfield, less euphoniously termed Frogtown, the bazar of the cantonment on the other side of the creek. During the days when Camp Floyd contained its full complement of camp followers—5000 souls—now reduced to 100 or 200 men, it must have been a delectable spot, teeming with gamblers and blacklegs, grog-house-keepers and prostitutes: the revolver and the bowie-knife had nightly work to do there, and the moral Saints were fond of likening Frogtown to certain Cities of the Plains. Of late years it has become more respectable, and now it contains some good stores.

We removed from the wagon the mail-bags containing letters for the camp, and made ourselves at home with the hospitable Gilbert. On the next day, after "morning glory" and breakfast, we called upon the officer commanding the department, Colonel P. St. G. Cooke, of the 2d Dragoons, and upon the commandant of the cantonment, Lieutenant Colonel C. F. Smith. They introduced us to the greater part of the officers, and, though living in camp fashion, did not fail to take in the strangers after the ancient, not the modern, acceptation of the term. It is a sensible pleasure, which every military man has remarked, to exchange the common run of civilian for soldier society in the United States. The reveillé in the morning speaks of discipline; the guard-mounting has a wholesome military sound; there is a habit of 'tention and of saluting which suggests some subordination; the orderlies say "Sir," not Sirree nor Sirree-bob. The stiffness and ungeniality of professionals, who are all running a race for wealth or fame, give way in a service of seniority, and where men become brothers, to the frankness which belongs to the trade of arms. The Kshatriya, or fighting caste, in the States is distinctly marked. The officers, both of the navy and the army, are, for the most part, Southerners, and are separated by their position from general society. The civilian, as was the case in England twenty years ago, dislikes the uniform. His principal boasts are, that he pays his fighting servants well, and that he—a militia-man—is far superior to the regular. A company of Cadets, called the Chicago Zouaves, during the summer of 1860, made a sensation throughout the land. The newspaper writers spoke of them in terms far higher than have been lavished upon the flower of the French army; even the military professionals were obliged to join in the cry. As a republican, the citizen looks upon a soldier as a drone. "I hate those cormorants," said to me an American diplomat, who, *par parenthèse*, had made a fortune by the law, as he entered a Viennese café. *L'arte della guerra presto s' impara* is his motto, and he evinces his love of the civilian element by giving away a considerable percentage of commissions in the army to those whose political influence enables them to dispense with the preparation of West Point.

I am here tempted to a few words concerning the cheap defense and the chief pride of the United States, viz., her irregular army. The opposite table shows the forces of the militia to be three millions, while the regular army does not number 19,000. The institution is, therefore, a kind of public, a writing, speaking, voting body, which makes itself heard and felt, while the existence of the regulars is almost ignored. To hint aught against the militia in the United States is sure seriously to "rile up" your civil audience, and Elijah Pogram will perhaps let you know that you can not know what you are talking about. The outspoken Britisher, despite his title and his rank as a general officer, had a "squeak" for his commission when, in the beginning of the volunteer mania, he spoke of the new levies as a useless body of men: it is on the same principle in the United States. Thus also the liberal candidate declares to his electors his "firm belief that, with all our enormous expenditure, the country had not felt itself secure, and straightway a noble arm of defense, springing unbought from the patriotism of the people, had crept into existence, forming a better shield for our national liberties than all that we had been able to buy with our mounds of gold." (Cheers.) The civilian in the United States boasts of his military institutions, his West Point and his regular army, and never fails to inform a stranger that it is better paid than any force in Europe. On the other hand, he prides himself upon, as he is probably identified with, the militia.

That writing, speaking, and voting have borne fruit in favor of the militia, may be read in the history of the Americo-Mexican War. The fame of the irregulars penetrated to Calcutta and China: it was stopped only by the Orient sun. But who ever heard of the regulars? The "newspaper heroes" were almost all militiamen, rangers, and other guerrillas: "keeping an editor in pay" is now a standing sarcasm. The sages of the Revolution initiated a yeo-

MILITIA FORCE OF THE UNITED STATES.

General Abstract of the Militia Force of the United States, according to the latest Returns received at the Office of the Adjutant General.

States and Territories.	For the Year	General Officers.	General Staff Officers.	Field Officers, etc.	Company Officers.	Total commissioned Officers.	Non-commissioned Officers, Musicians, Artificers, and Privates.	Aggregate.
Maine	1856	13	52	36	230	340	73,248	73,552
New Hampshire	1854	11	202	119	895	1,227	32,311	33,538
Massachusetts	1859	10	47	111	353	521	157,347	157,868
Vermont	1843	12	51	224	801	1,088	22,827	23,915
Rhode Island	1858	2	22	106	26	156	16,555	16,711
Connecticut	1858	3	9	82	199	293	51,312	51,605
New York	1856	93	299	1,531	5,495	7,388	329,847	337,235
New Jersey	1852	...	......	......	......	......	....	81,984
Pennsylvania	1858	...	......	......	......	......	....	350,000
Delaware	1827	4	8	71	364	447	8,782	9,229
Maryland	1838	22	68	544	1,763	2,397	44,467	46,864
Virginia	1858	...	......	......	......	......	....	150,000
North Carolina	1845	28	133	657	3,449	4,267	75,181	79,448
South Carolina	1856	20	135	535	1,909	2,599	33,473	36,072
Georgia	1850	39	91	624	4,296	5,050	73,649	78,699
Florida	1845	3	14	95	508	620	11,502	12,122
Alabama	1851	32	142	775	1,883	2,832	73,830	76,662
Louisiana	1859	16	129	542	2,105	2,792	88,532	91,324
Mississippi	1838	15	70	856	348	825	35,259	36,084
Tennessee	1840	25	79	392	2,644	3,607	67,645	71,252
Kentucky	1852	43	145	1,165	3,517	4,870	84,109	88,979
Ohio	1858	...	......	......	......	......	....	279,809
Michigan	1854	30	123	147	2,358	2,858	94,236	97,094
Indiana	1832	31	110	566	2,154	2,861	51,052	53,913
Illinois	1855	...	......	......	......	......	....	257,420
Wisconsin	1855	15	8	215	904	1,142	50,179	51,321
Iowa								
Missouri	1853	...	17	4	67	88	117,959	118,047
Arkansas	1859	10	39	179	911	1,139	46,611	47,750
Texas	1847	15	45	248	940	1,248	18,518	19,766
California	1857	18	126	11	175	330	207,400	207,730
Minnesota	1859	...	......	......	......	......	....	23,972
Oregon								
Washington Territory								
Nebraska Territory								
Kansas Territory								
Territory of Utah	1853	2	......	48	235	285	2,536	2,821
Territory of N. Mexico								
District of Columbia	1852	3	10	28	185	226	7,975	8,201
Grand aggregate	......	515	2,374	9,884	38,687	51,460	1,876,342	3,070,987

manry second to none in the world : they had, however, among them crowds of frontiersmen accustomed to deal with the bear and the Indian, not with the antelope and the deer. The Texan Rangers in later times were a first-rate body of men for irregular purposes, not to be confounded with the militia, yet always put forward as a proof how superior to the " sweepings of cities," as the regular army was once called in the Senate, are the irregulars, who "never fire a random shot, never draw trigger till their aim is sure," and are "here to-night and to-morrow are fifty miles off." But the true modern militia is pronounced by the best authorities

Y

—indeed, by all who hold it no economy to be ill served, for any but purely defensive purposes, a humbug, which costs in campaigns more blood and gold—neglect of business is perhaps the chief item of the expenditure—than a standing army would. As a "Garde Nationale" it is quite efficient. When called out for distant service, as in the Mexican War, every *pekin* fault becomes apparent. Personally the men suffer severely from unaccustomed hardship and exposure; in dangerous climates they die like sheep; half are in hospital, and the other half must nurse them: Nature soon becomes stronger than martial law; under the fatigue of the march they will throw away their rations and military necessaries rather than take the trouble to carry them: improvident and wasteful, their convoys are timid and unmanageable. Mentally they are in many cases men ignoring the common restraints of society, profoundly impressed with insubordination, which displays equality, which has to learn all the wholesome duty of obedience, and which begins with as much respect for discipline as for the campaigns of Frederick the Great. If inclined to retire, they can stay at home and obtain double or treble the wages: not a few are driven to service by that enthusiasm which, as Sir Charles Napier well remarked, readily makes men run away. Their various defects make organization painfully slow. In camp they amuse themselves with drawing rations, target practice, asking silly questions, electing officers, holding meetings, issuing orders, disobeying orders, "'cussing and discussing:" the sentinels will sit down to a quiet *euchre* after planting their bayonets in the ground, and to all attempts at dislodging them the reply will be, " You go to ——, Cap.! I'm as good a man as you." In the field, like all raw levies, they are apt to be alarmed by any thing unaccustomed, as the sound of musketry from the rear, or a threatened flank attack: they can not reserve their fire; they aim wildly, to the peril of friend and foe, and they have been accused of unmilitary cruelties, such as scalping and flaying men, shooting and killing squaws and children. And they never fail, after the fashion of such men, to claim that they have done all the fighting.[*]

Such is, I believe, the United States militia at the beginning of a campaign. After a reasonable time, say a year, which kills off the weak and sickly, and rubs out the brawler and the mutineer; when men have learned to distinguish the difference between the often Dutch courage of a bowie-knife squabble and the moral fortitude that stands firm in presence of famine or a night attack, then they become regulars. The American—by which I understand a man whose father is born in the United States—is a first-rate soldier, distinguished by his superior intelligence from his compeers in other lands; but he rarely takes to soldiering. There are not more than five of these men per company, the rest being

* These remarks were penned in 1860; I see no reason to alter them in 1861.

all Germans and Irishmen. The percentage in the navy is greater, yet it is still inconsiderable. The Mexican War, as History
writes it, is the triumph of the militia, whom old "Rough and
Ready" led to conquest as to a "manifest destiny."* On the other hand, the old and distinguished officer who succeeded General
Taylor has occasionally, it is said, given utterance to opinions concerning the irregulars which contrast strongly with those generally attributed to him.

At Camp Floyd I found feeling running high against the Mormons. "They hate us, and we hate them," said an intelligent
officer; consequently, every statement here, as in the city, must
be received with many grains of salt. At Camp Floyd one hears
the worst version of every fact, which, as usual hereabouts, has its
many distinct facets. These anti-Mormons declare that ten murders per annum during the last twelve years have been committed without punishment in New Zion, whereas New York averages
18·33. They attribute the phenomenon to the impossibility of
obtaining testimony, and the undue whitewashing action of juries,
which the Mormons declare to be "punctual and hard-working in
sustaining the dignity of the law," and praise for their "unparalleled habits of industry and sobriety, order, and respect to just
rights." Whatever objection I made was always answered by the
deception of appearances, and the assertion that whenever a stranger enters Great Salt Lake City, one or two plausible Mormons
are told off to amuse and hoodwink him. Similarly the Mormons
charge the Christians with violent injustice. On a late occasion,
the mayor of Springville, Mr. H. F. Macdonald, and the bishop
were seized simply because they were Church dignitaries, on the
occasion of a murder, and the former, after durance vile of months
at Camp Floyd, made his escape and walks about a free man,
swearing that he will not again be taken alive. In 1853, Captain
J. W. Gunnison and seven of his party were murdered near Nicollet on Sevier River, twenty-five miles south of Nephi City. The
anti-Mormons declare that the deed was done under high counsel,
by "white Indians," to prevent the exploration of a route to California, and the disclosures which were likely to be made. The
Mormons point to their kind treatment of the previous expedition
upon which the lamented officer was engaged, to the friendliness
of his book, to the circumstance that an Indian war was then raging, and that during the attack an equal number of Yuta Indians
were killed. M. Remy distinctly refers the murder to the Pahvant
Indians, some of whom had been recently shot by emigrants to
California.† The horrible "Mountain Meadow Massacre"‡ was,

---

* And it will be remembered, the Mexicans were not Austrians or Russians.

† See Translation, vol. i., p. 463.

‡ The following is the account of that affair, officially given, of course, by anti-
Mormons: On the 4th or 5th of September, 1857, a large emigrant train from Arkansas, proceeding to California with horses, mules, and ox-wagons, conveying stores
of clothing and valuables, was suddenly attacked near a spring at the west end of

according to the anti-Mormons, committed by the Saints to revenge the death of an esteemed apostle—Parley P. Pratt—who,
in the spring of 1857, when traveling through Arkansas, was
knived by one Hector M'Lean, whose wife he had converted and
taken unto himself. The Mormons deny that the massacre was
committed by their number, and ask the Gentiles why, if such be
the case, the murderers are not brought to justice? They look
upon Mr. P. P. Pratt's proceeding—even in El Islam, the women
of the infidels are, like their property, *halal*, or lawful to those who
win them—as perfectly justifiable.* In February, 1859, occurred

Mountain Meadow Valley. The Indians, directed by white men, cut off from water
the travelers, who had fortified themselves behind the vehicles, which they filled with
earth, and killed and wounded several. When the attacked party, distressed by
thirst and a galling fire, showed symptoms of surrender, several Mormons, among
whom the leaders, John D. Lee and Elder Isaac C. Haight, are particularly mentioned, approached them with a white flag, and by soft words persuaded them that if
they would give up their weapons they should be safely forwarded to Panther Creek
and Cedar City. The emigrants unwisely disarmed themselves, and flocked toward
the spring. The work of murder and robbery began near a patch of scrub-oak brush,
about one mile and a half from water. Between 115 and 120 adults were slain.
Three emerged from the valley; of these, two were soon overtaken and killed, and
the third was slaughtered at Muddy Creek, distant about fifty miles. One of the
Mormons — the name has been variously given — is accused of a truly detestable
deed; a girl, sixteen years old, knelt to him, imploring mercy; he led her away into
the thicket—and then cut her throat. Seventeen children, aged from two months
to seven years, were taken from the Indians by the whites, and were distributed
among the several Mormon families in Cedar City, Fort Harmony, Santa Clara, etc.
Of these, sixteen were recovered, and the seventeenth was found in the April of 1858.
Mr. Jacob Forney, the late Superintendent of Indian Affairs, conducted the investigation on the part of the federal government; he reported that white men joined in
the murder and the robbery. The Mormons of course deny, *in toto*, complicity with
the Indians, and remark that many trains—for instance, to quote no others, the emigrants at Sublette's Cut-off, Oregon, in August, 1858—have similarly suffered, and
that they can not be responsible for the misfortunes which men who insult and ill-
treat the natives bring upon themselves.

    * The following is an extract from the "Millennial Star," July 25th, 1857. The
article is headed "More of the Assassination:" "We publish the following extract
from a letter written by two gentlemen to the editor of a New York paper. The letter was dated Flint-Cherokee Nation, Arkansas, May 17th, 1857, and says that after
Elder Pratt was arrested in the Indian country, he was 'placed under a strong
guard, and by a military escort conveyed in chains to the Supreme Court, Van Buren, Arkansas. The case being promptly investigated, and there being no evidence
upon which a bill of indictment could be found, he was liberated on the 13th instant.
Brother Pratt, being without arms, and without friends to protect him, and knowing
that M'Lean was thirsting for his blood, and that he had the aid of a mass of the
corrupt, money-bought citizens of Van Buren, endeavored to make his escape on
horseback, unmolested; but every road and passway being under strict watch, he did
not succeed in getting far till his path was discovered. M'Lean and half a dozen
other armed fiends pursued him; and Brother Pratt being totally unarmed, they succeeded in killing him without being hurt. Two of the party in advance intercepted
his road, and brought him to a halt, while M'Lean and the others came up in the
rear. M'Lean discharged a six-shooter at him, but the balls took no effect: some
passed through his clothes, others lodged in his saddle. The parties now being in
immediate contact, M'Lean stabbed him (both being on horseback) with a heavy
bowie-knife twice under the left arm. Brother Pratt dropped from his horse, and
M'Lean dismounted, and probed the fatal wounds still deeper; he then got a Der-
ringer from one of his aids, and, as Brother Pratt lay dying upon his back, shot him
in the upper part of the breast, dropping the pistol by the side of the victim. The
assassin then mounted his horse and fled. This occurred within a few steps of the

sundry disturbances between the soldiers and citizens at Rush Valley, thirty-five miles west of Great Salt Lake City, in which Mr. Howard Spencer, nephew to Mr. Daniel Spencer, a squatter, while being removed from a government reservation by First Sergeant Ralph Pike of the 10th Infantry, raised a pitchfork, and received in return a broken head.   Shortly afterward the sergeant, having been summoned to Great Salt Lake City, was met in Main Street and shot down before all present.   The anti-Mormons, of course, declare the deed to have been done by Mr. Spencer, and hold it, under the circumstances—execution of duty and summons of justice—an unpardonable outrage; and the officers assert that they could hardly prevent their men arming and personally revenging the foul murder of a comrade, who was loved as an excellent soldier and an honest man.*   The Mormons assert that the "shooting" was done by an unknown hand; that the sergeant had used unnecessary violence against a youth, who, single-handed and surrounded by soldiers, had raised a pitchfork to defend his head, and that the provocation thus received converted the case from murder to one of justifiable homicide.   In the month of June before my arrival, a Lieutenant Saunders and Assistant Surgeon Covey had tied to a cart's tail and severely flogged Mr. Hennefer, a Mormon.   The opposition party assert that they recognized in him the man who two years before had acted as a spy upon them when sitting in Messrs. Livingston's store, and, when ordered to "make tracks," had returned with half a dozen others, and had shot Dr. Covey in the breast.   The Mormons represent Mr. Hen-

residence of a farmer by the name of Wire.   Two gentlemen, being at the house at the time, saw the whole affair, and have made oath to what they witnessed before a coroner's jury.   Brother Pratt survived the work of this assassin two hours and a half, and was enabled to tell those who came to his assistance who he was, that he had been murdered by a fiend for doing his duty, and gave full instructions as to what course should be pursued in interring his body, and the disposition of the means and property connected with his person.   His instructions were fully attended to by Elder Higginson and Mrs. M'Lean, who reached the place of his assassination the same evening.   Those who saw his last moments state that Brother Pratt died without a murmur or a groan, and apparently without a pain, perfectly resigned to the will of Heaven.   Brother Pratt told Elder Higginson, the morning after his arrest, that his enemies would kill him, and requested Elder Higginson to go through with this spring's emigration to Utah, and carry the news of his death to the Church and his family.   This Elder Higginson will do, the Lord helping.   After perpetrating this heaven-daring deed, M'Lean returned to Van Buren and made it known.   After remaining in town several hours, and walking the streets with impunity, he was escorted by a number of citizens of Van Buren to the boat, and took his leave of the place.   Verily we had long thought that the bloodthirsty mobocrats of Missouri and Illinois were without a parallel in the world, but we now yield the palm to the Church-going citizens of Van Buren, for they have proven to the world that they are a den of murderers and assassins.   GEORGE HIGGINSON.
                                                                                      GEORGE CROUCH.'"

* On this occasion, Cedar Fort, a neighboring settlement, with cultivation, and a few huts, near Camp Floyd, was attacked at night by camp-followers (soldiers); a single calf was killed (the whole place was burned to the ground), and the damages speedily rose from a dozen to $10,000, claimed from Congress (which did not half repay the injury done).

nefer to be a peaceful citizen, and quiet, unoffending man, thus brutally outraged by tyrannical servants of government, and, moreover, prove for him an *alibi* from the original cause of quarrel. I have given but a few instances: all are equally contradictory, and *tantas componere lites quis audet?*

Strongly disclaiming the idea that the officers who discussed with me the subject at Camp Floyd had any tendency to exaggeration or to set down aught in malice, and quite conscious, as they never failed to remark, that a stranger is allowed to see only the *beau côté* of the New Faith, I can not but think that their views are greatly warped by causes external to it. This is to be expected. Who, after the massacre of Cawnpore, would have admitted into his mind a shadow of excuse for Nana Sahib? Among so many, however blinded and fanatic, and however fond of polygamy—this is ever the first reproach—there must be some good men. Yet from the "chief impostor" to the last "acolyte," all are represented to be a gang of miscreants. The Mormons are far more tolerant; they have praise for those Gentiles, even federal officers, who have abstained from injuring them. They speak well of Lieutenant Colonel E. J. Steptoe, 9th Regiment of Infantry, and the officers of his force;* of General Wilson, afterward the Navy Agent at San Francisco; and of the present commandant, Colonel Cooke. They have nothing to say against Judge Reed, or Mr. John J. Kinney, the Chief Justice of the Supreme Court; and when Judge Leonidas Shaver died in 1855, they put the papers in mourning, and buried the Gentile in their cemetery. They do not abuse even their merchant rivals. Mr. J. B. Kimball, to mention no other, is generally praised and trusted. But when they find it necessary or advisable to take away a man's character, they can do it, "and no mistake." At the same time, their tolerance and discipline are, to say the least, remarkable. Judge Brocchus,† to quote but one, would run the risk of being torn to pieces in almost any fanatical meeting in Europe.

At Camp Floyd I was introduced to Colonel G. H. Crossman, Department Quarter-master General, and Major Montgomery of the same department; to Dr. Porter, who was uncommonly and unnecessarily shy upon the subject of a "sick certificate;" and to Lieutenant N. A. M. Dudley, when we passed many a merry time over "simpkin." It is hardly necessary to say that the judge, having no authority to demand, did not obtain either escort or carriage. Colonel Cooke frankly told him that he had neither men nor conveyance at liberty, and even if they were that he could not exceed orders. The Secretary of War is ready to "be down" upon such offenses, and in the United States Army prob-

---

* Mr. Hyde (chap. vi.) gives the official document in which these officers petitioned President Pierce to reappoint Mr. Brigham Young as Governor and Superintendent of Indian Affairs in Utah Territory, and it speaks volumes in praise of the much-abused Saints.   † Chap. vi.

ably more officers throw up the service from distress for leave than in the English army. It was clear that we must travel without the dignities, so we inspected an ambulance and a four-mule team, for which the Hungarian refugee, its owner, asked $1000— but little beyond its worth. After an exceedingly satisfactory day in a private sense, I passed the evening at Captain Gove's, and watched with astonishment the game of Boston. Invented by the French prisoners in the islands of the American Liverpool, and abounding in "grand misery," "little misery," and other appropriate terms, it combines all the difficulties of whist, écarté, piquet, brag, and cribbage, and seems to possess the same attractions which beam upon the mind of the advanced algebraic scholar. Fortunately there was an abundance of good commissariat whisky and excellent tobacco, whose attractions were greater than that of Boston. On the morrow, a gloomy morning, with cold blasts and spatters of rain from the southwest, and the tameness of the snowbirds—which here represent

> "Cock Robin and Jenny Wren,
> God Almighty's cock and hen"—

warned us that the fine season was breaking up, and that we had no time to lose. So, inspanning Julia and Sally, we set out, and after six hours reached once more the City of the Saints.

CHAPTER VIII.

Excursions continued.

I HAD long been anxious to visit the little chain of lakes in the Wasach Mountains, southeast of the city, and the spot where the Saints celebrate their "Great Twenty-fourth of July." At dinner the subject had been often on the carpet, and anti-Mormons had informed me, hinting at the presence of gold, that no Gentile was allowed to enter Cotton-wood Kanyon without a written permit from the President Prophet. Through my friend the elder I easily obtained the sign manual; it was explained to me that the danger of fires in a place which will supply the city with lumber for a generation, and the mischievousness of enemies, were at the bottom of the precaution. . Before starting, however, two Saints were chosen to accompany me, Mr. S——, and Mr., or rather Colonel, Feramorz, popularly called Ferry, Little. This gentleman, a partner, relative, and connection of Mr. Brigham Young, is one of the "Seventies;" of small and spare person, he is remarkable for pluck and hardihood, and in conjunction with Ephe Hanks, the Danite, he has seen curious things on the Prairies.

A skittish, unbroken, stunted, weedy three-year-old for myself, and a tall mule for my companion, were readily lent by Mr. Kennedy, an Irish Gentile and stock-dealer, who, being bound on business to California, was in treaty with us for reward in case of safe-conduct. We chose the morning of the 14th of September, after the first snow had whitened the peaks, and a glorious cool, clear day it was — a sky diaphanous, as if earth had been roofed with rock crystal. While awaiting the hour to depart under the veranda of the hotel, Governor Cumming pointed out to me Bill Hickman, once the second of the great "Danite" triumvirate, and now somewhat notorious for meddling with Church property. He is a good-looking fellow, about forty-five, rather stout and square, with high forehead, open countenance, and mild, light blue eye, and owns, I believe, to only three deaths. On the last Christmas-day, upon occasion of a difficulty with a youth named Lot Huntingdon, the head of the youngster party, he had drawn his "bowie," and a "shooting" took place, both combatants exchanging contents of revolvers across the street, both being well filled with slugs, and both living to tell the tale.

"Do you know what that fellow is saying to himself?" asked the governor, reading the thoughts of a fiercely frowning youth who swaggered past us.

I confessed to the negative.

"He is only thinking, 'D—d gov'rnor, wonder if he's a better man than me,'" said my interlocutor.

About 4 P.M. we mounted and rode out of the city toward the mouth of the kanyon, where we were to meet Mr. Little. Passing by the sugar-mills and turning eastward, after five or six miles we saw at a distance a block of buildings, which presently, as if by enchantment, sank into the earth; an imperceptible wave of ground — a common prairie formation — had intervened. From the summit of the land we again sighted the establishment. It is situated in the broad bed of a dry *fiumara*—which would, by-the-by, be a perilous place in the tropics—issuing from Parley's Kanyon. The ravine, which is sometimes practiced by emigrant trains, is a dangerous pass, here and there but a few rods wide, and hemmed in by rocks rising perpendicularly 2000 feet. The principal house was built for defense, the garden was walled round, and the inclosure had but two small doors.

We were met at the entrance by Mr. Little, who, while supper was being prepared, led us to the tannery and the grist-mill, of which he is part proprietor. The bark used for the process is the red fir, costing $25 per cord, and the refuse is employed in composts. The hides are received unsalted; to save labor, they are pegged to soak upon wheels turned by water-power. The leather is good, and under experienced European workmen will presently become cheaper than that imported from England.

Beyond the tannery was an adobe manufacture. The brick in this part splits while burning, consequently the sun-dried article is preferred; when the wall is to be faced, pegs are driven into it to hold the plaster. The material is clay or silt from the creek, puddled with water, and if saltish it is better than sweet soil; unity of color and formation are the tests of goodness. Each brick weighs, when dry, 16 lbs., and the mould is mostly double. On the day after making they are stacked, and allowed to stand for two months; the season is June, July, and August, after which it becomes too cold. The workman is paid 75 per cent.; 400 per diem would be tolerable, 700 good work; thus an able-bodied bricklayer can make twenty-one shillings a day—rather a contrast to the wages of an unfortunate laborer in England.

Returning home, we walked through Mr. Little's garden, and admired its neatness. The fruit-trees were mostly barren; in this year the city sets down a loss of $100,000 by frost. I tasted, for the first time, the Californian grape, "uvas·admodum maturas, ita voluit anni intemperies;" they not a little resembled the northern French. A single vine sometimes bears $100 worth. There was a little rhubarb, but it is not much used where sugar costs forty-five cents per pound. After supping with Mr. Little, his wife and family, we returned to the *andronitis*, and prepared for the night with a chat. The principal point illustrated was the curious amount of connection caused by polygamy; all men, calling each other brothers, become cousins, and it is hardly possible, among the old Mormons, to stop a child in the street without finding that it is a relative. I was surprised at the comfort, even the luxury, of a Mormon householder in these remote wilds, and left it with a most favorable impression.

At the dawn of the next day we prepared to set out; from the city to the mouth of the kanyon the distance is about thirteen, and to the lakelets twenty-seven miles. Mr. Little now accompanied us on horseback, and his son James, whom I may here safely call a boy, was driving a buck-board. This article is a light gig-body mounted upon a thin planking, to which luggage is strapped; it can go where a horse can tread, and is easier to both animals than riding down steep hills. The boy, like Mormon juveniles generally, had a great aptitude at driving, riding, and using the axe; he attended a school, but infinitely preferred that of Nature, and showed all the disposition to become the father of a stout, brave Western man. As in the wilder parts of Australia, where the pedagogue has less pay than the shepherd, "keep a school" is here equivalent to semi-starvation; there is no superstitious aversion, as the Gentiles have asserted, to a modicum of education, but the state of life renders manual labor more honored and profitable. While the schoolmaster gains $2 50 per mensem, a ditcher would make the same sum per diem. Besides impatience of study, the boys are ever anxious to become men—"bring up a child and away it goes," says the local proverb—and literature will not yet enable a youth to marry and to set up housekeeping in the Rocky Mountains.

Our route lay over the bench; on our right was a square adobe fort, that had been used during the Indian troubles, and fields and houses were scattered about. Passing the mouth of Parley's Kanyon, we entered the rich bottom-land of the Great Cottonwood, beautified with groves of quaking asp, whose foliage was absolute green, set off by paper-white stems. After passing through an avenue of hardheads, *i. e.*, erratic granite boulders, which are carted to the city for building the Temple, we turned to the left and entered the mouth of the kanyon, where its sides flare out into gentler slopes.

A clear mountain stream breaks down the middle. The bed is a mass of pebbles and blocks: hornblende; a white limestone, almost marble, but full of flaws; red sandstone, greenstone, and a conglomerate like mosaic-work. The bank is thick with the poplar, from which it derives its name; willow clumps; the alder, with its dry, mulberry-like fruit; the hop vine, and a birch whose bark is red as the cherry-tree's. Above the stream the ravine sides are in places too steep for growth; as a rule, the northern is never wooded save where the narrowness of the gorge impedes the action of the violent south winds. On the lower banks the timber is mostly cleared off. Upon the higher slopes grow the mountain mahogany and the scrub maple wherever there is a foot of soil. There is a fine, sturdy growth of abies. The spruce, or white pine, rises in a beautifully regular cone often 100 feet high; there are two principal varieties of fir, one with smooth light bark, and the other, which loves a higher range, and looks black as it bristles out of its snowy bed, is of a dun russet. Already appeared the splendid tints which make the American autumn a fit subject "*pictoribus atque poetis.*" An atmosphere of blue seemed to invest the pines; the maple blushed bright red; and the willow clumps of the bed and the tapestry of ferns had turned to vegetable gold, while snow, bleached to more than usual whiteness by intervals of deep black soil, flecked the various shade of the poison hemlocks and balsam firs, and the wild strawberry, which the birds had stripped of fruit.

Great Cotton-wood Kanyon, like the generality of these ravines in the western wall of the Wasach, runs east and west till near the head, when it gently curves toward the north, and is separated from its neighbor by a narrow divide. On both sides the continuity of the gap is cut by deep jagged gullies, rendering it impossible to crown the heights. The road, which winds from side to side, was worked by thirty-two men, directed by Mr. Little, in one season, at a total expense of $16,000. After exhausting Red Buttes, Emigration, and other kanyons, for timber and fuel, Great Cotton-wood was explored in 1854, and in 1856 the ascent was made practicable. In places where the gorge narrows to a gut there were great difficulties, but rocks were removed, while tree-trunks and boughs were spread like a corduroy, and covered

over with earth brought from a distance: Mormon energy overcame every obstacle. It is repaired every summer before the anniversary festival; it suffers during the autumn, and is preserved
from destruction by the winter snows. In many places there are
wooden bridges, one of which pays toll, and at the end of the season they become not a little rickety. As may be imagined, the
water-power has been utilized. Lines and courses carefully leveled, and in parts deeply excavated, lest the precious fluid should
spread out in basins, are brought from afar, and provided with
water-gates and coffer-dams. The mills are named after the letters C, B, A, D, and lastly E. Already 700,000 square feet of
lumber have been cut during this summer, and a total of a million is expected before the mills are snowed up; you come upon
these ugly useful erections suddenly, round a sharp turn in the
bed; they have a queer effect with their whirring saws and crash
of timber, forming a treble to the musical bass of the water-gods.

We halted at the several mills, when Mr. Little overlooked
his accounts, and distributed stores of coffee, sugar, and tobacco.
After the first five miles we passed flecks of snow; the thermometer, however, in the shade never showed less than 60° F. In
places the hill sides were bald from the effect of avalanches, and
we saw where a house had lately been swept away. In others a
fine white limestone glistened its deception. After passing Mill
D, we debouched upon the basin also called the Big Prairie, a
dwarf turfy savanna, about 100 yards in diameter, rock and tree
girt, and separated from Parley's Kanyon on the north by a tall,
narrow wall. We then ascended a slope of black, viscid, slippery
mud, in which our animals were nearly mired, with deep slush-
holes and cross-roots: as we progressed the bridges did not improve. On our left, in a pretty grove of thin pines, stood a bear-
trap. It was a dwarf hut, with one or two doors, which fall when
Cuffy tugs the bait from the figure of 4 in the centre. These
mountaineers apparently ignore the simple plan of the Tchuvash,
who fill up with corn-brandy a hollow in some tree lying across
"old Ephraim's" path, and catch him dead drunk. In many
places the quaking-asp trunks were deeply indented with claw-
scars, showing that the climbing species is here common. Shortly
before, a bear had been shot within a few miles of Great Salt
Lake City, and its paws appeared upon the hotel *table d'hôte*.

About mid afternoon we dismounted, and left our nags and
traps at Mill E, the highest point, where we were to pass the
night. Mr. Little was suffering from a severe neuralgia, yet he
insisted upon accompanying us. With visions of Albano, Killar-
ney, and Windermere, I walked up the half mile of hill separating
us from Great Cotton-wood Lake. In front rose tall pine-clad
and snow-strewed peaks, a *cul de sac* formed by the summit of the
Wasach. We could not see their feet, but instinct told me that
they dropped around the water. The creek narrowed to a jump.

Presently we arrived at a kind of punch-bowl, formed by an amphitheatre of frowning broken mountains, highest and most snowy on the southeast and west, and nearly clear of snow and trees on the east. The level ground, perhaps one mile in diameter, was a green sward, dotted with blocks and boulders, based on black humus and granite detritus. Part of it was clear, the rest was ivy-grown, with pines, clumps, and circlets of tall trees, surrounded by their young in bunches and fringes, as if planted by the hand of man. There were signs of the last season's revelry—heaps of charcoal and charred trunks, rough tables of two planks supported by trestles, chairs or rail-like settles, and the brushy remnants of three "boweries." Two skulls showed that wolves had been busy with the cattle. Freshly-caught trout lay upon the table, preserved in snow, and in the distance the woodman's axe awoke with artful sound the echoes of the rocks.

At last we came upon the little tarn which occupies the lowest angle, the western ridge of the punch-bowl or prairie basin. Unknown to Captain Stansbury, it had been visited of old by a few mountain-men, and since 1854 by the mass of the Mormons. According to my informants it is the largest of a chaplet of twelve pools, two to the S.W. and ten to the S.E., which are probably independent bulges in the several torrent beds. Some are described as having no outlet, yet all are declared to be sweet water. The altitude has not been ascertained scientifically. It is roughly set down between 9500 and 10,000 feet. It was then at its smallest—about half a mile long by one quarter broad. After the melting of the snow it spreads out over the little savanna. The bottom is sandy and gravelly, sloping from ten to twenty feet deep. It freezes over in winter, and about 25–30 May the ice breaks up and sinks. The runnel which feeds it descends from the snow-capped peak to the south, and copious supplies trickle through the soppy margin at the base of the dripping hills around. The surplus escapes through a head to the north, where a gated dam is thrown across to raise the level, and to regulate the water-power. The color is a milky white; the water is warm, and its earthy vegetable taste, the effect of the weeds that margin it, contrasts with the purity of the creek which drains it. The fish are principally mountain trout and the gymnotus eel. In search of shells we walked round the margin, now sinking in the peaty ground, then clambering over the boulders—white stones that, rolled down from the perpendicular rocks above, simulated snow—then fighting our way through the thick willow clumps. Our quest, however, was not rewarded. After satisfying curiosity, we descended by a short cut of a quarter of a mile under tall trees whose shade preserved the snow, and found ourselves once more in Mill E.

The log hut was of the usual make. A cold wind—the mercury had fallen to 50° F.—rattled through the crannies, and we prepared for a freezing night by a blazing fire. The furniture—two bunks, with buffalo robes, tables and chairs, which were bits of plank mounted on four legs—was of the rudest. I whiled away the last hours of light by adding to my various accomplishments an elementary knowledge of felling trees. Handling the timber-axe is by no means so simple a process as it appears. The woodman does it by instinct; the tyro, who is always warned that he may easily indent or slice off a bit of his leg, progresses slowly and painfully. The principal art is to give the proper angle to the blade, to whirl the implement loosely round the head, and to let it fall by the force of its own weight, the guiding hand gliding down the haft to the other, in order not to break the blow. We ate copiously; appetite appeared to come by eating, though not in the Parisian sense of the phrase—what a treasure would be such a sanitarium in India! The society was increased by two sawyers, gruff and rugged men, one of whom suffered from ophthalmia, and two boys, who successfully imitated their elders.

Our fireside chat was sufficiently interesting. Mr. S—— described the ceremonies of the last Mormon Independence Day. After the preliminaries had been settled as below,* the caravans

---

* Extract from the Great Salt Lake correspondent of that amiable and conscientious periodical, the "New York Herald."

"*The Great Twenty-fourth of July.*

"In my last I gave your readers a full account of the Mormon demonstrations on the anniversary of American independence. That done, they have now before them the celebration of their own independence. Adhesiveness is largely developed in the Mormon cranium. They will hold on to their notions. On the 24th of July, 1847, Brigham, at the head of the pioneers, entered this now beautiful valley—then a barren wilderness. Forgetful of the means that forced them here, the day was set apart for rejoicing. They laid aside the weeds of mourning, and consecrated the day to feasting and dancing. The Twenty-fourth is the day of deliverance that will be handed down to generations when the Fourth is immeasurably forgotten. Three years ago, two thousand persons were congregated at the head-waters of Big Cotton-wood, commemorating independence, when messengers from the East arrived with the intelligence that the troops were on the plains. I need not farther allude to what was then said and done; suffice it, things have been so disjointed since that Big Cotton-wood has been left alone in solitude. Setting aside the restraint of years, it seems that the faithful are to again enjoy themselves. The following card tells the marching orders; the interstices will be filled up with orations, songs, prayers, dances, and every kind of athletic game that the young may choose to indulge in:

"*Twenty-fourth of July at the Head-quarters of Big Cotton-wood.*—President Brigham Young respectfully invites —— to attend a picnic excursion to the lake in Big Cotton-wood Kanyon, on Tuesday, the 24th of July.

"*Regulations.*—You will be required to start so as to pass the first mill, about four miles up the kanyon, before twelve o'clock on Monday, the 23d, as no person will be allowed to pass that point after two o'clock P.M. of that day. All persons are forbidden to smoke segars or pipes, or kindle fires at any place in the kanyon, except on the camp-ground. The bishops are requested to accompany those invited from their respective wards, and see that each person is well fitted for the trip with good, substantial, steady teams, wagons, harness, hold-backs and locks, capable of completing the journey without repair, and a good driver, so as not to endanger the life of any individual. Bishops, heads of families, and leaders of small parties will, before passing the first mill, furnish a full and complete list of all persons accompanying them, and hand the same to the guard at the gate.

"*Committee of Arrangements.*—A. O. Smoot, John Sharp, L. W. Hardy, A. Cun-

set out from the Holy City.   In 1860 there were 1122 souls, 56
carriages, 163 wagons, 235 horses, 159 mules, and 168 oxen.   They
bivouacked for the night upon the road, and marched with a certain ceremony.   The first President issued an order allowing any
one to press forward, though not at the expense of others; still
no one would precede him; nor would the second advance before
the third President — a good example to some who might want
teaching.   Moreover, the bishops had the privilege of inviting,
or, rather, of permitting the people of their several wards, even
Gentiles, to attend.   The "pioneers"—the survivors of the noble
143 who, guided by their Joshua, Mr. Brigham Young, first attempted the Promised Land—were distinguished by their names
on banners, and the bands played lustily "God save the King,"
and the "Star-spangled Banner," "Happy Land," and "Du-dah."
At six on the fine morning of the 24th, which followed ugly
weather, a salute of three guns, in honor of the First Presidency,
was fired, with music in the intervals, the stars and the stripes
floating on the top of the noblest staff, a tall fir-tree.   At 9 A.M.
a salute of thirteen guns, denoting the age of New Zion, and at
6 P.M. twelve guns, corresponding with the number of the apostles, were discharged with similar ceremonies.   The scene must
have been lively and picturesque around the bright little tarn, and
under the everlasting hills — a holiday crowd, with wagons and
ambulances drawn up, tents and marquees pitched under the
groves, and horse-races, in which the fair sex joined, over the soft
green sward.   At 10 P.M., after the dancing in the boweries had
flagged, the bands finished with "Home, sweet Home," and the
Saints returned to their every-day occupations.

Mr. Little also recounted to us his experiences among the Indians, whom he, like all the Mormons, firmly believed to be children of Israel under a cloud.   He compared the medicine lodge
to a masonic hall, and declared that the so-called Red Men had
signs and grips like ourselves; and he related how an old chief,
when certain symbolic actions were made to him, wept and wail-
ed, thinking how he and his had neglected their observances.
The Saints were at one time good masons; unhappily they wanted to be better.   The angel of the Lord brought to Mr. Joseph
Smith the lost key-words of several degrees, which caused him,
when he appeared among the brotherhood of Illinois, to "work
right ahead" of the highest, and to show them their ignorance of
the greatest truths and benefits of masonry.   The natural result
was that their diploma was taken from them by the Grand Lodge,
and they are not admitted to a Gentile gathering.   Now heathens
without the gate, they still cling to their heresy, and declare that
other masonry is, like the Christian faith, founded upon truth, and

ningham, E. F. Sheets, F. Kesler, Thomas Callister, A. H. Raleigh, Henry Moon.
J. C. Little, Marshal of the Day;   Colonel R. T. Burton will arrange the Guard.
   "Great Salt Lake City, July 10, 1860."

originally of the eternal Church, but fallen away and far gone in
error.   There is no race, except perhaps antiquaries, more credulous than the brethren of the mystic craft.   I have been told by
one who may have deceived himself, but would not have deceived
me, that the Royal Arch, notoriously a corruption of the Royal
Arras, is known to the Bedouins of Arabia; while the dairy of
the Neilgherry Todas, with its exclusion of women, and its rude
ornamentation of crescents, circles, and triangles, was at once identified with the "old religion of the world whose vestiges survive
among all people."   But these are themes unfit for an "entered
apprentice."   Mr. Little corroborated concerning the Prairie Indians and the Yutas what is said of the settled tribes, namely, that
the comforts of civilization tend to their destruction.   The men,
enervated by indoor life for half the year, are compelled at times
to endure sudden privation, hardship, and fatigue, of which the
results are rheumatism, consumption, and fatal catarrhs.   Yet he
believed that the "valleys of Ephraim" would yet be full of them.
He spoke freely of the actualities and prospects of Mormonism.
My companions asserted with truth that there is not among their
number a single loafer, rich or poor, an idle gentleman or a lazy
vagabond, a drunkard or a gambler, a beggar or a prostitute.
Those honorable professions are membered by the Gentiles.   They
boasted, indeed, of what is sometimes owned by their enemies,
that there are fewer robberies, murders, arsons, and rapes in Utah
than in any other place of equal population in the world.   They
held that the laws of the United States are better adapted to secure the happiness of a small community than to consolidate the
provinces of a continent into one huge empire, and they looked
confidently forward to the spread of Mormonism over the world.
They claimed for themselves, like other secessionists, " le droit sa-
cré d'insurrection," against which in vain the Gentiles raged and
the federal government devised vain things.   They declared themselves to be the salt of the Union, and that in the fullness of time
they shall break the republic in pieces like a potter's vessel.   Of
Washington, Jefferson, and the other sages of the Revolution they
speak with all respect, describing them as instruments in the hand
of the Almighty, and as Latter-Day Saints in will if not in deed.
I was much pleased by their tolerance; but tolerance in the West
is rather the effect of climate and occupation than of the reasoning faculty.   Gentiles have often said before me that Mormonism
is as good as any other religion, and that Mr. Joseph Smith "had
as good a right to establish a Church as Luther, Calvin, Fox,
Wesley, or even bluff King Hal."   The Mormons are certainly
the least fanatical of our faiths, owning, like Hindoos, that every
man should walk his own way, while claiming for themselves superiority in belief and politics.   At Nauvoo they are said to have
been puffed up by the rapid growth of their power, and to have
been presumptuous, haughty, insolent, and overbearing; to have

assumed a jurisdiction independent of, and sometimes hostile to, the nine counties around them and to the States; to have attached penalties to speaking evil of the Prophet; and to have denied the validity of legal documents, unless countersigned by him who was also mayor and general. They are certainly changed for the better in these days. With respect to their future views, the anti-Mormons assert that Saints have now been driven to the end of their tether, and must stand to fight or deliver; that the new Territory of Nevada will presently be a fatal rival to them; that the States will no longer tolerate this theocratic despotism in the bosom of a democracy; and that presently they must be wiped out. The Mormons already discern the dawning of a brighter day. In the reaction which has taken place in their favor they fear no organized attack by the United States on account of lobby influence at Washington, and the *vis inertiæ* inherent in so slow and unwieldy a body as the federal government. They count upon secession, quoting a certain proverb touching conjunctures when honest men come in. They believe that the supernatural aid of God, plus their vote, will presently make them a state. "Some time this side of the great millennium" they will realize their favorite dream, restoration (which might indeed happen in ten years) to their quondam Zion—Independence, Mo., the centre of the old terrestrial Paradise. Of this promised land their President said, with "something of prophetic strain," "while water runs and grass grows, while virtue is lovely and vice hateful, and while a stone points out a sacred spot where a fragment of American liberty once was"—Lord Macaulay's well-known Zealander shall apparently take his passage by Cunard's—"I or my posterity will plead the cause of injured innocence, until Missouri makes atonement for all her sins, or sinks disgraced, degraded, and damned to hell, where the worm dieth not, and the fire is not quenched." Then shall the Jews of the Old World rebuild the Temple of Solomon, and the Jews of the New World (the Mormons) recover their own Zion. Gog and Magog—that is to say, the kings of the Gentiles—and their hosts shall rise up against the Latter-Day Saints, who, guided by a prophet that wields the sword of Laban, shall mightily overthrow them at the battle of Armageddon. Then the spears, bows, and arrows (probably an abstruse allusion to the descendants of our Miniés and Armstrongs) shall be burned with fire seven years; the earth and its fullness shall be theirs, and the long-looked-for millennium shall come at last. And as prophecy without date is somewhat liable to be vague and indefinite, these great events are fixed in Mr. Joseph Smith's Autobiography for the year of grace 1890. Meantime they can retire, if forbidden the Saskatchewan River and Vancouver's Island, to the rich "minerales" in "Sonora of the Gold Mountains."

On the morning of the next day, Sunday, the 16th of Septem-

ber, we mounted and rode slowly on. I had neglected to take
"leggins," and the loss of cuticle and cutis was deplorable. Once
at the Tabernacle was enough: on this occasion, however, non-at-
tendance was a mistake. There had been a little "miff" between
Mr. President and the "Gauge of Philosophy," Mr. O. Pratt. The
latter gentleman, who is also an apostle, is a highly though probably a self-educated man, not, as is stated in an English work, a
graduate of Trinity College, Dublin. The Usman of the New
Faith, writer, preacher, theologian, missionary, astronomer, philosopher, and mathematician—especially in the higher branches—he
has thrust thought into a faith of ceremony which is supposed to
dispense with the trouble of thinking, and has intruded human
learning into a scheme whose essence is the utter abrogation of
the individual will. He is consequently suspected of too much
learning; of relying, in fact, rather upon books and mortal paper
than that royal road to all knowledge, inspiration from on high,
and his tendencies to let loose these pernicious doctrines often
bring him into trouble and place him below his position. In his
excellent discourse delivered to-day he had declared the poverty
of the Mormons, and was speedily put down by Mr. Brigham
Young, who boasted the Saints to be the wealthiest (i. e., in good
works and post-obit prospects) people in the world. I had tried
my best to have the pleasure of half an hour's conversation with
the Gauge, who, however, for reasons unknown to me, declined.
At the same meeting Mr. Heber C. Kimball solemnly consigned
to a hotter place than the tropics Messrs. Bell and Livingston, the
cause being their supposed complicity in bringing in the federal
troops. I write it with regret, but both of these gentlemen, when
the sad tidings were communicated to them, showed a quasi-Pha-
raonic hardening of the carnal heart. A measure, however, was
on this occasion initiated, which more than compensated for these
small *ridicules*. To the present date missionaries were sent forth,
to Canton even, or Kurrachee, like the apostles of Judea, working
their passages and supporting themselves by handiwork; being
wholly without purse or scrip, baggage or salary, they left their
business to languish, and their families to want. When man has
no coin of his own, he is naturally disposed to put his hand into
his neighbor's pocket, and the greediness of a few unprincipled
propagandists, despite the prohibitions of the Prophet, had caused
a scandal by the richness of their "plunder." A new ordinance
was therefore issued to the thirty new nominees.* The mission-

* The following is a copy of the elder's certificate, officially signed by the president and his two councilors, and supplied to the departing missionary:

" *To all Persons to whom this Letter shall come:*

"This certifies that the bearer, Elder A. B., is in full faith and fellowship with
the Church of Jesus Christ of Latter-Day Saints, and by the general authorities of
said Church has been duly appointed a mission to Liverpool to preach the Gospel,
and administer in all the ordinances thereof pertaining to his office.

"And we invite all men to give heed to his teachings and counsels as a man of

Z

aries were forbidden to take from their converts, and in compensation they would receive regular salaries, for which funds were to be collected in the several wards. On the same evening I was informed a single ward, the 13th, subscribed $3000. That Sunday was an important day to myself also; I posted a "sick certificate," advising extension of leave for six months, signed by W. F. Anderson, M.D., of the University of Maryland. It was not wholly *en règle;* it required two signatures and the counter-signature of H. B. M.'s consul to affirm that the signatures were *bonâ fide,* not "bogus." But the signer was the only M.D. in the place, H. B. M.'s nearest consul was distant about 600 miles, and to suggest that a gentleman may be quietly forging or falsifying his signature is to incur an unjustifiable personal risk in the Far West.

Still bent upon collecting the shells of the Basin, I accepted Mr. S——'s offer of being my guide to Ensign Peak, where they are said to be found in the greatest number. Our route lay through the broken wall which once guarded the land against Lemuel, and we passed close by the large barn-like building called the Arsenal, where the military school will also be. Motives of delicacy prevented my asking questions concerning the furniture of the establishment. Anti-Mormons, however, whisper that it contains cannon, mortars, and other large-scaled implements of destruction, prepared, of course, for treasonable purposes. The Arsenal naturally led us into conversation concerning the Nauvoo Legion, the Mormon Battalion, the Danite band, and other things military, of which the reader may not be undesirous of knowing "some."

The Nauvoo Legion was organized in 1840, and was made to include all male Saints between the ages of sixteen and fifty. In 1842 it numbered 2000 men, well officered, uniformed, armed, and drilled. It now may amount throughout the Territory to 6000—8000 men: the Utah militia, however, is officially laid down in the latest returns at 2821. In case of war, it would be assisted by 30,000 or 40,000 Indian warriors. The Legion is commanded by a lieutenant general, at present Mr. Daniel C. Wells, the Martin Hofer of this Western Tyrol; the major general is Mr. C. D. Grant, who, in case of vacancy, takes command. The lieutenant general is elected by a majority of the commissioned officers, and is then commissioned by the governor: he organizes the Legion into divisions, brigades, regiments, battalions, companies, and districts: his staff, besides heads of departments—adjutant, commissary quarter-master, paymaster, and surgeon general

God, sent to open to them the door of life and salvation, and assist him in his travels, in whatsoever things he may need.

"And we pray God, the Eternal Father, to bless Elder A. B., and all who receive him and minister to his comfort, with the blessings of heaven and earth, for time and for all eternity, in the name of Jesus Christ: Amen.

"Signed at Great Salt Lake City, Territory of Utah, ——, 186-, in behalf of said Church."

—consists of three aids and two topographical engineers with the rank of colonel, a military secretary with the rank of lieutenant colonel, and two chaplains. The present adjutant general is Mr. William Ferguson, one of the few Irish Saints, originally sergeant-major in the Mormon battalion, who, after the fashion of the Western world, combines with the soldier the lawyer and the editor. The minutest directions are issued to the Legion in "An Act to provide for the farther Organization of the Militia of the Territory of Utah (Territorial Laws, chap. 35), and it is divided into military districts as below.* There is, moreover, an independent battalion of Life Guards in Great Salt Lake County not attached to any brigade or division, but subject at all times to the call of the governor and lieutenant general. There are also minute-men, picked fighters, ready to mount, at a few minutes' notice, upon horses that range near the Jordan, and to take the field in pursuit of Indians or others, under their commandant Colonel Burton. These corps form the nuclei of what will be, after two generations, formidable armies. The increase of Saintly population is rapid, and from their childhood men are trained to arms: each adult has a rifle and a sabre, a revolver and a bowie-knife, and he wants only practice to become a good, efficient, and well-disciplined soldier. Grants amounting to a total of $5000 have at different times been apportioned to military purposes, buildings, mounting ordnance, and schools: Gentiles declare that it was required for education, but I presume that the Mormons, like most people, claim to know their own affairs best. As in the land of Liberty generally, there is a modified conscription; "all free male citizens"—with a few dignified exceptions and exempts —are subject to soldier's duty within thirty days after their arrival at any military district in the Territory.

* There are eleven originally established, viz. :

1st. The Great Salt Lake Military District shall include all the militia within the boundaries of Great Salt Lake City.

2d. The Davis Military District shall include all the militia within the limits of Davis County.

3d. The Weber Military District shall include all the militia within the limits of Weber County.

4th. The Western Jordan Military District shall include all the militia in Great Salt Lake County west of the Jordan River.

5th. The Tooele Military District shall include all the militia within the limits of Tooele County.

6th. The Cotton-wood Military District shall include all the militia in Great Salt Lake County south of the south line of Great Salt Lake City and east of the Jordan River.

7th. The Utah Military District shall include all the militia in Utah County.

8th. The San Pete Military District shall include all the militia within the limits of San Pete County.

9th. The Parovan Military District shall include all the militia within the limits of Millard County.

10th. The Iron Military District shall include all the militia within the limits of Iron County.

11th. The Green River Military District shall include all the militia within the limits of Green River County.

That the Mormon battalion did good service in the Mexican War of 1847 is a matter of history. It was sent at a most critical conjuncture. Application was made to the Saints, when upon the point of commencing their exodus from Egypt, through the deserts of Paran and Sin, where the red Amalekite and the Moabite lay in wait to attack them, and when every male was wanted to defend the old and sick, the women and children, and the valuables of which the Egyptian had not despoiled them. Yet the present Prophet did not hesitate to obey the call: he sent off 500 of his best men, who fought through the war and shared in the triumph. Providence rewarded them. It was a Mormon—James W. Marshall—who, when discharged from service, entered with some comrades the service of a Swiss land-owner, Captain Suter—a remnant of Charles X.'s guard—near Sacramento, on the American River, and who, in January, 1848, when sinking a mill-run or water-run, discovered the shining metal which first made California a household word. On the return of the battalion to Great Salt Lake City, laden with nearly half a million of gold, a mint was established, and a $5 piece was added to the one million dollars which forms the annual circulation of the United States. It bears on the reverse, "Holiness to the Lord," surmounting a three-cornered cap, placed over a single eye: the former alludes, I was told, mystically to the first Presidency; the obverse having two hands clasped over the date (1849), and the words "Five Dollars, G. S. L. C. P. G." The $5 appeared somewhat heavier, though smaller than an English sovereign. Anti-Mormons adduce this coinage as an additional proof of saintly presumption; but it was legally done: a Territory may not stamp precious metal with the federal arms, but it has a right to establish its own. They adduce, moreover, a severe charge, namely, that the $5 piece was 15–20 per cent. under weight, and yet was forcibly made current. One remarkable effect the gold certainly had. When the Kirtland Safety Savings Bank, established by Mr. Joseph Smith in February, 1831, broke, he stout-heartedly prophesied that before twenty years should elapse the worthless paper should be again at par. The financial vaticination was true to the letter.*

---

* The Mormons quote two other prophecies both equally offensive to the United States, and both equally well known.

On the 26th of April, 1843, Mr. Joseph Smith distinctly declared, in the name of the Lord, that before the arrival of the Son of Man the "question of slavery would cause a rebellion in South Carolina," and effect a "division of the Southern against the Northern States." It was a calamity easy to be foreseen, but we look with anxiety to the unfulfilled portion, the "terrible bloodshed" which will result.

In 1846, when, humanly speaking, want and destitution stared the Saints in the face, Mr. Brigham Young predicted that within five years they would be wealthier than before. This was palpably fulfilled in 1849, when the passage of emigrants to California enabled the Saints to exchange their supplies of food for goods and valuables at enormous profits.

I commend these "uninspired prophecies" to the simple-minded translator of "Forewarnings, Prophecies on the Church, Antichrist (who was born, we are told,

ENSIGN PEAK.   (North End of Great Salt Lake City.)

The "Danite band," a name of fear in the Mississippi Valley, is said by anti-Mormons to consist of men between the ages of seventeen and forty-nine. They were originally termed Daughters of Gideon, Destroying Angels—the Gentiles say Devils—and, finally, Sons of Dan, or Danites, from one of whom it was prophesied that he should be a serpent in the path. They were organized about 1837, under D. W. Patten, popularly called Captain Fearnot, for the, purpose of dealing as avengers of blood with Gentiles; in fact, they formed a kind of "Death Society," Desperadoes, Thugs, Hashshashiyun—in plain English, assassins in the name of the Lord. The Mormons declare categorically the whole and every particular to be the calumnious invention of the impostor and arch apostate Mr. John C. Bennett, whilom mayor of Nauvoo; that the mystery and horror of the idea made it equally grateful to the knave and fool who persecuted them, and that not a trader could be scalped, nor a horse-stealer shot, nor a notorious villain of a Gentile knived without the deed of blood being attributed to Danite hands directed by prophetic heads. It was supposed that the Danites assume savage disguises: "he has met the Indians" was a proverbial phrase, meaning that a Gentile has fallen into the power of the destroying angels. I but express the opinion of sensible and moderate neutrals in disbelieving the existence of an organized band of "Fidawi;" where every man is ready to be a Danite, Danites are not wanting. Certainly, in the terrible times of Missouri and Illinois, destroying angels were required to smite secretly, mysteriously, and terribly the first-born of Egypt; now the necessity has vanished. This, however, the Mormons deny, declaring the existence of the Danites, like that of spiritual wives, to be, and ever to have been, literally and in substance totally and entirely untrue.

Meanwhile we had nearly ascended the Jebel Nur of this new Meccah, the big toe of the Wasach Mountains, and exchanged the sunny temperature below for a cold westerly wind, that made us feel snow: the air improved in purity, as we could judge by the effects of carcasses lying at different heights. The bench up which we trod was gashed by broad ravines, and bore upon its red soil a growth of thin sage and sunflower. A single fossil and two varieties of shells were found: iron and quartz were scattered over the surface, and there is a legend of gold having been discovered here. Presently, standing upon the topmost bluff, we sat down to enjoy a view which I have attempted to reproduce in a sketch. Below the bench lay the dot-like houses of Zion. We could see with bird's-eye glance the city laid out like a chessboard, and all the length and breadth of its bee-line streets and

four years ago), and Revelations in the Last Times." Messrs. Smith and Young's vaticinations will be found quite as respectable as the "Visions of an Aged Nun" and the "Predictions of Sister Rosa Columba." Prophecy, being the highest aim of human induction, is apparently universally and equally diffused.

crow-flight avenues, which, bordered by distance-dwarfed trees, narrowed to threads as they drew toward a vanishing point. Beyond the suburbs stretched the valley plain, sprinkled with little plantations clustering round the smaller settlements, and streaked by the rivulets which, arising from the frowning pine-clad heights on the left, flowed toward the little Jordan of this young Judea on the right. The extreme south was bounded by the denticulated bench which divided like a mole the valleys of the Great Salt and Utah Lakes. Already autumn had begun: the purpling plain and golden slopes shed a dying glory over the departing year, while the mellowing light of evening, and aerial blue from above, toned down to absolute beauty each harsher feature of the scene.

After lingering for a while over the fair *coup d'œil*, we descended, holding firm the sage-bushes, the abrupt western slope, and we passed by the warm Harrowgate spring, with its sulphury blue waters, white lime-like bed, and rushy margins in dark earth, snow-capped with salt efflorescence. As we entered the city we met a noted Gentile innocently driving out a fair Saint: both averted their faces as they passed us, but my companion's color darkened. All races have their pet prohibitions and aversions, their likes and dislikes in matters of sin. Among the Mormons, a suspicion of immorality is more hateful than the reputation of bloodshed. So horse-thieving in the Western States is a higher crime than any other—in fact, the sin which is never forgiven. An editor thus unconcernedly sums up the history of one lately shot when plundering stock: "He was buried by those who meted out to him summary justice, not exactly attending to law, but upon a more speedy, economical, and salutary principle, and a stake was placed at the head of his grave, on which was inscribed 'A. B. B——, shot for horse-stealing, July 1, 1860.'"

Entering the city by the northwest, we passed the Academy of the 7th Ward. Standing in a 10-acre block, it is a large adobe building with six windows, built for a hotel, and bought for educational purposes by the Prophet. Forms and tables, scattered with the usual school-books, were the sole furniture, and the doors were left open as if they had nothing to defend. My companion had a truly brotherly way of treating his co-religionists; he never met one, however surly-looking, without a salute, and when a door was opened he usually walked in. Thus we visited successively a water-power-mill, a tannery, and an English coachmaker, painter, and varnisher. Some of the houses which we passed were neat and cleanly curtained, especially that belonging to an Englishwoman whose husband, Captain R——, had lately left her in widowhood. We finished with the garden of Apostle Woodruff, who introduced us to his wife, and showed us work of which he had reason to be proud. Despite the hard, ungrateful soil which had required irrigation for the last ten years, there were apricots from Malta, the Hooker strawberries, here worth $5 the plant, plum-trees from Kew Gardens, French and Californian grapes, wild plum and buffalo berry, black currants, peaches, and apples —with which last we were hospitably loaded—in numbers. The kitchen garden contained rhubarb, peas, potatoes, Irish and sweet, asparagus, white and yellow carrots, cabbages, and huge beets: the sugar-cane had been tried there, but it was not, like the sweet holcus, a success.

The last time I walked out of Great Salt Lake City was to see the cemetery, which lies on the bench to the northeast of the settlement. There is but one cemetery for saint and sinner, and it has been prudently removed about three miles from the abodes of the living. The tombs, like the funeral ceremonies, are simple, lacking the "monumental mockery" which renders the country church-yard in England a fitter study for farce than for elegy. On occasions of death, prayers are offered in the house, and the corpse is carried at once to its last home. The grave-yard is walled round, and contains a number of occupants, the tombs being denoted by a stone or board, with name and date, and sometimes a religious sentence, at the head and foot.

CHAPTER IX.

Latter-Day Saints.—Of the Mormon Religion.

No less an authority than Alexander von Humboldt has characterized positive religions in general as consisting of an historical novelette more or less interesting, a system of cosmogony more or less improbable, and a code of morals mostly pure.* Two thirds of this description apply to the faith of the Latter-Day Saints: they have, however, escaped palæological criticism by adopting Genesitic history, and by "swallowing Eve's apple" in the infancy of their spiritual life.

Before proceeding to comment upon the New Dispensation— for such, though not claiming or owning to be, it *is*—I may compare the two leading interpretations of the word "Mormon," which, as has been well remarked,† truly convey the widely diverging opinions of the opposers and supporters of Mormonism. Mormon (μορμών) signifies literally a lamia, a maniola, a female spectre; the mandrill, for its ugliness, was called Cynocephalus mormon. "Mormon," according to Mr. Joseph Smith's Mormonic, or rather Pantagruelic interpretation, is the best—*scil.*, of mankind. "We

* A somewhat free version of "toutes les religions positives offrent trois parties distinctes; un traité de mœurs partout le même et très pur, un rêve géologique, et un mythe ou petit roman historique : le dernier élément obtient le plus d'importance." —LX. Letter, Dec. 3d, 1841.

† The Mormons, or Latter-Day Saints, by Lieutenant J. W. Gunnison, of the United States Topographical Engineers. Philadelphia, 1852.

say from the Saxon *good*, the Dane *god*, the Goth *goder*, the German *gut*, the Dutch *goed*, the Latin *bonus*, the Greek *kalos*, the Hebrew *tob*, and the Egyptian *mon*. Hence, with the addition of More, or the contraction Mor, we have the word Mormon, which means literally "more good." By faith it is said man can remove mountains: perhaps it will also enable him to believe in the spirit of that philology that revealed unto Mr. Joseph Smith his derivation, and rendered it a shibboleth to his followers. This is not the place to discuss a subject so broad and so long, but perhaps— the idea will suggest itself—the mind of man most loves those errors and delusions into which it has become self-persuaded, and is most fanatic concerning the irrationalities and the supernaturalities to which it has bowed its own reason.

Unaccountably enough, seeing that it means "more good," *scil.*, the best of mankind, the word Mormon is distasteful to its disciples, who look upon it as Jew by a Hebrew, Mohammedan by a Moslem, and Romanist or Puseyite by the sectarian Christian. They prefer to be called Latter-Day Saints, or, to give them their title in full, the Church of Jesus Christ of Latter-Day Saints, in contradistinction to the Former-Day Saints. Latter Day alludes to the long-looked-for convulsion that will end the present quiescent geologic epoch. Its near approach has ever been a favorite dogma and improvement subject of the Christian Church, from the time of St. Paul to that of Mr. Joseph Smith, and Drs. Wolff and Cumming;[*] for who, inquires Panurge, "is able to tell if the world shall last yet three years?" Others read it as a prophecy that "Gentilism," alias "the corrupted Christianity of the age," is "on its last legs." Even as "Saints" is a term which has been applied from time immemorial in the Apocalypse and elsewhere to the orthodox, *i. e.*, those of one's own doxy, and as Enoch speaks of "saints" before the Flood or Noachian cataclysm, so the honorable title has in these days been appropriated by seers, revelators, and prophets, and conferred upon the Lord's chosen people, *i. e.*, themselves and their followers. According to anti-Mormons, the name Latter-Day Saints was assumed in 1835 by the Mormons at the suggestion of Sidney Rigdon.

Before beginning a description of what Mormonism really is, I would succinctly lay down a few positions illustrating its genesis.

1. The religious as well as the social history of the progressive Anglo-Saxon race is a succession of contrasts, a system of reactions; at times retrogressive, it has a general onward tendency toward an unknown development. The Unitarians of New England, for instance, arose out of Calvinism. The Puritanism of the present generation is the natural consequence of the Rationalism which preceded it.

2. In what a French author terms "le triste état de dissolution

* The Mormon Prophet fixed "the end of the world" for A.D. 1890; Dr. Cumming, I believe, in 1870.

dans lequel gît le Chrétienté de nos jours"—the splitting of the Church into three grand divisions, Roman, Greek, and Eastern, the convulsion of the Northern mind, which created Protestantism, and the minute subdivision of the latter into Episcopalians and Presbyterians, Lutherans and Calvinists, Quakers and Shakers, the multiform Methodists and various Baptists, and, to quote no farther *variétés des églises*, the Congregationalists, Unitarians, and Universalists — a rationalistic race finds reason to inquire, "What is Christianity?" and holds itself prepared for a new faith, a regeneration of human thought — in fact, a religious and social change, such as the Reformation of the sixteenth century represented and fondly believed itself to be.*

3. Mormonism boasts of few Roman Catholic or Greek converts; the French and Italians are rare, and there is a remarkable deficiency of Germans and Irish — those wretched races without nationality or loyalty — which have overrun the Eastern American States. It is, then, to Protestantism that we must look for the origin of the New Faith.

4. In 1800–1804, and in 1820, a mighty Wesleyan "revival," which in Methodism represents the missions and retreats of Catholicism, had disturbed and excited the public mind in America, especially in Kentucky and Tennessee. The founder of Mormonism, Mr. Joseph Smith, his present successor, and his principal disciples and followers, were Campbellites, Millerites, Ranters, or other Methodists. Wesleyan sectarianism, like the old Arab pagan-

---

* *Religious Denominations in the United States, according to the Census of 1861.*
(From the " American Almanac" of 1861.)

Denominations.	No. of Churches.	Aggregate Accommodation.	Average Accommodation.	Total Value of Church Property.	Average Value of Property.
Baptist...............	8,791	3,130,878	356	$10,931,382	$1,244
Christian............	812	296,050	365	845,810	1,041
Congregational	1,674	795,177	475	7,973,962	4,763
Dutch Reformed ...	324	181,986	561	4,096,730	12,644
Episcopal	1,422	625,213	440	11,261,970	7,919
Free...................	361	108,605	300	251,255	698
Friends..............	714	282,823	396	1,709,867	2,395
German Reformed.	327	156,932	479	965,880	2,953
Jewish..............	31	16,575	534	371,600	11,987
Lutheran............	1,203	531,100	441	2,867,886	2,383
Mennonite..........	110	29,900	272	94,245	856
Methodist...........	12,487	4,209,333	337	14,636,671	1,174
Moravian............	331	112,185	338	443,347	1,339
Presbyterian........	4,584	2,040,316	445	14,369,889	3,135
Roman Catholic....	1,112	620,950	558	8,973,838	8,069
Swedenborgian	15	5,070	338	108,100	7,206
Tunker	52	35,075	674	46,025	885
Union................	619	213,552	345	690,065	1,114
Unitarian...........	243	137,367	565	3,268,122	13,449
Universalist.........	494	205,462	415	1,766,015	3,576
Minor sects.........	325	115,347	354	741,980	2,283
Total............	36,011	13,849,896	384	$86,416,639	$2,400

ism in El Islam, still shows its traces in the worship and various observances of a doxology which by literalism and exaggeration has wholly separated itself from the older creeds of the world. Thus we find Mormonism to be in its origin English, Protestant, anti-Catholic, Methodistic.

It may be advisable briefly to trace the steps by which we arrive at this undesirable end. The birth of Romanism, according to the Reformed writers, dates from certain edicts issued by Theodosius II. and by Valentinian III., and constituting the Bishop of Rome "Rector of the whole Church." The newly-born hierarchy found tender nurses in Justinian, Pepin, and Charlemagne, and in the beginning of the eleventh century St. Gregory VII. (Hildebrand the Great) supplied the prime want of the age by establishing a visible theocracy, with a vicar of Jesus Christ at its head. To the existence of a mediatorial priestly caste, the officials of a spiritual despotism, claiming power of censure and excommunication, and the gift of the crown terrestrial as well as celestial, antipapistical writers trace the various vices and corruptions inherent in a semi-barbarous age, the "melancholy duality" of faith and works of religion and morality which seems to belong to the Southern mind, and the Oriental semi-Pelagianism which taught that man might be self-sanctified or vicariously saved, with its logical deductions, penance, benefices, indulgences. An excessive superstition endured for a season. Then set in the inevitable reaction : the extreme religiousness, that characteristic of the earnest quasi-pagan age of the Christian Church, in the fullness of time fell into the opposite excess, Rationalism and its natural consequences, infidelity and irreligion.

Reformers were not wanting before the Reformation. As early as 1170, Pierre Vaud, or Valdo, of Lyons, sold off his merchandise, and appealing from popery to Scripture and to primitive Christianity, as in a later day did Jeremy Bentham from St. Paul to his Master, attacked the Roman hierarchy. John Wicliffe (1310–1385) is claimed by his countrymen to have originated the "liberal ideas" by which British Protestantism was matured; it is owned even by foreigners that he influenced opinion from Oxford to far Bohemia. He died peaceably, but the Wicliffites, who presently were called Lollards—"tares" sown by the fiend—though supported by the Commons against Henry IV. and his party, the dignified clergy, suffered, until the repeal of the Act " de hæreticis comburendis," the fiercest persecution. During the reign of Henry V. they gained strength, as the pronunciamento of 20,000 men in St. Giles's Fields under Sir John Oldcastle proves : the cruel death of their leader only served to strengthen them, supported as they were by the lower branch of the Legislature in their opposition to the crown. On the Continent of Europe the great follower of Wicliffe was John Huss, who preached in Bohemia about a century before the days of Luther, and who, condemned by the

Councils of Constance and Basle, perished at the stake in 1432. Jerome Savonarola, tortured and burnt in 1498, and other minor names, urged forward the fatal movement until the Northern element once more prevailed, in things spiritual as in things temporal, over the Southern; the rude and violent German again attacked the soft, sensuous Italian, and Martin Luther hatched the egg which the schools of Rabelais and Erasmus had laid. It was the work of rough-handed men; the reformer Zuingle emerged from an Alpine shepherd's hut; Melancthon, the theologian, from an armorer's shop, as Augustine, the monk, from the cottage of a poor miner. Such, in the 16th century, on the Continent of Europe, were the prototypes and predecessors of Messrs. Joseph Smith, Oliver Cowdery, Sidney Rigdon, and Brigham Young, who arose nearly three centuries afterward in the New World.

In England, when the unprincipled tyranny of Henry VIII. had established, by robbing and confiscating, hanging and quartering, that "reformed new-cast religion," of which Sir Thomas Brown "disliked nothing but the name," the bigotry of the ultra-reformatory school lost no time in proceeding to extremes. William Chillingworth, born A.D. 1602, and alternately Protestant, Catholic, Socinian, and Protestant, put forth in his "Religion of Protestants a safe Way of Salvation," that Chillingworthi Novissima, "the Bible and nothing but the Bible." This dogma swept away ruthlessly all the cherished traditions of a past age—the ancient observed customs of the Church—all, in fact, that can beautify and render venerable a faith, and substituted in their stead a bald Bibliolatry which at once justifies credulity and forbids it; which tantalizes man with the signs and wonders of antiquity, and yet which, with an unwise contradictoriness, forbids him to revise or restore them. And as each man became, by Bible-reading, his own interpreter, with fullest right of private judgment, and without any infallible guide—the inherent weakness of reformation—to direct him, the broad and beaten highway of belief was at once cut up into a parcel of little footpaths which presently attained the extreme of divergence.

One of the earliest products of such "religious freedom" in England was Methodism, so called from the Methodistic physicians at Rome. The founder and arch-priest of the schism, the Rev. John Wesley, son of the Rector of Epworth in Lincolnshire, and born in 1703, followed Luther, Calvin, and other creedmongers in acting upon his own speculation and peculiar opinions. One of his earliest disciples—only eleven years younger than his master—was the equally celebrated George Whitfield, of Gloucester. Suffice it to remark, without dwelling upon their history, that both these religionists, and mostly the latter, who died in 1770 at Newberry, New England, converted and preached to thousands in America, there establishing field-services and camp-meetings, revivals and conferences, which, like those of the French Convulsionists in the last century, galvanized Christianity with a wild and feverish life. Falling among uneducated men, the doctrine, both in England and the colonies, was received with a bewilderment of enthusiasm, and it soon produced the usual fruits of such phrensy — prophecies that fixed the end of the world for the 28th of February, 1763, miraculous discernment of angels and devils, mighty comings of the power of God and outpourings of the Spirit, rhapsodies and prophecies, dreams and visions, accompanied by rollings, jerks, and barks, roarings and convulsions, syncope, catalepsy, and the other hysterical affections and obscure disorders of the brain, forming the characteristic symptoms of religious mania.

Thus, out of the semi-barbarous superstitions of the Middle Ages, succeeded by the revival of learning, which in the 15th century followed the dispersion of the wise men of the East from captured Byzantium, proceeded " Protestant Rationalism," a system which, admitting the right of private judgment, protested against the religion of Southern Europe becoming that of the whole world. From Protestantism sprung Methodism, which restored to man the grateful exercise of his credulity—a leading organ in the human brain—his belief in preternatural and supernatural agencies and appearances, and his faith in miraculous communication between God and man; in fact, in that mysticism and marvel-love, which are the columns and corner-stones of religion. Mormonism thus easily arose. It will be found to contain little beyond a literal and verbal interpretation of the only book which Chillingworth recognizes as the rule for Christians, and a pointed condemnation of those who make the contents of the Bible typical, metaphysical, or symbolical, "as if God were not honest when he speaks with man, or uses words in other than their true acceptation," or could " palter in a double sense." It proposed as its three general principles, firstly, total immersion in the waters of baptism in the name of the three sacred names; secondly, the commissioning of prophets, apostles, and elders to administer in things holy the revelation and authority of heaven; and, thirdly, the ministering of angels. New Tables of the Law appeared in the Golden Plates. Another Urim and Thummim revealed to Mr. Joseph Smith that he was of the house of Israel and the tribe of Joseph, the inheritor of all things promised to that favored seed. It tempered the superstitions of popery with the rationalism of the Protestant; it supplied mankind with another sacred book and with an infallible interpreter. Human belief had now its weight to carry: those pining for the excitement of thaumaturgy felt satisfied. The Mormons were no longer compelled to ask " what made miracles cease," and "why and in which A.D. was the power taken from the Church." It relieved them from holding an apparent absurdity, viz., that the voices and visitations, the signs, miracles, and interventions—in fact, all that the Bible submitted to human faith had ended without reason about the time when one Constantine became king, and do not recommence now when they are most wanted. The Mormons are not forced to think that God is virtually dead in the world; the eminently practical tendencies of the New-World race cause them to develop into practice their contradiction of an inference from which human nature revolts. They claim to be the true Protestants, *i. e.*, those who protest against the doctrines of a ceased fellowship between the Creator and the creature made in his image; they gratify their self-esteem by sneering at those who confine themselves to the old and obsolete revelation, and by pitying the blindness and ignorance that can not or will not open its eyes to the new light. Hence it follows that few Catholics become Mormons, and that those few become bad Mormons. Man's powers of faith grow, like his physical force, with exercise. He considers over-belief a venial error compared with under-belief, and he progresses more easily in belief than he can retrograde into disbelief. Thus Catholicism has spread more widely over the world than the less credulous Protestantism, and the more thaumaturgic Mormonism is better adapted to some minds—the Hindoo's, for instance—than Catholicism.

In Mormonism, or, rather, in Mormon sacred literature, there are three epochs which bring us down to the present day. The first is the monogamic age, that of the books of Mormon, and of Doctrines and Covenants—1830–1843. The second is the polygamic, from the first revelation of "celestial marriage" to Mr. Joseph Smith in 1843, and by him communicated to three followers only, until its final establishment by Mr. Brigham Young in 1852, when secrecy was no longer deemed necessary. The third is the materialistic period; the doctrine, "not founded on modern supernatural revelation, but on reason and common sense," was the work of 1848–1849.

The first epoch laid the foundations of the Faith. It produced the Book of Mormon, "an abridgment written by the hand of Mormon upon plates taken from the plates of Nephi. Wherefore it is an abridgment of the record of the people of Nephi, and also of the Lamanites; written to the Lamanites, who are a remnant of the house of Israel, and also to Jew and Gentile: written by way of commandment, and also by the spirit of prophecy and of revelation. Written and sealed up, and hid up unto the Lord, that they might not be destroyed: to come forth by the gift and power of God unto the interpretation thereof: sealed by the hand of Mormon, and hid up unto the Lord, to come forth in due time by the way of Gentile; the interpretation thereof by the gift of God!"

"An abridgment taken from the Book of Ether also, which is a record of the people of Jared, who were scattered at the time the Lord confounded the language of the people, when they were building a tower to get (!) to heaven; which is to show unto the remnant of the house of Israel what great things the Lord hath done for their fathers; and that they may know the covenants of the Lord, that they are not cast off forever; and also to the convincing of the Jew and Gentile that JESUS is the CHRIST, the ETERNAL GOD, manifesting himself to all nations; and now, if there are faults, they are the mistakes of men; therefore condemn not the things of God, that ye may be found spotless at the judgment-seat of Christ. Moroni."

"Translated by Joseph Smith, Jun."

This extract is followed by the testimony of three witnesses, Oliver Cowdery, David Whitmer, and Martin Harris, who declare to have seen the Golden Plates with their engravings, which were shown to them by the power of God, not of man; and that they knew by the voice of God that the records had been translated by the gift and power of God. Furthermore they "declare with words of solemnness that an angel of God came down from heaven, and he brought and laid before our eyes, that we beheld and saw the plates and the engravings thereon." They conclude with these solemn words: "And the honor be to the Father, and to the Son, and to the Holy Ghost, which is one God, Amen." Then comes "also the testimony of eight witnesses"—four Whitmers, three Smiths, and one Page*—who make it "known unto all nations, kindred, tongues, and people, unto whom this work shall come, that Joseph Smith, Jun., the translator of this work, has shown unto us the plates of which hath been spoken, which have the appearance of gold; and as many of the leaves as the said Smith has translated we did handle with our hands; and we also saw the engravings thereon, all of which has the appearance of ancient work and of curious workmanship. And this we bear record with words of soberness that the said Smith has shown unto us, for we have seen and hefted, and know of a surety that the said Smith has got the plates of which we have spoken. And we give our hands unto the world, to witness unto the world that which we have seen; and we lie not, God bearing witness of it."

The nature of the Latter-Day Saints' Biblion will best be understood from the subjoined list of contents.†

---

* The total witnesses are thus eleven, exactly the number that bore evidence to the original Christian miracles.

† At the end of this chapter I have inserted a synopsis of Mormon chronology.

FIRST BOOK OF NEPHI.
Language of the Record.
Nephi's Abridgment.
Lehi's Dream.
Lehi departs into the Wilderness.
Nephi slayeth Laban.
Sariah complains of Lehi's Vision.
Contents of the brass Plates.
Ishmael goes with Nephi.
Nephi's Brethren rebel, and bind him.
Lehi's Dream of the Tree, Rod, etc.

Messiah and John prophesied of.
Olive-branches broken off.
Nephi's Vision of Mary.
Do. the Crucifixion of Christ.
Do. Darkness and Earthquake.
Great abominable Church.
Discovery of the Promised Land.
Bible spoken of.
Book of Mormon and Holy Ghost promised.
Other Books come forth.
Bible and Book of Mormon one.
Promises to the Gentiles.

Two Churches.
The Work of the Father to commence.
A Man in white Robes (John).
Nephites come to Knowledge.
Rod of Iron.
The Sons of Lehi take Wives.
Director found (Ball).
Nephi broke his Bow.
Directors work by Faith.
Ishmael died.
Lehi and Nephi threatened.
Nephi commanded to build a Ship.

The Book of Covenants and Doctrines is what the Vedanta is to the Vedas, the Talmud to the Old Testament, the Traditions to

Nephi about to be worshiped by his Brethren.
Ship finished and entered.
Dancing in the Ship.
Nephi bound; Ship driven back.
Arrived on the Promised Land.
Plates of Ore made.
Zenos, Neum, and Zenock.
Isaiah's Writings.
Holy One of Israel.

SECOND BOOK OF NEPHI.
Lehi to his Sons.
Opposition in all Things.
Adam fell that Men might be.
Joseph saw our Day.
A choice Seer.
Writings grow together.
Prophet promised to the Lamanites.
Joseph's Prophecy on brass Plates.
Lehi buried.
Nephi's Life sought.
Nephi separated from Laman.
Temple built.
Skin of Blackness.
Priests, etc., consecrated.
Make other Plates.
Isaiah's Words (by Jacob).
Angels to a Devil.
Spirits and Bodies reunited.
Baptism.
No Kings upon this Land.
Isaiah prophesieth.
Rod of the Stem of Jesse.
Seed of Joseph perish not.
Law of Moses kept.
Christ shall show himself.
Signs of Christ, Birth and Death.
Whisper from the Dust; Book sealed up.
Priestcraft forbidden.
Sealed Book to be brought forth.
Three Witnesses behold the Book.
The Words [read this, I pray thee].
Seal up the Book again.
Their Priests shall contend.
Teach with their Learning, and deny the Holy Ghost.
Rob the Poor.
A Bible, a Bible.
Men judged of the Books.
White and a delightsome People.
Work commence among all People.
Lamb of God baptized.
Baptism by water and Holy Ghost.

BOOK OF JACOB.
Nephi anointed a King.
Nephi died.
Nephites and Lamanites.
A righteous Branch from Joseph.
Lamanites shall scourge you.
More than one Wife forbidden.
Trees, Waves, and Mountains obey us.
Jews looked beyond the Mark.
Tame Olive-tree.
Nethermost Part of the Vineyard.
Fruit laid up against the Season.
Another Branch.
Wild Fruit had overcome.
Lord of the Vineyard wept.
Branches overcome the Roots.
Wild Branches plucked off.
Sherem the Anti-Christ.

A Sign; Sherem smitten.
Enos takes the Plates from his Father.

THE BOOK OF ENOS.
Enos, thy Sins are forgiven.
Records threatened by Lamanites.
Lamanites eat raw Meat.

THE BOOK OF JAROM.
Nephites waxed strong.
Lamanites drink Blood.
Fortify Cities.
Plates delivered to Omni.

THE BOOK OF OMNI.
Plates given to Amaron.
Plates given to Chemish.
Mosiah warned to flee.
Zarahemla discovered.
Engravings on a Stone.
Coriantumr discovered.
His Parents came from the Tower.
Plates delivered to King Benjamin.

THE WORDS OF MORMON.
False Christs and Prophets.

BOOK OF MOSIAH.
Mosiah made King, and received.
The Plates of Brass, Sword, and Director.
King Benjamin teacheth the People.
Their Tent Doors toward the Temple.
Coming of Christ foretold.
Beggars not denied.
Sons and Daughters.
Mosiah began to reign.
Ammon, etc., bounded and imprisoned.
Limhi's Proclamation.
Twenty-four Plates of Gold.
Seer and Translator.

RECORD OF ZENIFF.
A Battle fought.
King Laman died.
Noah made King.
Abinadi the Prophet.
Resurrection.
Alma believed Abinadi.
Abinadi cast into Prison and scourged with fagots.
Waters of Mormon.
The Daughters of the Lamanites stolen by King Noah's Priests.
Records on Plates of Ore.
Last Tribute of Wine.
Lamanites' deep Sleep.
King Limhi baptized.
Priest and Teachers labor.
Alma saw an Angel.
Alma fell (dumb).
King Mosiah's Sons preach to the Lamanites.
Translation of Records.
Plates delivered by Limhi.
Translated by two Stones.
People back to the Tower.
Records given to Alma.
Judges appointed.
King Mosiah died.
Alma died.
Kings of Nephi ended.

THE BOOK OF ALMA.
Nehor slew Gideon.
Amlici made King.
Amlici slain in Battle.
Amlicites painted red.
Alma baptized in Sidon.
Alma's Preaching.
Alma ordained Elders.
Commanded to meet often.
Alma saw an Angel.
Amulek saw an Angel.
Lawyers questioning Amulek.
Coins named.
Zeezrom the Lawyer.
Zeezrom trembles.
Election spoken of.
Melchizedek Priesthood.
Alma and Amulek stoned.
Records burned.
Prison rent.
Zeezrom healed and baptized.
Nehor's Desolation.
Lamanites converted.
Flocks scattered at Sebus.
Ammon smote off Arms.
Ammon and King Lamoni.
King Lamoni fell.
Ammon and the Queen.
King and Queen prostrate.
Aaron, etc., delivered.
Jerusalem built.
Preaching in Jerusalem.
Lamoni's Father converted.
Land Desolation and Bountiful.
Anti-Nephi-Lehies.
General Council.
Swords buried.
1005 massacred.
Lamanites perish by Fire.
Slavery forbidden.
Anti-Nephi-Lehies removed to Jershon, called Ammonites.
Tremendous Battle.
Anti-Christ, Korihor.
Korihor struck dumb. [gel.
The Devil in the Form of an Angel.
Korihor trodden down.
Alma's Mission to Zoramites.
Rameumptom (holy Stand).
Alma on Hill Onidah.
Alma on Faith.
Prophecy of Zenos.
Prophecy of Zenock.
Amulek's Knowledge of Christ.
Charity recommended.
Same Spirit possess your Body.
Believers cast out.
Alma to Helaman.
Plates given to Helaman.
24 Plates and Directors.
Gazelem, a Stone (secret).
Liahona, or Compass.
Alma to Shiblon.
Alma to Corianton.
Unpardonable Sin.
Resurrection.
Restoration.
Justice in Punishment.
If, Adam, took, Tree, Life.
Mercy rob Justice.
Moroni's Stratagem.
Slaughter of Lamanites.
Moroni's Speech to Zerahemnah.
Prophecy of a Soldier.
Lamanites' Covenant of Peace.
Alma's Prophecy 400 years after Christ.

A A

the Gospel, and the Ahadis to the Koran—a necessary supplement of amplifications and explanations. It contains two parts.

The first, of sixty-four pages, is entitled " Lectures on Faith;" although published in the name of the Prophet Joseph, it was written, men say, by Sidney Rigdon.   The second, which, with the Appendix, concludes the book, is called Covenants and Commandments (*scil.*, of the Lord to his servants of the Church of Jesus Christ of Latter-Day Saints).

Of the Lectures, the first is upon " Faith itself—what it is." It treats the subject in the normal way, showing how much faith is unconsciously exercised by man in his every-day life, and making it " the principle by which Jehovah acts."   The second is concerning " the subject on which Faith rests," and contains an ancient chronology from Adam to Abraham, showing how the knowledge of God was preserved.   The third, on the attributes of God, enlarges upon the dogma that " correct ideas of the character of God are necessary in order to the exercise of faith in him for life and salvation."   The fourth shows the " connection there is between correct ideas of the attributes of God, and the exercise of faith in him unto eternal life."   The fifth, following those that treat of the being, character, perfection, and attributes of God, "speaks of the Godhead"—meaning the Father, Son, and Holy Ghost—and explains the peculiarities of the " personage of tabernacle."   The sixth " treats of the knowledge which persons must have, that the tenor of life which they preserve is according to the will of God, in order that they may be enabled to exercise faith in him unto life and salvation."   The seventh and last discusses the effects of faith.   Each lecture is followed by " questions and answers on the foregoing principles," after the fashion of school catechisms, and to asterisk'd sentences a note is appended: " Let the student commit the paragraph to memory."   There is one merit in the lectures: like Wesley's Hymns, they are written for the poor and simple; consequently, they are read where a higher tone of thought and style would remain unheeded.

The " Index in order of date to Part Second" will explain its contents.*   The Appendix contains twelve pages of revelation on

* Index in the order of date to Part Second :

marriage, government, and laws in general, and finally the "martyrdom of Joseph Smith" (no longer junior) "and his brother Hy-

rum." Respecting the connubial state, the Gentile and exoteric reads with astonishment the following sentence (no date, but between 1842 and 1843): "Inasmuch as this Church of Christ has been reproached with the crime of fornication and polygamy, we declare that we believe that one man should have one wife, and one woman but one husband, except in case of death, when either is at liberty to marry again."

The polygamic era directly followed the monogamic: it became the custom of the Church when, on their toil-conquered oasis in the Great Desert, the Mormons found themselves in comparative security. I give *in extenso* the sole command of heaven upon the subject of

CELESTIAL MARRIAGE:

A REVELATION ON THE PATRIARCHAL ORDER OF MATRIMONY, OR PLURALITY OF WIVES.

Given to Joseph Smith, the Seer, in Nauvoo, July 12th, 1843.

1. Verily, then saith the Lord unto you, my servant Joseph, that inasmuch as you have inquired of my hand to know and understand wherein I, the Lord, justified my servants Abraham, Isaac, and Jacob, as also Moses, David, and Solomon, my servants, as touching the principle and doctrine of their having many wives and concubines: Behold, and lo, I am the Lord thy God, and will answer thee as touching this matter: therefore prepare thy heart to receive and obey the instructions which I am about to give unto you; for all those who have this law revealed unto them must obey the same; for behold, I reveal unto you a new and an everlasting covenant; and if ye abide not that covenant, then are ye damned ; for no one can reject this covenant, and be permitted to enter into my glory; for all who will have a blessing at my hands shall abide the law which was appointed for that blessing, and the conditions thereof, as was instituted from before the foundations of the world; and as pertaining to the new and everlasting covenant, it was instituted for the fullness of my glory; and he that receiveth a fullness thereof must and shall abide the law, or he shall be damned, saith the Lord God.

2. And verily I say unto you, that the conditions of this law are these: All covenants, contracts, bonds, obligations, oaths, vows, performances, connections, associations, or expectations that are not made and entered into, and sealed by the Holy Spirit of promise, of him who is anointed, both as well for time and for all eternity, and that, too, most holy, by revelation and commandment, through the medium of mine anointed, whom I have appointed on the earth to hold this power (and I have appointed unto my servant Joseph to hold this power in the last days, and there is never but one on the earth at a time on whom this power and the keys of the priesthood are conferred), are of no efficacy, virtue, or force in and after the res-

urrection from the dead; for all contracts that are not made unto this end have an end when men are dead.

3. Behold, mine house is a house of order, saith the Lord God, and not a house of confusion. Will I accept of an offering, saith the Lord, that is not made in my name? Or will I receive at your hands that which I have not appointed? And will I appoint unto you, saith the Lord, except it be by law, even as I and my Father ordained unto you before the world was? I am the Lord thy God, and I give unto you this commandment, that no man shall come unto the Father but by me, or by my word which is my law, saith the Lord; and every thing that is in the world, whether it be ordained of men, by thrones, or principalities, or powers, or things of name, whatsoever they may be, that are not by me, or by my word, saith the Lord, shall be thrown down, and shall not remain after men are dead, neither in nor after the resurrection, saith the Lord your God; for whatsoever things remaineth are by me, and whatsoever things are not by me shall be shaken and destroyed.

4. Therefore, if a man marry him a wife in the world, and he marry her not by me, nor by my word, and he covenant with her so long as he is in the world, and she with him, their covenant and marriage is not of force when they are dead, and when they are out of the world; therefore they are not bound by any law when they are out of the world; therefore, when they are out of the world, they neither marry nor are given in marriage, but are appointed angels in heaven, which angels are ministering servants, to minister for those who are worthy of a far more and an exceeding and an eternal weight of glory; for these angels did not abide my law, therefore they can not be enlarged, but remain separately and singly, without exaltation, in their saved condition, to all eternity, and from henceforth are not gods, but are angels of God forever and ever.

5. And again, verily I say unto you, if a man marry a wife, and make a covenant with her for time and for all eternity, if that covenant is not by me or by my word, which is my law, and is not sealed by the Holy Spirit of promise, through him whom I have anointed and appointed unto this power, then it is not valid, neither of force, when they are out of the world, because they are not joined by me, saith the Lord, neither by my word; when they are out of the world, it can not be received there, because the angels and the gods are appointed there, by whom they can not pass: they can not, therefore, inherit my glory, for my house is a house of order, saith the Lord God.

6. And again, verily I say unto you, if a man marry a wife by my word, which is my law, and by the new and everlasting covenant, and it is sealed unto them by the Holy Spirit of promise, by him who is anointed, unto whom I have appointed this power, and the keys of this priesthood, and it shall be said unto them, ye shall come forth in the first resurrection; and if it be after the first resurrection, in the next resurrection; and shall inherit thrones, kingdoms, principalities, and powers, dominions, all heights and depths, then shall it be written in the Lamb's Book of Life that he shall commit no murder whereby to shed innocent blood; and if ye abide in my covenant, and commit

no murder whereby to shed innocent blood, it shall be done unto them in all things whatsoever my servant hath put upon them, in time and through all eternity, and shall be of full force when they are out of the world; and they shall pass by the angels, and the gods which are set there, to their exaltation and glory in all things, as hath been sealed upon their heads, which glory shall be a fullness and a continuation of the seeds forever and ever.

7. Then shall they be gods, because they have no end; therefore shall they be from everlasting to everlasting, because they continue; then shall they be above all, because all things are subject unto them. Then shall they be gods, because they have all power, and the angels are subject unto them.

8. Verily, verily I say unto you, except ye abide my law, ye can not attain to this glory; for straight is the gate and narrow the way that leadeth unto the exaltation and continuation of the lives, and few there be that find it, because ye receive me not in the world, neither do ye know me. But if ye receive me in the world, then shall ye know me, and shall receive your exaltation, that where I am ye shall be also. This is eternal life, to know the only wise and true God, and Jesus Christ whom he hath sent. I am he. Receive ye, therefore, my law. Broad is the gate and wide the way that leadeth to death, and many there are that go in thereat, because they receive me not, neither do they abide in my law.

9. Verily, verily I say unto you, if a man marry a wife according to my word, and they are sealed by the Holy Spirit of promise according to mine appointment, and he or she shall commit any sin or transgression of the new and everlasting covenant whatever, and all manner of blasphemies, and if they commit no murder wherein they shed innocent blood, yet they shall come forth in the first resurrection, and enter into their exaltation, but they shall be destroyed in the flesh, and shall be delivered unto the buffetings of Satan unto the day of redemption, saith the Lord God.

10. The blasphemy against the Holy Ghost, which shall not be forgiven in the world nor out of the world, is in that ye commit murder wherein ye shed innocent blood, and assent unto my death after ye have received my new and everlasting covenant, saith the Lord God; and he that abideth not this law can in nowise enter into my glory, but shall be damned, saith the Lord.

11. I am the Lord thy God, and will give unto thee the law of my holy priesthood, as was ordained by me, and my Father before the world was. Abraham received all things, whatsoever he received, by revelation and commandment, by my word, saith the Lord, and hath entered into his exaltation, and sitteth upon his throne.

12. Abraham received promises concerning his seed and of the fruit of his loins—from whose loins ye are, viz., my servant Joseph—which were to continue so long as they were in the world; and as touching Abraham and his seed out of the world, they should continue; both in the world and out of the world should they continue as innumerable as the stars; or, if ye were to count the sand upon the sea-shore, ye could not number them. This promise is yours also, because ye are of Abraham, and the promise was made unto Abraham; and by

this law are the continuation of the works of my Father, wherein he glorifieth himself. Go ye, therefore, and do the works of Abraham; enter ye into my law, and ye shall be saved. But if ye enter not into my law ye can not receive the promises of my Father which he made unto Abraham.

13. God commanded Abraham, and Sarah gave Hagar to Abraham to wife. And why did she do it? Because this was the law, and from Hagar sprang many people. This, therefore, was fulfilling, among other things, the promises. Was Abraham, therefore, under condemnation? Verily, I say unto you, *Nay ;* for I, the Lord, commanded it. Abraham was commanded to offer his son Isaac; nevertheless, it was written, Thou shalt not kill. Abraham, however, did not refuse, and it was accounted unto him for righteousness.

14. Abraham received concubines, and they bare him children, and it was accounted unto him for righteousness, because they were given unto him for righteousness, because they were given unto him, and he abode in my law; as Isaac also, and Jacob did none other things than that which they were commanded, and because they did none other things than that which they were commanded, they have entered into their exaltation, according to the promises, and sit upon thrones; and are not angels, but are gods. David also received many wives and concubines, as also Solomon, and Moses my servant; and also many others of my servants, from the beginning of creation until this time; and in nothing did they sin save in those things which they received not of me.

15. David's wives and concubines were given unto him, of me, by the hand of Nathan, my servant, and others of the prophets who had the keys of this power; and in none of these things did he sin against me, save in the case of Uriah and his wife; and therefore he hath fallen from his exaltation, and received his portion; and he shall not inherit them out of the world; for I gave them unto another, saith the Lord.

16. I am the Lord thy God, and I gave unto thee, my servant Joseph, an appointment, and to restore all things; ask what ye will, and it shall be given unto you, according to my word; and as ye have asked concerning adultery, verily, verily I say unto you, if a man receiveth a wife in the new and everlasting covenant, and if she be with another man, and I have not appointed unto her by the holy anointing, she hath committed adultery, and shall be destroyed. If she be not in the new and everlasting covenant, and she be with another man, she has committed adultery; and if her husband be with another woman, and he was under a vow, he hath broken his vow, and hath committed adultery; and if she hath not committed adultery, but is innocent, and hath not broken her vow, and she knoweth it, and I reveal it unto you, my servant Joseph, then shall you have power, by the power of my holy priesthood, to take her and give her unto him that hath not committed adultery, but hath been faithful, for he shall be made ruler over many; for I have conferred upon you the keys and power of the priesthood, wherein I restore all things, and make known unto you all things in due time.

17. And verily, verily I say unto you, that whatsoever you seal on

earth shall be sealed in heaven; and whatsoever you bind on earth, in my name and by my word, saith the Lord, it shall be eternally bound in the heavens; and whosesoever sins you remit on earth, shall be remitted eternally in the heavens; and whosesoever sins ye retain on earth, shall be retained in heaven.

18. And again, verily I say, whomsoever you bless I will bless, and whomsoever you curse I will curse, saith the Lord; for I, the Lord, am thy God.

19. And again, verily I say unto you, my servant Joseph, that whatsoever you give on earth, and to whomsoever you give any one on earth, by my word, and according to my law, it shall be visited with blessings, and not cursings, and with my power, saith the Lord, and shall be without condemnation on earth and in heaven; for I am the Lord thy God, and will be with thee even unto the end of the world, and through all eternity; for verily I seal upon you your exaltation, and prepare a throne for you in the kingdom of my Father with Abraham your father. Behold, I have seen your sacrifices, and will forgive all your sins; I have seen your sacrifices in obedience to that which I have told you: go, therefore, and I make a way for your escape, as I accepted the offering of Abraham of his son Isaac.

20. Verily I say unto you, a commandment I give unto mine handmaid, Emma Smith, your wife, whom I have given unto you, that she stay herself, and partake not of that which I commanded you to offer unto her; for I did it, saith the Lord, to prove you all, as I did Abraham, and that I might require an offering at your hand by covenant and sacrifice; and let mine handmaid, Emma Smith, receive all those that have been given unto my servant Joseph, and who are virtuous and pure before me; and those who are not pure, and have said they are pure, shall be destroyed, saith the Lord God; for I am the Lord thy God, and ye shall obey my voice: and I give unto my servant Joseph that he shall be made ruler over many things, for he hath been faithful over a few things, and from henceforth I will strengthen him.

21. And I command mine handmaid, Emma Smith, to abide and cleave unto my servant Joseph, and to none else. But if she will not abide this commandment, she shall be destroyed, saith the Lord; for I am the Lord thy God, and will destroy her if she abide not in my law; but if she will not abide this commandment, then shall my servant Joseph do all things for her, even as he hath said; and I will bless him, and multiply him, and give unto him an hundred-fold in this world, of fathers and mothers, brothers and sisters, houses and lands, wives and children, and crowns of eternal lives in the eternal worlds. And again, verily I say, let mine handmaid forgive my servant Joseph his trespasses, and then shall she be forgiven her trespasses wherein she has trespassed against me; and I, the Lord thy God, will bless her and multiply her, and make her heart to rejoice.

22. And again I say, let not my servant Joseph put his property out of his hands, lest an enemy come and destroy him, for Satan seeketh to destroy; for I am the Lord thy God, and he is my servant; and behold, and lo, I am with him, as I was with Abraham thy father, even unto his exaltation and glory.

23. Now, as touching the law of the priesthood, there are many things pertaining thereunto. Verily, if a man be called of my Father, as was Aaron, by mine own voice, and by the voice of him that sent me, and I have endowed him with the keys of the power of this priesthood, if he do any thing in my name, and according to my law, and by my word, he will not commit sin, and I will justify him. Let no one, therefore, set on my servant Joseph; for I will justify him; for he shall do the sacrifice which I require at his hands, for his transgressions, saith the Lord your God.

24. And again, as pertaining to the law of the priesthood: If any man espouse a virgin, and desire to espouse another, and the first give her consent; and if he espouse the second, and they are virgins, and have vowed to no other man, then is he justified; he can not commit adultery, for they are given unto him; for he can not commit adultery with that that belongeth unto them, and to none else: and if he have ten virgins given unto him by this law, he can not commit adultery, for they belong to him, and they are given unto him; therefore is he justified. But if one, or either of the ten virgins, after she is espoused, shall be with another man, she has committed adultery, and shall be destroyed; for they are given unto him to multiply and replenish the earth, according to my commandment, and to fulfill the promise which was given by my Father before the foundation of the world, and for their exaltation in the eternal worlds, that they may bear the souls of men; for herein is the work of my Father continued, that he may be glorified.

25. And again, verily, verily I say unto you, if any man have a wife who holds the keys of this power, and he teaches unto her the law of my priesthood as pertaining to these things, then shall she believe, and administer unto him, or she shall be destroyed, saith the Lord your God; for I will destroy her; for I will magnify my name upon all those who receive and abide in my law. Therefore it shall be lawful in me, if she receive not this law, for him to receive all things whatsoever I, the Lord his God, will give unto him, because she did not believe and administer unto him, according to my word; and she then becomes the transgressor, and he is exempt from the law of Sarah, who administered unto Abraham according to the law, when I commanded Abraham to take Hagar to wife. And now, as pertaining to this law: Verily, verily I say unto you, I will reveal more unto you hereafter; therefore let this suffice for the present. Behold, I am Alpha and Omega. Amen.

Following the revelation is this explanation:

PLURALITY OF WIVES is a doctrine very popular among most of mankind at the present day. It is practiced by the most powerful nations of Asia and Africa, and by numerous nations inhabiting the islands of the sea, and by the aboriginal nations of the great western hemisphere. The one-wife system is confined principally to a few small nations inhabiting Europe, and to those who are of European origin inhabiting America. It is estimated by the most able historians of our day that about four fifths of the population of the globe believe and practice, according to their respective laws, the doctrine of a plurality of wives. If the popularity of a doctrine is in proportion to the numbers who believe in it, then it follows that the *plurality system* is four times more popular among the inhabitants of the earth than the *one-wife system.*

Those nations who practice the plurality doctrine consider it as virtuous and as right for one man to have many wives as to have one only. Therefore they have enacted laws not only giving this right to their citizens, but also protecting them in it, and punishing all those who infringe upon the chastity of the marriage covenant by committing adultery with any one of the wives of his neighbor. Those nations do not consider it possible for a man to commit adultery with any one of those women to whom he has been legally married according to their laws. The posterity raised up unto the husband through each of his wives are all considered to be legitimate, and provisions are made in their laws for those children the same as if they were the children of one wife. Adulteries, fornications, and all unvirtuous conduct between the sexes are severely punished by them. Indeed, plurality among them is considered not only virtuous and right, but a great check or preventive against adulteries and unlawful connections, which are among the greatest evils with which nations are cursed, producing a vast amount of suffering and misery, devastation and death; undermining the very foundations of happiness, and destroying the frame-work of society and the peace of the domestic circle.

Some of the nations of Europe who believe in the one-wife system have actually forbidden a plurality of wives by their laws, and the consequences are that the whole country among them is overrun with the most abominable practices; adulteries and unlawful connections prevail through all their villages, towns, cities, and country places to a most fearful extent. And among some of these nations these sinks of wickedness, wretchedness, and misery are licensed by law, while their piety would be wonderfully shocked to authorize by law the plurality system, as adopted by many neighboring nations.

The Constitution and laws of the United States, being founded upon the principles of freedom, do not interfere with marriage relations, but leave the nation free to believe in and practice the doctrine of a plurality of wives, or to confine themselves to the one-wife system, just as they choose. This is as it should be: it leaves the conscience of man untrammeled, and, so long as he injures no person, and does not infringe upon the rights of others, he is free by the Constitution to marry one wife, or many, or none at all, and becomes accountable to God for the righteousness or unrighteousness of his domestic relations.

The Constitution leaves the several States and Territories to enact such laws as they see proper in regard to marriages, provided that they do not infringe upon the rights of conscience and the liberties guaranteed in that sacred document. Therefore, if any State or Territory feels disposed to enact laws guaranteeing to each of its citizens the right to marry many wives, such laws would be perfectly constitutional; hence the several States and Territories practice the one-wife system out of choice, and not because they are under any obligations so to do by the national Constitution. Indeed, we doubt very much whether any State or Territory has the constitutional right to make laws prohibiting the plurality doctrine in cases where it is practiced by religious societies as a matter of conscience or as a doctrine of their religious faith. The first Article of the Amendments to the Constitution says expressly that " Congress shall make no law respecting an establishment of religion, or *prohibiting the free exercise thereof.*" Now, if even Congress itself has no power to pass a law " prohibiting the free exercise of religion," much less has any State or Territory power to pass such an act.

The doctrine of a plurality of wives was believed and practiced by Abraham, the father of the faithful; and we find that, while in this practice, the angels of God frequently ministered to him, and at one time dined with him; and God manifested himself to him, and entered into familiar conversation with him. Neither God nor his angels reproved Abraham for being a polygamist, but, on the contrary, the Almighty greatly blessed him, and made promises unto him, concerning both Isaac and Ishmael, clearly showing that Abraham practiced what is called polygamy under the sanction of the Almighty. Now if the father of the faithful was thus blessed, certainly it should not be considered irreligious for the faithful, who are called his children, to walk in the steps of their father Abraham. Indeed, if the Lord himself, through his holy prophets, should give more wives unto his servants, as he gave them unto the prophet David, it would be a great sin for them to refuse that which he gives. In such a case, it would become a matter of conscience with them, and a part of their religion, and they would be bound to exercise their faith in this doctrine, and practice it, or be condemned; therefore Congress would have no power to prohibit the free exercise of this part of their religion, neither would the States or Territories have power constitutionally to pass a law " prohibiting the free exercise thereof." Now a certain religious society, called Shakers, believe it to be wrong for them to marry even one wife; it certainly would be unconstitutional for either the Congress or the States to pass a law compelling all people to marry at a certain age, because it would infringe upon the rights of conscience among the Shakers, and they would be prohibited the free exercise of their religion.

From the foregoing revelation, given through Joseph the Seer, it will be seen that God has actually commanded some of his servants to take more wives, and has pointed out certain duties in regard to the marriage ceremony, showing that they must be married for time and for all eternity, and showing the advantages to be derived in a future state by this eternal union; and showing still farther that, if they refused to obey this command, after having the law revealed to them, they should be damned. This revelation, then, makes it a matter of conscience among all the Latter-Day Saints; and they embrace it as a part and portion of their religion, and verily believe that they can not be saved and reject it. Has Congress power, then, to pass laws " prohibiting" the Church of Jesus Christ of Latter-Day Saints " *the free exercise*" of this article of their religion? Have any of the States or Territories a constitutional right to pass laws " prohibiting the free exercise of the religion" which the Church of the Saints conscientiously and sincerely believe to be essential to their salvation? No, they have no such right.

The Latter-Day Saints have the most implicit confidence in all the revelations given through Joseph the Prophet, and they would much sooner lay down their lives and suffer martyrdom than to deny the least revelation that was ever given to him. In one of the revelations through him, we read that God raised up wise men and inspired them to write the Constitution of our country, that the freedom of the people might be maintained, according to the free agency which he had given to them; that every man might be accountable to God and not to man, so far as religious doctrines and conscience are concerned. And the more we examine that sacred instrument, framed by the wisdom of our illustrious fathers, the more we are compelled to believe that an invisible power controlled, dictated, and guided them in laying the foundation of liberty and freedom upon this great western hemisphere. To this land the Mohammedan—the Hindoo —the Chinese can emigrate, and each bring with him his score of wives and his hundred children, and the glorious Constitution of our country will not interfere with his domestic relations. Under the broad banner of the Constitution, he is protected in all his family associations; none have a right to tear any of his wives or his children from him. So, likewise, under the broad folds of the Constitution, the Legislative Assembly of the Territory of Utah have the right to pass laws regulating their matrimonial relations, and protecting each of their citizens in the right of marrying one or many wives, as the case may be. If Congress should repeal those laws, they could not do so on the ground of their being unconstitutional. And even if Congress should repeal them, there still would be no law in Utah prohibiting the free exercise of that religious right; neither do the citizens of Utah feel disposed to pass such an unconstitutional act which would infringe upon the most sacred rights of conscience.

Tradition and custom have great influence over nations. Long-established customs, whether right or wrong, become sacred in the estimation of mankind. Those nations who have been accustomed from time immemorial to the practice of what is called polygamy would consider a law abolishing it as the very height of injustice and oppression; the very idea of being limited to the one-wife system would be considered not only oppressive and unjust, but absolutely absurd and ridiculous; it would be considered an innovation upon the long-established usages, customs, and laws of numerous and powerful nations; an innovation of the most dangerous character, calculated to destroy the most sacred rights and privileges of family associations—to upset the very foundations of individual rights, rendered dear and sacred by being handed down to them from the most remote ages of antiquity.

On the other hand, the European nations who have been for centuries restricted by law to the one-wife theory would consider it a shocking innovation upon the customs of their fathers to abolish their restrictive laws, and to give freedom and liberty according to the plurality system. It is custom, then, in a great degree, that forms the conscience of nations and individuals in regard to the marriage relationships. Custom causes four fifths of the population of the globe to decide that polygamy, as it is called, is a good, and not an evil practice; custom causes the balance, or the remaining fifth, to decide in opposition to the great majority.

Those individuals who have strength of mind sufficient to divest themselves entirely from the influence of custom, and examine the doctrine of a plurality of wives under the light of reason and revelation, will be forced to the conclusion that it is a doctrine of divine origin; that it was embraced and practiced under the divine sanction by the most righteous men who ever lived on the earth: holy prophets and patriarchs, who were inspired by the Holy Ghost—who were enrapt in the visions of the Almighty—who conversed with holy angels—who saw God face to face, and talked with him as a man talks with his friend—were " polygamists," that is, they had many wives—raised up many children by them—and were never reproved by the Holy Ghost, nor by angels, nor by the Almighty, for believing in and practicing such a doctrine; on the contrary, each one of these "polygamists" received by revelation promises and blessings for himself, for his wives, and for his numerous children born unto him by his numerous wives. Moreover, the Lord himself gave revelation to different wives belonging to the same man, revealing to them the great blessings which should rest upon their posterity; angels also were sent to comfort and bless them; and in no instance do we find them reproved for having joined themselves in marriage to a " polygamist." Indeed, the Lord himself gave laws not to prohibit " polygamy," but showing his will in relation to the children raised up by the different wives of the same man; and, furthermore, the Lord himself actually officiated in giving David all the wives of Saul; this occurred, too, when David already had several wives which he had previously taken: therefore, as the Lord did actually give into David's own bosom all the wives of Saul, he must not only have sanctioned " polygamy," but established and instituted it upon a sure foundation, by giving the wives himself, the same as he gave Eve to Adam. Therefore those who are completely divested from the influence of national customs, and who judge concerning this matter by the Word of God, are compelled to believe that the plurality of wives was once sanctioned for many ages by the Almighty; and by a still farther research of the divine oracles they find no intimations that this divine institution was ever repealed. It was an institution, not originated under the law of Moses, but of a far more ancient date; and instead of being abolished by that law, it was sanctioned and perpetuated; and when Christ came to fulfill that law, and to do away by the introduction of a better covenant, he did not abolish the plurality system: not being originated under that law, it was not made null and void when that law was done away. Indeed, there were many things in connection with the law that were not abolished when the law was fulfilled; as, for instance, the Ten Commandments, which the people under the Gospel covenant were still obliged to obey; and until we can find some law of God abolishing and prohibiting a plurality of wives, we are compelled to believe it a divine institution; and we are furthermore compelled to believe, that if this institution be entered into now, under the same principles which governed the holy prophets and patriarchs, that God will approbate it now as much as he did then; and that the persons who do thus practice it conscientiously and sincerely are just as honorable in the sight of God as those who have but one wife. And that which is honorable before God should be honorable before men; and no one should be despised when he acts in all good conscience upon any principle of doctrine; neither should there be laws in any of these States or Territories to compel any individual to act in violation to the dictates of his own conscience; but every one should be left in all matters of religion to his own choice, and thus become accountable to God, and not to his fellow-man.

If the people of this country have generally formed different conclusions from us upon this subject, and if they have embraced religions which are more congenial to their minds than the religion of the Saints, we say to them that they are welcome to their own religious views; the laws should not interfere with the exercise of their religious rights. If we can not convince you by reason nor by the Word of God that your religion is wrong, we will not persecute you, but will sustain you in the privileges guaranteed in the great Charter of American Liberty: we ask from you the same generosity—protect us in the exercise of our religious rights—convince us of our errors of doctrine, if we have any, by reason, by logical arguments, or by the Word of God, and we will be ever grateful for the information, and you will ever have the pleasing reflection that you have been the instruments in the hands of God of redeeming your fellow-beings from the darkness which you may see enveloping their minds. Come, then, let us reason together, and try to discover the true light upon all subjects connected with our temporal or eternal happiness; and if we disagree in our judgments, let us impute it to the weakness and imperfections of our fallen natures, and let us pity each other, and endeavor with patience and meekness to reclaim from error, and save the immortal soul from an endless death.

Mormonism, it will be observed, claims at once to be, like Christianity, a progressive faith, with that development of spiritualism which the "Tracts for the Times" exemplified, and, like El Islam, to be a restoration by revelation of the pure and primeval religion of the world. Convinced that plurality was unforbidden by the founders of the former faiths, the Mormons, as well as the followers of the Arabian Prophet, have obeyed the command of their God to restore it, and that, too, although the Anglo-Scandinavian race every where agrees, after the fashion of pagan and monogamic Rome, to make it a common-law crime. Politically considered, the Mormons deem it necessary to their existence as a people. Contrary to the scientific modern economist, from Mr. Malthus to Mr. Mill, they hold population, not wealth, learning, civilization, nor virtue, to be the strength of a nation; they believe that numbers decide the rise and fall of empires, and that, as Nature works the extinction of her doomed races by infecundity, and as the decline of a people's destiny is first detected in the diminution of its census, so they look upon the celestial promises of prolificity made to the patriarchs of old as the highest temporal blessing. They admit in the lawgiver only a right to legislate for the good of those who are to obey his laws, not to gratify his "whimsy whamsies," and that the liberty which man claims by the dignity of his nature permits him to choose the tie, whether polyandric, monogamic, or polygamic, that connects him with the opposite sex. Mr. Parley P. Pratt ("Marriage and Morals in Utah," p. 3) is explicit upon this subject:

"If we find laws, statutes, covenants, and precedents emanating from God; sworn to by himself to be everlasting; as a blessing to all nations—if we find these have to do with exceeding multiplicity of race, and with family and national organization and increase—if such institutions are older than Moses, and are found perpetuated and unimpaired by Moses and the prophets, Jesus and the apostles, then it will appear evident that no merely human legislation or authority, whether proceeding from emperor, king, or people, has a right to change, alter, or pervert them."

The third epoch is that of Materialism. In this the Mormons are preceded, to quote but a few schools, by the classic Academics—by the Jews, who believed in a material and personal Demiurgus, and by many fathers of the Christian Church, who held the soul of man, while immortal, to be material. Matter with them, as with Newton, is an aggregate of "solid, massy, hard, impenetrable, and movable particles." Respecting the intelligence of its units and molecules—the test of true materialism—they are somewhat hazy; they deride the peripatetic dogma of perception by species or phantasms, and at the same time ignore the doctrine of Hobbes, Spinoza, Priestley, and others, who recognize no separate existence for the mind or spirit* except as a union of atoms or particles, which, unorganized, have neither feeling nor thought. They define matter as a something that exists in and occupies space between any two instants, and is susceptible of division, and of being removed from one portion of space to another. Unlike other metaphysicians, who confess ignorance as to the substratum of mind and matter, they boast acquaintance with the essence of all substances, solidity, which with them is not a mere property. Although the ultimate atoms of matter can not come under the cognizance of the senses, they are none the less assured of their solidity, viz., that they fill a certain amount of space, and

---

* "If man," says Dr. Priestley, "be a material being, and the power of thinking the result of a certain organization of the brain, does it not follow that all his functions must be regulated by the laws of mechanism, and that, of consequence, all his actions proceed from an irresistible necessity?" It is the glory of the present age, the highest result of our nineteenth century physiological and statistic studies, brought to bear by a master-mind of the age upon the History of Civilization—to establish the fact that mankind progresses by investigating the laws of phenomena; in fact, to prove, not to conjecture, that such mechanism really exists. I need hardly name Mr. Buckle.

are unable ever to fill a greater or a lesser—in fact, to believe otherwise would be impossible. They hold to different kinds of matter, for instance, the fleshly body and the spiritual body, which differ in quality as iron and oxygen. Mind and spirit, therefore, are real, objective, positive substances, which, like the astral spirit of the old alchymists, exists in close connection with the component parts of the porous, material body. Immaterialism is, with them, simply absurd; it is a belief which requires a man to put faith in a negation of time, space, and matter; in fact, in the zero of existence, in an entity whose ens admits no proof, and which can be described only by negative conditions and qualities, by saying what it is not. They contend that the materiality of spirit once taken away would negative its existence; that an "immaterial being" is a contradiction in terms; and that immateriality is another name for nothing;' therefore, that the spirituality of spirit "is an unphilosophical, unscriptural, and atheistical doctrine." The theses supported by Mr. Orson Pratt, the apostle of materialism, are the following:

I. That Immaterialism is irrational opposed to true philosophy.

II. That an Immaterial substance (i. e., a something existing which is not matter and is distinct from matter, which is not dependent upon matter for its existence, which possesses no properties nor qualities in common with matter, and which possesses properties and qualities all entirely different from those of matter) can not exist.

III. That a real material unchangeable spirit, possessing parts and extension, inhabits the body.

Immaterialists who believe in "an inexplicable, incomprehensible, imaginary something without extension or parts, as taught in the first of the Thirty-nine Articles," are therefore the worshipers of an immortal Nihil—of a Nothing clothed with almighty powers.

It is abundantly evident that the partition between the spiritualist and the materialist is mainly philological, a dispute of words, a variation of terms, spirit and matter differing about as much as azote and nitrogen. The deductions, however, from the Mormon's premises lead him, as the following extracts prove, far.*

"The Godhead consists of the Father, the Son, and the Holy Spirit. The Father is a material being. The substance of which he is composed is wholly material. It is a substance widely different in some respects from the various substances with which we are more immediately acquainted. In other respects, it is precisely like all other materials. The substance of his person occupies space the same as other matter. It has solidity, length, breadth, and thickness, like other matter. The elementary mate-

---

* From Mr. Apostle Orson Pratt's "Absurdities of Immaterialism," and his treatise on the "Kingdom of God." It is hardly possible not to believe that the author has borrowed most of his theories from Mr. Carlyle's "Republican."

B B

rials of his body are not susceptible of occupying at the same time the same identical space with other matter. The substance of his person, like other matter, can not be in two places at the same instant. It requires *time* for him to transport himself from place to place. It matters not how great the velocity of his movement, *time* is an essential ingredient to all motion, whether rapid or slow. It differs from other matter in the superiority of its powers, being intelligent, all-wise, and possessing the property of self-motion to a far greater extent than the coarser materials of nature. 'God is a spirit;' but that does not make him an immaterial being, a being that has no properties in common with matter." . . . .

" All the foregoing statements in relation to the person of the Father are equally applicable to the person of the Son.

" The Holy Spirit, being one part of the Godhead, is also a material substance, of the same nature and properties in many respects as the Spirits of the Father and Son. It exists in vast, immeasurable quantities, in connection with all material worlds. This is called God in the Scriptures, as well as the Father and Son. God the Father and God the Son can not be every where present; indeed, they can not be even in two places at the same instant; but God the Holy Spirit is omnipresent: it extends through all space, intermingling with all other matter, yet no one atom of the Holy Spirit can be in two places at the same instant, which in all cases is an absolute impossibility. It must exist in inexhaustible quantities, which is the only possible way for any substance to be omnipresent. All the innumerable phenomena of universal nature are produced in their origin by the actual presence of this intelligent, all-wise, and all-powerful material substance called the Holy Spirit. It is the most active matter in the universe, producing all its operations according to fixed and definite laws enacted by itself, in conjunction with the Father and the Son. What are called the laws of nature are nothing more nor less than the fixed method by which this spiritual matter operates. Each atom of the Holy Spirit is intelligent, and, like other matter, has solidity, form, and size, and occupies space. Two atoms of this Spirit can not occupy the same space at the same time, neither can one atom, as before stated, occupy two separate spaces at the same time. In all these respects it does not differ in the least from all other matter. Its distinguishing characteristics from other matter are its almighty powers and infinite wisdom, and many other glorious attributes which other materials do not possess. If several of the atoms of this Spirit should exist united together in the form of a person, then this person of the Holy Spirit would be subject to the same necessity" (N.B., this out-anagkes anagke) " as the other two persons of the Godhead—that is, it could not be every where present. No finite number of atoms can be omnipresent. An infinite number of atoms is requisite to be *every where* in infinite space. Two persons receiving the gift of the Holy Spirit do not receive at the same time the same identical particles, though they each receive a substance exactly similar in kind. It would be as impossible for them to receive the same identical atoms at the same instant as it would be for two men at the same time to drink the same identical pint of water."

I will offer another instance of the danger of meddling with such edged tools as mind and matter—concerning which mankind knows nothing beyond certain properties—in the following answer addressed by Mr. Pratt to the many who have been "traditionated in the absurd doctrines of immaterialism." "The resemblance between man and God has reference, as we have already observed, to the shape or figure: other qualities may or may not resemble each other. Man has legs, so has God, as is evident from his appearance to Abraham. Man walks with his legs; so does God sometimes, as is evident from his going with Abraham toward Sodom. God can not only walk, but he can move up or down through the air without using his legs as in the process of walking (Gen., xvii., 22, and xi., 5, and xxxv., 13)—'a man wrestled with Jacob until the breaking of day;' after which Jacob says, 'I have seen God face to face, and my life is preserved' (Gen., xxxii., 24–30). That this person had legs is evident from his wrestling with Jacob. His image and likeness was so much like man's, that Jacob at first supposed him to be a man. God, though in the figure of a man, has many powers that man has not got. He can go upward through the air. He can waft himself from world to world by his own self-moving powers. These are powers not possessed by man, only through faith, as in the instances of Enoch and Elijah. Therefore, though in the figure of a man, he has powers far superior to man."

This part of the subject may profitably be concluded by quoting the venerable adage, " *Qui nescit ignorare nescit sciri.*"

I now offer to the reader a few remarks upon the fourteen articles of the Mormon doxology,* leaving him to settle whether it be a kakodoxy or a kakistodoxy.

I. " WE BELIEVE IN GOD, THE ETERNAL FATHER, AND HIS SON JESUS CHRIST, AND IN THE HOLY GHOST."—Of the thousand sects and systems that have used this venerable Kalmah or formula of Christian faith, none have interpreted it more peculiarly than the Mormons.

The First Person is a perfected man, once a dweller upon earth: advancing in intelligence and power, he became such that in comparison with man he may be called the Infinite. Mr. Joseph Smith, in his last sermon preached at Nauvoo, thus develops his remarkable anthropomorphosis: " First, God himself, who sits enthroned

* From an article published in the " Frontier Guardian," then edited by the Apostle Orson Hyde.

in yonder heavens, is a man like one of yourselves; that is the great secret. If the veil was rent to-day, and the great God who holds this world in its orbit, and upholds all things by his power, if you were to see him to-day, you would see him in all the person, image, and very form as a man; for Adam was created in the very fashion and image of God; Adam received instruction, walked, talked, and conversed with Him, as one man talks and communes with another."

The Second Person is the "Son Jesus Christ," the material offspring of the First by the Virgin Mary, who was duly married, after betrothal by the angel Gabriel, to the Eternal Father, on the plains of Palestine: the Holy Babe was the "tabernacle" prepared for and assumed by the Spirit Son. The Son is the Creator: when in the material spirit still, he took of the "unformed chaotic matter element which had an existence from the time God had, and in which dwells all the glory," and formed and peopled this planetary world, which he afterward redeemed. He is to be worshiped as Lord of all, heir of the Father in power, creation, and dominion. · "What did Jesus do?" "Why, I do the things that I saw my Father do when worlds came rolling into existence. I saw my Father work out his kingdom with fear and trembling, and I must do the same." ("Last Sermon," p. 61.)

The Paraclete has already been described: it differs from the other two Persons in being a merely spirit-material soul or existence without a "tabernacle." Thus the Mormons mingle with a Trinity a very distinct, though not a conflicting Duality.

The Mormon Godhead may be illustrated by a council composed of three men, possessing equal wisdom, knowledge, and truth, together with equal qualifications in every other respect: each would be a separate person or a substance distinct from the other two, and yet the three would compose but one body. This body consists of three, viz., Eloheim, Jehovah, and Michael, which is Adam. From the Christian apostles and the Apocalypse, the Mormons deduce the dogma of gods in an *ad infinitum* ascending series: man, however, must limit his obedience to the last heavenly Father and Son revealed by the Holy Spirit. And as God is perfect man, so is perfect man God: any individual, by faith and obedience, can, as the Brahminical faith asserts, rise to the position of a deity, until, attaining the power of forming a planet, peopling, redeeming it, and sitting there enthroned in everlasting power. The Mormons, like the Moslems, believe that—"things of earth, customs, and ceremonies, being patterned after things in the Spirit world and future abodes of the gods"—there are inferior glories and pleasures for "hewers of wood and drawers of water." In the eternal heavens there are three great mansions, the celestial of the sun, the celestial of the stars, and the terrestrial: the other state is called the Lake of Fire, or the Burning Caldron.

II. "WE BELIEVE THAT MEN WILL BE PUNISHED FOR THEIR OWN SINS, AND NOT FOR ADAM'S TRANSGRESSIONS."—Yet the Mormons hold the Son to be necessary to reconcile fallen man to the Father and the Holy Spirit, to sanctify and purify the affections of men, and also to dwell in them as a teacher of truth. "The spiritual substance of man was formed in the beginning after the same image as the spiritual substance of the persons of the Father and the Son. Previously to the fall, these spirits were all moral in their nature; by the fall the spirits of men lost their morality and virtue, but not their essence—that continued the same: by the new birth man regains his morality and virtue, while the essence remains the same; it now becomes a moral, virtuous image, whereas the same substance was before immoral. Paul (1 Cor., xv., 49), in speaking of the resurrection, says, 'As we have borne the image of the earthly, let us bear also the image of the heavenly!'" Unlike the more advanced faiths—El Islam and Unitarianism—the Mormons retain the doctrine of a "fall." It contrasts strangely with their dogma of man's perfectibility. They have not attempted to steer clear between the Scylla and Charybdis of predestination and free will.

III. "WE BELIEVE THAT THROUGH THE ATONEMENT OF CHRIST ALL MANKIND MAY BE SAVED BY OBEDIENCE TO THE LAWS AND ORDINANCES OF THE GOSPEL."—After Adam had fallen from his primal purity, a council was held in heaven to debate how man should be saved or redeemed from the state of evil. The elder brother Lucifer, son of the morning, the bright star in glory, and the leader of heavenly hosts, declared, when appealed to, that he would save man *in* his sins. But he who is emphatically called "the Son"—Christ—answered, I will save him *from* his sins. Lucifer, the "archangel ruined," rebelled, was cast out from the planetary abode of the Father, and became, under the name of Satan, the great ruler and "head devil" of evil spirits, and of the baser sort of imps and *succubi*. I can not say whether in their mysteries the Mormons represent Sathanas as the handsome man of El Islam, or the horned, tailed, and cloven-footed monster which monkish Europe fashioned probably after pagan Pan.

IV. "WE BELIEVE THESE ORDINANCES ARE, 1ST. FAITH IN THE LORD JESUS; 2D. REPENTANCE; 3D. BAPTISM BY IMMERSION FOR THE REMISSION OF SINS; 4TH. LAYING ON OF HANDS BY THE GIFT OF THE HOLY SPIRIT; 5TH. THE LORD'S SUPPER." —Faith is not only the "evidence of things that appear not, the substance of things to be hoped for," the first principle of action, and an exercise of the will in intelligent beings toward accomplishing holy works and purposes, with a view to celestial glory; it is also the source of power both on earth and in heaven. We find that by faith God created the world (Heb., xi., 3); and, "take this principle or attribute away from the Deity, he would cease to exist." ("Lectures on Faith," sec. 1.) "Faith, then, is the first great governing principle which has power, dominion, and authority over all things." (Ibid.) Of the second ordinance, it was revealed, "Say nothing but repentance unto this generation" ("Covenants and Commandments," sec. 37); a very comprehensive and valuable rule to those under whom their brethren must sit. As regards the third, the child succeeds its parent in moral responsibility at eight years of age, when it must be baptized "in the name of the Father, and of the Son, and of the Holy Ghost, Amen," into the Church. Infant baptism is regarded as a Bida'at or innovation—a sin. Baptism by immersion—any other method being considered a vain ceremony—remits our peccata, but it must be repeated after each mortal act. ("Covenants and Commandments," sec. 2, par. 21.) Vicarious baptism for the dead is founded upon St. Paul's saying concerning the fathers, that they can not without us be made perfect, and "otherwise what shall they do that are baptized for the dead, if the dead rise not again at all? Why are they then baptized for them?" (1 Cor., xv., 29.) Immersion in water is the symbol of death, emersion of the resurrection, and the baptismal font is a simile of the grave; but baptism for the dead is acceptable only in the Temple. ("Covenants and Commandments," sec. 103.) There being a probationary state while the earth endures in the Spirit world—the purgatorial doctrine of Virgil and others—the dead can by proxy "fulfill all righteousness;" and the Saints are enjoined that "the greatest responsibility that God has laid upon us is to look after our dead;" so Mr. Joseph Smith, in his "Last Sermon," says, "Every man who has got a friend in the eternal world can save him, unless he has committed the unpardonable sin; so you can see how you can be a Savior." A man baptized for deceased relations traces back the line to one that held the priesthood among his progenitors, who, being a saint, will take the place of sponsor, and relieve him of farther responsibility. All thus admitted to salvation will be added at the resurrection to the household of the baptized person, who will reign as a patriarch forever, his rank and power among kingly spirits being proportioned to his wives and his children—adopted or begotten—and his baptizées. The fourth ordinance, or laying on of hands by the water's side, is a perfection of the regeneration begun in baptism, and whereby the recipient is promoted to the Melchisedek priesthood; the order was revealed, or rather renewed, in 1831. ("Covenants and Commandments," sec. 66.) The fifth ordinance, touching the Eucharist, is instituted "in remembrance of the Lord Jesus:" the elder or priest administers it kneeling with the Church, praying and blessing first the bread and then the wine. ("Covenants and Commandments," sec. 2.) The second element was changed by a direct revelation (Sept., 1830), saying, "You shall not purchase wine nor strong drink of your enemies," since which time water has been substituted. Mormons, young and old, equally take the sacrament every Sabbath.

V. "WE BELIEVE THAT MAN MUST BE CALLED OF GOD BY INSPIRATION, AND BY LAYING ON OF HANDS FROM THOSE WHO ARE DULY COMMISSIONED TO PREACH THE GOSPEL AND ADMINISTER IN THE ORDINANCES THEREOF."—The Mormons hold to a regular apostolic succession. "Every elder" (which includes the apostles), "priest, teacher, or deacon, is to be ordained according to the gifts and callings of God unto him; and he is to be ordained by the power of the Holy Ghost, which is the one who ordains him."

VI. "WE BELIEVE IN THE SAME ORGANIZATION THAT EXISTED IN THE PRIMITIVE CHURCH, VIZ., APOSTLES, PROPHETS, PASTORS, EVANGELISTS, ETC."—The proper signification of these words will be explained when treating of the Mormon hierarchy.

VI. "WE BELIEVE IN THE POWERS AND GIFTS OF THE EVERLASTING GOSPEL, VIZ., THE GIFT OF FAITH, DISCERNING OF SPIRITS, PROPHECY, REVELATIONS, VISIONS, HEALING, TONGUES, AND THE INTERPRETATION OF TONGUES, WISDOM, CHARITY, BROTHERLY LOVE, ETC."—The everlasting Gospel means the universal order and arrangement of things springing from the "two self-existing principles of intelligence and element, or matter," and forming the law under which the primordial gods came into being. According to Mr. Joseph Smith, "God himself could not create himself," and "Intelligence exists upon a self-existent principle: it is a spirit from age to age, and there is no creation about it." In the far eternity two of the elementary material æons met, compared intelligence, and calling in a third to council, united in what became the first power, superior because prior to all others, and ever-enduring by the union of other æons. Under this union arose a "law governing itself and all things"—the everlasting Gospel. The seer has not left on record the manner in which the head god originated: the other gods, however, sprung from him as children. Heaven has not only kings, but queens—the Sakti of Hindooism, and the various Ario-pagan faiths—who are the mothers of gods, of men's souls, and of all spiritual existences. St. John saw a portion of the everlasting Gospel in the "little book" in the hand of the angel "coming down from heaven" to proclaim again on earth the Church of Christ, a type of Moroni, who taught the fullness of knowledge to Joseph the Seer, that the gladder tidings might be preached to men with the "signs following" which were promised to the primitive apostles.

As regards the discerning of spirits, the human soul is not visible to mortal eyes without a miracle, nor is it ponderable: it passes through the body as the electric fluid through the earth. Yet, in reality, it is more substantial than the body, for it can not be changed nor destroyed; it "coexisted equal with God," and had no beginning, which would argue the possibility of an end, and "it is immortal as God himself." It is uncreate: "God never did have power to create the spirit of man at all—the very idea lessens man in my estimation—I know better." ("Last Sermon," p. 62.) Spiritual existences have a choice of two paths. Either they must remain cribbed, cabined, and confined in their own ethereal order and proper sphere, to be called and sent as angels, heralds, or ministers from one planet or planetary system to another; and thus the Mormon, as the Moslem, places angelic nature below human, saying with St. Paul (1 Cor., vi., 3), "Know you not that we shall judge angels?" or they may choose, like the precreated spirits of El Islam in the Yaum i Alast—the Day of Am-I-Not (thy God)?—the probation of an earthly tabernacle; and, ignoring their past existence, descend below all things to attain a higher than celestial glory, and perfection in the attributes of power and happiness. As with the metempsychosist, there are grades of tabernacles. The lowest of humans is the African, who, being a "servant of servants unto his brethren," is "cursed as to the priesthood," and therefore can not "attain to any thing above a dim-shining glory." Above him is the Indian, for the Red Men, through repentance, obedience, and acceptance of the new Evangelism, can rebecome a "fair and delightsome people," worthy of their Hebrew sires. Below the negro is the brute tabernacle, into which the still rebellious spirit descends, until, yielding to Gospel law, it is permitted to retrace its course through the successive changes to splendor and perfection. So, "when we are tormented by a refractory horse or an obstinate ass, it may not be amiss to reflect that they were actuated by an apostate soul, and exemplifying a few of the human infirmities." The same words might be spoken orthodoxically by a Jain or a Banyan.

The soul is supposed to take possession of the tabernacle at the quickening of the embryon. At baptism the Saint may ask in faith for some particular spirit or genius—an idea familiar to the adepts and spiritualists of this generation. Every one also has evil, false, and seducing spirits at variance with the good, a fancy reminding us of the poetical Moslem picture of the good guardian sitting upon man's right shoulder, and whispering into his ear suggestions against which the bad spirit on the left contends. Revelations are received by prayer and mighty faith, but only when diligence and sagacity fail to secure the desired information —where God has appointed means he will not work by miracles, nor will a "*de profundis*" act without a more concrete action. Heavenly communications vouchsafed to the seer must be registered, and kept for promulgation when the Saints can bear them;

for many " would be offended and turn back if the whole truth"
—polygamy, for instance—" were dashed down in a mass before
them." Of prophetic times it may be observed that the habitat
of God the Father is the planet Kolob, whose revolutions—one
of which is the beginning and the end of a day equal to 1000 terrestrial years—are the measure of heavenly time. The Deity, being finite, employs agents and auxiliaries, e. g., light, sound, electricity, inspiration, to communicate knowledge to his world of
worlds. An angel commissioned as a messenger to earth is taken
either from the chief or from a minor planet, and it naturally
measures time by the days and weeks, the months and years, of
its own home—a style of computation which must not a little
confuse our poor human chronology.

" Tongues" does not signify, as at the date of the first Pente-
cost, an ability to address heteroglottists in their several languages, which would render the gift somewhat too precise and
Mezzofantian for these days. It means that man moved by the
Spirit shall utter any set of sounds unintelligible even to himself,
but which, being known to the Lord, may, by special permission
to exercise the " gift of interpretation of tongues," be explained
by another to those addressed. The man gravid with " tongues"
must " rise on his feet, lean in faith on Christ, and open his lips,
utter a song in such cadence as he chooses, and the Spirit of the
Lord will give an interpreter, and make it a language." The linguistic feat has of late years been well known in England, where
it was, of course, set down to imposture. It may more charitably
be explained by an abnormal affection of the organ of language
on the part of the speaker of " tongues," and in the interpreter
by the effect of a fervent and fooling faith.

VIII. " WE BELIEVE THE WORD OF GOD RECORDED IN THE
BIBLE; WE ALSO BELIEVE THE WORD OF GOD RECORDED IN THE
BOOK OF MORMON, AND IN ALL OTHER GOOD BOOKS."—Some
Christians have contended that the Biblia of the Jews have been
altered; that the last chapter (verse 5) of Deuteronomy, for instance, recording the death and burial of Moses, was not written
by Moses. The Moslems assert that the Scripture of both Hebrew and Christian has not only been misunderstood, but has designedly been corrupted by Baulús (St. Paul) and other Greekish
Jews; that the Gospel of Infancy, and the similar compositions
now banished into the apocryphal New Testament, are mere ex-
crescences upon the pure commands of Jesus. The Mormons
hold with the latter. They believe, however, that the infinite
errors and interpretations have been removed by " Joseph the
Seer," to whom was given the " key of all languages"—he has
quoted in his writings only 15 out of 3500—and the following
specimen of his ultra-Bentleian emendations, borrowed from the
" Last Sermon," may suffice :

" I will make a comment on the very first sentence of the history of the creation in the Bible" (*i. e.*, "in King James's version;" he had probably never seen even the Douay translation). "It first read, 'The head one of the gods brought forth the gods.'* If you do not believe it, you do not believe *the learned* man of God. And, in farther explanation, it means, 'The head god called together the gods, and sat in grand council. The grand councilors sat in yonder heavens, and contemplated the worlds that were created at that time.' The Bible is, therefore, held to be the foundation book." Mr. Joseph Smith's inspired translation or impudent *rifacciamento* is believed to exist in MS.: in due time it will probably be promulgated. But the Word of God is not confined to the Bible; the Book of Mormon and the Doctrines and Covenants are of equal authority, strands of the "three-fold cord," connecting by the Church God and man. If these revelations contradict one another, the stumbling-block to the weak in faith is easily removed by considering the "situations" under which they were vouchsafed: "heaven's government is conducted on the principle of adapting revelation to the varied circumstances of the children of the kingdom"—a dogma common to all revelationists. Additional items may be supplied to the Mormons from day to day, a process by which a "flood of light has poured into their souls, and raised them to a view of the glorious things above." The present seer, revelator, translator, and prophet, however, shows his high wisdom by seeing, revealing, translating, and prophesying as little as possible. Yet he even repeats, and probably believes, that revelation is the rock upon which the Church is founded.

IX. " WE BELIEVE ALL THAT GOD HAS REVEALED, ALL THAT HE DOES NOW REVEAL, AND WE BELIEVE THAT HE WILL REVEAL MANY MORE GREAT AND IMPORTANT THINGS PERTAINING TO THE KINGDOM OF GOD AND MESSIAH'S SECOND COMING."—Much of this has been explained above. The second coming of Christ is for the restoration or restitution of all things, as foretold by the prophet Isaiah. When the living earth was created, the dry land emerged from the waters, which gathered by command into one place. The " Voice of Warning" draws an interesting picture of a state of things hitherto unknown to geologist and palæogeographer. "There was one vast ocean rolling around a single immense body of land, unbroken as to continents and islands; it was a beautiful plain, interspersed with gently rising hills and sloping vales; its climate delightfully varied with heat and cold, wet and dry; crowning the year with productions grateful to men and animals, while from the flowery plain or spicy grove sweet odors were wafted on every breeze, and all the vast creation

* I need hardly say that in the original the words are " at its head (beginning) the gods (he) created the earth and the heaven."

of animated beings breathed naught but health, peace, and joy."
Over this paradise, this general garden, "man reigned, and talked
face to face with the Supreme, with only a dimming veil between."
After the diffusion of sin, which followed the fall, came the puri-
fication of the Noachian cataclysm, and in the days of Peleg "the
earth was divided," *i. e.*, the Homeric circumambient sea was in-
terposed between portions of land rent asunder, which earthquakes
and upheavals subsequently broke into fragments and islands.
We learn from the whole and varied Scriptures that before the
second coming of Christ the several pieces shall be dovetailed into
one, as they were in the morn of creation, and the retiring sea
shall reassume its pristine place, when Samudra Devta was enthroned by the Rishis. The earth is thus restored for a people
purified to innocence, and is fitted for the first resurrection of the
body to reign with the Savior for a thousand years.

X. "WE BELIEVE IN THE LITERAL GATHERING OF ISRAEL, AND
IN THE RESTORATION OF THE TEN TRIBES; THAT ZION WILL BE
ESTABLISHED UPON THE WESTERN CONTINENT; THAT CHRIST
WILL REIGN PERSONALLY UPON THE EARTH A THOUSAND YEARS;
AND THAT THE EARTH WILL BE RENEWED AND RECEIVE ITS PAR-
ADISIACAL GLORY."—The only novelty in this article is the "location" of Zion, which has already been transferred from Palestine
to the celestial regions in the Valley of the Mississippi; this, in
the present era, when the old cradles of civilization upon the Gan-
ges and Indus, the Euphrates and the Nile, have been well-nigh
depopulated or exhausted, promises to become one of the vast
hives from which the human swarm shall issue. The American
continent, as the Book of Mormon informs us, was, at the time of
the Crucifixion, shaken to its foundation: towns and cities, lakes
and mountains, were buried and formed when "the earth writhed
in the convulsive throes of agonizing nature." After all the seed
of Israel shall have been raised from the dead, they shall flock to
Zion in Judea, and the saints of other races shall be gathered to
New Jerusalem in America: both these cities shall be "built with
fine stones, and the beauty of all precious things." At the end
of the millennium comes the great sabbath of rest and enjoyment;
the earth shall become celestial through the baptism of fire, while
the two holy cities shall be caught up (literally) into heaven, to
descend with the Lord God for their light and their temple, and
shall remain forever on the new earth "under the bright canopy
of the new heavens."

XI. "WE BELIEVE IN THE LITERAL RESURRECTION OF THE
BODY, AND THAT THE REST OF THE DEAD LIVE NOT AGAIN UNTIL
THE THOUSAND YEARS ARE EXPIRED."—Man, it has been shown,
is a duality of elements. The body is gross, the spirit—under
which the intellect or mind is included—is refined matter, perme-

ating, vivifying, and controlling the former: the union or fusion of the two constitutes the "living soul" alluded to by Moses (Gen., ii., 7) in the Adamical creation. Death followed the fall of the great patriarch, who, we are told, is called in Scripture Michael, the Ancient of Days, with hair like wool, etc. But in technical Mormon phrase, "Adam fell that man might be," and ate the forbidden fruit with a full foreknowledge of the consequences—a Shiah belief. The "fall," therefore, was a matter of previous arrangement, in order that spirits choosing to undertake their probations might be fitted with "tabernacles," and be born of women. Death separates the flesh and the spirit for a useful purpose, but the latter keeps guard over every particle of the former, until, at the fiat of resurrection, the body is again "clothed upon," and perfect man is the result—a doctrine familiar to the mediums. Such is also the orthodox Sunnite faith. The heretical peculiarity of the Mormon resurrection is this: the body will be the same as before, "except the blood," which is the natural life, and, consequently, the principle of mortality. A man restored to flesh and blood would be subject to death; "flesh and bones," therefore, will be the constitution of the "resurrected" body. This idea clearly derives from the Genesitic physiology, which teaches that "the life of the flesh is in the blood" (Levit., xvii., 14); life being, according to the moderns, not an absolute existence nor objective entity, but a property or condition of the corporeal mechanism—the working, as it were, of the engine until arrested by material lesion. It is confirmed in the Mormon mind by the Savior bidding his disciples to handle his limbs, and to know that he had flesh and bones, not blood.

XII. "WE CLAIM THE PRIVILEGE OF WORSHIPING ALMIGHTY GOD ACCORDING TO THE DICTATES OF CONSCIENCE UNMOLESTED, AND ALLOW ALL MEN THE SAME PRIVILEGE, LET THEM WORSHIP HOW OR WHERE THEY MAY."—This article embodies the tenets of Roger Williams, who, in establishing his simple democracy, provided that the will of the majority should rule, but "only in civil things." The charter of Rhode Island (1644) contains the memorable words: "No person within the said colony shall be molested, punished, disquieted, or called in question for any differences of opinion in matters of religion who does not actually disturb the public peace." But how often has this been mouthed —how little it has affected mankind! Would London—boasting in the nineteenth century to be the most tolerant of cities—allow the Cardinal of Westminster to walk in procession through her streets?

XIII. "WE BELIEVE IN BEING SUBJECT TO KINGS, QUEENS, PRESIDENTS, RULERS, AND MAGISTRATES, IN OBEYING, HONORING, AND SUSTAINING THE LAW."—When treating of the hierarchy, it will be made apparent that subjection to temporals and Gentiles must be purely nominal. At the same time, it must be owned that, throughout North America, I may say throughout the New World, the Mormon polity is the only fixed and reasonable form of government. The "turnpike-road of history," which Fisher Ames, nearly a century ago, described as "white with the tombstones of republics," is in a fair way to receive fresh accessions, while the land of the Saints promises continuance and progress.

XIV. "WE BELIEVE IN BEING HONEST, TRUE, CHASTE, TEMPERATE, BENEVOLENT, VIRTUOUS, AND UPRIGHT, AND IN DOING GOOD TO ALL MEN; INDEED, WE MAY SAY THAT WE FOLLOW THE ADMONITION OF PAUL; WE 'BELIEVE ALL THINGS,' WE 'HOPE ALL THINGS,' WE HAVE ENDURED VERY MANY THINGS, AND HOPE TO BE ABLE TO 'ENDURE ALL THINGS.' EVERY THING LOVELY, VIRTUOUS, PRAISEWORTHY, AND OF GOOD REPORT, WE SEEK AFTER, LOOKING FORWARD TO THE 'RECOMPENSE OF REWARD.' BUT AN IDLE OR LAZY PERSON CAN NOT BE A CHRISTIAN, NEITHER HAVE SALVATION. HE IS A DRONE; AND DESTINED TO BE STUNG TO DEATH, AND TUMBLED OUT OF THE HIVE." — All over the American Union there is an apotheosis of labor; the Latter-Day Saints add to it the damnation of osiosity.

This brief outline of Mormon faith will show its strange, but, I believe, spontaneous agglomeration of tenets which, were its disciples of a more learned and philosophical body, would suggest extensive eclecticism. But, as I have already remarked, there is a remarkably narrow limit to religious ideas: the moderns vainly attempt invention when combination is now the only possible process. In the Tessarakai Decalogue above quoted, we find syncretized the Semitic Monotheism, the Persian Dualism, and the Triads and Trinities of the Egyptians and the Hindoos. The Hebrews also have a personal Theos, the Buddhists avataras and incarnations, the Brahmans self-apotheosis of man by prayer and penance, and the East generally holds to quietism, a belief that repose is the only happiness, and to a vast complication of states in the world to be. The Mormons are like the Pythagoreans in their precreation, transmigration, and exaltation of souls; like the followers of Leucippus and Democritus in their atomic materialism; like the Epicureans in their pure atomic theories, their *summum bonum*, and their sensuous speculations; and like the Platonists and Gnostics in their belief of the Æon, of ideas, and of moving principles in element. They are fetichists in their ghostly fancies, their *evestra*, which became souls and spirits. They are Jews in their theocracy, their ideas of angels, their hatred of Gentiles, and their utter segregation from the great brotherhood of mankind. They are Christians inasmuch as they base their faith upon the Bible, and hold to the divinity of Christ, the fall of man, the atonement, and the regeneration. They are Arians inasmuch as they hold Christ to be "the first of God's creatures," a "perfect creature, but still a creature." They are Moslems in their views of the inferior status of womankind, in their polygamy, and in their resurrection of the material body: like the followers of the Arabian Prophet, they hardly fear death, because they have elaborated "continuation." They take no leap in the dark; they spring from this sublunary stage into a known, not into an unknown world: hence also their worship is eminently secular, their sermons are political or commercial, and — religion being with them not a thing apart, but a portion and parcel of every-day life — the intervention of the Lord in their material affairs becomes natural and only to be expected. Their visions, prophecies, and miracles are those of the Illuminati, their mysticism that of the Druses, and their belief in the Millennium is a completion of the dreams of the Apocalyptic sects. Masonry has evidently entered into their scheme; the Demiurgus whom they worship is "as good at mechanical inventions as at any other business." With their later theories, Methodism, Swedenborgianism — especially in its view of the future state—and Transcendentalism are curiously intermingled. And, finally, we can easily discern in their doctrine of affinity of minds and sympathy of souls the leaven of that faith which, beginning with the Mesmer, and progressing through the Rochester Rappers and the Poughkeepsie Seer, threatens to extend wherever the susceptible nervous temperament becomes the characteristic of the race.

The Latter-Day Saints do not deny this agglomeration.* They maintain that, being guided by the Spirit unto all truth, they have sifted it out from the gross mass of error that obscures it, and that whatever knowledge has been vouchsafed to man may be found in their possession. They assert that other sects were to them what the Platonists and the Essenes were to Christianity. Moreover, as has been seen, they declare their faith to be still in its infancy, and that many dark and doubtful subjects are still to be decided by better experience or revelation.

I borrow the following *résumé* of Mormonism from Lieutenant Gunnison—a Christian writer—of course, without endorsing any one of his opinions.

"In Mormonism we recognize an intuition of Transcendentalism—intuition, we say, for its founder was no scholar in the idealistic philosophy. He trampled under foot creeds and formulas, and soared away for perpetual inspiration from the God; and by the will, which he calls faith, he won the realms of truth, beauty, and happiness. Such things can only be safely confided to the

---

* "One of the grand fundamental principles of Mormonism" (says Mr. Joseph Smith in his sermon preached on the 9th of July, 1843) "is to receive truth, come whence it may." . . . . "Presbyterians, Baptists, Methodists, Catholics, Mohammedans, etc., are they in possession of any truth? Yes, they have all a little truth mixed with error. We ought to gather together all the good and true principles which are in the world, and keep them, otherwise we shall never become pure Mormons."

strong and pure-minded, and even they must isolate themselves in self-idolatry, and be 'alone with the alone,' and seek converse with the spirit of man's spirit.

"But this prophet was educated by passion, and sought to be social with the weak; he therefore baptized spiritually in the waters of materialism. Instead of evolving the godlike nature of the human spirit, he endeavored to prove that humanity was already divinity by investing Deity with what is manlike—men were to be like gods by making gods men."

The form of Mormon government is not new: it is the theocracy of the Jews, of the Jesuit missions in Brazil, Paraguay, and elsewhere, and briefly of all communities in which, contrary to the fitness of things, Church is made to include, or, rather, exclude State. In opposition to El Islam, they maintain that a hieratic priesthood is necessary to the well-being of a religion. They divide it into two grand heads, of which all other officers and authorities are appendages. The first is called the Melchisedek priesthood, "because Melchisedek was such a great high priest."* The second, which is a supplement to the former, and administers outward ordinances, is the Aaronic or Levitical, "because it was conferred upon Aaron and his seed throughout all their generations." To the Melchisedek belong the high priest, priests, and elders; to the Aaronic the bishops, the teachers or catechists, and the deacons.

"The power and authority of the higher, or Melchisedek priesthood, is to hold the keys of all the spiritual blessings of the Church, to have the privilege of receiving the mysteries of the kingdom of heaven, to have the heavens opened unto them, to commune with the general assembly and Church of the first-born, and to enjoy the communion and presence of God the Father, and Jesus the Mediator of the New Covenant.

"The power and authority of the lesser, or Aaronic priesthood, is to hold the keys of the ministering of angels, and to administer in outward ordinances the letter of the Gospel—the baptism of repentance for the remission of sins—agreeable to the covenants and commandments."

The apex of the Mormon hierarchy is the First Presidency, now Messrs. Young, Kimball, and Wells, who have succeeded to Peter, James, and John in the Gospel Church, and who correspond on earth to the Trinity in heaven—*numero Deus impare gaudet*. The presiding high priest over the high priesthood of the Church —*par excellence, "the"* President, also *ex-officio* seer, revelator, translator, and prophet, is supreme. The two sub-chiefs or counselors are *quasi*-equal: the first, however, takes social precedence of the second. This quorum of the presidency of the Church, elected by the whole body, is the centre of temporal as of ecclesiastical

---

* These and the following quotations are borrowed from sections 2 and 3 of "Covenants and Commandments."

power. It claims, under God, the right of life and death; it holds the keys of heaven and hell, and from its decrees there is no appeal except to the general assembly of all the quorums which constitute the spiritual authorities of the Church.

The second in rank is the Patriarch. The present incumbent is a nephew of the first seer, who succeeded Mr. Joseph Smith, sen., the father of Mr. Joseph Smith, jun.* As the sire of the Church, his chief duty is to administer blessings: it is an office of dignity held for life, whereas all others expire after the semestre.

Follows the "Second Presidency," the twelve traveling counselors, "called to be the twelve apostles or special witnesses of the name of Christ in all the world," modeled with certain political modifications after the primitive Christian Church, and abbreviatively termed "The Twelve." The President of the High Apostolic College, or, in his default, one of the members, acts as coadjutor, in the absence of a member of the First Presidency. The Twelve come nearer the masses, and, acting under direction of the highest authority, build up the Church, ordain and set in order all other officers, elders, priests, teachers, and deacons: they are empowered to baptize, and to administer bread and wine—the emblems of the flesh and blood of Christ; to confirm those who are baptized into the Church by the laying on of hands for the baptism of fire and the Holy Ghost; to teach, expound, exhort, baptize, and watch over the Church, and to take the lead in all meetings. They preside over the several "Stakes of Zion;" there is one, for instance, to direct, under the title of president, the European, and another the Liverpool mission. If there be several together, the eldest is the standing president of the quorum, and they act as councilors to one another.

The fourth body in rank is the Seventies. The "Seventy" act in the name of the Lord, under direction of the "Twelve," in building up the Church, and, like them, are traveling ministers, sent first to the Gentiles, and then to the Jews. Out of the "Seventy" are chosen seven presidents, of whom one presides over the other six councilors: these seven choose other seventy besides the first seventy, "and also other seventy, until seven times seventy, if the labor in the vineyard of necessity requires it." In 1853 the minutes of the Mormon General Conference enumerated the "Seventies" at 1572. Practically the seventy members are seldom complete. The chief of these traveling propagandists, the working bees of the community, is the "President of all the Seventies."

The fifth body is composed of "high priests after the order of the Melchisedek priesthood, who have a right to officiate in their own standing, under the direction of the Presidency, in administering spiritual things," and to "officiate in all the offices of the Church when there are no higher authorities present." Thus charged with the execution of spiritual affairs, they are usually

* So called in revelation until the death of Mr. Joseph Smith, sen.

aged and fatherly men.   Among the high priests are included, *ex-officio*, the bishops and the high council.

The Mormon ἐπίσκοπος is a steward, who renders an account of his stewardship both in time and eternity, and who superintends the elders, keeps the Lord's store-house, receives the funds of the Church, administers to the wants of those beneath him, and supplies assistance to those who manage the "literary concerns," probably editors and magazine publishers.   The bishopric is the presidency of the Aaronic priesthood, and has authority over it.   No man has a legal right to the office except a literal descendant of Aaron.   As these, however, are *non inventi*, and as a high priest of the Melchisedek order may officiate in all lesser offices, the bishop, who never affects a *nolo episcopari*, can be ordained by the First Presidency, or Mr. Brigham Young.   Thus the episcopate is a local authority in stakes, settlements, and wards, with the directorship of affairs temporal as well as spiritual.   This "overseer" receives the tithes on the commutation-labor, which he forwards to the public store-house ; superintends the registration of births, marriages, and deaths, makes domiciliary visits, and hears and determines complaints either laical or ecclesiastic.

The High Council was organized by revelation in Kirtland (Feb. 17, 1834) for the purpose of settling, when the Church or the "Bishop's" council might fail, important difficulties that might arise between two believers.   Revelation directed it to consist of twelve high priests, ascertained by lots or ballot, and one or three presidents, as the case might require.   The first councilors, when named, were asked if they would act in that office according to the law of heaven : they accepted, and at once, *more Americano*—"voted."   After deciding that the President of the Church should also be President of the Council, it was laid down that the duty of the twelve councilors should be to cast lots by numbers, and thereby ascertain who of the twelve shall speak first, commencing with number one, and so in succession to number twelve.   In an easy case only two speak ; in a difficult one, six.   The defendant has a right to one half of the council, and "those who draw even numbers, that is, 2, 4, 6, 8, 10, and 12, are the individuals who are to stand up in behalf of the accused, and to prevent insult or injustice."   After the evidence is heard, and the councilors, as well as the accuser and the accused, have " said their say," the president decides, and calls upon the "twelve" to sanction his decision by their vote.   When error is suspected, the case is subject to a "careful rehearing ;" and in peculiar difficulties the appeal is to revelation.   I venture to recommend this form of special jury to those who have lost faith in a certain effete and obsolete "palladium of British liberty" that dates from the days of Ethelbert. After all, it is sometimes better, *jurare in verba magistri*, especially of an inspired master.

The High Council is a standing council.   It bears the same relationship to the federal power as the university Sex viri to a court of civil law in England, and it saves the saints the expense of Gentile proceedings, which may roughly be set down at fifty per cent. The sessions take place in the Social Hall. Such an institution, which transfers to St. Peter all the duties, salaries, and honors which Justinianus gives, is, of course, most unpopular among the anti-Mormons, who call it Star-Chamber, and other ugly names. I look upon it rather as the Punchayat (*quinque viri*) Court of East India, a rough but ready instrument of justice, which, like spontaneous growths generally, have been found far superior to the exotic institutions forced upon the popular mind by professional improvers.

The Latter-Day Saint, when in a foreign land, can be punished for transgression by his own people. The presiding authority calls a council to examine the evidence for and against the offense; and if guilt be proven, the offender, after being officially suspended from his missionary functions and the fellowship of the Church, is sent, with a special report, to be tried by his own presidency at Great Salt Lake City.

The elders are those from whom the apostles are taken; they are, in fact, promoted priests charged with all the duties of that order, and with the conduct of meetings, "as they are led by the Holy Ghost, according to the commandments and revelations of God." They hold Conferences once in every three months, receive their licenses from the elders or from the Conferences; they are liable to be sent on missions, and are solemnly enjoined, by a revelation of January, 1832, to "gird up their loins and be sober."

The priest is the master mason of the order. It is his duty to preach, teach, expound, exhort, baptize, administer the sacrament, visit domiciliarily, exhort the saints to pray "vocally and in secret," ordain other priests, teachers, and deacons, take the lead of meetings when there is no elder present, and assist the elder when occasion requires.

Of the Aaronic order, the head are the bishops; under them are two ranks, who form the entered apprentices of the Mormon lodge.

1st. The teachers, who have no authority to baptize, to administer the sacrament, or to lay on hands, but who "warn, expound, exhort, teach, and invite all to come unto Christ, watch over the Church, and take the lead of meetings in the absence of the elder or priest." Of these catechists one or two is usually attached to each bishop.

2d. The deacon, or διάκονος, an assistant teacher. He also acts as treasurer to the missions in the several branches of the Church, collects money for the poor, and attends to the temporal wants of converts.

The rise of the "Church of Christ in these last days dates from 1830, since the coming of our Lord and Savior Jesus Christ:"

thus, A.D. 1861 is Annus Josephi Smithii 31.   In that year Mirabilis the book of Mormon appeared, the Church of Jesus Christ of Latter-Day Saints was organized, and the Body Ecclesiastic, after the fashion of those preceding it, was exodus'd or hegira'd to Kirtland, Ohio.

The actual composition of the Mormon hierarchy is that of a cadre of officers to a skeleton army of saints and martyrs, which may be filled up *ad infinitum*.   It is inferior in simplicity, and therefore in power, to that which the Jesuit organization is usually supposed to be, yet it is not deficient in the wherewithal of a higher grasp.   It makes state government, especially that of Gentile communities, an excrescence upon the clerical body.   The first president is the governor; the second is the lieutenant governor; the third is the secretary of state; the High Council is the Supreme Court; the bishops are justices of peace: briefly, the Church is legislative, judiciary, and executive—what more can be required?   It has evidently not neglected the masonic, monotheistic, and monocratic element, as opposed to, and likely to temper the tripartite rule of Anglo-American civil government.   The first president is the worshipful master of the lodge, the second and third are the senior and junior wardens, while the inferior ranks represent the several degrees of the master and apprentice. It symbolizes the leveling tendencies of Christianity and progressiveism, while its civil and ecclesiastical despotism and its sharp definition of rank are those of a disciplined army—the model upon which socialism has loved to form itself.   In society, while all are brothers, there is a distinct aristocracy, called west of the Atlantic "upper crust;" not of titles and lands, nor of bales and boxes, but of hierarchical position; and, contrary to what might be expected, there is as little real social fusion among Mormons as between the "sixties," the "forties," and the "twenties" of silly Guernsey.

Having now attempted, after the measure of my humble capacity, to show what Mormonism is, I will try to explain what Mormonism is not.   The sage of Norwich ("Rel. Med.," sect. vi.) well remarked that "every man is not a proper champion of truth, nor fit to take up the gauntlet in the cause of verity;" and that "many, from the ignorance of these maxims, have too rashly charged the troops of error, and remain as trophies to the enemies of truth."   The doctrine may fitly be illustrated by pointing out the prodigious aid lent to Mormonism by the self-inflicted defeats of anti-Mormonism.

The Jaredite exodus to America in dish-like "barges, whose length was the length of a tree," and whose voyage lasted 344 days, is certainly a trial of faith.   The authority of Mormonic inspiration is supposed to be weakened by its anachronisms and other errors: the mariner's compass, for instance, is alluded to long before the fourteenth century.   The Mormons, however, reply that the "Liahona" of their Holy Book is not a compass, and that if it were, nothing could be said against it: the Chinese claim the invention long before the days of Flavio, and the Moslems attribute it to one of their own saints.* The "reformed Egyptian" of the Golden Bible is ridiculed on the supposition that the Hebrew authors would write either in their own tongue, in the Syrian, or in the Chaldaic, at any rate in a Semitic, not in a Coptic language. But the first disciples of the Gospel Church were Jews, and yet the Evangel is now Greek. As regards the Golden Plates, it is contended that the Jews of old were in the habit of writing upon papyrus, parchment, and so on, not upon metal, and that such plates have never been found in America. But of late years Himyaritic inscriptions upon brass tablets have been forwarded from Yemen to the British Museum. Moreover, in 1843, six brass plates of a bell shape, covered with ancient glyphs, were discovered by a "respectable merchant" near Kinderhook," United States, proving that such material was not unknown to the ancient Semites and to the American aborigines. The word "Christ" often occurs ("Book of Mormon," p. 8, etc.) long before the coming of the Savior. But the Book of Mormon was written in the "reformed Egyptian:" the proper noun in question was translated "Christ" in English by the prophet, an "unlearned young man," according to his own understanding, and for the better comprehension of his readers. The same argument applies to such words as "synagogues," "alpha and omega," "steel," "S.S.E.," etc.; also to "elephant," "cow," "horse," "ass," "swine," and other pachyderms and solidunguls, which were transported to America after the Columbian discovery: they are mere translations, like the fabulous unicorn of the Old Testament and the phœnix of the apocryphal New Testament (Clement I., xii., 2): elephant, for instance, manifestly means mastodon, and swine, peccary. Ptolemy's theory of a moving earth is found anticipated. But who shall limit revelation? and has not the Mosaic Genesis, according to a multitude of modern divines, anticipated all the latest discoveries? The Lord describes America to Jared ("Book of Mormon," p. 78) as an "isle of the sea," and the accuracy of the geography is called in question. But in the Semitic and other Eastern tongues, insula and peninsula are synonymous. Moreover, if Dr. Kane's open circumpolar ocean prove aught but a myth, the New World is wholly insulated even by ice from the Old. Other little contradictions and inaccuracies, which abound in the inspired books, are as easily pooh-pooh'd as objections to the conflicting genealogies, and the contradictory accounts of the Crucifixion by the professors of the elder faith.

The "vulgarity" of Mormonism is a favorite theme with the anti-Mormon. The low origin and "plebbishness" of the apostles' names and of their institutions (e. g., the "Twelve," the "Seven-

* First Footsteps in East Africa, chap. i.

ties"), the snuffling Puritanic style which the learned Gibbon hated, and execrable grammar (*e. g.*, in the first page, "Nephi's brethren rebelleth against him"), and the various Yankeeisms of the New Scriptures, are cited as palpable proofs of fraud. But the primitive apostles of Christianity were of inferior social rank and attainments to the first Mormon converts, and of the reformers of Luther's age it may be asked, " Where was then the gentleman?" The Syriac-Greek of the New Testament, with its manifold flaws of idiom and diction, must have produced upon the polite philosophers and grammarians of Greece and Rome an effect even more painful than that which the Americanisms of the Book of Mormon exercise upon English nerves. These things are palpably stumbling-blocks disposed sleeper-wise upon the railroad of faith, lest Mr. Christian's progress should become a mere excursion. Gentiles naturally feel disposed to smile when they find in the nineteenth century prophets, apostles, saints; but the Church only gains by the restoration and reformation of her primitive discipline. The supernatural action of the Holy Spirit believed in by the Mormons as by the Seekers (1645), the Camisards (1688), the Leeites and Wilkinsonians (1776), is the best answer to that atheistic school which holds that God who once lived is now dead to man. As of the Ayat of El Islam, so of the revelations with which Mr. Joseph Smith was favored, it is remarked that their exceeding opportuneness excites suspicion. But of what use are such messages from Heaven unless they arrive *à propos?* Mr. O. Hyde contends, after the fashion of wiser men, that ambiguity, and, if I may use the word, a certain achronology, characterize inspired prophecy: it is evident that only a little more inspiration is wanted to render it entirely unambiguous.

The other sentimental objections to Mormonism may briefly be answered as follows:

" *That the holiest of words is profanely applied to man.*" But as Moses (Ex., iv., 16) was "instead of God to Aaron" (Ex., vii., 1), and was "made a god" to Pharaoh, and as the Savior declared that "he called them gods unto whom the word of God came" (John, xi., 35), the Mormons evidently use the word in its old and scriptural sense. Thus they assert that Mr. Joseph Smith is the god of this generation, Jesus is his god, Michael or Adam is the god of Jesus, Jehovah is the god of Adam, and Eloheim is the god of Jehovah.

" *That credible persons have testified to the bad character of Mr. Joseph Smith, junior, as a money-digger, a cheat, a liar, a vulgar impostor, or, at best, a sincere and ignorant fanatic.*" The Mormons reply that such has been the history of every prophet. They point with triumph and yearning love to the story of their martyr's life, to his intense affection for his family, and to their devotion to him. They boast of his invincible boldness, energy, enthusiasm, and moral courage; that he never flinched from his allotted tasks, from the duties which he was commissioned to perform; that he was fifty times dragged by his enemies before the tribunals, and was as often acquitted; that he never hesitated for a moment, when such act was necessary, to cut off from the Church those who, like Oliver Cowdery, had been the depositaries of his intimate secrets; that his career was one long Bartholomew's Day, and that his end was as glorious as his life was beautiful. In America Mr. Joseph Smith has by the general suffrage of anti-Mormons been pronounced to be a knave, while his successor, Mr. Brigham Young, has been declared by the same high authority—*vox diaboli*, the Mormons term it—to be a self-deluded but true man. I can scarcely persuade myself that great events are brought about by mere imposture, whose very nature is feebleness: zeal, enthusiasm, fanaticism, which are of their nature strong and aggressive, better explain the abnormal action of man on man. On the other hand, it is impossible to ignore the dear delights of fraud and deception, the hourly pleasure taken by some minds in finessing through life, in concealing their real selves from the eyes of others, and in playing a part till by habit it becomes a nature. In the estimation of unprejudiced persons Mr. Joseph Smith is a man of rude genius, of high courage, of invincible perseverance, fired by zeal, of great tact, of religious fervor, of extraordinary firmness, and of remarkable talent in governing men. It is conceded that, had he not possessed "strong and invincible faith in his own high pretensions and divine mission," he would probably have renounced the unprofitable task of prophet, and sought refuge from persecution and misery in private life and honorable industry. Be that as it may, he has certainly taken a place among the notabilities of the world—he has left a footprint upon the sands of time.

"*That Mr. Joseph Smith prophesied lies*," and that "*through greed of gain he robbed the public by appropriating the moneys of the Kirtland Bank.*" The Mormons reply that many predictions of undoubted truth undeniably passed their prophet's lips, and that some—*e. g.*, those referring to the Mormon Zion and to the end of the world—may still prove true. With reference to the fact that Martin Harris was induced by the seer to pay for the publication of the Book of Mormon, it is pleaded that the Christian apostles (Acts, iv., 35) also received money from their disciples. The failure of the Kirtland Bank (A.D. 1837) is thus explained: During the Prophet's absence upon a visit to the Saints at Toronto, the cashier, Warren Parrish, flooded the district with worthless paper, and, fearing discovery on his master's return, decamped with $25,000, thereby causing a suspension of payment. Regarding other peccadilloes, the Mormons remark that no prophet was ever perfect or infallible. Moses, for instance, was not suffered for his sins to enter the Promised Land, and Saul lost by his misconduct the lasting reign over Israel.

"*That the three original witnesses to the 'Book of Mormon' apostatized and denied its truth.*" To this the Mormons add, that after a season those apostates duly repented and were rebaptized; one has died; the second, Martin Harris, is now a Saint in Kirtland, Ohio; and the third, Sidney Rigdon, to whom the faith owed so much, left the community after the Prophet's martyrdom, saying that it had chosen the wrong path, but never rejecting Mormonism nor accusing it of fraud. The witnesses to those modern tables of the law (the Golden Plates) were but eleven *in toto*, and formed only three families interested in the success of the scheme. The same paucity, or rather absence of any testimony which would be valid in a modern court of justice, marks the birth of every new faith, not excluding the Christian. And, finally, wickedness proved against the witnesses does not invalidate the value of their depositions. The disorders in the conduct of David and Solomon, for instance, do not affect the inspiration of the Psalms and Canticles.

"*That Mormon apostles and elders, as Parley P. Pratt and John Taylor, denied the existence of polygamy, even after it was known and practiced by their community.*" The Mormons reply that they never attempted to evade the imputation of the true patriarchal marriage: they merely asserted their innocence of the "spiritual wifedom," the Free Loveism and the Fanny Wrightism of the Eastern States—charges brought against them by the anti-Mormons.

Having thus disposed of the principal allegations, I will more briefly allude to the minor.

"*That the Mormons do not allow monogamy.*" This I know not to be the fact, as several of my acquaintances had and have but one wife. "*That a multitude of saints, prophets, and apostles are in full chase after a woman, whom the absence of her husband releases from her vows; that the missionary on duty appoints a proxy or vicarious head to his house, and that his spouses are married* pro tempore *to elders and apostles at home.*" Mrs. Ferris has dreamed out this "abyss of abomination," and then uses it to declaim against. But is it at all credible? Would not such conduct speedily demoralize and demolish a society which even its enemies own to be peculiarly pure? "*That the Mormons are 'jealous fellows'*"—a curious contradiction of the preceding charges. The Saints hold to the semi-seclusion of Athens, Rome, and Syria, where "she was the best of women of whom least is said, either of good or harm," believing with the world generally that opportunity often makes the thief. "*That the Mormons 'swap,' sell, exchange, and transfer their wives to Indians.*" Mrs. Ferris started the story, which carries its own refutation, by chronicling a report of the kind; and Mr. Ward improves upon it by supplying false instances and names. "*That the utmost latitude of manners is allowed in the ballroom and the theatre,*" which are compared to the private *réunions* of Rosanna Townsend and other Aspasias. The contrary is notoriously the case. "*That the young Mormons are frequently guilty of the crimes of Absalom and other horrible offenses.*" Unprejudiced Gentiles always deny the truth of such accusations. "*That the Mormon has no home, and that Mormon houses are dirty, slovenly, and uncomfortable.*" The Far West is not remarkable for neatness: the only exceptions to the rule of filth which I have seen are in the abodes of the Mormons. "*That 'plurality-families' are in a state of perpetual storm.*" I believe that many a "happy English home" is far stormier, despite the holy presence of monogamy. Even Mrs. Ferris tells of two wives, one young, the other old, "who treated each other with that degree of affectionate cordiality which properly belongs to the intercourse between mother and daughter," and—naïvely wonder-struck by what she could not understand—exclaims, "What a strange spectacle!" "*That women must be married to be saved.*" The orthodox Mormon belief is that human beings are sent into the world to sow seed for heaven; that a woman who wittingly, and for stupid social Belgravian-mother motives, fails in so doing, neglects a vital duty, and that whoso gives not children to the republic has lived in vain—an opinion which the Saints are contented to share with Moses and Mohammed, Augustus Cæsar and Napoleon Bonaparte. "*That the Mormons marry for eternity.*" They believe that Adam and Eve, when wholly pure, were so married, and that redemption signifies a complete restoration to all the privileges lost by the fall. "*That Mormons are 'sealed' to rich old women.*" The *vetula beata* exists, I believe, almost universally. "*That Mormons marry and seal for the dead.*" As has been seen, it is a principle of faith that all ordinances for the living may vicariously be performed for those departed. "*That Mormon women are pale, thin, badly and carelessly dressed, and poorly fed—that they exhibit a sense of depression and degradation.*" I found them exceedingly pretty and attractive, especially Miss ——. "*That it is dangerous to be the rival of a Mormon elder in love and business.*" This is true only so far that the Saint is probably a better man than the Gentile. I have been assured by Gentiles that they would rather trust the followers of Mr. Joseph Smith than their own people, and that, under Mormon rule, there never has been, and never can be, a case of bankruptcy. The hunters and Indian traders dislike the Saints for two chief reasons: in the first place, the hunting-grounds have been narrowed; and, secondly, industry and sobriety have taken the place of rollicking and dare-devilism. "*That the Mormons are bigoted and intolerant.*" The Mormon's golden rule is, "Mind your own business, and let your neighbor mind his." At Great Salt Lake City I found all the most violent anti-Mormon books, and have often heard Gentiles talk in a manner which would not be tolerated in Paris, London, and Rome. "*That the Church claims possession of, and authority over, a dead disciple's goods and chattels.*" This is done only in cases when heirs fail. "*That it is the Mor-*

mon's duty to lay all his possessions at the apostles' feet." The Mormons believe that the Lord has ordered his Church to be established on earth; that its success involves man's salvation; that the apostles are the pillars of the sacred edifice, and that the disciple is bound, like Barnabas, when called upon, to lay his all at the apostles' feet; practically, however, the measure never takes place. "*That the high dignitaries are enriched by tithes and by plundering the people.*" I believe, for reasons before given, this assertion to be as wholly destitute of fact as of probability. "*That the elders borrow money from their Gentile disciples, and that the Saints 'milk the Gentiles.'*" The Mormons, like sensible men, do not deny that their net has drawn up bad fish as well as good; they assert, however, and I believe with truth, that their community will bear comparison in point of honesty with any other.

I have already remarked how thoroughly hateful to the petulant fanatical republican of the New World is the Mormon state within state, their absolute aristocracy clothed in the wolf-skin of democracy; and I have also shown how little of that "largest liberty," concerning which the traveler in the United States hears so often and sees so seldom, has been extended to them or to their institutions. Let us now consider a few of the political objections to Mormonism.

"*That the Mormon Church overshadows and controverts the actions and opinions, the property, and even the lives of its members.*" The Mormons boast that their Church, which is their state, does so legitimately, and deny any abuse of its power. "*That the Church usurps and exercises the legislative and political business of the Territory.*" The foregoing pages disprove this. "*That the Church organizes and commands a military force.*" True, for her own protection. "*That the Church disposes of public lands on her own terms.*" The Mormons reply that, as squatters, they have earned by their improvements the right of pre-emption, and as the federal government delays to recognize their title, they approve of the Church so doing. "*That the Church has coined money and forced its circulation.*" The former clause is admitted, and the excellence of the Californian gold is warranted; the latter is justly treated with ridicule. "*That the Church levies the tenth part of every thing from its members under the charge of tithing.*" The Mormons derive this practice from the laws of Moses, and assert that the gift is purely a free-will offering estimated by the donor, and never taken except from those who are in full communion. "*That the Church imposes enormous taxes upon Gentile citizens.*" The Mormons own that they levy a large octroi, in the form of a regulated license system, upon ardent spirits, but they deny that more is taken from the Gentile than from the Saint. "*That the Church supervises and penetrates into the domestic circle, and enjoins and inculcates obedience to her own counsels, as articles of faith paramount to all the obligations of society and morality, allegiance and law.*"

The Mormons reply that the counsel and the obligations run in the same grooves.

Mormonism in England would soon have fallen to the level of Leeism or Irvingism; its teachers to the rank of the South-coteans and Muggletonians. Its unparalleled rise and onward march could have taken place only in a new hemisphere, in another world. Its genius is essentially Anglo-American, without one taint of Gallic, Teutonic, or Keltic. It is Rationalistic: the analytic powers, sharpened by mundane practice, and wholly unencumbered by religious formal discipline, are allowed, in things ultra mundane, a scope, a perfect freedom, that savors of irreverence: thus the Deity is somewhere spoken of as a "right-hand man." It is Exaggerative in matter as in manner: the Pentateuch, for instance, was contented with one ark, Mormonism required eight. It is Simplificative: its fondness for facilitation has led it through literalism into that complete materialism which, to choose one point only, makes the Creator of the same species as his creature. It is Imitative to an extent that not a vestige of originality appears: the Scripture names are carefully moulded in Hebrew shape; and, to quote one of many instances, the death-bed of the first patriarch ("Life of Joseph Smith, the Prophet," chap. xlii.) is a travestie of that of Israel, with his prayers, prophecies, and blessings; while the titles of the apostles, e. g., Lion of the Lord, are literally borrowed from El Islam. It has a mystic element the other side of its severe rationalism, even as the American character mixes transcendentalism with the purest literalism, as Mr. Emerson, the Sufi, contrasts with the Pilgrim fathers and Sam Slick. It is essentially Practical, though commonplaces and generalisms are no part of its composition. Finally, it is admirably puffed, as the note upon Mormon bibliography proves—better advertised than Colonel Colt's excellent revolvers.

I had proposed to write a chapter similar to this upon the Mormon annals. After sundry attempts, the idea was abandoned in despair. It would be necessary to give two distinct or rather opposite versions—according to the Mormons and the anti-Mormons —of every motive and action which have engendered and produced history. Such a style would not be lively. Moreover, the excessive positivism with which each side maintains its facts, and the palpable sacrifice of truth to party feeling, would make it impossible for any but an eye-witness, who had lived through the scenes, and had preserved his impartiality, to separate the wheat from the chaff. The Mormons declare that if they knew their prophet to be an impostor, they could still love, respect, and follow him in this life to the next. The Gentiles, I can see, would not accept him, even if he were proposed to them by a spirit from the other world. There is little inducement in this case to break the scriptural injunction, "Judge not."

Under these considerations, I have added to the Appendix

(No. V.) a detailed chronological table of Mormon events: it is compiled from both parties, and has at least one merit—impartiality.

CHRONOLOGY OF THE MOST IMPORTANT EVENTS RECORDED IN THE BOOK OF MORMON.

(*By Elder James Marsden, and printed in the Compendium of Faith and Doctrines.*)

B.C.

600. Lehi, Sariah, and their four sons, Laman, Lemuel, Sam, and Nephi, left Jerusalem by the commandment of God, and journeyed into the wilderness of Arabia (p. 17, 44, 97, pars. 3, 47, 4).

592. Lehi and his family arrived at the land Bountiful, so called because of its much fruit. Its modern name is Arabia Felix, or Arabia the Happy (p. 36, par. 17).

570. Jacob and Joseph were consecrated priests and teachers over the people of Nephi (p. 66, par. 5).

560. Nephi was commanded to make a second volume of plates (p. 67, par. 6).

545. Nephi commanded Jacob to write on the small plates such things as he considered most precious (p. 114, par. 1).

421. Jacob having committed the records into the hands of his son Enos, and Enos being old, he gave the records into the hands of his son Jarom (p. 133, 136, pars. 9, 7).

400. The people of Nephi kept the law of Moses, and they rapidly increased in numbers, and were greatly prospered (p. 137, par. 3).

362. Jarom being old, delivered the records into the hands of his son Omni (p. 138, par. 6).

324. Omni was a wicked man, but he defended the Nephites from their enemies (p. 138, par. 2).

280. Amaron delivered the plates to his brother Chemish (p. 139, par. 3).

124. After Abinadom, the son of Chemish, Amaleki,* the son of Abinadom, King Benjamin, and Mosiah had successively kept the records, Mosiah, the son of King Benjamin, was consecrated king (p. 157, par. 2).

121. Mosiah sent sixteen men to the land of Lehi-Nephi to inquire concerning their brethren (p. 158, par. 2).

91. Mosiah died, having conferred the records upon Alma, who was the son of Alma. Mosiah also established a republican form

---

* While Amaleki was keeping the records, Mosiah, the father of King Benjamin, and as many as would hearken to the voice of God, were commanded to go into the wilderness, and were led by the power of the Almighty to the Land of Zarahemla, where they discovered a people who left Jerusalem at the time that Zedekiah was carried away captive into Babylon. They were led by Mulek, the only surviving son of Zedekiah; and on their arrival in America, met with Coriantumr, the late king of the Jaredites, who were slain a little previous to the immigration of Mulek and his people (p. 139, 40, 411, 549, pars. 6, 9).

B.C.

of government, and appointed Alma the first and chief judge of the land (p. 205, 209, pars. 1, 7).

90. Nehor suffered an ignominious death for apostasy and for killing Gideon (p. 210, pars. 3, 4).

86. The usurper Amlici was slain by Alma. In this year many battles were fought between the Nephites on the one hand, and the Amlicites, who were Nephite revolutionists, and the Lamanites on the other. The Nephites were mostly victorious (p. 215, 217, pars. 14, 18).

85. Peace was restored and many were baptized in the waters of Sidon, and became members of the Church (p. 218, par. 1).

84. Peace continued, and three thousand five hundred became members of the Church of God (p. 218, par. 2).

83. The members of the Church became proud because of their great riches (p. 218, par. 3).

82. Alma delivered up the office of chief judge to Nephilah, and confined himself wholly to the high priesthood, after the holy order of God (p. 219, par. 5).

81. Alma performed a mission to the land of Melek, and to the City Ammonihah (p. 230, pars. 2, 3).

80. Alma and Amulek were delivered from prison by the mighty power of God (p. 251, par. 11).

79. The Lamanites destroyed the people of Ammonihah (p. 253, par. 2).

76. There was peace during three years, and the Church was greatly prospered (p. 254, par. 8).

75. Ammon performed a successful mission among the Lamanites (p. 288, par. 10).

73. Korihor, the great anti-Christ, made his appearance (p. 290, par. 2).

72. Alma committed the record to the keeping of his son Helaman, and commanded him to continue the history of his people (p. 310, par. 5).

71. The Nephites obtained a complete victory over the Lamanites in the borders of Manti (p. 331, par. 16).

71. Helaman performed a successful mission among the Nephites. (p. 333, par. 4).

69. Moroni commanded that the Nephites should fortify all their cities. They also built many cities (p. 346, par. 1).

68. This was the most comfortable, prosperous, and happy year that the Nephites had ever seen (p. 348, par. 3).

65. The people of Morianton prevented from escaping to the North or Lake Country. Also Nephilah died, and his son Pahoran succeeded him as chief judge of the land (p. 348, pars. 5, 8).

64. A contention between the advocates of monarchy on the one hand, and of republicanism on the other, was peaceably settled by the voice of the people. But 4000 of the monarchy men were slain for refusing to take up arms in defense of their country against the Lamanites (p. 350, par. 3).

63. Preparations for war between the Nephites and the Lamanites were made (p. 354, par. 4).

B.C.
62. The same continued (p. 355, par. 4).

61. Moroni retook the city of Melek, and obtained a complete victory over the Lamanites (p. 356, par. 12).

60. Moroni, by stratagem, overcame the Lamanites, and liberated his people from prison (p. 363, par. 7).

59. Moroni received an epistle from Helaman, of the city of Judea, in which is set forth the wonderful victories obtained in that part of the land over the Lamanites (p. 364, par. 1).

58. Moroni obtained possession of the city of Nephilah (p. 386, par. 18).

54. Peace having been restored, the Church became very prosperous, and Helaman died (p. 387, par. 3).

53. Shiblon took possession of the sacred records, and Moroni died (p. 387, pars. 1, 2).

52. 5400 men, with their wives and children, left Zarahemla for the North country (p. 388, par. 3).

50. Shiblon conferred the sacred records upon Helaman, the son of Helaman, and then died (p. 388, par. 5).

49. Pahoran, the chief judge, having died, his son Pahoran was appointed to succeed him. This Pahoran was murdered by Kisheumen, and his brother Pacumeni was appointed by his successor (p. 389, par. 3).

48. Coriantumr led a numerous host against Zarahemla, took the city, and killed Pacumeni; but Moronihah retook the city, slew Coriantumr, and obtained a complete victory over the Lamanites (p. 390, par. 5).

47. Helaman was appointed chief judge, and the band of Gadianton robbers was organized (p. 392, par. 8).

46. Peace reigned among the Nephites (p. 393, par. 1).

45. Peace continued (p. 393, par. 1).

44. Peace continued (p. 393, par. 1).

43. Great contention among the Nephites; many of them traveled northward (p. 394, par. 2).

36. Helaman died, and his son Nephi was appointed chief judge.

31. The Nephites, because of their wickedness, lost many of their cities, and many of them were slain by the Lamanites (p. 397, par. 8).

28. The Nephites repented at the preaching of Moronihah (p. 397, par. 10).

27. Moronihah could obtain no more possessions from the Lamanites. Nephi vacated the office of chief judge in favor of Cezoram (p. 398, 399, pars. 11, 13). The greater part of the Lamanites became a righteous people (p. 403, par. 25).

26. Nephi and Lehi went northward to preach unto the people (p. 404, par. 26).

23. Cezoram was murdered by an unknown hand as he sat on the judgment-seat. His son, who was appointed to succeed him, was also murdered (p. 404, par. 28).

22. The Nephites became very wicked (p. 406, par. 31).

21. The Lamanites observed the laws of righteousness, and utterly destroyed the Gadianton robbers from among them (p. 406, par. 32).

B.C.

20. Men belonging to the Gadianton band usurped the judgment-seat (p. 407, par. 1).

18. Nephi prophesied many important things against his people (p. 416, par. 15).

14. Three years' famine brought the people to repentance, and caused them to destroy the Gadianton robbers (p. 417, pars. 2, 3).

13. Peace being restored, the people spread themselves abroad, to repair their waste places (p. 418, par. 4).

12. The majority of the people, both Nephites and Lamanites, became members of the Church (p. 418, par. 4).

9. Certain dissenters among the Nephites stirred up the Lamanites against their brethren, and they revived the secrets of Gadianton (p. 419, par. 5).

5. The Lamanites prevailed against the Nephites, because of their great wickedness (p. 420, par. 7).

4. Samuel the Lamanite performed a mission among the Nephites (p. 422, par. 1).

1. Great signs and wonders were given unto the people, and the words of the Prophets began to be fulfilled (p. 431, par. 10).

Lachoneus was the chief judge and governor of the land. Nephi gave the records into the hands of his son Nephi (p. 432, par. 1).

The Lord revealed to Nephi that he would come into the world the next day, and many signs of his coming were given (p. 433, par. 3).

A.C.

3. The Gadianton robbers committed many depredations (p. 434, par. 6).

4. The Gadianton robbers greatly increased (p. 434, par. 6).

9. The Nephites began to reckon their time from the coming of Christ (p. 435, par. 8).

13. The Nephites were joined by many of the Lamanites in defense against the robbers, who had now become very numerous and formidable (p. 436, par. 9).

15. The Nephites were worsted in several engagements (p. 436, par. 10).

16. Gidgidoni, who was a chief judge and a great prophet, was appointed commander-in-chief (p. 438, par. 3).

17. The Nephites gathered themselves together for the purpose of mutual defense, and provided themselves with seven years' provisions (p. 439, par. 4).

19. A great battle was fought between the Nephites and the Gadianton robbers, in which the latter were defeated, and their leader, Giddianhi, was slain (p. 440, pars. 6, 8).

21. The Nephites slew tens of thousands of the robbers, and took all that were alive prisoners, and hanged their leader, Femnarihah (p. 441, 442, pars. 9, 10).

25. Mormon made new plates, upon which he made a record of what

A.C.

took place from the time Lehi left Jerusalem until his own day, and also a history of his own times (p. 443, par. 11).

26. The Nephites spread themselves abroad on their former possessions (p. 445, par. 1).

30. Lachoneus, the son of Lachoneus, was appointed governor of the land. He was murdered, and the people became divided into numerous tribes (p. 446, 447, pars. 3, 4).

31. Nephi having great faith in God, angels did minister to him daily (p. 449, par. 8).

32. The few who were converted through the preaching of Nephi were greatly blessed of God (p. 449, par. 10).

33. Many were baptized into the Church (p. 449, par. 10).

34. A terrible tempest took place, which changed and deformed the whole face of the land. Three days elapsed during which no light was seen.
   The voice of Jesus Christ was heard by all the people of the land, declaring that he had caused this destruction, and commanding them to cease to offer burnt-offerings and sacrifices (p. 453, pars. 7, 8).

35. In this year Jesus Christ appeared among the Nephites, and unfolded to them at large the principles of the Gospel (p. 455, pars. 11, 1). The apostles of Christ formed a Church of Christ (p. 492, par. 1).

36. Both the Nephites and the Lamanites were all converted, and had all things in common (p. 492, par. 2).

37. Many miracles were wrought by the disciples of Jesus (p. 492, par. 3).

59. The people rebuilt the city of Zarahemla, and were very prosperous (p. 493, par. 3).

100. The disciples of Jesus, whom he had chosen, had all gone to Paradise except the three who obtained the promise that they should not taste of death (p. 493, par. 5).

110. Nephi died, and his son Amos kept the record (p. 493, par. 6).

194. Amos died, and his son Amos kept the record (p. 494, par. 7).

201. The people ceased to have all things in common; they became proud, and were divided into classes (p. 494, par. 7).

210. There were many churches who were opposed to the true Church of Christ (p. 494, par. 8).

230. The people dwindled in unbelief and wickedness from year to year (p. 494, par. 8).

231. A great division took place among the people (p. 495, par. 8).

244. The wicked part of the people became stronger and more numerous than the righteous (p. 495, par. 9).

260. The people began to build up the secret oaths and combinations of Gadianton (p. 495, par. 9).

300. The Gadianton robbers spread themselves all over the face of the land (p. 496, par. 10).

305. Amos died, and his brother Ammaron kept the record in his stead (p. 496, par. 11).

320. Ammaron hid up all the sacred records unto the Lord, and gave

commandment unto Mormon concerning them (p. 496, pars. 11, 1).

321. A war commenced between the Nephites and Lamanites, in which the former were victorious (p. 497, par. 2).

325. Mormon was restrained from preaching to the people, and because of their wickedness, and the prevalence of sorceries, witchcrafts, and magic, their treasures slipped away from them (p. 497, par. 2).

326. Mormon was appointed leader of the Nephite armies (p. 498, par. 3).

330. A great battle took place in the land of Joshua, in which the Nephites were victorious (p. 498, par. 3).

344. Thousands of the Nephites were hewn down in their open rebellion against God (p. 499, par. 4).

345. Mormon had obtained the plates according to commandment of Ammaron, and he made an account of the wickedness and abominations of his people (p. 499, par. 5).

346. The Nephites were driven northward to the land of Shem, and there fought and beat a powerful army of the Lamanites (p. 500, par. 6).

349. The Nephites obtained by treaty all the land of their inheritance, and a ten years' peace ensued (p. 500, par. 6).

360. The king of the Lamanites sent an epistle to Mormon indicating that they were again preparing for war (p. 501, par. 7).

361. A battle took place near the City of Desolation. The Nephites were victorious (p. 501, par. 8).

362. A second battle ensued with the like result (p. 501, par. 8). Mormon now gave up the command of the Nephite army (p. 501, par. 9).

363. The Lamanites obtained a signal victory over the Nephites, and took possession of the City of Desolation (p. 502, par. 1).

364. The Nephites retook the City of Desolation (p. 503, par. 2).

366. The Lamanites again took possession of the City of Desolation, and also succeeded in taking the City of Teancum (p. 503, par. 3).

367. The Nephites avenged the murder of their wives and children, and drove the Lamanites out of their land; and ten years' peace ensued (p. 503, par. 3).

375. The Lamanites came again to battle with the Nephites, and beat them (p. 504, par. 3).
The Nephites from this time forth were prevailed against by the Lamanites; Mormon therefore took all the records which Ammaron had hid up unto the Lord (p. 504, par. 3).

379. Mormon resumed the command of the Nephite armies (p. 504, par. 4).

380. Mormon wrote an abridged account of the events which he had seen (p. 505, par. 5).

384. The Nephites encamped around the hill Cumorah. Mormon hid up in the hill Cumorah all the plates that were committed to his trust, except a few which he gave to his son Moroni (p. 507, pars. 1, 2).

A.C.

The battle of Cumorah was fought, in which two hundred and thirty thousand of the Nephites were slain (p. 507, pars. 2, 3).

400. All the Nephites, as a distinct people, except Moroni, were destroyed (p. 509, par. 1).

421. Moroni finished and sealed up all the records, according to the commandment of God (p. 561, par. 1).

CHAPTER X.

Farther Observations at Great Salt Lake City.

ONE of my last visits was to the court-house on an interesting occasion. The *Palais de Justice* is near where the old fort once was, in the western part of the settlement. It is an unfinished building of adobe, based on red sandstone, with a flag-staff and a tinned roof, which gives it a somewhat Muscovite appearance, and it cost $20,000. The courts and Legislature sit in a neat room, with curtains and chandeliers, and polished pine-wood furniture, all as yet unfaded. The occasion which had gathered together the notabilities of the place was this: Mr. Peter Dotson, the United States Marshal of the Territory, living at Camp Floyd, and being on the opposition side, had made himself—the Mormons say—an unscrupulous partisan. In July, 1859, he came from the cantonment armed with a writ issued by Mr. Delana R. Eckels, Chief Justice of the Supreme Court, and accompanied by two officers of the United States Army, to the Holy City for the purpose of arresting a Mr. Mackenzie—now in the Penitentiary for counterfeiting "quarter-masters' drafts"—an engraver by profession, and then working in the Deserét store of Mr. Brigham Young. Forgery and false coining are associated in the Gentile mind with Mormonism, and inveterately so; whether truly or not, I can not say: it is highly probable that Mr. Bogus's* habitat is not limited by latitude, altitude, or longitude; at the same time, the Saints are too much *en évidence* to entertain him publicly. The marshal, probably not aware that the Territory had passed no law enabling the myrmidons of justice to seize suspicious implements and apparatus made *main forte*, levied, despite due notice, upon what he found appertaining to Mr. Mackenzie, a Bible, a Book of Mormon, and—here was the rub—the copper plates of the Deserét Currency Association. This plunder was deposited for the night with the governor, and was carried in a

----

* Bogus, according to Mr. Bartlett, who quotes the "Boston Courier" of June 12, 1857, is a Western corruption of Borghese, "a very corrupt individual, who, twenty years ago or more, did a tremendous business in the way of supplying the great West and portions of the Southwest with counterfeit bills and drafts on fictitious banks." The word is now applied in the sense of sham, forged, counterfeit, and so on; there are bogus laws and bogus members; in fact, bogus enters every where.

D D

sack on the next day to Camp Floyd. Then the anti-Mormons sang Io pæans; they had—to use a Western phrase—"got the dead wood on Brigham;" letters traced back to officials appeared in the Eastern and other papers, announcing to the public that the Prophet was a detected forger. Presently, the true character of the copper plates appearing, they were generously offered back; but, as trespass had been committed, to say nothing of libel, and as all concerned in the affair were obnoxious men, it was resolved to try law. A civil suit was instituted, and a sum of $1600 was claimed for damage done to the plates by scratching, and for loss of service, which hindered business in the city. The unfortunate marshal, who was probably a "cat's-paw," had "caught a Tartar;" he possessed a house and furniture, a carriage and horses, all of which were attached, and the case of "Brigham Young, sen., vs. P. K. Dotson," ended in a verdict for the plaintiff, viz., value of plates destroyed, $1668; damages, $648 66. The anti-Mormons declared him a martyr; the Mormons, a vicious fool; and sensible Gentiles asserted that he was rightly served for showing evil animus. The case might have ended badly but for the prudence of the governor. Had a descent been made for the purpose of arrest upon the Prophet's house, the consequences would certainly have been serious to the last degree.

The cause was tried in the Probate Court, which I have explained to be a Territorial, not a federal court. The Honorable Elias Smith presided, and the arguments for the prosecution and the defense were conducted by the ablest Mormon and anti-Mormon lawyers. I attended the house, and carefully watched the proceedings, to detect, if possible, intimidation or misdirection; every thing was done with even-handed justice. The physical aspect of the court was that which foreign travelers in the Far West delight to describe and ridicule, wholly forgetting that they have seen the same scene much nearer home. His honor sat with his chair tilted back and his boots on the table, exactly as if he had been an Anglo-Indian collector and magistrate, while by a certain contraction and expansion of the dexter corner of his well-closed mouth I suspected the existence of the quid. The position is queer, but not more so than that of a judge at Westminster sleeping soundly, in the attitude of Pisa's leaning monster, upon the bench. By the justice's side sat the portly figure of Dr. Kay, opposite him the reporters, at other tables the attorneys; the witnesses stood up between the tables, the jury were on the left, and the public, including the governor, was distributed like wall-flowers on benches around the room.

There is a certain monotony of life in Great Salt Lake City which does not render the subject favorable for description. Moreover, a Moslem gloom, the result of austere morals and manners, of the semi-seclusion of the sex, and, in my case, of a reserve arising toward a stranger who appeared in the train of federal officials, hangs over society.   There is none of that class which, according to the French author, *repose des femmes du monde.*   We rose early—in America the climate seems to militate against slugabedism—and breakfasted at any hour between 6 and 9 A.M. Ensued "business," which seemed to consist principally of correcting one's teeth, and walking about the town, with occasional "liquoring up."   Dinner was at 1 P.M., announced, not by the normal gong of the Eastern States, which lately so direfully offended a pair of Anglo-Hibernian ears, but by a hand-bell which sounded the *pas de charge.*   Jostling into the long room of the ordinary, we took our seats, and, seizing our forks, proceeded at once to action, after the fashion of Puddingburn House, where

> "They who came not the first call,
> Got no meat till the next meal."

Nothing but water was drunk at dinner, except when a gentleman preferred to wash down roast pork with a tumbler of milk; wine in this part of the world is of course dear and bad, and even should the Saints make their own, it can scarcely be cheap on account of the price of labor.   Feeding ended with a glass of liquor, not at the bar, because there was none, but in the privacy of one's chamber, which takes from drinking half its charm.   Most wellto-do men found time for a siesta in the early afternoon.   There was supper, which in modern English parlance would be called dinner, at 6 P.M., and the evening was easily spent with a friend.

One of my favorite places of visiting was the Historian and Recorder's Office, opposite Mr. Brigham Young's block.   It contained a small collection of volumes, together with papers, official and private, plans, designs, and other requisites, many of them written in the Deserét alphabet, of which I subjoin a copy.*   It is, as will readily be seen, a stereographic modification of Pitman's and other systems.   Types have been cast for it, and articles are printed in the newspapers at times; as man, however, prefers two alphabets to one, it will probably share the fate of the "Fonetik Nuz."   Sir A. Alison somewhere delivers it as his opinion that the future historian of America will be forced to Europe, where alone his material can be found; so far from this being the case, the reverse is emphatically true : every where in the States, even in the newest, the Historical Society is an institution, and men pride themselves upon laboring for it.   At the office I used to meet Mr. George A. Smith, the armor-bearer to the Prophet in the camp of Zion, who boasts of having sown the first seed, built the first saw-mill, and ground the first flour in Southern Utah, whence the nearest settlements, separated by terrible deserts, were distant 200 miles.   His companions were Messrs. W. Woodruff, Bishop Bentley, who was preparing for a missionary visit to England, and Wm. Thomas Bullock, an intelligent Mormon, who has had the honor to be soundly abused in Mrs. Ferris's 11th letter.

* See next page.

THE DESERÉT ALPHABET.

VOCAL SOUNDS.			
Long.	Double.	Ꝺ . . Ga	
ə . . E	ᴧ . . I	ᴘ . . F	
3 . . A	ϴ . . Ow	ᴕ . . V	
ɘ . . Ah	ω . . Woo	L . . Eth	
Ө . . Aw	⅄ . . Ye	ᵹ . . The	The sounds of the letters ✦, ᴧ, ✓, ɯ, ⌐, q, are heard in the words fit, net, fat, cot, nut, foot.
	Aspirate.		
O . . O	Ψ . . H	8 . . S	
	Articulate Sounds.	6 . . Z	
Φ . . Oo	˥ . . P	ᴅ . . Esh	Ϲ, Ꝺ, L, ᵹ, ᴅ, are heard in the words chee-se, ga-te, s-eth, the, fl-esh.
Short.	ᴚ . . B	ꜱ . . Zhe	ɋ is like ir in st-ér; are is made by the combination of √ɋ; И is heard in l-eng-th.
✦	ᴨ . . T	ᴣ . . Ur	
⌐	ᴇⅼ . . D	ᴜ . . L	
✓	Ϲ . . Che	ꭗ . . M	Learn this Alphabet and appreciate its advantages.
ɯ	ϥ . . G	ᴴ . . N	
ſ	ᴑ . . K	И . . Eng	
q			

This column of letters are the short sounds of the above.

The lady's "wicked Welshman"—I suppose she remembered the well-known line anent the sons of the Cymri—

"Taffy is a Welshman, Taffy is a thief"—

is no Cambrian, but an aborigine of Leek, Staffordshire, England, and was from 1838 to 1843 an excise officer in her majesty's Inland Revenue; he kindly supplied me with a plan of the city, and other information, for which he has my grateful thanks.

At the office, the undying hatred of all things Gentile-federal had reached its climax; every slight offered to the faith by anti-Mormons is there laid up in lavender, every grievance is carefully recorded. There I heard how, at a general conference of the Church of Jesus Christ of Latter-Day Saints, in September, 1851, Perry E. Brocchus, a judge of the Supreme Court, having the design of becoming Territorial delegate to Congress, ascended the rostrum and foully abused their most cherished institution, polygamy.* He was answered with sternness by Mr. Brigham Young, and really, under the circumstances, the Saints behaved very well in not proceeding to *voies de faits*. Mr. Brocchus, seeing personal danger, left the city in company with Chief Justice L. C. Brandenburg and Mr. Secretary Harris, whom the Mormons very naturally accused of carrying away $24,000, the sum appropriated by Congress for the salary and the mileage of the local Legislature, thus putting a clog upon the wheels of government. I also heard how Judge Drummond, in 1856, began the troubles by falsely reporting to the federal authority that the Mormons were in a state of revolt; that they had burned the public library, and were, in fact, defying the Union—how, bigotry doing its work, the officials at Washington believed the tale without investigation, and sent an army which was ready to renew the scenes of St. Bartholomew and Nauvoo. The federal troops were rather pitied than hated; had they been militia they would have been wiped out; but "wretched Dutchmen, and poor devils of Irishmen," acting under orders, were simply despised. Their *fainéantise* was contrasted most unfavorably with the fiery Mormon youth that was spoiling for a fight; that could ride, like part of the horse, down places where no trooper dared venture; that picked up a dollar at full gallop, drove off the invaders' cattle, burned wagons, grass, and provisions, offered to lasso the guns, and, when they had taken a prisoner, drank with him and let him go—how Governor Cumming, after his entry, at once certified the untruthfulness of the scandal spread by Judge Drummond, especially that touching the library and archives, and reported that no federal officer had ever been killed or even assaulted by the Saints—how the effects of these misrepresentations have been and still are serious. In 1857, for instance, the mail was cut off, and a large commercial community was left without postal communication for a whole year: the ostensible reason was the troubled state of the Territory; the real cause was the desire of the Post-office Department to keep the advance of the troops dark. The Mormons

---

* On the 5th of April, 1860, the Chamber of Representatives at Washington passed a projected law to repress polygamy by a majority of 149 to 60. Fortunately, the Committee of the Senate had no time to report upon it, and the slave discussion assumed dimensions which buried Mormonism in complete oblivion.

complain that they have ever been made a subject of political capital. President Van Buren openly confessed to them, "Gentlemen, your cause is just, but I can do nothing for you; if I took your part I should lose the vote of Missouri." Every grievance against them, they say, is listened to and readily believed: as an example, a Mr. John Robinson, of Liverpool, had lately represented to her Britannic majesty's Secretary for Foreign Affairs that his mother and sister were detained in Utah Territory against their will; the usual steps were taken; the British minister applied to the United States Secretary of State, who referred the affair to the governor of the Territory; after which process the tale turned out a mere *canard*. This sister had been married to Mr. Ferguson, adjutant general of the Nauvoo Legion; the mother had left the City of the Saints for Illinois, and had just written to her son-in-law for means by which she could return to a place whence she was to be rescued by British interference. To a false prejudice against themselves the Mormons attribute the neglect with which their project of colonizing Vancouver's Island was treated by the British government, and the active opposition to be expected should they ever attempt to settle in the Valley of the Saskatchewan. And they think it poor policy on the part of England to "bluff off" 100,000 moral, industrious, and obedient subjects, who would be a bulwark against aggression on the part of the States, and tend materially to prepare the thousand miles of valley between the Mississippi and the Pacific for the coming railway.

At the office I also obtained details concerning education in Great Salt Lake City. Before commencing the subject it will be necessary to notice certain statements relating to the ingenuous youth of Utah Territory. It is generally asserted that juvenile mortality here ranks second only to Louisiana, and the fault is, of course, charged upon polygamy. A French author talks of the *mortalité effrayante* among the newly-born, while owning, anomalously, that the survivors *sont braves et robustes*. I "doubt the fact." Mr. Ferris, moreover, declares that there is "nowhere out of the Five Points of New York City a more filthy, miserable, and disorderly rabble of children than can be found in the streets of Great Salt Lake City." As far as my experience goes, it is the reverse. I was surprised by their numbers, cleanliness, and health, their hardihood and general good looks. They are bold and spirited. The Mormon father, like the Indian brave, will not allow the barbarous use of the stick; but this is perhaps a general feeling throughout the States, where the English traveler first observes the docility of the horses and the indocility of the children. But, as regards rudeness, let a man "with whiskers under his snout," *i. e.*, mustaches, ride through a village in Essex or Warwickshire, and he will suffer more contumely at the hands of the infant population in half an hour than in half a year in the

United States or in Utah. M. Remy, despite a "*vif désir*" to judge favorably of the Saints, could not help owning that the children are mostly *grossiers, menteurs, libertins avant l'âge;* that they use *un langage honteux, comme si les mystères de la polygamie leur avaient été révélés dès l'âge de raison.* Apparently since 1855 *cette corruption précoce* has disappeared. I found less premature depravity than in the children of European cities generally. Mr. J. Hyde also brings against the juvenile Saints severe charges, too general, however, not to be applicable to other lands. "Cheating the confiding is called smart trading;" the same has been said of New England. "Mischievous cruelty, evidences of spirit;" the attribute of Plato's boys and of the Western frontiers generally. "Pompous bravado, manly talk;" not unusual in New York, London, and Paris. "Reckless riding, fearless courage;" so apparently thinks the author of "Guy Livingstone." "And if they outtalk their fathers, outwit their companions, whip their schoolteacher, outcurse a Gentile, they are thought to be promising greatness, and are praised accordingly. Every visitor to Salt Lake will recognize the portrait, for every visitor proclaims them to be the most whisky-loving, tobacco-chewing, saucy, and precocious children he ever saw." This is the glance of the anti-Mormon eye pure and simple. Tobacco and whisky are too dear for childhood at the City of the Saints; moreover, twenty years ago, before Tom Brown taught boys not to be ashamed of being called good, a youth at many an English public school would have been "cock of the walk" if gifted with the rare merits described above. I remarked that the juveniles had all the promptness of reply and the peremptoriness of information which characterizes the Scotch and the people of the Eastern States. A half-educated man can not afford to own ignorance. He must answer categorically every question, however beyond his reach; and the result is fatal to the diaries of those travelers who can not diagnostize the disease.

Mormon education is of course peculiar. The climate predisposes to indolence. While the emigrants from the Old Country are the most energetic and hard-working of men, their children, like the race of backwoodsmen in mass, are averse to any but pleasurable physical exertion. The object of the young colony is to rear a swarm of healthy working bees. The social hive has as yet no room for drones, book-worms, and gentlemen. The work is proportioned to their powers and inclinations. At fifteen a boy can use a whip, an axe, or a hoe—he does not like the plow—to perfection. He sits a bare-backed horse like a Centaur, handles his bowie-knife skillfully, never misses a mark with his revolver, and can probably dispose of half a bottle of whisky. It is not an education which I would commend to the generous youth of Paris and London, but it is admirably fitted to the exigencies of the situation. With regard to book-work, there is no difficulty to obtain in Great Salt Lake City that "mediocrity of knowledge between learning and ignorance" which distinguished the grammar-schools of the Western Islands in the days of Samuel Johnson. Amid such a concourse of European converts, any language, from Hebrew to Portuguese, can be learned. Mathematics and the exact sciences have their votaries. There are graduates of Harvard, Dartmouth, and other colleges. I saw one gentleman who had kept a school in Portsmouth, and another, who had had a large academy in Shropshire, taught in the school of the 14th ward. Music, dancing, drawing, and other artlets, which go by the name of accomplishments, have many votaries. Indefatigable travelers there are in abundance. Almost every Mormon is a missionary, and every missionary is a voyager. Captain Gibson, a well-known name for "personal initiative" in the Eastern Main, where he was seized by the Dutch of Java, lately became a convert to Mormonism, married his daughter to Mr. Brigham Young, and in sundry lectures delivered in the Tabernacle, advised the establishment of a stake of Zion in the "Islands of the Seas," which signified, I suppose, his intention that the Netherlands should "smell H—ll." Law is commonly studied, and the practice, as I have shown, is much simplified by the absence of justice. A solicitor from London is also established here. Theology is the growth of the soil. Medicine is represented by two graduates—one of Maryland; the other, who prefers politics to practice, of New York. I am at pains to discover what gave rise to the Gentile reports that the Mormons, having a veritable horror of medicine, leave curing to the priests, and dare not arrogate the art of healing. Masterships and apprenticeships are carefully regulated by Territorial law. Every one learns to read and write; probably the only destitutes are the old European pariahs, and the gleanings from the five or six millions of English illiterati. The Mormons have discovered, or, rather, have been taught, by their necessities as a working population in a state barely twelve years old, that the time of school drudgery may profitably be abridged. A boy, they say, will learn all that his memory can carry during three hours of book-work, and the rest had far better be spent in air, exercise, and handicraft. To their eminently practical views I would offer one suggestion, the advisability of making military drill and extension movements, with and without weapons, a part of scholarhood. For "setting up" the figure, forming the gait, and exercising the muscles, it is the best of gymnastic systems, and the early habit of acting in concert with others is a long stride in the path of soldiership.

While it is the fashion with some to deride the attempts of this painstaking and industrious community of hard-handed men to improve their minds, other anti-Mormons have taken the popular ground of representing the Saints as averse to intellectual activity, despisers of science, respecters only of manual labor, and "*singulièrement épris de la force brutale.*" It is as ungenerous as to ridicule the proceedings of an English Mechanics' Institute, or the compositions of an " Ed. Mechanics' Magazine." The names of their literary institutions are, it is true, somewhat pretentious and grandiloquent; but in these lands there is every where a leaning toward the grandiose. Humility does not pay. Modesty *laudatur et alget*.

As early as December, 1854, an act was approved enabling the Chancellor and Board of Regents of the University of the State of Deserét to appoint a superintendent of common schools for the Territory of Utah, and duly qualified trustees were elected to assess and collect for educational purposes a tax upon all taxable property. In the same year a pathetic memorial was dispatched to Congress, requesting that honorable body to appropriate the sum of $5000 to advance the interests of the University established by law in the City of Great Salt Lake. I know not whether it was granted. As yet there is no educational tax leviable throughout the Territory. Each district makes its own regulations. A city rate supports a school in each ward. The buildings are of plain adobe, thirty feet by twenty. They also serve as meeting-places on Sabbath evenings. There are tutoresses in three or four of the school-houses, who teach all the year round, whereas male education is usually limited by necessity to the three winter months. A certain difficulty exists in finding instructors. As in Australia, the pedagogue is cheaper than a porter, and " turning schoolmaster" is a proverbial phrase about equivalent to coming upon the parish.

The principal educational institutions in Great Salt Lake City have been the following:

1. The Deserét Universal Scientific.
2. The " Polysophical Society," a name given by Judge Phelps.
3. The Seventies' Variety Club.
4. The Council of Health, a medico-physiologio-clinical and matronly establishment, like the Dorcas Societies of the Eastern States.
5. The Deserét Theological Institution, whose President was Mr. Brigham Young.
6. The Deserét Library and Musical Society.
7. The Phrenological and Horticultural Society.
8. The Deserét Agricultural and Manufacturing Society, which has already been alluded to. It has many branch societies, whose members pay an annual subscription of $1.
9. The Academy founded in April, 1860, with an appropriation by the local Legislature of Church money to the extent of $2500. Science and art are to be taught gratis to all who will pledge themselves to learn thoroughly and to benefit the Territory by their exertions. The superintendent is Mr. Orson Pratt; and his son, Mr. O. Pratt, junior, together with Mr. Cobb, a Gentile, acts as teacher. At present those educated are males; in

course of time a girl class will be established for accomplishments and practical education.

The Historian's Office was ever to me a place of pleasant resort; I take my leave of it with many expressions of gratitude for the instructive hours passed there.

It will, I suppose, be necessary to supply a popular view of the "peculiar institution," at once the bane and blessing of Mormonism—plurality. I approach the subject with a feeling of despair, so conflicting are opinions concerning it, and so difficult is it to naturalize in Europe the customs of Asia, Africa, and America, or to reconcile the habits of the 19th century A.D. with those of 1900 B.C. A return to the patriarchal ages, we have seen, has its disadvantages.

There is a prevailing idea, especially in England, and even the educated are laboring under it, that the Mormons are Communists or Socialists of Plato's, Cicero's, Mr. Owen's, and M. Cabet's school; that wives are in public, and that a woman can have as many husbands as the husband can have wives—in fact, to speak colloquially, that they "all pig together." The contrary is notably the case. The man who, like Messrs. Hamilton and Howard Egan, murders, in cold blood, his wife's lover, is invariably acquitted, the jury declaring that civil damages mark the rottenness of other governments, and that "the principle, the only one that beats and throbs through the heart of the *entire inhabitants* (!) of this Territory, is simply this: *The man who seduces his neighbor's wife must die, and her nearest relation must kill him.*" Men, like Dr. Vaughan and Mr. Monroe, slain for the mortal sin, perish for their salvation; the Prophet, were they to lay their lives at his feet, would, because unable to hang or behead them, counsel them to seek certain death in a righteous cause as an expiatory sacrifice,* which may save their souls alive. Their two mortal sins are: 1. Adultery; 2. Shedding innocent blood.

This severity of punishing an offense which modern and civilized society looks upon rather in the light of a sin than of a crime, is clearly based upon the Mosaic code. It is also, *lex loci*, the "common mountain law," a "religious and social custom," and a point of personal honor. Another idea underlies it: the Mormons hold, like the Hebrews of old, "children of shame" in extreme dishonor. They quote the command of God, Deuteronomy (xxiii., 2), "a mamzer shall not enter into the Church of the Lord till the tenth generation," and ask when the order was repealed. They would expel all impurity from the Camp of Zion, and they adopt every method of preventing what they consider a tremendous evil, viz., the violation of God's temple in their own bodies.

---

* The form of death has yet to be decided. They call this a scriptural practice, viz., "to deliver such a one unto Satan for the destruction of the flesh, that the spirit may be saved in the day of the Lord Jesus Christ" (1 Cor., v., 5).

The marriage ceremony is performed in the temple, or, that being impossible, in Mr. Brigham Young's office, properly speaking by the Prophet, who can, however, depute any follower, as Mr. Heber C. Kimball, a simple apostle, or even an elder, to act for him. When mutual consent is given, the parties are pronounced man and wife in the name of Jesus Christ, prayers follow, and there is a patriarchal feast of joy in the evening.

The first wife, as among polygamists generally, is *the* wife, and assumes the husband's name and title.   Her "plurality"-partners are called sisters—such as Sister Anne or Sister Blanche—and are the aunts of her children.   The first wife is married for time, the others are sealed for eternity.   Hence, according to the Mormons, arose the Gentile calumny concerning spiritual wifedom, which they distinctly deny.   Girls rarely remain single past sixteen—in England the average marrying age is thirty—and they would be the pity of the community if they were doomed to a waste of youth so unnatural.

Divorce is rarely obtained by the man who is ashamed to own that he can not keep his house in order; some, such as the President, would grant it only in case of adultery: wives, however, are allowed to claim it for cruelty, desertion, or neglect.   Of late years, Mormon women married to Gentiles are cut off from the society of the Saints, and, without uncharitableness, men suspect a sound previous reason.   The widows of the Prophet are married to his successor, as David took unto himself the wives of Saul; being generally aged, they occupy the position of matron rather than wife, and the same is the case when a man espouses a mother and her daughter.

It is needless to remark how important a part matrimony plays in the history of an individual, and of that aggregate of individuals, a people; or how various and conflicting has been Christian practice concerning it, from the double marriage, civil and religious, the former temporary, the latter permanent, of the Coptic or Abyssinian Church, to the exaggerated purity of Mistress Anna Lee, the mother of the Shakers, who exacted complete continence in a state established according to the first commandment, *crescite et multiplicamini*.   The literalism with which the Mormons have interpreted Scripture has led them directly to polygamy.   The texts promising to Abraham a progeny numerous as the stars above or the sands below, and that "in his seed (a polygamist) all the families of the earth shall be blessed," induce them, his descendants, to seek a similar blessing.   The theory announcing that "the man is not without the woman, nor the woman without the man," is by them interpreted into an absolute command that both sexes should marry, and that a woman can not enter the heavenly kingdom without a husband to introduce her.   A virgin's end is annihilation or absorption, *nox est perpetua una dormienda;* and as baptism for the dead—an old rite, revived and founded upon the writings of St. Paul quoted in the last chapter—has been made a part of practice, vicarious marriage for the departed also enters into the Mormon scheme. Like certain British Dissenters of the royal burgh of Dundee, who in our day petitioned Parliament for permission to bigamize, the Mormons, with Bossuet and others, see in the New Testament no order against plurality,* and in the Old dispensation they find the practice sanctioned in a family, ever the friends of God, and out of which the Redeemer sprang. Finally, they find throughout the nations of the earth three polygamists in theory to one monogame.

The "chaste and plural marriage," being once legalized, finds a multitude of supporters. The anti-Mormons declare that it is at once fornication and adultery — a sin which absorbs all others. The Mormons point triumphantly to the austere morals of their community, their superior freedom from maladive influences, and the absence of that uncleanness and licentiousness which distinguish the cities of the civilized world. They boast that, if it be an evil, they have at least chosen the lesser evil; that they practice openly as a virtue what others do secretly as a sin—how full is society of these latent Mormons!—that their plurality has abolished the necessity of concubinage, cryptogamy, contubernium, celibacy, *mariages du treizième arrondissement*, with their terrible consequences, infanticide, and so forth; that they have removed their ways from those "whose end is bitter as wormwood, and sharp as a two-edged sword." Like its sister institution Slavery, the birth and growth of a similar age, Polygamy acquires *vim* by abuse and detraction: the more turpitude is heaped upon it, the brighter and more glorious it appears to its votaries.

There are rules and regulations of Mormonism—I can not say whether they date before or after the heavenly command to pluralize—which disprove the popular statement that such marriages are made to gratify licentiousness, and which render polygamy a positive necessity. All sensuality in the married state is strictly forbidden beyond the requisite for insuring progeny—the practice, in fact, of Adam and Abraham. During the gestation and nursing of children, the strictest continence on the part of the mother is required—rather for a hygienic than for a religious reason. The same custom is practiced in part by the Jews, and in whole by some of the noblest tribes of savages; the splendid physical development of the Kaffir race in South Africa is attrib-

---

* Histoire des Variations, liv. iv. "L'Evangile n'a ni révoqué ni défendu ce qui avait été permis dans la loi de Moïse à l'égard du mariage : Jesus Christ n'a pas changé la police extérieure, mais il a ajouté seulement la justice et la vie éternelle pour récompense." So, in 1539, the Landgrave Philip of Hesse, wishing to marry a second wife while the first was alive, was permitted to "commit bigamy" by the eminent reformers, M. Luther, Kuhorn (M. Bucer), Melancthon, and others, with the sole condition of secrecy. In the present age, the Right Rev. J. W. Colenso, D.D. and Bishop of Natal, "not only tolerates polygamy in converts, but defends it on the ground of religion and humanity."

uted by some authors to a rule of continence like that of the Mormons, and to a lactation prolonged for two years. The anomaly of such a practice in the midst of civilization is worthy of a place in De Balzac's great repertory of morbid anatomy: it is only to be equaled by the exceptional nature of the Mormon's position, his past fate and his future prospects. Spartan-like, the Faith wants a race of warriors, and it adopts the best means to obtain them.

Besides religious and physiological, there are social motives for the plurality. As in the days of Abraham, the lands about New Jordan are broad and the people few. Of the three forms that unite the sexes, polygamy increases, while monogamy balances, and polyandry diminishes progeny. The former, as Montesquieu acutely suggested, acts inversely to the latter by causing a preponderance of female over male births: "Un fait important à noter," says M. Remy, "c'est qu'il y a en Utah beaucoup plus de naissances de filles que de garçons, resultat opposé à ce qu'on observe dans tous les pays où la monogamie est pratiquée, et parfaitement conforme à ce qu'on a remarqué chez les polygames Mussulmans." M. Remy's statement is as distinctly affirmed by Mr. Hyde, the Mormon apostate. In the East, where the census is unknown, we can judge of the relative proportions of the sexes only by the families of the great and wealthy, who invariably practice polygamy, and we find the number of daughters mostly superior to that of sons, except where female infanticide deludes the public into judging otherwise. In lands where polyandry is the rule, for instance, in the Junsar and Bawur pergunnahs of the Dhun, there is a striking discrepancy in the proportions of the sexes among young children as well as adults: thus, in a village where 400 boys are found, there will be 120 girls; and, on the other hand, in the Gurhwal Hills, where polygamy is prevalent, there is a surplus of female children. The experienced East Indian official who has published this statement* is "inclined to give more weight to nature's adaptability to national habit than to the possibility of infanticide," for which there are no reasons. If these be facts, Nature then has made provision for polygamy and polyandry: our plastic mother has prepared her children to practice them all. Even in Scotland modern statists have observed that the proportion of boys born to girls is greater in the rural districts; and, attributing the phenomenon to the physical weakening of the parents, have considered it a rule so established as to "afford a valuable hint to those who desire male progeny." The anti-Mormons are fond of quoting Paley: "It is not the question whether one man will have more children by five wives, but whether these five women would not have had more children if they had each a husband." The Mormons reply that — setting aside the altered rule of production—their colony, unlike all oth-

* Hunting in the Himalaya, by R. H. W. Dunlop, C.B., B.C.S., F.R.G.S., London, Richard Bentley, 1860.

ers, numbers more female than male immigrants; consequently that, without polygamy, part of the social field would remain untilled.*

To the unprejudiced traveler it appears that polygamy is the rule where population is required, and where the great social evil has not had time to develop itself. In Paris or London the institution would, like slavery, die a natural death; in Arabia and in the wilds of the Rocky Mountains it maintains a strong hold upon the affections of mankind. Monogamy is best fitted for the large, wealthy, and flourishing communities in which man is rarely the happier because his quiver is full of children, and where the Hetæra becomes the succedaneum of the "plurality-wife." Polyandry has been practiced principally by priestly and barbarous tribes,† who fear most for the increase of their numbers, which would end by driving them to honest industry. It reappears in a remarkable manner in the highest state of social civilization, where excessive expenditure is an obstacle to freehold property, and the practice is probably on the increase.

The other motive for polygamy in Utah is economy. Servants are rare and costly; it is cheaper and more comfortable to marry them. Many converts are attracted by the prospect of becoming wives, especially from places where, like Clifton, there are sixty-four females to thirty-six males. The old maid is, as she ought to be, an unknown entity. Life in the wilds of Western America is a course of severe toil: a single woman can not perform the manifold duties of housekeeping, cooking, scrubbing, washing, darning, child-bearing, and nursing a family. A division of labor is necessary, and she finds it by acquiring a sisterhood. Throughout the States, whenever a woman is seen at manual or outdoor work, one is certain that she is Irish, German, or Scandinavian. The delicacy and fragility of the Anglo-American female nature is at once the cause and the effect of this exemption from toil.

The moral influence diffused over social relations by the presence of polygyny will be intelligible only to those who have studied the workings of the system in lands where seclusion is practiced in its modified form, as among the Syrian Christians. In

---

* I am sure of the correctness of this assertion, which is thus denied in general terms by M. Reclus, of the Revue des Deux-Mondes. "A la fin de 1858, on comptait sur le Territoire 3617 maris polygames, dont 1117 ayant cinque femmes où d'avantage: mais un grand nombre de Mormons n'avaient encore pu trouver d'épouses; il est probable même que le chiffre des hommes depasse celui des femmes, comme dans tous les pays peuplés d'emigrans. L'équilibre entre les sexes n'est pas encore établi."

† The Mahabharata thus relates the origin of the practice in India. The five princely Pandava brothers, when contending for a prize offered by the King of Drona to the most successful archer, agreed to divide it if any of them should prove the winner. Arjun, the eldest, was declared victor, and received in gift Draupadi, the king's daughter, who thus became the joint-stock property of the whole fraternity. They lived en famille for some years at the foot of Bairath, the remains of which, or rather a Ghoorka structure on the same site, are still visible on a hill near the N.W. corner of the Dhun. (Hunting in the Himalaya, chap. vii.)

America society splits into two parts—man and woman—even more readily than in England; each sex is freer and happier in the company of its congeners. At Great Salt Lake City there is a gloom like that which the late Professor H. H. Wilson described as being cast by the invading Moslem over the innocent gayety of the primitive Hindoo. The choice egotism of the heart called Love—that is to say, the propensity elevated by sentiment, and not undirected by reason, subsides into a calm and unimpassioned domestic attachment: romance and reverence are transferred, with the true Mormon concentration, from love and liberty to religion and the Church. The consent of the first wife to a rival is seldom refused, and a *ménage à trois*, in the Mormon sense of the phrase, is fatal to the development of that tender tie which must be confined to two. In its stead there is household comfort, affection, circumspect friendship, and domestic discipline. Womanhood is not petted and spoiled as in the Eastern States; the inevitable cyclical revolution, indeed, has rather placed her below par, where, however, I believe her to be happier than when set upon an uncomfortable and unnatural eminence.

It will be asked, What view does the softer sex take of polygyny? A few, mostly from the Old Country, lament that Mr. Joseph Smith ever asked of the Creator that question which was answered in the affirmative. A very few, like the Curia Electa, Emma, the first wife of Mr. Joseph Smith—who said of her, by-the-by, that she could not be contented in heaven without rule—apostatize, and become Mrs. Bridemann. The many are, as might be expected of the easily-moulded weaker vessel, which proves its inferior position by the delicate flattery of imitation, more in favor of polygyny than the stronger.

For the attachment of the women of the Saints to the doctrine of plurality there are many reasons. The Mormon prophets have expended all their arts upon this end, well knowing that without the hearty co-operation of mothers and wives, sisters and daughters, no institution can live long. They have bribed them with promises of Paradise—they have subjugated them with threats of annihilation. With them, once a Mormon always a Mormon. I have said that a modified reaction respecting the community of Saints has set in throughout the States; people no longer wonder that their missionaries do not show horns and cloven feet, and the federal officer, the itinerant politician, the platform orator, and the place-seeking demagogue, can no longer make political capital by bullying, oppressing, and abusing them. The tide has turned, and will turn yet more. But the individual still suffers: the apostate Mormon is looked upon by other people as a scamp or a knave, and the woman worse than a prostitute. Again, all the fervor of a new faith burns in their bosoms with a heat which we can little appreciate, and the revelation of Mr. Joseph Smith is considered on this point as superior to the Christian as the latter is in others to the Mosaic Dispensation. Polygamy is a positive command from heaven: if the flesh is mortified by it, *tant mieux*—"no cross, no crown;" "blessed are they that mourn." I have heard these words from the lips of a well-educated Mormon woman, who, in the presence of a Gentile sister, urged her husband to take unto himself a second wife. The Mormon household has been described by its enemies as a hell of envy, hatred, and malice—a den of murder and suicide. The same has been said of the Moslem harem. Both, I believe, suffer from the assertions of prejudice or ignorance. The temper of the New is so far superior to that of the Old Country, that, incredible as the statement may appear, rival wives do dwell together in amity, and do quote the proverb "the more the merrier." Moreover, they look with horror at the position of the "slavey" of a pauper mechanic at being required to "nigger it" upon love and starvation, and at the necessity of a numerous family. They know that nine tenths of the miseries of the poor in large cities arise from early and imprudent marriages, and they would rather be the fiftieth "sealing" of Dives than the toilsome single wife of Lazarus. The French saying concerning motherhood—"*le premier embellit, le second détruit, le troisième gâte tout,*" is true in the Western world. The first child is welcomed, the second is tolerated, the third is the cause of tears and reproaches, and the fourth, if not prevented by gold pills or some similar monstrosity, causes temper, spleen, and melancholy, with disgust and hatred of the cause. What the Napoleonic abolition of the law of primogeniture, combined with centralization of the peasant class in towns and cities, has effected on this side of the Channel, the terrors of maternity, aggravated by a highly nervous temperament, small cerebellum, constitutional frigidity, and extreme delicacy of fibre, have brought to pass in the older parts of the Union.

Another curious effect of fervent belief may be noticed in the married state. When a man has four or five wives, with reasonable families by each, he is fixed for life: his interests, if not his affections, bind him irrevocably to his new faith. But the bachelor, as well as the monogamic youth, is prone to backsliding. Apostasy is apparently so common that many of the new Saints form a mere floating population. He is proved by a mission before being permitted to marry, and even then women, dreading a possible renegade, with the terrible consequences of a heavenless future to themselves, are shy of saying yes. Thus it happens that male celibacy is mixed up in a curious way with polygamy, and that also in a faith whose interpreter advises youth not to remain single after sixteen, nor girls after fourteen. The celibacy also is absolute; any infraction of it would be dangerous to life. Either, then, the first propensity of the phrenologist is poorly developed in these lands—this has been positively stated of the ruder sex in California—or its action is to be regulated by habit to a greater degree than is usually believed.

I am conscious that my narrative savors of incredibility; the fault is in the subject, not in the narrator. *Exoneravi animan meam.* The best proof that my opinions are correct will be the following quotation. It is a letter addressed to a sister in New Hampshire by a Mrs. Belinda M. Pratt, the wife of the celebrated apostle. M. Remy has apparently dramatized it (vol. ii., chap. ii.) by casting it into dialogue form, and placing it in the mouth of *une femme distinguée.* Most readers, feminine and monogamic, will remark that the lady shows little heart or natural affection; the severe calm of her judgment and reasoning faculties, and the soundness of her physiology, can not be doubted.

"Great Salt Lake City, Jan. 12, 1854.

" DEAR SISTER,—Your letter of October 2 was received on yesterday. My joy on its reception was more than I can express. I had waited so long for your answer to our last, that I had almost concluded my friends were offended, and would write to me no more. Judge, then, of my joy when I read the sentiments of friendship and of sisterly affection expressed in your letter.

"We are all well here, and are prosperous and happy in our family circle. My children, four in number, are healthy and cheerful, and fast expanding their physical and intellectual faculties. Health, peace, and prosperity have attended us all the day long.

"It seems, my dear sister, that we are no nearer together in our religious views than formerly. Why is this? Are we not all bound to leave this world, with all we possess therein, and reap the reward of our doings *here* in a never-ending hereafter? If so, do we not desire to be undeceived, and to *know and to do the truth?* Do we not all wish in our very hearts to be sincere with ourselves, and to be honest and frank with each other?

"If so, you will bear with me patiently while I give a few of my reasons for embracing and holding sacred that particular point in the doctrine of the Church of the Saints to which you, my dear sister, together with a large majority of Christendom, so decidedly object. I mean, a '*plurality of wives.*'

"I have a Bible which I have been taught from my infancy to hold sacred. In this Bible I read of a holy man named Abraham, who is represented as the friend of God, a faithful man in all things, a man who kept the commandments of God, and who is called in the New Testament 'the father of the faithful.' See James, ii., 23; Rom., iv., 16; Gal., iii., 8, 9, 16, 29.

"I find this man had a plurality of wives, some of which were called concubines. See Book of Genesis; and for his concubines, see xxv., 6.

"I also find his grandson Jacob possessed of four wives, twelve sons, and a daughter. These wives are spoken very highly of by the sacred writers as honorable and virtuous women. '*These,*' say the Scriptures, '*did build the house of Israel.*'

"Jacob himself was also a man of God, and the Lord blessed him and his house, and commanded him to be fruitful and multiply. See Gen., xxx. to xxxv., and particularly xxxv., 10, 11.

E E

" I find also that the twelve sons of Jacob by these four wives became princes, heads of tribes, patriarchs, whose names are had in everlasting remembrance to all generations.

" Now God talked with Abraham, Isaac, and Jacob frequently, and his angels also visited and talked with them, and blessed them and their wives and children. He also reproved the sins of some of the sons of Jacob for hating and selling their brother, and for adultery. But in all his communications with them he never condemned their family organization, but, on the contrary, always approved of it, and blessed them in this respect. He even told Abraham that he would make him the father of many nations, and that in him and his seed all the nations and kindreds of the earth should be blessed. See Gen., xviii., 17–19; also xii., 1–3. In later years I find the plurality of wives perpetuated, sanctioned, and provided for in the law of Moses.

" David the Psalmist not only had a plurality of wives, but the Lord himself spoke by the mouth of Nathan the prophet, and told David that *he* (the Lord) had given his master's wives into his bosom; but because he had committed adultery with the wife of Uriah, and had caused his murder, *he* would take *his* wives and give them to a neighbor of his, etc. See 2 Sam., xii., 7–11.

" Here, then, we have the Word of the Lord not only sanctioning polygamy, but actually giving to King David the wives of his master (Saul), and afterward taking the wives of David from him, and giving them to another man. Here we have a sample of severe reproof and punishment for adultery and murder, while polygamy is authorized and approved by the Word of God.

" But to come to the New Testament. I find Jesus Christ speaks very highly of Abraham and his family. He says, '*Many shall come from the east, and from the west, and from the north, and from the south, and shall sit down with Abraham, Isaac, and Jacob in the kingdom of God.*' Luke, xiii., 28, 29.

" Again he said, '*If ye were Abraham's seed ye would do the works of Abraham.*'

" Paul the apostle wrote to the saints of his day, and informed them as follows : ' As many of you as have been baptized into Christ have put on Christ; and if ye are Christ's, then are ye Abraham's seed, and heirs according to the promise.

" He also sets forth Abraham and Sarah as patterns of faith and good works, and as the father and mother of faithful Christians, who should, by faith and good works, aspire to be counted the sons of Abraham and daughters of Sarah.

" Now let us look at some of the works of Sarah, for which she is so highly commended by the apostles, and by them held up as a pattern for Christian ladies to imitate. '*Now Sarah, Abram's wife, bare him no children ; and she had a handmaid, an Egyptian, whose name was Hagar. And Sarah said unto Abram, Behold now, the Lord hath restrained me from bearing : I pray thee, go in unto my maid : it may be that I may obtain children of her. And Abram hearkened unto the voice of Sarah. And Sarah, Abram's wife, took Hagar her maid, the Egyptian, after Abram had dwelt ten years in the land of Canaan, and gave her to her husband Abram to be his wife.'* See Gen., xvi., 1–3.

"According to Jesus Christ and the apostles, then, the only way to be saved is to be adopted into the great family of polygamists by the Gospel, and then strictly follow their examples.

"Again, John the Revelator describes the Holy City of the heavenly Jerusalem, with the names of the twelve sons of Jacob inscribed on the gates. Rev., xxi., 12.

"To sum up the whole, then, I find that polygamists were the friends of God; that the family and lineage of a polygamist were selected in which all nations should be blessed; that a polygamist is named in the New Testament as the father of the faithful Christians of after ages, and cited as a pattern for all generations; that the wife of a polygamist, who encouraged her husband in the practice of the same, and even urged him into it, and officiated in giving him another wife, is named as an honorable and virtuous woman, a pattern for Christian ladies, and the very mother of all holy women in the Christian Church, whose aspiration it should be to be called her daughters; that Jesus Christ has declared that the great fathers of the polygamic family stand at the head in the kingdom of good; in short, that all the saved of after generations should be saved by becoming members of a polygamic family; that all those who do not become members of it are strangers and aliens to the covenant of promise, the commonwealth of Israel, and not heirs according to the promise made to Abraham; that all people from the east, west, north, or south, who enter into the kingdom, enter into the society of polygamists, and under their patriarchal rule and government; indeed, no one can even approach the gates of heaven without beholding the names of twelve polygamists (the sons of four different women by one man) engraven in everlasting glory upon the pearly gates.

"My dear sister, with the Scriptures before me, I could never find it in my heart to reject the heavenly vision which has restored to man the fullness of the Gospel, or the Latter-Day prophets and apostles, merely because in this restoration is included the ancient law of family organization and government preparatory to the restoration of all Israel.

"But, leaving all Scripture, history, or precedent out of the question, let us come to Nature's law. What, then, appears to be the great object of the marriage relations? I answer, the multiplying of our species, the rearing and training of children.

"To accomplish this object, natural law would dictate that a husband should remain apart from his wife at certain seasons, which, in the very constitution of the female, are untimely; or, in other words, indulgence should be not merely for pleasure or wanton desires, but mainly for the purpose of procreation.

"The mortality of nature would teach a mother that, during Nature's process in the formation and growth of embryo man, her heart should be pure, her thoughts and affections chaste, her mind calm, her passions without excitement, while her body should be invigorated with every exercise conducive to health and vigor, but by no means subjected to any thing calculated to disturb, irritate, weary, or exhaust any of its functions.

" And while a kind husband should nourish, sustain, and comfort the wife of his bosom by every kindness and attention consistent with her situation and with his most tender affection, still he should refrain from all those untimely associations which are forbidden in the great constitutional laws of female nature, which laws we see carried out in almost the entire animal economy, human animals excepted.

" Polygamy, then, as practiced under the patriarchal law of God, tends directly to the chastity of women, and to sound health and morals in the constitutions of their offspring.

" You can read in the law of God, in your Bible, the times and circumstances under which a woman should remain apart from her husband, during which times she is considered unclean; and should her husband come to her bed under such circumstances, he would commit a gross sin both against the laws of nature and the wise provisions of God's law, as revealed in his word; in short, he would commit an abomination; he would sin both against his own body, against the body of his wife, and against the laws of procreation, in which the health and morals of his offspring are directly concerned.

" The polygamic law of God opens to all vigorous, healthy, and virtuous females a door by which they may become honorable wives of virtuous men, and mothers of faithful, virtuous, healthy, and vigorous children.

" And here let me ask you, my dear sister, what female in all New Hampshire would marry a drunkard, a man of hereditary disease, a debauchee, an idler, or a spendthrift; or what woman would become a prostitute, or, on the other hand, live and die single, or without forming those inexpressibly dear relationships of wife and mother, if the Abrahamic covenant, or patriarchal laws of God, were extended over your State, and held sacred and honorable by all?

" Dear sister, in your thoughtlessness you inquire, 'Why not a plurality of husbands as well as a plurality of wives?' To which I reply, 1st. God has never commanded or sanctioned a plurality of husbands; 2d. '*Man is the head of the woman*,' and no woman can serve two lords; 3d. Such an order of things would work death and not life, or, in plain language, it would multiply disease instead of children. In fact, the experiment of a plurality of husbands, or rather of one woman for many men, is in active operation, and has been for centuries, in all the principal towns and cities of '*Christendom!*' It is the genius of '*Christian institutions*,' falsely so called. It is the result of '*Mystery Babylon, the great whore of all the earth*.' Or, in other words, it is the result of making void the holy ordinances of God in relation to matrimony, and introducing the laws of Rome, in which the clergy and nuns are forbidden to marry, and other members only permitted to have one wife. This law leaves females exposed to a life of single '*blessedness*,' without husband, child, or friend to provide for or comfort them; or to a life of poverty and loneliness, exposed to temptation, to perverted affections, to unlawful means to gratify them, or to the necessity of selling themselves for lucre. While the man who has abundance of means is tempted to spend it on a mistress in secret, and in a lawless way, the law of God would have given her to him as an honorable wife. These circumstances give rise to murder, infanticide, suicide, disease, remorse, despair, wretchedness, poverty, untimely death, with all the attendant train of jealousies, heartrending miseries, want of confidence in families, contaminating disease, etc.; and, finally, to the horrible license system, in which governments called Christian license their fair daughters, I will not say to play the beast, but to a degradation far beneath them; for every species of the animal creation, except man, refrain from such abominable excesses, and observe in a great measure the laws of nature in procreation.

"I again repeat that Nature has constituted the female differently from the male, and for a different purpose. The strength of the female constitution is designed to flow in a stream of *life*, to nourish and sustain the embryo, to bring it forth, and to nurse it on her bosom. When Nature is not in operation within her in these particulars and for these heavenly ends, it has wisely provided relief at regular periods, in order that her system may be kept pure and healthy, without exhausting the fountain of life on the one hand, or drying up its river of life on the other, till mature age and an approaching change of worlds render it necessary for her to cease to be fruitful, and give her to rest a while, and enjoy a tranquil life in the midst of that family circle, endeared to her by so many ties, and which' may be supposed, at this period of her life, to be approaching the vigor of manhood, and therefore able to comfort and sustain her.

"Not so with man. He has no such drawback upon his strength. It is his to move in a wider sphere. If God shall count him worthy of a hundred fold in this life of wives and children, and houses, and lands, and kindreds, he may even aspire to patriarchal sovereignty, to empire; to be the prince or head of a tribe or tribes; and, like Abraham of old, be able to send forth, for the defense of his country, hundreds and thousands of his own warriors, born in his own house.

"A noble man of God, who is full of the Spirit of the Most High, and is counted worthy to converse with Jehovah or with the Son of God, and to associate with angels and the spirits of just men made perfect—one who will teach his children, and bring them up in the light of unadulterated and eternal truth—is more worthy of a hundred wives and children than the ignorant slave of passion, or of vice and folly, is to have one wife and one child. Indeed, the God of Abraham is so much better pleased with one than with the other, that he would even take away the one talent, which is habitually abused, neglected, or put to an improper use, and give it to him who has ten talents.

"In the patriarchal order of family government the wife is bound to the law of her husband. She honors, ' *calls him lord*,' even as Sarah obeyed and honored Abraham. She lives for him, and to increase his glory, his greatness, his kingdom, or family. Her affections are centred in her God, her husband, and her children.

"The children are also under his government worlds without end. ' *While life, or thought, or being lasts, or immortality endures*,' they are bound to obey him as their father and king.

"He also has a head to whom he is responsible. He must keep

the commandments of God and observe his laws. He must not take a wife unless she is given to him by the law and authority of God. He must not commit adultery, nor take liberties with any woman except his own, who are secured to him by the holy ordinances of matrimony.

"Hence a nation organized under the law of the Gospel, or, in other words, the law of Abraham and the patriarchs, would have no institutions tending to licentiousness; no adulteries, fornications, etc., would be tolerated. No houses or institutions would exist for traffic in shame, or in the life-blood of our fair daughters. Wealthy men would have no inducement to keep a mistress in secret, or unlawfully. Females would have no grounds for temptation in any such lawless life. Neither money nor pleasure could tempt them, nor poverty drive them to any such excess, because the door would be open for every virtuous female to form the honorable and endearing relationships of wife and mother in some virtuous family, where love, and peace, and plenty would crown her days, and truth and the practice of virtue qualify her to be transplanted with her family circle in that eternal soil where they might multiply their children without pain, or sorrow, or death, and go on increasing in numbers, in wealth, in greatness, in glory, might, majesty, power, and dominion, in worlds without end.

"Oh my dear sister, could the dark veil of tradition be rent from your mind—could you gaze for a moment on the resurrection of the just—could you behold Abraham, Isaac, and Jacob, and their wives and children, clad in the bloom, freshness, and beauty of immortal *flesh and bones*—clothed in robes of fine white linen, bedecked with precious stones and gold, and surrounded with an offspring of immortals as countless as the stars of the firmament or as the grains of sand upon the sea-shore, over which they reign as kings and queens forever and ever, you would then know something of the weight of those words of the sacred writer which are recorded in relation to the four wives of Jacob, the mothers of the twelve patriarchs, namely, '*These did build the house of Israel.*'

"Oh that my dear kindred could but realize that they have need to repent of the sins, ignorance, and traditions of those perverted systems which are misnamed '*Christianity*,' and be baptized—*buried* in the water, in the likeness of the death and burial of Jesus Christ, and rise to newness of life in the likeness of his resurrection; receive his Spirit by the laying on of the hands of an apostle, according to promise, and forsake the world and the pride thereof. Thus they would be adopted into the family of Abraham, become his sons and daughters, see and enjoy for themselves the visions of the Spirit of eternal truth, which bear witness of the family order of heaven, and the beauties and glories of eternal kindred ties, for my pen can never describe them.

"Dear, *dear* kindred: remember, according to the New Testament, and the testimony of an ancient apostle, if you are ever saved in the kingdom of God, it must be by being adopted into the family of polygamists—the family of the great patriarch Abraham; for in his seed, or family, and not out of it, '*shall all the nations and kindreds of the earth be blessed.*'

"You say you believe polygamy is '*licentious;*' that it is '*abominable,*' '*beastly,*' etc.; 'the practice only of the most barbarous nations, or of the Dark Ages, or of some great or good men who were left to commit gross sins.' Yet you say you are anxious for me to be converted to your faith; and that we may see each other in this life, and be associated in one great family in that life which has no end.

"Now, in order to comply with your wishes, I must renounce the Old and New Testaments; must count Abraham, Isaac, and Jacob, and their families, as licentious, wicked, beastly, abominable characters; Moses, Nathan, David, and the prophets, no better. I must look upon the God of Israel as partaker in all these abominations, by holding them in fellowship; and even as a minister of such iniquity, by giving King Saul's wives into King David's bosom, and afterward by taking David's wives from him, and giving them to his neighbor. I must consider Jesus Christ, and Paul, and John, as either living in a dark age, as full of the darkness and ignorance of barbarous climes, or else willfully abominable and wicked in fellowshiping polygamists, and representing them as fathers of the faithful and rulers in heaven. I must doom them all to hell, with adulterers, fornicators, etc., or else, at least, assign to them some nook or corner in heaven, as ignorant persons, who, knowing but little, were beaten with few stripes; while, by analogy, I must learn to consider the Roman popes, clergy, and nuns, who do not marry at all, as foremost in the ranks of glory, and those Catholics and Protestants who have but one wife as next in order of salvation, glory, immortality, and eternal life.

"Now, dear friends, much as I long to see you, and dear as you are to me, I can never come to these terms. I feel as though the Gospel had introduced me into the right family, into the right lineage, and into good company. And, besides all these considerations, should I ever become so beclouded with unbelief of the Scriptures and heavenly institutions as to agree with my kindred in New Hampshire in *theory*, still my practical circumstances are different, and would, I fear, continue to separate us by a wide and almost impassable gulf.

"For instance, I have (as you see, in all good conscience, founded on the Word of God) formed family and kindred ties which are inexpressibly dear to me, and which I can never bring my feelings to consent to dissolve. I have a good and virtuous husband whom I love. We have four little children which are mutually and inexpressibly dear to us. And, besides this, my husband has seven other living wives, and one who has departed to a better world. He has in all upward of twenty-five children. All these mothers and children are endeared to me by kindred ties, by mutual affection, by acquaintance and association; and the mothers in particular, by mutual and long-continued exercises of toil, patience, long-suffering, and sisterly kindness. We all have our imperfections in this life; but I know that these are good and worthy women, and that my husband is a good and worthy man; one who keeps the commandments of Jesus Christ, and presides in his family like an Abraham. He seeks to provide for them with all diligence; he loves them all, and seeks to comfort them and make them happy. He teaches them the commandments of Jesus Christ, and gathers them about him in the family circle to call upon his God, both morning and evening. He and his family have the confidence, esteem, good-will, and fellowship of this entire Territory, and of a wide circle of acquaintances in Europe and America. He is a practical teacher of morals and religion, a promoter of general education, and at present occupies an honorable seat in the Legislative Council of this Territory.

"Now, as to visiting my kindred in New Hampshire, I would be pleased to do so were it the will of God. But, first, the laws of that State must be so modified by enlightened legislation, and the customs and consciences of its inhabitants, and of my kindred, so altered, that my husband can accompany me with all his wives and children, and be as much respected and honored in his family organization and in his holy calling as he is at home, or in the same manner as the patriarch Jacob would have been respected had he, with his wives and children, paid a visit to his kindred. As my husband is yet in his youth, as well as myself, I fondly hope we shall live to see that day; for already the star of Jacob is in the ascendency; the house of Israel is about to be restored; while '*Mystery Babylon*,' with all her institutions, awaits her own overthrow. Till this is the case in New Hampshire, my kindred will be under the necessity of coming here to see us, or, on the other hand, we will be mutually compelled to forego the pleasure of each other's company.

"You mention in your letter that Paul the apostle recommended that bishops be the husband of one wife. Why this was the case I do not know, unless it was, as he says, that while he was among Romans he did as Romans did. Rome at that time governed the world, as it were; and, although gross idolaters, they held to the one-wife system. Under these circumstances, no doubt, the apostle Paul, seeing a great many polygamists in the Church, recommended that they had better choose for this particular temporal office men of small families, who would not be in disrepute with the government. This is precisely our course in those countries where Roman institutions still bear sway. Our elders there have but one wife, in order to conform to the laws of men.

"You inquire why Elder W., when at your house, denied that the Church of this age held to the doctrine of plurality. I answer that he might have been ignorant of the fact, as our belief on this point was not published till 1852. And had he known it, he had no right to reveal the same until the full time had arrived. God kindly withheld this doctrine for a time, because of the ignorance and prejudice of the nations of mystic Babylon, that peradventure he might save some of them.

"Now, dear sister, I must close. I wish all my kindred and old acquaintances to see this letter, or a copy thereof, and that they will consider it as if written to themselves. I love them dearly, and greatly desire and pray for their salvation, and that we may all meet with Abraham, Isaac, and Jacob in the kingdom of God.

"Dear sister, do not let your prejudices and traditions keep you from believing the Bible, nor the pride, shame, or love of the world keep you from your seat in the kingdom of heaven, among the royal family of polygamists. Write often and freely.

" With sentiments of the deepest affection and kindred feeling, I remain, dear sister, your affectionate sister,

" BELINDA MARDEN PRATT."

CHAPTER XI.

Last Days at Great Salt Lake City.

I NOW terminate my observations upon the subject of Mormonism. It will be remarked that the opinions of others—not my own—have been recorded as carefully as my means of study have permitted, and that facts, not theories, have been the object of this dissertation.

It will, I think, be abundantly evident that Utah Territory has been successful in its colonization. Every where, indeed, in the New World, the stranger wonders that a poor man should tarry in Europe, or that a rich man should remain in America; nothing but the strongest chains of habit and *vis inertiœ* can reconcile both to their miserable lots. I can not help thinking that, morally and spiritually, as well as physically, the *protégés* of the Perpetual Emigration Fund gain by being transferred to the Far West. Mormonism is emphatically the faith of the poor, and those acquainted with the wretched condition of the English mechanic, collier, and agricultural laborer—it is calculated that a million of them exist on £25 per annum—who, after a life of ignoble drudgery, of toiling through the year from morning till night, are ever threatened with the work-house, must be of the same opinion. Physically speaking, there is no comparison between the conditions of the Saints and the class from which they are mostly taken. In point of mere morality, the Mormon community is perhaps purer than any other of equal numbers.* I have no wish to commend their spiritual, or, rather, their materialistic vagaries—a materialism so leveling in its unauthorized deductions that even the materialist must reject it; but with the mind as with the body, bad food is better than none. When wealth shall be less unequally distributed in England, thus doing away with the contrast of excessive splendor and utter destitution, and when Home Missions shall have done their duty in educating and evangelizing the unhappy pariahs of town and country, the sons of the land which boasts herself to be the foremost among the nations will blush no more to hear that the Mormons or Latter-Day Saints are mostly English.

About the middle of September the time of my departure drew nigh. Judge Flennikin found a change of *venue* to Carson Valley necessary; Thomas, his son, was to accompany him, and the

* I refer the reader to Appendix IV.

Territorial marshal, Mr. Grice—a quondam volunteer in the Mexican War—was part of the cortége. Escort and ambulance had been refused; it was imperative to find both. Several proposals were made and rejected. At last an eligible presented himself. Mr. Kennedy, an Irishman from the neighborhood of Dublin, and an *incola* of California, where evil fate had made him a widower, had "swapped" stock, and was about to drive thirty-three horses and mules to the "El Dorado of the West." For the sum of $150 each he agreed to convey us, to provide an ambulance which cost him $300, and three wagons which varied in price from $25 to $75. We had reason to think well of his probity, concerning which we had taken counsel; and as he had lost a horse or two, and had received a bullet through the right arm in an encounter with the Yuta Indians near Deep Creek on the 3d of July of the same year, we had little doubt of his behaving with due prudence. He promised also to collect a sufficient armed party; and as the road had lately seen troubles—three drivers had been shot and seventeen Indians had been reported slain in action by the federal troops—we were certain that he would keep his word. It was the beginning of the hungry season, when the Indians would be collecting their pine nuts and be plotting onslaughts upon the spring emigrants.

I prepared for difficulties by having my hair "shingled off" till my head somewhat resembled a pointer's dorsum, and deeply regretted having left all my wigs behind me. The marshal undertook to lay in our provisions: we bought flour, hard bread or biscuit, eggs and bacon, butter, a few potted luxuries, not forgetting a goodly allowance of whisky and korn schnapps, whose only demerit was that it gave a taste to the next morning. The traveling canteen consisted of a little china, tin cups and plates, a coffee-pot, frying-pan, and large ditto for bread-baking, with spoons, knives, and forks.

The last preparations were soon made. I wrote to my friends. among others to Dr. Norton Shaw, who read out the missive *magno cum risu audientium*, bought a pair of leather leggins for $5, settled with M. Gebow, a Gamaliel at whose feet I had sat as a student of the Yuta dialect, and defrayed the expenses of living, which, though the bill was curiously worded,* were exemplarily

---

* The bill in question :

Gt. S. L. City, Septeber 18th, 1860.

Captain Burten to James Townsend, Dr.

Aug. 27.	14 Bottle Beer	600
	Belt & Scabbard	500
	Cleaning Vest and Coat	250
	2 Bottles Branday	450
	Washing	525
	to Cash, five dollars	500
	to 3 weaks 3 days Bord	3425
		62·50
	Cash, five dollars	500
		67·50

inexpensive.   Colonel Stambaugh favored me with a parting gift, the "Manual of Surveying Instructions," which I preserve as a reminiscence, and a cocktail whose aroma still lingers in my olfactories.   My last evening was spent with Mr. Stambaugh, when Mr. John Taylor was present, and where, with the kindly aid of Madam, we drank a *café au lait* as good as the *Café de Paris* affords.   I thanked the governor for his frank and generous hospitality, and made my acknowledgments to his amiable wife.   All my adieux were upon an extensive scale, the immediate future being somewhat dark and menacing.

The start in these regions is coquettish as in Eastern Africa. We were to depart on Wednesday, the 19th of September, at 8 A.M.—then 10 A.M.—then 12 A.M.—then, after a deprecatory visit, on the morrow.   On the morning of the eventful next day, after the usual amount of "smiling," and a repetition of adieux, I found myself "all aboord," wending southward, and mentally ejaculating *Hierosolymam quando revisam?*

MOUNT NEBO.

CHAPTER XII.

To Ruby Valley.

MOUNTED upon a fine mule, here worth $240, and "bound" to fetch in California $400, and accompanying a Gentile youth who answered to the name of Joe, I proceeded te take my first lesson in stock-driving. We were convoying ten horses, which, not being wild, declined to herd together, and, by their straggling, made the task not a little difficult to a tyro. The road was that leading to Camp Floyd before described. At the Brewery near Mountain Point we found some attempts at a station, and were charged $1 50 for frijoles, potatoes, and bread: among other decorations on the wall was a sheet of prize-fighters, in which appeared the portraiture of an old man, once the champion of the light weights in the English ring, now a Saint in Great Salt Lake City. The day was fine and wondrous clear, affording us a splendid back view of the Happy Valley before it was finally shut out from sight, and the Utah Lake looked a very gem of beauty, a diamond in its setting of steely blue mountains. After fording the Jordan we were overtaken by Mr. Kennedy, who had been delayed by more last words, and at the dug-out we drank beer with Shropshire Joe the Mormon, who had been vainly attempting to dig water by a divining rod of peach-tree. When moonlight began to appear, Joe the Gentile was ordered by the "boss" to camp out with the horses, where fodder could be found gratis, a commandment which he obeyed with no end of grumbling. It was deep in the night before we entered Frogtown, where a creaking little Osteria supplied us with supper, and I found a bed at the quarters of my friend Captain Heth, who obligingly insisted upon my becoming his guest.

The five days between the 20th and the 26th of September sped merrily at my new home, Camp Floyd; not pressed for time, I embraced with pleasure the opportunity of seeing the most of my American brothers in arms. My host was a son of that Old Dominion of Queen Elizabeth, where still linger traces of the glorious Cavalier and the noble feudal spirit, which (alas!) have almost disappeared from the mother country; where the genealogical tree still hangs against the wall; where the principal families, the Nelsons, Harrisons, Pages, Seldens, and Allens, intermarry and bravely attempt to entail; and where the houses, built of brick brought out from England, still retain traces of the seventeenth century. A winter indeed might be passed most pleasantly on the banks of James River and in the west of Virginia—a refreshing winter to those who love, as I do, the traditions of our ancestors.

From Captain Heth I gathered that in former times, in Western America as in British India, a fair aborigine was not unfrequently the copartner of an officer's hut or tent. The improved communication, however, and the frequency of marriage, have abolished the custom by rendering it unfashionable. The Indian squaw, like the Beebee, seldom looked upon her "mari" in any other light but her banker. An inveterate beggar, she would beg for all her relations, for all her friends, and all her tribe, rather than not beg at all, and the lavatory process required always to be prefaced with the bribe. Officers who were long thrown among the Prairie Indians joined, as did the Anglo-Indian, in their nautches and other amusements, where, if whisky was present, a cut or stab might momentarily be expected. The skin was painted white, black, and red, the hair was dressed and decorated, and the shirt was tied round the waist, while broadcloth and blanket, leggins and moccasins completed the costume. The "crack thing to do" when drinking with Indians, and listening to their monotonous songs and tales, was to imitate Indian customs; to become, under the influence of the jolly god, a Hatim Tai; exceedingly generous; to throw shirt to one man, blanket to another, leggins to a third—in fact, to return home in breech-cloth. Such sprees would have been severely treated by a highly respectable government; they have now, however, like many a pleasant hour in British India, had their day, and are sunk, many a fathom deep, in the genuine Anglo-Scandinavian gloom.

I heard more of army grievances during my second stay at Camp Floyd. The term of a soldier's enlistment, five years, is too short, especially for the cavalry branch, and the facilities for desertion are enormous. Between the two, one third of the army disappears every year. The company which should number 84 has often only 50 men. The soldier has no time to learn his work; he must drive wagons, clear bush, make roads, and build huts and stables. When thoroughly drilled he can take his discharge, and having filled a purse out of his very liberal pay ($11 per mensem), he generally buys ground and becomes a landed proprietor. The officers are equally well salaried; but marching, countermarching, and contingent expenses are heavy enough to make the profession little better than it is in France. The Secretary of War being a civilian, with naturally the highest theoretical idea of discipline and command combined with economy, is always a martinet; no one can exceed the minutest order, and leave is always obtained under difficulties. As the larger proportion of the officers are Southern men, especially Virginians, and as the soldiers are almost entirely Germans and Irish—the Egyptians of modern times—the federal army will take little part in the ensuing contest. It is more than probable that the force will disband, break in two like the nationalities from which it is drawn. As far as I could judge of American officers, they are about as republican in mind and tone of thought as those of the British army. They are aware of the fact that the bundle of sticks requires a tie, but they prefer, as we all do, King Stork to King Log, and King Log to King Mob.

I took sundry opportunities of attending company inspections, and found the men well dressed and tolerably set up, while the bands, being German, were of course excellent. Mr. Chandless and others talk of the United States army discipline as something Draconian; severity is doubtless necessary in a force so constituted, but—a proof of their clemency—desertion is the only crime punishable by flogging. The uniform is a study. The States have attempted in the dress of their army, as in the forms of their government, a moral impossibility. It is expected to be at once cheap and soldier-like, useful and ornamental, light and heavy, pleasantly hot in the arctic regions, and agreeably cool under the tropics. The "military tailors" of the English army similarly forget the number of changes required in civilian raiment, and, looking to the lightness of the soldier's kit, wholly neglect its efficiency, its capability of preserving the soldier's life. The federal uniform consists of a brigand-like and bizarre sombrero, with Mephistophelian cock-plume, and of a blue broadcloth tunic, imitated from the old Kentuckian hunter's surtout or wrapper, with terminations sometimes made to match, at other times too dark and dingy to please the eye. Its principal merit is a severe republican plainness, very consistent with the prepossessions of the people, highly inconsistent with the customs of military nations. Soldiers love to dress up Mars, not to clothe him like a butcher's boy.

The position of Camp Floyd is a mere brick-yard, a basin surrounded by low hills, which an Indian pony would have little difficulty in traversing; sometimes, however, after the fashion of the land, though apparently easy from afar, the summits assume a mural shape, which would stop any thing but a mountain sheep. The rim shows anticlinal strata, evidencing upheavals, disruption, and, lastly, drainage through the kanyons which break the wall. The principal vegetation is the dwarf cedar above, the sage greenwood and rabbit-bush below. The only animals seen upon the plain are jackass-rabbits, which in places afford excellent sport. There are but few Mormons in the valley; they supply the camp with hay and vegetables, and are said to act as spies. The officers can not but remark the coarse features and the animal expression of their countenances. On the outskirts of camp are a few women that have taken sanctuary among the Gentiles, who here muster too strong for the Saints. The principal amusement seemed to be that of walking into and out of the sutlers' stores, the hospitable Messrs. Gilbert's and Livingston's — a *passe temps* which I have seen at "Sukkur Bukkur Rohri"—and in an evening ride, dull, monotonous, and melancholy, as if we were in the vicinity of Hyderabad, Sindh.

I had often heard of a local lion, the Timpanogos Kanyon, and my friends Captains Heth and Gove had obligingly offered to show me its curiosities. After breakfast on the 23d of September —a bright warm day—we set out in a good ambulance, well provided with the materials of a two days' picnic, behind a fine team of four mules, on the road leading to the Utah Lake. After passing Simple Joe's dug-out we sighted the water once more; it was of a whitish-blue, like the milky waves of Jordan, embosomed in the embrace of tall and bald-headed hills and mountains, whose monarch was Nebo of the jagged cone.   Where the wind current sets there are patches of white sand strewn with broken shells and dried water-weed.   Near Pelican Point, a long, projecting rocky spit, there is a fine feeding-ground for geese and ducks, and swimmers and divers may always be seen dotting the surface. On the south rises a conspicuous buttress of black rock, and thirty miles off we could see enormous dust columns careering over the plain.   The western part of the valley, cut with suncracks and nullahs, and dotted with boulders, shelves gradually upward from the selvage of the lake to small divides and dwarf-hill ranges, black with cedar-bush, and traversed only by wood roads.   On the east is the best wheat country in this part of the Territory ; it is said to produce 106 bushels per acre.

After seventeen miles we crossed Jordan Bridge, another rickety affair, for which, being Mormon property, we paid 50 cents; had we been Saints the expense would have been one half.   Two more miles led us to Lehi, a rough miniature of Great Salt Lake City, in which the only decent house was the bishop's ; in British India it would have been the collector and magistrate's.   My companions pointed out to me a hut in which an apostate Mormon's throat had been cut by blackened faces.   It is gratifying to observe that throughout the United States, as in the Old Country, all historical interest pales before a barbarous murder.   As we advanced a wall of rock lay before us ; the strata were in confusion as if a convulsion had lately shuddered through their frame, and tumbled fragments cumbered the base, running up by precipitous ascents to the middle heights.   The colors were as grotesque : the foreground was a mass of emerald cane, high and bushy ; beyond it, the near distance was pink with the beautiful bloom most unpoetically termed " hogweed," and azure with a growth like the celebrated blue-grass of Kentucky ; while the wall itself was a bloodstone dark green with cedar—which, 100 feet tall, was dwarfed to an inch — and red stained with autumnal maple, and below and around the brightest yellow of the faded willow formed the bezel, a golden rim.

Two miles and a half from Lehi led us to American Fork, a soft sweet spring of snow-water, with dark shells adhering to white stones, and a quantity of trout swimming the limpid wave. The bridge was rickety and loose planked—in fact, the worst I ever saw in the United States, where, as a rule, the country bridges can never be crossed without fear and trembling ; the moderate toll was $1 both ways.   Three miles and a half more placed us at Battle Creek, where in 1853 the Yuta Indians fled precipitately from a Mormon charge.   Six miles over a dusty beach conducted us to the mouth of the kanyon, a brown tract crossed by a dusty road and many a spring, and showing the base of the opposite wall encumbered with degraded masses, superimposed upon which were miniature castles. The mouth of the ravine was a romantic spot: the staples were sister giants of brown rock—here sheer, their sloping—where pines and firs found a precarious roothold, and ranged in long perspective lines, while between them, through its channel, verdant with willow, and over a clear pebbly bed, under the screes and scaurs, coursed a mountain torrent more splendid than Ruknabad.

We forded the torrent and pursued the road, now hugging the right, then the left side of the chasm. The latter was exceedingly beautiful, misty with the blue of heaven, and rising till its solidity was blent with the tenuity of ether. The rest of the scenery was that of the great Cotton-wood Kanyon; painting might express the difference, language can not. After six miles of a narrow winding road, we reached the place of Cataracts, the principal lion of the place, and found that the season had reduced them to two thin milky lines coursing down bitumen-colored slopes of bare rock, bordered by shaggy forests of firs and cedars. The shrinking of the water's volume lay bare the formation of the cascades, two steps and a slope, which at a happier time would have been veiled by a continuous sheet of foam.

After finding a suitable spot we outspanned, and, while recruiting exhausted nature, allowed our mules to roll and rest. After dining and collecting a few shells, we remounted and drove back through a magnificent sunset to American Fork, where the bishop, Mr. Lysander Dayton, of Ohio, had offered us bed and board. The good episkopos was of course a Mormon, as we could see by his two pretty wives; he supplied us with an excellent supper as a host, not as an innkeeper. The little settlement was Great Salt Lake City on a small scale—full of the fair sex; every one, by-the-by, appeared to be, or about to be, a mother. Fair, but, alas! not fair to us; it was verily

"Water, water every where,
And not a drop to drink!"

Before setting out homeward on the next day we met O. Porter Rockwell, and took him to the house with us. This old Mormon, in days gone by, suffered or did not suffer imprisonment for shooting or not shooting Governor Boggs, of Missouri: he now herds cattle for Messrs. Russell and Co. His tastes are apparently rural; his enemies declare that his life would not be safe in the City of the Saints. An attempt had lately been made to assassinate him in one of the kanyons, and the first report that reached my ears when *en route* to California was the murder of the old Danite by a certain Mr. Marony. He is one of the triumvirate, the First Presidency of "executives," the two others being Ephe Hanks and Bill Hickman—whose names were loud in the land; they are now, however, going down; middle age has rendered them comparatively inactive, and the rising generation, Lot Huntington, Ike Clawson, and other desperadoes, whose teeth and claws are full grown, are able and willing to stand in their stead. Peter Rockwell was a man about fifty, tall and strong, with ample leather leggins overhanging his huge spurs, and the saw-handles of two revolvers peeping from his blouse. His forehead was already a little bald, and he wore his long grizzly locks after the ancient fashion of the United States, plaited and gathered up at the nape of the neck; his brow, puckered with frowning wrinkles, contrasted curiously with his cool, determined gray eye, jolly red face, well touched up with "paint," and his laughing, good-humored mouth. He had the manner of a jovial, reckless, devil-may-care English ruffian. The officers called him Porter, and preferred him to the "slimy villains" who will drink with a man and then murder him. After a little preliminary business about a stolen horse, all conducted on the amiable, he pulled out a dollar, and sent to the neighboring distillery for a bottle of Valley Tan. The *aguardiente* was smuggled in under a cloth, as though we had been respectables in a Moslem country, and we were asked to join him in a "squar' drink," which means spirits without water. The mode of drinking was peculiar. Porter, after the preliminary sputation, raised the glass with cocked little finger to his lips, with a twinkle of the eye ejaculated "Wheat!" that is to say, "good," and drained the tumbler to the bottom: we acknowledged his civility with a "here's how," and drank Kentucky-fashion, which in English is midshipman's grog. Of these "squar' drinks" we had at least four, which, however, did not shake Mr. Rockwell's nerve, and then he sent out for more. Meanwhile he told us his last adventure — how, when ascending the kanyon, he suddenly found himself covered by two long rifles; how he had thrown himself from his horse, drawn his revolver, and crept behind a bush, and how he had dared the enemy to come out and fight like men. He spoke of one Obry, a Frenchman, lately killed in a street-quarrel, who rode on business from Santa Fé to Independence, about 600 miles, in 110 hours. Porter offered, for the fun of the thing, to excel him by getting over 900 in 144. When he heard that I was preparing for California, he gave me abundant good advice—to carry a double-barreled gun loaded with buck-shot; to "keep my eyes skinned," especially in kanyons and ravines; to make at times a dark camp —that is to say, unhitching for supper, and then hitching up and turning a few miles off the road; ever to be ready for attack when the animals were being inspanned and outspanned, and never to trust to appearances in an Indian country, where the red varmint will follow a man for weeks, perhaps peering through a wisp of grass on a hill-top till the time arrives for striking the blow. I observed that, when thus speaking, Porter's eyes assumed the expression of an old mountaineer's, ever rolling as if set in quicksilver. For the purpose of avoiding "White Indians," the worst of their kind, he advised me to shun the direct route, which he

F F

represented to be about as fit for traveling as is h—ll for a powder magazine, and to journey *viâ* Fillmore and the wonder-bearing White Mountains;* finally, he comforted me with an assurance that either the Indians would not attempt to attack us and our stock—ever a sore temptation to them—or that they would assault us in force and "wipe us out."

When the drinking was finished we exchanged a cordial *poignée de main* with Porter and our hospitable host, who appeared to be the *crême de la crême* of Utah County, and soon found ourselves again without the limits of Camp Floyd.

On the evening of the 25th of September, the judge, accompanied by his son and the Marshal of the Territory, entered the cantonment, and our departure·was fixed for the next day. The morning of the start was spent in exchanging adieux and little gifts with men who had now become friends, and in stirrup-cups which succeeded one another at no longer intervals than quarter hours. Judge Crosby, who had arrived by the last mail, kindly provided me with fishing-tackle which could relieve a diet of eggs and bacon, and made me regret that I had not added to my outfit a Maynard. This, the best of breech-loading guns, can also be loaded at the muzzle; a mere carbine in size, it kills at 1300 yards, and in the United States costs only $40=£8. The judge, a remarkable contrast to the usual Elijah Pogram style that still affects bird's-eye or speckled white tie, black satin waistcoat, and swallow-tailed coat of rusty broadcloth, with terminations to match, had been employed for some time in Oregon and at St. Juan: he knew one of my expatriated friends — poor J. de C., whose exile we all lament—and he gave me introductions which I found most useful in Carson Valley. Like the best Americans, he spoke of the English as brothers, and freely owned the deficiencies of his government, especially in dealing with the frontier Indians.

We started from Lieutenant Dudley's hospitable quarters, where a crowd had collected to bid us farewell. The ambulance, with four mules driven by Mr. Kennedy in person, stood at the door, and the parting stirrup-cup was exhibited with a will. I bade farewell with a true regret to my kind and gallant hosts, whose brotherly attentions had made even wretched Camp Floyd a pleasant *séjour* to me. At the moment I write it is probably desolate, the "Secession" disturbances having necessitated the withdrawal of the unhappies from Utah Territory.

About 4 P.M., as we mounted, a furious dust-storm broke over the plain; perhaps it may account for our night's *méprise*, which

* An emigrant company lately followed this road, and when obliged by the death of their cattle to abandon their kit, they found on the tramp a lump of virgin silver, which was carried to California: an exploring party afterward dispatched failed, however, to make the lead. At the western extremity of the White Mountains there is a mammoth cave, of which one mile has been explored: it is said to end in a precipice, and the enterprising Major Egan is eager to trace its course.

a censorious reader might attribute to our copious libations of whisky. The road to the first mail station, " Meadow Creek," lay over a sage barren; we lost no time in missing it by forging to the west. After hopelessly driving about the country till 10 P.M. in the fine cool night, we knocked at a hut, and induced the owner to appear. He was a Dane who spoke but little English, and his son, "skeert" by our fierceness, began at once to boo-hoo. At last, however, we were guided by our "foreloper" to "Johnston's settlement," in Rock Valley, and we entered by the unceremonious process of pulling down the zigzag fences. After some trouble we persuaded a Mormon to quit the bed in which his wife and children lay, to shake down for us sleeping-places among the cats and hens on the floor, and to provide our animals with oats and hay. Mr. Grice, the marshal, one of the handiest of men, who during his volunteer service in Mexico had learned most things from carrying a musket to cooking a steak, was kind enough to prepare our supper, after which, still sorely laden with whisky dying within us, we turned in.

To Meadow Creek.   27th September.

We rose with the dawn, the cats, and the hens, sleep being impossible after the first blush of light, and I proceeded to inspect the settlement. It is built upon the crest of an earth-wave rising from grassy hollows; the haystacks told of stock, and the bunch-grass on the borders of the ravines and nullahs rendered the place particularly fit for pasturage. The land is too cold for cereals: in its bleak bottoms frost reigns throughout the year; and there is little bench-ground. The settlement consisted of half a dozen huts, which swarmed, however, with women and children. Mr. Kennedy introduced us to a Scotch widow of mature years, who gave us any amount of butter and buttermilk in exchange for a little tea. She was but a lukewarm Mormon, declaring polygamy to be an abomination, complaining that she had been inveigled to a mean place, and that the poor in Mormondom were exceedingly poor. Yet the canny body was stout and fresh, her house was clean and neat, and she washed her children and her potatoes.

We had wandered twenty-five miles out of the right road, and were still distant fifteen to sixteen from the first mail station. For the use of the floor, flies, and permission to boil water, we paid our taciturn Mormon $2, and at noon, a little before the bursting of the dusty storm-gusts, which reproduced the horrors of Sindh, we found ourselves once more in the saddle and the ambulance. We passed by a cattle track on rolling ground dotted with sage and greasewood, which sheltered hosts of jackass-rabbits, and the sego with its beautiful lily-like flowers. After crossing sundry nullahs and pitch-holes with deep and rugged sides, we made the mail station at the west end of Rush Valley, which is about twenty miles distant from Camp Floyd. The little green bottom, with its rush-bordered sinking spring, is called by Captain Simpson "Meadow Creek." We passed a pleasant day in revolver practice with Al. Huntington, the renowned brother of Lot, who had lately bolted to South California, in attempts at rabbit-shooting — the beasts became very wild in the evening — and in dining on an antelope which a youth had ridden down and pistoled. With the assistance of the station-master, Mr. Faust, a civil and communicative man, who added a knowledge of books and drugs to the local history, I compiled an account of the several lines of communication between Great Salt Lake City and California.

Three main roads connect the land of the Saints with the El Dorado of the West—the northern, the central, and the southern.

The northern road rounds the upper end of the Great Salt Lake, and falls into the valleys of the Humboldt and Carson Rivers. It was explored in 1845 by Colonel Frémont,* who, when passing over the seventy waterless miles of the western, a continuation of the eastern desert, lost ten mules and several horses. The "first overland trip" was followed in 1846 by a party of emigrants under a Mr. Hastings, who gave his name to the "cut-off" which has materially shortened the distance. The road has been carefully described in Kelly's California, in Horn's "Overland Guide," and by M. Remy. It is still, despite its length, preferred by travelers, on account of the abundance of grass and water: moreover, there are now but two short stretches of desert.

The southern road, *via* Fillmore and San Bernardino, to San Pedro, where the traveler can embark for San Francisco, is long and tedious; water is found at thirty-mile distances; there are three deserts; and bunch and other grasses are not plentiful. It has one great merit, namely, that of being rarely snowed up, except between the Rio Virgen and Great Salt Lake City : the best traveling is in Spring, when the melting snows from the eastern hills fill the rivulets. This route has been traveled over by

---

* Explored is used in a modified sense. Every foot of ground passed over by Colonel Frémont was perfectly well known to the old trappers and traders, as the interior of Africa to the Arab and Portuguese pombeiros. But this fact takes nothing away from the honors of the man who first surveyed and scientifically observed the country. Among those who preceded Colonel Frémont, the most remarkable, perhaps, was Sylvester Pattie, a Virginian, who, having lost his wife in his adopted home on the Missouri, resolved to trap upon and to trace out the head-waters of the Yellow River. The little company of five persons, among whom were Pattie and his son, set out on the 20th of June, 1824, and on the 22d of August arrived at the head-waters of the Platte, where they found General Pratt proceeding toward Santa Fé. Pattie, in command of 116 men, crossed the dividing ridge, descended into the valley of the Rio Grand del Norto, entered Santa Fé, and trapped on the Gila River. The party broke up on the 27th of November, 1826, when Pattie, accompanied by his son and six others, descended the Colorado, and, after incredible hardships, reached the Hispano-American missions, where they were received with the customary inhumanity. The father died in durance vile ; the son, after being released and vaccinated at San Diego, reached San Francisco, whence he returned home *via* Vera Cruz and New Orleans, after an absence of six years. The whole tale is well told in "Harper's Magazine."

Messrs. Chandless and Remy, who have well described it in their picturesque pages. I add a few notes, collected from men who have ridden over the ground for several years, concerning the stations : the information, however, it will be observed, is merely hearsay.*

The central route is called Egan's by the Mormons, Simpson's by the Gentiles. Mr. or Major Howard Egan is a Saint and well-known guide, an indefatigable mountaineer, who for some time drove stock to California in the employ of Messrs. Livingston, and who afterward became mail-agent under Messrs. Chorpenning and Russell. On one occasion he made the distance in twelve days, and he claims to have explored the present post-office route between 1850 and the winter of 1857–1858. Captain J. H. Simpson, of the federal army, whose itinerary is given in Appendix I., followed between May and June, 1859. He traveled along Egan's path, with a few unimportant deviations, for 300 miles, and left it ten miles west of Ruby Valley, trending southward to the suite of the Carson River. On his return he pursued a more southerly line, and fell into Egan's route about thirty miles west of Camp Floyd. The *employés* of the route prefer Egan's line, declaring that on Simpson's there is little grass, that the springs are mere fiumaras of melted snow, and that the wells are waterless. Bad, however, is the best, as the following pages will, I think, prove.

To Tophet. 28th September.

On a cool and cloudy morning, which at 10 A.M. changed into a clear sunny day, we set out, after paying $3 for three feeds, to make the second station. Our road lay over the seven miles of plain that ended Rush Valley: we saw few rabbits, and the sole vegetation was stunted sage. Ensued a rough divide, stony and

---

* The distance from Great Salt Lake City to San Bernardino is, according to my informant, about 750 miles, and has been accomplished in fourteen days. The road runs through Provo to Salt Cruz, formed by a desert of 50–60 miles, and making Sevier River the half-way point to the capital. At Corn Creek is an Indian farm, and Weaver is 64 miles from Fillmore. Cedar Spring is the entrance to Paravan Valley, where as early as 1806 there was a fort and a settlement. Then comes Fillmore, the territorial capital, and 96 miles afterward it passes through Paravan City in Little Salt Lake Valley. At Cold Creek it forks, the central road being that mostly preferred. The next station is Mountain Meadows, the Southern Rim of the Basin, celebrated for its massacre ; ensues the Santa Clara River, and thence a total of 70 miles, divided into several stages, lead to the Rio Virgen. After following the latter for 20–30 miles, the path crosses the divide of Muddy River, and enters a desert 55–67 miles in breadth leading to Las Vegas. Thirty miles beyond that point lies a pretty water called " Mountain Springs," a preliminary to "Dry Lake," a second desert 40–45 miles broad, and ending at an alkaline water called Kingston Springs. The third desert, 40 miles broad, leads to a post established for the protection of emigrants, and called Bitter or Bidder's Springs, 115 miles from Las Vegas. The next stage of 35 is to the Indian River, a tributary of the Colorado, whence there is another military establishment : the land is now Californian. Thence following and crossing the course of the stream, the traveler sights the Sierra Nevada. After 50 miles down the Mohave Kanyon is San Bernardino, once a thriving Mormon settlement, 90 miles from San Pedro and 120 from San Diego, where water conveyance is found to San Francisco.

dusty, with cahues and pitch-holes: it is known by the name of
General Johnston's Pass.   The hills above it are gray and bald-
headed, a few bristles of black cedar protruding from their breasts,
and the land wears an uninhabitable look.   After two miles of
toil we halted near the ruins of an old station.   On the right side
of the road was a spring half way up the hill: three holes lay
full of slightly alkaline water, and the surplus flowed off in a
black bed of vegetable mud, which is often dry in spring and
summer.   At "Point Look-out," near the counterslope of the divide, we left on the south Simpson's route, and learned by a sign-
post that the distance to Carson is 533 miles.   The pass led to
Skull Valley, of ominous sound.   According to some, the name
is derived from the remains of Indians which are found scattered
about a fine spring in the southern parts.   Others declare that the
mortal remains of bison here lie like pavement-stones or cannon
balls in the Crimean Valley of Death.   Skull Valley stretches
nearly southwest of the Great Salt Lake plain, with which it communicates, and its drainage, as in these parts generally, feeds the
lake.   Passing out of Skull Valley, we crossed the cahues and
pitch-holes of a broad bench which rose above the edge of the
desert, and after seventeen miles beyond the Pass reached the
station which Mormons call Egan's Springs, anti-Mormons Simpson's Springs, and Gentiles Lost Springs.

  Standing upon the edge of the bench, I could see the Tophet
in prospect for us till Carson Valley: a road narrowing in perspective to a point spanned its grisly length, awfully long, and
the next mail station had shrunk to a little black knob.   All was
desert: the bottom could no longer be called basin or valley: it
was a thin fine silt, thirsty dust in the dry season, and putty-like
mud in the spring and autumnal rains.   The hair of this unlove-
ly skin was sage and greasewood: it was warted with sand-heaps;
in places mottled with bald and horrid patches of salt soil, while
in others minute crystals of salt, glistening like diamond-dust in
the sunlight, covered tracts of moist and oozy mud.   Before us,
but a little to the right or north, and nearly due west of Camp
Floyd, rose Granite Mountain, a rough and jagged spine or hog's-
back, inhabited only by wolves and antelopes, hares and squirrels,
grasshoppers, and occasionally an Indian family.   Small sweet
springs are found near its northern and southern points.   The
tradition of the country declares it to be rich in gold, which, however, no one dares to dig.   Our road is about to round the southern extremity, wheeling successively S. and S.E., then W. and
N.W., then S.W. and S.E., and S.W. and N.W.—in fact, round
three quarters of the compass; and for three mortal days we shall
sight its ugly frowning form.   A direct passage leads between it
and the corresponding point of the southern hill: we contemplate,
through the gap, a blue ridge where lies Willow-Spring Station,
the destination of our party after to-morrow; but the straight line

which saves so much distance is closed by bogs for the greater part of the year, and the size of the wild sage would impede our wagon-wheels.

The great desert of Utah Territory extends in length about 300 miles along the western side of the Great Salt Lake. Its breadth varies: a little farther south it can not be crossed, the water, even where not poisonous, being insufficient. The formation is of bottoms like that described above, bench-lands, with the usual parallel and perfectly horizontal water-lines, leaving regular steps, as the sea settled down, by the gradual upheaval of the land. They mark its former elevation upon the sides of the many detached ridges trending mostly N. and S. Like the rim of the Basin, these hills are not a single continuous mountain range which might be flanked, but a series of disconnected protrusions above the general level of the land. A paying railway through this country is as likely as a profitable canal through the Isthmus of Suez: the obstacles must be struck at right angles, with such assistance as the rough kanyons and the ravines of various levels afford.

We are now in a country dangerous to stock. It is a kind of central point, where Pávant, Gosh Yuta (popularly called Gosh Ute), and Panak (Bannacks) meet. Watches, therefore, were told off for the night. Next morning, however, it was found that all had stood on guard with unloaded guns.

To Fish Springs. 29th September.

At Lost Springs the party was mustered. The following was found to be the material. The Ras Kafilah was one Kennedy, an Irishman, whose brogue, doubly Dublin, sounded startlingly in the Great American Desert. On a late trip he had been victimized by Indians. The savages had driven off two of his horses into a kanyon within sight of the Deep-Creek Station. In the hurry of pursuit he spurred up the ravine, followed by a friend, when, sighting jerked meat, his own property, upon the trees, he gave the word *sauve qui peut*. As they whirled their horses the Yutas rushed down the hill to intercept them at the mouth of the gorge, calling them in a loud voice dogs and squaws, and firing sundry shots, which killed Kennedy's horse and pierced his right arm. Most men, though they jest at scars before feeling a wound, are temporarily cowed by an infliction of the kind, and of that order was the good Kennedy.

The next was an excellent traveler, by name Howard. On the road between Great Salt Lake City and Camp Floyd I saw two men, who addressed me as Mr. Kennedy the boss, and, finding out their mistake, followed us to the place of rendezvous. The party, with one eye gray and the other black, mounted upon a miserable pony, was an American. After a spell at the gold diggings of California he had revisited the States, and he now wished to return to his adopted country without loss of time. He was a hardy, fine-tempered fellow, exceedingly skilled in driving stock. His companion was a Frenchman and ex-Zouave, who, for reasons best known to himself, declared that he came from Cuba, and that he had forgotten every word of Spanish. Like foreigners among Anglo-Scandinavians generally, the poor devil fared badly. He could not hold his own. With the most labor, he had the worst of every thing. He felt himself *mal placé*, and before the end of the journey he slunk away.

At Lost Springs we were joined by two Mormon fugitives, "pilgrims of love," who had, it was said, secretly left the city at night, fearing the consequences of having "loved not wisely, but too well." The first of the Lotharios was a Mr. R——, an English farrier-blacksmith, mounted upon an excellent horse and leading another. He soon took offense at our slow rate of progress, and, afflicted by the thought that the avenger was behind him, left us at Deep Creek, and "made tracks" to Carson City in ten days, with two horses and a total traveling kit of two blankets. We traced him to California by the trail of falsehoods which he left on the road. His comrade, Mr. A——, a New Englander, was also an apostate Mormon, a youth of good family and liberal education, who, after ruining himself by city sites and copper mines on Lake Superior, had permanently compromised himself with society by becoming a Saint. Also a Lothario, he had made his escape, and he proved himself a good and useful member of society. I could not but admire the acuteness of both these youths, who, flying from justice, had placed themselves under the protection of a judge. They reminded me of a debtor friend who found himself secure from the bailiff only within the walls of Spike Island or Belvidere Place, Southwark.

Another notable of the party was an apostate Jew and *soi disant* apostate Mormon who answered to the name of Rose. He had served as missionary in the Sandwich Islands, and he spoke Kanaka like English. His features were those which Mr. Thackeray loves to delineate; his accents those which Robson delights to imitate. He denied his connection with the Hebrews. He proved it by eating more, by driving a better bargain, by doing less work than any of the party. It was truly refreshing to meet this son of old Houndsditch in the land of the Saints, under the shadow of New Zion, and the only drawback to our enjoyment was the general suspicion that the honorable name of apostate covered the less respectable calling of spy. He contrasted strongly with Jim Gilston of Illinois, a lath-like specimen of humanity, some six feet four in length—a perfect specimen of the Indianized white, long hair, sun-tanned, and hatchet-faced; running like an ostrich, yelping like a savage, and ready to take scalp at the first provocation. He could not refrain, as the end of the journey drew nigh, from deserting without paying his passage. Mr. Colville, a most determined Yankee, far advanced in years, was equally remarkable. He had $90 in his pocket. He shivered for want of a blanket, and he lived on hard bread, bacon, and tea, of which no man was ever seen to partake. Such were the seven "free men," the independent traders of the company. There were also six "broths of boys," who paid small sums up to $40 for the benefit of our escort, and who were expected to drive and to do general work. Traveling soon makes friends. No illusions of *amicitia*, however, could blind my eyes to the danger of entering an Indian country with such an escort. Untried men for the most part, they would have discharged their weapons in the air and fled at the whoop of an Indian, all of them, including Jake the Shoshonee, who had been permitted to accompany us as guide, and excepting our stanch ones, Howard, "Billy" the colt, and "Brandy" the dog.

The station was thrown somewhat into confusion by the presence of a petticoat, an article which in these regions never fails to attract presents of revolvers and sides of bacon. "Gentle Annie," attended by three followers, was passing in an ambulance from California to Denver City, where her "friend" was. To most of my companions' inquiries about old acquaintances in California, she replied, in Western phrase, that the individual subject of their solicitude had "got to git up and git," which means that he had found change of air and scene advisable. Most of her sentences ended with a "you *bet*," even under circumstances where such operation would have been quite uncalled for. So it is related that when Dr. P——, of Camp Floyd, was attending Mrs. A. B. C. at a most critical time, he asked her tenderly, "Do you suffer much, Mrs. C. ?" to which the new matron replied, "You *bet!*"

We set out about noon, on a day hot as midsummer by contrast with the preceding nights, for a long spell of nearly fifty miles. Shortly after leaving the station the road forks. The left-hand path leads to a grassy spring in a dwarf kanyon near the southern or upper part of a river bottom, where emigrants are fond of camping. The hills scattered around the basin were of a dark metallic stone, sunburnt to chocolate. The strata were highly tilted up and the water-lines distinctly drawn. After eight miles we descended into the yellow silty bed of a bald and barren fiumara, which was not less than a mile broad. The good judge sighed when he contrasted it with Monongahela, the "river of the falling banks." It flows northward, and sinks near the western edge of the lake. At times it runs three feet of water. The hills around are white-capped throughout the winter, but snow seldom lies more than a week in the bottoms.

After twenty miles over the barren plain we reached, about sunset, the station at the foot of the Dugway. It was a mere "dug-out"—a hole four feet deep, roofed over with split cedar trunks, and provided with a rude adobe chimney. The tenants were two rough young fellows—station-master and express rider

—with their friend, an English bull-dog.   One of them had amused himself by decorating the sides of the habitation with niches and Egyptian heads.   Rude art seems instinctively to take that form which it wears on the banks of Nilus, and should some Professor Rafinesque discover these traces of the aborigines after a sepulture of a century, they will furnish materials for a rich chapter on anti-Columbian immigration.   Water is brought to the station in casks.   The youths believe that some seven miles north of the " Dugway" there is a spring, which the Indians, after the fashion of that folk, sensibly conceal from the whites.   Three wells have been sunk near the station.   Two soon led to rock; the third has descended 120 feet, but is still bone dry.   It passes first through a layer of surface silt, then through three or four feet of loose, friable, fossilless, chalky lime, which, when slaked, softened, and, mixed with sand, is used as mortar.   The lowest strata are of quartz gravel, forming in the deeper parts a hard conglomerate.   The workmen complained greatly of the increasing heat as they descend.   Gold now becomes uppermost in man's mind.   The youths, seeing me handle the rubbish, at once asked me if I was prospecting for gold.

After roughly supping we set out, with a fine round moon high in the skies, to ascend the " Dugway Pass" by a rough dusty road winding round the shoulder of a hill, through which a fiumara has burst its way.   Like other Utah mountains, the highest third rises suddenly from a comparatively gradual incline, a sore formation for cattle, requiring draught to be at least doubled.   Arriving on the summit, we sat down, while our mules returned to help the baggage-wagons, and amused ourselves with the strange aspect of the scene.   To the north, or before us, and far below, lay a long broad stretch, white as snow — the Saleratus Desert, west of the Great Salt Lake.   It wore a grisly aspect in the silvery light of the moon.   Behind us was the brown plain, sparsely dotted with shadows, and dewless in the evening as in the morning.   As the party ascended the summit with much noisy shouting, they formed a picturesque group—the well-bred horses wandering to graze, the white-tilted wagons with their panting mules, and the men in felt capotes and huge leather leggins.   In honor of our good star which had preserved every hoof from accident, we "liquored up" on that summit, and then began the descent.

Having reached the plain, the road ran for eight miles over a broken surface, with severe pitch-holes and wagon-tracks which have lasted many a month; it then forked.   The left, which is about six miles the longer of the two, must be taken after rains, and leads to the Devil's Hole, a curious formation in a bench under " High Mountain," about ninety miles from Camp Floyd, and south, with a little westing, of the Great Salt Lake.   The Hole is described as shaped like the frustrum of an inverted cone, forty feet in diameter above, twelve to fifteen below. As regards the depth, four lariats of forty feet each, and a line at the end, did not, it is said, reach the bottom. Captain Simpson describes the water as brackish. The drivers declare it to be half salt. The Devil's Hole is popularly supposed to be an air-vent or shaft communicating with the waters of the Great Salt Lake in their subterraneous journey to the sea (Pacific Ocean). An object cast into it, they say, is sucked down and disappears; hence, if true, probably the theory.

We chose the shorter cut, and, after eight miles, rounded Mountain Point, the end of a dark brown butte falling into the plain. Opposite us and under the western hills, which were distant about two miles, lay the station, but we were compelled to double, for twelve miles, the intervening slough, which no horse can cross without being mired. The road hugged the foot of the hills at the edge of the saleratus basin, which looked like a furrowed field in which snow still lingers. In places, warts of earth tufted with greasewood emerged from hard, flaky, curling silt-cakes; in others, the salt frosted out of the damp black earth like the miniature sugar-plums upon chocolate bonbons. We then fell into a saline resembling freshly-fallen snow. The whiteness changes to a slaty blue, like a frozen pond when the water still underlies it; and, to make the delusion perfect, the black rutted path looked as if lately cut out after a snow-storm. Weird forms appeared in the moonlight. A line of sand-heaps became a row of railroad cars; a raised bench was mistaken for a paling; and the bushes were any thing between a cow and an Indian. This part of the road must be terrible in winter; even in the fine season men are often compelled to unpack half a dozen times.

After ascending some sand-hills we halted for the party to form up in case of accident, and Mr. Kennedy proceeded to inspect while we prepared for the worst part of the stage—the sloughs. These are three in number, one of twenty and the two others of 100 yards in length. The tule, the bayonet-grass, and the tall rushes enable animals to pass safely over the deep slushy mud, but when the vegetation is well trodden down, horses are in danger of being permanently mired. The principal inconvenience to man is the infectious odor of the foul swamps. Our cattle were mad with thirst; however, they crossed the three sloughs successfully, although some had nearly made Dixie's Land in the second.

Beyond the sloughs we ascended a bench, and traveled on an improved road. We passed sundry circular ponds garnished with rush; the water is sulphury, and, according to the season, is warm, hot, or cold. Some of these debord, and send forth what the Somal would call Biya Gora, "night-flowing streams." About 3 A.M., cramped with cold, we sighted the station, and gave the usual "Yep! yep!" A roaring fire soon revived us; the strong ate supper and the weak went to bed, thus ending a somewhat fatiguing day.

To Willow Creek. 30th September.

On this line there are two kinds of stations—the mail station, where there is an agent in charge of five or six "boys," and the express station—every second—where there is only a master and an express rider. The boss receives $50—$75 per mensem, the boy $35. It is a hard life, setting aside the chance of death—no less than three murders have been committed by the Indians during this year—the work is severe; the diet is sometimes reduced to wolf-mutton, or a little boiled wheat and rye, and the drink to brackish water; a pound of tea comes occasionally, but the droughty souls are always "out" of whisky and tobacco. At "Fish Springs," where there is little danger of savages, two men had charge of the ten horses and mules; one of these was a German Swiss from near Schaffhausen, who had been digging for gold to little purpose in California.

A clear cool morning succeeding the cold night aroused us betimes. Nature had provided an ample supply of warm water, though slightly sulphury, in the neighboring pot-holes, and at a little distance from the station was one conveniently cool. The fish from which the formation derives its name is a perch-like species, easily caught on a cloudy day. The men, like the citizens of Suez, accustom themselves to the "rotten water," as strangers call it, and hardly relish the purer supplies of Simpson's Springs or Willow Springs: they might have built the station about one mile north, near a natural well of good cool water, but apparently they prefer the warm bad.

The saleratus valley looked more curious in daylight than in moonlight. The vegetation was in regular scale; smallest, the rich bunch-grass on the benches; then the greasewood and the artemisia, where the latter can grow; and largest of all, the dwarf cedar. All was of lively hue, the herbage bright red, yellow, and sometimes green, the shrubs were gray and glaucous, the cedars almost black, and the rim of hills blue-brown and blue. We had ample time to contemplate these curiosities, for Kennedy, whose wits, like those of Hiranyaka, the mouse, were mightily sharpened by the possession of wealth, had sat up all night, and wanted a longer sleep in the morning. After a breakfast which the water rendered truly detestable, we hitched up about 10 A.M., and set out *en route* for Willow Springs.

About an hour after our departure we met the party commanded by Lieutenant Weed, two subaltern officers, ninety dragoons, and ten wagons; they had been in the field since May, and had done good service against the Gosh Yutas. We halted and "liquored up," and, after American fashion, talked politics in the wilderness. Half an hour then led us to what we christened "Kennedy's Hole," another circular bowl, girt with grass and rush, in the plain under a dark brown rock, with black bands and scatters of stone. A short distance beyond, and also on the right of the road, lay the "Poison Springs," in a rushy bed: the water was temptingly clear, but the bleached bones of many a quadruped skeleton bade us beware of it. After turning a point we saw in front a swamp, the counterpart of what met our eyes last night; it renewed also the necessity of rounding it by a long southerly sweep. The scenery was that of the Takhashshua near Zayla, or the delicious land behind Aden, the Arabian sea-board. Sand-heaps—the only dry spots after rain—fixed by tufts of metallic green salsolæ, and guarded from the desert wind by rusty cane-grass, emerged from the wet and oozy plain, in which the mules often sank to the fetlock. The unique and snowy floor of thin nitre, bluish where deliquescent, was here solid as a sheet of ice; there a net-work of little ridges, as if the salt had expanded by crystallization, with regular furrows worked by rain. After heavy showers it becomes a soft, slippery, tenacious, and slushy mud, that renders traveling exceeding laborious; the glare is blinding by day, and at night the refrigerating properties of the salt render the wind bitterly cold, even when the mercury stands at 50° F.

We halted to bait at the half-way house, the fork of the road leading to Pleasant Valley, an unpleasant place, so called because discovered on a pleasant evening. As we advanced the land improved, the salt disappeared, the grass was splendidly green, and, approaching the station, we passed Willow Creek, where gophar-holes and snipes, willows and wild roses, told of life and gladdened the eye. The station lay on a bench beyond the slope. The express rider was a handsome young Mormon, who wore in his felt hat the effigy of a sword; his wife was an Englishwoman, who, as usual under the circumstances, had completely thrown off the Englishwoman. The station-keeper was an Irishman, one of the few met among the Saints. Nothing could be fouler than the log hut; the flies soon drove us out of doors; hospitality, however, was not wanting, and we sat down to salt beef and bacon, for which we were not allowed to pay. The evening was spent in setting a wolf-trap, which consisted of a springy pole and a noose: we strolled about after sunset with a gun, but failed to bag snipe, wild-fowl, or hare, and sighted only a few cunning old crows, and black swamp-birds with yellow throats. As the hut contained but one room, we slept outside. The Gosh Yuta are apparently not a venturesome people; still, it is considered advisable at times to shift one's sleeping quarters, and to acquire the habit of easily awaking.

To Deep Creek and halt. 1st and 2d of October, 1860.

A "little war" had been waging near Willow Springs. In June the station was attacked by a small band of Gosh Yuta, of whom three were shot and summarily scalped; an energetic proceeding, which had prevented a repetition of the affair. The savages, who are gathering their pine-nut harvest, and are driven by destitution to beg at the stations, to which one meal a week will attach them, are now comparatively peaceful: when the emigration season recommences they are expected to be troublesome, and their numbers — the Pa Yutas can bring 12,000 warriors into the field — render them formidable. "Jake," the Shoshonee, who had followed us from Lost Springs, still considered his life in danger; he was as unwilling to wend his way alone as an Arab Bedouin or an African negro in their respective interiors. With regard to ourselves, Lieutenant Weed had declared that there was no danger; the station people thought, on the contrary, that the snake, which had been scotched, not killed, would recover after the departure of the soldiers, and that the work of destruction had not been carried on with sufficient vigor.

At 6 A.M. the thermometer showed 45° F.; we waited two hours, till the world had time to warm. After six miles we reached "Mountain Springs," a water-sink below the bench-land, tufted round with cotton-wood, willow, rose, cane, and grass. On our right, or eastward, lay Granite Rock, which we had well-nigh rounded, and through a gap we saw Lost-Springs Station, distant apparently but a few hours' canter. Between us, however, lay the horrible salt plain—a continuation of the low lands bounding the western edge of the Great Salt Lake—which the drainage of the hills over which we were traveling inundates till June.

After twelve miles over the bench we passed a dark rock, which protects a water called Reading's Springs, and we halted to form up at the mouth of Deep-Creek Kanyon. This is a dangerous gorge, some nine miles long, formed by a water-course which sheds into the valley of the Great Salt Lake. Here I rode forward with "Jim," a young express rider from the last station, who volunteered much information upon the subject of Indians. He carried two Colt's revolvers, of the dragoon or largest size, considering all others too small. I asked him what he would do if a Gosh Yuta appeared. He replied that if the fellow were civil he might shake hands with him, if surly he would shoot him; and, at all events, when riding away, that he would keep a "stirrup eye" upon him: that he was in the habit of looking round corners to see if any one was taking aim, in which case he would throw himself from the saddle, or rush on, so as to spoil the shooting—the Indians, when charged, becoming excited, fire without effect. He mentioned four Red Men who could "draw a bead" against any white; usually, however, they take a minute to load; they require a long aim, and they stint their powder. He pointed out a place where Miller, one of the express riders, had lately been badly wounded, and lost his horse. Nothing, certainly, could be better fitted for an ambuscade than this gorge, with its caves and holes in snow-cuts, earth-drops, and lines of strata, like walls of rudely-piled stone; in one place we saw the ashes of an Indian encampment; in another, a whirlwind, curling, as smoke would rise, from behind a projecting spur, made us advance with the greatest caution.

As we progressed the valley opened out, and became too broad to be dangerous.   Near the summit of the pass the land is well lined with white sage, which may be used as fodder, and a dwarf cedar adorns the hills.   The ground gives out a hollow sound, and the existence of a spring in the vicinity is suspected.   Descending the western water-shed, we sighted, in Deep-Creek Valley, St. Mary's County, the first patch of cultivation since leaving Great Salt Lake.   The Indian name is Aybá-pá, or the Clay-colored Water; pity that America and Australia have not always preserved the native local terms.   It is bisected by a rivulet in which three streamlets from the southern hills unite; like these features generally, its course is northward till it sinks: fields extend about one mile from each bank, and the rest of the yellow bottom is a tapestry of wire grass and wheat grass.   An Indian model farm had been established here; the war, however, prevented cultivation; the savages had burned down the house, and several of them had been killed by the soldiers.   On the west of the valley were white rocks of the lime used for mortar: the hills also showed lias and marble-like limestones.   The eastern wall was a grim line of jagged peaks, here bare with granite, there black with cedar; they are crossed by a short cut leading to the last station, which, however, generally proves the longest way, and in a dark ravine Kennedy pointed out the spot where he had of late nearly left his scalp.   Coal is said to be found there in chunks, and gold is supposed to abound; the people, however, believing that the valley can not yet support extensive immigration, conceal it probably by "counsel."

At 4 P.M. we reached the settlement, consisting of two huts and a station-house, a large and respectable-looking building of unburnt brick, surrounded by fenced fields, water-courses, and stacks of good adobe.   We were introduced to the Mormon station-master, Mr. Sevier, and others.   They are mostly farm-laborers, who spend the summer here and supply the road with provisions: in the winter they return to Grantsville, where their families are settled.   Among them was a Mr. Waddington, an old Pennsylvanian and a bigoted Mormon.   It is related of him that he had treasonably saved 300 Indians by warning them of an intended attack by the federal troops.   He spoke strongly in favor of the despised Yutas, declared that they are ready to work, and can be led to any thing by civility.   The anti-Mormons declared that his praise was for interested motives, wishing the savages to labor for him gratis; and I observed that when Mr. Waddington started to cut wood in the kanyon, he set out at night, lest his dust should be seen by his red friends.

The Mormons were not wanting in kindness; they supplied us

with excellent potatoes, and told us to make their house our home. We preferred, however, living and cooking afield. The station was dirty to the last degree: the flies suggested the Egyptian plague; they could be brushed from the walls in thousands; but, though sage makes good brooms, no one cares to sweep clean. This, I repeat, is not Mormon, but Western: the people, like the Spaniards, apparently disdain any occupation save that of herding cattle, and will do so till the land is settled. In the evening Jake the Shoshonee came in, grumbling loudly because he had not been allowed to ride; he stood cross-legged like an African, ate a large supper at the station, and a second with us. No wonder that the savage in civilization suffers, like the lady's lapdog, from "liver." He was, however, a first-rate hand in shirking any work except that of peering and peeping into every thing; neither Gospel nor gunpowder can reform this race. Mr. R——, the English farrier and Lothario, left us on this day, after a little quarrel with Kennedy. We were glad to receive permission to sleep upon the loose wheat in an inner room: at 8 A.M. the thermometer had shown 59° F., but on this night ice appeared in the pails.

The next day was a halt; the stock wanted rest and the men provisions. A "beef"—the Westerns still retain the singular of "beeves"—was killed, and we obtained a store of potatoes and wheat. Default of oats, which are not common, this heating food is given to horses—12 lbs. of grain to 14 of long forage—and the furious riding of the Mormons is the only preventive of its evil effects. The people believe that it causes stumbling by the swelling of the fetlock and knee joint; similarly every East Indian ghorewalla will declare that wheaten bread makes a horse tokkar khana—"eat trips." The *employés* of the station were quiet and respectable, a fact attributed by some of our party to the want of liquor, which is said to cause frequent fights. Our party was less peaceable; there had been an extensive prigging of blankets; the cold now made them valuable, and this drove the losers "fighting mad."

En route again. 3d October.

The severity of the last night made us active; the appearance of deep snow upon the mountains and of ice in the valleys was an intelligible hint that the Sierra Nevada which lay before us would be by no means an easy task. Despite, therefore, the idleness always engendered by a halt, and the frigid blasts which poured down from the eastern hills, where rain was falling in torrents, we hitched up, bade adieu to our Mormon host, and set out about 4 P.M. Antelope Springs, the next station, was 30 miles distant; we resolved, therefore, to divide it, after the fashion of Asia and Africa, by a short forenoon march.

The road runs to the southwest down the Deep-Creek Valley, and along the left bank of the western rivulet. Near the divide we found a good bottom, with plenty of water and grass; the only fuel was the sage-bush, which crackled merrily, like thorns, under the pot, but tainted the contents with its medicinal odor. The wagons were drawn up in a half circle to aid us in catching the mules; the animals were turned out to graze, the men were divided into watches, and the masters took up their quarters in the wagons. Age gave the judge a claim to the ambulance, which was admitted by all hands; I slept with "Scotch Joe," an exceedingly surly youth, who apparently preferred any thing to work. At 8 P.M. a storm of wind and rain burst upon us from the S.W.: it was so violent that the wagons rocked before the blast, and at times the chance of a capsize suggested itself. The weather was highly favorable for Indian plundering, who on such nights expect to make a successful attack.

To the Wilderness. 4th October.

We awoke early in the frigid S.W. wind, the thermometer showing 39° F. After a few hundred yards we reached "Eight-mile Springs," so called from the distance to Deep Creek. The road, which yesterday would have been dusty to the hub, was now heavy and viscid; the rain had washed out the saleratus, and the sight and scent, and the country generally, were those of the environs of a horse-pond. An ugly stretch of two miles, perfectly desert, led to Eight-mile-Spring Kanyon, a jagged little ravine about 500 yards long, with a portaled entrance of tall rock. It is not, however, considered dangerous.

Beyond the kanyon lay another grisly land, if possible more deplorable than before; its only crops were dust and mud. On the right hand were turreted rocks, around whose base ran Indian trails, and a violent west wind howled over their summits. About 1 30 P.M. we came upon the station at Antelope Springs: it had been burned by the Gosh Yutas in the last June, and had never been rebuilt. "George," our cook, who had been one of the inmates at the time, told us how he and his *confrères* had escaped. Fortunately, the corral still stood: we found wood in plenty, water was lying in an adjoining bottom, and we used the two to brew our tea.

Beyond Antelope Springs was Shell Creek, distant thirty miles by long road and eighteen by the short cut. We had some difficulty in persuading Kennedy to take the latter; property not only sharpens the intellect, it also generates prudence, and the ravine is a well-known place for ambush. Fortunately two express riders came in and offered to precede us, which encouraged us. About 3 P.M. we left the springs and struck for the mouth of the kanyon, which has not been named; Sevier and Farish are the rival claimants. Entering the jagged fir and pine-clad breach, we found the necessity of dismounting. The bed was dry—it floods in spring and autumn—but very steep, and in a hole on the right stood water, which we did not touch for fear of poison. Reach-

G G

ing the summit in about an hour we saw below the shaggy foreground of evergreens, or rather ever-blacks, which cast grotesque
and exaggerated shadows in the last rays of day, the snowy-white
mountains, gloriously sunlit, on the far side of Shell Creek.   Here
for the first time appeared the piñon pine (*P. Monophyllus*), which
forms the principal part of the Indian's diet; it was no beauty to
look upon, a dwarfish tree, rendered shrub-like by being feathered
down to the ground.   The nut is ripe in early autumn, at which
time the savages stow away their winter provision in dry ravines
and pits.   The fruit is about the size of a pistachio, with a decided flavor of turpentine, tolerably palatable, and at first laxa-
tive.   The cones are thrown upon the fire, and when slightly
burnt the nuts are easily extracted; these are eaten raw, or like
the Hindoo's toasted grains.   The harvest is said to fail every
second year.   Last season produced a fine crop, while in this autumn many of the trees were found, without apparent reason but
frost, dead.

We resumed the descent along a fiumara, which presently
"sank," and at 5 P.M. halted in a prairillon somewhat beyond.
Bunch-grass, sage-fuel, and water were abundant, but the place
was favorable for an attack.   It is a golden rule in an Indian
country never to pitch near trees or rocks that can mask an approach, and we were breaking it in a place of danger.   However,
the fire was extinguished early, so as to prevent its becoming a
mark for Indians, and the pickets, placed on both sides of the ravine, were directed to lie motionless a little below the crest, and
to fire at the first comer.   I need hardly say we were not mur-
dured; the cold, however, was uncommonly piercing.

To "Robber's Roost." 5th October.

We set out at 6 A.M. the next morning, through a mixture of
snow and hail and howling wind, to finish the ravine, which was
in toto eight miles long.   The descent led us to Spring Valley, a
bulge in the mountains about eight miles broad, which a sharp
divide separates from Shell Valley, its neighbor.   On the summit
we fell into the line of rivulet which gives the low lands a name.
At the foot of the descent we saw a woodman, and presently the
station.   Nothing could more want tidying than this log hut,
which showed the bullet-marks of a recent Indian attack.   The
master was a Français de France, Constant Dubail, and an ex-
Lancier: his mother's gossip had received a remittance of 2000
francs from a son in California, consequently he had torn himself
from the *sein* of *sa pauvre mère*, and with three others had started
in search of fortune, and had nearly starved.   The express riders
were three roughs, of whom one was a Mormon.   We passed our
time while the mules were at bait in visiting the springs.   There
is a cold creek 200 yards below the station, and close by the hut
a warm rivulet, said to contain leeches.   The American hirudo,

however, has a serious defect in a leech—it will not bite; the faculty, therefore, are little addicted to hirudination; country doctors rarely keep the villainous bloodsuckers, and only the wealthy can afford the pernicious luxury, which, imported from Spain, costs $12 per dozen, somewhat the same price as oysters at Nijni Novgorod.

The weather, which was vile till 10 A.M., when the glass showed 40° (F.), promised to amend, and as the filthy hole—still full of flies, despite the cold—offered no attraction, we set out at 2 P.M. for Egan's Station, beyond an ill-omened kanyon of the same name. We descended into a valley by a regular slope—in proportion as we leave distance between us and the Great Salt Lake the bench formation on this line becomes less distinct—and traversed a barren plain by a heavy road. Hares and prairie-hens seemed, however, to like it, and a frieze of willow thicket at the western end showed the presence of water. We in the ambulance halted at the mouth of the kanyon; the stock and the boys had fallen far behind, and the place had an exceedingly bad name. But the cold was intense, the shades of evening were closing in, so we made ready for action, looked to the priming of gun and revolver, and then *en avant!* After passing that kanyon we should exchange the land of the Gosh Yuta for those of the more friendly Shoshonee.

An uglier place for sharp-shooting can hardly be imagined. The floor of the kanyon is almost flush with the bases of the hills, and in such formations, the bed of the creek which occupies the sole is rough and winding. The road was vile — now winding along, then crossing the stream—hedged in with thicket and dotted with boulders. Ahead of us was a rocky projection which appeared to cross our path, and upon this Point Dangerous every eye was fixed.

Suddenly my eye caught sight of one fire—two fires under the black bunch of firs half way up the hill-side on our left, and as suddenly they were quenched, probably with snow. Nothing remained but to hear the war-whoop, and to see a line of savages rushing down the rocks. We loosed the doors of the ambulance, that we might jump out, if necessary, and tree ourselves behind it; and knowing that it would be useless to return, drove on at our fastest speed, with sleet, snow, and wind in our faces. Under the circumstances, it was cold comfort to find, when we had cleared the kanyon, that Egan's Station at the farther mouth had been reduced to a chimney-stack and a few charred posts. The Gosh Yutas had set fire to it two or three days before our arrival, in revenge for the death of seventeen of their men by Lieutenant Weed's party. We could distinguish the pits from which the wolves had torn up the corpses, and one fellow's arm projected from the snow. After a hurried deliberation, in which Kennedy swore, with that musical voice in which the Dublin swains delight, that "shure we were all kilt"—the possession of property not only actuates the mind, and adds industry to its qualities, it also produces a peculiar development of cautiousness—we un-hitched the mules, tethered them to the ambulance, and planted ourselves behind the palisade, awaiting all comers, till the boys could bring re-enforcement. The elements fought for us: al-though two tongues of high land directly in front of us would have formed a fine mask for approach, the snow lay in so even a sheet that a prowling coyote was detected, and the hail-like sleet which beat fiercely on our backs would have been a sore incon-venience to a party attacking in face. Our greatest disadvantage was the extreme cold; it was difficult to keep a finger warm enough to draw a trigger. Thomas, the judgeling, so he was called, was cool as a cucumber, mentally and bodily : youths gen-erally are. Firstly, they have their "*preuves*" to make; second-ly, they know not what they do.

After an hour's freezing, which seemed a day's, we heard with quickened ears the shouts and tramp of the boys and the stock, which took a terrible load off the exile of Erin's heart. We threw ourselves into the wagons, numbed with cold, and forgot, on the soft piles of saddles, bridles, and baggage, and under heaps of blankets and buffalos, the pains of Barahut. About 3 A.M. this enjoyment was brought to a close by arriving at the end of the stage, Butte Station. The road was six inches deep with snow, and the final ascent was accomplished with difficulty. The good station-master, Mr. Thomas, a Cambrian Mormon, who had, he informed me, three brothers in the British army, bade us kind-ly welcome, built a roaring fire, added meat to our supper of cof-fee and doughboy, and cleared by a summary process among the snorers places for us on the floor of "Robber's Roost," or "Thieves' Delight," as the place is facetiously known throughout the coun-try-side.

Halt at "Robber's Roost." 6th October.

The last night's sound sleep was allowed to last through the morning. This day was perforce a halt: the old white mare and her colt had been left at the mouth of the kanyon, and one of the Shoshonee Indian servants of the station had been persuaded by a bribe of a blanket and some gunpowder to return for them. About noon we arose, expecting a black fog, and looked down upon Butte Valley, whose northern edge we had traversed last night. Snow still lay there—that bottom is rarely without frost —but in the fine clear sunny day, with the mercury at 43° F. in the shade, the lowest levels re-became green, the hill cedars turn-ed once more black, earth steamed like a garment hung out to dry, and dark spots here and there mottled the hills, which were capped with huge turbans of muslin-like mist. While the Sho-shonee is tracking and driving the old mare, we will glance around the " Robber's Roost," which will answer for a study of the West-ern man's home.

It is about as civilized as the Galway shanty, or the normal dwelling-place in Central Equatorial Africa. A cabin fronting east and west, long walls thirty feet, with port-holes for windows, short ditto fifteen; material, sandstone and bog ironstone slabs compacted with mud, the whole roofed with split cedar trunks, reposing on horizontals which rested on perpendiculars. Behind the house a corral of rails planted in the ground; the inclosed space a mass of earth, and a mere shed in one corner the only shelter. Outside the door—the hingeless and lockless backboard of a wagon, bearing the wounds of bullets—and resting on lintels and staples, which also had formed parts of locomotives, a slab acting stepping-stone over a mass of soppy black soil strewed with ashes, gobs of meat offals, and other delicacies. On the right hand a load of wood; on the left a tank formed by damming a dirty pool which had flowed through a corral behind the "Roost." There was a regular line of drip distilling from the caked and hollowed snow which toppled from the thick thatch above the cedar braces.

The inside reflected the outside. The length was divided by two perpendiculars, the southernmost of which, assisted by a half-way canvas partition, cut the hut into unequal parts. Behind it were two bunks for four men: standing bedsteads of poles planted in the ground, as in Australia and Unyamwezi, and covered with piles of ragged blankets. Beneath the frame-work were heaps of rubbish, saddles, cloths, harness, and straps, sacks of wheat, oats, meal, and potatoes, defended from the ground by underlying logs, and dogs nestled where they found room. The floor, which also frequently represented bedstead, was rough, uneven earth, neither tamped nor swept, and the fine end of a spring oozing through the western wall kept part of it in a state of eternal mud. A redeeming point was the fireplace, which occupied half of the northern short wall: it might have belonged to Guy of Warwick's great hall; its ingle nooks boasted dimensions which one connects with an idea of hospitality and jollity; while a long hook hanging down it spoke of the bouillon-pot, and the iron oven of hot rolls. Nothing could be more simple than the furniture. The chairs were either posts mounted on four legs spread out for a base, or three-legged stools with reniform seats. The tables were rough-dressed planks, two feet by two, on rickety trestles. One stood in the centre for feeding purposes; the other was placed as buffet in the corner near the fire, with eating apparatus—tin coffee-pot and gamelles, rough knives, "pitchforks," and pewter spoons. The walls were pegged to support spurs and pistols, whips, gloves, and leggins. Over the door, in a niche, stood a broken coffee-mill, for which a flat stone did duty. Near the entrance, on a broad shelf raised about a foot from the ground, lay a tin skillet and its "dipper." Soap was supplied by a handful of gravel, and evaporation was expected to act towel. Under the board was a pail of water with a floating can, which enabled the inmates to supply the drainage of everlasting chaws. There was no sign of Bible, Shakspeare, or Milton; a Holywell-Street romance or two was the only attempt at literature. *En revanche,* weapons of the flesh, rifles, guns, and pistols, lay and hung all about the house, carelessly stowed as usual, and tools were not wanting—hammers, large borers, axe, saw, and chisel. An almost invariable figure in these huts is an Indian standing cross-legged at the door, or squatting uncomfortably close to the fire. He derides the whites for their wastefulness, preferring to crouch in parties of three or four over a little bit of fuel than to sit before a blazing log. These savages act, among other things, as hunters, bringing home rabbits and birds. We tried our revolvers against one of them, and beat him easily; yet they are said to put, three times out of four, an arrow through a keyhole forty paces off. In shooting they place the thumb and forefinger of the right hand upon the notch, and strengthen the pull by means of the second finger stretched along the bowstring. The left hand holds the whipped handle, and the shaft rests upon the knuckle of the index.

From Mr. Thomas we heard an account of the affair which took place near Egan's Kanyon. In the last August, Lieutenant Weed happened to be "on a scout," with seventeen mounted riflemen, after Indians. An express rider from the West had ridden up to the station, which, being in a hollow, can not be seen from afar, and found it surrounded by Gosh Yuta Indians. The fellows had tied up the master and the boy, and were preparing with civilized provisions a good dinner for themselves, to be followed by a little treat in the form of burning down the house and roasting their captives. The Indians allowed the soldiers brought up by the express rider to draw near, thinking that the dust was raised by fresh arrivals of their own people; and when charged, at once fled. The mounted riflemen were armed with revolvers, not with sabres, or they would have done considerable execution; as it was, seventeen of the enemy remained upon the field, besides those who were carried off by their friends. The Indian will always leave a scalped and wounded fellow-tribesman in favor of an unscalped corpse.

In the evening the Shoshonee returned, bringing with him the white mare and her colt, which he had recovered *selon lui* from the hands of two Gosh Yutas. The weather still held up; we had expected to be snowed up in five days or so; our departure, therefore, was joyfully fixed for the morrow.

To Ruby Valley.   7th October.

A frosty night was followed by a Tuscan day: a cold tramontana from the south, and a clear hot sun, which expanded the mercury at 10 A.M. to 70° F. After taking leave of the hospitable station-master, we resumed the road which ran up the short

and heavy ascent, through a country here and there eighteen
inches deep in snow, and abounding in large sage and little rabbits. A descent led into Long Valley, whose northern end we
crossed, and then we came upon a third ascent, where, finding a
sinking creek, a halt was called for lunch. The formation of the
whole country is a succession of basins and divides. Ensued another twelve miles' descent, which placed us in sight of Ruby Valley, and a mile beyond carried us to the station.

Ruby Valley is a half-way house, about 300 miles from Great
Salt Lake City, and at the same distance from Carson Valley. It
derives its name from the small precious stones which are found
like nuggets of gold in the crevices of primitive rock. The
length of the valley is about 100 miles, by three or four broad,
and springs are scattered in numbers along the base of the western mountains. The cold is said to be here more severe than in
any place on the line of road, Spring Valley excepted. There is,
however, excellent bench-land for grazing. In this season the
scenery is really pretty. The white peaks tower over hill-land
black with cedar, and this looks down upon the green bottom
scattered over with white sage—winter above lying by the side
of summer below.

We were received at the Ruby-Valley Station by Colonel Rogers,
better known as "Uncle Billy." He had served in the troublous
days of California as marshal, and has many a hairbreadth escape
to relate. He is now assistant Indian agent, the superintendent
of a government model farm, and he lives *en garçon*, having left
his wife and children at Frogtown. We were soon introduced to
the chief of the country, Chyŭkŭpĭchyă (the "old man"), a word
of unpronounceable slur, changed by whites into Chokop ("earth").
His lands are long to the north and south, though of little breadth.
He commands about 500 warriors, and, as Uncle Billy is returning to Frogtown, he is collecting a large hunting-party for the autumnal battue. In 1849 his sister was wantonly shot by emigrants
to California. He attacked the train, and slew in revenge five
men, a fact with which we were not made acquainted till after our
departure. His father and grandfather are both alive, but they
have abdicated under the weight of years and infirmities, reserving their voices for the powwow.

We dined in the colonel's stone hut, and then saw the lions
feed ; after us, Chokop and five followers sat down with knife
and fork before a huge tureen full of soft pie, among which they
did terrible execution, champing and chewing with the noisiness
of wild beasts, and eating each enough for three able-bodied sail-
ors. The chief, a young man twenty-five years old, had little to
denote the Indian except vermilion where soap should have been ;
one of his companions, however, crowned with eagle's feathers disposed in tulip shape, while the claws depended gracefully down
his back, was an object worthy of Guinea. All were, however, to

appearance, happy, and for the first time I heard an Indian really laugh outright. Outside squatted the common herd in a costume which explains the prevalence of rheumatism. The men were in rags, yet they had their coquetry, vermilion streaked down their cheeks and across their foreheads—the Indian fashion of the omnilocal rouge. The women, especially the elders, were horrid objects, shivering and half dressed in breech-cloths and scanty capes or tippets of wolf and rabbit skin : the existence of old age, however, speaks well for the race. Both are unclean; they use no water where Asiatics would; they ignore soap, and rarely repair to the stream, except, like animals, in hot weather.

We then strolled about the camp and called upon the two Mistresses Chokop. One was a buxom dame, broad and strong, with hair redolent of antelope marrow, who boasted of a "wikeap" or wigwam in the shape of a conical tent. The other, much her junior, and rather pretty, was sitting apart in a bower of bushes, with a newly-born pappoose in a willow cage to account for her isolation : the poor thing would have been driven out even in the depth of winter, and were she to starve, she must do without meat. As among the Jews, whenever the Great Father is angry with the daughters of Red Men, they sit apart; they never touch a cooking utensil, although it is not held impure to address them, and they return only when the signs of wrath have passed away. The abodes of the poorer clansmen were three-quarter circles of earth, sticks, and sage-bush to keep off the southerly wind. A dog is usually one of the occupants. Like the African, the Indian is cruel to his brute, starves it and kicks it for attempting to steal a mouthful: "Love me, love my dog," however, is his motto, and he quarrels with the stranger that follows his example. The furniture was primitive. Upon a branch hung a dried antelope head used in stalking: concerning this sport Uncle Billy had a story of his nearly being shot by being mistaken for the real animal; and tripods of timber supporting cloths and moccasins, pans, camp-kettles, stones for grinding grass-seed, and a variety of baskets. The material was mostly willow twig, with a layer of gum, probably from the pine-tree. Some were watertight like the "Hán" of Somaliland; others, formed like the Roman amphora, were for storing grain; while others, in giant cocked-hat shape, were intended for sweeping in crickets and the grass-seeds upon which these Indians feed. The chief gramineæ are the atriplex and chenopodaceous plants. After inspecting the camp we retired precipitately : its condition was that of an Egyptian army's last nighting-place.

About two miles from the station there is a lake covered with water-fowl, from the wild swan to the rail. I preferred, however, to correct my Shoshonee vocabulary under the inspection of Mose Wright, an express rider from a neighboring station. None of your "one-horse" interpreters, he had learned the difficult dialect in his youth, and he had acquired all the intonation of an Indian. Educated beyond the reach of civilization, he was in these days an oddity; he was convicted of having mistaken a billiard cue for a whip handle, and was accused of having mounted the post supporting the electric telegraph wire in order to hear what it was saying. The evening was spent in listening to Uncle Billy's adventures among the whites and reds. He spoke highly of his *protégés*, especially of their affection and fidelity in married life: they certainly appeared to look upon him as a father. He owed something to legerdemain; here, as in Algeria, a Houdin or a Love would be great medicine-men with whom nobody would dare to meddle. Uncle Billy managed to make the post pay by peltries of the mink, wolf, woodchuck or ground-hog, fox, badger, antelope, black-tailed deer, and others. He illustrated the peculiarities of the federal government by a curious anecdote. The indirect or federal duties are in round numbers $100,000,000, of which $60,000,000 are spent, leaving a surplus of forty for the purpose of general corruption: the system seems to date from the days of the "ultimus Romanorum," President Jackson. None but the largest claimants can expect to be recognized. A few years ago one of the Indian agents in —— was asked by a high official what might be about the cost of purchasing a few hundred acres for a government farm. After reckoning up the amount of beads, wire, blankets, and gunpowder, the total was found to be $240. The high official requested his friend to place the statement on paper, and was somewhat surprised the next morning to see the $240 swollen to $40,000. The reason given was characteristic: "What great government would condescend to pay out of £8,000,000 a paltry £48, or would refuse to give £8000?"

CHAPTER XIII.

To Carson Valley.

Before resuming the Itinerary, it may be advisable briefly to describe the various tribes tenanting this Territory.

We have now emerged from the Prairie Indians, the Dakotah, Crow, Kiowa, Comanche, Osage, Apache, Cheyenne, Pawnee, and Arapaho. Utah Territory contains a total of about 19,000 souls of two great kindred races, the Shoshonee or Snake, and the Yuta, called Uche by the Spaniards and Ute by the Anglo-American trappers. Like the Comanche and Apache, the Pimas, the Lipans, and the people of the Pueblos, they are of the Hispano-American division, once subject to the Conquistadores, and are bounded north by the Pánák* (Bannack) and the once formidable Black-

* The Panak is a small tribe of 500 souls, now considered dangerous: the greater

feet. The Shoshonee own about one third of the Territory; their principal settlements lie north of the Great Salt Lake, and on the line of the Humboldt or Mary River, some 400 miles west, and 100 to 125 south of the Oregon line. They number about 4500 souls, and are wildest in the southeast parts of their motherland. The Yuta claim the rest of the Territory between Kansas, the Sierra Nevada, New Mexico, and the Oregon frontier. Of course the two peoples are mortal foes, and might be well pitted against each other. The Snakes would form excellent partisan warriors.

The Shoshonee number fourteen tribes regularly organized; the principal, which contains about 12,000 souls, is commanded by Washaki, assisted, as usual, by sub-chiefs, four to six in number. Five bands, numbering near 1000 each, roam about the mountains and kanyons of Great Salt Lake County, Weber, Bear, Cache, and Malad Valleys, extending eighty miles north from the Holy City. These have suffered the most from proximity with the whites, and no longer disdain agriculture. One band, 150 to 180 in number, confines itself to the North Californian Route from Bear and Malad Valleys to the Goose-Creek Mountains. Seven bands roam over the country from the Humboldt River to 100 miles south of it, and extend about 200 miles from east to west: the principal chief, Wanamuka, or "the Giver," had a band of 155 souls, and lived near the Honey Lake.

The Yuta claim, like the Shoshonee, descent from an ancient people that immigrated into their present seats from the northwest. During the last thirty years they have considerably decreased according to the mountaineers, and have been demoralized mentally and physically by the emigrants: formerly they were friendly, now they are often at war with the intruders. As in Australia, arsenic and corrosive sublimate in springs and provisions have diminished their number. The nation is said to contain a total of 14,000 to 15,000 souls, divided into twenty-seven bands, of which the following are the principal:

The Pá Yuta (Pey Utes) are the most docile, interesting, and powerful, containing twelve bands;* those in the west of the Ter-

part resides in Oregon, the smaller about ninety miles in the N.E. of the Territory, where they hunt the bison and the elk. For thirty years they have traded with Fort Bridger, and when first known they numbered 1200 lodges. "Horn," their principal chief, visited the place in April, 1858. Mr. Forney, the late Superintendent of Indian Affairs in Utah Territory, granted them a home in the lands of Washaki, and they have intermarried and lived peaceably with the Shoshonee.

* These are, 1. Wanamuka's; 2. San Joaquim, near the forks of that river in Carson Valley, numbering 170; 3. Hadsapoke, or Horse-stopper band, of 110, in Gold Kanyon, on Carson River; 4. Wahi or Fox band, on Big Bend of Carson River, 130 in number; 5 and 6. Odakeo, "Tall-man band," and Petodseka, "White-Spot band," round the lakes and sinks of the Carson and Walker Rivers, numbering 484 men, 372 women, and 405 children; 7. Tosarke, "Gray-head band," their neighbors; 8. Tonoziet, "Woman-helper band," on the Truckee River, below Big Meadows, numbering 280 souls; 9. Torape, or "Lean-man band," on the Truckee River, near Lone Crossing, 360 souls; 10. Gonega, the "Dancer band," 290 souls, near the mouth of the Truckee River; 11. Watsequendo, the "Four Crows," along the shores of Pyra-

ritory, on the Humboldt River, number 6000, and in the south 2200 souls; they extend from forty miles west of Stony Point to the Californian line, and northwest to the Oregon line, and inhabit the valley of the Fenelon River, which, rising from Lake Bigler, empties itself into Pyramid Lake. The term means Water Yuta, that is to say, those who live upon fish which they take from lakes and rivers in wiers and traps of willow, perferring that diet to roots, grass-seed, lizards, and crickets, the food of the other so-called Digger tribes.

Gosh Yuta, or Gosha Ute, is a small band, once *protégés* of the Shoshonee, who have the same language and limits. Their principal chief died about five years ago, when the tribe was broken up. A body of sixty, under a peaceful leader, were settled permanently on the Indian farm at Deep Creek, and the remainder wandered 40 to 200 miles west of Great Salt Lake City. Through this tribe our road lay; during the late tumults they have lost fifty warriors, and are now reduced to about 200 men. Like the Ghuzw of Arabia, they strengthen themselves by admitting the outcasts of other tribes, and will presently become a mere banditti.

Pavant, or Parovan Yuta, are a distinct and self-organized tribe, under one principal and several sub-chiefs, whose total is set down at 700 souls. Half of them are settled on the Indian farm at Corn Creek; the other wing of the tribe lives along Sevier Lake, and the surrounding country in the northeast extremity of Fillmore Valley, fifty miles from the city, where they join the Gosh Yuta. The Pavants breed horses, wear clothes of various patterns, grow grain, which the Gosh Yutas will not, and are as brave and improvable as their neighbors are mean and vile.

Timpenaguchyă,* or Timpana Yuta, corrupted into Tenpenny Utes, who dwell about the kanyon of that name, and on the east of the Sweetwater Lake. Of this tribe was the chief Wakara, who so called himself after Walker, the celebrated trapper; the notorious horse-stealer proved himself a friend to the Latter-Day Saints. He died at Meadow Creek, six miles from Fillmore City, on the 29th of January, 1855, and at his obsequies two squaws, two Pa Yuta children, and fifteen of his best horses composed the "customs."

Uinta Yuta, in the mountains south of Fort Bridger, and in the country along the Green River. Of this tribe, which contains a total of 1000, a band of 500, under four chiefs, lately settled on the Indian reservations at Spanish Fork.

Sampichyă, corrupted to San Pete Utas; about eighty warriors, settled on the Indian farm at San Pete. This and the Spanish-Fork Farm number 900 inhabitants.

Elk-Mountain Yutas, who are set down at 2000 souls, by some

mid Lake, 320 souls; 12. The second Wanamuka's band, 500 in number, along the shores of the Northern Mud Lake.

* In the Yuta language meaning "water among the stones."

even 3000; they wander over the southeast portion of the Territory, and, like the Uinta Yutas, are the most independent of white settlers.

Weber-River Yutas are those principally seen in Great Salt Lake City; they are a poor and degraded tribe. Their chief settlement is forty miles to the north, and, like the Gosh Yutas, they understand Shoshonee.

Among the Yutas are reckoned the Washoe, from 500 to 700 souls. They inhabit the eastern slopes of the Sierra Nevada, from Honey Lake to the West Fork of Walker's River in the south. Of this troublesome tribe there are three bands: Captain Jim's, near Lake Bigler, and Carson, Washoe, and Eagle Valleys, a total of 342 souls; Pasuka's band, 340 souls, in Little Valley; and Deer Dick's band, in Long Valley, southeast of Honey Lake. They are usually called Shoshoko,* or "Digger Indians"—a term as insulting to a Shoshonee as nigger to an African.

Besides the Parawat Yutas, the Yampas, 200—300 miles south, on the White River; the Tabechyă, or Sun-hunters, about Tête de Biche, near Spanish lands; and the Tash Yuta, near the Navajoes: there are scatters of the nation along the Californian road from Beaver Valley, along the Santa Clara, Virgen, Las Vegas, and Muddy Rivers to New Mexico.

The Indian Bureau of Utah Territory numbers one superintendent, six agents, and three to six farm-agents. The annual expenditure is set down at $40,000; the Mormons declare that it is iniquitously embezzled, and that the total spent upon the Indians hardly exceeds $1000 per annum. The savages expect blankets and clothing, flour and provisions, arms and ammunition: they receive only a little tobacco, become surly, and slay the settlers. It is understood that the surveyor general has recommended to the federal government the extinction of the Indian title—somewhat upon the principle of the English in Tasmania† and New Zealand—to grounds in the Utah Territory, and the establishment of a land-office for the sale of the two millions of acres already surveyed. Until the citizens can own their farms and fields under the existing pre-emption laws, and until the troublesome Indians can be removed by treaty to reservations remote from white settlements, the onward march of progress will be arrested. The savage and the civilized man, like crabbed age and youth, like the black and gray rat, can not live together: the former starves unless placed in the most fertile spots, which the latter of course covets; the Mormons attempt a peace policy, but

---

* It is said to mean "one who goes on foot."

† Van Diemen's Land, in the days of Captain Flinders (A.D. 1800, two generations ago), had a population of 100,000 souls, now well-nigh annihilated by strong waters and corrosive sublimate. Neither man nor woman was safe in the vicinity of a native tribe; the Anglo-Scandinavian race thus found it necessary to wipe out a people that could not be civilized—a fair instance of the natural selection of species. And New Zealand now threatens to walk the path of Tasmania.

the hunting-grounds are encroached upon, and terrible massacres are the result. Here, as elsewhere, the battle of life is fiercely fought. It has been said,

> "Man differs more from man
> Than beast from beast."

Yet every where we trace the mighty resemblance.

The three principal farms which now form the nuclei of future reservations are those at Spanish Fork, San Pete, and Corn Creek. The two latter have often been denuded by the grasshopper; the former has fared better. Situated in Utah Valley, under the shelter of lofty Nebo, it extends northward within four miles of the Sweetwater Lake, and on the northeast is bounded by the Spanish-Fork Creek, rich in trout and other fish. It was begun five years ago for the Yutas, who claim the land, and contains a total of 13,000 acres, of which 500 have been cultivated; 900 have been ditched to protect the crop, and 1000 have been walled round with a fence six feet high. Besides other improvements, they have built a large adobe house and two rail corrals, and dug dams and channels for irrigation, together with a good stone-curbed well. Under civilized superintendence the savages begin to labor, and the chiefs aspire to erect houses. Yet the crops have been light, rarely exceeding 2500 bushels. San Pete Farm, in the valley and on the creek of the same name, lies 150 miles south of Great Salt Lake City; it supports, besides those who come for temporary assistance, a band of thirty souls; 200 acres have been planted with wheat and potatoes, two adobe houses and a corral have been made, and irrigating trenches have been dug. Corn-Creek Farm, in Fillmore Valley, was begun about four years ago; 300 acres have been broken up, several adobe houses have been built for the Indians and the farm agent, with the usual adjuncts, corral and fences. The crickets and grasshoppers have committed sad havoc among the wheat, corn, and potatoes. It is now tenanted by a Pahvant chief. The Uinta Farm is near Fort Bridger. Those lately opened in Deep Creek and Ruby Valleys have this year lain fallow in consequence of Indian troubles; the soil, however, is rich, and will produce beets, potatoes, onions, turnips, and melons. It is proposed to place the Pa Yutas and Washoes in the Truckee Meadows, on the lands "watered by the majestic Kuyuehup, or Salmon-Trout River," where, besides fish and piñon forests, there are 15,000 acres fit for cultivation and herding. The Indian agents report that the cost will be $150,000, from which the Mormons deduct at least two 0's.

The Yuta, though divided into many tribes and bands, is a distinct race from its prairie neighbors, speaking a single *langue mère* much diversified by dialect. They are a superstitious brood, and have many cruel practices—human sacrifices and vivisepulture—like those of Dahomey and Ashantee. Their religion is the usual African and Indian fetichism, that germal faith which, under fa-

vorable influences and among higher races, developed itself by
natural means—or as explained by a mythical, distinct, and independent revelation—into the higher forms of Judaism, Christianity, and El Islam. In the vicinity of the Mormons many savages
have been baptized, and have become nominal Saints. They divide white men into Shwop or Americans and Mormons. Their
learned men have heard of Washington, but, like the French peasant's superstition concerning Napoleon, they believe him to be
still alive. They have a name for the Book of Mormon, and have
not learned, like their more civilized Eastern neighbors, to look
upon it as the work of Mujhe Manitou, the bad god, who, like
Wiswakarma of the Hindoos, amuses himself by caricaturing and
parodying the creatures of the good god. They are not cannibals
—the Wendigo is a giant man-eater of a mythologic type, not an
actual anthropophage—but, like all Indians, especially those of
New England, they "feel good" after eating a bit of the enemy,
a natural display of destructiveness: they will devour the heart
of a brave man to increase their courage, or chop it up, boil it in
soup, engorge a ladleful, and boast they have drunk the enemy's
blood. They are as liable to caprice as their Eastern neighbors.
A prisoner who has distinguished himself in battle is as often dismissed unhurt as porcupined with arrows and killed with cruel
tortures; if they yield in ingenuity of inflicting pain to the Algonquins and Iroquois, it is not for want of inclination, but by
reason of their stupidity. Female captives who fall into their
hands are horribly treated; I was told of one who, after all manner of atrocities, scalping included, escaped with life. They have
all the savage's improvidence; utility is not their decalogue. Both
sexes, except when clothed by a charitable Mormon, are nearly
naked, even in the severest weather; they sleep in sleet and snow
unclothed, except with a cape of twisted rabbits' furs and a miserable attempt at moccasins, lined with plaited cedar bark: leggins are unknown, even to the women. Their ornaments are vermilion, a few beads, and shell necklaces. They rarely suffer from
any disease but rheumatism, brought on by living in the warm
houses of the whites, and various consequences of liver complaint,
produced by overgorging: as with strong constitutions generally,
they either die at once or readily recover. They dress wounds
with pine gum after squeezing out the blood, and their medicine-
men have the usual variety of savage nostrums. In the more desert parts of the Territory they are exceedingly destitute. South
of Cedar City, even ten years ago they had fields of wheat and
corn of six acres each, and supported emigrants; some of them
cultivate yearly along the stream-banks peas, beans, sweet potatoes, and squashes. They live upon the flesh of the bear, elk,
antelope, dog, wolf, hare, snake, and lizard, besides crickets, grasshoppers, ants, and other vermin. The cactus leaf, piñon nut, and
various barks; the seed of the bunch-grass and of the wheat or

yellow grass, somewhat resembling ryĕ; the rabbit-bush twigs, which are chewed, and various roots and tubers; the soft sego bulb, the rootlet of the cat-tail flag, and of the tule, which, when sun-dried and powdered to flour, keeps through the winter, and is palatable even to white men, conclude the list of their dainties. When these fail they must steal or starve, and the dilemma is easily solved, to the settler's cost.

The Yutas in the vicinity of the larger white settlements continually diminish; bands of 150 warriors are now reduced to 35. Some of the minor tribes in the southern part of the Territory, near New Mexico, can scarcely show a single squaw, having traded them off for horses and arms; they go about killing one another, and on kidnapping expeditions, which farther diminish the breed. The complaint which has devastated the South Sea Islands rages around the City of the Saints, and extends to the Rio Virgen. In six months six squaws were shot by red Othellos for yielding their virtue to the fascinations of tobacco, whisky, and blankets; the Lotharios were savage as well as civilized. The operation of courting is performed by wrapping a blanket round one's beloved; if she reciprocates, it is a sign of consent. A refusal in these lands is often a serious business; the warrior collects his friends, carries off the recusant fair, and, after subjecting her to the insults of all his companions, espouses her. There is little of the shame which Pliny attributes to the "Barrus." When a death takes place they wrap the body in a skin or hide, and drag it by the leg to a grave, which is heaped up with stones as a protection against wild beasts. They mourn till the end of that moon, allow a month to elapse, and then resume their lamentations for another moon: the interval is gradually increased till the grief ends. It is usual to make the dead man's lodge appear as desolate as possible.

The Yuta is less servile, and, consequently, has a higher ethnic status than the African negro; he will not toil, and he turns at a kick or a blow. The emigrant who addresses him in the usual phrase, "D— your eyes, git out of the road or I'll shoot you!" is pretty sure to come to grief. Lately the Yutas demanded compensation for the use of their grass upon the Truckee River, when the emigrants fired, killing Wanamuka the chief. After the death of two or three whites, Mayor Ormsby, of the militia at Carson Valley, took the field, was decoyed into a kanyon by Indian cunning, and perished with all his men.

To " Chokop's" Pass. 8th October, 1860.

The morning was wasted in binding two loose tires upon their respective wheels; it was past noon before we were *en route.* We shook hands cordially with Uncle Billy, whose generosity—a virtue highly prized by those who, rarely practicing, expect it to be practiced upon them—has won for him the sobriquet of the "Big-hearted Father." He had vainly, however, attempted to rescue my silver pen-holder, whose glitter was too much for Indian virtue. Our route lay over a long divide, cold but not unpicturesque, a scene of light-tinted mountain mahogany, black cedar, pure snowy hill, and pink sky. After ten miles we reached the place where the road forks; that to the right, passing through Pine Valley, falls into the gravelly ford of the Humboldt River, distant from this point eighty to eighty-five miles. After surmounting the water-shed we descended over bench-land into a raw and dreary plain, in which greasewood was more plentiful than sage-bush. "Huntingdon Valley" is traversed by Smith's Fork, which flows northward to the Humboldt River; when we crossed it it was a mere rivulet. Our camping-ground was at the farther end of the plain, under a Pass called after the chief Chokop; the kanyon emitted a cold draught like the breathing caves of Kentucky. We alighted at a water near the entrance, and found bunch-grass, besides a little fuel. After two hours the wagon came up with the stock, which was now becoming weary, and we had the usual supper of dough, butter, and coffee. I should have slept comfortably enough upon a shovel and a layer of carpet-bags had not the furious south wind howled like the distant whooping of Indians.

To the Wilderness again. 9th October.

The frosty night was followed by a thaw in the morning. We hastened to ascend Chokop's Pass by a bad, steep dugway: it lies south of "Railroad Kanyon," which is said to be nearly flat-soled. A descent led into "Moonshine," called by the Yutas Pahannap Valley, and we saw with pleasure the bench rising at the foot of the pass. The station is named Diamond Springs, from an eye of warm, but sweet and beautifully clear water bubbling up from the earth. A little below it drains off in a deep rushy ditch, with a gravel bottom, containing equal parts of comminuted shells: we found it an agreeable and opportune bath. Hard work had begun to tell upon the temper of the party. The judge, who ever preferred monologue to dialogue, aweary of the rolling prairies and barren plains, the bald and rocky ridges, the muddy flats, saleratus ponds, and sandy wastes, sighed monotonously for the woodland shades and the rustling of living leaves near his Pennsylvanian home. The marshal, with true Anglo-American impetuosity, could not endure Paddy Kennedy's "slow and shyure" style of travel; and after a colloquy, in which the holiest of words were freely used as adjectives, participles, and exclamations, offered to fight him by way of quickening his pace. The boys—four or five in number—ate for breakfast a quarter of beef, as though they had been Kaffirs or Esquimaux, and were threatened with ration-cutting. The station folks were Mormons, but not particularly civil: they afterward had to fly before the savages, which, perhaps, they will be pleased to consider a "judg-ment" upon them.

Shortly after noon we left Diamond Springs, and carried on for a stretch of seven miles to our lunching-ground, a rushy water, black where it overlies mud, and bluish-green where light gravel and shells form the bottom: the taste is sulphury, and it abounds in confervæ and animalculæ like leeches and little tadpoles. Aft-er playing a tidy bowie-knife, we remounted, and passed over to the rough divide lying westward of Moonshine Valley. As night had closed in, we found some difficulty in choosing a camping-place: at length we pitched upon a prairillon under the lee of a hill, where we had bunch-grass and fuel, but no water. The wind blew sternly through the livelong night, and those who suffered from cramps in cold feet had little to do with the "sweet restorer balmy sleep."

To Sheawit Creek. 10th October.

At 6 A.M. the mercury was sunk only to 29° F., but the ele-vation and rapid evaporation, with the fierce gusty wind cours-ing through the kanyon, rendered the sensation of cold painful. As usual on these occasions, "George," our chef, sensibly pre-ferred standing over the fire, and enwrapping himself with smoke. to the inevitable exposure incurred while fetching a coffee-pot or a tea-kettle. A long divide, with many ascents and descents, at length placed in front of us a view of the normal "distance"— heaps of hills, white as bridal cakes, and, nearer, a sand-like plain, somewhat more yellow than the average of those salt-bottoms: instinct told us that there lay the station-house. From the hills rose the smokes of Indian fires: the lands belong to the Tusa-wichya, or White-Knives, a band of the Shoshonees under an in-dependent chief. This depression is known to the Yutas as Shea-wit, or Willow Creek: the whites call it, from Mr. Bolivar Rob-erts, the Western agent, "Roberts' Springs Valley." It lies 286 miles from Camp Floyd: from this point "Simpson's Road" strikes off to the S.E., and as Mr. Howard Egan's rule here termi-nates, it is considered the latter end of Mormondom. Like all the stations to the westward, that is to say, those now before us, it was burned down in the late Indian troubles, and has only been partially rebuilt. One of the *employés* was Mr. Mose Wright, of Illinois, who again kindly assisted me with correcting my vocab-ulary.

About the station loitered several Indians of the White-Knife tribe, which boasts, like the old Sioux and the modern Flatheads, never to have stained its weapons with the blood of a white man. They may be a respectable race, but they are an ugly: they re-semble the Diggers, and the children are not a little like juvenile baboons. The dress was the usual medley of rags and rabbit furs: they were streaked with vermilion ; and their hair—con-trary to, and more sensibly than the practice of our grandfathers

H H

—was fastened into a frontal pigtail, to prevent it falling into the eyes. These men attend upon the station and herd the stock for an occasional meal, their sole payment. They will trade their skins and peltries for arms and gunpowder, but, African-like, they are apt to look upon provisions, beads, and tobacco in the light of presents.

A long march of thirty-five miles lay before us. Kennedy resolved to pass the night at Sheawit Creek, and, despite their grumbling, sent on the boys, the stock, and the wagons, when rested from their labor, in the early afternoon. We spent a cosy, pleasant evening—such as I have enjoyed in the old Italian days before railroads—of travelers' tittle and Munchausen tattle, in the ingle corner and round the huge hearth of the half-finished station, with its holey walls. At intervals, the roarings of the wind, the ticking of the death-watch (a well-known xylophagus), boring a home in the soft cotton-wood rafters, and the howlings of the Indians, who were keening at a neighboring grave, formed a rude and appropriate chorus. Mose Wright recounted his early adventures in Oregon; how, when he was a greenhorn, the Indians had danced the war-dance under his nose, had then set upon his companions, and, after slaying them, had displayed their scalps. He favored us with a representation of the ceremony, an ursine performance—the bear seems every where to have been the sire of Terpsichore—while the right hand repeatedly clapped to his lips quavered the long loud howl into broken sounds: "Howh! howh! howh! ow! ow! ough! ough! aloo! aloo! loo! loo! oo!" We talked of a curious animal, a breed between the dog and the bear, which represents the semi-fabulous jumard in these regions: it is said to be a cross far more savage than that between the dog and the wolf. The young grizzly is a favorite pet in the Western hut, and a canine graft is hardly more monstrous than the progeny of the horse and the deer lately exhibited in London. I still believe that in Africa, and indeed in India, there are accidentally mules bimanous and quadrumanous, and would suggest that such specimens should be sought as the means of settling on a rational basis the genus and species of "homo sapiens."

Mose Wright described the Indian arrow-poison. The rattlesnake—the copperhead and the moccasin he ignored—is caught with a forked stick planted over its neck, and is allowed to fix its fangs in an antelope's liver. The meat, which turns green, is carried upon a skewer when wanted for use: the flint-head of an arrow, made purposely to break in the wound, is thrust into the poison, and when withdrawn is covered with a thin coat of glue. Ammonia is considered a cure for it, and the Indians treat snake-bites with the actual cautery. The rattlesnake here attains a length of eight to nine feet, and is described as having reached the number of seventy-three rattles, which, supposing (as the theory is) that after the third year it puts forth one per annum, would raise its age to that of man: it is much feared in Utah Territory. We were also cautioned against the poison oak, which is worse than the poison vine east of the Mississippi. It is a dwarf bush with quercine leaves, dark colored and prickly like those of the holly: the effect of a sting, of a touch, or, it is said, in sensitives of its proximity, is a painful itching, followed by a rash that lasts three weeks, and other highly inconvenient consequences. Strong brine was recommended to us by our prairie doctor.

Among the *employés* of the station was an intelligent young mechanic from Pennsylvania, who, threatened with consumption, had sought and soon found health in the pure regions of the Rocky Mountains. He looked forward to revisiting civilization, where comforts were attainable. In these wilds little luxuries like tea and coffee are often unprocurable; a dudeen or a cutty pipe sells for a dollar, consequently a hollowed potato or corn-cob with a reed tube is often rendered necessary; and tobacco must be mixed with a myrtaceous leaf called by the natives "timaya," and by the mountaineers "larb"—possibly a corruption of "l'herbe" or "la yerba." Newspapers and magazines arrive sometimes twice a year, when they have weathered the dangers of the way. Economy has deprived the stations of their gardens, and the shrinking of emigration, which now dribbles eastward, instead of flowing in full stream westward, leaves the exiles to amuse themselves.

To Dry Creek. 11th October.

We arose early, and found that it had not "frosted;" that flies were busy in the station-house; and that the snow, though thick on the northern faces, had melted from the southern shoulders of the hills—these were so many indices of the St. Martin's, or Indian summer, the last warm glow of life before the cold and pallid death of the year. At 6 A.M. we entered the ambulance, and followed a good road across the remains of the long, broad Sheawit Valley. After twelve miles we came upon a water surrounded by willows, with dwarf artemisia beyond—it grows better on the benches, where the subsoil is damper, than in the bottoms—and there we found our lazy boys, who, as Jim Gilston said, had been last night "on a drunk." Resuming our way, after three miles we reached some wells whose alkaline waters chap the skin. Twenty miles farther led to the west end of the Sheawit Valley, where we found the station on a grassy bench at the foot of low rolling hills. It was a mere shell, with a substantial stone corral behind, and the inmates were speculating upon the possibility of roofing themselves in before the winter. Water is found in tolerable quantities below the station, but the place deserved its name, "Dry Creek."

A fraternal recognition took place between Long Jim and his brother, who discovered each other by the merest accident. Gilston, the *employé,* was an intelligent man: at San Francisco he had learned a little Chinese, and at Deep Creek he was studying the Indian dialects. He had missed making a fortune at Carson Valley, where, in June or July, 1859, the rich and now celebrated silver mines were discovered; and he warned us against the danger of tarrying in Carson City, where revolvers are fired even into houses known to contain "ladies." Colonel Totten, the station-master, explained the formation of the gold diggings as beds of gravel, from one to 120 feet, overlying slate rock.

Dry-Creek Station is on the eastern frontier of the western agency ; as at Roberts' Creek, supplies and literature from Great Salt City east and Carson City west are usually exhausted before they reach these final points. After a frugal feed, we inspected a grave for two, which bore the names of Loscier and Applegate, and the date 21st of May. These men, *employés* of the station, were attacked by Indians — Panaks or Shoshonees, or possibly both : the former was killed by the first fire ; the latter, when shot in the groin, and unable to proceed, borrowed, under pretext of defense, a revolver, bade good-by to his companions, and put a bullet through his own head : the remainder then escaped. Both these poor fellows remain unavenged. The Anglo-American, who is admirably protected by the officials of his government in Europe, Asia, and Africa, is systematically neglected — *teste* Mexico—in America. The double grave, piled up with stones, showed gaps where the wolves had attempted to tunnel, and blue-bottle flies were buzzing over it in expectation. Colonel Totten, at our instance, promised that it should be looked to.

The night was comfortably passed at Dry Creek, under the leeward side of a large haystack. The weather was cold, but clear and bright. We slept the sleep of the just.

To Simpson's Park. 12th October.
At the time of the cold clear dawn, whose gray contrasted strongly with the blush of the most lovely evening that preceded it, the mercury stood at 45° F. Shortly after 8 A.M. we were afield, hastening to finish the long divide that separates Roberts' Creek Valley from its western neighbor, which, as yet unchristened, is known to the b'hoys as Smoky Valley. The road wound in the shape of the letter U round the impassable part of the ridge. Crossing the north end of Smoky Valley, we came upon rolling ground, with water-willows and cedars "blazed"—barked with a gash—for sign-posts. Ensued a long kanyon, with a flat sole, not unlike Egan's, a gate by which the swift shallow stream had broken through the mountains: in places it was apparently a *cul de sac ;* in others, shoulder after shoulder rose in long perspective, with points and projections behind, which an enemy might easily turn. The granite walls were of Cyclopean form, with regular lines of cleavage, as in the Rattlesnake Hills, which gave a false air of stratification. The road was a mere path along and across

the rivulet bed, and the lower slopes were garnished with the pep-
per-grass and the everlasting bunch-grass, so truly characteristic
of the "Basin State." Above us, in the pellucid sky, towered the
eagle in his pride of place; the rabbit ran before us from the
thicket; the ground-squirrel cached himself in the sage-bush; and
where distance appeared, smokes upcurling in slow, heavy masses
told us that man was not far distant. A second divide, more abrupt than the former, placed us in sight of Simpson's Park—and
such a park! a circlet of tawny stubble, embosomed in sage-grown
hills, the "Hiré" or "Look-out," and others, without other tree
but the deformed cedars. The bottom is notorious for cold; it
freezes even in June and July; and our night was, as may be
imagined, none of the pleasantest.

The station-house in Simpson's Park was being rebuilt. As
we issued from Mormondom into Christendom, the civility of our
hosts perceptibly diminished; the judge, like the generality of
Anglo-Americans, did unnecessary kow-tow to those whom republicanism made his equals, and the "gentlemen," when asked
to do any thing, became exceedingly surly. Among them was
one Giovanni Brutisch, a Venetian, who, flying from conscription,
had found a home in Halifax: an unfortunate fire, which burned
down his house, drove him to the Far West. He talked copiously of the Old Country, breathed the usual aspirations of *Italia una*,
and thought that Garibaldi would do well "*se non lo molestano*"—
a euphuism accompanied by a look more expressive than any nod.
The station was well provided with good miniés, and the men apparently expected to use them; it was, however, commanded by
the neighboring heights, and the haystacks were exposed to fire
at a time of the year when no more forage could be collected.
The Venetian made for us some good light bread of wheaten
flour, started or leavened with hop-water, and corn-bread "shortened" with butter, and enriched with two or three eggs. A hideous Pa Yuta and surly Shoshonee, whom I sketched, loitered
about the station: they were dressed in the usual rabbit-skin
cape, and carried little horn bows, with which they missed small
marks at fifteen paces. The boys, who were now aweary of
watching, hired one of these men for a shirt—tobacco was not to
be had, and a blanket was too high pay—to mount guard through
the night. Like the Paggi or Ramoosee of Western India, one
thief is paid to keep off many: the Indian is the best of wardens,
it being with him a principle not to attack what the presence of
a fellow-tribesman defends.

To Reese's River.   13th October.

Simpson's Park lies 195 miles from Carson City, where we
might consider the journey at an end; yet the cold of night did
not allow us to set out before 10 A.M. Our route lay across the
park, which was dotted with wheat-grass and broom-like reeds
rising from a ground saupoudré like salt. Presently we began

to ascend Simpson's Pass, a long kanyon whose sloping sides and benches were dotted with the green bunch-grass. At the divide we found the "Sage Springs," whose position is too elevated for the infiltration of salt: they are consequently sweet and wholesome. Descending by a rugged road, we sighted every where on the heights the fires of the natives. They were not symbols of war, but signals—for which smokes are eminently adapted—made by tribes telegraphing to one another their being *en route* for their winter quarters. Below us, " Reese's River" Valley might have served for a sketch in the African desert: a plain of saleratus, here yellow with sand or hay, there black with fire, there brown where the skin of earth showed through her garb of rags, and beyond it were chocolate-colored hills, from whose heads curled blue smokes of volcanic appearance.

Bisecting the barren plain ran a bright little stream, whose banks, however, had been stripped of their "salt grass:" pure and clear it flows over a bed of gravel, sheds in a northerly direction, and sinks at a distance of about twenty miles. From afar we all mistook the course, deceived, as travelers often are, by the horizontality of the lines. Leaving on the right the road which forks to the lower ford, we followed that on the left hand leading to the station. There can not be much traveling upon these lines: the tracks last for years, unaffected by snow: the carcasses of animals, however, no longer mummified us as in the Eastern prairies, are readily reduced to skeletons.

The station-house in the Reese-River Valley had lately been evacuated by its proprietors and burnt down by the Indians: a new building of adobe was already assuming a comfortable shape. The food around it being poor and thin, our cattle were driven to the mountains. At night, probably by contrast with the torrid sun, the frost appeared colder than ever: we provided against it, however, by burrowing into the haystack, and, despite the jackal-like cry of the coyote and the near tramping of the old white mare, we slept like tops.

To Smith's Creek.   14th October.
Before 8 A.M. we were under way, bound for Smith's Creek. Our path stretched over the remainder of Reese's River Valley, an expanse of white sage and large rabbit-bush which affords fuel even when green. After a long and peculiarly rough divide, we sighted the place of our destination. It lay beyond a broad plain or valley, like a huge white "splotch" in the centre, set in dirty brown vegetation, backed by bare and rugged hills, which are snow-topped only on the north; presently we reached the "splotch," which changed its aspect from that of a muddy pool to a yellow floor of earth so hard that the wheels scarcely made a dent, except where a later inundation had caused the mud to cake, flake, and curl—smooth as ice without being slippery. Be-

yond that point, guided by streams meandering through willow-thickets, we entered a kanyon—all are now wearying of the name—and presently sighted the station deep in a hollow. It had a good stone corral and the usual haystack, which fires on the hill-tops seemed to menace. Among the station-folks we found two New Yorkers, a Belfast man, and a tawny Mexican named Anton, who had passed his life riding the San Bernardino road. The house was unusually neat, and displayed even signs of decoration in the adornment of the bunks with osier-work taken from the neighboring creek. We are now in the lands of the Pa Yuta, and rarely fail to meet a party on the road: they at once propose "shwop," and readily exchange pine nuts for "white grub," i. e., biscuits. I observed, however, that none of the natives were allowed to enter the station-house, whereas in other places, especially among the Mormons, the savages squeezed themselves into the room, took the best seats near the fire, and never showed a symptom of moving.

To Cold Springs. 15th October.

After a warmer night than usual—thanks to fire and lodging—we awoke, and found a genial south wind blowing. Our road lay through the kanyon, whose floor was flush with the plain; the bed of the mountain stream was the initiative of vile traveling, which, without our suspecting it, was to last till the end of the journey. The strain upon the vehicle came near to smashing it, and the prudent Kennedy, with the view of sparing his best animals, gave us his worst—two aged brutes, one of which, in consequence of her squealing habits, had won for herself the title of "ole Hellion." The divortia aquarum was a fine water-shed to the westward, and the road was in V shape, whereas before it had oscillated between U and WW. As we progressed, however, the valleys became more and more desert, the sage more stunted, and the hills more brown and barren. After a midday halt, rendered compulsory by the old white mare, we resumed our way along the valley southward, over a mixture of pitch-hole and boulder, which forbids me to forget that day's journey. At last, after much sticking and kicking on the part of the cattle, and the mental refreshment of abundant bad language, self-adhibited by the men, we made Cold-Springs Station, which, by means of a cut across the hills, could be brought within eight miles of Smith's Creek.

The station was a wretched place, half built and wholly unroofed; the four boys, an exceedingly rough set, ate standing, and neither paper nor pencil was known among them. Our animals, however, found good water in a rivulet from the neighboring hills, and the promise of a plentiful feed on the morrow, while the humans, observing that a "beef" had been freshly killed, supped upon an excellent steak. The warm wind was a pleasant contrast to the usual frost, but, as it came from the south, all the weather-wise predicted that rain would result. We slept, however, without such accident, under the haystack, and heard the loud howling of the wolves, which are said to be larger on these hills than elsewhere.

To Sand Springs. 16th October.

In the morning the wind had shifted from the south to a more pluvial quarter, the southeast—in these regions the westerly wind promises the fairest—and stormy cirri mottled the sky. We had a long stage of thirty-five miles before us, and required an early start, yet the lazy b'hoys and the weary cattle saw 10 A.M. before we were *en route*. Simpson's road lay to our south; we could, however, sight, about two miles distant from the station, the easternmost formation, which he calls Gibraltar Gate. For the first three miles our way was exceedingly rough; it gradually improved into a plain cut with nullahs, and overgrown with a chapparal, which concealed a few "burrowing hares." The animals are rare; during the snow they are said to tread in one another's trails after Indian fashion, yet the huntsman easily follows them. After eight miles we passed a spring, and two miles beyond it came to the Middle Gate, where we halted from noon till 5 15 P.M. Water was found in the bed of a river which fills like a mill-dam after rain, and a plentiful supply of bunch-grass, whose dark seeds it was difficult to husk out of the oat-like capsules. We spent our halt in practicing what Sorrentines call *la caccia degl' uccelluzzi*, and in vain attempts to walk round the. uncommonly wary hawks, crows, and wolves.

Hitching to as the sun neared the western horizon, we passed through the Gate, narrowly escaping a "spill" down a dwarf precipice. A plain bounded on our left by cretaceous bluffs, white as snow, led to the West Gate, two symmetrical projections like those farther eastward. After that began a long divide broken by frequent chuck-holes, which, however, had no cunette at the bottom. An ascent of five miles led to a second broad basin, whose white and sounding ground, now stony, then sandy, scattered over with carcass and skeleton, was bounded in front by low dark ranges of hill. Then crossing a long rocky divide, so winding that the mules' heads pointed within a few miles to N., S., E., and W., we descended by narrow passes into a plain. The eye could not distinguish it from a lake, so misty and vague were its outlines: other senses corrected vision, when we sank up to the hub in the loose sand. As we progressed painfully, broken clay and dwarf vegetation assumed in the dim shades fantastic and mysterious forms. I thought myself once more among the ruins of that Arab village concerning which Lebid sang,

"Ay me! ay me! all lone and drear the dwelling-place, the home—
On Mina, o'er Rijam and Ghool, wild beasts unheeded roam."

Tired out and cramped with cold, we were torpid with what the Bedouin calls El Rakl—la Ragle du Désert, when part of the

FIRST VIEW OF CARSON LAKE.

brain sleeps while the rest is wide awake. At last, about 2 30
A.M., thoroughly "knocked up"—a phrase which I should advise the Englishman to eschew in the society of the fair Columbian—we sighted a roofless shed, found a haystack, and, reckless
of supper or of stamping horses, fell asleep upon the sand.

To Carson Lake. 17th October.

Sand-Springs Station deserved its name. Like the Brazas de
San Diego and other *mauvaises terres* near the Rio Grande, the
land is cumbered here and there with drifted ridges of the finest
sand, sometimes 200 feet high, and shifting before every gale.
Behind the house stood a mound shaped like the contents of an
hour-glass, drifted up by the stormy S.E. gale in esplanade shape,
and falling steep to northward or against the wind. The water
near this vile hole was thick and stale with sulphury salts : it
blistered even the hands. The station-house was no unfit object
in such a scene, roofless and chairless, filthy and squalid, with a
smoky fire in one corner, and a table in the centre of an impure
floor, the walls open to every wind, and the interior full of dust.
Hibernia herself never produced aught more characteristic. Of
the *employés*, all loitered and sauntered about *desœuvrés* as cretins,
except one, who lay on the ground crippled and apparently dying
by the fall of a horse upon his breast-bone.

About 11 A.M. we set off to cross the ten miles of valley that
stretched between us and the summit of the western divide still
separating us from Carson Lake. The land was a smooth saleratus plain, with curious masses of porous red and black basalt protruding from a ghastly white. The water-shed was apparently
to the north, the benches were distinctly marked, and the bottom
looked as if it were inundated every year. It was smooth except
where broken up by tracks, but all off the road was dangerous
ground : in one place the horses sank to their hocks, and were
not extricated without difficulty. After a hot drive—the glass
at 9 A.M. showed 74° F.—we began to toil up the divide, a sand
formation mixed with bits of granite, red seeds, and dwarf shells,
whose lips were for the most part broken off. Over the fine loose
surface was a floating haze of the smaller particles, like the film
that veils the Arabian desert. Arrived at the summit, we sighted
for the first time Carson Lake, or rather the sink of the Carson
River. It derives its name from the well-known mountaineer
whose adventurous roamings long anticipated scientific exploration. Supplied by the stream from the eastern flank of the Sierra
Nevada, it is just such a lake as might be formed in any of the
basins which we had traversed—a shallow sheet of water, which,
in the cloudy sky and mitigated glare of the sun, looked pale and
muddy. Apparently it was divided by a long, narrow ruddy
line, like ochre-colored sand ; a near approach showed that water
on the right was separated from a saleratus bed on the left by a

thick bed of tule rush.   Stones imitated the sweep of the tide, and white particles the color of a wash.

Our conscientious informant at Sand-Springs Station had warned us that upon the summit of the divide we should find a perpendicular drop, down which the wagons could be lowered only by means of lariats affixed to the axle-trees and lashed round strong "stubbing-posts."   We were not, however, surprised to find a mild descent of about 30°.   From the summit of the divide five miles led us over a plain too barren for sage, and a stretch of stone and saleratus to the watery margin, which was troublesome with sloughs and mud.   The cattle relished the water, although tainted by the rush; we failed, however, to find any of the fresh-water clams, whose shells were scattered along the shore.

Remounting at 5 15 P.M. we proceeded to finish the ten miles which still separated us from the station, by a rough and stony road, perilous to wheel conveyances, which rounded the southern extremity of the lake.   After passing a promontory whose bold projection had been conspicuous from afar, and threading a steep kanyon leading toward the lake, we fell into its selvage, which averaged about one mile in breadth.   The small crescent of the moon soon ceased to befriend us, and we sat in the sadness of the shade, till presently a light glimmered under Arcturus, the road bent toward it, and all felt "jolly."   But,

> " Heu, heu! nos miseros, quam totus homuncio nil est!"

A long dull hour still lay before us, and we were approaching civilized lands.   "Sink Station" looked well from without; there was a frame house inside an adobe inclosure, and a pile of wood and a stout haystack promised fuel and fodder.   The inmates, however, were asleep, and it was ominously long before a door was opened.   At last appeared a surly cripple, who presently disappeared to arm himself with his revolver.   The judge asked civilly for a cup of water; he was told to fetch it from the lake, which was not more than a mile off, though, as the road was full of quagmires, it would be hard to travel at night.   Wood the churl would not part with: we offered to buy it, to borrow it, to replace it in the morning; he told us to go for it ourselves, and that after about two miles and a half we might chance to gather some.   Certainly our party was a law-abiding and a self-governing one; never did I see men so tamely bullied; they threw back the fellow's sticks, and cold, hungry, and thirsty, simply began to sulk.   An Indian standing by asked $20 to herd the stock for a single night.   At last, George the Cordon Blue took courage; some went for water, others broke up a wagon-plank, and supper after a fashion was concocted.

I preferred passing the night on a side of bacon in the wagon to using the cripple's haystack, and allowed sleep to steep my senses in forgetfulness, after deeply regretting that the Mormons do not extend somewhat farther westward.

To Fort Churchill. 18th October.

The b'hoys and the stock were doomed to remain near the Carson Lake, where forage was abundant, while we made our way to Carson Valley—an arrangement not effected without excessive grumbling. At last the deserted ones were satisfied with the promise that they should exchange their desert quarters for civilization on Tuesday, and we were permitted to start. Crossing a long plain bordering on the Sink, we "snaked up" painfully a high divide which a little engineering skill would have avoided. From the summit, bleak with west wind, we could descry, at a distance of fifty miles, a snowy saddle-back—the Sierra Nevada. When the deep sand had fatigued our cattle, we halted for an hour to bait in a patch of land rich with bunch-grass. Descending from the eminence, we saw a gladdening sight: the Carson River, winding through its avenue of dark cotton-woods, and afar off the quarters and barracks of Fort Churchill. The nearer view was a hard-tamped plain, besprinkled with black and red porous stones and a sparse vegetation, with the ruddy and yellow autumnal hues; a miserable range of low, brown, sunburnt rocks and hills, whose ravines were choked with white sand-drifts, bounded the basin. The farther distance used it as a foil; the Sierra developed itself into four distinct magnificent tiers of snow-capped and cloud-veiled mountain, whose dissolving views faded into thin darkness as the sun disappeared behind their gigantic heads.

While we admired these beauties night came on; the paths intersected one another, and, despite the glow and gleam of a camp-fire in the distance, we lost our way among the tall cotton-woods. Dispersing in search of information, the marshal accidentally stumbled upon his predecessor in office, Mr. Smith, who hospitably insisted upon our becoming his guests. He led us to a farm-house already half roofed in against the cold, fetched the whisky for which our souls craved, gave to each a peach that we might be good boys, and finally set before us a prime beefsteak. Before sleeping we heard a number of "shooting stories." Where the corpse is, says the Persian, there will be the kites. A mining discovery never fails to attract from afar a flock of legal vultures— attorneys, lawyers, and judges. As the most valuable claims are mostly parted with by the ignorant fortunate for a song, it is usual to seek some flaw in the deed of sale, and a large proportion of the property finds its way into the pockets of the acute professional, who works on half profits. Consequently, in these parts there is generally a large amount of unscrupulous talent. One gentleman judge had knived a waiter and shot a senator; another, almost as "heavy *on* the shyoot," had in a single season killed one man and wounded another. My informants declared that in and about Carson a dead man for breakfast was the rule; besides accidents perpetually occurring to indifferent or to peace-making parties, they reckoned per annum fifty murders. In a peculiar

fit of liveliness, an intoxicated gentleman will discharge his revolver in a ballroom, and when a "shyooting" begins in the thin-
walled frame houses, those not concerned avoid bullets and splin-
ters by jumping into their beds.   During my three days' stay at
Carson City I heard of three murders.   A man "heavy *on* the
shoulder," who can "hit out straight from the hip," is a valuable
acquisition.   The gambler or professional player, who in the Eastern States is exceptionably peaceful, because he fears the publicity
of a quarrel, here must distinguish himself as a fighting-man.   A
curious story was told to illustrate how the ends of justice might,
at a pinch, in the case of a popular character, be defeated.   A
man was convicted of killing his adversary after saying to the by-
standers, "Stoop down while I shoot the son of a dog (female)."
Counsel for the people showed *malice prepense;* counsel for defense
pleaded that his client was *rectus in curia,* and manifestly couldn't.
mean a man, but a dog.   The judge ratified the verdict of acquittal.

Such was the state of things, realizing the old days of the Californian gold-diggings, when I visited in 1860 Carson City.   Its
misrule, or rather want of rule, has probably long since passed
away, leaving no more traces than a dream.   California has been
transformed by her Vigilance Committee, so ignorantly and un-
justly declaimed against in Europe and in the Eastern States of
the Union, from a savage autonomy to one of the most orderly of
the American republics, and San Francisco, her capital, from a den
of thieves and prostitutes, gamblers and miners, the offscourings
of nations, to a social status not inferior to any of the most favored cities.

Hurrah again—in! 19th *October.*
This day will be the last of my diary.   We have now emerged
from the deserts of the Basin State, and are debouching upon
lands where coaches and the electric telegraph ply.

After a cold night at the hospitable Smith's, and losing the cattle, we managed to hitch to, and crossed, not without difficulty,
the deep bed of the Carson River, which runs over sands glittering with mica.   A little beyond it we found the station-house,
and congratulated ourselves that we had escaped a twelve hours'
durance vile in its atmosphere of rum, korn schnapps, stale tobacco, flies, and profane oaths, not to mention the chance of being
"wiped out" in a "difference" between a soldier and a gambler, or
a miner and a rider.

From the station-house we walked, accompanied by a Mr. O.—
who, after being an editor in Texas, had become a mail-rider in
Utah Territory — to the fort.   It was, upon the principle of its
eastern neighbors, a well-disposed cantonment, containing quarters
for the officers and barracks for the men.   Fort Churchill had
been built during the last few months: it lodged about two companies of infantry, and required at least 2000 men.   Captain F. F.

Flint (6th Regiment) was then commanding, and Lieutenant Colonel Thomas Swords, a deputy quarter-master general, was on a tour of inspection. We went straight to the quarter-master's office, and there found Lieutenant Moore, who introduced us to all present, and supplied us with the last newspapers and news. The camp was Teetotalist, and avoided cards like good Moslems: we were not, however, expected to drink water except in the form of strong waters, and the desert had disinclined us to abstain from whisky. Finally, Mr. Byrne, the sutler, put into our ambulance a substantial lunch, with a bottle of cocktail, and another of cognac, especially intended to keep the cold out.

The dull morning had threatened snow, and shortly after noon the west wind brought up cold heavy showers, which continued with intervals to the end of the stage. Our next station was Miller's, distant 15 to 16 miles. The road ran along the valley of Carson River, whose trees were a repose to our eyes, and we congratulated ourselves when we looked down the stiff clay banks, 30 feet high, and wholly unfenced, that our journey was by day. The desert was now "done." At every few miles was a drinking "calaboose:"* where sheds were not a kettle hung under a tree, and women peeped out of the log huts. They were probably not charming, but, next to a sea voyage, a desert march is the finest cosmetic ever invented. We looked upon each as if

> "Her face was like the Milky Way i' the sky,
> A meeting of gentle lights without a name."

At Miller's Station, which we reached at 2 30 P.M., there really was one pretty girl—which, according to the author of the Art of Pluck, induces proclivity to temulency. While the rain was heavy we sat round the hot stove, eating bread and cheese, sausages and anchovies, which Rabelais, not to speak of other honest drinkers, enumerates among provocatives to thirst. When we started at 4 P.M. through the cold rain, along the bad road up the river bed, to "liquor up" was manifestly a duty we owed to ourselves. And, finally, when my impatient companions betted a supper that we should reach Carson City before 9 P.M., and sealed it with a "smile," I knew that the only way to win was to ply Mr. Kennedy, the driver, with as many *pocula* as possible.

Colder waxed the weather and heavier the rain as, diverging from the river, we ascended the little bench upon which China-town lies. The line of ranches and frame houses, a kind of length-without-breadth place, once celebrated in the gold-digging days, looked dreary and grim in the evening gloom. At 5 30 P.M. we were still fourteen miles distant from our destination. The benches and the country round about had been turned topsy-turvy in the search for precious metal, and the soil was still burrowed

---

* The Spanish is calabozo, the French calabouse. In the Hispano-American countries it is used as a "common jail" or a "dog-hole," and, as usual, is converted into a verb.

with shaft and tunnel, and crossed at every possible spot by flumes, at which the natives of the Flowery Land still found it worth their while to work. Beyond China-town we quitted the river, and in the cold darkness of night we slowly began to breast the steep ascent of a long divide.

We had been preceded on the way by a young man, driving in a light cart a pair of horses, which looked remarkable by the side of the usual Californian teams, three pair with the near wheeler ridden. Arriving at a bad place, he kindly called out to us, but before his warning could be taken a soft and yielding sensation, succeeded by a decided leaning to the right, and ending with a loud crash, announced an overturn. In due time we were extricated, the pieces were picked up, and, though the gun was broken, the bottle of cocktail fortunately remained whole. The judge, probably and justly offended by my evil habit of laughing out of season, informed us that he had never been thrown before, an announcement which made us expect more "spills." The unhappy Kennedy had jumped off before the wheels pointed up hill; he had not lost a hoof, it is true, on the long march, but he wept spirits and water at the disappointing thought that the ambulance, this time drawn by his best team, and laden with all the dignities, had come to grief, and would not be fit to be seen. After 100 yards more another similar series of sensations announced a repetition of the scene, which deserved the epitaph,

"Hic jacet amphora vini."

This time, however, falling down a bank, we "came to smash;" the bottle (eheu!) was broken, so was the judge's head, while the ear of the judgeling—serve him right for chaffing!—was cut, the pistols and powder-flasks were half buried in the sand, a variety of small objects were lost, and the flying gear of the ambulance was a perfect wreck. Unwilling to risk our necks by another trial, we walked over the rest of the rough ground, and, conducted by the good Croly, found our way to "Dutch Nick's," a ranch and tavern apparently much frequented by the teamsters and other roughs, who seemed, honest fellows! deeply to regret that the accident had not been much more serious.

Remounting after a time, we sped forward, and sighted in front a dark line, but partially lit up about the flanks, with a brilliant illumination in the centre, the Kursaal of Mr. Hopkins, the local Crockford. Our entrance to Penrod House, the Fifth Avenue of Carson City, was by no means of a triumphal order; Nature herself seemed to sympathize with us, besplashing us with tears heavier than Mr. Kennedy's. But after a good supper and change of raiment, a cigar, "something warm," and the certainty of a bed, combined to diffuse over our minds the calm satisfaction of having surmounted our difficulties *tant bien que mal.*

* * * * * *

VIRGINIA CITY.   (From the Northeast.)

CONCLUSION.

THE traveler and the lecturer have apparently laid down a law that, whether the journey does or does not begin at home, it should always end at that "hallowed spot." Unwilling to break through what is now becoming a time-honored custom, I trespass upon the reader's patience for a few pages more, and make my final *salaam* in the muddy-puddly streets, under the gusty, misty sky of the "Liverpool of the South."

After a day's rest at Carson City, employed in collecting certain necessaries of tobacco and raiment, which, intrinsically vile, were about treble the price of the best articles of their kind in the Burlington Arcade, I fell in with Captain Dall, superintendent of the Ophir mines, for whom I bore a recommendation from Judge Crosby, of Utah Territory. The valuable silver leads of Virginia City occupied me, under the guidance of that hospitable gentleman, two days, and on the third we returned to Carson City, *viâ* the Steam-boat Springs, Washoe Valley, and other local lions. On the 24th appeared the boys driving in the stock from Carson Lake: certain of these youths had disappeared; Jim Gilston, who had found his brother at Dry-Creek Station, had bolted, of course forgetting to pay his passage. A stage-coach, most creditably horsed, places the traveler from Carson City at San Francisco in two days; as Mr. Kennedy, however, wished to see me safely to the end, and the judge, esteeming me a fit Mentor for youth, had intrusted to me Telemachus, alias Thomas, his son, I resolved to cross the Sierra by easy stages. After taking kindly leave of and a last "liquor up" with my old *compagnons de voyage*, the judge and the marshal, we broke ground once more on the 25th of October. At Genoa, pronounced Ge-nóa, the county town, built in a valley thirteen miles south of Carson, I met Judge Cradlebaugh, who set me right on grounds where the Mormons had sown some prejudices. Five days of a very dilatory travel placed us on the western slope of the Sierra Nevada; the dugways and zigzags reminded me of the descriptions of travelers over the Andes; the snow threatened to block up the roads, and our days and nights were passed among teamsters *en route* and in the frame-house inn. On the 30th of November, reaching Diamond Springs, I was advised by a Londoner, Mr. George Fryer, of the "Boomerang Saloon," to visit the gold diggings at Placerville, whither a coach was about to start. At "Hangtown," as the place was less euphoniously termed, Mr. Collum, of the Cary House, kindly put me through the gold washing and "hydraulicking," and Dr. Smith, an old East Indian practitioner, and Mr. White, who had collected some fine specimens of minerals, made the evenings pleasant. I started on the 1st of November by coach to Folsom, and there found the railroad, which in two hours conducts to Sacramento: the negro coachmen driving hacks and wagons to the station, the whistling of the steam, and the hurry of the train, struck me by the contrast with the calm travel of the desert.

At Sacramento, the newer name for New Helvetia—a capital mass of shops and stores, groggeries and hotels—I cashed a draught, settled old scores with Kennedy, who almost carried me off by force to his location, shook hands with Thomas, and transferred myself from the Golden Eagle on board the steamer Queen City. Eight hours down the Sacramento River, past Benicia—the birthplace of the Boy—in the dark to the head-waters of the glorious bay, placed me at the "El Dorada of the West," where a tolerable opera, a superior supper, and the society of friends made the arrival exceptionably comfortable.

I spent ten pleasant days at San Francisco. There remained some traveler's work to be done: the giant trees, the Yosemite or Yohamite Falls—the highest cataracts yet known in the world—and the Almaden cinnabar mines, with British Columbia, Vancouver's Island, and Los Angelos temptingly near. But, in sooth, I was aweary of the way; for eight months I had lived on board steamers and railraod cars, coaches and mules; my eyes were full of sight-seeing, my pockets empty, and my brain stuffed with all manner of useful knowledge. It was far more grateful to *flaner* about the stirring streets, to admire the charming faces, to enjoy the delicious climate, and to pay quiet visits like a "ladies' man," than to front wind and rain, muddy roads, *arrieros*, and rough teamsters, fit only for Rembrandt, and the solitude of out-stations. The presidential election was also in progress, and I wished to see with my eyes the working of a system which has been facetiously called "universal suffering and vote by bullet." Mr. Consul Booker placed my name on the lists of the Union Club, which was a superior institution to that of Leamington; Colonel Hooker, of Oregon, and Mr. Tooney, showed me life in San Francisco; Mr. Gregory Yale, whom I had met at Carson City, introduced me to a quiet picture of old Spanish happiness, fast fading from California; Mr. Donald Davidson, an old East Indian, talked East Indian with me; and Lieutenants Macpherson and Brewer accompanied me over the forts and batteries which are intended to make of San Francisco a New-World Cronstadt. Mr. Polonius sensibly refused to cash for me a draught not authorized by my circular letter from the Union Bank. Mr. Booker took a less prudential and mercantile view of the question, and kindly helped me through with the *necessaire*—£100. My return for all this kindness was, I regret to say, a temperate but firm refusal to lecture upon the subject of Meccah and El Medinah, Central Africa, Indian cotton, American politics, or every thing in general. I nevertheless bade my adieux to San Francisco and the hospitable San Franciscans with regret.

On the 15th of November, the Golden Age, Commodore Watkins, steamed out of the Golden Gates, bearing on board, among some 520 souls, the body that now addresses the public. She was a model steamer, with engines and engine-rooms clean as a club kitchen, and a cuisine whose terrapin soup and deviled crabs à la Baltimore will long maintain their position in my memory— not so long, however, as the kindness and courtesy of the ancient mariner who commanded the Golden Age. On the 28th we spent the best part of a night at Acapulco, the city of Cortez and of Doña Marina, where any lurking project of passing through ill-conditioned Mexico was finally dispelled. The route from Acapulco to Vera Cruz, over a once well-worn highway, was simply and absolutely impassable. Each sovereign and independent state in that miserable caricature of the Anglo-American federal Union was at daggers drawn with all and every of its next-door neighbors; the battles were paper battles, but the plundering and the barbarities—cosas de Méjico!—were stern realities. A rich man could not travel because of the banditti ; a poor man would have been enlisted almost outside the city gates; a man with many servants would have seen half of them converted to soldiers under his eyes, and have lost the other half by desertion, while a man without servants would have been himself press-gang'd; a Liberal would have been murdered by the Church, and a Churchman—even the frock is no protection—would have been martyred by the Liberal party. For this disappointment I found a philosophical consolation in various experiments touching the influence of Mezcal brandy, the Mexican national drink, upon the human mind and body.

On the 15th of December we debarked at Panama; horridly wet, dull, and dirty was the "place of fish," and the "Aspinwall House" and its Mivart reminded me of a Parsee hotel in the fort, Bombay. Yet I managed to spend there three pleasant circlings of the sun. A visit to the acting consul introduced me to M. Hurtado, the Intendente or military governor, and to a charming countrywoman, whose fascinating society made me regret that my stay there could not be protracted. Though politics were running high, I became acquainted with most of the officers of the United States squadron, and only saw the last of them at Colon, alias Aspinwall. Messrs. Boyd and Power, of the "Weekly Star and Herald," introduced me to the officials of the Panama Railroad, Messrs. Nelson, Center, and others, who, had I not expressed an aversion to "dead-headism," or gratis traveling, would have offered me a free passage. Last, but not least, I must mention the venerable name of Mrs. Seacole, of Jamaica and Balaklava.

On the 8th of December I passed over the celebrated Panama Railway to Aspinwall, where Mr. Center, the superintendent of the line, made the evening highly agreeable with conversation aided by "Italia," a certain muscatel cognac that has yet to reach Great Britain.   We steamed the next morning, under charge of Captain Leeds, over the Caribbean Sea or Spanish Main, bound for St. Thomas.   A hard-hearted E.N.E. wind protracted the voyage of the Solent for six days, and we reached the Danish settlement in time, and only just in time, to save a week's delay upon that offensive scrap of negro liberty-land.   On the 9th of December we bade adieu with pleasure to the little dungeon-rock, and turned the head of the good ship Seine, Captain Rivett, toward the Western Islands.   She played a pretty wheel till almost within sight of Land's End, where Britannia received us with her characteristic welcome, a gale and a pea-soup fog, which kept us cruising about for three days in the unpleasant Solent and the Southampton Water.

IN THE SIERRA NEVADA.

APPENDICES.

APPENDICES.

I. EMIGRANT'S ITINERARY,

Showing the distances between camping-places, the several mail-stations where mules
are changed, the hours of travel, the character of the roads, and the facilities for
obtaining water, wood, and grass on the route along the southern bank of the
Platte River, from St. Joseph, Mo., *viâ* Great Salt Lake City, to Carson Valley.
From a Diary kept between the 7th of August and the 19th of October, 1860.

No. of Mail.		Miles.	Start.	Arrival.	Date.
1.	Leave St. Joseph, Missouri, in N. lat. 39° 40′, and W. long. 94° 50′. Cross Missouri River by steam ferry. Five miles of bottom land, bend in river and settlements. Over rolling prairie 2000 feet above sea level. After 6 miles, Troy, capital of Doniphan Co., Kansas Territory, about a dozen shanties. Dine and change mules at Cold Spring —good water and grass	20– 24	A.M. 9 30	P.M. 3	Aug. 7
	Road from Fort Leavenworth (N. lat. 39° 21′ 14″, and W. long. 94° 44′) falls in at Cold Spring, distant 15 miles.				
	From St. Jo to Cold Spring there are two routes, one lying north of the other, the former 20, the latter 24 miles in length.				
2.	After 10 miles, Valley Home, a whitewashed shanty. At Small Branch on Wolf River, 12 miles from Cold Spring, is a fiumara on the north of the road, with water, wood, and grass. Here the road from Fort Atchinson falls in. Kennekuk Station, 44 miles from St. Joseph. Sup and change mules...	22– 23	P.M. 4	P.M. 8	Aug. 7
3.	Two miles beyond Kennekuk is the first of the three Grasshopper Creeks, flowing after rain to the Kansas River. Road rough and stony; water, wood, and grass. Four miles beyond the First Grasshopper is Whitehead, a young settlement on Big Grasshopper; water in pools, wood, and grass. Five and a half miles beyond is Walnut Creek, in Kickapoo Co.: pass over corduroy bridge; roadside dotted with shanties. Thence to Locknan's, or Big Muddy Station	25	P.M. 9	A.M. 1	Aug.7,8
4.	Seventeen miles beyond Walnut Creek, the Third Grasshopper, also falling into the Kansas River. Good camping-ground. Ten miles beyond lies Richland, deserted site. Thence to Seneca, capital of Nemehaw Co. A few shanties on the N. bank of Big Nemehaw Creek, a tributary of the Missouri River, which affords water, wood, and grass	18	A.M. 3	A.M. 6	Aug. 8
5.	Cross Wildcat Creek and other nullahs. Seven miles beyond Seneca lies Ash Point, a few wood-				

No. of Mail.		Miles.	Start.	Arrival.	Date.
	en huts, thence to "Uncle John's Grocery," where liquor and stores are procurable. Eleven miles from Big Nemehaw, water, wood, and grass are found at certain seasons near the head of a ravine. Thence to Vermilion Creek, which heads to the N.E., and enters the Big Blue 20 miles above its mouth. The ford is miry after rain, and the banks are thickly wooded. Water is found in wells 40–43 feet deep. Guittard's Station......	20	A.M. 8	NOON. 12	Aug. 8
6.	Fourteen miles from Guittard's, Marysville, capital of Washington Co., affords supplies and a blacksmith. Then ford the Big Blue, tributary to Kansas River, clear and swift stream. Twelve miles W. of Marysville is the frontier line between Kansas and Nebraska. Thence to Cotton-wood Creek, fields in hollow near the stream.	25	P.M. 1	P.M. 6	Aug. 8
7.	Store at the crossing very dirty and disorderly. Good water in spring 400 yards N. of the road; wood and grass abundant. Seventeen and a half miles from the Big Blue is Walnut Creek, where emigrants encamp. Thence to West Turkey or Rock Creek in Nebraska Territory, a branch of the Big Blue: its approximate altitude is 1485 feet......	26	P.M. 6	P.M. 11	Aug. 8
8.	After 19 miles of rough road and musquetoes, cross Little Sandy, 5 miles E. of Big Sandy; water and trees plentiful. There Big Sandy deep and heavy bed. Big Sandy Station......	23	P.M. 12	A.M. 4	Aug. 9
9.	Cross hills forming divide of Little Blue River, ascending valley 60 miles long. Little Blue fine stream of clear water falling into Kansas River; every where good supplies and good camping-ground. Along the left bank to Kiowa.........	19	A.M. 6	A.M. 10	Aug. 9
10.	Rough road of spurs and gullies runs up a valley 2 miles wide. Well wooded chiefly with cotton-wood, and grass abundant. Ranch at Liberty Farm, on the Little Blue......	25	A.M. 11	P.M. 3	Aug. 9
11.	Cross divide between Little Blue and Platte River; rough road, musquetoes troublesome. Approximate altitude of dividing ridge 2025 feet. Station at Thirty-two-Mile Creek, a small wooded and winding stream flowing into the Little Blue..	24	P.M. 4	P.M. 9	Aug. 9
12.	After 27 miles strike the Valley of the Platte, along the southern bank of the river, over level ground, good for camping, fodder abundant. After 7 miles Fort Kearney in N. lat. 40° 38′ 45″, and W. long. 98° 58′ 11″: approximate altitude 2500 feet above sea level. Groceries, cloths, provisions, and supplies of all kinds are to be procured from the sutler's store. Beyond Kearney a rough and bad road leads to "Seventeen-Mile Station"......	34	P.M. 10 30	A.M. 8	Aug. 10
13.	Along the south bank of the Platte. Buffalo chips used for fuel. Sign of buffalo appears. Plum-Creek Station on a stream where there is a bad crossing in wet weather......	21	A.M. 9 30	P.M. 1 15	Aug. 10
14.	Beyond Plum Creek, Willow-Island Ranch, where supplies are procurable. Road along the Platte, wood scarce; grass plentiful, buffalo abounds; after 20 miles "Cold-Water Ranch." Halt and change at Midway Station......	25	P.M. 2 30	P.M. 8	Aug. 10

No. of Mail.		Miles.	Start.	Arrival.	Date.
15.	Along the Valley of the Platte, road muddy after rain, fuel scarce, grass abundant, camp traces every where. Ranch at Cotton-wood Station, at this season the western limit of buffalo............	27	P.M. 9	A.M. 1 45	Aug. 11
16.	Up the Valley of the Platte. No wood; buffalo chips for fuel. Good camping-ground; grass on small branch of the Platte. To Junction-House Ranch, and thence to station at Frémont Springs	30	A.M. 6 15	A.M. 11	Aug. 11
17.	Road passes O'Fallon's Bluffs. "Half-way House," a store and ranch, distant 120 miles from Fort Kearney, 400 from St. Joseph, 40 from the Lower Crossing, and 68 from the Upper Crossing of the South Fork (Platte River). The station is called Alkali Lake.................................	25	NOON. 12	P.M. 5	Aug. 11
18.	Road along river ; no timber ; grass, buffalo chips, and musquetoes. Station at Diamond Springs near Lower Crossing ......:......................	25	P.M. 6	P.M. 10 15	Aug. 11
19.	Road along river. Last 4 miles very heavy sand, avoided by Lower Crossing. Poor accommodation at Upper Ford or Crossing on the eastern bank, where the mail passes the stream en route to Great Salt Lake City, and the road branches to Denver City and Pike's Peak....................	25	P.M. 11	A.M. 3 15	Aug. 12
20.	Ford Platte 600 yards wide, 2·50 feet deep, bed gravelly and solid, easy ford in dry season. Cross divide between North and South Forks, along the bank of Lodge-Pole Creek. Land arid ; wild sage for fuel. Lodge-Pole Station.................	35	A.M. 6 30	P.M. 12 45	Aug. 12
21.	Up Lodge-Pole Creek over a spur of table-land ; then, striking over the prairie, finishes the high divide between the Forks. Approximate altitude 3500 feet. On the right is Ash Hollow, where there is plenty of wood and a small spring. The station is Mud Springs, a poor ranch.........	25	P.M. 3	P.M. 5 45	Aug. 12
22.	Route lies over a rolling divide between the Forks, crossing Omaha, Lawrence, and other creeks, where water and grass are procurable. Cedar is still found in hill-gullies. About half a mile north of Chimney Rock is a ranch where the cattle are changed.....................	25	A.M. 8	P.M. 12 30	Aug. 13
23.	Road along the south bank of North Ford of Platte River. Wild sage the only fuel in the valley; small spring on top of first hill. Rugged labyrinth of paths abreast of Scott's Bluffs, which lie 5 miles S. of river, in N. lat. 41° 48′ 26″, and W. long. 103° 45′ 02″. Water found in first ravine of Scott's Bluffs 200 yards below the road, cedars on heights. To station..............................	24	P.M. 1 30	P.M. 5 30	Aug. 13
24.	Road along the river ; crosses Little Kiowa Creek, a tributary to Horse Creek, which flows into the Platte. Ford Horse Creek, a clear shallow stream with a sandy bottom. No wood below the hills..	16	P.M. 6 30	P.M. 8 30	Aug. 13
25.	Route over sandy and heavy river bottom and rolling ground, leaving the Platte on the right : cotton-wood and willows on the banks. Ranch at Laramie City kept by M. Badeau, a Canadian, who sells spirits, Indian goods, and outfit.........	26	A.M. 6	P.M. 10 20	Aug. 14
26.	After 9 miles of rough road cross Laramie Fork and enter Fort Laramie, N. lat. 42° 12′ 38″, and W. long. 104° 31′ 26″. Altitude 4519 feet. Military post, with post-office, sutler's stores, and				

No. of Mail.		Miles.	Start.	Arrival.	Date.
	other conveniences. Thence To Ward's Station on the Central Star, small ranch and store	18	P.M. 12 15	P.M. 4	Aug. 14
27.	Rough and bad road. After 14 miles cross Bitter Cotton-wood Creek; water rarely flows; after rain 10 feet wide and 6 inches deep; grass and fuel abundant. Pass Indian shop and store. At Bitter Creek branch of Cotton-wood the road to Salt Lake City forks. Emigrants follow the Upper or South road over spurs of the Black Hills, some way south of the river, to avoid kanyons and to find grass. The station is called Horseshoe Creek. Residence of road-agent, Mr. Slade, and one of the worst places on the line..................	25	P.M. 5	P.M. 9 30	Aug. 14
28.	Road forks; one line follows the Platte, the other turns to the left, over "cut-off;" highly undulating ridges, crooked and deeply dented with dry beds of rivers; land desolate and desert. No wood nor water till end of stage. La Bonté River and Station; unfinished ranch in valley; water and grass	25	A.M. 10 45	A.M. 2 45	Aug. 15
29.	Road runs 6 miles (wheels often locked) on rugged red land, crosses several dry beds of creeks, and springs with water after melting of snow and frosts in dry season, thence into the Valley of the Platte. After 17 miles it crosses the La Prêle (Rush River), a stream 16 feet wide, where water and wood abound. At Box-Elder Creek Station good ranch and comfortable camping-ground....	25	P.M. 4	P.M. 9	Aug. 15
30.	Along the Platte River, now shrunk to 100 yards. After 10 miles, M. Bissonette; at Deer Creek, a post-office, blacksmith's shop, and store near Indian Agency. Thence a waste of wild sage to Little Muddy, a creek with water. No accommodation nor provisions at station.....................	20	A.M. 8 30	NOON. 12	Aug. 16
31.	After 8 miles cross vile bridge over Snow Creek. Thence up the river valley along the S. bank of the Platte to the lower ferry. To Lower Bridge, old station of troops. To Upper Bridge, where the ferry has now been done away with............	18	P.M. 1 15	P.M. 4 15	Aug. 16
32.	Road ascends a hill 7 miles long; land rough, barren, and sandy in dry season. After 10 miles, red spring near the Red Buttes, an old trading-place and post-office. Road then leaves the Platte River and strikes over high, rolling, and barren prairie. After 18 miles, "Devil's Backbone." Station at Willow Springs; wood, water, and grass; good place for encampment, but no accommodation nor provisions. On this stage mineral and alkaline waters dangerous to cattle abound..	28	A.M. 6 30	P.M. 12 50	Aug. 17
33.	After 3 miles, Green Creek, not to be depended upon, and Prospect Hill, a good look-out. Then, at intervals of 3 miles, Harper's, Woodworth's, and Greasewood Creeks, followed by heavy sand. At 17 miles, "Saleratus Lake," on the west of the road. Four miles beyond is "Independence Rock," Ford Sweetwater, leaving the "Devil's Gate" on the right. Pass a blacksmith's shop. Sage the only fuel. Plante or Muddy Station; family of Canadians; no conveniences............	33	P.M. 2 30	P.M. 9 15	Aug. 17
34.	Along the winding banks of the Sweetwater. After 4 miles, "Alkali Lake" S. of the road. Land dry and stony; stunted cedars in hills. After 12				

No. of Mail.		Miles.	Start.	Arrival.	Date.
	miles, the "Devil's Post-office," a singular bluff on the left of the road, and opposite a ranch kept by a Canadian. Mail station "Three Crossings," at Ford No. 3; excellent water, wood, grass, game, and wild currants......................	25	A.M. 7	A.M. 11	Aug. 18
35.	Up a kanyon of the Sweetwater. Ford the river 5 times, making a total of 8. After 16 miles, "Ice Springs" in a swampy valley, and one quarter of a mile beyond "Warm Springs." Then rough descent and waterless stretch. Descend by "Lander's Cut-off" into fertile bottom. "Rocky Ridge Station;" at Muskrat Creek good cold spring, grass, and sage fuel.................................	35	A.M. 5 45	P.M. 12 45	Aug. 19
36.	Up the bed of the creek, and, ascending long hills, leave the Sweetwater. After 4 miles, 3 alkaline ponds S. of the road. Rough path. After 7 miles, "Strawberry Creek," 6 feet wide; good camping-ground; willows and poplars. One mile beyond is Quaking-Asp Creek, often dry. Three miles beyond lies M'Achran's Branch, 33 × 2. Then "Willow Creek," 10 × 2 ; good camping-ground. At Ford No. 9 is a Canadian ranch and store. A long table-land leads to "South Pass," dividing trip between the Atlantic and Pacific, and thence 2 miles to the station at "Pacific Springs;" water, tolerable grass, sage fuel, and musquetoes....	35	A.M. 7 45	P.M. 3	Aug. 20
37.	Cross Miry Creek. Road down Pacific Creek; water scarce for 20 miles. After 11 miles, "Dry Sandy Creek;" water scarce and too brackish to drink; grass little; sage and greasewood plentiful. After 16 miles, "Sublette's Cut-off," or the "Dry Drive," turns N.W. to Soda Springs and Fort Hall: the left fork leads to Fort Bridger and Great Salt Lake City. Four miles beyond the junction is "Little Sandy Creek," 20–25 × 2; grass, timber, and good camping-ground. Eight miles beyond is "Big Sandy Creek," clear, swift, and with good crossing, 110 × 2. The southern route is the best; along the old road, no water for 49 miles. Big Sandy Creek Station...........	33	A.M. 8	P.M. 12 50	Aug. 21
38.	Desolate road cuts off the bend of the river; no grass nor water. After 12 miles, "Simpson's Hollow." Fall into the Valley of Green River, half a mile wide, water 110 yards broad. After 20½ miles, Upper Ford ; Lower Ford 7 miles below Upper. Good camping-ground on bottom ; at the station in Green River, grocery, stores, and ferry-boat when there is high water.................	32	P.M. 1 45	P.M. 6 30	Aug. 21
39.	Diagonal ford over Green River ; a good camping-ground in bottom. Follow the valley for 4 miles; grass and fuel. Michel Martin's store and grocery. The road leaves the river and crosses a waterless divide to Black's Fork, 100 × 2; grass and fuel. Wretched station at Ham's Fork	24	A.M. 8	NOON. 12	Aug. 22
40.	Ford Ham's Fork. After 12 miles the road forks at the 2d striking of Ham's Fork, both branches leading to Fort Bridger. Mail takes the left-hand path. Then Black's Fork, 20 × 2, clear and pretty valley, with grass and fuel, cotton-wood and yellow currants. Cross the stream 3 times. After 12 miles, "Church Butte." Ford Smith's				

No. of Mail.		Miles.	Start.	Arrival.	Date.
	Fork, 30 feet wide and shallow, a tributary of Black's Fork. Station at Millersville on Smith's Fork; large store and good accommodation.....	20	P.M. 2	P.M. 5 15	Aug. 22
41.	Road runs up the valley of Black's Fork. After 12 miles, Fort Bridger, in N. lat. 41° 18′ 12″, and W. long. 110° 32′ 23″, on Black's Fork of Green River. Commands Indian trade, fuel, corn; little grass. Post-office, sutler's store, grocery, and other conveniences. Thence rough and rolling ground to Muddy Creek Hill; steep and stony descent. Over a fertile bottom to Big Muddy and Little Muddy Creek, which empties into Black's Fork below Fort Bridger. At Muddy Creek Station there is a Canadian, provisions, excellent milk; no stores....................	25	A.M. 8 30	P.M. 12 15	Aug. 23
42.	Rough country. The road winds along the ridge to Quaking-Asp Hill, 7900 (8400?) feet above sea level. Steep descent; rough and broken ground. After 18 miles, Sulphur Creek Valley; stagnant stream, flowing after rain; ford bad and muddy. Station in the fertile valley of Bear River, which turns northward and flows into the east side of the lake; wood, grass, and water. Poor accommodations at Bear River Station...................	20	NOON. 12	P.M. 5 30	Aug. 23
43.	Road runs by Needle Rocks; falls into the Valley of Egan's Creek. "Cache Cave" on the right hand. Three miles below the Cave is Red Fork in Echo Kanyon; unfinished station at the entrance. Rough road; steep ascents and descents along Red Creek Station on Weber River, which falls into Salt Lake south of Bear River...........	36	A.M. 8 15	P.M. 2 30	Aug. 24
44.	Road runs down the Valley of the Weber. Ford the river. After 5¼ miles is a salt spring, where the road leaves the river to avoid a deep kanyon, and turns to the left into a valley with rough paths, trying to wheels. Then crosses a mountain, and, ascending a long hill, descends to Bauchmin's Creek, tributary to Weber River. Creek 18 feet wide, swift, pebbly bed, good ford; grass and fuel abundant. The station is called Carson's House; accommodations of the worst.......	22	P.M. 4 30	P.M. 7 45	Aug. 24
45.	Ford Bauchmin's Creek 13 times in 8 miles. After 2 miles along a small water-course ascend Big Mountain, whence first view of Great Salt Lake City, 12 miles distant. After 14 miles, Big Kanyon Creek. Six miles farther the road leaves Big Kanyon Creek, and after a steep ascent and descent makes Emigration Creek. Cross Little Mountain, 2 miles beyond Big Mountain; road rough and dangerous. Five miles from Emigration Kanyon to Great Salt Lake City. Road through "Big Field" 6 miles square................	29	A.M. 7	P.M. 7 15	Aug. 28

GREAT SALT LAKE CITY, N. lat. 40° 46′ 08″
W. long. 112° 06′ 08″ (G.)
Altitude 4300 feet.

The variation of compass at Temple Block in 1849 was 15° 47′ 23″, and in 1860 it was 15° 54′, a slow progress toward the east. (In the Wind-River Mountains, as laid down by Colonel Frémont in 1842, it was E. 18°.) In Fillmore Valley it is now 18° 15′, and three years ago was about 17° east; the rapid progression to the east is accompanied with extreme irregularity, which the people attribute to the metallic constituents of the soil.

Total of days between St. Jo and Great Salt Lake City............	19
Total stages..	45
Distance in statute miles...	1136
From Fort Leavenworth to Great Salt Lake City....................	1168

ITINERARY OF THE MAIL-ROUTE FROM GREAT SALT LAKE CITY TO SAN FRANCISCO.

No. of Mail.		Miles.	Start.	Arrival.	Date.
1 and 2.	Road through the south of the city, due south along the right bank of the Jordan. Cross many creeks, viz., Kanyon Creek, 4¼ miles; Mill Creek, 2½; First or Great Cotton-wood Creek, 2; Second ditto, 4; Fork of road, 1¼; Dry Creek, 3½; Willow Creek, 2¾. After 22–23 miles, hot and cold springs, and half-way house, the brewery under the point of the mountain. Road across Ash-Hollow or Jordan Kanyon, 2 miles. Fords river, knee deep; ascends a rough divide between Utah Valley and Cedar Valley, 10 miles from camp, and finally reaches Cedar Creek and Camp Floyd............	44	10 30	9 30	Sept. 20
3.	Leaves Camp Floyd; 7 miles to the divide of Cedar Valley. Crosses the divide into Rush Valley; after a total of 18·2 miles reaches Meadow Creek; good grass and water. Rush Valley mail station 1 mile beyond; food and accommodation........	20	10 30	9 30	Sept. 27
4.	Crosses remains of Rush Valley 7 miles. Up a rough divide called General Johnston's Pass. Spring, often dry, 200 yards on the right of the road. At Point Look-out leaves Simpson's Road, which runs south. Cross Skull Valley ; bad road. To the bench on the eastern flank of the desert. Station called Egan's Springs, Simpson's Springs, or Lost Springs, grass plentiful, water good.....	27	A.M. 9 30	4 30	Sept. 28
5.	New station; road forks to S.E., and leads, after 5 miles, to grass and water. After 8 miles, river bottom, 1 mile broad. Long line over desert to express station, called Dugway ; no grass, and no water...	20	12	P.M. 5 30	Sept. 29
6.	Steep road 2½ miles to the summit of Dugway Pass. Descend by a rough incline; 8 miles beyond the road forks to Devil's Hole, 90 miles from Camp Floyd on Simpson's route, and 6 miles S. of Fish Springs. Eight miles beyond the fork is Mountain Point; road winds S. and W., and then N. to avoid swamp, and crosses 3 sloughs. Beyond the last is Fish-Spring Station, on the bench—a poor place; water plentiful, but bad. Cattle here drink for the first time after Lost Springs, distant 48 miles	28	P.M. 6 30	A.M. 3 30	Sept. 29
7.	Road passes many pools. Half way forks S. to Pleasant Valley (Simpson's line). Road again rounds the swamp, crossing S. end of Salt Plain. After 21 miles, "Willow Creek;" water rather brackish. Station "Willow Springs" on the bench below the hills, at W. end of desert; grass and hay plentiful	22	A.M. 10	3 30	Sept. 30
8.	Road ascending the bench, turns N. to find the pass. After 6 miles, Mountain Springs ; good water,				

No. of Mail.		Miles.	Start.	Arrival.	Date.
	grass, and fuel. Six miles beyond is Deep-Creek Kanyon, a dangerous ravine 9 miles long. Then descends into a fertile and well-watered valley, and after 7 miles enters Deep-Creek mail station. Indian farm....................................	28	A.M. 8	P.M. 4	Oct. 1
9.	Along Willow Creek. After 8 miles, "Eight-Miles Springs;" water, grass, and sage fuel. Kanyon after 2½ miles, 500 yards long and easy. Then 19 miles through Antelope Valley to the station of the same name, burnt in June, 1860, by Indians. Simpson's route from Pleasant Valley, distant 12·5 miles, falls into the E. end of Antelope Valley, from Camp Floyd 151 miles.........	30	A.M. 8	P.M. 4	Oct. 3, 4
10.	Road over the valley for 2 miles to the mouth of Shell-Creek Kanyon, 6 miles long. Rough road; fuel plentiful. Descends into Spring Valley, and then passes over other divides into Shell Creek, where there is a mail station; water, grass, and fuel abundant...............................	18	A.M. 6	P.M. 11	Oct. 5
11.	Descends a rough road. Crosses Steptoe Valley and bridged creek. Road heavy, sand or mud. After 16 miles, Egan's Kanyon, dangerous for Indians. Station at the W. mouth burned by Indians in October, 1860...............	18	P.M. 2	P.M. 6	Oct. 5
12.	Pass the divide, fall into Butte Valley, and cross its N. end. Bottom very cold. Mail station half way up a hill; a very small spring; grass on the N. side of the hill. Butte Station..................	18	P.M. 8	A.M. 3	Oct. 6
13.	Ascend the long divide; 2 steep hills and falls. Cross the N. end of Long Valley, all barren. Ascend the divide, and descend into Ruby Valley; road excellent; water, grass, and bottom; fuel distant. Good mail station....................	22	A.M. 8	P.M. 1 45	Oct. 7
14.	Long divide; fuel plenty; no grass nor water. After 10 miles the road branches to the right hand to Gravelly Ford of Humboldt River. Cross a dry bottom. Cross Smith's Fork of Humboldt River in Huntingdon Valley; a little stream; bunch-grass and sage fuel on the W. end. Ascend Chokop's Pass, Dugway, and hard hill; descend into Moonshine Valley. Station at Diamond Springs; warm water, but good...........	23	A.M. 8	P.M. 1 45	Oct. 8, 9
15.	Cross Moonshine Valley. After 7 miles a sulphurous spring and grass. Twelve miles beyond ascend the divide; no water; fuel and bunch-grass plentiful. Then a long divide. After 9 miles, the station on Roberts' Creek, at the E. end of Sheawit, or Roberts' Springs Valley..............	28	A.M. 8	P.M. 1 45	Oct. 10
16.	Down the valley to the west; good road; sage small; no fuel. After 12 miles, willows and water-holes; 3 miles beyond there are alkaline wells. Station on the bench; water below in a dry creek; grass must be brought from 15 miles.......................	35	A.M. 6 30	P.M. 12 30	Oct. 11
17.	Cross a long rough divide to Smoky Valley. At the northern end is a creek called "Wanahonop," or "Netwood," i. e., trap. Thence a long rough kanyon to Simpson's Park; grass plentiful; water in wells 10 feet deep. Simpson's Park in Shoshonee country, and, according to Simpson's Itinerary, 348 miles from Camp Floyd.............	25	A.M. 8 15	P.M. 2 25	Oct. 12
18.	Cross Simpson's Park. Ascend Simpson's Pass, a				

No. of Mail.		Miles.	Start.	Arrival.	Date.
	long kanyon, with sweet "Sage Springs" on the summit; bunch-grass plentiful. Descend to the fork of the road; right hand to the lower, left hand to the upper ford of Reese's River. Water perennial and good; food poor......................	15	A.M. 10	P.M. 2	Oct. 13
19.	Through the remainder of Reese's River Valley. After a long divide, the Valley of Smith's Creek; saleratus; no water nor grass. At last, the station, near a kanyon, and hidden from view. The land belongs to the Pa Yutas....................	28	A.M. 7 20	P.M. 2 45	Oct. 14
20.	Ascend a rough kanyon, and descend to a barren and saleratus plain. Toward the south of the valley over bench-land, rough with rock and pitch-hole. "Cold Springs Station" half built, near stream; fuel scarce............................	25	A.M. 8 15	P.M. 4 15	Oct. 15
21.	At the west gate, 2 miles from the station, good grass. After 8 miles, water. Two miles beyond is the middle gate; water in fiumara, and grass near. Beyond the gate are 2 basins, long divides, winding road to "Sand Springs Valley;" bad water; little grass............................	35	A.M. 9 50	P.M. 2 30	Oct. 16
22.	Cross the valley, 10 miles to the summit, over slough inundations and bad road. Summit shifting sand. Descend 5 miles to Carson Lake; water tolerable; tule abundant. Round the S. side of the lake to the sink of Carson River Station; no provisions; pasture good; fuel scarce.............	25	A.M. 11	P.M. 9	Oct. 17
23.	Cross a long plain. Ascend a very steep divide, and sight Sierra 50 miles distant. Descend to Carson River. Fort Churchill newly built. Sutler's stores, etc.	25	A.M. 9 30	P.M. 7 15	Oct. 18
24.	Carson City	35	11	10 30	Oct. 19
	Carson City lies on the eastern foot of the Sierra Nevada, distant 552 statute miles, according to Captain Simpson, from Camp Floyd. The present itinerary reduces it to 544, and, adding 44 miles, to a total of 588 from Great Salt Lake City.				

ITINERARY of Captain J. H. SIMPSON's Wagon-road from Camp Floyd to Genoa, Carson Valley, Utah Territory. Explored by direction of General A. G. JOHNSTON, commanding the Department of Utah, between the 2d of May and the 12th of June, 1859.

Places.	Intermediate Distances. Miles.	From Camp to Camp. Miles.	Total from Camp Floyd. Miles.	No. of Camp.	Wood.	Water.	Grass.
Camp Floyd, wood and grass in vicinity........						W	
Meadow Creek.....................................	18·2	18·2	18·2	1			
Cross Meadow Creek (Rush Valley), mail station ¼ mile.................................	1						
Spring ⅓ mile to the right of General Johnston's Pass, just after passing the summit. This spring furnishes but little water, even in the spring, and in the summer would be most probably dry..............................	8·9	9·9	28·1	2	W	W	G
Simpson's Springs, mail station	16·2	16·2	44·3	3	W { Willow	W	G
Summit, Short-cut Pass.............................	21·6						

K K

Places.	Intermediate Distances. Miles.	From Camp to Camp. Miles.	Total from Camp Floyd. Miles.	No. of Camp.	Wood.	Water.	Grass.
1·6 miles below summit	1·6	23·2	67·5	4	Sage		very little grass
Tolerable grass skirting a low range of rocks on the right of the road	7·8						G
A little grass; sage in valley	4·8				S		G
Devil's Hole; water slightly brackish	6·7					W	
Fish Springs, mail station	5·4	24·7	92·2	5	Ctw	W	G
Warm Springs	3·4				GW	W	G
Grass in considerable quantity of good character	26·4	29·7	121·9	6			G
Alkaline spring to the right of the road; water not drinkable	1·						
Sulphur springs; water abundant and palatable	1·5	2·5	125·	7	W,S	W	G
Spring, Pleasant Valley, mail station	13·4	13·4	138·4	8	W	W	G
East side of Antelope Valley		12·5	150·9	9	W	W	G
Spring Valley; good grass on the west bench and slopes		19·	169·9	10	GW	W	G
Cross a marsh; road takes up a fine stream; grass all along	3·5						
Leave Creek	3·5				W	W	G
Spring, copious; grass fine	2·8				W	W	G
East side of Steptoe Valley, mail station	1·3	11·1	181·0	11	W	W	G
Steptoe Creek; dry in summer	6·5						
Mouth of Egan Kanyon	6·8	13·3	194·3	12	W	W	G
Spring; source of Egan Creek	1·8				W	W	G
West side of Butte Valley. Mail station; a very small spring, barely sufficient for cooking purposes, near the top of the hill; grass on the N. side of same hill	16·2	18·1	212·4	13	W	W	G
Spring 1 mile west side of summit of range	12·	12·	224·4	14	W	W	G
Ruby Valley, mail station	9·2	9·2	233·6	15	GW	W	G
Smith's Fork, Humboldt River, Huntingdon's Creek	14·4						
Small mountain stream	3·3	17·6	251·2	16	GW	W	G
Spring left of the road	1·2				GW	W	G
Near west foot of Cho-kupe Pass	5·8	7·1	258·3	17	GW	W	G
Spring in Pah-hun-nupe Valley	7·8						
Do. west side of Pah-hun-nupe Valley	5·6	13·3	271·6	18	S,W GW	W	G
She-a-wi-te (Willow) Creek	14·9	14·9	286·5	19	S,W	W	G
Bed of Nash River; water in pools, probably not constant	11·6						
Small spring; grass on mountain side, 2 miles off	5·9	17·5	304·	20	S,W	W	G
Wons-in-dam-me, or Antelope Creek	7·	7·	311·	21	W	W	G
Creek	4·3				S,W	W	G
Creek west side of valley	9·5	13·7	324·7	22	S,W	W	G
Wan-a-ho-no-pe (Netwood trap) Creek	13·6						
Do. do. do	4·6	18·2	342·9	23	S,W	W	G
Simpson's Park, according to topographer, Lieutenant Putnam, and guide, Colonel Reese	4·9	4·9	347·8	24	S,W	W	G
Small spring in Simpson's Pass (same authority)	3·						
Ford of Reese's River	8·2					W	G
Reese's River	2·6	13·8	361·6	25		W	G
Leave Reese's River	3·4					W	G
Small spring to the left of the road, just before reaching the summit of the Pass	10·						
Lieutenant J. L. Kirby Smith's Creek	7·8	21·2	382·8	26	GW	W	G

Places.	Intermediate Distances. Miles.	From Camp to Camp. Miles.	Total from Camp Floyd. Miles.	No. of Camp.	Wood.	Water.	Grass.
Engleman's Creek	1·6					W	
Lieutenant Putnam's Creek	8·6	10·2	393·	27	S,W	W	G
Do. South Fork	2·7				W	W	G
Rock Creek	3·				W	W	G
Do.	3·1	8·7	401·7	28	W	W	G
Do. Sinks	1·7						
Spring-water kegs should be filled for 2 days. Camp from this in alkaline flat	5·4					W	
Gibraltar Gate	0·6					W	
Creek joins Gibraltar Creek	4·2						
Middle-Gate Spring	3·2	14·7	416·4	29	S,W	W	G
West Gate	3·5						
Dry wells; alkaline valley; very poor camp; water and grass alkaline, and little of either. Rabbit-bush fuel	21·0	24·5	440·9	30	Rab. bush	W	G
Creek connecting the two lakes of Carson. Road can be shortened some eight or ten miles by striking across the head of Alkaline Valley after getting about nine miles from Camp 30, and then proceeding directly to the shore of Carson Lake. It is not necessary to go so far north as the connecting creek referred to		16·6	457·5	31	Dry rush	W	R,G
Leave Carson Lake	9·7					W	R,G
Walker's River	21·5	31·2	488·7	32	W	W	G
Do. do.		10·	498·7	33	W	W	G
Do. North Bend		6·3	505·	34	W	W	G
Small spring, not sufficient for a large command; grass ½ mile south	14·1				S,W	W	G
Carson River	1·9						
Do. do.	3·0	19·0	524·	35	W	W	G
Pleasant Grove; cross Carson River and get into Old Emigrant Road. Mail station	9·0	9·0	533·	36	W	W	G
China Town. Gold diggings	7·4					W	
Carson City. East foot of Sierra Nevada	11·6	19·0	552·	37		W	G
Genoa. Do. do. do.	12·9	12·9	564·9	38	W	W	G

(Signed),   J. H. SIMPSON, Capt. Top. Engineers.

To Brevet Major F. J. Porter, Assist. Adj. Gen., Dept. Utah, Camp Floyd.

II. DESCRIPTION OF THE MORMON TEMPLE.

[Extracted from the Deserét News.]

THE following is a brief detail of the temple, taken from drawings in my office in Great Salt Lake City.

The Temple Block is 40 rods square, the lines running north and south, east and west, and contains 10 acres. The centre of the temple is 156 feet 6 inches due west from the centre of the east line of the block. The length of said house east and west is 186½ feet, including towers, and the width 99 feet. On the east end there are three towers, as also on the west. Draw a line north and south 118½ feet through the centre of the tower, and you have the north and south extent of ground-plan, including pedestal.

We depress into the earth at the east end to the depth of 16 feet, and enlarge all around beyond the lines of wall 3 feet for a footing. The north and south walls are 8 feet thick clear of pedestal; they stand upon a footing of 16 feet wall on its bearing, which slopes 3 feet on each side to the height of 7½ feet. The footing of the towers rise to the same height as the side, and is one solid piece of masonry of rough ashlars, laid in good lime mortar.

The basement of the main building is divided into many rooms by walls, all having footings. The line of the basement floor is 6 inches above the top of the footing. From the towers on the east to the towers on the west, the face of the earth slopes 6 feet; 4 inches above the earth on the east line begins a promenade walk from 11 to 22 feet wide around the entire building, and approached by stone steps as the earth slopes and requires them. There are four towers on the four corners of the building, each starting from their footing of 26 feet square; these continue 16½ feet high, and come to the line of the base string course, which is 8 feet above the promenade walk. At this point the towers are reduced to 25 feet square; they then continue to the height of 38 feet, or the height of the second string course. At this point they are reduced to 23 feet square; they then continue 38 feet high to the third string course. The string courses continue all around the building, except when separated by buttresses. These string courses are massive mouldings from solid blocks of stone.

The two east towers then rise 25 feet to a string course or cornice. The two west towers rise 19 feet, and come to their string course or cornice. The four towers then rise 9 feet to the top of battlements. These towers are cylindrical, having 17 feet diameter inside, within which stairs ascend around a solid column 4 feet in diameter, allowing landings at the various sections of the building. These towers have each five ornamental windows on two sides above the basement. The two centre towers occupy the centre of the east and west ends of the building, starting from their footings 31 feet square, and break off in sections in line with corner towers, to the height of the third string course. The east centre tower then rises 40 feet to the top of battlements; the west centre tower rises 34 feet to the top of battlements. All these towers have spires; the east centre tower rises 200 feet, while the west centre tower rises 190 feet. All these towers at their corners have octagon turrets, terminated by octagon pinnacles 5 feet diameter at base, 4 feet at first story, and three feet from there up. There are also on each side of these towers two buttresses, except where they come in contact with the body of the main building. The top of these buttresses show forty-eight in number, and stand upon pedestals. The space between the buttresses and turrets is 2 feet at the first story. On the front of the two centre towers are two large windows, each 32 feet high, one above the other, neatly prepared for that place.

On the two west corner towers, and on the west end a few feet below the top of battlements, may be seen in alto-relievo and bold relief the great dipper, or Ursa Major, with the pointers ranging nearly toward the north star. (Moral: the lost may find themselves by the priesthood.)

I will now glance at the main body of the house. I have before stated that the basement was divided into many rooms. The central one is arranged for a baptismal font, and is 59 feet long by 35 feet wide, separated from the main wall by four rooms, two on each side, 19 feet long by 12 feet wide. On the east and west sides of these rooms are four passages 12 feet wide; these lead to and from by outside doors, two on the north and two on the south. Farther east and west from these passages are four more rooms, two at each end, 28 feet wide by 38½ long. These two thin walls occupy the basement. All the walls start off their footings, and rise 16½ feet, and there stop with groin ceiling.

We are now up to the line of the base string course, 8 feet above the promenade or steps rising to the temple, which terminates at the cope of the pedestal, and to the first floor of said house. This room is joined to the outer courts, these courts being the width between towers 16 feet by 9 in the clear. We ascend to the floors of these courts (they being on a line with the first floor of the main house) by four flights of stone steps 9½ feet wide, arranged in the basement work, the first step ranging to the outer line of towers. From these courts doors admit to any part of the building.

The size of the first large room is 120 feet long by 80 feet wide; the height reaches nearly to the second string course. The room is arched over in the centre with an elliptical arch, which drops at its flank 10 feet, and has 38 feet span. The side ceilings have one fourth elliptical arches, which start from the side walls of the main building 16 feet high, and terminate at the capitals of the columns, or foot of centre arch, at the height of 24 feet. The columns obtain their bearings direct from the footings of the said house; these columns extend up to support the floor above. The outside walls of this story are 7 feet thick. The space, from the termination of the foot of the centre arch to the outer wall, is divided into sixteen compartments, eight in each side, making rooms 14 feet by 14, clear of partitions, and 10 feet high, leaving a passage of 6 feet wide next to each flank of the centre arch, which is approached from the ends. These rooms are each lighted by an elliptical or oval window, whose major axis is vertical.

The second large room is one foot wider than the room below; this is in consequence of the wall being but 6 feet thick, falling off 6 inches on the inner and 6 on the outer side. The second string course provides for this on the outer side. The rooms of this story are similar to those below. The side walls have nine buttresses on a side, and have eight tiers of windows, five in each tier.

The foot of the basement windows are 8 inches above the promenade, rise 3 feet perpendicular, and terminate in a semicircular head. The first-story windows have 12 feet long of sash to the top of the semicircular head. The oval windows have 6½ feet length of sash. The windows of the second story are the same as those below. All these frames have 4½ feet width of sash. The pedestals under all the buttresses project at their base 2 feet; above their base, which is 15 inches by 4½ feet wide, on each front is a figure of a globe 3 feet 11 inches across, whose axis corresponds with the axis of the earth.

The base string course forms a cope for those pedestals. Above this cope the buttresses are 3½ feet, and continue to the height of 100 feet. Above the promenade, close under the second string course on each of the buttresses, is the moon, represented in its different phases. Close under the third string course or cornice is the face of the sun. Immediately above is Saturn with his rings. The buttresses terminate with a projected cope.

The only difference between the tower buttresses and the one just described is, instead of Saturn being on them, we have clouds and rays of light descending.

All of these symbols are to be chiseled in bas-relief on solid stone. The side walls continue above the string course or cornice 8½ feet, making the walls 96 feet high, and are formed in battlements interspersed with stars.

This roof is quite flat, rising only 8 feet, and is to be covered with galvanized iron or some other metal. The building is to be otherwise ornamented in many places. The whole structure is designed to symbolize some of the great architectural work above. The basement windows recede in from the face of the outer wall to the sash frame 23 inches, and are relieved by a large cavetto, while on the inside they are approached by stone steps.

Those windows above the base recede from the face of the wall to the sash frame 3 feet, and are surrounded by stone jambs formed in mouldings, and surmounted by labels over each, which terminate at their horizon, excepting the oval windows, whose labels terminate as columns, which extend from an enriched string course at the foot of each window to the centre of the major axis. My chief object in the last paragraph is to show to the judgment of any who may be baffled how those windows can be come at, etc., etc. All the windows in the towers are moulded, and have stone jambs, each being crowned with label mouldings. The whole house covers an area of 21,850 feet.

For farther particulars, wait till the house is done, then come and see it.

(Signed),   Truman O. Angell, *Architect.*

III. THE MARTYRDOM OF JOSEPH SMITH.

BY APOSTLE JOHN TAYLOR.

Being requested by George A. Smith and Willford Woodruff, Church historians, to write an account of events that transpired before and took place at the time of the martyrdom of Joseph Smith, in Carthage jail, in Hancock County, State of Illinois, I write the following principally from memory, not having access to any public documents relative thereto farther than a few desultory items contained in Ford's "History of Illinois." I must also acknowledge myself considerably indebted to George A. Smith, who was with me when I wrote it, and who, although not there at the time of the bloody transaction, yet from conversing with several persons who were in the capacity of Church historians, and aided by an excellent memory, has rendered me a considerable service. These and the few items contained in the notes at the end of this account is all the aid I have had. I would farther add that the items contained in the letter, in relation to dates especially, may be considered strictly correct.

After having written the whole, I read it over to the Hon. J. M. Bernhisel, who, with one or two slight alterations, pronounced it strictly correct. Brother Bernhisel was present most of the time. I am afraid that, from the length of time that has transpired since the occurrence, and having to rely almost exclusively on my memory, there may be some slight inaccuracies, but I believe that in the general it is strictly correct; as I figured in those transactions from the commencement to the end, they left no slight impression on my mind.

In the year 1844, a very great excitement prevailed in some parts of the counties of Hancock, Brown, and other neighboring counties, in relation to the "Mormons," and a spirit of vindictive hatred and persecution was exhibited among the people, which was manifested in the most bitter and acrimonious language, as well as by acts of hostility and violence, frequently threatening the destruction of the citizens of Nauvoo and vicinity, and utter annihilation of the "Mormons" and "Mormonism," and in some instances breaking out in the most violent acts of ruffianly barbarity; persons were kidnapped, whipped, prosecuted, and falsely accused of various crimes; their cattle and houses injured, destroyed, or stolen; vexatious prosecutions were instituted to vex, harass, and annoy. In some remote neighborhoods they were expelled from their homes without redress, and in others violence was threatened to their persons and property, while in others every kind of insult and indignity was heaped upon them, to induce them to abandon their homes, the county, or the state.

These annoyances, prosecutions, and persecutions were instigated through different agencies and by various classes of men, actuated by different motives, but all uniting in the one object, prosecution, persecution, and extermination of the Saints.

There were a number of wicked and corrupt men living in Nauvoo and its vicinity who had belonged to the Church, but whose conduct was incompatible with the Gospel; they were accordingly dealt with by the Church and severed from its communion; some of these had been prominent members, and held official stations either in the city or Church. Among these was John C. Bennett, formerly Mayor; William Law, Councilor to Joseph Smith; Wilson Law, his natural brother, and general in the Nauvoo Legion; Dr. R. D. Foster, a man of some property, but with a very bad reputation; Francis and Chauncey Higbee, the latter a young lawyer, and both sons of a respectable and honored man in the Church, known as Judge Elias Higbee, who died about twelve months before.

Besides these, there were a great many apostates, both in the city and country, of less notoriety, who, for their delinquencies, had been expelled from the Church. John C. Bennett and Francis and Chauncey Higbee were cut off from the Church; the former was also cashiered from his generalship for the most flagrant acts of seduction and adultery; and such was the scandalous nature of the developments in their cases, that the high council before whom they were tried had to sit with closed doors.

William Law, although councilor to Joseph, was found to be his most bitter foe and maligner, and to hold intercourse, contrary to all law, in his own house, with a young lady resident with him, and it was afterward proved that he had conspired with some Missourians to take Joseph Smith's life, and was only saved by Josiah Arnold, who, being on guard at his house, prevented the assassins from seeing him. Yet, although having murder in his heart, his manners were generally courteous and mild, and he was well calculated to deceive.

General Wilson Law was cut off from the Church for seduction, falsehood, and defamation; both the above were also court-martialed by the Nauvoo Legion and expelled. Foster was also cut off, I believe, for dishonesty, fraud, and falsehood. I know he was eminently guilty of the whole, but whether these were the specific charges or not, I don't know, but I do know that he was a notoriously wicked and corrupt man.

Besides the above characters and "Mormonic" apostates, there were other three parties. The first of these may be called religionists, the second politicians, and the third counterfeiters, blacklegs, horse-thieves, and cut-throats.

The religious party were chagrined and maddened because "Mormonism" came in contact with their religion, and they could not oppose it from the Scriptures; and thus, like the ancient Jews, when enraged at the exhibition of their follies and hypocrisies by Jesus and his apostles, so these were infuriated against the Mormons because of their discomfiture by them; and instead of owning the truth and rejoicing in it, they were ready to gnash upon them with their teeth, and to persecute the believers in principles which they could not disprove.

The political party were those who were of opposite politics to us. There were always two parties, the Whigs and Democrats, and we could not vote for one without offending the other; and it not unfrequently happened that candidates for office would place the issue of their election upon opposition to the "Mormons," in order to gain political influence from religious prejudice, in which case the "Mormons" were compelled, in self-defense, to vote against them, which resulted almost invariably against our opponents. This made them angry; and, although it was of their own making, and the "Mormons" could not be expected to do otherwise, yet they raged on account of their discomfiture, and sought to wreak their fury on the "Mormons." As an instance of the above, when Joseph Duncan was candidate for the office of Governor of Illinois, he pledged himself to his party that, if he could be elected, he would exterminate or drive the "Mormons" from the state.* The consequence was that Governor Ford was elected. The Whigs, seeing that they had been outgeneraled by the Democrats in securing the "Mormon" vote, became seriously alarmed, and sought to repair their disaster by raising a kind of crusade against that people. The Whig newspapers teemed with accounts of the wonders and enormities of Nauvoo, and of the awful wickedness of a party which could consent to receive the support of such miscreants. Governor Duncan, who was really a brave, honest man, and who had nothing to do with getting the "Mormon" charters passed through the Legislature, took the stump on this subject in good earnest, and expected to be elected governor almost on this question alone. The third party, composed of counterfeiters, blacklegs, horse-thieves, and cut-throats, were a pack of scoundrels that infested the whole of the Western country at that time. In some districts their influence was so great as to control important state and county offices. On this subject Governor Ford says the following:

"Then, again, the northern part of the state was not destitute of its organized bands of rogues, engaged in murders, robberies, horse-stealing, and in making and passing counterfeit money. These rogues were scattered all over the north, but the most of them were located in the counties of Ogle, Winnebago, Lee, and De Kalb.

"In the county of Ogle they were so numerous, strong, and well organized that they could not be convicted for their crimes. By getting some of their numbers on the juries, by producing a host of witnesses to sustain their defense by perjured evidence, and by changing the venue of one county to another, by continuances from term to term, and by the inability of witnesses to attend from time to time at distant and foreign counties, they most generally managed to be acquitted."†

There was a combination of horse-thieves extending from Galena to Alton. There were counterfeiters engaged in merchandising, trading, and store-keeping in most of the cities and villages, and in some districts, I have been credibly informed by men to whom they have disclosed their secrets, the judges, sheriffs, constables, and jailers, as well as professional men, were more or less associated with them. These had in their employ the most reckless, abandoned wretches, who stood ready to carry into effect the most desperate enterprises, and were careless alike of human life and property. Their object in persecuting the "Mormons" was in part to cover their own rascality, and in part to prevent them from exposing and prosecuting them; but the principal reason was plunder, believing that if they could be removed or driven they would be made fat on Mormon spoils, besides having in the deserted city a good asylum for the prosecution of their diabolical pursuits.

This conglomeration of apostate Mormons, religious bigots, political fanatics, and combination of blacklegs, all united their forces against the "Mormons," and organized themselves into a party, denominated "anti-Mormons." Some of them, we have reason to believe, joined the Church in order to cover their nefarious practices, and when they were expelled for their unrighteousness only raged with greater violence. They circulated every kind of falsehood that they could collect or manufacture against the Mormons. They also had a paper to assist them in their propagations called the "Warsaw Signal," edited by a Mr. Thomas Sharp, a violent and unprincipled man, who shrunk not from any enormity. The anti-Mormons had public meetings, which were very numerously attended, where they passed resolutions of the most violent and inflammatory kind, threatening to drive, expel, and exterminate the "Mormons" from the state, at the same time accusing them of all the vocabulary of crime.

They appointed their meetings in various parts of Hancock, M'Donough, and other counties, which soon resulted in the organization of armed mobs, under the direction

---

* See his remarks as contained in his History of Illinois, p. 269.
† Ford's History of Illinois, p. 246.

of officers who reported to their head-quarters, and the reports of which were published in the anti-Mormon paper, and circulated through the adjoining counties. We also published in the "Times and Seasons" and the "Nauvoo Neighbor" (two papers published and edited by me at that time) an account, not only of their proceedings, but our own. But such was the hostile feeling, so well arranged their plans, and so desperate and lawless their measures, that it was with the greatest difficulty that we could get our papers circulated; they were destroyed by postmasters and others, and scarcely ever arrived at the place of their destination, so that a great many of the people, who would have been otherwise peaceable, were excited by their misrepresentations, and instigated to join their hostile or predatory bands.

Emboldened by the acts of those outside, the apostate "Mormons," associated with others, commenced the publication of a libelous paper in Nauvoo, called the "Nauvoo Expositor." This paper not only reprinted from the others, but put in circulation the most libelous, false, aud infamous reports concerning the citizens of Nauvoo, and especially the ladies. It was, however, no sooner put in circulation than the indignation of the whole community was aroused; so much so, that they threatened its annihilation; and I do not believe that in any other city in the United States, if the same charge had been made against the citizens, it would have been permitted to remain one day. As it was among us, under these circumstances, it was thought best to convene the City Council to take into consideration the adoption of some measures for its removal, as it was deemed better that this should be done legally than illegally. Joseph Smith, therefore, who was then mayor, convened the City Council for that purpose; the paper was introduced and read, and the subject examined. All, or nearly all present, expressed their indignation at the course taken by the "Expositor," which was owned by some of the aforesaid apostates, associated with one or two others: Wilson Law, Dr. Foster, Charles Ivins, and the Higbees before referred to, some lawyers, store-keepers, and others in Nauvoo who were not "Mormons," together with the "anti-Mormons" outside of the city, sustained it. The calculation was, by false statements, to unsettle the minds of many in the city, and to form combinations there similar to the anti-Mormon associations outside of the city. Various attempts had therefore been made by the party to annoy and irritate the citizens of Nauvoo; false accusations had been made, vexatious lawsuits instituted, threats made, and various devices resorted to to influence the public mind, and, if possible, to induce us to the commission of some overt act that might make us amenable to the law. With a perfect knowledge, therefore, of the designs of these infernal scoundrels who were in our midst, as well as of those who surrounded us, the City Council entered upon an investigation of the matter. They felt that they were in a critical position, and that any move made for the abating of that press would be looked upon, or at least represented, as a direct attack upon the liberty of speech, and that, so far from displeasing our enemies, it would be looked upon by them as one of the best circumstances that could transpire to assist them in their nefarious and bloody designs. Being a member of the City Council, I well remember the feeling of responsibility that seemed to rest upon all present; nor shall I soon forget the bold, manly, independent expressions of Joseph Smith on that occasion in relation to this matter. He exhibited in glowing colors the meanness, corruption, and ultimate designs of the "anti-Mormons;" their despicable characters and ungodly influences, especially of those who were in our midst; he told of the responsibility that rested upon us, as guardians of the public interest, to stand up in the defense of the injured and oppressed, to stem the current of corruption, and, as men and saints, to put a stop to this flagrant outrage upon this people's rights. He stated that no man was a stronger advocate for the liberty of speech and of the press than himself; yet, when this noble gift is utterly prostituted and abused, as in the present instance, it loses all claim to our respect, and becomes as great an agent for evil as it can possibly be for good; and notwithstanding the apparent advantage we should give our enemies by this act, yet it behooved us, as men, to act independent of all secondary influences, to perform the part of men of enlarged minds, and boldly and fearlessly to discharge the duties devolving upon us by declaring as a nuisance, and removing this filthy, libelous, and seditious sheet from our midst.

The subject was discussed in various forms, and after the remarks made by the mayor, every one seemed to be waiting for some one else to speak. After a considerable pause, I arose and expressed my feelings frankly, as Joseph had done, and numbers of others followed in the same strain; and I think, but am not certain, that I made a motion for the removal of that press as a nuisance. This motion was finally put, and carried by all but one ; and he conceded that the measure was just, but abstained through fear.

Several members of the City Council were not in the Church. The following is the bill referred to :

Bill for Removing of the Press of the "Nauvoo Expositor." *

" Resolved by the City Council of the City of Nauvoo, that the printing-office from whence issues the ' Nauvoo Expositor' is a public nuisance ; and also all of said ' Nauvoo Expositors' which may be or exist in said establishment ; and the mayor is instructed to cause said establishment and papers to be removed without delay, in such manner as he shall direct.

"Passed June 10th, 1844.   Geo. W. Harris, President *pro tem.*
  "W. Richards, Recorder."

After the passage of the bill, the marshal, John P. Green, was ordered to abate or remove, which he forthwith proceeded to do by summoning a posse of men for that purpose. The press was removed or broken, I don't remember which, by the marshal, and the types scattered in the street.

This seemed to be one of those extreme cases that require extreme measures, as the press was still proceeding in its inflammatory course. It was feared that, as it was almost universally execrated, should it continue longer, an indignant people might commit some overt act which might lead to serious consequences, and that it was better to use legal than illegal means.

This, as was foreseen, was the very course our enemies wished us to pursue, as it afforded them an opportunity of circulating a very plausible story about the "Mormons" being opposed to the liberty of the press and of free speech, which they were not slow to avail themselves of. Stories were fabricated, and facts perverted ; false statements were made, and this act brought in as an example to sustain the whole of their fabrications ; and, as if inspired by Satan, they labored with an energy and zeal worthy of a better cause. They had runners to circulate their reports, not only through Hancock Co., but in all the surrounding counties ; these reports were communicated to their "anti-Mormon" societies, and these societies circulated them in their several districts. The "anti-Mormon" paper, the "Warsaw Signal," was filled with inflammatory articles and misrepresentations in relation to us, and especially to this act of destroying the press. We were represented as a horde of lawless ruffians and brigands, anti-American and anti-republican, steeped in crime and iniquity, opposed to freedom of speech and of the press, and all the rights and immunities of a free and enlightened people ; that neither persons nor property were secure ; that we had designs upon the citizens of Illinois and of the United States, and the people were called upon to rise *en masse,* and put us down, drive us away, or exterminate us as a pest to society, and alike dangerous to our neighbors, the state, and commonwealth.

These statements were extensively copied and circulated throughout the United States. A true statement of the facts in question was published by us both in the "Times and Seasons" and the "Nauvoo Neighbor," but it was found impossible to circulate them in the immediate counties, as they were destroyed at the post-offices or otherwise by the agents of the anti-Mormons, and, in order to get the mail to go abroad, I had to send the papers a distance of thirty or forty miles from Nauvoo, and sometimes to St. Louis (upward of two hundred miles), to insure its proceeding on its route, and then one half or two thirds of the papers never reached the place of destination, being intercepted or destroyed by our enemies.

These false reports stirred up the community around, of whom many, on account of religious prejudice, were easily instigated to join the "anti-Mormons," and embark in any crusade that might be undertaken against the "Mormons ;" hence their ranks swelled in numbers, and new organizations were formed, meetings were held, resolutions passed, and men and means volunteered for the extirpation of the "Mormons."

These also were the active men in blowing up the fury of the people, in hopes that a popular movement might be set on foot, which would result in the expulsion or extermination of the "Mormon" voters. For this purpose public meetings had been called, inflammatory speeches had been made, exaggerated reports had been extensively circulated, committees had been appointed, who rode night and day to spread

* Des. News, No. 29, Sept. 23, 1857, p. 226.

the reports and solicit the aid of neighboring counties, and at a public meeting at Warsaw resolutions were passed to expel or exterminate the "Mormon" population. This was not, however, a movement which was unanimously concurred in. The county contained a goodly number of inhabitants in favor of peace, or who at least desired to be neutral in such a contest. These were stigmatized by the name of "Jack Mormons," and there were not a few of the more furious exciters of the people who openly expressed their intention to involve them in the common expulsion or extermination.

A system of excitement and agitation was artfully planned and executed with tact. It consisted in spreading reports and rumors of the most fearful character. As examples: On the morning before my arrival at Carthage I was awakened at an early hour by the frightful report, which was asserted with confidence and apparent consternation, that the "Mormons" had already commenced the work of burning, destruction, and murder, and that every man capable of bearing arms was instantly wanted at Carthage for the protection of the county.

We lost no time in starting; but when we arrived at Carthage we could hear no more concerning this story. Again, during the few days that the militia were encamped at Carthage, frequent applications were made to me to send a force here, and a force there, and a force all about the country, to prevent murders, robberies, and larcenies which, it was said, were threatened by the "Mormons." No such forces were sent, nor were any such offenses committed at that time, except the stealing of some provisions, and there was never the least proof that this was done by a "Mormon." Again, on my late visit to Hancock County, I was informed by some of their violent enemies that the larcenies of the "Mormons" had become unusually numerous and insufferable. They admitted that but little had been done in this way in their immediate vicinity, but they insisted that sixteen horses had been stolen by the "Mormons" in one night near Lima, and, upon inquiry, was told that no horses had been stolen in that neighborhood, but that sixteen horses had been stolen in one night in Hancock County. This last informant being told of the Hancock story, again changed the venue to another distant settlement in the northern edge of Adams.*

In the mean time legal proceedings were instituted against the members of the City Council of Nauvoo. A writ, here subjoined, was issued upon the affidavit of the Laws, Foster, Higbees, and Ivins, by Mr. Morrison, a justice of the peace in Carthage, the county seat of Hancock, and put into the hands of one David Bettesworth, a constable of the same place.

Writ issued upon affidavit by Thomas Morrison, J. P., State of Illinois, Hancock County, ss.

"The people of the State of Illinois, to all constables, sheriffs, and coroners of said state, greeting:

"Whereas complaint hath been made before me, one of the justices of the peace in and for the County of Hancock aforesaid, upon the oath of Francis M. Higbee, of said county, that Joseph Smith, Samuel Bennett, John Taylor, William W. Phelps, Hyrum Smith, John P. Green, Stephen Perry, Dimick B. Huntington, Jonathan Dunham, Stephen Markham, William Edwards, Jonathan Holmes, Jesse P. Harmon, John Lytle, Joseph W. Coolidge, Harvey D. Redfield, Porter Rockwell, and Levi Richards, of said county, did, on the 10th day of June instant, commit a riot at and within the county aforesaid, wherein they with force and violence broke into the printing-office of the 'Nauvoo Expositor,' and unlawfully and with force burned and destroyed the printing-press, type, and fixtures of the same, being the property of William Law, Wilson Law, Charles Ivins, Francis M. Higbee, Chauncey L. Higbee, Robert D. Foster, and Charles A. Foster.

"These are therefore to command you forthwith to apprehend the said Joseph Smith, Samuel Bennett, John Taylor, William W. Phelps, Hyrum Smith, John P. Green, Stephen Perry, Dimick B. Huntington, Jonathan Dunham, Stephen Markham, William Edwards, Jonathan Holmes, Jesse P. Harmon, John Lytle, Joseph W. Coolidge, Harvey D. Redfield, Porter Rockwell, and Levi Richards, and bring them before me, or some other justice of the peace, to answer the premises, and farther to be dealt with according to law.

"Given under my hand and seal at Carthage, in the county aforesaid, this 11th day of June, A.D. 1844. THOMAS MORRISON, J. P." (Seal.)†

---

* Ford's History of Illinois, p. 330, 331.   † Des. News, No. 30, Sept. 30, 1857, p. 233.

The council refused not to attend to the legal proceedings in the case, but, as the law of Illinois made it the privilege of the persons accused to go "or appear before the issuer of the writ, or any other justice of peace," they requested to be taken before another magistrate, either in the city of Nauvoo or at any reasonable distance out of it.

This the constable, who was a mobocrat, refused to do; and as this was our legal privilege, we refused to be dragged, contrary to law, a distance of eighteen miles, when at the same time we had reason to believe that an organized band of mobocrats were assembled for the purpose of extermination or murder, and among whom it would not be safe to go without a superior force of armed men. A writ of habeas corpus was called for, and issued by the municipal court of Nauvoo, taking us out of the hands of Bettesworth, and placing us in the charge of the city marshal. We went before the municipal court, and were dismissed. Our refusal to obey this illegal proceeding was by them construed into a refusal to submit to law, and circulated as such, and the people either did believe, or professed to believe, that we were in open rebellion against the laws and the authorities of the state. Hence mobs began to assemble, among which all through the country inflammatory speeches were made, exciting them to mobocracy and violence. Soon they commenced their prosecutions of our outside settlements, kidnapping some, and whipping and otherwise abusing others.

The persons thus abused fled to Nauvoo as soon as practicable, and related their injuries to Joseph Smith, then mayor of the city, and lieutenant general of the Nauvoo Legion; they also went before magistrates, and made affidavits of what they had suffered, seen, and heard. These affidavits, in connection with a copy of all our proceedings, were forwarded by Joseph Smith to Mr. Ford, then Governor of Illinois, with an expression of our desire to abide law, and a request that the governor would instruct him how to proceed in the case of the arrival of an armed mob against the city. The governor sent back instructions to Joseph Smith that, as he was lieutenant general of the Nauvoo Legion, it was his duty to protect the city and surrounding country, and issued orders to that effect. Upon the reception of these orders Joseph Smith assembled the people of the city, and laid before them the governor's instructions; he also convened the officers of the Nauvoo Legion for the purpose of conferring in relation to the best mode of defense. He also issued orders to the men to hold themselves in readiness in case of being called upon. On the following day General Joseph Smith, with his staff, the leading officers of the Legion, and some prominent strangers who were in our midst, made a survey of the outside boundaries of the city, which was very extensive, being about five miles up and down the river, and about two and a half back in the centre, for the purpose of ascertaining the position of the ground, and the feasibility of defense, and to make all necessary arrangements in case of an attack.

It may be well here to remark that numbers of gentlemen, who were to us strangers, either came on purpose or were passing through Nauvoo, who, upon learning the position of things, expressed their indignation against our enemies, and avowed their readiness to assist us by their council or otherwise; it was some of these who assisted us in reconnoitering the city, and finding out its adaptability for defense, and the best mode of protection against an armed force. The Legion was called together and drilled, and every means made use of for defense; at the call of the officers both old and young men came forward, both denizens from the city and from the outside regions, and I believe at one time they mustered to the number of about five thousand.

In the mean time our enemies were not idle in mustering their forces and committing depredations, nor had they been; it was, in fact, their gathering that called ours into existence; their forces continued to accumulate; they assumed a threatening attitude, and assembled in large bodies, armed and equipped for war, and threatened the destruction and extermination of the "Mormons." An account of their outrages and assemblages was forwarded to Governor Ford almost daily, accompanied by affidavits furnished by eyewitnesses of their proceedings. Persons were also sent out to the counties around with pacific intentions, to give them an account of the true state of affairs, and to notify them of the feelings and dispositions of the people of Nauvoo, and thus, if possible, quell the excitement. In some of the more distant counties these men were very successful, and produced a salutary influence upon the minds of many intelligent and well-disposed men. In neighboring counties, however, where "anti-Mormon" influence prevailed, they produced little effect. At the same time, guards were stationed around Nauvoo, and picket-guards in the distance. At length opposing forces gathered so near that more active measures were taken; reconnoitering parties were sent out, and the city proclaimed under martial law. Things now assumed a belligerent attitude, and persons passing through the city were questioned as to what they knew of the enemy, while passes were in some instances given to avoid difficulty with the guards. Joseph Smith continued to send on messengers to the governor (Philip B. Lewis and other messengers were sent). Samuel James, then residing at La Harpe, carried a message and dispatches to him, and in a day or two after Bishop Edward Hunter and others went again with fresh dispatches, representations, affidavits, and instructions; but as the weather was excessively wet, the rivers swollen, and the bridges washed away in many places, it was with great difficulty that they proceeded on their journeys. As the mobocracy had at last attracted the governor's attention, he started in company with some others from Springfield to the scene of trouble, and missed, I believe, both Brothers James and Hunter on the road, and of course did not see their documents. He came to Carthage, and made that place, which was a regular mobocratic den, his headquarters; as it was the county-seat, however, of Hancock County, that circumstance might, in a measure, justify his staying there.

To avoid the appearance of all hostility on our part, and to fulfill the law in every particular, at the suggestion of Judge Thomas, judge of that judicial district, who had come to Nauvoo at the time, and who stated that we had fulfilled the law, that, in order to satisfy all, he would counsel us to go before Esquire Wells,* who was not in our Church, and have a hearing. We did so, and after a full hearing we were again dismissed.

The governor on the road collected forces, some of whom were respectable; but on his arrival in the neighborhood of the difficulties he received as militia all the companies of the mob forces who united with him. After his arrival at Carthage he sent two gentlemen from there to Nauvoo as a committee to wait upon General Joseph Smith, informing him of the arrival of his excellency, with a request that General Smith would send out a committee to wait upon the governor and represent to him the state of affairs in relation to the difficulties that then existed in the county. We met this committee while we were reconnoitering the city, to find out the best mode of defense as aforesaid. Dr. J. M. Bernhisel and myself were appointed as a committee by General Smith to wait upon the governor. Previous to going, however, we were furnished with affidavits and documents in relation both to our proceedings and those of the mob; in addition to the general history of the transaction, we took with us a duplicate of those documents which had been forwarded by Bishop Hunter, Brother James, and others. We started from Carthage in company with the aforesaid gentleman at about 7 o'clock on the evening of the 21st of June, and arrived at Carthage at about 11 P.M. We put up at the same hotel with the governor, kept by a Mr. Hamilton; on our arrival we found the governor in bed, but not so with the other inhabitants. The town was filled with a perfect set of rabble and rowdies, who, under the influence of Bacchus, seemed to be holding a grand saturnalia, whooping, yelling, and vociferating as if Bedlam had broken loose.

On our arrival at the hotel, and while supper was preparing, a man came to me, dressed as a soldier, and told me that a man named David Carn had just been taken prisoner, and was about to be committed to jail, and wanted me to go bail for him. Believing this to be a ruse to get me out alone, and that some violence was intended, after consulting with Dr. Bernhisel, I told the men that I was well acquainted with Mr. Carn, that I knew him to be a gentleman, and did not believe that he had transgressed law, and, moreover, that I considered it a very singular time to be holding courts and calling for security, particularly as the town was full of rowdyism.

I informed him that both Dr. Bernhisel and myself would, if necessary, go bail for him in the morning, but that we did not feel ourselves safe among such a set at that late hour of the night.

After supper, on retiring to our room, we had to pass through another, which was separated from ours only by a board partition, the beds in each room being placed side by side, with the exception of this fragile partition. On the bed that was in the room which we passed through I discovered a man by the name of Jackson, a desperate character, and a reputed, notorious cut-throat and murderer. I hinted to the doctor that things looked rather suspicious, and looked to see that my arms were in order. The doctor and I both occupied one bed. We had scarcely laid down when

* Now a member of the First Presidency.—Ed.

a knock at the door, accompanied by a voice, announced the approach of Chauncey Higbee, the young lawyer and apostate before referred to.

He addressed himself to the doctor, and stated that the object of his visit was to obtain the release of Daniel Carn; that Carn he believed to be an honest man; that if he had done any thing wrong, it was through improper counsel, and that it was a pity that he should be incarcerated, particularly when he could be so easily released; he urged the doctor, as a friend, not to leave so good a man in such an unpleasant situation; he finally prevailed upon the doctor to go and give bail, assuring him that on his giving bail Carn would be immediately dismissed.

During this conversation I did not say a word. Higbee left the doctor to dress, with the intention of returning and taking him to the court. As soon as Higbee had left, I told the doctor that he had better not go; that I believed this affair was all a ruse to get us separated; that they knew we had documents with us from General Smith to show to the governor; that I believed their object was to get possession of those papers, and, perhaps, when they had separated us, to murder one or both. The doctor, who was actuated by the best of motives in yielding to the assumed solicitude of Higbee, coincided with my views; he then went to Higbee, and told him that he had concluded not to go that night, but that he and I would both wait upon the justice and Mr. Carn in the morning.

That night I lay awake with my pistols under my pillow, waiting for any emergency. Nothing more occurred during the night. In the morning we arose early, and after breakfast sought an interview with the governor, and were told that we could have an audience, I think, at 10 o'clock. In the mean time we called upon Mr. Smith, a Justice of the Peace, who had Mr. Carn in charge. We represented that we had been called upon the night before by two different parties to go bail for a Mr. Daniel Carn, whom we were informed he had in custody, and that, believing Mr. Carn to be an honest man, we had come now for that purpose, and were prepared to enter into recognizances for his appearance, whereupon Mr. Smith, the magistrate, remarked "that, under the present excited state of affairs, he did not think he would be justified in receiving bail from Nauvoo, as it was a matter of doubt whether property would not be rendered valueless there in a few days.

Knowing the party we had to deal with, we were not much surprised at this singular proceeding; we then remarked that both of us possessed property in farms out of Nauvoo in the country, and referred him to the county records. He then stated that such was the nature of the charge against Mr. Carn that he believed he would not be justified in receiving any bail. We were thus confirmed in our opinion that the night's proceedings before, in relation to their desire to have us give bail, was a mere ruse to separate us. We were not permitted to speak with Carn, the real charge against whom was that he was traveling in Carthage or its neighborhood: what the fictitious one was, if I then knew, I have since forgotten, as things of this kind were of daily occurrence.

After waiting the governor's pleasure for some time we had an audience; but such an audience! He was surrounded by some of the vilest and most unprincipled men in creation; some of them had an appearance of respectability, and many of them lacked even that. Wilson, and, I believe, William Law, were there, Foster, Frank and Chauncey Higbee, Mr. Mar, a lawyer from Nauvoo, a mobocratic merchant from Warsaw, the aforesaid Jackson, a number of his associates, among whom was the governor's secretary, in all some fifteen or twenty persons, most of whom were recreant to virtue, honor, integrity, and every thing that is considered honorable among men. I can well remember the feelings of disgust that I had in seeing the governor surrounded by such an infamous group, and on being introduced to men of so questionable a character; and had I been on private business, I should have turned to depart, and told the governor that if he thought proper to associate with such questionable characters, I should beg leave to be excused; but coming as we did on public business, we could not, of course, consult our private feelings.

We then stated to the governor that, in accordance with his request, General Smith had, in response to his call, sent us to him as a committee of conference; that we were acquainted with most of the circumstances that had transpired in and about Nauvoo lately, and were prepared to give him all information; that, moreover, we had in our possession testimony and affidavits confirmatory of what we should say, which had been forwarded to him by General Joseph Smith; that communications had been forwarded to his excellency by Mr. Hunter, James, and others, some of which had not reached their destination, but of which we had duplicates with us.

We then, in brief, related an outline of the difficulties, and the course we had pursued from the commencement of the troubles up to the present, and handing him the documents, respectfully submitted the whole. During our conversation and explanations with the governor we were frequently rudely and impudently contradicted by the fellows he had around him, and of whom he seemed to take no notice.

He opened and read a number of the documents himself, and as he proceeded he was frequently interrupted by "that's a lie," "that's a God damned lie," "that's an infernal falsehood," "that's a blasted lie," etc.

These men evidently winced at an exposure of their acts, and thus vulgarly, impudently, and falsely repudiated them. One of their number, Mr. Mar, addressed himself several times to me while in conversation with the governor. I did not notice him until after a frequent repetition of his insolence, when I informed him "that my business at that time was with Governor Ford," whereupon I continued my conversation with his excellency. During the conversation the governor expressed a desire that Joseph Smith, and all parties concerned in passing or executing the city law in relation to the press, had better come to Carthage; that, however repugnant it might be to our feelings, he thought it would have a tendency to allay public excitement, and prove to the people what we professed, that we wished to be governed by law. We represented to him the course he had taken in relation to this matter, and our willingness to go before another magistrate other than the Municipal Court; the illegal refusal of our request by the constable; our dismissal by the Municipal Court, a legally constituted tribunal; our subsequent trial before Squire Wells at the instance of Judge Thomas (the circuit judge), and our dismissal by him; that we had fulfilled the law in every particular; that it was our enemies who were breaking the law, and, having murderous designs, were only making use of this as a pretext to get us into their power. The governor stated that the people viewed it differently, and that, notwithstanding our opinions, he would recommend that the people should be satisfied. We then remarked to him that, should Joseph Smith comply with his request, it would be extremely unsafe, in the present excited state of the country, to come without an armed force; that we had a sufficiency of men, and were competent to defend ourselves, but that there might be danger of collision should our forces and that of our enemies be brought into such close proximity. He strenuously advised us not to bring any arms, and *pledged his faith as governor, and the faith of the state, that we should be protected, and that he would guarantee our perfect safety.*

We had at that time about five thousand men under arms, one thousand of which would have been amply sufficient for our protection.

At the termination of our interview, and previous to our withdrawal, after a long conversation and the perusal of the documents which we had brought, the governor informed us that he would prepare a written communication for General Joseph Smith, which he desired us to wait for. We were kept waiting for this instrument some five or six hours.

About 5 o'clock in the afternoon we took our departure with not the most pleasant feelings. The associations of the governor, the spirit that he manifested to compromise with these scoundrels, the length of time that he had kept us waiting, and his general deportment, together with the infernal spirit that we saw exhibited by those whom he had admitted to his councils, made the prospect any thing but promising.

We returned on horseback, and arrived at Nauvoo, I think, at about 8 or 9 o'clock at night, accompanied by Captain Yates in command of a company of mounted men, who came for the purpose of escorting Joseph Smith and the accused in case of their complying with the governor's request, and going to Carthage. We went directly to Brother Joseph's, when Captain Yates delivered to him the governor's communication. A council was called consisting of Joseph's brother Hyrum, Dr. Richards, Dr. Bernhisel, myself, and one or two others, when the following letter was read from the governor:

Governor Ford's Letter to the Mayor and Common Council of Nauvoo.

"Head Quarters, Carthage, June 21st, 1844.

"To the Hon. the Mayor and Common Council of the City of Nauvoo:

"GENTLEMEN,—Having heard of the excitement in this part of the country, and judging that my presence here might be necessary to preserve the peace and enforce the laws, I arrived at this place this morning. Both before and since my arrival, complaints of a grave character have been made to me of certain proceedings of your honorable body. As chief magistrate, it is my duty to see that impartial justice shall be done, uninfluenced by the excitement here or in your city.

"I think, before any decisive measure shall be adopted, that I ought to hear the allegations and defenses of all parties. By adopting this course I have some hope that the evils of war may be averted; and, at any rate, I will be enabled by it to understand the true merits of the present difficulties, and shape my course with reference to law and justice.

"For these reasons, I have to request that you will send out to me, at this place, one or more well-informed and discreet persons, who will be capable of laying before me your version of the matter, and of receiving from me such explanations and resolutions as may be determined on.

"Colonel Elam S. Freeman will present you this note in the character of a herald from the governor. You will respect his character as such, and permit him to pass and repass free from molestation.

"Your messengers are assured of protection in person and property, and will be returned to you in safety.

"I am, gentlemen, with high considerations, most respectfully your obedient servant, THOMAS FORD, Governor and Commander-in-Chief."*

We then gave a detail of our interview with the governor. Brother Joseph was very much dissatisfied with the governor's letter and with his general deportment, and so were the council, and it became a serious question as to the course we should pursue. Various projects were discussed, but nothing definitely decided upon for some time. In the interim two gentlemen arrived; one of them, if not both, sons of John C. Calhoun. They had come to Nauvoo, and were very anxious for an interview with Brother Joseph. These gentlemen detained him for some time; and as our council was held in Dr. Bernhisel's room in the Mansion House, the doctor lay down; and as it was now between 2 and 3 o'clock in the morning, and I had had no rest on the previous night, I was fatigued, and thinking that Brother Joseph might not return, I left for home and rest.

Being very much fatigued, I slept soundly, and was somewhat surprised in the morning by Mrs. Thompson entering my room about 7 o'clock, and exclaiming in surprise, "What, you here! the brethren have crossed the river some time since." "What brethren?" I asked. "Brother Joseph, and Hyrum, and Brother Richards." I immediately arose upon learning that they had crossed the river, and did not intend to go to Carthage. I called together a number of persons in whom I had confidence, and had the type, stereotype plates, and most of the valuable things removed from the printing-office, believing that, should the governor and his force come to Nauvoo, the first thing they would do would be to burn the printing-office, for I knew that they would be exasperated if Brother Joseph went away. We had talked over these matters the night before, but nothing was decided upon. It was Brother Joseph's opinion that, should we leave for a time, public excitement, which was then so intense, would be allayed; that it would throw on the governor the responsibility of keeping the peace; that, in the event of any outrage, the onus would rest upon the governor, who was amply prepared with troops, and could command all the forces of the state to preserve order; and that the acts of his own men would be an overwhelming proof of their seditious designs, not only to the governor, but to the world. He moreover thought that, in the East, where he intended to go, public opinion would be set right in relation to these matters, and its expression would partially influence the West, and that, after the first ebullition, things would assume a shape that would justify his return. I made arrangements for crossing the river, and Brother Elias Smith and Joseph Cain, who were both employed in the printing-office with me, assisted all that lay in their power, together with Brother Brower and several hands in the printing-office. As we could not find out the exact whereabouts of Joseph and the brethren, I crossed the river in a boat furnished by Brothers Cyrus H. Wheelock and Alfred Bell; and after the removal of the things of the printing-office, Joseph Cain brought the account-books to me, that we might make arrangements for their adjustment; and Brother Elias Smith, cousin to Brother Joseph, went to obtain money for the journey, and also to find out and report to me the location of the brethren. As Cyrus H. Wheelock was an active, enterprising man, and in the event of not finding Brother Joseph I calculated to go to Upper Canada for the time being, and should need a companion, I said to Brother Wheelock, "Can you go with me ten

* Des. News, No. 33, Oct. 21, 1857, p. 257.

or fifteen hundred miles?" He answered "Yes." "Can you start in half an hour?" "Yes." However, I told him that he had better see his family, who lived over the river, and prepare a couple of horses and the necessary equipage for the journey, and that, if we did not find Brother Joseph before, we would start at nightfall. A laughable incident occurred on the eve of my departure. After making all the preparations I could previous to leaving Nauvoo, and having bid adieu to my family, I went to a house adjoining the river owned by Brother Eddy. There I disguised myself so as not to be known, and so effectually was the transformation that those who had come after me with a boat did not know me. I went down to the boat and sat in it. Brother Bell, thinking it was a stranger, watched my moves for some time very impatiently, and then said to Brother Wheelock, "I wish that old gentleman would go away; he has been pottering around the boat for some time, and I am afraid Elder Taylor will be coming." When he discovered his mistake, he was not a little amused. I was conducted by Brother Bell to a house that was surrounded by timber on the opposite side of the river. There I spent several hours in a chamber with Brother Joseph Cain, adjusting my accounts; and I made arrangements for the stereotype plates of the "Book of Mormon," and "Doctrine and Covenants," to be forwarded East, thinking to supply the company with subsistence money through the sale of these books in the East.

My horses were reported ready by Brother Wheelock, and funds on hand by Brother Elias Smith. In about half an hour I should have started, when Brother Elias Smith came to me with word that he had found the brethren; that they had concluded to go to Carthage, and wished me to return to Nauvoo and accompany them. I must confess that I felt a good deal disappointed at this news, but I immediately made preparations to go. Escorted by Brother Elias Smith, I and my party went to the neighborhood of Montrose, where we met Brother Joseph, Hyrum, Brother Richards, and others. Dr. Bernhisel thinks that W. W. Phelps was not with Joseph and Hyrum in the morning, but that he met him, myself, Joseph, and Hyrum, W. Richards, and Brother Calhoun, in the afternoon, near Montrose, returning to Nauvoo. On meeting the brethren I learned that it was not Brother Joseph's desire to return, but that he came back by request of some of the brethren, and that it coincided more with Brother Hyrum's feelings than with those of Brother Joseph. In fact, after his return, Brother Hyrum expressed himself as perfectly satisfied with the course taken, and said that he felt much more at ease in his mind than he did before. On our return the calculation was to throw ourselves under the immediate protection of the governor, and to trust to his word and faith for our preservation.

A message was, I believe, sent to the governor that night, stating that we should come to Carthage in the morning, the party that came along with us to escort us back, in case we returned to Carthage, having returned. It would seem from the following remarks of General Ford that there was a design on foot, which was, that if we refused to go to Carthage at the governor's request, there should be an increased force called for by the governor, and that we should be destroyed by them. In accordance with this project, Captain Yates returned with his *posse*, accompanied by the constable who held the writ. The following is the governor's remark in relation to this affair: "The constable and his escort returned. The constable made no effort to arrest any of them, nor would he or the guard delay their departure one minute beyond the time, to see whether an arrest could be made. Upon their return they reported that they had been informed that the accused had fled, and could not be found. I immediately proposed to a council of officers to march into Nauvoo with the small force then under my command, but the officers were of opinion that it was too small, and many of them insisted upon a farther call of the militia. Upon reflection I was of opinion that the officers were right in the estimate of our force, and the project for immediate action was abandoned. I was soon informed, however, of the conduct of constable and guard, and then I was perfectly satisfied that a most base fraud had been attempted; that, in fact, it was feared that the 'Mormons' would submit, and thereby entitle themselves to the protection of the law. It was very apparent that many of the bustling, active spirits were afraid that there would be no occasion for calling out an overwhelming militia force, for marching it into Nauvoo, for probable mutiny when there, and for the extermination of the 'Mormon' race. It appeared that the constable and the escort were fully in the secret, and acted well their part to promote the conspiracy."*

In the morning Brother Joseph had an interview with the officers of the Legion,

* Ford's History of Illinois, page 333.

with the leading members of the City Council, and with the principal men of the city. The officers were instructed to dismiss their men, but to have them in a state of readiness to be called upon in any emergency that might occur.

About half past 6 o'clock the members of the City Council, the marshal, Brothers Joseph and Hyrum, and a number of others, started for Carthage, all on horseback. We were instructed by Brother Joseph Smith not to take any arms, and we consequently left them behind. We called at the house of Brother Fellows on our way out. Brother Fellows lived about four miles from Carthage. While at Brother Fellows' house, Captain Dunn, accompanied by Mr. Coolie, one of the governor's aid-de-camps, came up from Carthage *en route* for Nauvoo with a requisition from the governor for the state arms. We all returned to Nauvoo with them; the governor's request was complied with, and, after taking some refreshments, we all returned to proceed to Carthage. We arrived there late in the night. A great deal of excitement prevailed on and after our arrival. The governor had received into his company all of the companies that had been in the mob; these fellows were riotous and disorderly, hallooing, yelling, and whooping about the streets like Indians, many of them intoxicated; the whole presented a scene of rowdyism and lowbred ruffianism only found among mobocrats and desperadoes, and entirely revolting to the best feelings of humanity. The governor made a speech to them to the effect that he would show Joseph and Hyrum Smith to them in the morning. About here the companies with the governor were drawn up into line, and General Demming, I think, took Joseph by the arm and Hyrum (Arnold says that Joseph took the governor's arm), and as he passed through between the ranks, the governor leading in front, very politely introduced them as General Joseph Smith and General Hyrum Smith.* All were orderly and courteous except one company of mobocrats—the Carthage Grays—who seemed to find fault on account of too much honor being paid to the Mormons. There was afterward a row between the companies, and they came pretty near having a fight; the more orderly not feeling disposed to endorse or submit to the rowdyism of the mobocrats. The result was that General Demming, who was very much of a gentleman, ordered the Carthage Grays, a company under the command of Captain Smith, a magistrate in Carthage, and a most violent mobocrat, under arrest. This matter, however, was shortly afterward adjusted, and the difficulty settled between them. The mayor, aldermen, councilors, as well as the marshal of the city of Nauvoo, together with some persons who had assisted the marshal in removing the press in Nauvoo, appeared before Justice Smith, the aforesaid captain and mobocrat, to again answer the charge of destroying the press; but as there was so much excitement, and as the man was an unprincipled villain before whom we were to have our hearing, we thought it most prudent to give bail, and consequently became security for each other in $500 bonds each, to appear before the County Court at its next session. We had engaged as counsel a lawyer by the

---

* The "Deseret News" gives the following account of Joseph and Hyrum Smith's passing through the troops in Carthage:

"Carthage, June 25th, 1844.

"Quarter past 9. The governor came and invited Joseph to walk with him through the troops. Joseph solicited a few moment's private conversation with him, which the governor refused.

"While refusing, the governor looked down at his shoes, as though he was ashamed. They then walked through the crowd, with Brigadier General Miner, R. Demming, and Dr. Richards, to General Demming's quarters. The people appeared quiet until a company of Carthage Grays flocked round the doors of General Demming in an uproarious manner, of which notice was sent to the governor. In the mean time the governor had ordered the M'Donough troops to be drawn up in line, for Joseph and Hyrum to pass in front of them, they having requested that they might have a clear view of the General Smiths. *Joseph had a conversation with the governor for about ten minutes, when he again pledged the faith of the state that he and his friends should be protected from violence.*

"Robinson, the post-master, said, on report of martial law being proclaimed in Nauvoo, he had stopped the mail, and notified the post-master general of the state of things in Hancock County.

"From the general's quarters Joseph and Hyrum went in front of the lines, in a hollow square of a company of Carthage Grays; at seven minutes before 10 they arrived in front of the lines, and passed before the whole, Joseph being on the right of General Demming and Hyrum on his left, Elders Richards, Taylor, and Phelps following. Joseph and Hyrum were introduced by Governor Ford about twenty times along the line as General Joseph Smith and General Hyrum Smith, the governor walking in front on the left. The Carthage Grays refused to receive them by that introduction, and some of the officers threw up their hats, drew their swords, and said they would introduce themselves to the damned Mormons in a different style. The governor mildly entreated them not to act so rudely, but their excitement increased; the governor, however, succeeded in pacifying them by making a speech, and promising them that they should have 'full satisfaction.' General Smith and party returned to their lodgings at five minutes past 10."—*Des. News*, No. 35, Nov. 4, 1857, page 274.

L L

name of Wood, of Burlington, Iowa; and Reed, I think, of Madison, Iowa. After some little discussion the bonds were signed, and we were all dismissed.

Almost immediately after our dismissal, two men—Augustine Spencer and Norton—two worthless fellows, whose words would not have been taken for five cents, and the first of whom had a short time previously been before the mayor in Nauvoo for maltreating a lame brother, made affidavits that Joseph and Hyrum Smith were guilty of treason; and a writ was accordingly issued for their arrest, and the constable Bettesworth, a rough, unprincipled man, wished immediately to hurry them away to prison without any hearing. His rude, uncouth manner in the administration of what he considered the duties of his office made him exceedingly repulsive to us all. But, independent of these acts, the proceedings in this case were altogether illegal. Providing the court was sincere, which it was not, and providing these men's oaths were true, and that Joseph and Hyrum were guilty of treason, still the whole course was illegal.

The magistrate made out a mittimus, and committed them to prison without a hearing, which he had no right legally to do. The statute of Illinois expressly provides that "all men shall have a hearing before a magistrate before they shall be committed to prison;" and Mr. Robert H. Smith, the magistrate, had made out a mittimus committing them to prison contrary to law without such hearing. As I was informed of this illegal proceeding, I went immediately to the governor and informed him of it. Whether he was apprised of it before or not, I do not know; but my opinion is that he was.

I represented to him the characters of the parties who had made oath, the outrageous nature of the charge, the indignity offered to men in the position which they occupied, and declared to him that he knew very well it was a vexatious proceeding, and that the accused were not guilty of any such crime. The governor replied, "He was very sorry that the thing had occurred; that he did not believe the charges, but that he thought the best thing to be done was to let the law take its course." I then reminded him that we had come out there at his instance, not to satisfy the law, which we had done before, but the prejudices of the people, in relation to the affair of the press; that at his instance we had given bonds, which we could not by law be required to do to satisfy the people, and that it was asking too much to require gentlemen in their position in life to suffer the degradation of being immured in a jail at the instance of such worthless scoundrels as those who had made this affidavit. The governor replied "that it was an unpleasant affair, and looked hard; but that it was a matter over which he had no control, as it belonged to the judiciary; that he, as the executive, could not interfere with their proceedings, and that he had no doubt but that they would immediately be dismissed." I told him "that we had looked to him for protection from such insults, and that I thought we had a right to do so from the solemn promises which he had made to me and to Dr. Bernhisel in relation to our coming without guard or arms; that we had relied upon his faith, and had a right to expect him to fulfill his engagements after we had placed ourselves implicitly under his care, and complied with all his requests, although extra-judicial."

He replied "that he would detail a guard, if we required it, and see us protected, but that he could not interfere with the judiciary." I expressed my dissatisfaction at the course taken, and told him "that, if we were to be subject to mob rule, and to be dragged, contrary to law, into prison at the instance of every infernal scoundrel whose oaths could be bought for a dram of whisky, his protection availed very little, and we had miscalculated his promises."

Seeing there was no prospect of redress from the governor, I returned to the room, and found the constable Bettesworth very urgent to hurry Brothers Joseph and Hyrum to prison, while the brethren were remonstrating with him. At the same time a great rabble was gathered in the streets and around the door, and from the rowdyism manifested I was afraid there was a design to murder the prisoners on the way to jail.

Without conferring with any person, my next feeling was to procure a guard, and, seeing a man habited as a soldier in the room, I went to him and said, "I am afraid there is a design against the lives of the Messrs. Smith; will you go immediately and bring your captain; and, if not convenient, any other captain of a company, and I will pay you well for your trouble?" He said he would, and departed forthwith, and soon returned with his captain, whose name I have forgotten, and introduced him to me. I told him of my fears, and requested him immediately to fetch his company; he departed forthwith, and arrived at the door with them just at the time when the constable was hurrying the brethren down stairs. A number of the brethren went along, together with one or two strangers; and all of us, safely lodged in prison, remained there during the night.

At the request of Joseph Smith for an interview with the governor, he came the next morning, Thursday, June 26th, at half past 9 o'clock, accompanied by Colonel Geddes, when a lengthy conversation was entered into in relation to the existing difficulties; and after some preliminary remarks, at the governor's request, Brother Joseph gave him a general outline of the state of affairs in relation to our difficulties, the excited state of the country, the tumultuous mobocratic movements of our enemies, the precautionary measures used by himself (Joseph Smith), the acts of the city council, the destruction of the press, and the moves of the mob and ourselves up to that time.

The following report is, I believe, substantially correct:

Governor. "General Smith, I believe you have given me a general outline of the difficulties that have existed in the country in the documents forwarded to me by Dr. Bernhisel and Mr. Taylor; but, unfortunately, there seems to be a great discrepancy between your statements and those of your enemies. It is true that you are substantiated by evidence and affidavit, but for such an extraordinary excitement as that which is now in the country there must be some cause, and I attribute the last outbreak to the destruction of the 'Expositor,' and to your refusal to comply with the writ issued by Esquire Morrison. The press in the United States is looked upon as the great bulwark of American freedom, and its destruction in Nauvoo was represented and looked upon as a high-handed measure, and manifests to the people a disposition on your part to suppress the liberty of speech and of the press. This, with your refusal to comply with the requisitions of a writ, I conceive to be the principal cause of this difficulty; and you are moreover represented to me as turbulent, and defiant of the laws and institutions of your country."

General Smith. "Governor Ford, you, sir, as governor of this state, are aware of the persecutions that I have endured. You know well that our course has been peaceable and law-abiding, for I have furnished this state ever since our settlement here with sufficient evidence of my pacific intentions, and those of the people with whom I am associated, by the endurance of every conceivable indignity and lawless outrage perpetrated upon me and upon this people since our settlement here; and you yourself know that I have kept you well posted in relation to all matters associated with the late difficulties. If you have not got some of my communications, it has not been my fault.

"Agreeably to your orders, I assembled the Nauvoo Legion for the protection of Nauvoo and the surrounding country against an armed band of marauders; and ever since they have been mustered I have almost daily communicated with you in regard to all the leading events that have transpired; and whether in the capacity of mayor of the city, or lieutenant general of the Nauvoo Legion, I have striven, according to the best of my judgment, to preserve the peace and to administer evenhanded justice; but my motives are impugned, my acts are misconstrued, and I am grossly and wickedly misrepresented. I suppose I am indebted for my incarceration to the oath of a worthless man, who was arraigned before me and fined for abusing and maltreating his lame, helpless brother. That I should be charged by you, sir, who know better, of acting contrary to law, is to me a matter of surprise. Was it the Mormons or our enemies who first commenced these difficulties? You know well it was not us; and when this turbulent, outrageous people commenced their insurrectionary movements, I made you acquainted with them officially, and asked your advice, and have followed strictly your counsel in every particular. Who ordered out the Nauvoo Legion? I did, under your direction. For what purpose? To suppress the insurrectionary movements. It was at your instance, sir, that I issued a proclamation calling upon the Nauvoo Legion to be in readiness at a moment's warning to guard against the incursions of mobs, and gave an order to Jonathan Dunham, acting major general, to that effect.

"Am I, then, to be charged for the acts of others? and because lawlessness and mobocracy abound, am I, when carrying out your instructions, to be charged with not abiding law? Why is it that I must be made accountable for other men's acts? If there is trouble in the country, neither I nor my people made it; and all that we have ever done, after much endurance on our part, is to maintain and uphold the Constitution and institutions of our country, and to protect an injured, innocent, and persecuted people against misrule and mob violence.

"Concerning the destruction of the press to which you refer, men may differ somewhat in their opinions about it; but can it be supposed that after all the indignities to which they have been subjected outside, that people could suffer a set of worthless vagabonds to come into their city, and, right under their own eyes and protection, vilify and calumniate not only themselves, but the character of their wives and daughters, as was impudently and unblushingly done in that infamous and filthy sheet?

"There is not a city in the United States that would have suffered such an indignity for twenty-four hours. Our whole people were indignant, and loudly called upon our city authorities for a redress of their grievances, which, if not attended to, they themselves would have taken into their own hands, and have summarily punished the audacious wretches as they deserved. The principles of equal rights that have been instilled into our bosoms from our cradles as American citizens forbid us submitting to every foul indignity, and succumbing and pandering to wretches so infamous as these. But, independent of this, the course that we pursued we considered to be strictly legal; for, notwithstanding the result, we were anxious to be governed strictly by law, and therefore we convened the city council; and being desirous in our deliberations to abide by law, we summoned legal counsel to be present on the occasion. Upon investigating the matter, we found that our city charter gave us power to remove all nuisances. Furthermore, after consulting Blackstone upon what might be considered a nuisance, it appeared that that distinguished lawyer, who is considered authority, I believe, in all our courts, states among other things that 'a libelous and filthy press may be considered a nuisance, and abated as such.' Here, then, one of the most eminent English barristers, whose works are considered standard with us, declares that a libelous and filthy press may be considered a nuisance; and our own charter, given us by the Legislature of this state, gives us the power to remove nuisances; and by ordering that press to be abated as a nuisance, we conceived that we were acting strictly in accordance with law. We made that order in our corporate capacity, and the city marshal carried it out. It is possible there may have been some better way, but I must confess that I could not see it.

"In relation to the writ served upon us, we were willing to abide the consequences of our own acts, but were unwilling, in answering a writ of that kind, to submit to illegal exactions, sought to be imposed upon us under the pretense of law, when we knew they were in open violation of it. When that document was presented to me by Mr. Bettesworth, I offered, in the presence of more than twenty persons, to go to any other magistrate, either in our city, in Appanoose, or in any other place where we should be safe, but we all refused to put ourselves into the power of a mob. What right had that constable to refuse our request? He had none according to law; for you know, Governor Ford, that the statute law in Illinois is, that the parties served with the writ 'shall go before him who issued it, or some other justice of the peace.' Why, then, should we be dragged to Carthage, where the law does not compel us to go? Does not this look like many others of our persecutions with which you are acquainted? and have we not a right to expect foul play? This very act was a breach of law on his part, an assumption of power that did not belong to him, and an attempt, at least, to deprive us of our legal and constitutional rights and privileges. What could we do, under the circumstances, different from what we did do? We sued for, and obtained a writ of habeas corpus from the Municipal Court, by which we were delivered from the hands of Constable Bettesworth, and brought before and acquitted by the Municipal Court. After our acquittal, in a conversation with Judge Thomas, although he considered the acts of the party illegal, he advised that, to satisfy the people, we had better go before another magistrate who was not in our Church. In accordance with his advice, we went before Esquire Wells, with whom you are well acquainted; both parties were present, witnesses were called on both sides, the case was fully investigated, and we were again dismissed. And what is this pretended desire to enforce law, and wherefore are these lying, base rumors put into circulation but to seek through mob influence, under pretense of law, to make us submit to requisitions which are contrary to law and subversive of every principle of justice? And when you, sir, required us to come out here, we came, not because it was legal, but because you required it of us, and we were desirous of showing to you, and to all men, that we shrunk not from the most rigid investigation of our acts. We certainly did expect other treatment than to be immured in a jail at the instance of these men, and I think, from your plighted faith, we had a right so to expect, after disbanding our own forces, and putting ourselves entirely in your hands. And now, after having fulfilled my part, sir, as a man and an American citizen, I call upon you, Governor Ford, to deliver us from this place, and rescue us from this outrage that is sought to be practiced upon us by a set of infamous scoundrels."

Governor Ford. "But you have placed men under arrest, detained men as prisoners, and given passes to others, some of which I have seen."

John P. Green, City Marshal. "Perhaps I can explain. Since these difficulties have commenced, you are aware that we have been placed under very peculiar circumstances; our city has been placed under a very rigid police guard; in addition to this, frequent guards have been placed outside the city to prevent any sudden surprise, and those guards have questioned suspected or suspicious persons as to their business. To strangers, in some instances, passes have been given to prevent difficulty in passing these guards; it is some of these passes that you have seen. No person, sir, has been imprisoned without a legal cause in our city."

Governor. "Why did you not give a more speedy answer to the posse that I sent out?"

General Smith. "We had matters of importance to consult upon; your letter showed any thing but an amiable spirit. We have suffered immensely in Missouri from mobs, in loss of property, imprisonment, and otherwise. It took some time for us to weigh duly these matters; we could not decide upon matters of such importance immediately, and your posse were too hasty in returning; we were consulting for a large people, and vast interests were at stake. We had been outrageously imposed upon, and knew not how far we could trust any one; besides, a question necessarily arose, How shall we come? Your request was that we should come unarmed. It became a matter of serious importance to decide how far promises could be trusted, and how far we were safe from mob violence."

Colonel Geddes. "It certainly did look, from all I have heard, from the general spirit of violence and mobocracy that here prevails, that it was not safe for you to come unprotected."

Governor Ford. "I think that sufficient time was not allowed by the posse for you to consult and get ready. They were too hasty; but I suppose they found themselves bound by their orders. I think, too, there is a great deal of truth in what you say, and your reasoning is plausible, but I must beg leave to differ from you in relation to the acts of the city council. That council, in my opinion, had no right to act in a legislative capacity and in that of the judiciary. They should have passed a law in relation to the matter, and then the Municipal Court, upon complaint, could have removed it; but for the city council to take upon themselves the law-making and the execution of the law is in my opinion wrong; besides, these men ought to have had a hearing before their property was destroyed; to destroy it without was an infringement on their rights; besides, it is so contrary to the feelings of American people to interfere with the press. And, furthermore, I can not but think that it would have been more judicious for you to have gone with Mr. Bettesworth to Carthage, notwithstanding the law did not require it. Concerning your being in jail, I am sorry for that; I wish it had been otherwise. I hope you will soon be released, but I can not interfere."

Joseph Smith. "Governor Ford, allow me, sir, to bring one thing to your mind that you seem to have overlooked. You state that you think it would have been better for us to have submitted to the requisition of Constable Bettesworth, and to have gone to Carthage. Do you not know, sir, that that writ was served at the instance of an 'anti-Mormon' mob, who had passed resolutions, and published them, to the effect that they would exterminate the 'Mormon' leaders? and are you not informed that Captain Anderson was not only threatened when coming to Nauvoo, but had a gun fired at his boat by this said mob in Warsaw when coming up to Nauvoo, and that this very thing was made use of as a means to get us into their hands; and we could not, without taking an armed force with us, go there without, according to their published declarations, going into the jaws of death? To have taken a force would only have fanned the excitement, and they would have stated that we wanted to use intimidation; therefore we thought it the most judicious to avail ourselves of the protection of law."

Governor Ford. "I see, I see."

Joseph Smith. "Furthermore, in relation to the press, you say that you differ from me in opinion. Be it so; the thing, after all, is only a legal difficulty, and the courts, I should judge, are competent to decide on that matter. If our act was illegal, we are willing to meet it; and although I can not see the distinction that you draw about the acts of the city council, and what difference it could have made in point of fact, law, or justice between the city councils acting together or separate, or how much more legal it would have been for the Municipal Court, who were a part of the city council, to act separate instead of with the councilors, yet, if it is deemed that we did a wrong in destroying that press, we refuse not to pay for it; we are desirous to fulfill the law in every particular, and are responsible for our acts. You say that the parties ought to have had a hearing. Had it been a civil suit, this, of course, would have been proper; but there was a flagrant violation of every principle of right—a nuisance; and it was abated on the same principle that any nuisance, stench, or putrefied carcass would have been removed. Our first step, therefore, was to stop the foul, noisome, filthy sheet, and then the next in our opinion would have been to have prosecuted the man for a breach of public decency. And furthermore, again let me say, Governor Ford, I shall look to you for our protection. I believe you are talking of going to Nauvoo; if you go, sir, I wish to go along. I refuse not to answer any law, but I do not consider myself safe here."

Governor. "I am in hopes that you will be acquitted, and if I go I will certainly take you along. I do not, however, apprehend danger. I think you are perfectly safe either here or any where else. I can not, however, interfere with the law. I am placed in peculiar circumstances, and seem to be blamed by all parties."

Joseph Smith. "Governor Ford, I ask nothing but what is legal; I have a right to expect protection, at least from you; for, independent of law, you have pledged your faith and that of the state for my protection, and I wish to go to Nauvoo."

Governor. "And you shall have protection, General Smith. I did not make this promise without consulting my officers, who all pledged their honor to its fulfillment. I do not know that I shall go to-morrow to Nauvoo, but if I do I will take you along."

At a quarter past ten o'clock the governor left.

At about half past twelve o'clock, Mr. Reed, one of Joseph's counsel, came in, apparently much elated; he stated that, "upon an examination of the law, he found that the magistrate had transcended his jurisdiction, and that, having committed them without an examination, his jurisdiction ended; that he had him upon a pin-hook; that he ought to have examined them before he committed them, and that, having violated the law in this particular, he had no farther power over them; for, once committed, they were out of his jurisdiction, as the power of the magistrate extended no farther than their committal, and that now they could not be brought out except at the regular session of the Circuit Court, or by a writ of habeas corpus; but that if Justice Smith would consent to go to Nauvoo for trial, he would compromise matters with him, and overlook this matter."

Mr. Reed farther stated that "the 'anti-Mormons,' or mob, had concocted a scheme to get out a writ from Missouri, with a demand upon Governor Ford for the arrest of Joseph Smith and his conveyance to Missouri, and that a man by the name of Wilson had returned from Missouri the night before the burning of the press for this purpose."

At half past two o'clock Constable Bettesworth came to the jail with a man named Simpson, professing to have some order, but he would not send up his name, and the guard would not let him pass. Dr. Bernhisel and Brother Wasson went to inform the governor and council of this. At about twenty minutes to three Dr. Bernhisel returned, and stated that he thought the governor was doing all he could. At about ten minutes to three Hyrum Kimball appeared with news from Nauvoo.

Soon after Constable Bettesworth came with an order from Esquire Smith to convey the prisoners to the court-house for trial. He was informed that the process was illegal, that they had been placed there contrary to law, and that they refused to come unless by legal process. I was informed that Justice Smith (who was also Captain of the Carthage Grays) went to the governor and informed him of the matter, and that the governor replied, "You have your forces, and of course can use them." The constable certainly did return, accompanied by a guard of armed men, and by force, and under protest, hurried the prisoners to the court.

About four o'clock the case was called by Captain Robert F. Smith, J. P. The counsel of the prisoners called for subpœnas to bring witnesses. At twenty-five minutes past four he took a copy of the order to bring the prisoners from jail to trial, and afterward he took names of witnesses.

Counsel present for the state: Higbee, Skinner, Sharpe, Emmons, and Morrison. Twenty-five minutes to five the writ was returned as served, June 25th.

Many remarks were made at the court that I paid but little attention to, as I considered the whole thing illegal and a complete burlesque. Wood objected to the proceedings in toto, in consequence of its illegality, showing that the prisoners were not only illegally committed, but that, being once committed, the magistrate had no farther power over them; but as it was the same magistrate before whom he was pleading who imprisoned them contrary to law, and the same who, as captain, forced them from jail, his arguments availed but little. He then urged that the prisoners be remanded until witnesses could be had, and applied for a continuance for that purpose. Skinner suggested until twelve o'clock next day. Wood again demanded until witnesses could be obtained; that the court meet at a specified time, and that, if witnesses were not present, again adjourn, without calling the prisoners. After various remarks from Reed, Skinner, and others, the court stated that the writ was served yesterday, and that it will give until to-morrow at twelve M. to get witnesses.

We then returned to jail. Immediately after our return Dr. Bernhisel went to the governor, and obtained from him an order for us to occupy a large open room containing a bedstead. I rather think that the same room had been appropriated to the use of debtors; at any rate, there was free access to the jailer's house, and no bars or locks except such as might be on the outside door of the jail. The jailer, Mr. George W. Steghall, and his wife, manifested a disposition to make us as comfortable as they could; we ate at their table, which was well provided, and of course paid for it.

I do not remember the names of all who were with us that night and the next morning in jail, for several went and came; among those that we considered stationary were Stephen Markham, John S. Fulmer, Captain Dan Jones, Dr. Williard Richards, and myself. Dr. Bernhisel says that he was there from Wednesday in the afternoon until eleven o'clock next day. We were, however, visited by numerous friends, among whom were Uncle John Smith, Hyrum Kimball, Cyrus H. Wheelock, besides lawyers, as counsel. There was also a great variety of conversation, which was rather desultory than otherwise, and referred to circumstances that had transpired; our former and present grievances; the spirit of the troops around us, and the disposition of the governor; the devising for legal and other plans for deliverance; the nature of testimony required; the gathering of proper witnesses; and a variety of other topics, including our religious hopes, etc.

During one of these conversations Dr. Richards remarked: "Brother Joseph, it is necessary that you die in this matter, and if they will take me in your stead, I will suffer for you." At another time, when conversing about deliverance, I said, "Brother Joseph, if you will permit it, and say the word, I will have you out of this prison in five hours, if the jail has to come down to do it." My idea was to go to Nauvoo, and collect a force sufficient, as I considered the whole affair a legal farce, and a flagrant outrage upon our liberty and rights. Brother Joseph refused.

Elder Cyrus Wheelock came in to see us, and when he was about leaving drew a small pistol, a six-shooter, from his pocket, remarking at the same time, "Would any of you like to have this?" Brother Joseph immediately replied, "Yes, give it to me;" whereupon he took the pistol, and put it in his pantaloons pocket. The pistol was a six-shooting revolver, of Allen's patent; it belonged to me, and was one that I furnished to Brother Wheelock when he talked of going with me to the East, previous to our coming to Carthage. I have it now in my possession. Brother Wheelock went out on some errand, and was not suffered to return. The report of the governor having gone to Nauvoo without taking the prisoners along with him caused very unpleasant feelings, as we were apprised that we were left to the tender mercies of the Carthage Grays, a company strictly mobocratic, and whom we knew to be our most deadly enemies, and their captain, Esquire Smith, was a most unprincipled villain. Besides this, all the mob forces, comprising the governor's troops, were dismissed, with the exception of one or two companies, which the governor took with him to Nauvoo. The great part of the mob was liberated, the remainder was our guard.

We looked upon it not only as a breach of faith on the part of the governor, but also as an indication of a desire to insult us, if nothing more, by leaving us in the proximity of such men. The prevention of Wheelock's return was among the first of their hostile movements.

Colonel Markham then went out, and he was also prevented from returning. He was very angry at this, but the mob paid no attention to him; they drove him out of town at the point of the bayonet, and threatened to shoot him if he returned; he went, I am informed, to Nauvoo for the purpose of raising a company of men for our protection. Brother Fulmer went to Nauvoo after witnesses : it is my opinion that Brother Wheelock did also.

Some time after dinner we sent for some wine. It has been reported by some that this was taken as a sacrament. It was no such thing; our spirits were generally dull and heavy, and it was sent for to revive us. I think it was Captain Jones who went after it, but they would not suffer him to return. I believe we all drank of the wine, and gave some to one or two of the prison guards. We all of us felt unusually dull and languid, with a remarkable depression of spirits. In consonance with those feelings I sang the following song, that had lately been introduced into Nauvoo, entitled, "A poor wayfaring man of grief," etc.

1. A poor wayfaring man of grief
   Hath often cross'd me on my way,
   Who sued so humbly for relief
   That I could never answer Nay.

2. I had not power to ask his name,
   Whither he went, or whence he came;
   Yet there was something in his eye
   That won my love, I know not why.

3. Once, when my scanty meal was spread,
   He enter'd—not a word he spake!
   Just perishing for want of bread;
   I gave him all : he bless'd it, brake,

4. And ate, but gave me part again ;
   Mine was an angel's portion then,
   For while I fed with eager haste,
   The crust was manna to my taste.

5. I spied him where a fountain burst
   Clear from the rock—his strength was gone—
   The heedless water mock'd his thirst;
   He heard it, saw it hurrying on.

6. I ran and raised the suff'rer up;
   Thrice from the stream he drain'd my cup,
   Dipp'd, and return'd it running o'er ;
   I drank, and never thirsted more.

7. 'Twas night; the floods were out; it blew
   A winter hurricane aloof;
   I heard his voice abroad, and flew
   To bid him welcome to my roof.

8. I warm'd, I clothed, I cheer'd my guest,
   I laid him on my couch to rest;
   Then made the earth my bed, and seem'd
   In Eden's garden while I dream'd.

9. Stripp'd, wounded, beaten nigh to death,
   I found him by the highway side;
   I roused his pulse, brought back his breath,
   Revived his spirit, and supplied

10. Wine, oil, refreshment : he was heal'd ;
    I had myself a wound conceal'd,
    But from that hour forgot the smart,
    And peace bound up my broken heart.

11. In prison I saw him next, condemn'd
    To meet a traitor's doom at morn;
    The tide of lying tongues I stemm'd,
    And honor'd him 'mid shame and scorn.

12. My friendship's utmost zeal to try,
    He asked if I for him would die;
    The flesh was weak; my blood ran chill;
    But the free spirit cried " I will."

13. Then in a moment to my view
    The stranger started from disguise ;
    The tokens in his hands I knew;
    The Savior stood before mine eyes.

14. He spake—and my poor name he named—
    "Of me thou hast not been ashamed ;
    These deeds shall thy memorial be;
    Fear not ; thou didst them unto me.'

The song is pathetic, and the tune quite plaintive, and was very much in accordance with our feelings at the time, for our spirits were all depressed, dull, and gloomy, and surcharged with indefinite ominous forebodings. After a lapse of some time, Brother Hyrum requested me again to sing that song. I replied, " Brother Hyrum, I do not feel like singing;" when he remarked, " Oh ! never mind; commence singing, and you will get the spirit of it." At his request I did so. Soon afterward I was sitting at one of the front windows of the jail, when I saw a number of men, with painted faces, coming round the corner of the jail, and aiming toward the stairs. The other brethren had seen the same, for, as I went to the door, I found Brother Hyrum Smith and Dr. Richards already leaning against it; they both pressed against the door with their shoulders to prevent its being opened, as the lock and latch were comparatively useless. While in this position, the mob, who had come up stairs, and strove to open the door, probably thought it was locked, and fired a ball through the keyhole ; at this Dr. Richards and Brother Hyrum leaped back from the door, with their faces toward it; almost instantly another ball passed through the panel of the door, and struck Brother Hyrum on the left side of the nose, entering his face and head; simultaneously, at the same instant, another ball from the outside entered his back, passing through his body and striking his watch. The ball came from the back, through the jail window, opposite the door, and must, from its range, have been fired from the Carthage Grays, as the balls of fire-arms, shot close by the jail, would have entered the ceiling, we being in the second story, and there never was a time after that Hyrum could have received the latter wound. Immediately, when the balls struck him, he fell flat on his back, crying as he fell, " I am a dead man !" He never moved afterward.

I shall never forget the feeling of deep sympathy and regard manifested in the countenance of Brother Joseph as he drew nigh to Hyrum, and, leaning over him, exclaimed, "Oh! my poor, dear brother Hyrum." He, however, instantly arose, and with a firm, quick step, and a determined expression of countenance, approached the door, and pulling the six-shooter left by Brother Wheelock from his pocket, opened the door slightly, and snapped the pistol six successive times; only three of the barrels, however, were discharged. I afterward understood that two or three were wounded by these discharges, two of whom, I am informed, died. I had in my hands a large, strong hickory stick, brought there by Brother Markham, and left by him, which I had seized as soon as I saw the mob approach; and while Brother Joseph was firing the pistol, I stood close behind him. As soon as he had discharged it he stepped back, and I immediately took his place next the door, while he occupied the one I had done while he was shooting. Brother Richards, at this time, had a knotty walking-stick in his hands belonging to me, and stood next to Brother Joseph, a little farther from the door, in an oblique direction, apparently to avoid the rake of the fire from the door. The firing of Brother Joseph made our assailants pause for a moment; very soon after, however, they pushed the door some distance open, and protruded and discharged their guns into the room, when I parried them off with my stick, giving another direction to the balls.

It certainly was a terrible scene: streams of fire as thick as my arm passed by me as these men fired, and, unarmed as we were, it looked like certain death. I remember feeling as though my time had come, but I do not know when, in any critical position, I was more calm, unruffled, and energetic, and acted with more promptness and decision. It certainly was far from pleasant to be so near the muzzles of those fire-arms as they belched forth their liquid flame and deadly balls. While I was engaged in parrying the guns, Brother Joseph said, "That's right, Brother Taylor; parry them off as well as you can." These were the last words I ever heard him speak on earth.

Every moment the crowd at the door became more dense, as they were unquestionably pressed on by those in the rear ascending the stairs, until the whole entrance at the door was literally crowded with muskets and rifles, which, with the swearing, shouting, and demoniacal expressions of those outside the door and on the stairs, and the firing of guns, mingled with their horrid oaths and execrations, made it look like Pandemonium let loose, and was, indeed, a fit representation of the horrid deed in which they were engaged.

After parrying the guns for some time, which now protruded thicker and farther into the room, and seeing no hope of escape or protection there, as we were now unarmed, it occurred to me that we might have some friends outside, and that there might there be some chance of escape, but here there seemed to be none. As I expected them every moment to rush into the room — nothing but extreme cowardice having thus far kept them out — as the tumult and pressure increased, without any other hope, I made a spring for the window, which was right in front of the jail door, where the mob was standing, and also exposed to the fire of the Carthage Grays, who were stationed some ten or twelve rods off. The weather was hot, we all of us had our coats off, and the window was raised to admit air; as I reached the window, and was on the point of leaping out, I was struck by a ball from the door about midway of my thigh, which struck the bone, and flattened out almost to the size of a quarter of a dollar, and then passed on through the fleshy part to within about half an inch of the outside. I think some prominent nerve must have been severed or injured, for as soon as the ball struck me I fell like a bird when shot, or an ox struck by a butcher, and lost entirely and instantaneously all power of action or locomotion. I fell on to the window-sill, and cried out, "I am shot!" Not possessing any power to move, I felt myself falling outside of the window, but immediately I fell inside, from some, at that time, unknown cause; when I struck the floor my animation seemed restored, as I have seen sometimes squirrels and birds after being shot. As soon as I felt the power of motion I crawled under the bed, which was in a corner of the room, not far from the window where I received my wound. While on my way and under the bed I was wounded in three other places; one ball entered a little below the left knee, and never was extracted; another entered the forepart of my left arm, a little above the wrist, and, passing down by the joint, lodged in the fleshy part of my hand, about midway, a little above the upper joint of my little finger; another struck me on the fleshy part of my left hip, and tore away the flesh as large as my hand, dashing the mangled fragments of flesh and blood against the wall.

My wounds were painful, and the sensation produced was as though a ball had passed through and down the whole length of my leg. I very well remember my reflections at the time.   I had a very painful idea of becoming lame and decrepit, and being an object of pity, and I felt as though I had rather die than be placed in such circumstances.

It would seem that immediately after my attempt to leap out of the window, Joseph also did the same thing, of which circumstance I have no knowledge only from information.   The first thing that I noticed was a cry that he had leaped out of the window.   A cessation of firing followed, the mob rushed down stairs, and Dr. Richards went to the window.   Immediately afterward I saw the doctor going toward the jail door, and as there was an iron door at the head of the stairs adjoining our door which led into the cells for criminals, it struck me that the doctor was going in there, and I said to him, "Stop, doctor, and take me along."   He proceeded to the door and opened it, and then returned and dragged me along to a small cell prepared for criminals.

Brother Richards was very much troubled, and exclaimed, "Oh! Brother Taylor, is it possible that they have killed both Brother Hyrum and Joseph? it can not surely be, and yet I saw them shoot him;" and, elevating his hands two or three times, he exclaimed, "Oh Lord, my God, spare thy servants!"   He then said, "Brother Taylor, this is a terrible event;" and he dragged me farther into the cell, saying, "I am sorry I can not do better for you;" and, taking an old, filthy mattress, he covered me with it, and said, "That may hide you, and you may yet live to tell the tale, but I expect they will kill me in a few moments."   While lying in this position I suffered the most excruciating pain.

Soon afterward Dr. Richards came to me, informing me that the mob had precipitately fled, and at the same time confirming my worst fears that Joseph was assuredly dead.   I felt a dull, lonely, sickening sensation at the news.   When I reflected that our noble chieftain, the prophet of the living God, had fallen, and that I had seen his brother in the cold embrace of death, it seemed as though there was an open void or vacuum in the great field of human existence to me, and a dark, gloomy chasm in the kingdom, and that we were left alone.   Oh, how lonely was that feeling! how cold, barren, and desolate!   In the midst of difficulties he was always the first in motion; in critical position his counsel was always sought.   As our prophet he approached our God, and obtained for us his will; but now our prophet, our counselor, our general, our leader was gone, and, amid the fiery ordeal that we then had to pass through, we were left alone without his aid, and as our future guide for things spiritual or temporal, and for all things pertaining to this world or the next, he had spoken for the last time on earth.

These reflections and a thousand others flashed upon my mind.   I thought, Why must the good perish, and the virtuous be destroyed?   Why must God's nobility, the salt of the earth, the most exalted of the human family, and the most perfect types of all excellence, fall victims to the cruel, fiendish hate of incarnate devils?

The poignancy of my grief, I presume, however, was somewhat allayed by the extreme suffering that I endured from my wounds.

Soon afterward I was taken to the head of the stairs and laid there, where I had a full view of our beloved and now murdered brother Hyrum.   There he lay as I had left him; he had not moved a limb; he lay placid and calm, a monument of greatness even in death; but his noble spirit had left its tenement, and had gone to dwell in régions more congenial to its exalted nature.   Poor Hyrum! he was a great and a good man, and my soul was cemented to his.   If ever there was an exemplary, honest, and virtuous man, an embodiment of all that is noble in the human form, Hyrum Smith was its representative.

While I lay there a number of persons came around, among whom was a physician.   The doctor, on seeing a ball lodged in my left hand, took a penknife from his pocket and made an incision in it for the purpose of extracting the ball therefrom, and having obtained a pair of carpenter's compasses, made use of them to draw or pry out the ball, alternately using the penknife and compasses.   After sawing for some time with a dull penknife, and prying and pulling with the compasses, he ultimately succeeded in extracting the ball, which was about a half ounce one.   Some time afterward he remarked to a friend of mine that "I had nerves like the devil to stand what I did in its extraction."   I really thought I had need of nerves to stand such surgical butchery, and that, whatever my nerves may be, his practice was devilish.

This company wished to remove me to Mr. Hamilton's hotel, the place where we had staid previous to our incarceration in jail.   I told them, however, that I did not wish to go; I did not consider it safe.   They protested that it was, and that I was safe with them; that it was a perfect outrage for men to be used as we had been; that they were my friends; that it was for my good they were counseling me, and that I could be better taken care of there than here.

I replied, "I don't know you. Who am I among? I am surrounded by assassins and murderers; witness your deeds! Don't talk to me of kindness or comfort; look at your murdered victims. Look at me! I want none of your counsel nor comfort. There may be some safety here; I can be assured of none any where," etc.

They "God damned their souls to hell," made the most solemn asseverations, and swore by God and the devil, and every thing else that they could think of, that they would stand by me to death and protect me. In half an hour every one of them had fled to the town.

Soon after a coroner's jury were assembled in the room over the body of Hyrum. Among the jurors was Captain Smith, of the "Carthage Grays," who had assisted in the murder, and the same justice before whom we had been tried. I heard the name of Francis Higbee as being in the neighborhood; on hearing his name mentioned, I immediately rose and said, "Captain Smith, you are a justice of the peace; I have heard his name mentioned; I want to swear my life against him." I was informed that word was immediately sent to him to leave the place, which he did.

Brother Richards was busy during this time attending to the coroner's inquest, and to the removal of the bodies, and making arrangements for their removal from Carthage to Nauvoo.

When we had a little leisure, he again came to me, and at his suggestion I was removed to Hamilton's tavern; I felt that he was the only friend, the only person, that I could rely upon in that town. It was with difficulty that sufficient persons could be found to carry me to the tavern; for immediately after the murder a great fear fell upon all the people, and men, women, and children fled with great precipitation, leaving nothing nor any body in the town but two or three women and children, and one or two sick persons.

It was with great difficulty that Brother Richards prevailed upon Mr. Hamilton, hotel-keeper, and his family, to stay; they would not until Brother Richards had given a solemn promise that he would see them protected, and hence I was looked upon as a hostage. Under these circumstances, notwithstanding, I believe they were hostile to the "Mormons," and were glad that the murder had taken place, yet they did not actually participate in it; and, feeling that I should be a protection to them, they staid.

The whole community knew that a dreadful outrage had been perpetrated by those villains, and fearing lest the citizens of Nauvoo, as they possessed the power, might have a disposition to visit them with a terrible vengeance, they fled in the wildest confusion. And, indeed, it was with very great difficulty that the citizens of Nauvoo could be restrained; a horrid, barbarous murder had been committed, the most solemn pledge violated, and that, too, while the victims were, contrary to the requirements of the law, putting themselves into the hands of the governor to pacify a popular excitement. This outrage was enhanced by the reflection that we were able to protect ourselves against not only all the mob, but against three times their number and that of the governor's troops put together. These were exasperated by the speech of the governor in town. The whole events were so faithless, so dastardly, so mean, cowardly, and contemptible, without one extenuating circumstance, that it would not have been surprising if the citizens of Nauvoo had arisen *en masse*, and blotted the wretches out of existence. The citizens of Carthage knew they would have done so under such circumstances, and, judging us by themselves, they were all panic-stricken and fled. Colonel Markham, too, after his expulsion from Carthage, had gone home, related the circumstances of his ejectment, and was using his influence to get a company to go out. Fearing that when the people heard that their prophet and patriarch had been murdered under the above circumstances they might act rashly, and knowing that, if they once got roused, like a mighty avalanche they would lay the country waste before them and take a terrible vengeance—as none of the twelve were in Nauvoo, and no one, perhaps, with sufficient influence to control the people, Dr. Richards, after consulting me, wrote the following note, fearing that my family might be seriously affected by the news. I told him to insert that I was slightly wounded.

William Richards's Note from Carthage Jail to Nauvoo.*

"Carthage Jail, 8 o'clock 5 min. P.M., June 27th, 1844.

" Joseph and Hyrum are dead. Taylor wounded, not very badly. I am well. Our guard was forced, as we believe, by a band of Missourians from 100 to 200. The job was done in an instant, and the party fled toward Nauvoo instantly. This is as I believe it. The citizens here are afraid of the Mormons attacking them ; I promise them no. W. RICHARDS.

" N.B.—The citizens promise us protection ; alarm guns have been fired.
"JOHN TAYLOR."

I remember signing my name as quickly as possible, lest the tremor of my hand should be noticed, and their fears too excited.

A messenger was dispatched immediately with that note, but he was intercepted by the governor, who, on hearing a cannon fired at Carthage, which was to be the signal for the murder, immediately fled with his company, and fearing that the citizens of Nauvoo, when apprised of the horrible outrage, would immediately rise and pursue, he turned back the messenger, who was George D. Grant. A second one was sent, who was treated similarly ; and not until a third attempt could news be got to Nauvoo.

Samuel H. Smith, brother to Joseph and Hyrum, was the first brother that I saw after the outrage ; I am not sure whether he took the news or not ; he lived at the time at Plymouth, Hancock County, and was on his way to Carthage to see his brothers, when he was met by some of the troops, or rather mob, that had been dismissed by the governor, and who were on their way home. On learning that he was Joseph Smith's brother they sought to kill him, but he escaped, and fled into the woods, where he was chased for a length of time by them ; but, after severe fatigue, and much danger and excitement, he succeeded in escaping, and came to Carthage. He was on horseback when he arrived, and was not only very much tired with the fatigue and excitement of the chase, but was also very much distressed in feelings on account of the death of his brother. These things produced a fever, which laid the foundation for his death, which took place on the 30th of July. Thus another of the brothers fell a victim, although not directly, but indirectly to this infernal mob.

I lay from about five o'clock until two next morning without having my wounds dressed, as there was scarcely any help of any kind in Carthage, and Brother Richards was busy with the dead bodies, preparing them for removal. My wife Leonora started early the next day, having had some little trouble in getting a company or a physician to come with her ; after considerable difficulty she succeeded in getting an escort, and Dr. Samuel Bennet came along with her. Soon after my father and mother arrived from Quakie, near which place they had a farm at that time, and hearing of the trouble, hastened along.

General Demming, Brigadier General of the Hancock County Militia, was very much of a gentleman, and showed me every courtesy, and Colonel Jones also was very solicitous about my welfare.

I was called upon by several gentlemen of Quincy and other places, among whom was Judge Ralston, as well as by our own people, and a medical man extracted a ball from my left thigh that was giving me much pain : it lay about half an inch deep, and my thigh was considerably swollen. The doctor asked me if I would be tied during the operation ; I told him no ; that I could endure the cutting associated with the operation as well without, and I did so ; indeed, so great was the pain I endured that the cutting was rather a relief than otherwise.

A very laughable incident occurred at the time : my wife Leonora went into an adjoining room to pray for me, that I might be sustained during the operation. While on her knees at prayer, a Mrs. Bedell, an old lady of the Methodist association, entered, and, patting Mrs. Taylor on her back with her hand, said, "There's a good lady, pray for God to forgive your sins ; pray that you may be converted, and the Lord may have mercy on your soul."

The scene was so ludicrous that Mrs. Taylor knew not whether to laugh or be angry. Mrs. Taylor informed me that Mr. Hamilton, the father of the Hamilton who kept the house, rejoiced at the murder, and said in company "that it was done up in the best possible style, and showed good generalship ;" and she farther believed that the other branches of the family sanctioned it. These were the associates of the

* "Des. News," No. 38, Nov. 25, 1857, p. 297.

old lady referred to, and yet she could talk of conversion and saving souls in the midst of blood and murder : such is man and such consistency.

The ball being extracted was the one that first struck me, which I before referred to ; it entered on the outside of my left thigh, about five inches from my knee, and, passing rather obliquely toward my body, had, it would seem, struck the bone, for it was flattened out nearly as thin and large as a quarter of a dollar.

The governor passed on, staying at Carthage only a few minutes, and he did not stop until he got fifty miles from Nauvoo. There had been various opinions about the complicity of the governor in the murder, some supposing that he knew all about it, and assisted or winked at its execution. It is somewhat difficult to form a correct opinion ; from the facts presented it is very certain that things looked more than suspicious against him.

In the first place, he positively knew that we had broken no law.

Secondly. He knew that the mob had not only passed inflammatory resolutions, threatening extermination to the "Mormons," but that they had actually assembled armed mobs and commenced hostilities against us.

Thirdly. He took those very mobs that had been arrayed against us, and enrolled them as his troops, thus legalizing their acts.

Fourthly. He disbanded the Nauvoo Legion, which had never violated law, and disarmed them, and had about his person in the shape of militia known mobocrats and violators of the law.

Fifthly. He requested us to come to Carthage without arms, promising protection, and then refused to interfere in delivering us from prison, although Joseph and Hyrum were put there contrary to law.

Sixthly. Although he refused to interfere in our behalf, yet, when Captain Smith went to him and informed him that the persons refused to come out, he told him that "he had a command and knew what to do," thus sanctioning the use of force in the violation of law when opposed to us, whereas he would not for us interpose his executive authority to free us from being incarcerated contrary to law, although he was fully informed of all the facts of the case, as we kept him posted in the affairs all the time.

Seventhly. He left the prisoners in Carthage jail contrary to his plighted faith.

Eighthly. Before he went he dismissed all the troops that could be relied upon, as well as many of the mob, and left us in charge of the "Carthage Grays," a company that he knew were mobocratic, our most bitter enemies, and who had passed resolutions to exterminate us, and who had been placed under guard by General Demming only the day before.

Ninthly. He was informed of the intended murder, both before he left and while on the road, by several different parties.

Tenthly. When the cannon was fired in Carthage, signifying that the deed was done, he immediately took up his line of march and fled. How did he know that this signal portended their death if he was not in the secret ? It may be said some of the party told him. How could he believe what the party said about the gun-signal if he could not believe the testimony of several individuals who told him in positive terms about the contemplated murder ?

He has, I believe, stated that he left the "Carthage Grays" there because he considered that, as their town was contiguous to ours, and as the responsibility of our safety rested solely upon them, they would not dare suffer any indignity to befall us. This very admission shows that he did really expect danger ; and then he knew that these people had published to the world that they would exterminate us, and his leaving us in their hands and talking of their responsibilities was like leaving a lamb in charge of a wolf, and trusting to its humanity and honor for its safe-keeping.

It is said, again, that he would not have gone to Nauvoo, and thus placed himself in the hands of the "Mormons," if he had anticipated any such event, as he would be exposed to their wrath. To this it may be answered that the "Mormons" did not know their signals, while he did ; and they were also known in Warsaw, as well as in other places ; and as soon as the gun was fired, a merchant of Warsaw jumped upon his horse and rode directly to Quincy, and reported "Joseph and Hyrum killed, and those who were with them in jail." He reported farther "that they were attempting to break jail, and were all killed by the guard." This was their story ; it was anticipated to kill all, and the gun was to be the signal that the deed was accomplished. This was known in Warsaw. The governor also knew it and fled ;

and he could really be in no danger in Nauvoo, for the Mormons did not know it, and he had plenty of time to escape, which he did.

It is said that he made all his officers promise solemnly that they would help him to protect the Smiths; this may or may not be. At any rate, some of these same officers helped to murder them.

The strongest argument in the governor's favor, and one that would bear more weight with us than all the rest put together, would be that he could not believe them capable of such atrocity; and, thinking that their talk and threatenings were a mere ebullition of feeling, a kind of braggadocio, and that there was enough of good moral feeling to control the more violent passions, he trusted to their faith. There is, indeed, a degree of plausibility about this, but when we put it in juxtaposition to the amount of evidence that he was in possession of it weighs very little. He had nothing to inspire confidence in them, and every thing to make him mistrust them. Besides, why his broken faith? why his disregard of what was told him by several parties? Again, if he knew not the plan, how did he understand the signal? Why so oblivious to every thing pertaining to the "Mormon" interest, and so alive and interested about the mobocrats? At any rate, be this as it may, he stands responsible for their blood, and it is dripping on his garments. If it had not been for his promises of protection, they would have protected themselves; it was plighted faith that led them to the slaughter; and, to make the best of it, it was a breach of that faith and a non-fulfillment of that promise, after repeated warnings, that led to their death.

Having said so much, I must leave the governor with my readers and with his God. Justice, I conceive, demanded this much, and truth could not be told with less; as I have said before, my opinion is that the governor would not have planned this murder, but he had not sufficient energy to resist popular opinion, even if that opinion led to blood and death.

It was rumored that a strong political party, numbering in its ranks many of the prominent men of the nation, were engaged in a plot for the overthrow of Joseph Smith, and that the governor was of this party, and Sharp, Williams, Captain Smith, and others, were his accomplices, but whether this was the case or not I don't know. It is very certain that a strong political feeling existed against Joseph Smith, and I have reason to believe that his letters to Henry Clay were made use of by political parties opposed to Mr. Clay, and were the means of that statesman's defeat. Yet, if such a combination as the one referred to existed, I am not apprised of it.

While I lay at Carthage, previous to Mrs. Taylor's arrival, a pretty good sort of a man, who was lame of a leg, waited upon me, and sat up at night with me; after Mrs. Taylor, my mother and others waited upon me.

Many friends called upon me, among whom were Richard Ballantyne, Elizabeth Taylor, several of the Perkins family, and a number of the brethren from Macedonia and La Harpe. Besides these, many strangers from Quincy, some of whom expressed indignant feelings against the mob and sympathy for myself. Brother Alexander Williams called upon me, who suspected that they had some designs in keeping me there, and stated "that he had at a given point in some woods fifty men, and that if I would say the word he would raise other fifty, and fetch me out of there." I thanked him, but told him I thought there was no need. However, it would seem that I was in some danger; for Colonel Jones, before referred to, when absent from me, left two loaded pistols on the table in case of an attack, and some time afterward, when I had recovered and was publishing the affair, a lawyer, Mr. Backman, stated that he had prevented a man by the name of Jackson, before referred to, from ascending the stairs, who was coming with a design to murder me, and that now he was sorry he had not let him do the deed.

There were others, also, of whom I heard that said I ought to be killed, and they would do it, but that it was too damned cowardly to shoot a wounded man; and thus, by the chivalry of murderers, I was prevented from being a second time mutilated or killed. Many of the mob, too, came around and treated me with apparent respect, and the officers and people generally looked upon me as a hostage, and feared that my removal would be the signal for the rising of the Mormons.

I do not remember the time that I staid there, but I think three or four days after the murder, when Brother Marks with a carriage, Brother James Aldred with a wagon, Dr. Ells, and a number of others on horseback, came for the purpose of taking me to Nauvoo. I was very weak at the time, occasioned by the loss of blood and the great discharge of my wounds, so that when Mrs. Taylor asked me if I could talk I could barely whisper no. Quite a discussion arose as to the propriety of my removal, the physicians and people of Carthage protesting that it would be my death, while my friends were anxious for my removal if possible.

I suppose the former were actuated by the above-named desire to keep me. Colonel Jones was, I believe, sincere; he has acted as a friend all the time, and he told Mrs. Taylor she ought to persuade me not to go, for he did not believe I had strength enough to reach Nauvoo. It was finally agreed, however, that I should go; but as it was thought that I could not stand riding in a wagon or carriage, they prepared a litter for me; I was carried down stairs and put upon it. A number of men assisted to carry me, some of whom had been engaged in the mob. As soon as I got down stairs, I felt much better and strengthened, so that I could talk; I suppose the effect of the fresh air.

When we had got near the outside of the town I remembered some woods that we had to go through, and telling a person near to call for Dr. Ells, who was riding a very good horse, I said, " Doctor, I perceive that the people are getting fatigued with carrying me; a number of Mormons live about two or three miles from here, near our route; will you ride to their settlement as quietly as possible, and have them come and meet us?" He started off on a gallop immediately. My object in this was to obtain protection in case of an attack, rather than to obtain help to carry me.

Very soon after the men from Carthage made one excuse after another, until they had all left, and I felt glad to get rid of them. I found that the tramping of those carrying me produced violent pain, and a sleigh was produced and attached to the hind end of Brother James Aldred's wagon, a bed placed upon it, and I propped up on the bed. Mrs. Taylor rode with me, applying ice and ice-water to my wounds. As the sleigh was dragged over the grass on the prairie, which was quite tall, it moved very easily and gave me very little pain.

When I got within five or six miles of Nauvoo the brethren commenced to meet me from the city, and they increased in number as we drew nearer, until there was a very large company of people of all ages and both sexes, principally, however, men.

For some time there had been almost incessant rain, so that in many low places in the prairie it was from one to three feet deep in water, and at such places the brethren whom we met took hold of the sleigh, lifted it, and carried it over the water; and when we arrived in the neighborhood of the city, where the roads were excessively muddy and bad, the brethren tore down the fences, and we passed through the fields.

Never shall I forget the difference of feeling that I experienced between the place that I had left and the one that I had now arrived at. I had left a lot of reckless, bloodthirsty murderers, and had come to the City of the Saints, the people of the living God; friends of truth and righteousness, thousands of whom stood there with warm, true hearts to offer their friendship and services, and to welcome my return. It is true it was a painful scene, and brought sorrowful remembrances to mind, but to me it caused a thrill of joy to find myself once more in the bosom of my friends, and to meet with the cordial welcome of true, honest hearts. What was very remarkable, I found myself very much better after my arrival at Nauvoo than I was when I started on my journey, although I had traveled eighteen miles.

The next day, as some change was wanting, I told Mrs. Taylor that if she could send to Dr. Richards, he had my purse and watch, and they would find money in my purse.

Previous to the doctor leaving Carthage, I told him that he had better take my purse and watch, for I was afraid the people would steal them. The doctor had taken my pantaloons' pocket, and put the watch in it with the purse, cut off the pocket, and tied a string round the top; it was in this position when brought home. My family, however, were not a little startled to find that my watch had been struck with a ball. I sent for my vest, and, upon examination, it was found that there was a cut, as if with a knife, in the vest pocket which had contained my watch. In the pocket the fragments of the glass were found literally ground to powder. It then occurred to me that a ball had struck me at the time I felt myself falling out of the window, and that it was this force that threw me inside. I had often remarked to Mrs. Taylor the singular fact of finding myself inside the room, when I felt a moment before, after being shot, that I was falling out, and I never could account for it until then; but here the thing was fully elucidated, and was rendered plain to my mind. I was indeed falling out, when some villain aimed at my heart. The ball struck my watch, and forced me back; if I had fallen out I should assuredly have been killed, if not by the fall, by those around, and this ball, intended to dispatch me, was turned by an overruling Providence into a messenger of mercy, and saved my life. I shall never forget the feelings of gratitude that I then experienced toward my heavenly Father; the whole scene was vividly portrayed before me, and my heart melted before the Lord. I felt that the Lord had preserved me by a special act of mercy; that my time had not yet come, and that I had still a work to perform upon the earth.

(Signed), JOHN TAYLOR.

NOTES.

In addition to the above I give the following:

Dr. Bernhisel informed me that Joseph, looking him full in the face, and as solemn as eternity, said, "I am going as a lamb to the slaughter, but I am as calm as a summer's morning. I have a conscience void of offense toward God and man." I heard him state, in reply to an interrogatory, made either by myself or some one in my hearing, in relation to the best course to pursue, "I am not now acting according to my judgment; others must counsel, and not me, for the present," or in words to the same effect.

The governor's remarks about the press may be partially correct, so far as the legal technicality was concerned, and the order of administering law. The proper way would perhaps have been for the City Council to have passed a law in regard to the removal of nuisances, and then for the Municipal Court to have ordered it to be abated on complaint. Be this as it may, it was only a variation in form, not in fact, for the Municipal Court formed part of the City Council, and all voted; and, furthermore, some time after the murder, Governor Ford told me that the press ought to have been removed, but that it was bad policy to remove it as we did; that if we had only let a mob do it, instead of using the law, we could have done it without difficulty, and no one would have been implicated. Thus the governor, who would have winked at the proceedings of a mob, lent his aid to, or winked at, the proceedings of mob violence in the assassination of Joseph and Hyrum Smith, for removing a nuisance according to law, because of an alleged informality in the legal proceedings or a legal technicality.

I must here state that I do not believe Governor Ford would have planned the murder of Joseph and Hyrum Smith; but, being a man that courted popular opinion, he had not the firmness to withstand the mob, even when that mob were seeking to imbrue their hands in the blood of innocence; he lent himself to their designs, and thus became a partaker of their evil deeds.

I will illustrate this vexed question with the following official paper, which appeared in the "Deseret News," No. 30:

"Two of the brethren arrived this evening (June 13th, 1844), from Carthage, and said that about 300 mobbers were assembled there, with the avowed intention of coming against Nauvoo. Also that Hamilton was paying a dollar per bushel for corn to feed their animals."

The following was published in the Warsaw Signal Office; I insert it as a specimen of the unparalleled corruption and diabolical falsehood of which the human race has become capable in this generation:

"At a mass meeting of the citizens of Hancock County, convened at Carthage on the 11th day of June, 1844, Mr. Knox was appointed President, John Doty and Lewis F. Evans, Vice-Presidents, and William Y. Head, Secretary.

"Henry Stephens, Esq., presented the following resolutions, passed at a meeting of the citizens of Warsaw, and urged the adoption of them as the sense of this meeting:

"PREAMBLE AND RESOLUTIONS.

"WHEREAS information has reached us, about which there can be no question, that the authorities of Nauvoo did recently pass an ordinance declaring a printing-press and newspaper published by the opponents of the Prophet a nuisance, and in pursuance thereof did direct the marshal of the city and his adherents to enter by force the building from whence the paper was issued, and violently (if necessary) to take possession of the press and printing materials, and thereafter to burn and destroy the same; and whereas, in pursuance of said ordinance, the marshal and his adherents, together with a mob of Mormons, did, after sunset on the evening of the 10th inst., violently enter said building in a tumultuous manner, burn and destroy the press and other materials found on the premises;

" And whereas Hyrum Smith did, in presence of the City Council and the citizens of Nauvoo, offer a reward for the destruction of the printing-press and materials of the ' Warsaw Signal,' a newspaper also opposed to his interest;

"And whereas the liberty of the press is one of the cardinal principles of our government, firmly guaranteed by the several Constitutions of the states as well as the United States ;

"And whereas Hyrum Smith has within the last week publicly threatened the life of one of our valued citizens, Thos. C. Sharp, the editor of the ' Signal:'

"Therefore be it solemnly *Resolved* by the citizens of Warsaw in public meeting assembled,

"That we view the recent ordinance of the city of Nauvoo, and the proceedings thereunder, as an outrage of an alarming character, revolutionary and tyrannical in its tendency, and, being under color of law, as calculated to subvert and destroy in the minds of the community all reliance on the law.

"*Resolved*, That as a community we feel anxious, when possible, to redress our grievances by legal remedies ; but the time has now arrived when the law has ceased to be a protection to our lives and property ; a mob at Nauvoo, under a city ordinance, has violated the highest privilege in our government, and to seek redress in the ordinary mode would be utterly ineffectual.

"*Resolved*, That the public threat made in the council of the city not only to destroy our printing-press, but to take the life of its editor, is sufficient, in connection with the recent outrage, to command the efforts and the services of every good citizen to put an immediate stop to the career of the mad Prophet and his demoniac coadjutors. We must not only defend ourselves from danger, but we must resolutely carry the war into the enemy's camp. We do therefore declare that we will sustain our press and the editor at all hazards. That we will take full vengeance—terrible vengeance, should the lives of any of our citizens be lost in the effort. That we hold ourselves at all times in readiness to co-operate with our fellow-citizens in this state, Missouri, and Iowa, *to exterminate*—UTTERLY EXTERMINATE, the wicked and abominable Mormon leaders, the authors of our troubles.

"*Resolved*, That a committee of five be appointed forthwith to notify all persons in our township *suspected* of being the tools of the Prophet to leave immediately on pain of INSTANT VENGEANCE. And we do recommend the inhabitants of the adjacent townships to do the same, hereby pledging ourselves to render all the assistance they may require.

"*Resolved*, That the time, in our opinion, has arrived when the adherents of Smith, as a body, should be driven from the surrounding settlements into Nauvoo; that the Prophet and his miscreant adherents should then be demanded at their hands, and if not surrendered, A WAR OF EXTERMINATION SHOULD BE WAGED, to the entire destruction, if necessary for our protection, of his adherents. And we do hereby recommend this resolution to the consideration of the several townships, to the Mass Convention to be held at Carthage, hereby pledging ourselves to aid to the utmost the complete consummation of the object in view, that we may thereby be utterly relieved of the alarm, anxiety, and trouble to which we are now subjected.

"*Resolved*, That every citizen arm himself, to be prepared to sustain the resolutions herein contained.

"Mr. Roosevelt rose and made a brief but eloquent speech, and called upon the citizens throughout the country to render efficient aid in carrying out the spirit of the resolutions. Mr. Roosevelt then moved that a committee of seven be appointed by the chair to draft resolutions expressive of our action in future.

"Mr. Catlin moved to amend the motion of Mr. Roosevelt so that the committee should consist of one from each precinct; which motion, as amended, was adopted.

"The chair then appointed the following as said committee: Colonel Levi Williams, Rocky Run Precinct; Joel Catlin, Augusta; Samuel Williams, Carthage; Elisha Worrell, Chili; Captain Maddison, St. Mary's; John M. Ferris, Fountain Green; James Rice, Pilot Grove; John Carns, Bear Creek; C. L. Higbee, Nauvoo; George Robinson, La Harpe; and George Rockwell, Warsaw.

"On motion of Mr. Sympson, Walter Bagby, Esq., was requested to address the meeting during the absence of the committee. He spoke long and eloquently upon the cause of our grievances, and expressed his belief that the time was now at hand when we were individually and collectively called upon to repel the innovations upon our liberties, and suggested that points be designated as places of encampment at which to rendezvous our forces, that we may be ready, when called upon, for efficient action.

M M

"Dr. Barns, one of the persons who went with the officers to Nauvoo for the purpose of arresting the rioters, having just arrived, came into the meeting, and reported the result of their proceedings, which was, that the persons charged in the writs were duly arrested, but taken from the officer's hands on a writ of *habeas corpus* from the Municipal Court, and discharged, and the following potent words entered upon the records—HONORABLY DISCHARGED.

"On motion of O. C. Skinner, Esq., a vote of thanks was tendered to Dr. Barns for volunteering his services in executing said writs.

"Francis M. Higbee was now loudly called for. He stated his personal knowledge of the Mormons from their earliest history, throughout their hellish career in Missouri and this state, which had been characterized by the darkest and most diabolical deeds which had ever disgraced humanity.

"The committee appointed to draft resolutions brought in the following report, which, after some considerable discussion, was unanimously adopted:

"'Whereas the officer charged with the execution of a writ against Joseph Smith and others, for riot in the County of Hancock, which said writ said officer has served upon said Smith and others; and whereas said Smith and others refuse to obey the mandate of said writ; and whereas, in the opinion of this meeting, it is impossible for the said officer to raise a posse of sufficient strength to execute said writ; and whereas it is the opinion of this meeting that the riot is still progressing, and that violence is meditated and determined on, it is the opinion of this meeting that the circumstances of the case require the interposition of executive power: Therefore,

"'*Resolved*, That a deputation of two discreet men be sent to Springfield to solicit such interposition.

"'2d. *Resolved*, That said deputation be furnished with a certified copy of the resolution, and be authorized to obtain evidence by affidavit and otherwise in regard to the violence which has already been committed and is still farther meditated.'

"Dr. Evans here rose and expressed his wish that the above resolutions would not retard our operations, but that we would each one arm and equip ourselves forthwith.

"The resolutions passed at Warsaw were again read by Dr. Barns, and passed by acclamation.

"On motion of A. Sympson, Esq., the suggestion of Mr. Bagby, appointing places of encampment, was adopted, to wit: Warsaw, Carthage, Green Plains, Spilman's Landing, Chili, and La Harpe.

"On motion, O. C. Skinner and Walter Bagby, Esqrs., were appointed a committee to bear the resolutions adopted by this meeting to his excellency the governor, requiring his executive interposition.

"On motion of J. H. Sherman, a Central Corresponding Committee was appointed.

"Ordered, That J. H. Sherman, H. T. Wilson, Chauncy Robinson, Wm. S. Freeman, Thomas Morrison, F. M. Higbee, Lyman Prentiss, and Stephen H. Tyler be said committee.

"On motion of George Rockwell,

"*Resolved*, That constables in the different precincts hold themselves in readiness to obey the officer in possession of the writs, whenever called upon, in summoning the posse.

"On motion, the meeting adjourned.

"JOHN KNOX, President.

"JOHN DOTY,   } Vice-Presidents.
"LEWIS F. EVANS, }

"W. Y. HEAD, Secretary."

The following will conclude the "Expositor Question:"

"Nauvoo, June 14th, 1844.

"SIR,—I write you this morning briefly to inform you of the facts relative to the removal of the press and fixtures of the 'Nauvoo Expositor' as a nuisance.

"The 8th and 10th instant were spent by the City Council of Nauvoo in receiving testimony concerning the character of the 'Expositor,' and the character and designs of the proprietors.

"In the investigation it appeared evident to the Council that the proprietors were a set of unprincipled, lawless debauchees, counterfeiters, bogus-makers, gamblers, peace-disturbers, and that the grand object of said proprietors was to destroy our constitutional rights and chartered privileges; to overthrow all good and wholesome regulations in society; to strengthen themselves against the municipality; to fortify themselves against the Church of which I am a member, and destroy all our religious rights and privileges by libels, slanders, falsehoods, perjury, etc., and sticking at no corruption to accomplish their hellish purposes; and that said paper of itself was libelous of the deepest dye, and very injurious as a vehicle of defamation, tending to corrupt the morals, and disturb the peace, tranquillity, and happiness of the whole community, and especially that of Nauvoo.

"After a long and patient investigation of the character of the 'Expositor,' and the characters and designs of its proprietors, the Constitution, the Charter (see Addenda to Nauvoo Charter from the Springfield Charter, sec. 7), and all the best authorities on the subject (see Blackstone, iii., 5, and n., etc., etc.), the City Council decided that it was necessary for the 'peace, benefit, good order, and regulations' of said city, 'and for the protection of property,' and for 'the happiness and prosperity of the citizens of Nauvoo,' that said 'Expositor' should be removed; and declaring said 'Expositor' a nuisance, ordered the mayor to cause them to be removed without delay, which order was committed to the marshal by due process, and by him executed the same day, by removing the paper, press, and fixtures into the streets, and burning the same; all which was done without riot, noise, tumult, or confusion, as has already been proved before the municipality of the city; and the particulars of the whole transaction may be expected in our next 'Nauvoo Neighbor.'

"I send you this hasty sketch that your excellency may be aware of the lying reports that are now being circulated by our enemies, that there has been a 'mob at Nauvoo,' and 'blood and thunder,' and 'swearing that two men were killed,' etc., etc., as we hear from abroad, are false—false as Satan himself could invent, and that nothing has been transacted here but what has been in perfect accordance with the strictest principles of law and good order on the part of the authorities of this city; and if your excellency is not satisfied, and shall not be satisfied, after reading the whole proceedings, which will be forthcoming soon, and shall demand an investigation of our municipality before Judge Pope, or any legal tribunal at the Capitol, you have only to write your wishes, and we will be forthcoming; we will not trouble you to file a writ or send an officer for us.

"I remain, as ever, a friend to truth, good order, and your excellency's humble servant, (Signed), JOSEPH SMITH.
"His Excellency Thomas Ford."

IV.

I THINK that the unpalatable assertion in the text will be proved by the following contrasted extracts from the London "Times" and the "Deserét News."

THE BLACK COUNTRY.—The reports of the assistant commissioners engaged in the recent education inquiry contain some very painful notices of the state of morals in some parts of the kingdom. In collier villages in Durham, where the men earn high wages, which they know no way of spending but in the gratification of animal appetites, the condition of the people in respect to morals and manners, it is said, may not be described. Adultery is made a matter of mere jest, and incest also is frightfully common, and seems to excite no disgust. In some of those parts girls mingle with boys at school till 13, 14, or 15 years of age, and that in schools not superintended by women; it is impossible to state the coarseness of manners that prevails in these schools. Coming south, into Staffordshire, we are told that in the union of Dudley, where boys and girls can earn high wages, their independence of their parents' aid to maintain them leads to a remarkable independence of conduct, and, in fact, no restraint is put upon their inclinations either by their parents or the opinion of the neighborhood. It is held rather a shame to an unmarried woman not to have had a child; and the assistant commissioner, Mr. Coode, says that the details given to him by the most respectable and trustworthy witnesses would, if they could be reported, be discredited by most men of the world only acquainted with the ordinary profligacy of the poor; but he adds that, notwithstanding all this, the behavior and manners in other respects of girls and women is not in public less decent than that in places of better repute, and it is generally asserted that this early corruption of females does not hinder them from being very good neighbors, and excellent, hard-working, and affectionate wives and mothers. Education in this district is not much prized; it is a common saying, "The father went to the pit and he made a fortune, the son went to school and he lost it." But so much has been done by the upper classes in providing schools for the lower that education is gradually making its way, and many who can not read are ashamed of their deficiency, and desirous to have their children taught. In a village where an energetic clergyman, who has adopted a rough, strong style of preaching, has succeeded in filling his church, Mr. Coode noticed during the service that all the people affected to find the place in the books furnished to them, but full half the books were held upside down, and within his observation not one was open at the right place, except where some young person taught to read in the school was by to find it.

An Ordinance relating to Houses of Ill-fame and Prostitution.

Sec. 1. Be it ordained by the City Council of Great Salt Lake City, that any person or persons who shall be found guilty of keeping, or shall be an inmate of any house of ill-fame, or place for the practice of fornication or adultery, or knowingly own or be interested as proprietor or landlord of any such house, or any person or persons harboring or keeping about his, her, or their private premises any whore-master, strumpet, or whore, knowing them to be guilty of following a lewd course of life, shall be liable to a fine for each offense not exceeding one hundred dollars, or imprisonment not exceeding six months, or both fine and imprisonment, at the discretion of the court having jurisdiction. In a prosecution under this section, the person having charge of any house or place shall be deemed the keeper thereof.

Sec. 2. It shall be lawful, on the trial of any person before said court charged with either of the offenses named in the preceding section, for the city to introduce in support of such charge testimony of the general character and reputation of the person or place touching the offense or charge set forth in the complaint, and the defendant may likewise resort to testimony of a like nature for the purpose of disproving such charge.

Sec. 3. No person shall be incapacitated or excused from testifying touching any offense committed by another against any of the provisions set forth in the first section of this ordinance by reason of his or her having participated in such crime, but the evidence which may be given by such person shall in no case be used against the person so testifying.

Sec. 4. The word adultery, as made use of in this ordinance, shall be construed to mean the unlawfully cohabiting together of two persons when either one or both of such persons are married; and the word fornication shall be construed to mean the cohabiting together of two unmarried persons.

Passed December 30th, 1860.   A. O. SMOOT, Mayor.
ROBERT CAMPBELL, City Recorder.

V. CHRONOLOGICAL ABSTRACT OF MORMON HISTORY.

1801. June 1. Birth of Mr. Brigham Young, at Wittingham, Vermont, U. S. In this year Mr. Heber C. Kimball also was born (June 14th).

1805. Dec. 23. Mr. Joseph Smith, jun., son of Mr. Joseph Smith, sen., generally called "Old Father Smith," and Lucy Mack, known as "Mother Smith," born at Sharon, Windsor Co., Vermont.

1812. A book called the "Manuscript Found" was presented to Mr. Patterson, a bookseller at Pittsburgh, Penn., by Mr. Solomon Spalding or Spaulding, of Crawford, Penn.; born in Ashford Co., and a graduate of Dartmouth College. The author died, the bookseller followed him in 1826, and the book fell into the hands of a printer's compositor, Sidney Rigdon, one of the earliest Mormon converts. Anti-Mormons identify parts of the "Book of Mormon" with the "Manuscript Found." The Saints deny the existence of a Patterson, and assert that Mr. Spaulding's book was a mere historical and idolatrous romance concerning the Ten Lost Tribes, altogether different from their Biblion. They trace the calumny to a certain Doctor (so called because a seventh son) Philastus Hurlbert or Hurlbut, an apostate excommunicated for gross immorality, and bound over in $500 to keep the peace, after threatening to murder Mr. Joseph Smith, jun.; and they observe that in those early days their Prophet was too unlearned a man to adapt or to alter a manuscript.

1814. Mr. Joseph Smith, jun., powerfully awakened by the preaching of Mr. Lane, an earnest Methodist minister.

1815. Mr. and Mrs. Smith removed with their family—Alvin, Hyrum, Sophronia, Joseph, Samuel, Ephraim, William, and Catharine, from Vermont to New York. They first lived at Palmyra, Wayne Co., for ten years, and then passed on to Manchester, Ontario Co., the site of the Hill Cumorah, where they tarried eleven or twelve years.

1820. Many religious revivals in Western New York. Mr. Joseph Smith becomes partial to Methodism (J. Hyde, chap. viii.). Early in the spring of the year occurred Mr. Joseph Smith, jun.'s first or preparatory vision announcing his ministry.

1823. Sept. 20. Second vision; the Angel of the Lord revealed in rather a solemn way to Mr. Joseph Smith, jun., the existence of the Gold Plates, which, according to anti-Mormons, he and his brother Hyrum had been employed in forging and fabricating for some years. On the next day (22d) Mr. Joseph Smith, jun., opened the place where the Plates were deposited and saw them.

1825. Mr. Joseph Smith, jun., was employed by a person called Stroude to dig for him, near Hartwich, Oswego City, N. Y. Money-diggers were then common in that part of the state, seeking the buried treasures of Captain Kidd, the buccaneer. Near Hartwich, between the years 1818–1832, lived Mrs. Spaulding, and Mr. Joseph Smith, jun., stole the "Manuscript Found" from a trunk full of papers (J. H.).

1827. Jan. 18. Mr. Joseph Smith, jun., married Miss Emma Hale, daughter of Isaac Hale, of South Bainbridge, Chenango Co., N. Y. This person afterward became the Cyria Electa, or Elect Lady, and ended by apostatizing and marrying a Gentile.

Sept. 22. The Golden Plates which the angel announced were taken up from the Hill Cumorah with a mighty display of celestial machinery, and the Breastplate and the Urim and Thummim were found. According to Gentiles, the latter was a "peep-stone stolen from Willard Chase."

1828. February. Martin Harris, a farmer from whom Mr. Joseph Smith, jun., had borrowed $50 to defray expenses of printing the "Book of Mormon," submitted a transcript of the characters to Professor Anthon and Dr. Mitchell of New York. The former pronounced them to be a " singular scroll," and "evidently copied after the Mexican Calendar given by Humboldt."

July. Translation of the " Book of Mormon" suspended in consequence of Martin Harris stealing (116–118?) pages of the manuscript, which were never replaced. For this reason he was not enrolled among the glorious first six converts to Mormonism.

1829. April 16. Mr. Joseph Smith, jun., saw O. Cowdery the first time. Translation of the " Book of Mormon" resumed, O. Cowdery acting as secretary.

May 15. John the Baptist ordained into the Aaronic priesthood Mr. Joseph Smith, jun., and O. Cowdery, his amanuensis, who forthwith baptized each other.

June or July. The Plates of the " Book of Mormon" were shown by the Angel of God to the three earthly witnesses—Oliver Cowdery, David Whitmer, and Martin Harris.

1830. The " Book of Mormon" was translated and published, and this year is No. 1 of the Mormon Æra.

April 6. The Church of Jesus Christ of Latter-Day Saints was organized at Manchester, N. Y. It began with six members or elders being ordained, viz., Mr. Joseph Smith, sen., Mr. Hyrum Smith, Mr. Joseph Smith, jun., Mr. Samuel Smith, Mr. Oliver Cowdery, and Mr. Joseph Knight. The Sacrament was administered, and hands were laid on for the gift of the Holy Ghost on this first occasion in the Church.

April 11. Oliver Cowdery preached the first public discourse on this dispensation, and the principles of the Gospel as revealed to Mr. Joseph Smith, jun. During this month the first miracle was performed by the power of God in Colesville, Broome Co., N. Y.

June 1, First Conference of the Church at Fayette, Seneca Co., N. Y. During this month Mr. Joseph Smith, jun., was twice arrested on false pretenses, tried, and acquitted; while his wife, by special revelation, was entitled "Elect Lady" and " Daughter of God."

August. Parley P. Pratt and Sidney Rigdon were converted.

Sept. 19. O. Pratt baptized.

October. The first missionaries to the Lamanites were appointed.

December. Sidney Rigdon visited the Prophet.

1831. January. Mr. Joseph Smith, jun., set out for Kirtland, the birthplace of Sidney Rigdon.

Feb. 1. Mr. Joseph Smith, jun., arrived at Kirtland, Ohio, the first of his many Hegiras.

Feb. 9. God commanded the elders to go forth in pairs and preach.

March 8. John Whitmer was appointed Church recorder and historian by revelation.

June 6. The Melchizedek, or Superior Priesthood, was first conferred upon the elders.

June 10–19. Mr. Joseph Smith, jun., and sundry Saints transferred themselves from Kirtland, Ohio, to Jackson County, Missouri, where they arrived in the middle of July. The Land of Zion was dedicated and consecrated for the gathering of the Saints, and the first log was laid in Kaw township, twelve miles west of Independence, Missouri.

Aug. 2–3. Site for the temple of New Zion dedicated, a little west of Independence.

Aug. 4. First Conference of the Church in the land of Zion held.

Aug. 9. Mr. Joseph Smith, jun., returned from Independence to Kirtland, and, arriving about the end of the month (27th?), established the fatal "Kirtland Safety Society Bank."

1832. March 25. Mr. Joseph Smith, jun., and Sidney Rigdon were tarred and feathered by a mob for attempting to establish communism and dishonorable dealing, forgery, and swindling (J. H.).

March 26. Mr. Joseph Smith, jun., acknowledged the President of the High Priesthood at a General Council of the Church; visited his flock in Missouri.

April 2. Mr. Joseph Smith, jun., left Ohio for Missouri, and arrived at Independence on the 24th.

April 14. Mr. Brigham Young, converted by Elder Samuel Smith, and baptized by Eleazar Millard, in this year went to Kirtland, Ohio, and became a devoted follower of the Prophet.

May 1. At an Œcumenical Council held at Independence, Mo., it was decided to print the "Book of Doctrines and Covenants."

May 6. Mr. Joseph Smith, jun., left Missouri for Kirtland, where he arrived in June.

June. The first Mormon periodical, the "Evening and Morning Star," was published by the Church, under the superintendence of Mr. W. W. Phelps, at Independence, Mo., where the Saints numbered 1200 souls.

Nov. 6. Mr. Joseph Smith, jun.'s, son Joseph born at Kirtland, Ohio.

In this year Mr. Heber C. Kimball was baptized.

1833. Jan. 22. Gift of tongues conferred.

Feb. 2. Mr. Joseph Smith, jun., finished his inspired retranslation of the New Testament.

March 18. The Quorum of Three High Priests, viz., Mr. Joseph Smith, jun., Sidney Rigdon, a Campbellite or reformed Baptist preacher, and Frederick G. Williams, an early convert, was organized as a Presidency of the Church in Kirtland, and forthwith proceeded to have visions of the Savior, of concourses of angels, etc., etc.

July 2. Mr. Joseph Smith, jun., finished the translation of the Bible.

July 20. A mob of Missourians in Jackson City tore down the new newspaper office, tarred, feathered, and whipped the Saints. Thereupon, three days afterward, the Saints agreed with their persecutors to leave Jackson Co., and laid the corner-stone of the Lord's House in Kirtland.

Sept. 11. A printing-press was established at Kirtland for the publication of the "Latter-Day Saints' Messenger and Advocate," Bishop Partridge being at the head of the Church in Zion.

Oct. 8. Elders W. W. Phelps and O. Hyde presented to the governors of Missouri a petition from the Saints of Jackson City praying for redress.

Oct. 31. Ten Mormon houses destroyed by the populace in Jackson Co.

Two of a mob were killed by the Saints. "This was the first blood shed, and the Mormons shed it" (J. H.). Until Nov. 4, the persecutions continued till the Saints evacuated Jackson Co., and fled to Clay Co.

December. Persecutions raged against the Saints in Van Buren Co., Mo.

Dec. 18. Mr. Joseph Smith, sen., was ordained Patriarch.

Dec. 27. The mob permitted Messrs. Davis and Kelley to carry the establishment of the "Evening and Morning Star" to Liberty, Clay Co., Mo., where they began to publish the "Missouri Enquirer."

1834. Feb. 17. A First Presidency of Three and a High Council of Twelve were first organized.

Feb. 20. Mr. Joseph Smith, jun., began to raise a small army for carrying out his dreams of physical conquest and temporal sovereignty (J. H.); also to defend himself against the Missourian mob.

May 3. At a Conference of Elders in Kirtland, the body ecclesiastic was first named "The Church of Jesus Christ of Latter-Day Saints." The body of Zelph, the Lamanite, was dug up by Mr. Joseph Smith, jun., in Illinois.

May 5. Mr. Joseph Smith, jun., marched on Missouri with 150 Mormons (?). In other words, left Kirtland for Missouri with a company for the redemption of Zion.

June 19. The cholera broke out in "Zion's camp" soon after its arrival in Missouri, and a terrible storm scattered the mob.

June 23. The camp, after suffering from cholera, arrived at Liberty, Clay Co., Missouri.

June 29 (or Nov. 29 ?). Mr. Joseph Smith, jun., and Oliver Cowdery first make a "Conditional Covenant with the Lord" that they would pay tithing. This was its first introduction among the Latter-Day Saints.

July 9. Mr. Joseph Smith, jun., left Clay Co. and returned to Kirtland, where he arrived about the end of the month.

1835. Feb. 14. A Quorum of Twelve Apostles was organized, among whom were Brigham Young and Heber C. Kimball. The former, being then thirty-four years old, was appointed the head of the Apostolic College, and, receiving the gift of tongues, was sent on a missionary tour toward the east.

Feb. 21. First meeting of the Twelve Apostles.

Feb. 28. The organization of the Quorum of Seventies began.

May 3. The Twelve left Kirtland on their first mission.

July. The rolls of Egyptian papyrus, which contained the writings of Abraham and Joseph in Egypt,* were obtained in the early part of this month.

Aug. 17. At a General Assembly at Kirtland, the "Book of Doctrines and Covenants" was accepted as a rule of faith and practice, including the "Lectures on Faith" delivered by Sidney Rigdon.

1836. Jan. 4. A Hebrew professorship established at Kirtland.

Jan. 21. The authorities of the Church in Kirtland met in the Temple school-room, and anointed and blessed one another, when visions of heaven were opened to many.

March 24–27. The House of the Lord in Kirtland, costing $40,000, was dedicated.

April 3. In the House of the Lord, the Savior, Moses, Elias, and Elijah appeared to Mr. Joseph Smith, jun., and O. Cowdery, and delivered the keys of the several priesthoods, and unlimited power in things temporal and spiritual.

May. The Mormons were requested by the citizens to remove from Clay Co., Mo., to Carroll, Davies, and Caldwell Counties, and founded the city of "Far West" in Caldwell Co.

1837. June 12. Messrs. H. C. Kimball and O. Hyde, and on the 13th W. Richards,. set out to convert England (returned in July, 1838). This was the first organized foreign mission.

July 20. Elders H. C. Kimball, O. Hyde, W. Richards, J. Goodson, T. Russell, and Priest J. Fielding, leaving Kirtland on June 13, sailed from New

* "Nemo mortalium omnibus horis sapit" is well proved by the Mormon attempts to decipher hieroglyphics. M. Remy has given, with the assistance of M. Théodule Devéria, a terrible blow to the Book of Abraham in the seventeenth note at the end of his second volume.

York in the ship "Garrick" (July 1), and landed at Liverpool. Three days afterward Preston had the honor of first hearing the preaching of the Gospel as revealed to Mr. Joseph Smith, jun. The first baptism by divine authority was performed by immersion in the River Ribble (July 30), and the first confirmation of members took place at Walkerford Chaidgey (Aug. 4).

July 27. Mr. Joseph Smith, jun., was prosecuted with a vexatious lawsuit at Painesville, Ohio.

Sept. 27. Mr. Joseph Smith, jun., left Kirtland to establish gathering-places and visit the Saints in Missouri, and arrived in Far West about the last of October or the first of November.

Dec. 10. Mr. Joseph Smith, jun., arrived in Kirtland from Missouri.

Dec. 25. The first Conference of Mormons in England was held in the Cock-pit, Preston. An extensive apostasy befell during this month in Kirtland, Ohio; and the "Safety Society Bank" failed, to the great scandal of Mormondom.

1838. Jan. 12. Mr. Joseph Smith, jun., and Sidney Rigdon fled from Kirtland to escape mob violence, and arrived at Far West on March 14.

April 12 and 13. Martin Harris, Oliver Cowdery, and David Whitmer, the three witnesses to the "Book of Mormon" (others say O. Cowdery, D. Whitmer, and L. E. Johnson), charged with lying, theft, counterfeiting, and defaming the Prophet's character, were cut off from the Church (J. H.). Orson Hyde, Thos. B. Marsh, W. W. Phelps, and others apostatized, accused the Prophet of being accessory to several thefts and murders, and of meditating a tyranny over that part of Missouri, and eventually over the whole republic (J. H.).

April 20. Elders H. C. Kimball and O. Hyde sailed from Liverpool on their return home.

July 4. Sidney Rigdon, in an anniversary discourse called "Sidney's Last Sermon," threatened Gentiles and apostates with violence; the "Danite Band," according to anti-Mormons, was at once organized.

July 6. The Saints were again persecuted; 565 Saints left Kirtland for Missouri, and Mr. Joseph Smith, jun., was carried before Judge King.

Aug. 6. Troubles in Gallatin Co. occasioned by elections. The Mormons say that persecutions of the Saints commenced in Davies Co., Mo.

Aug. and Sept. Emeutes between the mob and the Mormons: the latter seized sixty to eighty stand of arms at Richmond, and fired on the militia, mistaking them for the mob. The militia, after losing several of their number, returned the fire, killing Mr. D. W. Patten (J. H.).

Sept. 7. Mr. Joseph Smith, jr., was tried before Judge King, of Davies Co.

Sept. 25. The Saints, attempting political rule in Davies Co., were attacked by the citizen mob, who murmured at being placed under Mormon rule (J. H.), and forced the intruders to vacate. Mr. Brigham Young fled for his life to Quincy, Ill.

Oct. 1. After a battle in Carroll Co., Mo., the Saints agreed to evacuate the town of De Witt, Carroll Co. (Oct. 11).

Oct. 25. At the battle of Crooked River, D. W. Patten, alias Captain Fear-not, the head of the Danites, was killed (Mormon Calendar).

Oct. 27. General Lilburn W. Boggs, of Missouri, issued his "extermination order" to General J. B. Clark.

Oct. 30. The militia (mob), to revenge the death of their comrades, slaughtered sixteen Mormons and two boys at Haun's Mills.

Oct. 31. Mr. Joseph Smith, jun., and others, were betrayed by J. M. Hinckle.

Nov. 1. General J. B. Clark, with a military force, surrounded Far West, and took prisoners (by stratagem) Mr. Joseph Smith, jun., Mr. Hyrum Smith, and forty others, who were placed in jail, tried by court-martial, and sentenced to be shot—a catastrophe prevented by General Doniphan. The Saints gave up their arms, and Far West was plundered by the mob.

Nov. 2. Mr. Joseph Smith, jun., and his fellow-prisoners left Far West for Independence.

Nov. 4. Mr. Joseph Smith, jun., and his fellow-prisoners were kindly received at Independence.

Nov. 12. Mr. Joseph Smith and 52 others were tried at Richmond, Ray

Co., Mo., and, after a narrow escape from being shot by the militia, were handed to the civil authorities, placed in close confinement in Liberty jail, and released.

December. The Saints withdrew into Illinois.

1839. Feb. 14 and March 26. Mr. Brigham Young and others fled from Far West to Illinois, and attempted to relay the foundations of the Temple at the New Jerusalem, twelve miles west of Independence, Jackson Co., Missouri.

April 6. Mr. Joseph Smith, jun., and his fellow-prisoners were removed for trial from Richmond to Gallatin, Davies Co.

April 9. The trial of the prisoners commenced before Judge King.

April 15. Mr. Joseph Smith, jun., and his companions left Davies for Boone Co., and on the way escaped from their jailor-guards.

April 18–22. The Saints evacuated Far West, and arrived with Mr. Joseph Smith, jun., at Quincy, Illinois.

April 26. Mr. Brigham Young privily laid the foundation of a Temple at Independence (M. Remy). A Conference was held at the Temple Lot, in Far West, in fulfillment of a revelation given July 8th, 1838. (Appendix to "Compendium of Faith and Doctrines," etc.)

May 9. Mr. Joseph Smith, jun., visited Commerce, Hancock Co., Illinois, at the invitation of Dr. Isaac Galland, of whom he obtained, gratis, a large tract of land to induce the Mormons to immigrate, and upon the receipt of revelation called his people around him, and sold them the town lots (J. H.).

June 11. The first house was built by the Saints at Commerce, a new "State of Zion," afterward called Nauvoo—the beautiful site—which presently contained 15,000 souls.

June 27. Orson Hyde, the Apostle, returned to the Church.

July 4. P. P. Pratt and Morris Phelps escaped from the jail in Columbia, Boone Co., Missouri.

Aug. 29. Elders P. P. Pratt and O. Pratt set out on their first mission to England, followed on Sept. 18 by Elders Brigham Young and H. C. Kimball, and on Sept. 20, 21, by Elders G. A. Smith, R. Hedlock, and T. Turley: O. Hyde, though previously appointed by revelation, did not accompany them (J. H.). The result was a body of 769 converts.

Oct. 29. Mr. Joseph Smith, jun., S. Rigdon, E. Higbee, and O. P. Rockwell, the chief of the Danites, set out from Nauvoo as delegates from the Church to the general government, and arrived on the 28th of November at Washington, D. C., seeking to obtain redress from Congress for their losses in Missouri.

1840. March 4. Mr. Joseph Smith, jun., returned from Washington to Nauvoo.

March 9. Elders Young, Kimball, P. P. Pratt, O. Pratt, Smith, and Hedlock sailed from New York for England.

April 6. The English mission from New York landed at Liverpool.

April 15. Elder O. Hyde set out from Nauvoo on a mission to Jerusalem.

April 21. Commerce was finally named Nauvoo.

May 27. The first number of the "Latter-Day Saints' Millennial Star" was published at Manchester.

June 6. The first company of emigrating Saints sailed from Liverpool, and reached New York in July 20. About the 1st of June appeared the first English edition of the "Latter-Day Saints' Hymn Book."

Aug. 7. The first regular company of 200 emigrants, conducted by Elders Theodore Turley, a returning missionary, and William Clayton, an early English convert, sailed from Liverpool to New York.

Sept. 14. Mr. Joseph Smith, sen., died at Nauvoo.

Oct. 3. The Mormons began to build their Temple, and petitioned the Legislature of Illinois for the incorporation of Nauvoo.

Dec. 16. The municipal charter of the city of Nauvoo became law.

1841. January. The first English edition of the "Book of Mormon" was published.

Feb. 4. The Nauvoo Corporation Act, passed in the preceding winter, began to be in force. The Nauvoo Legion was organized by Mr. Joseph Smith, who made himself its lieutenant general.

April 6. The corner-stone of the House of the Lord in Nauvoo was laid. A second mission, composed of Elders B. Young, H. C. Kimball, O. Pratt,

W. Woodruff, J. Taylor, G. A. Smith, and W. Richards left New York on April 2d, and landed at Liverpool on May 20.

June 5. Mr. Joseph Smith was arrested under a requisition from the Governor of the State of Missouri, was tried at Monmouth, Illinois, on the 9th, and was acquitted on the next day.

July 1. Messrs. Brigham Young and Heber C. Kimball returned from England.

Nov. 8. The baptismal font in Nauvoo Temple was dedicated.

1842. March 1. "Book of Abraham" translated and published in "Times and Seasons."

May 6. Attempt to assassinate Lieutenant Governor Boggs, attributed to O. P. Rockwell.

May 19. Mr. Joseph Smith made Mayor of Nauvoo.

Aug. 6. Mr. Joseph Smith prophesied that the Saints would be driven to the Rocky Mountains.

Aug. 8. Mr. Joseph Smith arrested a second time under circumstances similar to those of the first.

Dec. 7. Mr. O. Hyde returned from his mission to Palestine.

Dec. 26. Mr. Joseph Smith, charged with assassination, was arrested a third time under a requisition from the Governor of the State of Missouri. In this year polygamy began to be whispered about Nauvoo (J. H.).

1843. Jan. 5. Mr. Joseph Smith acquitted at Springville.

Jan. 20. Mr. O. Pratt received back into the Church.

May 6. Lieutenant Governor L. W. Boggs (under Governor D. Dunklin), of Missouri (who had offended the Mormons by driving them from the state in 1838), was shot in the mouth through an open window—an act generally attributed to O. P. Rockwell, Chief of the Danites, "with the connivance and under the instructions of Joseph Smith" (J. H.). In this year Mr. Joseph Smith became Mayor of Nauvoo, vice J. C. Bennett, "cut off for imitating Smith in his spiritual wifedom" (J. H.). Anti-Mormons declare that in 1843 polygamy was enjoined a second time, but not practiced till 1852.

June 23. Mr. Joseph Smith again arrested, and released on July 2.

July 12. Revelation enjoining polygamy received.

Aug. 30. General J. A. Bennett baptized.

Nov. 4. Mr. Joseph Smith sent his letters to the candidates for the Presidency of the United States.

Nov. 28. Mr. Joseph Smith addresses a memorial to Congress respecting the transactions at Missouri.

1844. Feb. 7. Mr. Joseph Smith issued his address as candidate for the Presidency of the United States.

May 17. Mr. Joseph Smith was carried in triumph through the streets of Nauvoo.

May 4. Francis M. Higbee, expelled for disobedience from the Church, prosecuted Mr. Joseph Smith for slander, and arrested him under a capias: the defendant then sued out a habeas corpus before the Municipal Court of Nauvoo, of which he was mayor.

May 6. Dr. R. D. Foster and Mr. William Law, having libeled, in the "Expositor" paper, Mr. Joseph Smith, accusing him of having taken to spiritual wife Mrs. Foster, were punished by the marshal and municipal officers, who, with a posse, broke the press as a nuisance, and burned the types. The libelers fled, and took out a warrant against Mr. Joseph Smith and others, who resisted and repelled the officer in charge, whereupon the militia was ordered out.

June 13. The Gentiles armed against the Mormons.

June 17. Mr. Joseph Smith arrested and released.

June 24. Governor Ford, of Illinois, persuaded the Smiths, under the pledge of his word, and the faith and honor of the state, to yield up their arms, and sent them prisoners under the charge of sixty militia-men, the Carthage Grays, a highly hostile body, commanded by Captain Smith, to Carthage, the capital of Hancock Co., eighteen to twenty miles from Nauvoo, where 5000 Mormons were in arms.

June 25. The prisoners were arrested by the constable on a charge of treason.

June 26. The governor again pledged himself for the personal safety of his prisoners.

June 27 (Thursday). A body of 200 armed Missourians, with their faces painted and blackened, broke into Carthage jail, and at 5 P.M. murdered, in a most cowardly and brutal manner, Mr. Joseph Smith and his brother Hyrum, and desperately wounded Mr. John Taylor; Dr. Willard Richards alone escaping.

Aug. 15. The Twelve Apostles, with Mr. Brigham Young at the head, assumed the Presidency of the Church, and addressed an Encyclical to "all the Saints in the world."

Oct. 7. Mr. Brigham Young, the President of the Twelve Apostles, came from Boston, and succeeded to the Presidency of the Church, defeating Sidney Rigdon, who was forthwith cut off, and delivered over to the buffetings of Satan.

Nov. 17. Mr. David Smith, son of the Prophet, born at the Nauvoo Mansion.

1845. The Mormon leaders determined to abandon Nauvoo.

May. The capstone of the Mormon Temple was laid, and endowments began.

Sept. 11. Twenty-nine Mormon houses burnt by the Gentiles.

Sept. 24. The charter of Nauvoo was repealed by the State Legislature. The authorities of the Church made a treaty with the mob to evacuate the "Beautiful City" on the following spring. Several places were proposed: Vancouver's Island by Mr. John Taylor, Texas by Mr. Lyman Wight, California by others; at last they chose some valley in the Rocky Mountains (J. H.).

1846. January. Baptism for the dead was administered in the Mississippi River; on the 20th a band of Mormon pioneers left Nauvoo, and "located" at Council Bluffs, Iowa.

February. The first Mormon exodus began with this month; 2000 souls crossed the frozen Mississippi *en route* for Council Bluffs.

April 24. The exiled Saints arrived at Garden Grove, Iowa Territory.

May 1. Dedication of the Temple at Nauvoo.

May 16. The pioneer camp of the Saints arrived at Mount Pisgah, Iowa Territory.

June–July. The Mormon battalion (500 men), on being called for by the general government, set out for the Mexican campaign. "Mr. Brigham Young sells a company of his brethren for $20,000" (J. H.). "You shall have your battalion at once, if it has to be a class of our elders," said Mr. Brigham Young (Captain H. Stansbury).

Sept. 10–13. After three days of fighting the few surviving Saints were expelled from Nauvoo in a "cruel, cowardly, and brutal manner."

Sept. 16. The trustees of the Church in Nauvoo made a treaty with the mob for the surrender of their city, and its immediate evacuation by the remnant of the Saints. Toward the end of this year and the beginning of the next, the Quorum of Three was reorganized at a special conference, held at Council Bluffs, Iowa, Mr. Brigham Young nominating his coadjutors. The "Twelve" delivered themselves of an epistle to the Saints, urging them to recommence the gathering.

1847. April 14. The pioneer band, 143 men, headed by Mr. Brigham Young, and driving seventy wagons, left winter quarters, Omaha Nation, on the west bank of the Missouri River, and followed Colonel Frémont's trail over the Rocky Mountains.

July 23. Messrs. O. Pratt, W. Woodruff, and a few others arrived at the valley of the Great Salt Lake.

July 24. Mr. Brigham Young and the main body entered the valley on this day, which became a solemn anniversary in the Church. The Mormons proceeded to lay the foundations of the city.

Oct. 31. Mr. Brigham Young returned to Council Bluffs.

1848. Feb. 20. The emigration from England reopened after a suspension of two years.

May. Mr. Brigham Young (whose appointment had been confirmed by a General Conference held at Kanesville, Iowa) left winter quarters the second time, and, followed by Mr. H. C. Kimball and the mass of the Saints, reached the Promised Land in September.

September. Some Mormons who had started from New York for San Francisco, expecting to find the Church in California or Vancouver's Island, arrived in Great Salt Lake City from the West.

Nov. 10. The Temple in Nauvoo burnt.

1849. March 5. At a convention held in Great Salt Lake City the Constitution of the State of Deserét was drafted, and the Legislature was elected under its provisions.

July 2. Delegates sent to Washington petitioned for admission into the Union as a free, sovereign, and independent state.

August. Captain Stansbury and Lieutenant Gunnison, Topographical Engineers, by order of the federal government, surveyed Great Salt Lake Valley.

Sept. 9. A bill organizing Utah Territory was signed by President Fillmore. The Perpetual Emigration Fund was organized. Five Yutas were killed in battle by Captain John Scott and his Mormons.

1850. April 5. The Assembly met, and Utah Territory was duly organized.

May 27. The walls of the Temple at Nauvoo were blown down by a hurricane.

June 14. The first missionaries to Scandinavia landed in Copenhagen, Denmark.

June 15. The first number of the "Deserét News" appeared under the editorship of Dr. Willard Richards.

Aug. 12. The first baptisms in Denmark by legal authority in this Dispensation took place.

Sept. 9. The "Act" for organizing the Territory of Utah became a law. Mr. Brigham Young was appointed Governor and Superintendent of Indian Affairs in Utah Territory by President Fillmore, who signed the act. The judges, Brocchus, Day, and Brandeburg, and Mr. Secretary Harris, arrived at Great Salt Lake City.

Sept. 22. Judge Brocchus insulted the people, and, accompanied by the other federal officers, fled from the Territory.

Oct. 13. The first company of Perpetual Emigration Fund emigrants arrived in Great Salt Lake City from the United States.

Dec. 7. The first branch of the Church in France was organized at Paris.

In 1850 was the Indian War. Mr. Higbee was the first white settler slain, and many of the Yutas were killed.

1851. Jan. 9. Great Salt Lake City was incorporated.

Feb. 3. Mr. Brigham Young sworn in as Governor of Utah.

April 5. Legislature of Provisional State of Deserét dissolved. The Legislative Assembly was elected under the Territorial Bill. A memorial signed by 13,000 names was forwarded to her Britannic majesty's government, proposing for a relief by emigration of a portion of the poorer subjects to colonize Oregon or Vancouver's Island, the latter being about the dimensions of England.

April 7. The Tabernacle was built, and at a General Conference in Great Salt Lake City it was voted to build a Temple.

Sept. 22. Opening of the Legislature of Utah Territory. Great trouble with the government of the United States fomented by the federal officials' march. The Legislature forbade by ordinances the sale of arms, ammunition, and spirituous liquors to the Indians.

Dec. 13. Parovan City, on Centre Creek, Iron Co., Utah Territory, founded.

1852. June. Fifteen Frenchmen baptized in Paris.

Aug. 29. The revelation on the celestial law of marriage, alias polygamy (bearing date 1843), was published by Mr. Brigham Young.

Sept. 3. The first company of Perpetual Emigration Fund converts from Europe reached Great Salt Lake City.

Dec. 13. The Legislative Assembly of Utah Territory met for the first time. The judges and the Secretary of State appointed by President Pierce came to hand.

1853. Jan. 17. The Deserét Iron Company was chartered by the Legislature of Utah Territory.

Jan. 25. The missionary elders O. Spencer and J. Houtz arrived in Berlin, Prussia, and were banished on the 2d of February.

Feb. 14. Temple Block was consecrated, ground was broken for the foundation of the Temple, and the excavations began.

March 7. The first missionaries to Gibraltar arrived there.

April 6. Corner-stone of the new Temple laid with religious rites.

In the summer (July) and autumn of this year were serious Indian troubles. At 6 A.M., Oct. 26th, Lieutenant J. W. Gunnison and eight men of his party, including the botanist, M. Creutzfeldt, were massacred on the border of Sevier River, twenty miles north of Lake Sevier.

Nov. 1. The first number of the "Journal of Discourses" was published in England. This year Keokuk was made the outfitting place for emigrants.

1854. January. New alphabet adopted by the University of Deserét.

April 7. Mr. J. M. Grant was appointed to the First Presidency, *vice* W. Richards, deceased on March 11th.

May 23. The patriarch John Smith died, and was succeeded by another John Smith, son of Hyrum Smith, and nephew of the Prophet.

June 28. John Smith, son of Hyrum Smith, was appointed Patriarch over the Church.

August. Colonel Steptoe, commanding about 1000 federal troops, arrived at Great Salt Lake City.

Sept. 9. At the instance of Colonel Steptoe, who refused to resign his military commission, Mr. Brigham Young was reappointed governor, and held the office until 1857. Even the Gentiles memorialized in his favor.

1855. Jan. 29. Walchor, alias Wakara, alias Walker, chief of the Yuta Indians, died (was secretly put to death and buried by Jordan, Mr. Chandless).

May 5. Endowment House in Great Salt Lake City consecrated.

May 11. Treaty of peace concluded with the Yuta Indians.

May. Colonel Steptoe, after a stay of six months, marched with the United States cavalry to California.

August (July?). Judge Drummond, Surveyor General Burr, and other United States officials, arrived at Great Salt Lake City.

In the fall of this year one third of the crops was destroyed by drought and grasshoppers.

October. A branch of the Church was organized in Dresden (15th); Elder O. Spencer died on the 29th. The First Presidency of the Church proposed in a general epistle that Saints emigrating by the Perpetual Emigration Fund should cross the Prairies and Rocky Mountains with hand-carts.

Dec. 10. The local Legislature met for the first time at Fillmore, the Territorial capital, and passed a bill authorizing an election of delegates to a Territorial Convention for the purpose of forming a State Constitution, and to petition Congress for the admission of Utah into the Union. They also passed a bill authorizing a census.

Most of the Mormons became polygamists (J. H.).

1856. March 17. A convention of delegates met in Great Salt Lake City, and adopted a State Constitution, sending Messrs. John Taylor and George A. Smith, apostles, both as delegates to Washington, with a view to obtaining admission into the Union as a state. No answer was returned. During the very severe winter and spring half the stock perished by frost, and grain became very scarce.

May. Judge W. W. Drummond left Great Salt Lake City, after having forwarded false charges of rebellion, burning the library, and destroying the archives: these reports caused all the troubles with the United States.

The practice of tithe-paying was introduced among the Saints in Europe. Iowa City was made the outfit point for the Plains.

June. Lucy Mack, the Prophet's mother, died.

Sept. 26. The first hand-cart train crossed the Plains, and arrived at Great Salt Lake City.

1857. (The winter of Mormon discontent.) March. Judge Drummond reported calumnies against the Mormons.

April. Surveyor General Burr and other United States officials left Utah Territory and returned to the United States.

The Territorial Legislature petitioned Congress to send better officers, or to permit the Mormons to appoint *bonâ fide* citizens and residents.

Mail communication with the States—the "Y Express" established by Mr. Brigham Young—was cut off, to keep the Mormons ignorant of the steps taken against them, and this continued for nearly a year. The Press in the United States generally opined that the Mormons were to be "wiped out."

May 14. Apostle Parley P. Pratt killed by Hector M'Lean in Kansas.

June 29. Brigadier General W. S. Harney, commanding Fort Leavenworth, was ordered to take charge of the army of Utah. He was removed after declaring that he would "hang Brigham first and try him afterward," and was succeeded first by Colonel Alexander, and afterward by General Johnston.

Sept. 3, 4. Indians aided by white men massacred 115 to 120 emigrants at Mountain Meadow.

In this month 1400 men, artillery and liners of the 5th and 10th regiments, appeared upon the Sweetwater, followed by 1000 more, making the whole force amount to 2400 men, a kind of *posse comitatus* to enforce obedience to the federal laws.

Sept. 15. Mr. Brigham Young issued the remarkable document subjoined.* General Wells was ordered to occupy the passes in the Wasach Mountains, and 2016 Mormons prepared to defend their hearths and homes against the violence of the United States. Captain Van Vliet arrived at Great Salt Lake City.

Oct. 5–6. The Mormons, who were "spoiling for a fight," burned, without the orders of their governor, two provision trains, one of fifty-one and the other of twenty-three wagons, causing great want and violent exasperation in the army of Utah.

* *Proclamation by the Governor, proclaiming Martial Law in the Territory of Utah.*

"CITIZENS OF UTAH,—We are invaded by a hostile force, who are evidently assailing us to accomplish our overthrow and destruction.

"For the last twenty-five years we have trusted officials of the government, from constables and justices to judges, governors, and presidents, only to be scorned, held in derision, insulted, and betrayed. Our houses have been plundered and then burned, our fields laid waste, our principal men butchered while under the pledged faith of the government for their safety, and our families driven from their homes to find that shelter in the barren wilderness, and that protection among hostile savages, which were denied them in the boasted abodes of Christianity and civilization.

"The Constitution of our common country guarantees unto us all that we do now or have ever claimed.

"If the constitutional rights which pertain unto us as American citizens were extended to Utah, according to the spirit and meaning thereof, and fairly and impartially administered, it is all that we could ask—all that we have ever asked.

"Our opponents have availed themselves of prejudice existing against us because of our religious faith to send out a formidable host to accomplish our destruction. We have had no privilege, no opportunity of defending ourselves from the false, foul, and unjust aspersions against us before the nation. The government has not condescended to cause an investigating committee or other person to be sent to inquire into and ascertain the truth, as is customary in such cases.

"We know those aspersions to be false, but that avails us nothing. We are condemned unheard, and forced to an issue with an armed mercenary mob, which has been sent against us at the instigation of anonymous letter-writers ashamed to father the base, slanderous falsehoods which they have given to the public; of corrupt officials, who have brought false accusations against us to screen themselves in their own infamy; and of hireling priests and howling editors, who prostitute the truth for filthy lucre's sake.

"The issue which has been thus forced upon us compels us to resort to the great first law of self-preservation, and stand in our own defense—a right guaranteed unto us by the genius of the institutions of our country, and upon which the government is based.

"Our duty to ourselves, to our families, requires us not to tamely submit to be driven and slain without an attempt to preserve ourselves. Our duty to our country, our holy religion, our God, to freedom and liberty, requires that we should not quietly stand still and see those fetters forging around which are calculated to enslave and bring us in subjection to an unlawful military despotism, such as can only emanate [in a country of constitutional law] from usurpation, tyranny, and oppression.

"Therefore I, Brigham Young, Governor and Superintendent of Indian Affairs for the Territory of Utah, in the name of the people of the United States in the Territory of Utah,

"1st. Forbid all armed forces, of every description, from coming into this Territory under any pretense whatever.

"2d. That all the forces in said Territory hold themselves in readiness to march at a moment's notice, to repel any and all such invasion.

"3d. Martial law is hereby declared to exist in this Territory from and after the publication of this proclamation; and no person shall be allowed to pass or repass into, or through, or from this Territory without a permit from the proper officer.

"Given under my hand and seal at Great Salt Lake City, Territory of Utah, this fifteenth day of September, A.D. eighteen hundred and fifty-seven, and of the Independence of the United States of America the eighty-second (L. S.) BRIGHAM YOUNG."

November. Army of Utah encamped near Green River.

Nov. 21. Proclamation of Mr. Cumming, the new governor.

Dec. 15. Mr. Brigham Young's message to the Legislature of Utah.

1858. Jan. 16. Address of citizens of Great Salt Lake City sent to President Buchanan.

February. Colonel Kane reached Great Salt Lake City.

April 5. Governor A. Cumming appointed to Utah Territory after the thankless offer had been refused by sixteen or seventeen political persons; left Camp Scott, near Fort Bridger, and on the 12th of April entered Great Salt Lake City. The "rebellion in Utah" found to be a pure invention.

Mr. Brigham Young, followed by 25,000 souls, marched to Provo, with their stock, flocks, and chattels, even their furniture.

April 15. Governor Cumming officially reported a respectful reception, and the illumination of Echo Kanyon; also that the records of the United States Courts, then in charge of a Mormon, Mr. W. H. Hooper, Secretary *pro tem.*, the Territorial Library, in charge of Mr. W. C. Staines, and other public property, were all unimpaired, the contrary report having constituted the *causa belli.*

April 24. Governor Cumming issued a proclamation that he would assume effective protection of all persons illegally restrained of their liberty in Utah. Few availed themselves of his offer. The Indian agent, Dr. T. Garland Hurt, was accused of having incited the Uinta Indians to acts of hostility against the Mormons—a standing charge and counter charge in the United States.

May 21. The governor made a requisition that "no hinderance may be hereafter presented to the commercial, postal, or social communications throughout the Territory."

May 29. The "Peace Commissioners" from Washington, ex-Governor Lazarus W. Powell, of Kentucky, and Major Ben M'Culloch, of Texas, the celebrated Indian fighter, arrived at Great Salt Lake City (where they staid till June 2), and after proclaiming a general amnesty and free pardon, obtained permission for the army of Utah to enter the Territory, and to encamp at a place not nearer than forty miles from New Zion.

June 12. Mr. Brigham Young treated with the Peace Commissioners.

June 14. The President's pardon "for all treasons and seditions" was proclaimed by the governor, and accepted by the citizens.

June 26. The federal troops, having left Camp Scott, passed through the deserted City of the Saints, led by Lieutenant Colonel Cooke, who rode, according to Mormon report, with head uncovered: they remained for two days encamped on the Jordan, outside the settlement, and then moved twelve to fifteen miles westward for wood and grass.

1859. The Legislature sat at Great Salt Lake City.

Judge Charles S. Sinclair attempted to break faith by misinterpreting the amnesty, and nearly caused collision between the federal troops and the Mormons.

The Hon. John Cradlebaugh, ex-officio judge of the Second Judicial District Court, Utah Territory, quartered a company of 110 men in the court-house and public buildings of Provo, thereby causing disturbances: Governor Cumming protested against the proceeding.

The Deserét currency plates were seized at Mr. Brigham Young's house.

Jan. 2. Religious service, interrupted by the war, again performed in the Tabernacle.

Feb. 28. Troubles between the citizens at Rush Valley and the federal troops under General A. J. Johnston, commanding the Department of Utah.

March 25. Mr. Howard Spencer, nephew of Mr. Daniel Spencer, was severely wounded by First Sergeant Ralph Pike, Company I of the 10th Regiment.

Aug. 10. Sergeant Pike, summoned for trial to Great Salt Lake City, was shot in the street, it is supposed by Mr. H. Spencer.

In this month the citizens of Carson Valley declared themselves independent of Utah Territory.

1860. Mr. Forney, Indian Superintendent, Utah Territory, and highly hostile to the Mormons, was removed.

Troubles with the troops.   Mr. Heneage, a Mormon citizen, was flogged at a cart's tail by two federal officers under a little mistake.

June 20. Major Ormsby (militia) and his force destroyed by the Indians near Honey Lake.

1861. The federal troops evacuated the Land of the Saints.

INDEX.

N N

THE END.